THE MAKING OF THE
CONSTITUTION

By Charles Warren

The Supreme Court in United States History
Revised Edition. Two Volumes

Congress, the Constitution, and the Supreme Court

The Making of the Constitution

THE MAKING OF THE CONSTITUTION

BY

CHARLES WARREN

AUTHOR OF "THE SUPREME COURT IN UNITED STATES HISTORY"
"THE SUPREME COURT AND SOVEREIGN STATES"
"CONGRESS, THE CONSTITUTION, AND
THE SUPREME COURT"

BARNES & NOBLE, Inc.
NEW YORK
PUBLISHERS & BOOKSELLERS SINCE 1873

PREFACE TO 1937 EDITION

New economic, social, and political conditions, and new legislative proposals have renewed public interest in the conditions which led to, and which surrounded, the making of the Constitution (whose one hundred and fiftieth anniversary occurs on September 17, 1937). I have tried to make present-day readers realize that, like all works of wise statesmanship of modern times, the Constitution was a practical document, drafted by practical men — men of wide vision and high ideals but also of skill in adjustment of varying points of view. That is why it has lasted and proved adequate to the needs of our country. It was not the product of a class or of a section, and no single influence led either to its inception or to its adoption — as Part One and Part Three of this book amply show.

CHARLES WARREN

February, 1937.

INTRODUCTION

THIS book is intended for the student, the layman, and the lawyer, who may desire to know how and why the various clauses of the Constitution were framed, and the influences surrounding the men who framed them.

It may be asked: Why another book on the Constitution? But can there be a more important subject for an American than an adequate knowledge of the document on which his government is founded? The increase of attention to this subject in recent years is one of the healthiest signs of the fundamental soundness of American policies. It is interesting to read now what J. Franklin Jameson wrote, forty years ago, in his *Introduction to the Study of the Constitutional and Political History of the States.*

"Three years ago (1882) when I first visited the Library of the Department of State at Washington, the Constitution of the United States was kept folded up in a little tin box in the lower part of a closet, while the Declaration of Independence, mounted with all elegance, was exposed to the view of all in the central room of the library. It was evident that the former document was an object of interest to very few of the visitors of Washington. But when I was last in the library, I learned that the Constitution also was being mounted in order to be similarly placed upon exhibition, because, as I understood it, there was a more general desire to see it. It seemed to me that this incident is typical of a considerable change which the last few years have seen in our way of looking at American history. The interest which during most of the years of the republic has been nearly confined, so far as the popular mind is concerned, to the more dramatic episodes and portions of our history, and has made histories of discoveries, histories of settlements, and pictorial fieldbooks of our various wars the most popular historical works, is now at last being extended to our constitutional and political history. . . ."

Since those words were written, there has been a vast change in the attitude of the public towards a study of the Constitution. The original document has been brought into the light, and now has an honored and fittingly permanent public location in the Library of Congress. And both by legislation and otherwise, means are now provided by which every one may become familiar with its provisions. Knowledge, however, of its contents is imperfect without knowledge of the conditions and of the ideals which led to its formation.

In this book, I have attempted three things — first, to picture the necessity for the Constitution, through the letters and words of the statesmen who led in bringing about the Federal Convention of 1787; second, to bring together, as far as possible, the letters and newspaper articles written during the period of that Federal Convention, so as to show how it and its great work were viewed by the men of the time; third, to present the debates on the Constitution from day to day, in such a manner that one may easily trace in a continued story the way in which each of the important clauses of the Constitution reached its final shape.

There have been many histories of the Constitution; but no single book contains all the contemporary material. Most of the letters of the public men of that era, referring to the making of the Constitution, are of course to be found, either in Max Farrand's valuable work entitled *The Records of the Federal Convention;* in the *Documentary History of the Constitution;* in the

Diplomatic Correspondence of the United States; in George Bancroft's notable *History of the Formation of the Constitution;* in George Ticknor Curtis's *History of the Constitution;* or in the collected works of Washington, Madison, Hamilton, Monroe, Jay, King, and Jefferson, and the scattered correspondence of other statesmen. But most, if not all, of these books are voluminous, difficult of access, or out of print. It has seemed to me, therefore, that to assemble all these letters in a single volume in their proper sequence would deeply impress upon a student of the Constitution, the sentiments and motives and ideals which impelled and guided the framers in their great task. In themselves, these letters are history, as well as the material from which each reader may construct history for himself.

In the same way, I have attempted to bring before the reader the materials from the newspapers of the year 1787, which reflect the economic, social, and political conditions then prevailing, as well as the attitude of the correspondents of the papers. No book has hitherto attempted to reproduce these contemporary newspaper articles, the facts and sentiments contained in which constituted (in part at least) the influences which were brought to bear upon the members of the Federal Convention and upon the public. While contemporary newspaper articles do not always present facts with entire accuracy, they certainly contain what their readers, in general, then accepted as facts. J. A. Froude, in a much quoted passage, has said that: "Actions and words are carved upon eternity; opinions are but forms of cloud created by the prevailing currents of the moral air." This sentiment is contrary to human experience. What the people thought to be true has often been more important than the actual truth; and events of history have often been founded

on a belief as much as on a fact. If all the economic
and political conditions which led to the making of the
Constitution were not, in reality, quite as black or
quite as disastrous as they then seemed to many of the
statesmen of that day, those statesmen at least believed
them to be so, and acted on that belief.

In order to impress upon the reader the actual
sequence of events in the making of the Constitution
and the influences and conditions surrounding each
step taken by the Federal Convention which framed it,
I have set forth these materials for the history of the
formation of that document — letters and newspaper
articles — as they were written or appeared, day by
day. This method of treatment may be open to criticism; but I believe that in this manner the reader
can be led to appreciate the actual atmosphere in which,
from day to day, the framers were living — at least,
so far as materials are now available for its reproduction. I have presented the bald facts, leaving to the
reader himself to clothe them with fancy.[1]

Every American who wishes really to understand the
principles of the Constitution should, of course, read
the *Notes of Debates in the Federal Convention* made by
James Madison. It must be admitted, however, that
Madison's *Notes* are not easy reading. For the
delegates discussed the same subject on many different
days; they also discussed on the same day parts of
many subjects; they changed their views, as the Convention progressed and as compromises were entered
into or arguments against their views became more
convincing, or as the attitude of other delegates
changed; they altered and reversed their decisions
on a subject, in order to adjust their vote to other

---

[1] The editor and publisher of the first daily newspaper in England, *The Daily
Courant*, March 11, 1702, wrote: "Nor will he take upon him to give any comments
or conjectures of his own, but will relate any matters of fact, supposing other people
to have sense enough to make reflections for themselves."

votes previously taken. Hence, some sort of a guide to Madison's *Notes* is necessary, if one desires to gain a knowledge of how any particular clause in the Constitution reached its final shape. Moreover, the reasons which impelled the delegates to adopt a provision generally lay in political and economic experiences — in past history — which were not set forth in the debates; and the sources of many of these provisions were to be found in documents anterior to the Convention and not referred to in the discussions. I have attempted in this book, therefore, while depicting the proceedings and debates of the Convention as they occurred day by day, to trace at the same time a consecutive story of the source of each important clause of the Constitution, and of its progress to its final form, as well as its connection with previous history.

I have tried to keep this book within the bounds of its title and not to allow it to become a commentary on Constitutional law. So far as I have succeeded in this respect, I advance the claim made by Pope in the preface to his poems: " For what I have published, I can only hope to be pardoned; but for what I have burned, I deserve to be praised."

CHARLES WARREN.

WASHINGTON, D. C.
May, 1928.

CONTENTS

CONTENTS

APPENDICES

THE MAKING OF THE CONSTITUTION

PART ONE
BEFORE THE CONVENTION

"If not the greatest exertion of human understanding, the greatest single effort of National deliberation that the world has ever seen. . . ."
John Adams to Rufus King, December 26, 1787.

"The example of changing a Constitution, by assembling the wise men of the State, instead of assembling armies, will be worth as much to the world as the former examples we had given them. The Constitution, too, which was the result of our deliberations is unquestionably the wisest ever presented to men."
Thomas Jefferson to David Humphreys, March 18, 1789.

CHAPTER ONE

FEARS OF DISUNION

In recent years there has been a tendency to interpret all history in terms of economics and sociology and geography — of soil, of debased currency, of land monopoly, of taxation, of class antagonism, of frontier against seacoast, and the like — and to attribute the actions of peoples to such general materialistic causes. This may be a wise reaction from the old manner of writing history almost exclusively in terms of wars, politics, dynasties, and religions. But its fundamental defect is, that it ignores the circumstance that the actions of men are frequently based quite as much on sentiment and belief as on facts and conditions. It leaves out the souls of men and their response to the inspiration of great leaders. It forgets that there are such motives as patriotism, pride in country, unselfish devotion to the public welfare, desire for independence, inherited sentiments, and convictions of right and justice. The historian who omits to take these facts into consideration is a poor observer of human nature. No one can write true history who leaves out of account the fact that a man may have an inner zeal for principles, beliefs, and ideals. "It seems to me a great truth," wrote Thomas Carlyle, "that human things cannot stand on selfishness, mechanical utilities, economics, and law courts." Those who contend, for instance, that economic causes brought about the War of the Revolution will always find it difficult to explain away the fact that the men who did the fighting thought, themselves, that they were fighting for a belief — a principle. Sixty-two years after the battle of Concord and Lexington, an able American historian had an interview with one of the men who had been in that battle, and asked him the reasons which impelled him, a plain, simple working man, to take arms. And this was the colloquy between the historian and the man who fought.:[1]

"Why did you? . . . My histories tell me that you men of the Revolution took up arms against intolerable oppressions."

"What were they? Oppressions? I didn't feel them."

"What, were you not oppressed by the Stamp Act?"

"I never saw one of those stamps. . . . I am certain I never paid a penny for one of them."

"Well, what about the tea tax?"

"Tea tax, I never drank a drop of the stuff. The boys threw it all overboard."

"Then, I suppose, you had been reading Harrington, or Sidney and Locke, about the eternal principles of liberty?"

"Never heard of 'em."

"Well, then, what was the matter, what did you mean in going into the fight?"

"Young man, what we meant in going for those red-coats, was this: we always had governed ourselves and we always meant to. They didn't mean we should."

In other words, it was an idea, a principle — belief in self-government — for which this New England yeoman and his fellow-countrymen were fighting.

In the same manner, the men who urged and framed and advocated the Constitution were striving for an idea, an ideal — belief in a National Union, and a determination to maintain it, and the men who opposed

[1] *John Adams, the Statesman of the American Revolution* (1898), by Mellen Chamberlain, p. 248, interview with Capt. Levi Preston of Danvers, Mass., in 1837.

the Constitution were also fighting for the preservation of an idea — self-rule as opposed to control by a central government which they feared would destroy their local governments. Historians who leave these factors out of account and who contend that these men were moved chiefly by economic conditions utterly fail to interpret their character and their acts. To appreciate the patriotic sincerity of the motives which inspired the framing of the Constitution, it is necessary to read the hopes and fears of the leading American statesmen prior to 1787, as expressed in their own words. Thomas Jefferson wrote, one hundred years ago, that "the opening scenes of our present government" would not be "seen in their true aspect until the letters of the day, now held in private hoards, shall be broken up and laid open to public use." [1] Within the last thirty-five years, these letters have been very fully published; and unless their authors, in writing to intimate personal friends, were expressing one reason for desiring a change in the form of government, while in fact moved by other and more selfish reasons, then these letters must portray, with accuracy, the motives which led the writers to advocate a new Constitution. These letters, moreover, embody the principles on which the new Government was to be built — principles which were distinctively American and little connected with economics.

The actual evils which led to the Federal Convention of 1787 are familiar to every reader of history and need no detailed description here. As is well known, they arose, in general, first, from lack of power in the Government of the Confederation to legislate and enforce at home such authority as it possessed, or to maintain abroad its credit or position as a sovereign Nation; second, from State legislation unjust to

[1] Jefferson to William Johnson, June 12, 1823.

citizens and productive of dissensions with neighboring
States—the State laws particularly complained of being
those staying process of the Courts, making property
a tender in payment of debts, issuing paper money,
interfering with foreclosure of mortgages, setting aside
judgments of the Courts, interfering with private concerns, imposing commercial restrictions on goods and
citizens of other States.[1]   The Articles of Confederation
as agreed upon by the Continental Congress on November 15, 1777, had provided for a Government consisting
simply of a Congress with a single House, in which each
State had equal representation — a Government having
no Executive and no adequate Court — a Government
in which Congress had no power to tax, to raise troops,
to regulate commerce, or to execute or enforce its own
laws and treaties—a Government in which each of the
various States had power to tax, to make its own money,
to impose its own import and export duties, and to
conform or not, as it chose, to the acts or treaties of
Congress, or to its requisitions for money or troops.
Congress could only supplicate; it could not enforce.

> *Glendower.*   "I can call spirits from the vasty deep."
> *Hotspur.*   "Why, so can I, or so can any man.
> But will they come when you do call for them?"

Such a Government could not operate successfully for
any length of time and there could be no real Union of
the States, except in time of war when need of mutual
protection would prevent undue dissensions.   From

---

[1] For best descriptions of the disastrous conditions of the period 1781 to 1787,
see *Vices of the Political System of the United States, Writings of James Madison*
(Hunt's ed.), II, 361; *History of the United States* (1912), by Edward Channing,
III, and bibliography; *The American States During and After the Revolution 1775–
1789* (1924), by Allan Nevins; *The Rise of American Civilization* (1927), by Charles
A. Beard and Mary R. Beard; *History of the People of the United States*, by John
Bach McMaster, I, 423–427; *History of the Origin, Formation, and Adoption of the
Constitution* (1854–1858), by George Ticknor Curtis; *History of the Formation of the
Constitution* (1882), by George Bancroft; *Narrative and Critical History of America*
(ed. by Justin Winsor), VII, chap. 3 and authorities cited; *The Critical Period of
American History* (1888), by John Fiske.

the very outset, and long before economic disturbances had arisen in the States, the voices of American statesmen were heard urging upon the people the necessity of a change. Even before the whole thirteen States had decided to ratify the Articles, Alexander Hamilton formulated the additional authority which Congress ought to possess; and in this comprehensive document, written in 1780 (when he was only twenty-three years old), he anticipated most of the powers which were granted, seven years later, by the Constitution.[1] The ink was scarcely dry on the signatures of the delegates from Maryland — the last of the thirteen States to sign the Articles (on March 1, 1781) — when James Madison, James Duane of New York, and James M. Varnum of Rhode Island were appointed a Committee to report on needful changes.[2] This Committee

[1] Hamilton to James Duane, Sept. 3, 1780. Amongst other things, Hamilton wrote: "The Confederation, in my opinion, should give Congress complete sovereignty, except as to that part of internal police which relates to the rights of property and life among individuals and to raising money by internal taxes. It is necessary that everything belonging to this should be regulated by the State Legislatures. Congress should have complete sovereignty in all that relates to war, peace, trade, and finance; and to the management of foreign affairs, the right of declaring war; of raising armies, officering, paying them, directing their motions in every respect, of equipping fleets and doing the same with them; of building fortifications, arsenals, magazines, etc., etc.; of making peace on such conditions as they think proper; of regulating trade, determining with what countries it shall be carried on; granting indulgencies; laying prohibitions on all the articles of export or import; imposing duties, granting bounties and premiums for raising, exporting, or importing and applying to their own use, the product of these duties — only giving credit to the States on whom they are raised in the general account of revenues and expenses; instituting Admiralty Courts, etc.; of coining money; establishing banks on such terms and with such privileges as they think proper; appropriating funds, and doing whatever also relates to the operations of finance; transacting everything with foreign nations; making alliances, offensive and defensive, treaties of commerce, etc., etc." See also his series of essays entitled *The Continentalist*, published in Loudon's *New York Packet*, July 12, 1781, July 4, 1782, *Works of Alexander Hamilton* (Lodge's ed., 1903), I.

[2] It is interesting to note the convivial manner in which the final ratification of the Confederation was celebrated. The Committee which announced it, Feb. 28, 1781, recommended "that the Congress adjourn after completing the Confederation; and the President shall invite the Minister of France, the Speaker and Members of the General Assembly, the Vice President and Members of the Supreme Executive Council and the officers of the Army and Navy to drink a glass of wine to 'The United States of America', a keg of biscuits in the room of cakes. To be in the Hall where Congress sits." *Journals of the Continental Congress.*

recommended vesting power in Congress to employ the
Continental army and navy "to compel any delinquent
State to fulfill its Federal engagement, by restraining its
vessels, merchandise, and trade."[1] Another Committee, consisting of Edmund Randolph of Virginia,
Oliver Ellsworth of Connecticut and James M. Varnum,
five months later, in August, 1781, reported a long list
of additional powers for Congress, as necessary in order
to make the Government efficient, among which was the
important suggestion that Congress be authorized "to
distrain the property of a State delinquent in its assigned proportion of men and money." No action
was ever taken on this Report.[2] A year later a strong
appeal made by Robert Morris, Superintendent of
Finance, that Congress be granted power to levy excise,
land, and poll taxes, to discharge the Government debts
was adversely reported on by a Congressional Committee. In 1783, Congress rejected a motion by
Alexander Hamilton and James Wilson that that body
should be given power to levy a land tax; but, a month
later, Congress voted to ask the States to grant to it the
power to levy import duties.

It is also to be noted that the idea of a Convention
to revise and amend the Articles of Confederation was
no new thing in the year 1787. It had been in the
minds of the leading American statesmen, and long
before any economic evils appeared in the various
States.[3] It arose from their patriotic desire for a united

[1] *Journals of the Continental Congress*, March 1, 6, May 2, July 20, Aug. 22, 1781;
Aug. 5, 1782; April 18, 1783.

[2] As early as Jan. 20, 1778, Judge William Henry Drayton, in the South Carolina
Assembly, had noted the lack of any power in Congress to enforce its recommendations or requisitions, and had proposed as an amendment to the Articles of Confederation that: in case any of the States should in any respect violate the Articles,
"the Congress shall within one year thereafter declare such State under the ban of
the Confederacy, and by the utmost vigor of arms shall forthwith proceed against
such State until it shall have paid due obedience, upon which the ban shall be taken
off and the State shall be restored to the benefits of this Confederacy." See
Principles and Acts of the Revolution (1822), by Hezekiah Niles.

[3] See esp. *Magazine of American History* (1883), X, 410–411; *Constitutional*

Nation, able to take its place with the other Nations of the world. As Edmund Randolph of Virginia strikingly said: "The American spirit ought to be mixed with American pride, to see the Union magnificently triumphant." What they chiefly feared were dissensions of the States and dissolution of the Union, leaving the States open to attack by foreign power. What they desired was to frame some form of Government which, while safeguarding the liberties of the citizens and the rights of the States, should have power to maintain adequately its own authority and independence. These were the objects which occupied all their correspondence. Conventions of the delegates from various States had gathered several times prior to 1787. In 1777, a Convention from New York and the New England States met at Springfield; in 1778, at New Haven, New Jersey and Pennsylvania were represented in addition to New York and New England. In 1780, New York and New England met at Hartford and suggested a General Convention to revise the Articles.[1]

History of the United States (1901), by Francis N. Thorpe, I, 248–254. See also a pamphlet by a William Barton (a Philadelphia merchant) published in May, 1781, urging such a Convention; *Pelatiah Webster and the Constitution*, by Gaillard Hunt, *The Nation*, Dec. 28, 1911.

[1] Madison in his notes of the debates in Congress, April 1, 1783, wrote on the subject of Conventions: "Mr. Gorham called for the order of the day, to wit the Report on Revenue, etc., and observed, as a cogent reason for hastening that business, that the Eastern States at the invitation of the Legislature of Massachusetts were with N. Y. about to form a Convention for regulating matters of common concern. . . . Mr. Mercer expressed great disquietude at this information and considered it as a dangerous precedent. . . . Mr. Osgood said that the sole object was to guard against an interference of taxes among States whose local situation required such precaution. . . . that nothing was intended that could be drawn within the purview of the Federal Articles. Mr. Bland said he had always considered those Conventions as improper and contravening the spirit of the Federal Government. He said they had the appearance of young Congresses. Mr. Madison and Mr. Hamilton disapproved of these partial Conventions, not as absolute violations of the Confederacy but as ultimately leading to them, and in the mean time exciting pernicious jealousies; the latter observing that he wished instead of them to see a General Convention take place and that he should soon, in pursuance of instructions from his constituents, propose to Congress a plan for that purpose, the object would be to strengthen the Federal Constitution. Mr. White informed Congress that New Hampshire had declined to accede to a plan of Convention on foot. Mr. Higginson said that no gentleman would be alarmed, at

The earliest call for a General Convention came from the Legislature of New York in 1782, under the leadership of Alexander Hamilton and General Philip Schuyler. In 1783, the Continental Congress appointed a Committee to consider these New York resolutions for a Convention, but no further action was ever taken.[1] In 1783 also, Washington wrote to Dr. William Gordon suggesting a Convention of the People, as follows:[2]

"To suppose that the general concerns of this country can be directed by thirteen heads, or one head without competent powers, is a solecism, the bad effects of which every man who has had the practical knowledge to judge from, that I have, is fully convinced of; tho' none perhaps has felt them in so forcible and distressing a degree. The People at large, and at a distance from the theatre of action, who only know that the machine was kept in motion, and that they are at last arrived at the first object of their wishes, are satisfied with the event, without investigating the causes of the slow progress to it, or of the expenses which have accrued, and which they have been unwilling to pay — great part of which has arisen from that want of energy in the Federal Constitution, which I am complaining of, and which I wish to see given to it by a Convention of the People, instead of hearing it remarked that, as we have worked through an arduous contest with the powers Congress already have (but which, by the by, have been gradually diminishing) why should they be invested with more? . . . For Heaven's sake, who are Congress? Are they not the

any rate; for it was pretty certain that the Convention would not take place. He wished with Mr. Hamilton to see a General Convention for the purpose of revising and amending the Federal Government." *Writings of James Madison* (Hunt's ed.) I.

[1] The Congress postponed action on the proposal for a Convention, Sept. 2, 1783. George Bancroft in his *History of the Formation of the Constitution of the United States of America* (1882), I, cites Pennsylvania, Virginia, and Maryland papers of July, 1783, as endorsing a Continental Convention. Madison wrote to Jefferson as early as December 10, 1783, that George Mason of Virginia was "sound and ripe on the article of a Convention for revising our form of Government, and I think would not decline a participation in the work."

[2] Washington to Dr. William Gordon, July 8, 1783. *Writings of George Washington* (Ford's ed.) IX.

creatures of the People, amenable to them for their conduct, and dependent from day to day on their breath? Where then can be the danger of giving them such powers as are adequate to the great ends of Government and to all the general purposes of the Confederation (I repeat the word general, because I am no advocate for their having to do with the particular policy of any State, further than it concerns the Union at large)."

In 1784, Richard Henry Lee, then President of the Congress, wrote to Madison: "It is by many here suggested as a very necessary step for Congress to take, the calling on the States to form a Convention for the sole purpose of revising the Confederation so far as to enable Congress to execute with more energy, effect, and vigor the powers assigned to it," [1] and Madison replied to him: "I have not yet found leisure to scan the project of a Continental Convention with so close an eye as to have made up any observations worthy of being mentioned to you. In general, I hold it for a maxim that the Union of the States is essential to their safety against foreign danger and internal contention, and that the perpetuity and efficacy of the present system cannot be confided in." In 1785, the Massachusetts Legislature passed Resolutions, in response to a message from Governor James Bowdoin, recommending to Congress the calling of a General Convention.

Meanwhile, the sentiments and motives which inspired the desire for a change in the form of Government may be seen in the letters of Washington, Hamilton, Jay, Madison, Jefferson and many others, both in

[1] Richard Henry Lee to Madison, Nov. 26, 1784; Madison to R. H. Lee, Dec. 25, 1784. Mann Page of Fredericksburg, Va., wrote to R. H. Lee, Dec. 14, 1784: "I think it would be wise in Congress to recommend to the States the calling of a Convention for the sole purpose of amending the Confederation. At present, the Supreme Council of the Union is so feeble that they have no weight in Government. Their recommendations are slighted and their wisest plans are subject to be rejected by any one petty insignificant State refusing to accept them." *Omitted Chapters of History Disclosed in the Life and Papers of Edmund Randolph* (1881), by Moncure D. Conway, p. 61.

the South and the North. Washington, more than any other man, was responsible for calling the attention of the people to the defects of the Confederation. His letters were filled with appeals for a remedy.[1] As early as July, 1780, he wrote: "Our measures are not under the influence and direction of one Council, but thirteen, each of which is actuated by local views and politics. . . . We are attempting the impossible." In December, 1780, he wrote that "there are two things (as I have often declared) which, in my opinion, are indispensably necessary to the well-being and good government of our public affairs; these are greater powers to Congress and more responsibility and permanency in the Executive bodies." In 1782, he wrote that if the powers of Congress were not enlarged, "anarchy and confusion must ensue." In 1783, he wrote that: "The experience, which is purchased at the price of difficulties and distress, will alone convince us that the honor, power, and true interest of this country must be measured by a Continental scale, and that every departure therefrom weakens the Union, and may ultimately break the band which holds us together. To avert these evils, to form a Constitution that will give consistency, stability, and dignity to the Union and sufficient powers to the great Council of the Nation for general purposes, is a duty which is incumbent upon every man who wishes well to his Country, and will meet with my aid as far as it can be rendered in the private walks of life." On June 8, 1783, he sent

[1] From among the very numerous letters of Washington on the subject, the following should be especially noted: to Fielding Lewis, July 6, 1780; James Duane, Dec. 26, 1780; R. R. Livingston, Jan. 31, 1781; John Sullivan, Feb. 4, 1781; John Mathews, Feb. 14, 1781; Philip Schuyler, Feb. 20, 1781; John P. Custis, Feb. 28, 1781; William Gordon, March 9, 1781; Joseph Jones, March 24, 1781; Jacob Armstrong, March 26, 1781; Gen. Greene, March 31, 1781; Tench Tilghman, April 24, 1782; Archibald Cary, June 15, 1782; B. Harrison, March 4, 1783; A. Hamilton, March 4, 1783; Lafayette, April 5, 1783; William Gordon, July 8, 1783; B. Harrison, Jan. 18, 1784; James McHenry, Aug. 22, 1785; James Warren, Oct. 7, 1785; James Madison, Nov. 30, 1785; David Stuart, Nov. 30, 1785.

to the Governors of the States a message in which
he said :

"There are four things, which, I humbly conceive, are
essential to the well-being, I may even venture to say, to
the existence of the United States, as an independent power.
First.   An indissoluble union of the States under one Federal head; secondly.   A sacred regard to public justice;
thirdly.   The adoption of a proper peace establishment;
and, fourthly.   The prevalence of that pacific and friendly
disposition among the people of the United States, which
will induce them to forget their local prejudices and policies ;
to make those mutual concessions, which are requisite to
the general prosperity; and in some instances, to sacrifice
their individual advantages to the interest of the community.
These are the pillars on which the glorious fabric of our independency and National character must be supported."

And these views, he continued to express in the ensu-
ing years, through a voluminous correspondence with
friends in the various States.   The letters of other
leading Americans showed a realization that a truly
National Government which should promote the
Union of the States was imperative.   John Jay of New
York wrote to Gouverneur Morris of Pennsylvania,
September 24, 1783 : [1]

"I am perfectly convinced that no time is to be lost in
raising and maintaining a National spirit in America.
Power to govern the Confederacy, as to all general purposes,
should be granted and exercised.   The governments of the
different States should be wound up, and become vigorous.
America is beheld with jealousy, and jealousy is seldom idle.
Settle your boundaries without delay.   It is better that some
improper limits should be fixed, than any left in dispute.   In
a word, everything conducive to union and constitutional
energy of government should be cultivated, cherished and
protected, and all counsels and measures of a contrary com-

[1] See Jay to Robert R. Livingston, July 19, 1783; Jay to John Adams, Oct. 14,
1785.

plexion should at least be suspected of impolitic views and objects."

Governor John Hancock, in his Message to the Massachusetts Legislature in September, 1783, said: "How to strengthen and improve the Union so as to render it completely adequate, demands the immediate attention of these States. Our very existence as a free nation is suspended upon it." Thomas Jefferson wrote to Madison, in 1784: "I find the conviction growing strongly that nothing can preserve our Confederacy unless the bond of union, their common Council, be strengthened." [1] And to Monroe, Jefferson wrote in 1785: "The interests of the States ought to be made joint in every possible instance, in order to cultivate the idea of our being one Nation." [2] Stephen Higginson, a former Member of Congress from Massachusetts, wrote to John Adams, December 30, 1785, that: "Experience and observation most clearly evince that in their habits, manners, and commercial interests, the Southern and Northern States are not only very dissimilar, but in many instances directly opposed. Happy for America would it be if there was a greater coincidence of sentiment and interest among them. Then we might expect those National arrangements soon to take place which appear so essential to our safety and happiness." [3]

[1] Edward Bancroft wrote to W. W. Frazer, May 28, 1784: "In every one of the States, government is too feeble to command either respect or obedience; and the powers of Congress are still more inadequate to the support of the Confederation. Of this, all reasonable men in the Middle States are now convinced; and Mr. Jefferson is just now informed, as he tells me, that the great leader of the Virginians, Mr. Patrick Henry, who has been violently opposed to every idea of increasing the powers of Congress, is convinced of his error, and has within these few days pledged himself to Mr. Madison, Mr. Jones, and others, to support a plan which they are to prepare and propose to the Legislature of Virginia for amending the Confederation by a further concession of powers to Congress; but I do not believe that this or any other plan for this purpose will ever be adopted, even by a majority, much less by all the United States." *Bancroft*, II, 367.

[2] See also Monroe to Jefferson, June 16, 1784, Aug. 15, 1785; Monroe to Madison, June 26, 1785, Feb. 9, 11, 1786.

[3] *Letters of Stephen Higginson, Amer. Hist. Ass. Report* (1896), I, 704 *et seq.* Of the attitude of men of the different sections of the Union towards each other, the

Such were the sentiments which prevailed among the public men of the country, prior to the year 1786, as to the necessity of some alteration in the form of their Government which should promote a more perfect National Union. The first step towards a Convention to frame such an alteration was taken on January 21, 1786, when the Virginia Legislature, at the suggestion of James Madison, passed a Resolution inviting the States to send Commissioners to meet in Convention:

"to take into consideration the trade of the United States; to examine the relative situations and trade of the States; to consider how far a uniform system in their commercial regulations may be necessary to their common interest and their permanent harmony; and to report to the several States such an act relative to this great object, as, when unanimously ratified by them, will enable the United States in Congress effectually to provide for the same."

This was a very restricted step towards a thorough revision of the Articles of Confederation — but it was a step; and Madison wrote to James Monroe, March 19, 1786: "The efforts for bringing about a correction thro the medium of Congress have miscarried. Let a Convention, then, be tried. . . . If the present

following letters are illustrative. Elbridge Gerry of Massachusetts wrote to Rufus King, May 9, 1785: "What is the matter with Virginia? Their attachments to their opinions originate, I fear, from mistaken ideas of their own importance. They have certainly many good qualities; but has not their ambition been bribed by artifice and flattery to besiege and undermine their reason and good policy?" Gerry also wrote to King, May 27, 1785, as to Connecticut: "The Devil is in that State. They are like a young Puritan . . . who, having been trammeled with piety from his birth and been just freed from his domestic confinement, runs into every excess, religious, moral and political." *Life and Correspondence of Rufus King* (1894), I.

Ephraim Paine of Vermont, writing to Robert R. Livingston from Annapolis, May 24, 1784, as to the dissensions between the sections said: "I expected in Congress to find Justice sit enthroned, supported by all the virtues. Judge, then, how great was my disappointment when I found caballing, selfishness, and injustice reign almost perpetually. . . . The Southern nabobs behave as though they viewed themselves a superior order of animals when compared with those of the other end of the Confederacy; this, sir, you know, does not agree with the great spirits of the Northern gentry, and unless a new disposition takes place, some important matters must be left undone, or they will be ill done." *Bancroft*, II, 364.

paroxysm of our affairs be totally neglected, our case may become desperate. If anything comes of the Convention, it will probably be of a permanent not a temporary nature, which I think will be a great point."

To Jefferson, Madison wrote at the same time, March 18, 1786:

"The States are every day giving proofs that separate regulations are more likely to set them by the ears than to attain the common object. When Massachusetts set on foot a retaliation of the policy of Great Britain, Connecticut declared her ports free. New Jersey served New York in the same way. And Delaware I am told has lately followed the example in opposition to the commercial plans of Pennsylvania. A miscarriage of this attempt to unite the States in some effectual plan will have another effect of a serious nature. It will dissipate every prospect of drawing a steady revenue from our imposts. . . . Another unhappy effect of a continuance of the present anarchy of our commerce will be a continuance of the unfavorable balance on it, which, by draining us of our metals, furnishes pretexts for the pernicious substitution of paper money, for indulgences to debtors, for postponement of taxes. In fact most of our political evils may be traced up to our commercial ones, as most of our moral may to our political. . . . I almost despair of success. It is necessary, however, that something should be tried . . . and if the present crisis cannot effect unanimity, from what future concurrence of circumstances is it to be expected?"

To Washington, Jay set forth his views of the proposed Convention called by Virginia:[1]

"Experience has pointed out errors in our National Government which call for correction, and which threaten to blast the fruit we expected from our tree of liberty. The Convention proposed by Virginia may do some good and perhaps do more if it comprehended more objects. An opinion begins to prevail that a General Convention for

[1] See letters of Jay to Adams, Feb. 22, 1786, and to Washington, Jan. 16, March 16, 1786, June 27, 1786; letters of Washington to Jay, May 18, Aug. 1, 1786.

revising the Articles of Confederation would be expedient. Whether the people are yet ripe for such a measure, or whether the system proposed to be attained by it is only to be expected from calamity and commotion, is difficult to ascertain. I think we are in a delicate situation, and a variety of considerations and circumstances give me uneasiness. It is in contemplation to take measures for forming a General Convention; the plan is not matured. If it should be well concerted and take effect, I am fervent in my wishes that it may comport with the line of life you have marked out for yourself to favour your country with your counsels on such an important and signal occasion."

To this, Washington replied: "I scarcely know what opinion to entertain of a General Convention. That it is necessary to revise and amend the Articles of Confederation, I entertain no doubt; but what may be the consequences of such an attempt is doubtful. Yet something must be done or the fabric must fall; it is certainly tottering." A month later, June 27, Jay wrote to Washington, expressing a fear lest the evils of the existing form of Government might drive many men into anti-republican views, and he said: "What I most fear is that the better kind of people (by which I mean the people who are orderly and industrious, who are content with their situations, and not uneasy in their circumstances) will be led, by the insecurity of property, the loss of confidence in their rulers, and the want of public faith and rectitude, to consider the charms of liberty as imaginary and delusive. A state of fluctuation and uncertainty must disgust and alarm such men, and prepare their minds for almost any change that may promise them quiet and security." To this, Washington replied:

"Your sentiments, that our affairs are drawing rapidly to a crisis, accord with my own. What the event will be is also beyond the reach of my foresight. . . . I do not conceive we can exist long as a nation without having lodged

here for some time past, he will attend the Convention. He does not discover or propose any other plan than that of investing Congress with full powers for the regulation of commerce foreign and domestic. But this power will run deep into the authorities of the individual States, and can never be well exercised without a Federal Judicial. The reform must necessarily be extensive."

Meanwhile, Congress itself was alarmed at the growing dissensions among the States and the people.[1] On February 15, 1786, a Committee of Congress composed of Rufus King of Massachusetts, Charles Pinckney of South Carolina, James Monroe of Virginia, John Kean of South Carolina and Charles Pettit of Pennsylvania reported that "the crisis has arrived when the people of the United States . . . must decide whether they will support their rank as a nation, by maintaining the public faith at home and abroad; or whether, for want of a timely exertion in establishing a general revenue and thereby giving strength to the Confederacy, they will hazard not only the existence of the Union, but of those great and invaluable privileges for which they have so arduously and so honorably contended." And on May 13, Pinckney moved in Congress for the appointment of a general Committee on the affairs of the Nation. "Congress must be invested with greater powers," he said, "or the Federal Government must

[1] Francis N. Thorpe in his *Constitutional History of the United States*, I, 279, says: "The last blow was now struck against the credit of the Confederation. When New Jersey had approved the Articles, it had insisted that the sole and exclusive power of regulating the trade with foreign nations ought to be clearly vested in Congress, and from this opinion it had never receded. It resented the power of New York to collect taxes from the inhabitants of New Jersey through the port of New York City, and now its Assembly voted to pay no part of its quota, one hundred and sixty-six thousand dollars, until all the States had consented to the Federal impost. Fully aware of the irremedial and disastrous consequence of this decision, Congress speedily sent a committee [Charles Pinckney, Nathaniel Gorham and William Grayson] to the New Jersey Legislature to urge its compliance with the requisition. Charles Pinckney, the chairman of the committee, in a powerful speech to its Assembly urged it to call a General Convention of the States for the purpose of increasing the powers of the Federal Government and not to precipitate a dissolution of the Union by refusing to help carry it on."

fall. It is therefore necessary for Congress either to appoint a Convention for that purpose, or by requisition to call on the States for such powers as are necessary to enable it to administer the Federal Government." William Grayson, a Member of Congress from Virginia, wrote to Madison from New York, in March, 1786 : [1]

"There has been some serious thought in the minds of some of the Members of Congress to recommend the meeting of a General Convention to consider of an alteration of the Confederation, and there is a motion to this effect now under consideration. It is contended that the present Confederation is utterly inefficient and that if it remains much longer in its present state of imbecility, we shall be one of the most contemptible Nations on the face of the earth. For my own part, I have not yet made up my mind on the subject. I am doubtful whether it is not better to bear those ills we have, than fly to others we know not of. I am, however, in no doubt about the weakness of the Fœderal Government."

On August 7, 1786, a sub-Committee of Congress, headed by Charles Pinckney, reported a set of proposed amendments to the Articles of Confederation. As Congress, however, took no action on the matter, the Convention which had been called by Virginia and which was to meet at Annapolis in September was looked to by many as a source of hope. That it would be forced to deal with the political as well as the commercial situation was anticipated both in the North and the South. Stephen Higginson of Massachusetts wrote to John Adams, in July, 1786: "The ostensible object of that Convention is the regulation of commerce, but when I consider the men who are deputed from New York, Pennsylvania, and Virginia, and the source from whence the proposition was made, I am strongly in-

[1] *Writings of James Madison* (1901), II, 404 note, W. Grayson to Madison, March 22, 1786.

clined to think political objects are intended to be combined with commercial, if they do not principally engross their attention. . . . Few of them have been in the commercial line, nor is it probable they know or care much about commercial objects. . . . If it be practicable to effect a general regulation of trade and to harmonize the apparently variant interests of the States, it will probably be done by the Convention. I shall be happy to have it effected." William Grayson had already written to Madison in May, from New York : that even if "the Eastern people mean nothing more than to carry the commercial point," nevertheless, "the State of Virginia, having gone thus far, it is matter of great doubt to me whether she had not better go farther and propose to the other States to augment the powers of the delegates so as to comprehend all the grievances of the Union and to combine the commercial arrangements with them and make them dependent on each other." James Monroe wrote to Madison from New York, in September : "I consider the Convention at Annapolis as a most important era in our affairs. The Eastern men, be assured, mean it as leading further than the object originally comprehended. . . . I have always considered the regulation of trade in the hands of the United States as necessary to preserve the Union. Without it, it will infallibly tumble to pieces."[1] And Madison wrote to Jefferson, in August : "Many gentlemen both within and without Congress wish to make this meeting subservient to a plenipotentiary Convention for amending the Confederation. Tho my wishes are in favor of such

---

[1] Higginson to J. Adams, July, 1786, *Amer. Hist. Ass. Report* (1896), I; Grayson to Madison, May 28, 1786; Monroe to Madison, Sept. 3, 1786; Madison to Jefferson, Aug. 12, 1786. Monroe had written to Jefferson as to the Convention, May 11, 1786: "Of its success, I must confess I have some hopes. The investigation of the subject will always be of advantage, since truth and sound State policy in every instance will urge the commission of the power to the United States."

an event, yet I despair so much of its accomplishment at
the present crisis, that I do not extend my views beyond
a commercial reform. To speak the truth, I almost
despair even of this."

When the Convention assembled, it was found that
only New York, New Jersey, Pennsylvania, Delaware,
and Virginia were represented (by twelve delegates),
and that delegates from New England, Maryland, and
the other three Southern States had either failed to
arrive or to be appointed. Accordingly, the Convention adjourned on September 14, after having
adopted a Report drafted by Alexander Hamilton.
This Report stated that the National circumstances
were " of a nature so serious as, in the view of your Commissioners, to render the situation of the United
States delicate and critical, calling for an exertion of
the united virtue and wisdom of all the members of the
Confederacy"; and it concluded with the important
recommendation that the States should appoint Commissioners to meet at Philadelphia on the second
Monday of May in the succeeding year "to devise such
further provisions as shall appear to them necessary to
render the Constitution of the Fœderal Government
adequate to the exigencies of the Union." [1]

Meanwhile, all patriotic Americans who wished to
see a united country and a real National Union were
now given serious cause for alarm by the increase of
sentiment in many parts of the land for a division of the
States into two or more Confederacies. The fact that
such a dissolution of the existing Confederacy was
believed by many men to be the true remedy for the
unfortunate conditions prevailing in the Government
drove home to many, who had hitherto doubted, the
necessity of summoning together the representatives
of the States in Convention, in an effort to frame an

[1] See Madison to Monroe, Sept. 11, 1786.

adequate Government of the whole. During the past three years, this suggestion that the commercial and political interests and conditions of the Southern, Middle, and Eastern States were so divergent that they could be dealt with, fairly and justly, only by a separation, had been made on many occasions in letters and in newspaper articles.[1] In this year, 1786, the sentiment for such a division had been given great impetus by the serious dissension which arose in Congress, between the States of the South and of the East, over a proposal initiated by John Jay, then Secretary of Foreign Affairs, to relinquish (for a term of years) the right which the United States had long and persistently asserted against Spain to the free navigation of the Mississippi River. This right had been a cardinal principle with the Southern States and especially with Virginia; and the suggestion that its maintenance might now be abandoned, through the votes of the Northern States headed by Massachusetts, aroused hot excitement.[2] The dangerous situation was described by James Monroe (then a Member of Congress

[1] As early as 1783, Edward Bancroft wrote to William Frazier, from Philadelphia: "Should the Confederation be dissolved, it is a question whether we shall have thirteen separate States in alliance, or whether the New England, the Middle, and the Southern States will form three new Confederacies." *Bancroft*, I, 332. Madison wrote to E. Randolph, Feb. 25, 1783: "A respectable delegate from Massachusetts, a few days ago . . . said that if justice was not to be obtained thro general Confederacy, the sooner it was known, the better, that some States might be forming other Confederacies adequate to the purpose. . . . Unless some amenable and adequate arrangements be speedily taken for adjusting all the subsisting accounts and discharging the public engagements, a dissolution of the Union will be inevitable." In 1784, Richard D. Spaight of North Carolina wrote to Governor Martin that in his view, the New England States had tried to weaken the Union to increase their own importance, and that they were pressing so hard upon the national framework that "I imagine it will break before they are well aware of it." *North Carolina State Records*, XVII, 173–175. In 1785, Rufus King of Massachusetts expressed an opinion that the eight Northern States might quarrel decisively with the five Southern States over the Congressional regulation of trade, "and in the event must form a sub-Confederation, remedied of all their present embarrassment." *Life and Correspondence of Rufus King* (1894), I, 112–113.

[2] See especially letter of Madison to Jefferson, Aug. 12, 1786; and letters of Monroe to Madison, May 21, Aug. 10, 14, Sept. 3, 1786; to Jefferson, July 16, Aug. 19, 1786; to Patrick Henry, Aug. 12, 1786.

from Virginia). Writing to Madison, August 14, 1786, he said: "It is manifest here that Jay and his party in Congress are determined to pursue this business as far as possible, either as the means of throwing the Western people and territory without the government of the United States and keeping the weight of population and government here, or of dismembering the Government itself, for the purpose of a separate Confederacy. There can be no other object than one of these, and I am, from such evidence as I have, doubtful which hath the influence." And to Jefferson, he wrote August 19: "I am sorry to inform you that our affairs are daily falling into a worse situation, arising more from the intrigues of designing men than any real defect in our system or distress of our affairs. The same party who advocate this business [of the Mississippi River] have certainly held in this city Committees for dismembering the Confederacy, and throwing the States eastward the Hudson into one Government. As yet, this business hath not gone far, but that there should be a party in its favor, and a man heretofore so well respected but in my opinion so little known, engaged in it, is to me very alarming." [1] And to Patrick Henry he wrote:

"Certain it is that Committees are held, in this town, of Eastern men and others of this State upon the subject of a dismemberment of the States East of the Hudson from the Union and the erection of them into a separate government. To what lengths they have gone I know not, but have assurances as to the truth of the above position, with this addition

[1] Monroe wrote to Madison, Sept. 3, 1786: "They have even sought a dismemberment to the Potomack, and those of the party here have been sounding those in office thus far. . . . If a dismemberment takes place, that State (Pennsylvania) must not be added to the Eastern scale. It were as well to use force to prevent it as to defend ourselves afterwards." Monroe wrote to Jefferson, July 16, 1786: "The Massachusetts delegates, except the President [Nathaniel Gorham] whose talents and merits have been greatly overrated (tho preferable greatly in the latter instance to his brethren), are without exception the most illiberal I have ever seen from that State. Two of these men whose names are Dane and King are elected for the next year which is my motive for making known to you this circumstance."

to it that the measure is talked of in Mass. familiarly, and is supposed to have originated there. The plan of the Government in all its modifications has even been contemplated by them. I am persuaded these people who are in Congress from that State (at the head of the other business) mean that as a step toward the carriage of this, as it will so displease some of them as to prepare the States for this event. . . . Be assured as to all the subjects upon which I have given you information above, it hath been founded on authentic documents. I trust these intrigues are confined to a few only, but by these men I am assured are not."

Monroe was probably unjustified in believing that Jay of New York or Nathan Dane or Rufus King (the Massachusetts Congressmen) were in favor of division of the Union; but it was unquestionably true that an increasing number of men in the different States were coming to believe in such a dismemberment as the only solution for their political problems. As early as February 11, 1786, General Benjamin Lincoln of Massachusetts had written to King, describing at length the different interests of the States, and concluding : [1]

"If the observations I have made are just, the citizens of these States are deceiving themselves, in an expectation that any relief can, or will, be granted them by Congress, under our present system of government. . . . That our interests do and will clash, are troubles which will not be questioned. These are the necessary consequences of our great extent, of our difference of climate, productions, views, etc. I do not see how we shall surmount the evils under which we now labor, and prevent our falling into the utmost confusion, disgrace, and ruin, but by a division, which might be formed upon such principles as would secure our public creditors, and thereby our public faith, and our after-peace and safety by a firm alliance between the divisions."

[1] *Life and Correspondence of Rufus King* (1894), I, 156 *et seq.*; see also King to Gerry, Aug. 13, 1786.

And Theodore Sedgwick of Massachusetts wrote to Caleb Strong, August 6, 1786 : [1]

"No reasonable expectations of advantage can be formed from the Commercial Convention. The first proposers designed none. The measure was originally brought forward with an intention of defeating the enlargement of the powers of Congress. Of this, I have the most decisive evidence. It well becomes the Eastern and Middle States, who are in interest one, seriously to consider what advantages result to them from their connection with the Southern States. They can give us nothing, as an equivalent for the protection which they derive from us, but a participation in their commerce. This they deny to us. Should their conduct continue the same, and I think there is not any prospect of an alteration, an attempt to perpetuate our connection with them, which act too will be found ineffectual, will sacrifice everything to a mere chimera. Even the appearance of a Union, cannot, in the way we now are, be long preserved. It becomes us seriously to contemplate a substitute; for if we do not controul events we shall be miserably controulled by them. No other substitute can be devised than that of contracting the limits of the Confederacy to such as are natural and reasonable, and within those limits, instead of a nominal, to institute a real and an efficient Government."

Dr. Benjamin Rush wrote from Philadelphia to Dr. Richard Price, in London, October 27, 1786 : [2]

"Some of our enlightened men who begin to despair of a more complete union of the States in Congress have secretly proposed an Eastern, Middle and Southern Confederacy, to

[1] *American Historical Review* (1899), IV.

[2] *Price Papers* in *Mass. Hist. Soc. Proc. 2d Series* (1903), XVI. The *Pennsylvania Journal*, May 16, 1787, published Price's reply as follows: "The newspapers which you sent me were very acceptable; the essays and information they contain have contributed towards gratifying a curiosity which I am always feeling with respect to the affairs of the United States. Your Federal Government is a point of great difficulty and importance which I find still remains unsettled. I dread the thoughts of such a division of the States into three Confederacies, as you say had been talked of. It is a pity that some general controuling power cannot be established, of sufficient vigour to decide disputes, to regulate commerce, to prevent

be united by an alliance offensive and defensive. These
Confederacies, they say, will be united by nature, by interest, and by manners, and consequently they will be safe,
agreeable, and durable. The first will include the four New
England States and New York. The second will include
New Jersey, Pennsylvania, Delaware, and Maryland; and
the last Virginia, North and South Carolina, and Georgia.
The foreign and domestic debt of the United States they say
shall be divided justly between each of the new Confederations. This plan of a new Continental Government is at
present a mere speculation. Perhaps necessity, or rather
Divine Providence, may drive us to it."

Madison summed up the situation in his diary,
February 21, 1787, as follows:

"All [Members of Congress] agreed and owned that the
Federal Government in its existing shape was inefficient and
could not last. The members from the Southern and Middle
States seemed generally anxious for some republican organization of the system which should preserve the Union and
give due energy to the Government of it. Mr. Bingham (of
Pennsylvania) alone avowed his wishes that the Confederacy
might be divided into several distinct Confederacies, its
great extent and various interests being incompatible with
a single government. The Eastern Members were suspected
by some of leaning towards some anti-republican establishment (the result of their late confusions) or of being less desirous or hopeful of preserving the unity of the empire. For
the first time, the idea of separate Confederacies had got
into the newspapers. It appeared today under a Boston
head. Whatever the views of the leading men in the East-

wars, and to constitute a Union that shall have weight and credit. At present, the
power of Congress, in Europe, is an object of derision rather than respect. The
tumults in New England, the weakness of Congress, and the knavery of the Rhode
Island Legislature form subjects of triumph in this country. The conclusion is
that you are falling to pieces and will soon repent your independence."

James Madison wrote to Edmund Randolph, Jan. 10, 1788: "I have for some
time considered him (Patrick Henry) as driving at a Southern Confederacy." To
Jefferson, he wrote, Dec. 9, 1787, that Henry and his followers would probably
contend for such amendments " as strike at the essence of the system and must
lead to an adherence to the principles of the existing Confederation . . . or to a
partition of the Union into several Confederacies."

ern States may be, it would seem that the great body of the people, particularly in Connecticut, are equally indisposed either to dissolve or divide the Confederacy, or to submit to any anti-republican innovations."

This sentiment for dismemberment, however, continued to spread in the spring of 1787. In April, the newspapers in Philadelphia and many other cities published widely the following letter : [1]

"Instead of attempting to amend the present Articles of Confederation with a view to retain them as the form of Government, or instead of attempting one General Government for the whole community of the United States, would it not be preferable to distribute the United States into three Republics, who should enter into a perpetual league and alliance for mutual defence? . . . Reflections on the subject in the abstract would have suggested to us, and our experience has fully convinced us, that there can be only one sovereignty in a government; the notion therefore of a government by confederation between several independent States, each State still retaining its sovereignty, must be abandoned, and with it every attempt to amend the present Articles of Confederation. . . . The National concerns of a people so numerous with a territory so extensive will be proportionally difficult and important. This will require proportionate powers in the administration, especially in the Chief Executive; greater, perhaps, than will consist with the democratic form. ، Our fate, as far as it can depend on human means, is committed to the Convention; as they decide, so will our lot be. It must be the wish of the delegates, and it is certainly both our duty and interest to aid them in the arduous business intrusted to them."

And a Massachusetts newspaper stated that the same suggestion for a division of the Confederacy had appeared in Southern newspapers : [2]

---

[1] *Independent Gazetteer*, March 30; *Freeman's Journal*, April 11; *Pennsylvania Journal*, April 16; *Massachusetts Centinel*, April 18, 1787. See also *Pennsylvania Gazette*, June 29, 1787.

[2] *Massachusetts Centinel*, April 1, 1787. The *New York Daily Advertiser*, Feb. 23, 1787, quoted a Boston dispatch suggesting that Massachusetts refuses to let the

"A hint has, in the Southern papers, been suggested to the
Deputies to the Federal Convention on the propriety of
recommending a dissolution of the Confederation and a
division of the States into four Republicks — the first, to
contain the States of New Hampshire, Massachusetts,
Rhode Island and Connecticut, to which Vermont might
be added — the second to contain New York, New Jersey,
Delaware, Pennsylvania and Maryland — the third, Virginia, the two Carolinas and Georgia. And the fourth to
contain the State of Franklin, Kentucky and the lands lying
on the Ohio. This division seems to be pointed out by cli-
mates whose effect no positive law ever can surpass. The
religion, manners, customs, exports, imports and general
interest of each being then the same, no opposition arising
from difference in these (as at present) would any longer
divide their councils — unanimity would render it secure at
home and respected abroad and promote agriculture, manufactures and commerce."

In addition to their fears as to the growth of this
policy of division into separate Confederacies, those
who were anxious for preservation of the Union were
given a new cause for alarm, in the rise of the Shays
Rebellion in Massachusetts between September, 1786,
and February, 1787.[1] It afforded one more reason, in

jealousy of New York and Pennsylvania keep it bound. "Let the General Court
recall its delegates from the Convention, send its neighbors proposals for a new
Congress speaking for New England, and leave the rest of the Continent to pursue
their own imbecile and disjointed plans."

[1] As to the effect of the Shays Rebellion, see letters of Knox to Washington, Oct.
23, 1786; Jay to Adams, Oct. 4, 1786; Jay to Jefferson, Dec. 14, 1786; Adams to
Jay, Nov. 30, 1786; Jefferson to Carrington, Jan. 16, 1787. Throughout December, 1786, and January, February, and March, 1787, columns of despatches and
letters from Massachusetts appeared in all the leading newspapers. Among them,
there may be especially noted a letter widely copied from the Hampshire Gazette of
Dec. 27, 1786, by one Thomas Grover of Worcester who sympathized with the
insurgents and who accurately summed up their grievances and demands — a revision of the State Constitution so as to eliminate the Senate, members of which were
required to have a high property qualification and to be chosen by electors with
high property qualifications, and which, accordingly, was felt to be not responsive
to the needs of the people — no payment of the face value of Government securities
to speculators purchasing at a discount — the removal of the capital from Boston
into some place more responsive to the appeals of the farmers — reduction of taxes
through sale of the State lands in Maine; payment of the National foreign debt

addition to the many which already existed, for the
meeting of a Convention to consider an adequate
framework for a Government for a united Nation. As
General Henry Knox, then Secretary at War, wrote to
Washington in October:

"This dreadful situation has alarmed every man of principle and property in New England. They start as from a
dream and ask what has been the cause of our delusion?
What is to afford us security against the violence of lawless
men? Our Government must be braced, changed or altered
to secure our lives and property. . . . The men of reflection and principles are determined to endeavor to establish
a government which shall have a power to protect them in
their lawful pursuits, and which will be efficient in all cases
of internal commotions or foreign invasions. They mean
that liberty shall be the basis, a liberty resulting from the
equal and firm administration of the laws. They wish for
a General Government of unity, as they see the local Legislatures must naturally and necessarily tend to retard and
frustrate all General Government."

John Marshall wrote to James Wilkinson in the
succeeding January: [1]

"All is gloom in the Eastern States, Massachusetts is rent
into two factions, and an appeal, I fear, has by this time been
made to the God of battles. . . . Whatever may be the
cause of these dissensions or however they may terminate,
in their present operation they deeply affect the happiness
and reputation of the United States. They will, however,
I presume tend to people the Western world, if you can govern yourselves so wisely as to present a safe retreat to the

by import and excise taxes instead of by direct taxes on lands and polls; abolition of
the Courts of Common Pleas — abolition of deputy sheriffs, and authority to con-
stables to perform sheriff duty "by which means a large swarm of lawyers will be
banished from their wonted haunts, who have been more damage to the people at
large, especially the farmers, than the common, savage beasts of prey." Another
article, copied from a Boston paper, treating "the cause of the present commotion",
said that "the worm at the root of the tree . . . is the shocking mode of taxation,
which cramps industry by oppressing the poor." See *Freeman's Journal*, March 4;
Pennsylvania Gazette, April 8, 1787.

[1] Marshall to Wilkinson, Jan. 5, 1787. *Amer. Hist. Rev.* (1907), XII.

weaker party. These violent, I fear bloody, dissensions in a State I had thought inferior in wisdom and virtue to no one in the Union, added to the strong tendency which the politics of many eminent characters among ourselves have to promote private and public dishonesty, cast a deep shade over that bright prospect which the revolution in America and the establishment of our free Governments had opened to the votaries of liberty throughout the globe. I fear, and there is no opinion more degrading to the dignity of man, that these have truth on their side who say that man is incapable of governing himself, I fear we may live to see another revolution."

This Shays Rebellion, however, has been somewhat over-emphasized by historians as a moving cause of the Federal Convention and of the Constitution; and the desire to protect the propertied interests in the future against such assaults has been alleged by some writers to have been a leading motive inspiring the framers of the Constitution. The desire for the prevention of a recurrence of such a Rebellion was undoubtedly one of the causes for agreement upon the Constitution, but it was by no means the leading motive. It will be noted that the Rebellion did not really become serious before December, 1786; but long before that time, the leading statesmen of the country had determined that a change in the framework of the National Government was absolutely necessary, and they had agreed upon the general lines on which such a change must be made. The Shays Rebellion simply afforded one more proof of the disturbing conditions existing in the States and of the weakness of the Confederacy — which must be remedied if the United States were to continue in existence. As an object lesson, it shocked into action many men who had hitherto been lukewarm towards the subject of a Constitutional Convention.[1]

[1] Stephen Higginson of Massachusetts wrote to General Knox, Nov. 25, 1786: "I never saw so great a change in the public mind, on any occasion, as has lately

The first State to take action in conformity with the suggestions made by the Commissioners who met at Annapolis in September was Virginia. On October 16, 1786, the Assembly of that State voted to send delegates to a Convention to assemble in Philadelphia in the succeeding May. This action was taken largely on pressure from Madison and Washington; and the former wrote to Jefferson, December 4, 1786:

"The recommendation from the meeting at Annapolis of a plenipotentiary Convention in Philadelphia in May next has been well received by the Assembly here. Indeed the evidence of dangerous defects in the Confederation has at length proselyted the most obstinate adversaries to a reform. The unanimous sanction given by the Assembly to the inclosed compliance with the recommendation marks sufficiently the revolution of sentiment which the experience of one year has effected in this country."

To his intimate friend and former aide-de-camp, Col. David Humphreys of Connecticut, Washington now wrote, expressing surprise that the Massachusetts and other New England Governments had not been represented at the Annapolis Convention, especially in view of the civil disorders in those States, "for of all others, the distractions and turbulent tempers of the people would, I should have thought, have afforded the strongest evidence of the necessity of competent powers somewhere. That the Federal Government is nearly, if not quite, at a stand, none will deny. The first question then is, shall it be annihilated or supported? If the latter, the proposed Convention is an object of the first magnitude and should be supported by all the friends of the present Constitution. . . .

appeared in this State as to the expediency of increasing the powers of Congress, not merely as to commercial objects, but generally." And on Jan. 20, 1787, he wrote: "The friends of Government in the most seditious towns now venture to talk with firmness and in a manly tone. Should this spirit pervade the other States, it will give rise to sentiments favorable to the Union. . . ."

I would wish anything and everything essayed, to avert
the effusion of blood and to avert the humiliating and
contemptible figure we are about to make on the annals
of Mankind." [1]   A month later, he wrote to Humphreys
that if this "second attempt to convene the States . . .
should also prove abortive, it may be considered as an
unequivocal evidence that the States are not likely to
agree on any general measure which is to pervade the
Union, and of course that there is an end of Federal
Government." Writing to Madison, on November 5,
1786, Washington expressed the following patriotic
views, as to the attitude of mind in which the delegates to
such a Convention should approach the grave problem :

"Fain would I hope that the great and most important of
all subjects, the Federal Government, may be considered
with that calm and deliberate attention, which the magnitude of it so critically and loudly calls for at this critical
moment.   Let prejudices, unreasonable jealousies, and local
interests, yield to reason and liberality.   Let us look to
our National character, and to things beyond the present
moment.   No morn ever dawned more favorably than ours
did ; and no day was ever more clouded than the present.
Wisdom and good examples are necessary at this time to rescue the political machine from the impending storm.   Virginia has now an opportunity to set the latter, and has
enough of the former, I hope, to take the lead in promoting
this great and arduous work.   Without an alteration in our
political creed, the superstructure we have been seven years

[1] See Washington to Humphreys, Nov. 4, Dec. 26, 1786; Humphreys to Washington, Jan. 20, March 24, April 9, 1787, *Life and Times of David Humphreys* (1917),
by Frank Landon Humphreys.
    To Jefferson, Washington wrote, Nov. 12, 1786: "The want of energy in the
Federal Government; the pulling of one State and parts of States against another;
and the commotions among the Eastern people have sunk the National character
much below par, and have brought our politics and credit to the brink of a precipice.
A step or two more must plunge us into inextricable ruin."   To David Stuart, he
wrote, Nov. 19: "However delicate the revision of the Federal system may appear,
it is a work of indispensable necessity."   To Governor Randolph, he wrote, Nov.
19: "Our affairs seem to be drawing to an awful crisis; it is necessary, therefore,
that the abilities of every man should be drawn into action in a public line, to rescue
them, if possible, from impending ruin."

in raising, at the expense of so much treasure and blood, must fall. We are fast verging to anarchy and confusion. . . . To you, I am sure, I need not add aught on this subject. The consequences of a lax or inefficient government are too obvious to be dwelt upon. Thirteen sovereignties pulling against each other, and all tugging at the Federal head, will soon bring ruin on the whole; whereas a liberal and energetic Constitution, well guarded and closely watched to prevent encroachments, might restore us to that degree of respectability and consequences, to which we had a fair claim and the brightest prospect of attaining."

Humphreys replied in January, 1787, giving somewhat pessimistic views as to the attitude of Connecticut towards a Convention: "As to a Convention, it has not until lately engrossed but little share in the conversation here. I am induced to expect the only good it can do will be to demonstrate to the People that a number of characters in whom they repose confidence, believe seriously we cannot remain as a Nation much longer, in the present manner of administering our actual Government. The evil appears to me to consist more of the untowardly dispositions of the States (who make no hesitation in palpably violating the Confederacy whenever it suits their interests) rather than in the form of our National Compact as it exists on paper." He asserted that the demagogues in Connecticut were persuading the people that their liberties were being taken away "by an artful, designing aristocracy." And he added: "I am as confident as I am of my own existence, the States will not comply with the recommendation. They have a mortal reluctance to divest themselves of the smallest attributes of independent, separate sovereignty."[1] Similar views were

[1] Rufus King, then a Member of Congress from Massachusetts, in New York wrote to Elbridge Gerry, June 18, 1786, referring to the plans for reforming the Government, that: "Every man who wishes to strengthen the Federal Government and confirm the Union is represented as unfriendly to the liberties of the People. These expressions of anxiety for the liberties of the People come now from those

expressed by Jay, writing to Carmichael in January:
"The inefficiency of the Federal Government becomes
more and more manifest; and how it is to be amended
is a question that engages the serious attention of the
best people in all the States. Endeavors are making
to form a Convention for the purpose, but it is not clear
that all the States will join in that measure. On this
and some other great points the public mind is fluctuat-
ing, though uneasy; perhaps a few months more may
produce a greater degree of decision." [1]

To Washington, Jay wrote, January 7, that it was
not easy to say what should be done; that it was useless to give any further degree of power to the existing
Congress, but that he was doubtful about the proposed Convention consisting of delegates elected by the
State Legislatures, for, said he, "no alterations in the
Government should, I think, be made, nor if attempted
will easily take place, unless deducible from the only
source of just authority — the People"; moreover, he
felt that a Convention having power only to recommend
would "produce endless discussion, perhaps jealousies
and party heat"; hence, he favored popular Conventions in each State to appoint deputies to a General
Convention which should have power to alter and
amend the Articles of Confederation.

General Knox wrote from New York to General
Benjamin Lincoln in Massachusetts, that the topic of
a Convention "engrosses a great portion of the attention
of men of reflection"; and to Stephen Higginson, he
wrote that "the poor, poor, Federal Government is sick
almost to death" and that a Convention had been
proposed "to consult on some plan to prevent our utter
ruin." [2]

artful and venal miscreants who withdrew themselves from their country's support
and existed, her bitterest enemies."

[1] Jay to Carmichael, Jan. 4, 1787; Jay to Washington, Jan. 7, 1787.

[2] General Henry Knox to Benjamin Lincoln, January 28, 1787.

"Perhaps this Convention originated and has been imbued with ideas far short of a radical reform. Let this have been the case, may it, notwithstanding, be turned to an excellent purpose. Our views are limited in all things; we can only see from point to point. If men, great men, are sent to the Convention, might they not assist the vision of the Southern delegates, in such a manner as to induce the adoption of some energetic plan, in the prosecution of which we might rise to National dignity and happiness?"

Knox suggested that the Convention should submit a plan for a Constitution to State Conventions who should then choose delegates to a new Continental Convention having power to decide upon and put in force a more General Government; and he especially urged Massachusetts to join in the present Convention :[1]

". . . The Southern States are jealous enough already. If New England, and particularly Massachusetts, should decline sending delegates to the Convention, it will operate in a duplicate ratio to injure us, by annihilating the rising desire in the Southern States of effecting a better National system, and by adding to their jealousies of the designs of New England. I have dwelt on this subject to you, in order that if your sentiments should correspond with mine, that you should influence a choice of delegates of such characters as would possess the ability of pointing out the road to National glory and felicity."

Stephen Higginson, in reply to Knox, suggested that the Convention in Philadelphia be empowered to form a Federal Constitution to be submitted to the States in

[1] Knox to Higginson, Jan. 28, 1787. See also Knox to Lincoln, Feb. 14, 1787: "The Convention proposed by the commercial Convention this September, to meet in Philadelphia, in May next, engrosses a great portion of the attention of men of reflection. Some are for and some against it, but the preponderance of opinion is for it. None of the New England States have yet chosen, and it appears quite problematical whether any will choose, unless Massachusetts. The Convention will be at liberty to consider more diffusively the defects of the present system than Congress can, who are the executors of a certain system. . . . If a differently constructed republican government should be the object, the shortest road to it will be found to be the Convention. I hope, therefore, that Massachusetts will choose, and that you, Mr. King, and Mr. Higginson should be three of the delegates."

appointment be numerous, and if possible let the men have a good knowledge of the Constitutions and various interests of the several States, and of the good and bad qualities of the Confederation. Events are hurrying to a crisis; prudent and sagacious men should be ready to seize the most favourable circumstances to establish a more permanent and vigorous Government. I hope you will be at leisure to attend the Convention. Madison is here. I presume he will be preparing himself for the Convention; you know he is a delegate from Virginia; he professes great expectation as to the good effects of the measure."

William Livingston, Governor of New Jersey, wrote to Elijah Clarke, February 17, 1787 : [1]

"I am really more distressed by the posture of our public affairs than I ever was by the most gloomy appearances during the late war. We do not exhibit the virtue that is necessary to support a republican government; and without the utmost exertions of the more patriotic part of the community, and the blessing of God upon their exertions, I fear that we shall not be able, for ten years from the date of this letter, to support that independence which has lost us so much blood and treasure to acquire. . . . Our situation is truly deplorable, and without a speedy alteration of measures, I doubt whether you and I shall survive the existence of that liberty for which we have so strenuously contended."

Meanwhile, some of the States, without waiting for Congress to act upon the recommendation of the Annapolis Convention, had voted to elect delegates to

King had written to Gerry, notifying him that Virginia and Pennsylvania had appointed delegates to the coming Convention but that Jay and others in New York were opposed to the measure "not alone because it is unauthorized, but from an opinion that the result will prove inefficacious"; and he wrote: "If Massachusetts should send deputies, for God's sake, be careful who are the men; the times are becoming critical; a movement of this nature ought to be carefully observed by every member of the community."

[1] *Memoirs of the Life of William Livingston* (1833), by Theodore Sedgwick, p. 462. Edmund Randolph, Governor of Virginia, wrote to Governor William Livingston of New Jersey, December 6, 1786, transmitting to him a copy of the Virginia Act, appointing delegates to the new Convention and stating his "anxiety for the well being of the Federal Government", begged him to "give a zealous attention to the present American crisis."

attend the new Convention to be held in Philadelphia;
Virginia, on October 16, 1786; New Jersey, on No-
vember 3; New Hampshire, on November 27; Penn-
sylvania, on December 30; North Carolina, on
January 6, 1787; Delaware, on February 3, and
Georgia, on February 10. New York and the New
England States had delayed action, chiefly because of
their doubts of the legality of any action looking
towards amendment of the Confederation which did
not originate with Congress. Edward Carrington, a
Member of Congress from Virginia, wrote to Madison,
December 18, 1786, that the reasons given by the
Massachusetts Members for failure to support the idea
of a Convention were that "the mode of amending the
Confederation is provided by the Act itself. Amendments are to originate with Congress and be agreed to
by the States, and that it would derogate from the
dignity and weight of that body to take a secondary
position in the business"; but, he added, wisely:
"This is an elevated idea, and in an efficient sovereignty
would be a wise one. The truth is, we have not a
Government to wield and correct, but must pursue the
most certain means for obtaining one." Madison
wrote to Jefferson, February 15, as to the "respectable
appointments" already made, but adding that:

"New York has not yet decided on the point. Her
Assembly has just rejected the impost, which has an unpro-
pitious aspect. It is not clear, however, that she may not
yet accede to the other measure. Connecticut has a great
aversion to Conventions, and is otherwise habitually disinclined to abridge her State prerogatives. Her concurrence
nevertheless is not despaired of. Massachusetts, it is said,
will concur, though hitherto not well inclined. New Hampshire will probably do as she does. Rhode Island can be
relied on for nothing that is good. On all great points, she
must sooner or later bend to Massachusetts and Connecticut."

Jay, who until Congress should take action was doubtful as to the advisability or chance of success of the Convention, wrote to John Adams, February 21:

"Our Government is unequal to the task assigned it, and the people begin also to perceive its inefficiency. The Convention gains ground. New York has instructed her delegates to move in Congress for a recommendation to the States to form a Convention; for this State dislikes the idea of a Convention, unless countenanced by Congress. I do not promise myself much further immediate good from the measure, than that it will tend to approximate the public mind to the changes which ought to take place. It is hard to say what those changes should be, exactly. There is one, however, which I think would be much for the better, viz.: to distribute the Federal sovereignty into its three proper departments of Executive, Legislative, and Judicial; for that Congress should act in these different capacities was, I think, a great mistake in our policy."

On this same day (February 21), however, Congress passed the following Resolve:[1]

"That in the opinion of Congress, it is expedient, that on the second Monday in May next, a Convention of delegates, who shall have been appointed by the several States, be held at Philadelphia, for the sole purpose of revising the Articles of Confederation, and reporting to Congress and the several Legislatures, such alterations and provisions therein, as shall, when agreed to in Congress, and confirmed by the States, render the Federal Constitution adequate to the exigencies of Government, and the preservation of the Union."

[1] This Resolve was substituted, on motion of King and Dane from Massachusetts, for a more pronounced declaration originally moved by New York members as follows: "Congress, having had under consideration the letter of John Dickinson, Esq., chairman of the commissioners who assembled at Annapolis, during the last year; also the proceedings of the said commissioners, and entirely coinciding with them, as to the inefficiency of the Federal Government, and the necessity of devising such farther provisions as shall render the same adequate to the exigencies of the Union, do strongly recommend to the different Legislatures to send forward delegates, to meet the proposed Convention, on the second Monday in May next, at the city of Philadelphia."

This action by Congress changed the attitude of many who had hitherto opposed a Convention, and influenced the States which had hitherto been reluctant to appoint delegates — New York acting on February 28, Massachusetts on March 10, Maryland on April 23, and Connecticut on May 12.[1]

On the day when Congress passed its Resolve, Madison wrote from New York to General Washington that it had "been much divided and embarrassed on the question whether its taking an interest in the measure would impede or promote it. On one side, it has been urged that some of the backward States have scruples against acceding to it without some constitutional sanction; on the other, that other States will consider any interference of Congress as proceeding from the same views which have hitherto excited their jealousies. . . . I have not been here long enough to gather the general sentiments of leading characters touching our affairs and prospects. I am inclined to hope that they will gradually be concentered in the plan of a thorough reform of the existing system. Those who may lean towards a Monarchical Government, and who, I suspect, are swayed by very indigested ideas, will of course abandon an unattainable object whenever a prospect opens of rendering the Republican form competent to its purposes. Those who remain attached to the latter form must soon perceive that it cannot be preserved at all under any modification which does not redress the ills experienced from our present establishments." Washington replied to Madison's letter, March 31, expressing his doubts whether the Monarchi-

[1] In a letter from New York in *Independent Gazetteer* (Phil.), March 16, 1787, it was said: "You have seen the resolution of Congress approving a Convention for revising the Confederation. This measure was adopted to reconcile the five Eastern States to the sending deputies, which they thought *unconstitutional* without the recommendation of Congress. It is believed that all the States except Connecticut will appoint, and I think they will also."

cal tendencies extended far, and also his hopes that the
Convention would probe deep into the existing defects
of the Government and would essay a thorough reform:

"I am fully of opinion that those who lean to a Monarchical Government have either not consulted the public mind,
or that they live in a region, which (the levelling principles
in which they were bred being entirely eradicated) is much
more productive of Monarchical ideas, than are to be found
in the Southern States, where, from the habitual distinctions
which have always existed among the people, one would have
expected the first generation and the most rapid growth of
them. I am also clear, that even admitting the utility, nay,
necessity of the form, yet that the period is not arrived for
adopting the change without shaking the peace of this country to its foundation. That a thorough reform of the present system is indispensable, none who have capacities to
judge, will deny; and with hand (and heart) I hope the
business will be essayed in a full Convention. . . . I confess, however, that my opinion of public virtue is so far
changed, that I have my doubts whether any system, without the means of coercion in the sovereign, will enforce due
obedience to the ordinances of a General Government; without which every thing else fails. Laws or ordinances unob-
served, or partially attended to, had better never have been
made; because the first is a mere nihil, and the second is
productive of much jealousy and discontent. But what
kind of coercion, you may ask. This indeed will require
thought, though the non-compliance of the States with the
late requisition is an evidence of the necessity. It is somewhat singular that a State (New York) which used to be
foremost in all federal measures, should now turn her face
against them in almost every instance. . . . I am desirous
of knowing how this matter is, as my wish is that the Convention may adopt no temporizing expedients, but probe
the defects of the Constitution to the bottom, and provide
a radical cure, whether they are agreed to or not. A conduct of this kind will stamp wisdom and dignity on their

proceedings, and hold up a light which sooner or later will have its influence."

To Edmund Pendleton, Madison wrote, February 28, that it now seemed probable that the Convention would take place "and that it will be a pretty full one. What the issue of it will be, is among the other arcana of futurity and nearly as inscrutable as any of them. In general, I find men of reflection much less sanguine as to the new than despondent as to the present system." He then expressed the fear that was so prevalent, and which was a very leading motive in the desire for the formation of a new Constitution, the fear lest, otherwise, there might be a move towards Monarchy or division of the Confederacy.

"If the approaching Convention should not agree on some remedy, I am persuaded that some very different arrangement will ensue. The late turbulent scenes in Massachusetts and infamous ones in Rhode Island have done inexpressible injury to the republican character in that part of the United States; and a propensity towards Monarchy is said to have been produced by it in some leading minds. The bulk of the people will probably prefer the lesser evil of a partition of the Union into three more practicable and energetic Governments. The latter idea I find, after long confinement to individual speculations and private circles, is beginning to show itself in the newspapers. But tho' it is a lesser evil, it is so great a one that I hope the danger of it will rouse all the real friends of the Revolution to exert themselves in favor of such an organization of the Confederacy as will perpetuate the Union, and redeem the honor of the Republican name."

Meanwhile, many statesmen had been pondering on the nature of the necessary changes in the framework of Government and of the theory on which they must be based. That additional power must be given to Congress, especially power over commerce, was generally

acknowledged; and as Jefferson phrased it: "The
politics of Europe rendered it indispensably necessary
that with respect to everything external we be one
nation firmly hooped together; interior government is
what each State should keep to itself." [1] That the
three functions of Government — the Legislative,
Executive, and Judicial — must be vested in separate
bodies was the first principle agreed upon by several of
the leaders; and Jay wrote to Jefferson, as early as
August 18, 1786, that:

"I have long thought, and become daily more convinced,
that the construction of our Federal Government is fundamentally wrong. To vest Legislative, Judicial, and Executive power in one and the same body of men, and that too
in a body daily changing its members, can never be wise.
In my opinion, those three great departments of sovereignty
should be forever separated, and so distributed as to serve
as checks on each other. But these are subjects that have
long been familiar to you, and on which you are too well
informed not to anticipate everything that I might say on
them. . . ."

A development of this idea in greater detail was
written by Rufus King, a Member of Congress from
Massachusetts, to Jonathan Jackson of that State,
September 3: [2]

"It should be remembered that the pressure of a common
calamity which induced the present Confederation is now
removed, that the individual States are governed by their
particular interests. These stand, or are supposed to stand,
in opposition to each other, and, so long as the idea obtains,
will prevent unanimity in any opinion concerning the cor-
roboration of the Federal Constitution. Others, and by no
means the least respectable, answer that nothing can be

---

[1] Jefferson to Madison, Oct. 8, 1786. See *Life and Times of James Madison*
(1859) by William C. Rives, II, 31, 34, 41, 68, for views of the leaders as to power
over commerce.

[2] *Mass. Hist. Soc. Proc.* (1915), XLIX.

done in our present form, that the error lies in the original plan. Diminish, say they, the number of States, let those which are to be established be nearly equal, reform their Constitutions, give their Governments more energy, the laws more stability, the magistrates greater authority and responsibility. Let the State Governments be confined to concerns merely internal, and let there be a Federal Government, with a vigorous Executive, wise Legislature, and independent Judicial."

Jefferson, writing to Madison, December 16, 1786, presented the same ideas as follows:

"I find by the public papers that your Commercial Convention failed in point of representation. If it should produce a full meeting in May and a broader reformation, it will still be well. To make us one nation as to foreign concerns, and keep us distinct in domestic ones, gives the outline of the proper division of power between the general and particular Governments. But to enable the Federal head to exercise the power given it to best advantage, it should be organized, as the particular ones are, into Legislative, Executive, and Judiciary. The first and last are already separated. The second should also be. . . ."

To Jefferson in Paris, Madison wrote, March 19: [1]

"What may be the result of this political experiment cannot be foreseen. The difficulties which present themselves are on one side almost sufficient to dismay the most sanguine, whilst on the other side, the most timid are compelled to encounter them by the mortal diseases of the Constitution. . . . They are at present marked by symptoms which are truly alarming, which have tainted the faith of the most orthodox republicans, and which challenge from the votaries of liberty every concession in favor of stable Government,

[1] To James Madison, Sr., Madison wrote April 1, that: "Notwithstanding this prospect of a very full and respectable meeting, no very sanguine expectations can well be indulged. The probable diversity of opinions and prejudices and of supposed or real interests among the States renders the issue totally uncertain. The existing embarrassments and mortal diseases of the Confederacy form the only ground of hope that a spirit of concession on all sides may be produced by the general chaos, or at least partition of the Union which offer itself as the alternative."

not infringing fundamental principles, as the only security against an opposite extreme of our present situation."

He stated four principles which he believed essential to embody in a new Government: first, ratification by the people themselves rather than by State Legislatures; second, grant of power to the National Legislatures to negative any Act of a State Legislature in order to preserve the boundary between the Federal and the State powers; third, proportional instead of equal representation of the States; fourth, organization of the Federal powers so as not to blend those which ought to be exercised by distinct departments of Government.

On March 27, Edmund Randolph wrote to Madison, stating his views as to action the coming Convention might take:

"I have turned my mind somewhat to the business of May next, but am hourly interrupted. At present, I conceive — 1. that the alterations should be grafted on the old Confederation. 2. That what is best in itself, not merely what can be obtained from the Assemblies, be adopted. 3. That the points of power to be granted be so detached from each other, as to permit a State to reject one part, without mutilating the whole. With these objects, ought not some general proposition to be prepared for feeling the pulse of the Convention on the subject at large? Ought not an address to accompany the new Constitution?"

In reply to this, Madison wrote to Randolph, on April 8, elaborating his Jefferson letter, and setting forth a comprehensive scheme for a National Government, acting upon individuals and not upon States. The first plan for such a form of Government had been presented by Pelatiah Webster of Philadelphia, who, on February 16, 1783, published a pamphlet entitled, "A Dissertation on the Political Union and Constitution of the Thirteen States of North America, which is Necessary to Their Preservation and Happiness." There is no evidence, however, that Madison ever saw this pamphlet.[1] To Randolph, he now said: "I think with you it will be well to retain as much as possible of the old Confederation, tho' I doubt whether it may not be best to work the valuable articles into a new system, instead of engrafting the latter on the former." Madison thus took the bold step of announcing that the work of the Convention should be to frame a new Constitution and not merely to alter over the old one. And this idea he further developed in a long letter to Washington, a week later, April 16, in which he set forth "some outlines of a new system", and in which he stated succinctly the whole theory on which the Constitution, as finally drafted, was based:

"Conceiving that an individual independence of the States is utterly irreconcilable with their aggregate sovereignty, and that a consolidation of the whole into one simple republic would be as inexpedient as it is unattainable,

[1] Prof. Edward Channing in his *History of the United States*, III, 477, note, says that Prof. Max Farrand in a note to him states that he has "not a scrap of evidence that Webster's dissertation directly influenced a single member of the Convention. In fact, I have found practically no reference to it at that time." In *Amer. Hist. Rev.*, XVII, 162, Farrand states that students "have generally believed that the American Constitution would have taken its present form if the pamphlet in question had never been written, or indeed if Webster had never lived." Hannis Taylor in *The Science of Jurisprudence*, in 1908, stated that Pelatiah Webster's pamphlet was the direct source of the Constitution; but he paid no attention to the fact that Webster's only conception of enforcement of National laws in case of disobedience by individuals, and his only remedy was, for Congress to summon such individuals to appear before it and for Congress to fine and punish; and in case of resistance to National laws by a State, for Congress to employ force against the State. It is to be noted that Madison in his *Preface to Debates in the Convention*, written about 1835, admits that Noah Webster of Connecticut had in 1785 proposed in one of his publications "a new system of government which should act, not on the States, but directly on individuals, and vest in Congress full power to carry its laws into execution." Noah Webster's essay, entitled *Plan of Policy for Improving the Advantages and Perpetuating the Union of the American States* (1785), presented no detailed scheme of a Constitution, but it suggested the correct theory for a new Government as follows: "Let the Government of the United States be formed upon the general plan of government in laws of the several States. . . . The general concerns of the Continent may be reduced to a few heads; but in all the affairs that respect the whole, Congress must have the same power to enact laws and compel obedience throughout the Continent as the Legislatures of the several States have in their respective jurisdictions."

I have sought for some middle ground, which may at once support a due supremacy of the National authority and not exclude the local authorities wherever they can be subordinately useful."

To Edmund Pendleton, Madison wrote, April 22: [1]

"The absence of one or two States however will not materially affect the deliberations of the Convention. Disagreement in opinion among those present is much more likely to embarrass us. The nearer the crisis approaches, the more I tremble for the issue. The necessity of gaining the concurrence of the Convention in some system that will answer the purpose, the subsequent approbation of Congress, and the final sanction of the States, presents a series of chances, which would inspire despair in any case where the alternative was less formidable. The difficulty too is not a little increased by the necessity which will be produced by encroachments on the State Constitutions, of obtaining not merely the assent of the Legislatures, but the ratification of the people themselves. Indeed, if such encroachments could be avoided, a higher sanction than the Legislative authority would be necessary to render the laws of the Confederacy paramount to the acts of its members."

Meanwhile, other statesmen were expressing their views of the situation. Richard Henry Lee, in a letter to Randolph declining appointment as a delegate, wrote, March 26: that "there are so many gentlemen

[1] Madison wrote to Jefferson, April 23, 1787: "The prospect of a full and respectable Convention grows stronger every day. Rhode Island alone has refused to send Deputies. Maryland has probably appointed by this time. Of Connecticut alone doubts are entertained. The anti-federal party in that State is numerous and persevering. It is said that the elections which are now going on are rather discouraging to the advocates of the Convention. Pennsylvania has added Dr. Franklin to her deputation. There is some ground to calculate on the attendance of General Washington. Our Governor, Mr. Wythe, Mr. Blair, and Col. Mason will pretty certainly attend. The last, I am informed, is renouncing his errors on the subject of the Confederation, and means to take an active part in the amendment of it. Mr. (Patrick) Henry pretty soon resigned the undertaking. General Nelson was put into his place, who has also declined. He was succeeded by Mr. R. H. Lee, who followed his example. Doctor M'Clurg has been since appointed, and as he was on the spot must have been previously consulted." See also Madison to Washington, March 18, 1787, as to Henry's resignation.

of good hearts and sound heads appointed to the
Convention at Philadelphia that I feel a disposition
to repose with confidence in their determinations." [1]
Edward Rutledge of South Carolina wrote to Richard
Henry Lee, March 27:

"We have agreed to send deputies to the Continental
Convention. My brother, who is truly federal, is among
the number of gentlemen, none of whom, I am convinced,
will yield to him in zeal for Continental measures. . . . It
is said that the Eastern States will not send delegates to the
Convention. If this be their determination, they must
change it. What, although they have experienced domestic
convulsions from their State Conventions, can they not foresee that a restoration of their trade will afford an outlet for
their restless spirits and remove, with the poverty of their
situation, an inclination to disturb the Government? They,
of all others, are more immediately interested in vesting
powers in the United Council. Animate them, my good
Sir, to a sense of their duty and of their interest."

David Ramsay of South Carolina wrote to Jefferson,
April 7: [2]

"Our Governments in the Southern States are much more
quiet than in the Northern, but much of our quiet arises
from the temporizing of the Legislature in refusing legal
protection to the prosecution of the just rights of the creditors. Our eyes now are all fixed on the Continental Convention to be held in Philadelphia, in May next. Unless
they make an efficient Federal Government, I fear that the

---

[1] *Letters of Richard Henry Lee* (ed. by J. C. Ballagh, 1914) II, 415. See also Lee
to Thomas Lee Shippen, April 17, 1787: "I feel and see the unhappy state of
public affairs that you describe, but I hope for amendment. We have everywhere
young men coming forward with worth and talents that promise good things. In
May next a Convention is to meet in Philadelphia for the purpose of amending
our Federal Constitution — from this source, perhaps we may derive some good."

[2] Ralph Izard of South Carolina wrote to Jefferson, April 4, 1787: "If the powers
of Congress can be so extended as to give efficacy to the decisions of that body, the
measure will assuredly contribute to the security and happiness of the Continent.
At present, our affairs are by no means in a desirable state." *South Carolina Historical and Genealogical Magazine* (1901), II, 199.

end of the matter will be an American Monarchy, or rather three or more Confederacies."

Benjamin Franklin wrote to Jefferson, April 19:

"Our Federal Constitution is generally thought defective and a Convention, first proposed by Virginia, and since recommended by Congress, is to assemble here next month, to revise it and propose amendments. The delegates generally appointed, as far as I have heard of them, are men of character for prudence and ability, so that I hope good from their meeting. Indeed, if it does not do good, it must do harm, as it will show that we have not wisdom enough among us to govern ourselves; and will strengthen the opinion of some political writers, that popular governments cannot long support themselves."

James Dawson of Virginia wrote to Madison, April 15: "Much depends on the Convention in May. The attention of almost every person is fixed on that body; and should the issue not be successful, which I am sorry to find you suspect, I fear there will be an end to the General Confederacy." Rufus King wrote to Theophilus Parsons in Massachusetts, April 8:

"I wish it was in my power to say that the affairs of the Union bore a more favorable appearance than when I saw you last; but the contrary is the fact. What the Convention may do at Philadelphia is very doubtful. There are many well disposed men from the Southern States who will attend the Convention; but the projects are so various, and all so short of the best, that my fears are by no means inferior to my hopes on this subject."

Edward Carrington of Virginia wrote to Jefferson, April 24:

. . . "Rhode Island is at all points so antifederal and contemptible that her neglecting the invitation will probably occasion no demur whatever in the proceedings. . . . Various are the conjectures as to the issue of this meeting, and still more various are the suggested remedies to the defects of our system. I am rather a zealot in the measure, because it will operate, at least as an alarm; but whether it will be productive of any immediate effects may be doubtful. Perhaps that experiment has not yet been made of the present system, which could discover its defects or point to their remedies. I am certain it is very imperfect, but, at the same time, there was evident causes for their failure, other than those of defectiveness in the constructure. The best of governments, like other things, can prosper alone by due attention. America was placed in possession of peace and independence, under circumstances which have not only deprived her political systems of the necessary care of her citizens but exposed her to the injurious designs of men whose interest it has been to destroy the efficiency of Government. A great proportion of the people, being loaded with debt, have found an interest in promoting measures directly opposed to good government, and have been solicitous to direct the public affairs; whilst better men have been inactive or engrossed by the alluring invitations of ease and plenty in our vast Western and Southern regions. . . . Genl. Washington, it is hoped, will attend, but there is good reason to apprehend the contrary — his state of health is not a good one. . . . The Convention will be productive of things worth communicating to you and I will do myself the pleasure to write by the first opportunity that offers after its commencement."

Jay wrote to Jefferson, April 25, as to the Convention: "I wish their councils may better our situation; but I am not sanguine in my expectations. There is reason to fear that our errors do not proceed from want of knowledge; and, therefore, that reason and public spirit will require the aid of calamity to render their dictates effectual."[1] And John Adams wrote from London to Jay, May 8:

[1] Washington had written similarly to Knox, March 8, 1787, that "it is among the evils, and perhaps is not the smallest, of democratic Governments that the people must always *feel* before they will *see*."

"The Convention at Philadelphia is to consist of members of such ability, weight, and experience that the result must be beneficial to the United States. The settlement of so many great controversies such as those between Massachusetts and New York, Pennsylvania, and Connecticut, New York and Vermont, &c., show that the Union has great weight in the minds of the people. It is, indeed, an object of such magnitude that great sacrifices ought to be made to its preservation. The consequences of a division of the Continent cannot be foreseen fully, perhaps, by any man; but the most shortsighted must perceive such manifest danger, both from foreign Powers and from one another, as cannot be looked upon without terror."

Such were the sentiments of the public men of the day. Such were their alarms at the existing situation, and such were their hopes that some method might be found to preserve the Union. That they realized the disastrous economic conditions, that they feared the effect of prevailing unwise and unjust State legislation, and that they expected that a more adequate form of Government would bring an increase of economic prosperity for all classes in the community, cannot be doubted. But it is equally indubitable that their leading motive in desiring a new Constitution was their conviction that, without it, a dissolution of the Union and disappearance of republican government were inevitable.

NOTE. Unless special citations of authority are given in the footnotes, all letters quoted in the text of this book will be found in Bancroft's *History of the Formation of the Constitution;* Farrand's *Records of the Federal Convention; Documentary History of the Constitution;* or in one of the other collected editions of letters of American statesmen, contained in Appendix A *infra.*

CHAPTER TWO

The Delegates, the Public, and the Press

To attend the Federal Convention, the twelve States (other than Rhode Island) had appointed, through their Legislatures or their Governors, a total of seventy-four delegates, of whom nineteen had either declined to accept or failed to come to Philadelphia.[1] What had been the experience of the fifty-five men who actually attended? What fitted them for their great task?

In the first place, it is to be remarked that thirty-nine of them had already served in the Congress of the Confederation; eight of them had signed the Declaration of Independence;[2] eight had helped to form their State Constitutions; five had been members of the Annapolis Convention in September, 1786; seven had been Chief Executives of their States; and twenty-one had fought to maintain the independence of their country in the Revolutionary War.

At least thirty-three had been lawyers, of whom ten had served as State Judges; eight were engaged in mercantile or other business; six were planters; three had been physicians. About one half were graduates

[1] I accept the list as given in *The Records of the Federal Convention* (1911), by Max Farrand, III, 557–559. The list of delegates printed in the *Journal, Acts and Proceedings of the Convention* (1819), published officially by the Secretary of State, contained the names of only sixty-five delegates, but it omits one from Connecticut, five from Maryland, two from Virginia, and one from South Carolina, who were appointed but declined to serve. For full list, see Appendix B.

[2] Elbridge Gerry, Roger Sherman, Benjamin Franklin, Robert Morris, George Clymer, James Wilson, George Read, George Wythe. Roger Sherman had the unique distinction of signing all three of the great American documents — the Declaration of Independence, the Articles of Confederation, and the Constitution.

of Colleges — nine coming from Princeton, and Yale, Harvard, Columbia, University of Pennsylvania and William and Mary being also represented, as well as Oxford and the Scotch Universities.

It is interesting to note that the Convention was a meeting of comparatively young men; six of the fifty-five were under thirty-one years of age — Dayton (the youngest, being twenty-six), Mercer, Charles Pinckney, Spaight, Davie, and Hamilton; only twelve men were over fifty-four years of age — Read, Washington, Blair, Dickinson, Carroll, Johnson, Wythe, Mason, Livingston, and (regarded as the three Nestors) Jenifer aged sixty-four, Sherman aged sixty-six, and Franklin aged eighty-one.[1]

It is unnecessary to call the roll of these delegates in detail.[2] The ablest delegations came from five States and comprised among their number — Washington, Madison, and Randolph of Virginia; Rufus King, Nathaniel Gorham, and Elbridge Gerry of Massachusetts; Benjamin Franklin, James Wilson, Gouverneur Morris, and Robert Morris of Pennsylvania; Roger Sherman, Oliver Ellsworth, and William Samuel Johnson of Connecticut; and John Rutledge, Charles Pinckney, Gen. Charles C. Pinckney and Pierce Butler of South Carolina. These were the leaders in the formation of the Constitution. Amongst others who were prominent but had a less active part in its framing were Alexander Hamilton of New York, David Brearley and William Paterson of New Jersey, John Dickinson of Delaware, Hugh Williamson and William R. Davie of North

[1] Note the change in viewpoint as to age.   Richard Henry Lee, writing to George Mason, May 15, 1787, said: "I am glad . . . to find on this occasion that so many gentlemen of competent years are sent to the Convention, for certainly youth is the season of credulity, and confidence a slow plant in an aged bosom."

[2] For the most complete account of the delegates, see *History of the Celebration of the 100th Anniversary of the Constitution* (1889), by Hampton L. Carson; *History of the Formation of the Constitution* (1882), by George Bancroft.   See also *An Introduction to the Study of the American Constitution* (1926), by Charles E. Martin.

Carolina, and Abraham Baldwin of Georgia. The
most active opponent of the Constitution in the Convention was Luther Martin of Maryland. Of the other
delegates, many were men of talent and character;
others were of more mediocre calibre. Ten men stand
out as chiefly responsible for the form which the Constitution finally took — Madison, Randolph, Franklin,
Wilson, Gouverneur Morris, King, Rutledge, Charles
Pinckney, Ellsworth, and Sherman.

Madison, born in 1751, was thirty-six years old at the
time of the Convention. A graduate of Princeton, he
had originally studied for the ministry, but for eleven
years had devoted his life to deep and comprehensive
study of the theory, history, and practice of governments; he had been a member of the Virginia Assembly
which framed the first State Constitution; a Member
of Congress from Virginia from 1780 to 1784, and a
member of the Virginia Assembly from 1784 to 1787.
Of him, Fisher Ames, who served with him in Congress
a few years later, wrote that "he is a thorough master
of almost every public question that can arise, or he
will spare no pains to become so. He is well versed in
public life, was bred to it, and has no other profession.
. . . It is rather a science than a business with him."
A striking phrase — versed in the "science" rather
than the "business" of public life! No one who reads
Madison's letters and his speeches in the debates will
wonder that he has been termed, without dissent, the
"Father of the Constitution."

Edmund Randolph was born in 1753, being thirty-
four years old. He had been a member of the Virginia
Assembly which framed the first State Constitution,
Attorney General, and Governor of the State. Of
Randolph, his fellow delegate, William Pierce of
Georgia wrote that he united "all the accomplish-
ments of the scholar and the statesman. . . . He has

a harmonious voice, a fine person and striking manners"; and a Virginian later wrote that "his manner and disposition were formed alike to inspire and return lively sentiments of friendship and affection. . . . There was, however, one drawback . . . an instability of conduct and opinion resulting not from moral but intellectual causes."[1]

Benjamin Franklin was born in 1706, and was eighty-one years old. His long years of service in Colonial affairs in Pennsylvania, as agent of the Colonies in England, in the Continental Congress, as Minister to France, and now as President of Pennsylvania, preeminently fitted him as a sage adviser. He had been unanimously elected at the spring session of the Legislature, after a nomination by Robert Morris, who had said that "a Convention met on so important and interesting an occasion could not fail to derive great assistance and advantages from the knowledge and patriotism of that experienced statesman and philosopher."[2] Jefferson termed him "the greatest man and ornament of the age and country in which he lived", and Madison said of him that "he has written his own life and no man ever had a finer one to write."[3] Notwithstanding his advanced age and serious inflictions of gout and stone, Franklin took an active part in the proceedings, though his speeches were read for him by Wilson.[4]

[1] *Life and Times of James Madison* (1859), by William Cabell Rives, II, 242–243.

[2] *Pennsylvania Packet*, March 27, 1787.   Franklin wrote to the Duc de la Rochefoucauld, April 15, 1787: "There seems to be but little thought, at present, in the particular States, of mending their particular Constitutions; but the grand Federal Constitution is generally blamed as not having given sufficient powers to Congress, the Federal head.   A Convention is therefore appointed to revise that Constitution, and propose a better.   You will see by the enclosed paper that your friend is to be one in that business, though he doubts his malady may not permit his giving constant attendance."

[3] Jefferson to Samuel Smith, Aug. 22, 1798, *Writings of Thomas Jefferson* (Ford's ed.), VIII, 443; Madison to J. R. Paulding, April, 1831, *Writings of James Madison* (Hunt's ed.), IX, 451.

[4] Dr. Benjamin Rush gave the following picture of Franklin, a year earlier, in a letter to Richard Price, May 25, 1786. "Our venerable friend, Dr. Franklin, continues to enjoy as much health and spirits as are compatible with his time of his

James Wilson was born in Scotland in 1742, and was forty-five years old — a learned and skilful lawyer, a Member of Congress, and one of the signers of the Declaration of Independence, he was regarded as one of the foremost citizens of Philadelphia; and Washington termed him as "able, candid, and honest a member" as the Convention held.[1]

Gouverneur Morris was born in 1754, being thirty-three years of age — an eloquent and facile lawyer, a merchant and financier, who had served as Assistant to the Superintendent of Finance (Robert Morris) under the Confederation. "To the brilliancy and fertility of his genius, he added — what is too rare —" wrote Madison, "a candid surrender of his opinions when the lights of discussion satisfied him that they had been too hastily formed and a readiness to aid in making the best of measures in which he had been overruled."[2] The loss of a leg in his youth did not prevent him from taking the floor as the most frequent speaker in the Convention.

life. I dined with him a few days ago in a most agreeable circle where he appeared as cheerful and gay as a young man of five and twenty. But his conversation was full of the wisdom and experience of mellow old age. He has destroyed party rage in our State, or, to borrow an allusion from one of his discoveries, his presence and advice, like oil upon troubled waters, have composed the contending waves of faction which for so many years agitated the State of Pennsylvania." *Price Papers* in *Mass. Hist. Soc. Proc.*, 2d Series (1903), XVII.

[1] Washington to David Stuart, Oct. 17, 1787; see also *James Wilson and the Constitution*, by A. C. McLaughlin, *Pol. Sci. Qu.* (1897), XII.

[2] Madison to Jared Sparks, April 8, 1831. G. Morris wrote to Gen. Henry Knox, Jan. 9, 1787: "The newspapers will have informed you that Pennsylvania has appointed me a Commissioner on her part to meet in the Convention in May. Had the object been any other than it is, I would have declined. The appointment was the most unexpected thing that ever happened to me, for I have not only declared in general, but in this particular instance objected to being named; but it was done while I was at Trenton." Knox replied from New York, Jan. 16, 1787: "I am glad that you and Robert Morris are chosen as delegates to the Convention. I ardently wish, for many reasons, that the States would unanimously send delegates to it, but the various opinions respecting it prevent. I most exceedingly wish Massachusetts and the Eastern States would be at it, but they appear to think it an irregular step and inadequate to a critical situation. Will you muster up all your arguments in favor of it and forward them to me. I will not make a bad use of them." *Knox Papers MSS* in Massachusetts Historical Society Library.

Rufus King was born in 1755, being thirty-two years old. He was a business man, and had been in the Massachusetts Legislature and a Member of Congress from Massachusetts since 1784. "Distinguished for his eloquence and great parliamentary talents," wrote William Pierce.[1]

John Rutledge was born in 1739, being forty-eight years old. He had been the leading statesman of South Carolina during the Revolution, and Attorney General and a Member of Congress from that State.

Charles Pinckney was only twenty-nine years old — born in 1758. He was a lawyer and had been a Member of Congress from South Carolina in 1777–1778, and from 1784 to 1787. "Intimately acquainted with every species of polite learning, and has a spirit of application and industry beyond most men," wrote Pierce.

Oliver Ellsworth was born in 1745, being forty-two years old. He was a lawyer and had been a Member of Congress from Connecticut and Judge of the highest Court of that State from 1784 — "a gentleman of clear, deep and copious understanding, eloquent and connected in public debate" (in the words of Pierce), and as described later by a fellow diplomat "that man has a head of iron, just iron, that works with the precision of a mule without its quickness and giddy manner. profoundly admire the neatness and accuracy of his mind." [2]

Roger Sherman was born in 1721, being sixty-six

[1] T. P. Brissot de Warville in his *New Travels in the United States of America* recorded in August, 1788: "Mr. King whom I saw at this dinner passes for the most eloquent man of the United States. What struck me most in him was his modesty. He appears ignorant of his own worth. Mr. Hamilton has the determined air of a republican; Mr. Madison the meditative air of a profound politician. . . . His look announces a censor, his conversation discovers the man of learning, and his reserve was that of a man conscious of his talents and of his duties."

[2] *The Letters of John Quincy Adams* (1912), II., William Vans Murray to Adams, Nov. 7, 1800. As to his farming interests, see "Letters of a Landholder," *Connecticut Courant*, Nov. 5, 1787.

years old (next to Franklin in age).   He had originally been a shoemaker but had become a lawyer, he had been a signer of the Declaration of Independence, a Member of Congress from Connecticut, and a Judge of the highest Court of that State.   "No man has a better heart or a clearer head," wrote Pierce.

Of all the delegates, there was one whose presence in the Convention was absolutely essential to its success, and without whose approval, the work of the Convention would have failed of acceptance by the American people.[1]   In estimating the services of George Washington to his country, the part he played in this connection should rank next to his military service.   Of his familiarity with the defects of the existing form of Government and of his long insistence upon the necessity of a change, his correspondence (quoted in the

[1] When the Convention had finished its great task, Gouverneur Morris wrote to Washington, October 30, 1787, his views of the importance of the latter's participation : "I have observed that your name to the new Constitution has been of infinite service.   Indeed, I am convinced that if you had not attended the Convention, and the same paper had been handed out to the world, it would have met with a colder reception, with fewer and weaker advocates, and with more and more strenuous opponents.   As it is, should the idea prevail that you will not accept the Presidency, it would prove fatal in many parts.   The truth is, that your great and decided superiority leads men willingly to put you in a place which will not add to your personal dignity nor raise you higher than you already stand.   But they would not readily put any other person in the same situation."

Forty years later, a contemporary, writing his reminiscences of 1787 in the *Salem Gazette*, June 5, 1827, said that the Constitution was framed "by some of the greatest and best men of the country who were actuated by the purest patriotism, by a sincere and ardent desire to render their country great and happy," and that at the head of the Convention was "a man in whose wisdom, integrity and patriotism the whole people placed unbounded confidence; and let it be forever remembered, it is to George Washington, the United States are indebted for the establishment of the Federal Government.   Had not the Constitution come out under the sanction of his name, it never would have been adopted."   See, however, comments on this by Timothy Pickering.   *Pickering Papers MSS*, XLVI, 363.

William Livingston, Governor of New Jersey, writing in *Collins Gazette*, as early as April 1, 1778, had made the following interesting poetical prophecy of Washington's future part (*The Memoirs of the Life of William Livingston* (1833), by Theodore Sedgwick, Jr.) :

"And in the calm of life
Methinks I see thee, Solon-like, design
The future grandeur of Confederate States
High towering; or for legislation met,
Adjust in Senate what thou sav'dst in war."

preceding chapter) affords ample proof.[1] It is no exaggeration to say that without the support which he gave to the calling of the Convention and without the confidence inspired in the country by his participation in the Convention and by his earnest advocacy of its final work, the Constitution never would have been adopted. General Henry Knox rightly wrote, during this spring of 1787, that: "I am persuaded that your name has had already great influence to induce the States to come into the measure; that your attendance will be grateful and your absence chagrining; that your presence would confer on the Assembly a National complexion, and that it would more than any other measure induce a compliance to the propositions of the Convention"; and again that "the unbounded confidence the people have of your patriotism and wisdom would exceedingly facilitate the adoption of any important alterations that might be proposed." [2]

In spite of this general view as to the benefits to be derived from his attendance, Washington had been

---

[1] George Bancroft in his *History of the Formation of the Constitution* (1882), I, 278, said: "He made himself familiar with the reasonings of Montesquieu; and he obtained the opinions not of Madison only, but of Knox and of Jay. From their letters and his own experience, he drew three outlines of a new Constitution, differing in manifold ways, and yet each of the three designed to restore and consolidate the Union." This statement was slightly inaccurate as it was made by Bancroft on the authority of an article by Jared Sparks in *North American Review* (Oct. 1827), XXV, 263, in which Sparks simply stated that: "We are about to insert a document, which we possess, in General Washington's handwriting, and which is a summary of three letters received by him from Jay, Knox and Madison not long before the Convention at Philadelphia. . . . After obtaining the views of others in detail, it was his custom to draw out, arrange and note on paper the prominent points that he might bring them into a compass which his mind could more easily grasp. The following quotation is an exact transcript of such a summary."

[2] Knox to Washington, March 19, April 9, 1787. Writing March 19, he said: "Were the Convention to propose only amendments and patchwork to the present defective Confederation, your reputation would in a degree suffer. But were an energetic and judicious system to be proposed with your signature, it would be a circumstance highly honorable to your fame, in the judgment of the present and future ages; and doubly entitle you to the glorious republican epithet — The Father of your Country. But the men generally chosen being of the first information, great reliance may be placed on the wisdom and vigor of their councils and judgments, and therefore the balance of my opinion preponderates greatly in favor of your attendance."

extremely reluctant to accept the appointment as delegate which the Virginia Legislature had made, on December 4, 1786. In answer to a deluge of letters urging his acceptance, he had written to all that it would be "impracticable", giving as his reasons — first, that he was in very bad health, and second, that he had already declined attending a meeting of the General Society of the Cincinnati of which he was President and which was also to convene in Philadelphia in May.[1] Edmund Randolph as Governor of Virginia had, however, continued to entreat his acceptance. So had Madison, who wrote earnestly:

"It was the opinion of every judicious friend whom I consulted, that your name could not be spared from the Deputation to the Meeting in May at Philadelphia. It was supposed, in the first place, that the peculiarity of the mission, and its acknowledged pre-eminence over every other public object, may possibly reconcile your undertaking it with the respect which is justly due and which you wish to pay to the late officers of the army; and in the second place, that although you should find that or any other consideration an obstacle to your attendance on the service, the advantage of having your name in the front of the appointment as a mark of the earnestness of Virginia, and an invitation to the most select characters from every part of the Confederacy, ought at all events to be made use of."

To this Washington had replied:

"I have been thus particular, to show, that under circumstances like these, I should feel myself in an awkward situation to be in Philadelphia on another public occasion,

<hr>

[1] See Washington to Randolph, Nov. 14; Randolph to Washington, Dec. 6; Madison to Washington, Nov. 8, Dec. 7; Washington to Madison, Dec. 16; Washington to Randolph, Dec. 21, 1786; Randolph to Washington, Jan. 4, March 11, 1787, April 2, 1787; Washington to Humphreys, Dec. 26, 1786; Humphreys to Washington, Jan. 20, March 24, April 9, 1787; Washington to Knox, March 8, 1787; Knox to Washington, March 19; Washington to Knox, April 3; Knox to Washington, April 9; Washington to Knox, April 27, 1787.

during the sitting of this Society. That the present moment is pregnant of great and strange events, none who will cast their eyes around them can deny. What may be brought forth between this and the first of May, to remove the difficulties which at present labor in my mind against the acceptance of the honor, which has lately been conferred on me by the Assembly, is not for me to predict; but I should think it incompatible with that candor, which ought to characterize an honest mind, not to declare that under my present view of the matter, I should be too much embarrassed by the meeting of these two bodies in the same place at the same moment, after what I have written, to be easy in my situation, and therefore that it would be improper to let my appointment stand in the way of another."

While this correspondence was going on, Col. David Humphreys of Connecticut, who had been his military aide, was urging Washington not to accept, in view of the fact that the Convention was not likely to be a success and that participation in a failure would impair his influence on the country. "I know your personal influence and character is justly considered the last stake which America has to play. Should you not reserve yourself for the united call of a Continent entire?" he wrote in January, 1787.[1] On the other hand, Randolph wrote, in January, entreating Washington not to make an immediate or final decision; and in March, he wrote again with considerable urgency. On April 9, Humphreys wrote that circumstances had so changed, since Congress had determined to recommend the Convention, that he now was inclined to agree with General Knox and other friends that Washington's attendance might be advisable:

[1] On March 24, 1787, Humphreys wrote that Connecticut and New York were likely to elect to the Convention delegates "directly anti-federal", and he asked, "what chance is there then that entire unanimity will prevail? . . . I have heard few express any sanguine expectations concerning the successful issue of the meeting, and I think not one had judged it eligible for you to attend."

"Should you decide to be present at the Convention, it will be indispensable to arrive in Philadelphia the preceding week, in order to attend the General Meeting of the Cincinnati. This may palliate, perhaps obviate, one of my former objections. I mentioned in my last that I had not conversed with a single character of consideration who judged it proper for you to attend the Convention. I have now seen several who think it highly interesting that you should be here. Gouverneur Morris and some others have wished me to use whatever influence I might have to induce you to come. I could not have promised this without counteracting my own judgment. I will not, however, hesitate to say that I do not conceive your attendance can hazard such personal ill consequences as were to be apprehended, before the proposed meeting had been legitimated by the sanction of Congress. If the difference of opinion amongst the members of this National Assembly should be as great as the variety of sentiments concerning the results, the progress of business before it will be attended with infinite perplexity and embarrassment. Besides the two primary objects of discussion, viz., 1st, whether the old Constitution can be supported, or 2d, whether a new one must be established, I expect a serious proposal will be made for dividing the Continent into two or three separate Governments. Local politics and diversity of interest will undoubtedly find their way into the Convention. Nor need it be a matter of surprise to find there, as subjects of infinite disagreement, the whole Western country as well as the navigation of the Mississippi. Should you think proper to attend, you will indisputably be elected President. This would give the measures a degree of national consequence in Europe and with posterity; but how far, under some supposable case, your personal influence, unattended with other authority, may compose the jarring interest of a great number of discordant individuals and control events, I will not take upon me to determine. We cannot augur anything very favorable, if we are to judge of future dispositions by those exhibited since the War."

On March 28, however (before he received Humphrey's last letter), Washington wrote to Randolph, agreeing to attend: [1]

"I had entertained hopes that another had been, or soon would be, appointed in my place, inasmuch as it is not only inconvenient for me to leave home, but because there will be, I apprehend, too much cause to arraign my conduct with inconsistence in again appearing on a public theatre, after a public declaration to the contrary, and because it will, I fear, have a tendency to sweep me back into the tide of public affairs, when retirement and ease is so essentially necessary for and is so much desired by me. However, as my friends, with a degree of solicitude which is unusual, seem to wish for my attendance on this occasion, I have come to a resolution to go, if my health will permit. . . . I have of late been so much afflicted with a rheumatic complaint in my shoulder that at times I am hardly able to raise my hand to my head, or turn myself in bed."

It is interesting to note that Madison, himself, as the date of the Convention approached, was so pessimistic as to its chances of success that he suggested to Randolph, April 15, that Washington delay his attendance:

"The probability of General Washington's coming to Philadelphia, is, in one point of view, flattering. Would it

[1] His decision to attend the Federal Convention made it necessary for Washington to reconsider his declination to attend the meeting of the Society of the Cincinnati, and to accept reappointment as President — as he explained in a letter to Jefferson, May 30, 1787: "Happy in finding (so far as I could learn by assiduous inquiry) that all the clamors and jealousies, which had been excited against the original Association, had ceased, I judged it a proper time in the last autumn to withdraw myself from any farther agency in the business; and to make my retirement complete, agreeably to my original plan. I wrote circular letters to all the State Societies, announcing my wishes, informing that I did not propose to be at the General Meeting, and requested not to be reelected President. This was the last step of a public nature I expected ever to have taken. But, having since been appointed by my native State to attend the National Convention, and having been pressed to a compliance in a manner which it hardly becomes me to describe, I have, in a measure, been obliged to sacrifice my own sentiments, and to be present in Philadelphia, at the very time of the General Meeting of the Cincinnati. After which I was not at liberty to decline the presidency, without placing myself in an extremely disagreeable situation with relation to that brave and faithful class of men whose persevering patriotism and friendship I had experienced on so many trying occasions."

not, however, be well for him to postpone his actual attendance, until some judgment can be formed of the result of
the meeting? It ought not to be wished by any of his friends
that he should participate in any abortive undertaking. It
may occur, perhaps, that the delay would deprive the Convention of his presiding auspices, and subject him, on his
arrival, to a less conspicuous point of view than he ought on
all occasions to stand in. Against this difficulty must be
weighed the consideration above mentioned."

It is well known that historians — American,
English, and foreign — have long agreed that no
political assembly ever contained a larger proportion
of members possessing high character, intellectual
ability, political sagacity, and far-sighted statesmanship. It is sometimes forgotten, however, that the
men of their own times were equally unanimous in
recognizing the merit of the delegates, and in according
to those delegates disinterested, unselfish, and patriotic
motives in the performance of their great task. Thus,
Jefferson wrote from Paris of his "high opinion of the
abilities and honesty of the framers of the Constitution."

John Adams wrote from London before the Convention, that it was to consist of "members of such
ability, weight, and experience that the result must be
beneficial," and later he wrote that the Constitution
was the result "of good heads prompted by good
hearts." Franklin wrote that the delegates were
"men of character for prudence and ability." John
Jay wrote of their "patriotism and talents." President
Ezra Stiles of Yale College, wrote that "this Federal
Convention embosoms some of the most sensible and
great characters in America." [1] Leading opponents of
the Constitution itself paid tribute to the character of its
framers. Thus, George Mason of Virginia wrote that
"America has certainly upon this occasion drawn forth

[1] *The Literary Diary of Ezra Stiles* (1912), III, June 6, 1787.

her first characters . . . of the purest intentions."
Richard Henry Lee wrote that "America probably
never will see an assembly of men of a like number
more respectable"; and Patrick Henry spoke of the
States as having trusted "the great object of revising
the Confederation to the greatest, the best, and the
most enlightened of our citizens."[1] M. Otto, the
French diplomatic representative in this country,
wrote to the Foreign Office that: "If all the delegates
chosen for this Congress attend, one will never have
seen, even in Congress, an Assembly more respectable
for talents, knowledge, disinterestedness, and patriotism
in those who will compose it."[2] As will be amply seen
in succeeding chapters, the newspapers of the day paid
unanimous and unstinted tribute to the high motives
and character of the delegates. And James Madison
at the close of his life, stated that: "Whatever may be
the judgment pronounced on the competency of the
architects of the Constitution, or whatever may be the
destiny of the edifice prepared by them, I feel it a duty
to express my profound and solemn conviction, derived
from my intimate opportunity of observing and appre-
ciating the views of the Convention, collectively and
individually, that there never was an assembly of men,
charged with a great and arduous trust, who were more
pure in their motives or more exclusively or anxiously
devoted to the object committed to them to . . .
best secure the permanent liberty and happiness of
their country."[3]

[1] So also, George Clinton ("Cato") in *New York Journal*, Oct. 11, 1787, wrote
that he thought "that the wisdom of America in that Convention, was drawn to a
focus. I placed an unbounded confidence in some of the characters who were members of it, from the services they had rendered their country, without adverting to
the ambitions and interested views of others." And James Winthrop ("Agrippa")
in *Massachusetts Gazette*, Jan. 20, 1788, termed the members of the Convention
"men respectable for learning and ability."

[2] M. Otto to Comte de Montmorin, April 10, 1787, *Farrand*, III, 15.

[3] *Preface to Notes of Debates*, by James Madison, written in 1834 or 1835.
Charles Pinckney said in the House, Feb. 13, 1821 (*16th Cong., 2d Sess.*): "This

That these men possessed the confidence of the people of this country was shown by the fact that eight of them were elected as Representatives and ten of them as Senators of the First Congress of the United States, in 1789. And the other posts of honor to which they were later called mark these men as worthy of confidence. Two became Presidents of the United States (Washington and Madison); and one, Vice President (Gerry). Two became Chief Justices of the United States (Rutledge and Ellsworth), and three, Associate Justices of the Supreme Court (Blair, Wilson, and Paterson). Randolph became Attorney General and Secretary of State of the United States; and Hamilton, Secretary of the Treasury. Six became Governors of their States. Four became Ministers to foreign countries.

It has sometimes been contended, in recent years, that these fifty-five men who drafted the Constitution were not truly representative of the people of the States, because they came entirely from the mercantile, the professional, or the propertied classes, and included no immediate representatives of the small farmers or mechanics. It has also been insisted that because they were the owners, to a greater or less degree, of Government securities and of landed properties, or of personalty used for loans or for business purposes, that the form of government which they adopted was designed chiefly in the interests of property and that the Constitution was an economic document framed primarily to protect property.[1] Those who urge this view of the

Constitution of compromise was formed by a body of men at least as well informed and disinterested and as much lovers of freedom and humanity as may probably ever again be assembled in this country."

[1] See *An Economic Interpretation of the Constitution* (1913), by Charles A. Beard. In this book, after elaborate research, Prof. Beard arrived at the conclusion that of the fifty-five delegates, forty-five had investments in public securities; fourteen in land for speculation; twenty-four in money loaned at interest; eleven in personalty in mercantile, manufacturing, and shipping interests; and fifteen in personalty

work of the framers of the Constitution overlook many factors.

In the first place, it is to be noted that if these delegates were not truly representative of American beliefs, of American principles, and of American desires at the time, then the same thing is true of the statesmen who sat in the Continental Congresses in 1775 and 1776, of those who signed the Declaration of Independence, of those who framed the State Constitutions, who drafted the Articles of Confederation, and who sat in the Congress from 1781 to 1786. For not only did the delegates comprise many of the actual men who took part in all of those other political gatherings prior to the date of the Federal Convention, but they came from the same class of men from which most of the other members of those previous gatherings were elected. So that if this Federal Convention was not truly representative of American principles, then neither were any of the Continental bodies which had previously met. Moreover, these delegates were appointed by State Legislatures; and in most of the States, the small farmers, who formed a part of the debtor class at the time (if such a thing as a distinctively debtor class existed — which is doubtful), had a fully adequate representation in the Legislatures. This fact is frequently overlooked by historians — the

in slaves. As some of his data were of a later date than 1787, the figures cannot be taken as entirely accurate. Moreover, as Prof. Beard points out, sixteen out of the forty-five owning Governmental securities owned less than $5000; yet no line of distinction can be traced in their votes in the Convention between the holders of large amounts and holders of small amounts of securities. It should be carefully noted, however, for it has been often overlooked, that Prof. Beard himself was scrupulously careful to state that he did not intend to charge that the delegates made the Constitution for their personal benefit, for he said (p. 73): "The purpose of such an enquiry is not, of course, to show that the Constitution was made for the personal benefit of the members of the Convention. Far from it. . . . The only point here considered is: Did they represent distinct groups whose economic interests they understood and felt in concrete, definite form through their own personal experience with identical property rights, or were they working merely under the guidance of abstract principles of political service?"

fact that, since possession of freehold in land was then a property qualification for voting for members of the Legislature, it was peculiarly the small farmers who, in most States, were possessed of the requisite qualification to vote. Hence, it cannot accurately be stated that they had no part in choosing representatives to the Federal Convention.

In the second place, the delegates did not and could not, from the nature of things, act in behalf or in the interest of one particular class in the community solely, for the interests of each class varied very greatly in the different States. In a recent brilliant history, there has been repeated the theory that economic conditions accounted for the division of party lines in 1787; [1] and the following classes of people are described as having been those interested in promoting a new Constitution — all who held claims against the Government, original holders of securities and speculators in such securities, owners of warrants for land, the soldiers and officers who held Government notes, certificates, and warrants, the shipowners and agents engaged in foreign trade, the domestic merchants, the money lenders; and, it is said: "In short, the financial, creditor, commercial, and speculating classes, from every point of view, as they saw the matter, had valid reasons for wanting to establish under their own auspices, on American soil, a system of centralized political, judicial, and economic control." On the other hand, the agrarian interests, the small farmers, and the debtors are portrayed as the classes chiefly opposed to the Constitution. Similarly, in another recent book, it is said: "The Federal Constitution was a practical document, drawn up by representatives of the class of property owners, security holders, speculators in Western lands, merchants and

---

[1] *The Rise of American Civilization* (1927), by Charles A. Beard and Mary R. Beard, I, 303–306.

bankers, who wisely desired to escape from the economic and fiscal chaos of the Government under the Articles of Confederation.   The Constitution was opposed by the debtors, chiefly from the agricultural districts." [1]

Such an alignment of interests in favor of and against the Constitution is clearly imperfect.   The lines of the picture are altogether too neat, too simple.   Incidentally, it may be noted that the division of the community, above made, omits any mention of a considerable proportion of the population — all the physicians, clergymen, and small attorneys, all the small tradespeople, all the domestic servants, apprentices, and farm laborers, all the mechanics in the industrial and shipping business, and all the small manufacturing industries (woolen, iron, paper, cotton, and many others), which had grown up during the war and which were conducted by individual men.   But the fundamental error made by the economic historians is this — that no such division of the population into a debtor and a creditor class as they have contended, existed in fact.   The bulk of Americans, in 1787, were actually neither rich nor poor, but consisted of the plain, every-day citizen, hard working and possessing sufficient means to raise a family in reasonable comfort.   Richard Henry Lee of Virginia, the Antifederalist leader, rightly depicted the real situation when, writing in the fall of 1787, he said that there were "two very unprincipled parties in the United States, two fires between which the honest and substantial people have long found themselves situated. . . .   These two parties . . . are really insignificant, compared with the solid, free, and independent part of the community":

"One party is composed of little insurgents, men in debt who want no law and who want a share of the property of others; these are called levellers, Shaysites, etc.   The other

---

[1] *History and Social Intelligence* (1926), by Prof. Harry Elmer Barnes.

party is composed of a few, but more dangerous men, with their servile dependents; these avariciously grasp at all power and property; you may discover in the actions of these men an evident dislike to free and equal government, and they will go systematically to work to change, essentially, the forms of government in this country; these are called aristocrats, etc., etc. Between these two parties is the weight of the community; the men of middling property, men not in debt on the one hand, and men on the other, content with republican governments, and not aiming at immense fortunes, offices and power."

And James Madison wrote that while, in Virginia, the lawyers and propertied men were opposing the Constitution, "the body of sober and steady people, even of the lower order, are tired of the vicissitudes, injustice, and follies which have characterized public measures, and are impatient for some changes which promise stability and repose." [1]

It is this solid, free, independent part of the community — these "men of middling property, who were not in debt on the one hand and on the other content with republican governments" — that the economic historian leaves entirely out of account, or else wrongly classifies as a unit. In other words, an alignment of men as for or against a new Constitution, on the basis of property or non-property — credits or debts — is an attempted simplification of the political situation in 1787, which facts and human nature do not support. It is impossible to draw a hard and fast economic line with reference to the attitude of classes of men towards the Constitution, and omit all consideration of their political faiths, ideals, inherited sentiments, personal antagonisms, past experiences, and patriotic desires. The same class had different views in different parts of the country. The same class had different interests

---

[1] *Writings of James Madison* (Hunt's ed.), V, Madison to Jefferson, Dec. 9, 1787.

which would impel them in divergent directions, if they were to be moved purely by selfish causes. Thus, ownership of Government securities by the delegates or by others was certainly not a proof that they were devoted to property interests; for at that time (as recently during the Great War), there was probably not a single patriotic citizen of any means whatever, who had not invested in such securities, or who had not received them in payment for his military or other services to the Government. Moreover, large numbers of the small farmers and debtors were also holders of such Government paper received in payment for supplies to the army. So, too, large numbers of the soldiers and officers were also owners of Government paper and land warrants, and at the same time many of them were small farmers and debtors. According to the economic theory, all these men, in their capacity of Government creditors, were necessarily interested in the adoption of the Constitution, yet, equally according to the economic theory, as small farmers and debtors, they were necessarily opposed to its adoption. It may be noted that the leaders of the Shays Rebellion, themselves, were army officers holding such Government claims, and that two of them were actually members of the Society of the Cincinnati: while of the Massachusetts State Convention, which ratified the Constitution, fifty out of eighty-one members bearing military titles voted against the Constitution. In actual application, the attempted simple classification does not work. So too, if all the debtors were to be regarded as interested in opposing the Constitution and in upholding paper money and stay and tender laws favorable to them as a class, then a large number of the wealthy planters would, theoretically, be so included; for most men of property were then heavily in debt. Thus, George Washington himself was in grave financial difficulties at this time, and had written only three months before the Federal Convention, that he had had no crops for two years and that he could not pay his running expenses without selling some of his land at less than its value; and again he had written that unless a loan could be repaid, the sheriff might distrain his land for taxes.[1]   George Mason of Virginia, though owner of large landed estates, said that he could not come to the Convention unless the Legislature would advance his salary.   Hence, if impelled merely by economic motives, it would have been the interest of such men to vote in the Convention in favor of stay laws postponing payment of their debts.   In South Carolina, many of the wealthy planters heavily in debt *did*, in fact, oppose the Constitution because they favored paper money legislation as a means of paying their debts.[2]

The so-called "landed interest" were by no means united in their views, and were far from acting as a unit. This class was described by Charles Pinckney of South Carolina, as follows: "In the Eastern and Northern States, the landed property is nearly equally divided; very few have large bodies and there are few that have not small tracts.   The greater part of the people are employed in cultivating their own lands;   the rest in

---

[1] Washington wrote to Mrs. Mary Washington, Feb. 15, 1787, that he owed for taxes, that he had had no crops for two years and that he could not pay his expenses without selling some of his land at less than its value.   To John F. Mercer, he wrote, Jan. 11, 1788, that unless Mercer should pay two hundred pounds "which you assured me in Philadelphia, I might absolutely rely", he would be obliged to allow the sheriff to distrain his (Washington's) land for taxes; see also letter to Mercer, Sept. 9, 1787.

[2] See *History of the United States* (1912), by Edward Channing, III, 482–483. See also letter from Charleston, So. Car., in *Independent Gazetteer*, April 19, 1788, stating that John Rutledge, one of the leading advocates of the Constitution, "is principally concerned here in the paper money laws and in preventing the due execution of property for lawful debts. . . .   The back country interests (*i.e.*, the small farmer) is as large as the lower, and they are pretty unanimous in the opposition, and the lower is divided; the first opposed from principle, and the latter from paper money interests, as all the lower country are in favor of paper money, etc., except the city and some leading characters such as Aedanus Burke, Esq., who is the head of the opposition in the City."

handicraft and commerce. . . . Among the landed interest, it may be truly said there are few of them rich and few of them very poor." [1] In New York, the owners of large estates were opposed to the Constitution, because of their fear of new and heavy Federal direct taxes on land; in Virginia and South Carolina, many of the large planters were actuated by the same fears. Of the small farmers, it is true that many of those in Massachusetts, Connecticut, and North Carolina were opposed to the Constitution; but on the other hand, many of those in Pennsylvania and Western Virginia were active in support of the Constitution.[2]

As to the lawyers, it will be found that their views varied in the different States. In Massachusetts, they all favored the Constitution. In New York, they were divided, and in Virginia, they were largely opposed. Thus, James Madison wrote to Jefferson, December 9, 1787, that in Virginia: "The General and Admiralty Courts, with most of the Bar, oppose the Constitution", and "while in Virginia and some of the other States in the Middle and Southern Districts of the Union, the men of intelligence, patriotism, property, and independent circumstances are thus divided, all of this description in the Eastern States and most of the middle States are zealously attached to the Constitution." [3]

[1] *Elliot's Debates*, IV, 321.

Madison said in the Convention, July 26, 1787: "Landed possessions were no certain evidence of real worth. Many enjoyed them to a great extent who were more in debt than they were worth. The unjust laws of the States had proceeded more from this class of men than any other." G. Morris said, August 7, that $\frac{9}{10}$ of the people "are at present freeholders."

[2] In the *Pennsylvania Packet*, Dec. 25, 1787, a correspondent just returned from Virginia wrote that "at least $\frac{19}{20}$ of the yeomen of Virginia are on the side of General Washington, the man of the People, in favour of the new Government," and that "the nabobs or great men (falsely so called) of Virginia are its only enemies." On the other hand, Patrick Henry, in the Virginia State Convention in June, 1788, stated, as his belief, that "the great body of yeomanry are in decided opposition to it." *Elliot's Debates*, IV, 159. It is a fact, however, that it was the vote of the delegates from the small farming districts in the Western part of Virginia (other than Kentucky), which secured the adoption of the Constitution in Virginia.

[3] *Writings of James Madison* (Hunt's ed.), V, Madison to Jefferson, Dec. 9, 1787. A letter from a Representative in the Virginia Assembly who wrote from Richmond,

If there was any wealthy class at that time, it consisted probably of the importers, the merchants, and the shipowners in the sea-coast towns and cities; but these were divided in their views; in New York most of them opposed the Constitution, for fear of the loss to that State of its import taxes and its commercial monopoly; while in Pennsylvania and Massachusetts, they took a contrary view. From this class of persons, it is to be noted, there were but few delegates in the Federal Convention.

As to the labor class and its attitude towards the Constitution, no such class, as now understood, then existed. It was then composed chiefly of apprentices, domestic servants, farm laborers, mechanics and sailors. As to the mechanics and the other city workingmen, they favored the Constitution in New York, Philadelphia, and Boston, and wherever any note was taken of their action.[1] As to the farm laborers and domestic servants, there is no evidence extant as to their votes (even if many of them were entitled to any vote, which is doubtful). There were, in those days, no employees of business, manufacturing, public service, or municipal corporations, for no such corporations had then come into existence.[2] Hence, the Convention had no occasion to consider any of the problems affecting capital and labor, which give rise to so much of the social

Dec. 15, 1787: "The most respectable names appear in the number of pros and cons. . . . I will place at the head of the list for it, Judge Pendleton who is looked up to as the President of the Convention to be held in June. Nicholas, Wythe, Blair, the Pages, Johnson, Stuart, Harvie, Jones, Wood — and a multitude of others against it — first, as the leader of this party — Henry, Mason, Governor Randolph, Lawson, John Taylor, with most of the General Court lawyers and many of the Judges, R. H. Lee . . . and many others. In a word, the division of the multitude is great." *Maryland Journal*, Dec. 18, 1787.

[1] As to the Constitution as a benefit to the mechanics, see *New York Independent Journal*, Oct. 6, 1787; *American Herald* (Boston), Jan. 14, 1788.

[2] In 1787, the only business corporations in existence were as follows: in Massachusetts, 1 banking, 1 bridge corporation; in Connecticut, 1 mining; in Pennsylvania, 1 bank, 1 insurance company; in Maryland, 1 canal, 1 navigation; in Virginia, 2 navigation; in South Carolina, 1 navigation. See *Two Centuries of Growth of American Law* (1901), pp. 296–311.

legislation of today. Unless these things are borne in
mind in considering the work of the men of 1787, one
is constantly in danger of "reading into the past, con-
ceptions which are especially characteristic of the
present. The problems that the founders of the
Government faced were essentially problems of political
organization, while the problems that we have to face
today are essentially problems of industrial organization." [1] It is faulty history to describe the subjects of
division in 1787 in terms of class consciousness, for such
social phenomena did not then exist.

In view of the above, it is evident that if the picture
is to be drawn of a division of the American people on
economic lines, the lines would cross and recross and
break and twist and curve, so as to render the line of
division unrecognizable. And while, just as today as
well as in every epoch of history, there were undoubtedly numbers of voters who viewed the Constitution
according to the manner in which they considered its
adoption or rejection would benefit them personally,
these people could not be classified uniformly in any
single town, county, State, or section of the country.
So that the delegates to the Federal Convention, even
if they had selfishly desired to frame only such a Constitution as would protect the interests of the particular
class whom they were supposed to represent, would
have found themselves confronted with many conflicting
views and interests even within that class.

That the leaders, however, were not primarily actuated by economic or class interests, unconsciously or
consciously, must be evident to those who have read
the letters in the previous chapter. One cannot fail
to be impressed with the fact that the burning desire
and insistent determination pervading them was, that
the Union of the States must be preserved and that all

[1] John H. Latané in *Amer. Pol. Sci. Rev.* (1913), VII, pp. 698 *et seq.*

legislation or other conditions prevailing in the States which were impeding or undermining this possibility of Union must be remedied, in any new form of Government that might be adopted. Proof that economic conditions *per se* played a minor part in the plans for alteration of the old Articles of Confederation is to be found in the fact that, as before pointed out, their plans for a more efficient and adequate Union were being suggested and worked out, long before the economic evils developed as alarmingly as they did in the three years prior to the Federal Convention. It has also been shown, in the previous chapter, how the Shays Rebellion has been over-emphasized by historians as a leading factor in producing an agreement upon a new Constitution, and how the fears produced by the sentiment prevailing in so many States for a separation of the Confederacy into three separate Confederacies was a far more potent factor in arousing men to the necessity of a Government, which should, if possible, bind the country into a firm Union.

That many of the delegates were also greatly alarmed at the unwisdom and injustice of much of the State legislation dealing with property rights, and that they were resolved to remedy this evil, is undoubtedly true. Madison, indeed, later stated that such legislation "perhaps more than anything else produced this Convention." But it was not the economic effect of these State laws which chiefly alarmed them; it was the fact that these laws were creating State dissensions which placed the National Union and independence in vital danger, and all the delegates were anxious to remedy any conditions, economic or otherwise, which were promoting these dissensions.[1] It is to be noted, more-

---

[1] Thus Madison himself in his *Vices of the Political System of the United States*, written in the spring of 1787 (see *Writings of James Madison* (Hunt's ed.), II, 361), enumerated the State laws as to paper money, installments of debts, occlusion of the courts, legal tender, etc., as "aggressions on the rights of other States"; and,

over, that those statesmen who led in opposition to the
Constitution, like Patrick Henry, Richard Henry Lee,
and Samuel Adams, were equally opposed to State
laws issuing paper money and impairing obligation of
contracts and, had they been members of the Convention, would equally have voted to include restrictions on the States in these respects.   The desire to
protect individual rights (whether of property or otherwise and whether of the rich or poor) against the Governmental injustice was shared by the leaders of thought
on both sides.   It should further be noted that the
framers of the Constitution (even though holders of
Government securities) made no express provision in
the Constitution for the payment of the Government
securities; they simply provided that such securities
should remain as valid as under the Confederation;
and, while they vested the new Congress with power to
tax to pay debts, this was done in order to provide for
a stable Government in the interest of the prosperity
of all citizens, for it had been agreed by all — Federalists and Antifederalists alike — in 1787, that Congress
must be given such a taxing power and the only disagreement had been over its power to lay direct taxes.

The broad purpose of the delegates in respect to the
protection of property was eloquently set forth by the
veteran statesman, Edmund Pendleton, in the State
Convention of Virginia, in 1788.[1]

"I am an advocate of fixing our government in true republican principles, giving to the poor man free liberty in his
person and property.   Whether a man be great or small, he
is equally dear to me.   I wish for a regular government, in
order to secure and protect those honest citizens who have
been distinguished — I mean the industrious farmer and

he said, "the practice of many States in restricting the commercial intercourse with
other States . . . is certainly adverse to the spirit of the Union and tends to beget
retaliating regulations . . . destructive of the general harmony."

[1] *Elliot's Debates*, III, 295.

planter. I wish them to be protected in the enjoyment of
their honestly and industriously acquired property. I wish
commerce to be fully protected and encourage it. . . . I
presume that there can be no political happiness, unless
industry be cherished and protected, and property secured.
. . . In my mind, the true principle of republicanism and
the greatest security of liberty is a regular government."

To sum up, the chief aim of the delegates was to
establish an adequate Government which should promote the Union of the States and which should be able
to maintain itself at home and abroad. Economic
prosperity was but an incident. To represent it as
their leading aim is to attribute a sordid and selfish
purpose which neither their characters nor their principles warrant. And in the words of Robert Louis
Stevenson, "it is at best but a pettifogging, pickthank
business to decompose actions into little personal
motives, and explain heroism away." An able liberal
writer of today has struck the keynote in reply to those
who attribute economic motives to the class of men
which included Washington and his colleagues in the
Convention. "It was an aristocracy, and as such it
had inherited a concept of public duty, quite separate
and distinct from the universal concept of private
interest. There were things that Washington simply
would not do, even to serve Washington. He saw the
Nation that he had helped to set up, as something apart
from and superior to himself, or to any other man in
it — as something deserving and demanding a high
measure of devotion." [1] To the charge that they were
influenced by their economic conditions, the framers
would have made the same answer that Jefferson later
made as President, to the charge that he was influenced in his conduct of American affairs by his
predilections for France: "I must have had a mind

[1] Henry L. Mencken, in *American Mercury* (1927), XII, 251.

far below the duties of my station to have felt either
National partialities or antipathies in conducting the
affairs confided to me.   My affections were first for my
country, and then generally for all mankind."

The men who framed the Constitution conceived and
realized that they were building for a great Nation and
for a great and illimitable future.   They so stated in
the Convention.   Edmund Randolph of Virginia said
that "the salvation of the Republic was at stake."
James Wilson of Pennsylvania said that "when he
considered the amazing extent of country, the immense
population which is to fill it, the influence which the
Government we are to form will have, not only on the
present generation of our people and their multiplied
posterity but on the whole Globe, he was lost in the
magnitude of the object. . . .   We should consider
that we are providing a Constitution for future generations and not merely for the peculiar circumstance of
the moment."   And John Rutledge of South Carolina
said: "As we are laying the foundation for a great
empire, we ought to take a permanent view of the
subject and not look at the present moment only."
Furthermore, they believed that they were engaged
upon a work which would affect government not only
in this country but also in the whole world.   As
James Madison said, it was probable that they "were
now digesting a plan which in its operation would
decide forever the fate of republican government."
"Something must be done, or we shall disappoint not
only America but the whole world," said Elbridge
Gerry of Massachusetts. Men holding such broad
views as to the nature of their task and its effect upon
the whole future of their country and of the world were
not moved by selfish, personal, or class interests in
performing their great work.   They were not engaged
in constructing merely a guarantee of material prosper-

ity. Their object was the welfare of their country and not merely the welfare of their currency, their commerce, or their class. They were inspired by the determination to build a great Nation which should ensure the permanence of the liberty they had won on the battlefields of the Revolution.

To what extent were the people at large familiar with the political and economic conditions which prevailed in 1787, and which were leading to dissolution of the Union? To what extent were they inspired with the views of the leading statesmen of the times? The questions are difficult of answer. The people probably had slight acquaintance with theories of government; for, as John Adams wrote in 1790: "It is incredible how small is the number in any nation of those who comprehend any system of Constitution or administration." Undoubtedly, the nature of the remedy and the type of new government required under existing conditions were more clearly perceived by the great men whose ideas and motives have been described in the preceding chapter than by the mass of the people. It was the possession of that vision which made them leaders. A great leader is the man of intuition, the man who is the first to feel the movement of the age and to inspire others with a recognition of its significance. Such leaders, as Emerson said, "having hearts and minds in peculiar unison with their time and their country are able to point the way with the surest aim. . . . They are the lenses through which we read our own minds." And as Edmund Burke wrote: "As well may we fancy that, of itself, the sea will swell, and that without winds the billows will insult the adverse shore, as that the gross mass of the people will be moved and elevated, and continue by a steady and permanent direction to bear upon one point, without the influence of superior mind."

These days prior to the Federal Convention were peculiarly a time when a few men with insight and patriotic statesmanship led and moulded public opinion. But while perhaps not capable of formulating or deciding for themselves the changes in their Government needed to preserve their union, the people of the times were undoubtedly familiar with and deeply impressed by the Legislative and economic conditions, which made those changes imperative. They received their political education partly from almanacs, from pamphlets, from letters of leading American statesmen copied or passed from hand to hand, but chiefly from the newspapers.[1] The comments and correspondence appearing in the papers (whether containing accurate or inaccurate views) were prominent sources from which Americans drew their political opinions; and a survey of the papers, between January and May, 1787, affords a fairly accurate idea of the extent to which the minds of the reading public were directed towards the problems which gave rise to the Federal Convention. The newspapers of Philadelphia, Boston, and New York played the most important part in this political education of the country; for not only were they the leading papers in their respective States, but they were also the chief source from which the papers of the other States derived material to fill their columns; and comments and letters appearing in these three cities were reproduced or otherwise used by

[1] Politics formed the leading topic in a new monthly magazine issued by Matthew Carey called *The American Museum*, whose second number had appeared on February 1, 1787. Though containing poems, essays, fiction, and scientific articles, this first number presented seven articles on opportune political topics: "Comfort for America or remarks on her real situation, her interests and her politics" (by B. Franklin); "On the defects of the Confederation"; "Letter of a farmer aged 67 on the real cause of and cure for Hard Times"; "Causes of a country's growing rich"; "Letter on the propriety of investing Congress with power to regulate trade"; "Letter on American manufactures"; "Common Sense by Mr. Payne. Part the first, on the origin and design of government in general — with concise remarks on the English Constitution. Part the Second, on monarchy and hereditary succession."

editors throughout the country. Nothing in these papers is more striking than the amount of space devoted to the political situation, illuminating references being found to all the conditions which were factors in convincing the public of the necessity of a change in their form of Government — the proposals for division into three Confederacies, the paper money legislation, the situation in Rhode Island, the Shays Rebellion, the refusal of New York to grant to Congress power to levy import duties, the disordered state of the currency, the iniquitous State legislation violative of private contracts — all were commented on in numerous articles and letters.

One factor in the situation undoubtedly greatly influenced men to look favorably on proposals for a change in the form of Government — namely, the existence (or at least the belief in the existence) of "hard times." In parts of some of the States, seriously depressed conditions prevailed in agriculture and in commercial business. Paper money in some States had driven out specie, and debtors, even with the best intentions, found it difficult to pay their debts. Foreign commerce was burdened by the navigation laws of England, and interstate commerce by the restrictive laws of States like New York and Virginia. Taxes were inordinately high.[1] That the reports of "hard times"

[1] Some statesmen believed that the hard times were due to the people's own fault rather than to laws or lack of them. Thus, Noah Webster wrote to Timothy Pickering, Aug. 10, 1786, from Massachusetts: "It is a fact, demonstrated by correct calculations, that the common people in the country drink rum and tea sufficient every year to pay the interest of the public debt — articles of luxury, which, so far from doing them any good, injure their morals, impair health and shorten their lives. A man has a right, in a political view, to make himself sick or drunk when he pleases, provided he does not injure himself or his neighbors; but when, by these means, he renders himself unable to fulfill the duties of society, or comply with the laws of the State, very little indulgence should be granted to luxuries. The best way to redress grievances is, for every man when he gets a sixpence, instead of purchasing a pint of rum or two ounces of tea, to deposit his pence in a desk till he has accumulated enough to answer the calls of the Collector. Every man who does this soundly redresses his own grievances." *Pickering Papers MSS.*, XIX, 74. Richard Henry Lee, writing to George Mason, May 15, 1787, said: "Alas,

were somewhat exaggerated is probably true.   An
acute historian has recently pointed out that "between
1783 and 1787, the country had passed through a
period of economic adjustment.   This was now coming
to an end; and commerce and industry were beginning
to thrive; but this fact was not recognized at the time.
Contemporary evidence as to actual conditions is
always very misleading.   The onlooker sees only a
portion of any field, is influenced by local and personal
considerations, and is governed largely by his own
immediate experience.   Statistics that are accessible
to us, but were unattainable by the voters in 1786 and
1787, demonstrate the truth of the theory that com-
mercially and industrially the country had regained its
prosperity by 1788 and was on the highroad to it in
1786." [1]   That there were some statesmen who perceived that economic conditions were improving is seen
from letters written by Benjamin Franklin from
Philadelphia to English correspondents. [2]

Sir, I fear it is more in vicious manners than in mistakes in form (of government)
that we must seek for the causes of the present discontent."

[1] *History of the United States* (1912), by Edward Channing, III, 481.   Charles
A. Beard in *An Economic Interpretation of the Constitution* (1913), p. 48, makes a
similar suggestion: "Certainly the inflamed declarations of the Shaysites are not
to be taken as representing accurately the state of the people, and just as certainly
the alarmist letters and pamphlets of interested persons on the other side are not
to be accepted without discount.   When it is remembered that most of our history
has been written by Federalists, it will become apparent that great care should be
taken in accepting, without reserve, the gloomy pictures of the several conditions
prevailing under the Articles of Confederation.   In fact, a very learned, though
controversial historian, Henry B. Dawson, in an article published more than forty
years ago, makes out quite a plausible case (documented by minute research) for
the statement that the 'chaos' of which historians are wont to speak, when
dealing with the history of the years 1783–87, was a creation of their fancies."   See
The Historical Magazine (1871), Second Series, IX, pp. 157 *et seq.*

[2] Franklin to William Hunter, Nov. 24, 1786; to Edward Bancroft, Nov. 26,
1786; to Duke de Rochefoucauld, April 15, 1787.   These letters possibly are to be
received with caution as depicting with entire accuracy the real situation; for it
must be noted that there were many statesmen in England who were giving currency to statements that the United States was on the point of economic and political dissolution and nearly ready to rejoin the mother country, and who were using
such reports as a basis for their contention that no commercial treaty should be
entered into with the United States.   Franklin may possibly have been painting
the picture in too optimistic colors in order to counteract these misleading English

Whatever may have been the real facts, however, as to the advance towards recovery of prosperity in 1787, it is undoubtedly true that "this fact was not recognized at the time", by the general public.[1] This is one of the instances in which what the people believed was more important than what the actual fact was.[2] And undoubtedly, there was a very widespread belief, entertained not only by the mercantile and professional classes, but by the farmers as well, that return of prosperity would be promoted by a reform in the Government. And as William Bingham, a Member of Congress from Pennsylvania, wrote to Dr. Richard Price, December 1, 1786: "Our resources are great, the industry and intelligence of our people are not to be surpassed; and I do not believe there exists a greater fund of public and private virtue than in this country.

stories. James Winthrop ("Agrippa"), however, in *Massachusetts Gazette*, Nov. 30, 1787, wrote: "Let any man look around his own neighborhood, and see if the people are not with a very few exceptions, peaceable and attached to the Government, if the country had ever within their knowledge more appearance of industry, improvement and tranquillity. . . . Circumstances all denote a general prosperity. One class of citizens indeed suffer greatly. . . . The publick creditors . . . the ship carpenters."

[1] In *The Rise of American Civilization* (1927), by Charles A. Beard and Mary R. Beard, it is said (p. 302): "It has become the fashion to draw a doleful picture of the age, yet an analysis of the data upon which that view is built raises the specter of skepticism. The chief sources of information bearing on this thesis are the assertions and lamentations of but one faction in the great dispute, and they must, therefore, be approached with the same spirit of prudence as Whig editorials on Andrew Jackson or Republican essays on Woodrow Wilson." This analogy is inaccurate. For, certainly prior to the political campaign for and against the ratification of the Constitution, the newspapers of the period were open to correspondence from more than the "one faction"; and those who believed that prosperity existed were as able to make known their views as were those who believed that conditions were tending towards disaster and ruin.

[2] *Connecticut Gazette*, Nov. 9, 1787: "Hear the complaints of our farmers, whose unequal oppressive taxes in every part of the country amount to nearly the rent of their farms. Hear too the complaints of every class of public creditors. See the number of our bankruptcies. Look at the melancholy countenances of our mechanics who now wander up and down our streets without employment. See our ships rotting in our harbors or excluded from nearly all the ports in the world. Listen to the insults that are offered to the American name and character in every Court of Europe. See order and honor everywhere prostrate in the dust, and religion with all her attendant train of virtues about to quit this Continent forever. View these things, fellow citizens, and then say that we do not require a new, a protecting and efficient Federal Government, if you can."

Nothing is wanting but a good government to direct these advantages to public good and private benefit."

Unquestionably, there were many men who were opposed to increase of Executive power, to any tendency towards military domination, and to proposals to vest Congress with such powers as might overthrow the State Governments, and who feared lest the calling of a Convention should result in the suggestion of an aristocratical or monarchical form of Government. These men re-echoed the fears which Rufus King and Elbridge Gerry had expressed, two years before, in refusing to lay before Congress a memorial of the Massachusetts Legislature in favor of the calling of a Convention. Though both King and Gerry had, in 1787, changed their minds on the subject, they had, in 1785, apprehended that such a measure "would produce throughout the Union, an exertion of the friends of aristocracy to send members who would promote a change of Government":

"Plans have been artfully laid and vigorously pursued which, had they been successful, we think would inevitably have changed our Republican Governments into baleful aristocracies. Those plans are frustrated, but the same spirit remains in their abettors. And the Institution of the Cincinnati, honourable and beneficent as the views may have been of the officers who compose it, we fear, if not totally abolished will have the same fatal tendency. 'More power in Congress,' has been the cry from all quarters; but especially those whose views, not being confined to a Government that will best promote the happiness of the people, are extended to one that will afford lucrative employments, and military. Such a Government is an aristocracy, which would require a standing army and a numerous train of pensioners and placemen to prop and support its exalted administration."

But opposition to the Federal Convention on the above grounds had, by the spring of 1787, very greatly diminished, and there is little evidence of it in the newspapers or in the correspondence of the day.

It is a significant fact that the regions where antagonism chiefly existed were the frontier farming settlements and the small towns distant from the seaboard, which were little reached by the newspapers and which had few sources of information as to conditions prevailing outside. Where communities were ignorant of legislation in other States, productive of political or other evils, it was natural that they should feel a minor interest in the Union and a more active desire for the supremacy of their own particular State.[1] As a New Hampshire paper said, in the spring of 1787 : "One great cause of the discontents of the back country is their total want of regular intelligence. This gives designing men an opportunity of forging the grossest falsehoods and propagating them without fear of detection, there being no publick newspapers to stare them in the face, and contradict what they assert." [2] So, a Connecticut newspaper, commenting on the division of men into two parties over the question of imparting additional power to the Government, attributed the difference largely to lack of information :

[1] See *The Constitution of the United States — An Historical Survey of Its Formation* (1923), by Robert Livingston Schuyler, p. 27 : "Under such conditions, men's interests naturally centered in their own localities, and the patriotism of many a sturdy Revolutionist was bounded by the limits of his own State. Why should those who had taken up arms against the claim of Parliament to tax them, and who had'grumbled at the laws it passed for the regulation of their trade, promptly concede these very powers to another central and remote government?"

[2] See *Pennsylvania Packet*, Jan. 3, 1787; *New Hampshire Spy*, Feb. 16, 1787; *Connecticut Courant*, Nov. 20, 1786; see also *New York Gazette*, Jan. 1, 1787. Noah Webster wrote to Timothy Pickering from Boston, Sept. 13, 1786, as to the disturbances in Massachusetts: "The mob is headed by some desperate felons, without property or principle. Many well-meaning people are led into opposition merely by false information; and the truth, diffused among the people at large, would soon restore tranquillity." *Pickering Papers MSS.*, XIX, 78. A letter from Newburyport, Mass., in *Pennsylvania Packet*, Jan. 8, 1787, discussed the effect of the Massachusetts tax on newspapers which drove them out of business and prevented information from getting to the people, thus promoting the cause of the insurgents.

"There are two parties in this State, jealous of each other — federal and antifederal. The federal men suppose the antifederal to be knaves, artful, designing demagogues. The antifederal suppose the federal to be ambitious, tyrannical men who are aiming at power at the expense of the people at large. . . . The antifederal think as they have been bred — their education has been rather indifferent — they have been accustomed to think on the small scale — they can think on no other without an enlargement of their minds. Besides, most of them live remote from the best opportunities of information, the knowledge they acquire is late, and is longer in producing conviction in their minds than in more enlarged minds. . . . Were the antifederal men in this State to travel, to sit in Congress, to converse with men who understand foreign policy, in short, were they to view this State and the Continent in their true connection with other nations, they would think like the federal men and join in their measures."

That education in political conditions was necessary before effective reforms could be made, was interestingly commented upon by Dr. Benjamin Rush in writing to Dr. Richard Price, in 1786: "Republics are slow in discovering their interest, but when once they find it out, they pursue it with vigor and perseverance. Nothing can be done by our public bodies till they carry the people along with them, and as the means of propagating intelligence and knowledge in our country are as yet but scanty, all their movements are marked with appearances of delay and procrastination." [1]

It may be confidently stated, however, from a review of contemporary newspapers, that in the spring of 1787 the reading public of the several States were, in general, well-informed as to the conditions which the greater

[1] *Price Papers* in *Mass. Hist. Soc. Proc., 2d Series* (1903), XVII. Rush to Price, April 22; on May 25, 1786, he wrote: "An opinion seems to have pervaded all classes of people that an increase of power in Congress is absolutely necessary for our safety and independence."

part of their leaders believed rendered the calling of a Constitutional Convention imperative. Of the high hopes which were rested on that body and its performance, ample proof is given in the amount of space which the newspapers devoted to it and its members. Skepticism and distrust were entirely absent, and confidence in the results of the work of the delegates was apparent in all the papers. A letter published in December, 1786, and widely copied, expressed a view evidently generally felt : [1]

"A correspondent observes that every true patriot must be pleased with the very respectable delegation appointed by the State of Virginia to meet in Convention for Federal purposes in this city in May next. The names of Washington, Wythe, and Randolph will ever be held in the highest veneration by every lover of American history. It is to be hoped that the Assembly of Pennsylvania will appoint some of her first political characters to meet those illustrious statesmen and friends to their country before the present session expires. . . . A Convention composed of such and similar characters will, undoubtedly, be able to remove the defects of the Confederation, produce a vigorous and energetic Continental Government which will crush and destroy faction, subdue insurrections, revive public and private credit, disappoint our transatlantic enemies and their lurking emissaries among us, and finally (to use an Indian phrase) endure 'while the sun shines and the rivers flow.'"

As the date for its meeting approached, a very general interest in the Convention was evident through-

[1] *Independent Gazetteer*, Dec. 27, 1786; see also *Connecticut Courant*, Jan. 8, 1787, and many other papers. The lists of delegates appointed by Massachusetts, New York, Georgia, South Carolina, Delaware, Maryland, and Connecticut appeared successively in the Pennsylvania papers. *Pennsylvania Herald*, March 7, 14, May 2; *Pennsylvania Journal*, March 10, 28; *Independent Gazetteer*, Jan. 27, March 8, 17, April 3, 12, June 1; *Pennsylvania Packet*, May 17, 1787; see also *Massachusetts Centinel*, and *New York Daily Advertiser, passim*, in the spring of 1787. The *Pennsylvania Journal*, March 10, stated: "By a letter from Annapolis we are informed of several solemn conferences between both Houses of the Legislature of that State; deputies have been nominated to the Grand Convention . . . from whose united deliberations and wisdom so much dignity and benefit to the Confederation is expected by every well wisher to liberty and independence."

out the newspapers. In April, the Philadelphia and many other papers printed a Richmond despatch, giving the grateful news of Washington's decision to attend : [1]

"It is with peculiar satisfaction we inform the public that our illustrious fellow citizen, George Washington, Esquire, has consented to serve on the ensuing Federal Convention to be held in Philadelphia, the second Monday in May next, and that his Excellency, Edmund Randolph, Esquire, purposes leaving this city early in that month on the same business. Should a delegation attend from each or a majority of the States, chosen with that circumspection and wisdom which governed the Legislature of this Commonwealth, what happy consequences may not all the true friends to Federal Government promise themselves from the united zeal, policy and ability of so august an assembly."

A letter from Boston was printed by the Philadelphia papers, stating : [2]

"The political existence of the United States perhaps depends on the results of the Convention which is to be held in Philadelphia in May next, for the purpose of forming a National Government. The acknowledged necessity of the measure has induced nine States . . . to appoint delegates."

Another from Boston said :

"The States of America cannot be said to be under a Federal head, when they will not acknowledge any supremacy in Congress. In time of war, we were bound together by a principle of fear; that principle is gone. We are no longer United States because we are not under any firm and energetic compact. The breath of jealousy has blown the

[1] *Independent Gazetteer*, April 21, 26; *Pennsylvania Herald*, April 28; *Pennsylvania Journal*, April 28, 1787.

[2] *Pennsylvania Journal*, April 14; *Pennsylvania Herald*, April 14; *Independent Gazetteer*, April 30, 1787; *Massachusetts Centinel*, April 4, 11, 14, 1787; *New Hampshire Spy*, Feb. 6, April 30, 1787. A despatch from Worcester, Mass., in the *New York Daily Advertiser*, May 8, 1787, said: "It is now the general opinion that, unless some wise plan should be proposed by the Federal Convention and adopted by the several States, our republican Governments will speedily terminate — What will take their place, heaven only knows."

cobweb of our Confederation asunder. Every link of the
chain of union is separated from its companion. We live,
it is true, under the appearances of friendship, but we
secretly hate and envy and endeavor to thwart the interest
of each other. . . ."

A New Hampshire paper said:

"We are happy to hear that the citizens of the American
States begin to be more deeply impressed with the importance of having a *Federal head* — for we are headless at
present. We sincerely wish that this event, the vesting of
the United States in Congress assembled, with powers sufficient to regulate the internal and external police of the
States may speedily be effected — on it, in a great measure,
depends the political salvation of this country."

A letter from New York to Baltimore, in April, said:

"The effect of the Convention soon to be held at Philadelphia, creates much conjecture and political speculation.
The nature and excellency of the different kinds of governments that have ever existed or have ever been treated upon
is here every day discussed, explained, demonstrated, dis-
sected, reviewed and placed in every possible light, by everybody on every occasion; and we have as many predictions
of the fate of America as if the prophetic spirit of the ancient
Jews had remained among us."

Another Boston despatch commented on the hopes
entertained of the coming Convention, as follows:[1]

"Reasonably is it to be expected that the deliberations of
the sages and patriots who are to meet in Convention at
Philadelphia next month will be attended with much good.
An union of the abilities of so distinguished a body of men,
among whom will be a Franklin and Washington, cannot but
produce the most salutary measures. These last names
affixed to their recommendations (and it is to be hoped that
this will be the case) will stamp a confidence in them which
the narrow-souled antifederal politicians in the several

[1] *Independent Chronicle* (Boston), May 17, 1787.

States, who by their influence have hitherto damned us as a Nation, will not dare to attack or endeavour to nullify."

And the *Pennsylvania Journal* of May 11 emphasized the importance of the Convention : [1]

"A correspondent observes that, as the time approaches for opening the business of the Federal Convention, it is natural that every lover of his country should experience some anxiety for the fate of an expedient so necessary, yet so precarious. Upon the event of this great Council, indeed, depends everything that can be essential to the dignity and stability of the National character. . . . All the fortunes of the future are involved in this momentous undertaking. The imperfections and debility of the League, framed during a struggle for liberty and political existence, were obscured and concealed by the ardor of enterprise and the proximity of danger. The feelings of the people were then more obligatory than the positive injunction of law; and men in pursuit of an important object required no consideration to discharge their duty, but their interests and their passions. Though the Federal compact, therefore, thus fortified might be adequate to the acquisition, yet from the nature and disposition of human affairs, it becomes inadequate to the preservation, of sovereign power. Unless some rule is prescribed, some motive introduced which, in a state of tranquillity, will enforce a regard to the general interest equal to the voluntary enthusiasm arising from common suffering and apprehension, we have only exchanged tyranny for anarchy, we have idly preferred the prospect to the possession of a jewel, and have wasted our strength and riches in accomplishing the revolution, merely to furnish another memorable tale for the historian's pen."

One striking fact should be especially noted — that, during the six months prior to the meeting of the Convention, practically no comment appeared in the newspapers critical of or derogatory to the character or

---

[1] *Pennsylvania Journal*, May 11, 1787, reprinted in *Virginia Independent Chronicle*, May 23, 1787; *Massachusetts Centinel*, May 17, 1787, and in other papers.

motives of the delegates elected by the various States. It was clearly believed by their contemporaries, that they were wise and able men, who were to assemble with a pure and disinterested purpose — not for the sake of framing a Government in their own interests, but a Government which should be strong, National, and lasting, in the interests of the whole people. This continued to be the popular belief and sentiment throughout the sessions of the Convention itself. It was only after the ratification of the Constitution became the subject of a bitter, partisan, political campaign in the fall of 1787 and the spring of 1788, that any personal attacks on the framers were published.

In Part Two of this book, the actions of the Federal Convention, the views of the delegates and of other prominent statesmen as presented in their letters, and the sentiments of the correspondents and editors of the newspapers, are now to be described and reproduced, as they occurred or were written or published from day to day — presenting a daily picture of the political situation, both inside and outside the Convention, from its convening on May 14, until its adjournment on September 17, 1787.

PART TWO
DURING THE CONVENTION

CHAPTER ONE

THE OPENING OF THE CONVENTION

SUNDAY, MAY 13, 1787

On this day, General Washington, who had left Mount Vernon, a little after sunrise, Wednesday, May 9, arrived in Philadelphia. He occupied during the Convention the house owned by Robert Morris. Of his arrival, Madison wrote to Jefferson (May 15) that it was "amidst the acclamation of the people, as well as more sober marks of the affection and veneration which continues to be felt for his character." The *Journal* described the event as follows: "Sunday last, his Excellency General Washington a member of the grand Convention arrived here. He was met at some distance and escorted into the City, by the troop of horse and saluted at his entrance by the artillery. The joy of the people on the coming of this great and good man was shown by their acclamations, the ringing of bells, etc." The *New York Daily Advertiser* said that Washington's arrival "was announced by a salute of the United States from the train artillery and the ringing of bells. He was escorted from Chester by the City Light Dragoon, and has taken apartments at

Mrs. House's, one of the most genteel boarding houses in this city." [1]

Washington himself wrote in the diary which he kept from the date of his departure from Mount Vernon to the date of his return: [2]

"About 8 o'clock, Mr. Corbin and myself set out, and dined at Chester (Mrs. Withys), where I was met by Genls. Mifflin (now Speaker of the Pennsylvania Assembly), Knox and Varnum; the Colonels Humphreys and Minges; and Majors Jackson and Nicholas, with whom (after dinner) I proceeded to Philada. At Gray's Ferry, the city light horse, commanded by Colo. Miles, met me and (by whom and a large concourse I was escorted) escorted me in by the artillery officers who stood arranged at the entrance of the City and saluted as I passed. Alighted through a crowd at Mrs. House's, but being again warmly and kindly pressed by Mr. and Mrs. Robert Morris to lodge with them, I did so, and had my baggage removed thither. Waited on the President, Doctr. Franklin, as soon as I got to town. On my arrival the bells were chimed."

Robert Morris, as early as April 23, had invited Washington to be his guest while in Philadelphia: [3]

[1] *Pennsylvania Journal*, May 16; *Freeman's Journal*, May 16; *New York Daily Advertiser*, May 18, 1787. The boarding house of Mrs. Mary House was at Fifth and Market Streets. In the *American Museum*, for August, 1787, a magazine published in Philadelphia by Mathew Carey, there appears "Verses on General Washington's Arrival in Philadelphia", by Philip Freneau.

Jacob Hiltzheimer, a prominent German farmer and stock breeder of Philadelphia, wrote in his *Diary* (1893) on May 13, 1787: "Went twice to church. This evening his Excellency General Washington arrived in the city from his seat in Virginia. The City Troops of horse received him at Mr. Gray's Ferry; the artillery company saluted with firing their cannon."

Morris' house, on Market Street east of Sixth, was the finest private residence in the city. It was built of brick, three stories high, with three windows on the first floor and four windows on the second and third floors, two on either side of the main hall. The main building was forty-two feet wide by fifty-two feet deep, and the kitchen and washhouses twenty feet wide by fifty-five feet deep. The stables would accommodate twelve horses. On each side of the house were vacant lots used as a garden and containing trees and shrubbery. See *Manuscript of Robert Morris* (1876), by Henry A. Homes.

[2] Except in some matters of punctuation and abbreviation, I have followed, in general, the version of the diary given in *The Diaries of George Washington* (1925), edited by John C. Fitzpatrick.

[3] *Washington Papers MSS.* in Library of Congress.

"The public papers have announced your consent to serve as a member of the Convention to be held in this City. This is what I ardently wished for and I am truly rejoiced at it. I was only restrained from writing to you by motives of delicacy, thinking that your own judgment rather than the persuasion of friends ought to determine. I hope Mrs. Washington will come with you and Mrs. Morris joins me in requesting that you will, on your arrival come to our house and make it your home during your stay in this City. We will give you as little trouble as possible and endeavour to make it agreeable. It will be a charming season for travelling, and Mrs. Washington, as well as yourself will find benefit from the journey, change of air, etc. As I hope soon for the pleasure of seeing you, I will only add that you must not refuse our request and the honor you confer by acceptance shall ever be considered a great favour."

MONDAY, MAY 14, 1787

On this day, the date appointed for its assembling, the Federal Convention met in the State House (old Independence Hall). The official minutes state as follows:

"On Monday, the 14th day of May A.D. 1787, and in the eleventh year of the independence of the United States of America at the State House in the City of Philadelphia, in virtue of appointments from their respective States, sundry deputies to the Federal Convention appeared; but a majority of the States not being represented, the members present adjourned, from day to day, until Friday, the 25th of said month."

Washington noted in his diary:

"This being the day appointed for the Convention to meet, such members as were in town assembled at the State House, but only two States being represented, viz. Virginia and Pennsylvania, agreed to attend at the same place tomorrow (at 11 o'clock). Dined in a family way at Mr. Morris's (and drank tea there)."

The newspapers announced the opening of the Convention as follows: [1]

"Yesterday a number of the honorable the delegates from the States of Pennsylvania, Delaware, Virginia and North Carolina, to the Federal Convention appointed to be held in this city, met at the State House. The South Carolina members have arrived, and from every information we have reason to conclude that the representation will be complete in a few days."

TUESDAY, MAY 15, 1787

The Convention met and adjourned, as the requisite majority of the thirteen States were not yet represented by a sufficient number of delegates to act for the States respectively.

Washington noted in his diary:

"Repaired at the hour appointed to the State House, but no more States being represented than were yesterday tho' several more members had come in (viz. No. Carolina and Delaware, as also New Jersey) we agreed to meet again tomorrow. Gov. Randolph from Virginia came in today. Dined with the members, to the General Meeting of the Society of the Cincinnati."

Madison wrote to Jefferson, this day, that: "The Governor, Messrs. Wythe and Blair and Doctor McClurg are also here. . . . There is less punctuality on the outset than was to be wished. Of this, the late bad weather has been the principal cause."

---

[1] *Pennsylvania Packet*, May 15; *Pennsylvania Journal*, May 16, 1787. The Philadelphia newspapers quoted in this book are the two dailies — the *Pennsylvania Packet* and *Independent Gazetteer;* the two semi-weeklies, the *Pennsylvania Journal* and *Pennsylvania Herald;* and the two weeklies, the *Pennsylvania Gazette* and *Freeman's Journal.* For conciseness, when the names of these papers are used in the text, they are termed respectively, the *Packet, Gazetteer, Journal, Herald, Gazette,* and *Freeman's Journal.*

WEDNESDAY, MAY 16, 1787

The Convention again met and adjourned, a quorum of States not being present. The *Packet* said that representatives from seven States (New York, New Jersey, Virginia, Delaware, Maryland, North Carolina and South Carolina) were "now in town"; but the representation of no State was sufficiently full to allow the Convention to do business.

Washington noted in his diary :

"No more than two States being yet represented, agreed till a quorum of them should be formed to alter the hour of meeting at the State House to one o'clock (Dr. McClerg of Virginia came in). Dined at the President Doctor Franklin's, and drank tea, and spent the evening at Mr. Jno. Penn's."

As to this dinner, Franklin wrote to Thomas Jordan :

"I received your very kind letter of February 27th, together with the cask of porter you have been so good as to send me. We have here at present what the French call *une assemblée des notables,* a Convention composed of some of the principal people from the several States of our Confederation. They did me the honor of dining with me last Wednesday, when the cask was broached, and its contents met with the most cordial reception and universal approbation. In short, the company agreed unanimously, that it was the best porter they have ever tasted."

Of Franklin's active interest in discussion of the science of government, an interesting illustration may be found in the fact that in the preceding February, a "Society for Political Enquiries" had been formed in Philadelphia, consisting of fifty members, with Franklin as its President, and George Clymer and William Bingham as Vice Presidents, and with its object, the study of government. Its Rules and Regulations stated that: "While objects of subordinate importance have employed the associated labors of learned and ingenious men, the arduous and complicated science of government has been generally left to the care of practical politicians or the speculations of individual theorists. From a desire, therefore, of supplying this deficiency and of promoting the welfare of our country, it is now proposed to establish a society for mutual improvement in the knowledge of government and for the advancement of political science." [1] Only three days before the Federal Convention met, a paper was read at a meeting of this Society at Franklin's house on May 11, entitled "An Enquiry into the Principles on which a Commercial System for the United States of America Should be Founded." [2]

A portrayal of the political and economic situation, in general, appeared this day in a letter in *Freeman's Journal*, as follows: [3]

"It seems to be generally felt and acknowledged that the affairs of this country are in a ruinous situation. With a vast resource in our hands we are impoverished by the continual drain of money from us in foreign trade; our navigation is destroyed; our people in debt and unable to pay; industry is at a stand; our public treaties are violated, and

[1] *Pennsylvania Packet*, March 27, 1787. At this period, moreover, lectures on political topics were a frequent occurrence. Amongst those whose views were thus presented was Noah Webster, who, with Pelatiah Webster, had been among the earliest political writers to suggest the desirability of a Federal Convention to frame a new Constitution. Lectures by him were advertised in the *Pennsylvania Packet*, Jan. 18, 1787, as follows: "On Saturday evening, the 20th instant at 7 o'clock at the University, Mr. Webster proposes to read some remarks on the present state of our public affairs — on the connection between opinions, manners, and commerce. It will be considered how far our manners defeat the purposes of the Revolution, and how far the interest and taste of Americans are sacrificed to fashion and opinion. The public are most respectfully informed that this and another Lecture to be delivered upon a similar subject are not designed for amusement. They are designed for people who have leisure and inclination to devote one hour to serious reflection, as their object is to unfold some of the less visible causes of our political embarrassments. They are designed for thinking men of every denomination; and the first is particularly calculated for ladies of sentiment, who are very influential in manners. Tickets at 3/9 to be sold by Mr. Cruikshank and Mr. Bailey, printers, and at the door."

[2] See *American Museum* (June, 1787), I, 496. It was written by Tench Coxe.

[3] Printed also in *Pennsylvania Gazette*, June 13, 1787, as a despatch from New York.

National faith, solemnly plighted to foreigners and to our own citizens, is no longer kept. We are discontented at home, and abroad — we are insulted and despised. In this exigency, people naturally look up to the Continental Convention, in hopes that their wisdom will provide some effectual remedy for the complication of disorders. It is perhaps the last opportunity which may be presented to us of establishing a permanent system of Continental Government; and if this opportunity be lost, it is much to be feared that we shall fall into irretrievable confusion. How the great object of their meeting is to be attained is a question which deserves to be seriously considered. Some men, there is reason to believe, have indulged the idea of reforming the United States by some refined and complicated schemes of organizing a future Congress in a different form. These schemes . . . will be found to be merely visionary. . . . The source of all our misfortunes is evidently in the want of power of Congress. . . . To remedy these only, some have weakly imagined that it is necessary to annihilate the several States and vest Congress with the absolute direction and government of the Continent as one single republic. This, however, would be impracticable and mischievous. In so extensive a country, many local and internal regulations would be required, which Congress could not possibly attend to, and to which the States individually are fully competent; but those things which alike concern all the States, such as our foreign trade and foreign transactions, Congress should be fully authorized to regulate, and should be invested with the power of enforcing their regulations. . . . Would it not then be right to vest Congress with the sole and exclusive right of regulating trade . . . and deciding all questions by their own authority which concern foreign trade and navigation upon the high seas?"

THURSDAY, MAY 17, 1787

The Convention again met and adjourned; and Washington noted: [1]

[1] Mr. Samuel Powell was Mayor of Philadelphia.

tion was evinced most clearly by her pathetic recitation of the prayer of Demosthenes to the immortal Gods."

The *Gazetteer*, this day, printed a poem in fourteen stanzas "on the Meeting of the Grand Convention," in which the following optimistic expression occurred:

> "Faction shall cease.   Industry smile.
> Nor next door neighbours each revile,
> But friendly bands combine.
> The powerful league will all unite,
> Destroy invidious smiles and spite
> As harmony both join."

Benjamin Franklin wrote, this day, to Richard Price in England: "We have now meeting here a Convention of the principal people in the several States, for the purpose of revising the Federal Constitution, and proposing such amendments as shall be thoroughly necessary. It is a most important business, and I hope will be attended with success." [1]

SATURDAY, MAY 19, 1787

The Convention met and adjourned; and Washington noted:

"No more States represented.   Agreed to meet at one o'clock on Monday.   Dined at Mr. [Jared] Ingersoll's, spent the evening at my lodgings and retired to my room soon."

The *Journal* and *Herald* printed a list of the delegates appointed, and noted the arrival of only four-

[1] Franklin began this letter: "My health continues as when Mr. Vaughan left us.   My malady does not grow perceptibly worse, and I hope may continue tolerable to my life's end, which cannot now be far distant, being in my 82d year." Dr. Benjamin Rush had written to Richard Price, Oct. 27, 1786: "Our venerable friend, Dr. Franklin, has found considerable benefit from the use of the remedy you recommended to him, joined with the blackberry jam.   He informed me a few days ago that he had not enjoyed better health for the last 30 years of his life than he does at present.   His faculties are in full vigor.   He amuses himself daily in superintending two or three houses which he is building in the neighborhood of his dwelling house.   One of them is for a printing office for his grandson, a promising youth who was educated by him in France (Benjamin Franklin Bache)." *Price Papers* in *Mass. Hist. Soc. Proc., 2d Series* (1903), XVII.

teen from outside of Pennsylvania.[1] They also said:
"Perhaps this city affords the most striking picture
that has been exhibited for ages. Here at the same
moment, the collective wisdom of the Continent
deliberates upon the extensive politics of the confederated empire, two religious conventions clear and
distribute the streams of religion through the American
world, and those veterans whose valour accomplished
a mighty revolution are once more assembled to
recognize their fellowship in arms and to communicate
to their distressed brethren the blessings of peace."

The reference to the "veterans" was to the fact that
the Society of the Cincinnati had been holding its
third General Meeting at Carpenter's Hall in Philadelphia, since May 14. Among the delegates present
were the following Members of the Federal Convention,
— Washington, Alexander Hamilton, Jonathan Dayton,
and Thomas Mifflin, while the following Members —
Nicholas Gilman, David Brearley, and Charles C.
Pinckney — were also delegates of the Society; and
probably about one half of the Members of the Convention also belonged to the Society. These facts must
be borne in mind, in considering the attacks which were
later made upon the Constitution as the work of a
military caste. Though organized, in 1783, as a
fraternal and benevolent society to foster patriotic
efforts, the Cincinnati (and especially its provision that
membership should descend to the "eldest male
posterity") had, for four years before the Federal
Convention, been the object of antagonism and ex-
travagant denunciation. Four Legislatures — South
Carolina, Massachusetts, Pennsylvania, and Rhode
Island — had passed resolves against its institution.

[1] From New York — Yates, Lansing, Hamilton; New Jersey — Brearley; Dela-
ware — Read, Broom; Virginia — Washington, Randolph, Madison, Wythe; North
Carolina — Spaight; South Carolina — Rutledge, Charles Pinckney; Georgia — Few.
See also *Massachusetts Centinel*, May 26, 1787, and numerous other newspapers.

Jefferson, Jay, John Adams, Franklin, Samuel Adams, Elbridge Gerry, Madison, Rufus King, and many other prominent statesmen had opposed it. And there was a general fear among the people against anything bearing the aspect of military domination or of hereditary nobility, whether based on army service or otherwise. The meeting of this Society adjourned on this day, having elected Washington as President General, Thomas Mifflin as Vice President General, and Henry Knox as Secretary General.

SUNDAY, MAY 20, 1787

Washington noted in his diary:

"(Went into the country with Mr. and Mrs. Morris.) Dined with Mr. and Mrs. Morris and other company at their farm (called the Hills). Returned in the evening and drank tea at Mr. Powell's."

Washington wrote, this day, to Arthur Lee:

"My rheumatic complaint having very much abated . . . I have yielded to what appeared to be the wishes of many of my friends, and am now here as a delegate to the Convention. Not more than four States were represented yesterday. If any have come in since, it is unknown to me. These delays greatly impede public measures, and serve to sour the temper of the punctual members, who do not like to idle away their time."

George Mason of Virginia wrote to his son, describing the situation in Philadelphia:[1]

"Upon our arrival here on Thursday evening, seventeenth May, I found only the States of Virginia and Pennsylvania fully represented; and there are at this time only five — New York, the two Carolinas, and the two before mentioned. . . . The expectations and hopes of all the Union centre in this Convention. God grant that we may be able to

[1] See *Pennsylvania Packet*, May 26, 1787.

concert effectual means of preserving our country from the evils which threaten us. The Virginia deputies (who are all here) meet and confer together two or three hours every day, in order to form a proper correspondence of sentiments; and for form's sake, to see what new deputies are arrived, and to grow into some acquaintance with each other, we regularly meet every day at three o'clock. These and some occasional conversations with the deputies of different States, and with some of the general officers of the late army (who are here upon a general meeting of the Cincinnati), are the only opportunities I have hitherto had of forming any opinion upon the great subject of our mission, and consequently, a very imperfect and indecisive one. Yet, upon the great principles of it, I have reason to hope, there will be greater unanimity and less opposition, except from the little States, than was at first apprehended. The most prevalent idea in the principal States seems to be a total alteration of the present federal system, and substituting a great National Council or Parliament, consisting of two branches of the Legislature, founded upon the principles of equal proportionate representation, with full legislative powers upon all the subjects of the Union; and an Executive; and to make the several State Legislatures subordinate to the National, by giving the latter the power of a negative upon all such laws as they shall judge contrary to the interest of the Federal Union. It is easy to foresee that there will be much difficulty in organizing a government upon this great scale, and at the same time reserving to the State Legislatures a sufficient portion of power for promoting and securing the prosperity and happiness of their respective citizens; yet with a proper degree of coolness, liberality, and candor (very rare commodities, by the bye), I doubt not but it may be effected. There are among a variety some very eccentric opinions upon this great subject; and what is a very extraordinary phenomenon, we are likely to find the republicans, on this occasion, issue from the Southern and Middle States, and the anti-republicans from the Eastern; however extraordinary this may at first seem, it may, I think, be accounted for from a very common and natural impulse of the human mind. Men disappointed in expectations too hastily and sanguinely formed, tired and disgusted with the unexpected evils they have experienced, and anxious to remove them as far as possible, are very apt to run into the opposite extreme; and the people of the Eastern States, setting out with more republican principles, have consequently been more disappointed than we have been."

The early attendance of the Virginia delegation had been urged by Madison in a letter to Governor Edmund Randolph, April 15, 1787:

"I am sorry that punctuality on your part will oblige you to travel without the company of Mrs. Randolph. But the sacrifice seems to be the more necessary, as Virginia ought not only to be on the ground in due time, but to be prepared with some materials for the work of the Convention. In this view, I could wish that you might be able to reach Philadelphia some days before the second Monday in May."

Accordingly, Madison arrived on May 3; Washington, May 13: Wythe, Blair, and McClurg before May 14; Randolph, May 15, and Mason, May 17. This delegation being first on the field held daily conferences over the plan to be presented.[1] As Madison wrote later:

. . . "When the Convention as recommended at Annapolis took place at Philadelphia, the deputies from Virginia supposed that, as that State had been first in the successive steps leading to a revision of the Federal system, some introductory propositions might be expected from them. They accordingly entered into consultation on the subject and having agreed among themselves on the outline of a plan, it was laid before the Convention by Mr. Randolph. . . .

[1] See *Life and Times of James Madison* (1859), by William Cabell Rives, II, 206, 273: "Judges Wythe and Blair, owing to the 'badness of their cavalry', as Governor Randolph wrote to Mr. Madison, were furnished by his orders with a 'Stateboat' to convey them to the head of Chesapeake Bay and sailed from Yorktown for their destination on the seventh of May. They arrived in Philadelphia, as their colleague, Dr. McClurg, did also, in full time for the meeting of the Convention, making five of the delegates of Virginia present the first day."

This project was the basis of its deliberations, and after passing through a variety of changes in its important, as well as its lesser features, was developed and amended into the form finally agreed upon."

It was a striking fact that Edmund Randolph should have been entrusted to propose this Virginia Plan, for it favored a much stronger National Government than most of the delegates were at first prepared for, and Randolph himself had apparently come to the Convention with the belief that amendments to the Articles of Confederation were all that were necessary. Writing to Madison, March 27, 1787, he had said:

"I have turned my mind somewhat to the business of May next, but am hourly interrupted. At present I conceive — 1. That the alterations should be grafted on the old Confederation. 2. That what is best in itself, not merely what can be obtained from the Assemblies, be adopted. 3. That the points of power to be granted be so detached from each other, as to permit a State to reject one part, without mutilating the whole. With these objects, ought not some general proposition to be prepared for feeling the pulse of the Convention on the subject at large? Ought not an address to accompany the new Constitution?"

Undoubtedly, the conferences of the Virginia delegates after their arrival in Philadelphia (referred to by Mason and Madison) led Randolph to change his opinion; for in his letter to the speaker of the Virginia House of Delegates, in the following October, he described his conversion: [1]

"Before my departure for the Convention, I believed that the Confederation was not so eminently defective as it had been supposed. But after I had entered into a free communication with those who were best informed of the condition and interest of each State; after I had compared the intelligence derived from them with the properties which

---

[1] Randolph to the Speaker, Oct. 10, 1787, *Elliot's Debates*, I, 482.

ought to characterize the Government of our Union, I became persuaded that the Confederation was destitute of every energy which a Constitution of the United States ought to possess. For the objects proposed by the institution were, that it should be a shield against foreign hostility, and a firm resort against domestic commotion; that it should cherish trade and promote the prosperity of the States under its care. But these are not the attributes of our present Union. Several experiences under the pressure of war, a ruinous weakness manifested since the return of peace, and the contemplation of those dangers which darken the future prospect, have condemned the hope of grandeur and safety under the auspices of the Confederation."

MONDAY, MAY 21, 1787

The Convention met and adjourned; and Washington noted:

"Delaware State was represented. Dined and drank tea at Mr. Bingham's in great splendor."

The *Packet* said that: "Various opinions are propagated respecting the probable results of the Federal Convention; but whatever means are pursued it seems to be unanimously agreed that a strong and efficient Executive must be somewhere established." [1]

George Read of Delaware wrote to his fellow delegate from that State, John Dickinson:

"I have now seen Mr. Bassett, being from my lodgings when he called last evening. He stopt at the Indian Queen, where Mr. Mason of Virginia stays, the last of their seven deputies who came in. We have now a quorum from six States to wit, South and North Carolina, Virginia, Delaware, Pennsylvania and New York, and single deputies from three others — Georgia, New Jersey and Massachusetts — whose

[1] See also *Pennsylvania Gazette*, May 23; *American Herald*, May 28, 1787 (and other papers), adding: "How widely different would have been the character of the Union, if in Congress resided a power to controul the selfish interests of single States and to compel the sacrifice of partial views in order to promote the common weal."

additional ones are hourly expected, and also the Connecticut delegates who have been appointed within the last ten
days by the Legislature there. We have no particular
accounts from New Hampshire, other than that the delegates to Congress were appointed deputies to this Convention. Maryland, you may probably have heard more certain accounts of than we who are here. Rhode Island hath
made no appointment yet. The gentlemen who came here
early, particularly Virginia, that had a quorum on the first
day, express much uneasiness at the backwardness of individuals in giving attendance. It is meant to organize the
body as soon as seven States' quorums attend. I wish you
were here. I am in possession of a copied draft of a Federal
system intended to be proposed, if something nearly similar
shall not precede it. Some of its principal features are taken
from the New York system of Government. A House of
Delegates and Senate for a General Legislature, as to the
great business of the Union. The first of them to be chosen
by the Legislature of each State, in proportion to its number
of white inhabitants, and three-fifths of all others, fixing a
number for sending each representative. The second, to
wit, the Senate, to be elected by the delegates so returned,
either from themselves or the people at large, in four great
districts, into which the United States are to be divided for
the purpose of forming this Senate from, which, when so
formed, is to be divided into four classes for the purpose of
an annual rotation of a fourth of the members. A President having only Executive powers for seven years. By
this plan, our State may have a representation in the House
of Delegates of one member in eighty. I suspect it to be of
importance to the small States that their deputies should
keep a strict watch upon the movements and propositions
from the larger States, who will probably combine to swallow
up the smaller ones by addition, division, or impoverish-
ment; and if you have any wish to assist in guarding against
such attempts, you will be speedy in your attendance."

The draft of the Constitution referred to by Read as
in his possession was undoubtedly the one prepared by

Charles Pinckney of South Carolina, which he was about to present to the Convention on May 29. Both Pinckney and Madison, as well as Read and Governor Randolph, boarded at Mrs. House's; and the various plans for the new Government were early talked over. For, as Madison wrote later: [1]

"All who regarded the objects of the Convention to be a real and regular Government, as contradistinguished from the old Federal system, looked to a division of it into Legislative, Executive, and Judiciary branches, and of course would accommodate their plans to their organization. This was the view of the subject generally taken and familiar in conversation, when Mr. Pinckney was preparing his plan. I lodged in the same house with him, and he was fond of conversing on the subject."

George Mason wrote to Arthur Lee of Virginia as to a similar plan:

"The most prevalent idea, I think at present, is a total change of the Federal system, and instituting a great National Council or Parliament upon the principles of equal, proportionate representation, consisting of two branches of the Legislature invested with full legislative powers upon the objects of the Union; and to make the State Legislatures subordinate to the National by giving to the latter a negative upon all such laws as they judge contrary to the principles and interest of the Union; to establish also a National Executive, and a Judiciary system with cognizance of all such matters as depend upon the law of nations, and such other objects as the local courts of justice may be inadequate to."

The news that New Hampshire was hesitating to join in the Convention was so disturbing that several delegates now asked General Henry Knox (then in Philadelphia attending the meeting of the Society of Cincinnati) to urge his friend, General John Sullivan,

---

[1] Madison to Jared Sparks, Nov. 25, 1831.

Governor of New Hampshire, to hasten, if possible, the departure of its delegates.[1] Knox wrote, this day, that he was impressed with the belief that:

"We are verging fast to anarchy and that the present Convention is the only means of avoiding the most flagitious evils that ever inflicted three millions of people. . . . There are here a number of the most respectable characters from several States, among which is our illustrious friend, General Washington, who is extremely anxious on the subject of the New Hampshire delegates. . . . Endeavor, then, my dear Sir, to push this matter with all your powers. I am persuaded, from the present complexion of opinions, that the issue will prove that you have highly served your country in promoting the measure."

The living conditions for the delegates in Philadelphia were interestingly described in the letter from Read to Dickinson, quoted above:

"It is rather unlucky that you had not given me a hint of your wish to be in a lodging house at an earlier day. Mrs. House's, where I am, is very crowded, and the room I am presently in so small as not to admit of a second bed. That which I had heretofore on my return from New York was asked for Governor Randolph, it being then expected he would have brought his lady with him, which he did not, but she is expected to follow some time hence. I have not seen Mr. Bassett, being from my lodgings when he called last evening. He stopt at the Indian Queen, where Mr. Mason of Virginia stays, the last of the seven deputies who came in."

And, in a letter to Dickinson, three days later, Read said:[2]

---

[1] On June 1, a despatch from Portsmouth, New Hampshire, dated May 19, was printed in the *Independent Gazetteer*: "We are authorized to inform our readers that the probability of the Honorable delegates from this State not attending the Convention in Philadelphia, causes great uneasiness in the minds of the true Whigs of New Hampshire, and will cause a considerable inspection into the state of our finances."

[2] Read to Dickinson, May 24, 1787, *Book of the Signers* (1861), by William Brotherhead; George Mason to George Mason, Jr., May 20, 1787.

E. Trist wrote to Jefferson, June 6, 1787: "Our family is much enlarged by

"Being told last evening by Governor Randolph of his having engaged a couple of rooms in a house at a small distance from our present lodgings and that he will move to them tomorrow evening, I renewed my application on your behalf this morning, and am told that the room here which Mr. Randolph leaves, you may have.   It is on the first floor, up one pair of stairs on 5th Street — the same which I used theretofore, and you have seen me in.   My present lodging room is behind it, and there are doors which form a communication between the two.   As Mr. Randolph expects his lady, his situation is too confined in this house.   He is to dine at our table.   Since my application on your behalf here on Monday last, another has been made for Mr. Gerry who is expected daily; but mine being first, I now have the offer for you."

George Mason of Virginia described conditions, as follows:

"We found travelling very expensive — from eight to nine dollars per day.   In this city, the living is cheap.   We are at the old Indian Queen in Fourth Street, where we are very well accommodated, have a good room to ourselves, and are charged only twenty five Pennsylvania currency per day, including our servants and horses, exclusive of club in liquors and extra charges; so that I hope I shall be able to defray my expenses with my public allowance, and more than that, I do not wish."

TUESDAY, MAY 22, 1787

The Convention met and adjourned; and Washington noted:

the meeting of the Convention of the States.   Gov. Randolph, Dr. McClurg, Mr. Madison and Mr. Beckley all of your State, make a part.   Mrs. Randolph did not accompany her husband.   She has lately presented Mr. Randolph another little one, but is now so well recovered as to undertake the journey, and in a short time, I hope to have the happiness of seeing her in this City."   *Jefferson Papers MSS*, in *Massachusetts Historical Society*.   Randolph wrote to Lieut. Gov. Beverly Randolph, June 6, 1787: "The prospect of a very long sojournment here has determined me to bring up my family.   They will want about thirty pounds (about $105) for the expense of travelling."   *Calendar of Virginia State Papers*, IV.

"The representation from No. Carolina was compleated and made a representation for five States. [Pennsylvania, Virginia, New York, Delaware, North Carolina.] Dined and drank tea at Mr. Morris's."

WEDNESDAY, MAY 23, 1787

The Convention met and adjourned; and Washington noted:

"No more States being represented, I rid to Gen'l. Mifflin's to breakfast. After which, in company with him, Mr. Madison, Mr. Rutledge and others, I crossed the Schuylkill above the Falls, visited Mr. Peter's — Mr. Penn's seat, and Mr. Wm. Hamilton's (and repaired at the hour of one to the State House). Dined at Mr. Chew's with the wedding guests (Colo. Howard of Baltimore having married his daughter, Peggy). Drank tea there in a very large circle of ladies."

James Monroe, this day, wrote from Fredericksburg, Virginia, to Madison that "we all look with great anxiety to the result of the Convention."

"Indeed, it seems to be the sole point on which all future movements will turn. If it succeeds wisely and of course happily, the wishes of all good men will be gratified. The arrangements must be wise, and every way well concerted, for them to force their way through the States. The experience of the Federal Government hath taught Congress, or rather those who have composed it, the sentiments of the several States upon the subject of the powers it should possess. Yet it may by some be thought doubtful, whether it hath not taught them that it will be almost impossible to adopt any plan that will have the concurrence of all the States; or if it hath, that will be of any duration afterwards. It is, however, the business of every passenger to do what he thinks right and to hope that others will act on the same principle."

THURSDAY, MAY 24, 1787

The Convention met and adjourned; and General Washington noted:

"No more States represented. Dined and drank tea at Mr. John Ross's. One of my postillion boys (Paris) being sick, requested Doctr. Jones to attend him."

Rufus King, a delegate from Massachusetts, wrote, this day, to Jeremiah Wadsworth of Connecticut: "I am mortified that I alone am from New England. The backwardness may prove unfortunate. Pray hurry on your delegates." William Grayson, a Member of Congress from Virginia, then in New York, wrote to Madison: "Entre nous. I believe the Eastern people have taken ground they will not depart from respecting the Convention — one Legislature composed of a lower house triennially elected, and an Executive and Senate for a good number of years. I shall see Gerry and Johnson as they pass and may perhaps give you a hint."

FRIDAY, MAY 25, 1787

IN CONVENTION

On this day, twelve days after its call, the Convention perfected its organization, a quorum of States having at last been present, through the advent of the South Carolina delegation, and of Paterson and William Churchill Houston of the New Jersey delegation. Robert Morris of Pennsylvania proposed Washington for President, and John Rutledge of South Carolina seconded the motion, "expressing his confidence that the choice would be unanimous, and observing that the presence of General Washington forbade any observation on the occasion which might otherwise be proper." Madison, in his *Notes* of the Convention proceedings, observed that: "The nomination came with particular grace from Pennsylvania, as Doctor Franklin alone could have been thought of as a competitor. The Doctor was himself to have made the nomination of General Washington, but the state of the weather and his health confined him to his house." Washington was unanimously elected, and was conducted to the Chair by Morris and Rutledge. The Convention proceeded to elect as Secretary, Major William Jackson (nominated by Alexander Hamilton) against William Temple Franklin (nominated by James Wilson).[1] A Committee was then appointed to prepare standing rules and orders and the Convention adjourned.

Washington noted in his diary:

"Another delegate coming in from the State of New Jersey gave it a representation and encreased the number to seven, which forming a quorum of the 13, the members present resolved to organize the body; when by a unanimous vote, I was called up to the Chair as President of the body, Major William Jackson was appointed Secretary and a committee was chosen consisting of (Mr. Wythe, Mr. Hamilton, and Mr. Charles Pinckney chosen) 3 members to prepare rules and regulations for conducting the business. And after appointing doorkeepers the Convention adjourned till Monday (10 o'clock) to give time to the Committee to report the matters referred to them.

Returned many visits (in the forenoon) today. Dined at Mr. Thomas Willing's, and spent the evening at my lodgings."

Of Washington's address to the Convention, Madison noted that he "thanked the Convention for the honor they had conferred upon him, reminded them of the

---

[1] Major Jackson, who was chosen Secretary, had been formerly Assistant Secretary of War. George Mason wrote, May 26, to Arthur Lee, who urged Jackson: "I have received your favor by Major Jackson. Nothing that I have heard has yet been mentioned upon the subject among the deputies here, though I understand there are several candidates, which I am surprised at, as the office will be of so short duration, and merely honorary, or possibly introductory to something substantial." The letter is of interest as showing Mason's opinion that the Convention would not be long in session. It appears that John Beckley, Clerk of the Virginia House of Delegates, was also a candidate.

novelty of the scene of business in which he was to act, lamented his want of better qualifications, and claimed the indulgence of the House towards the involuntary errors which his inexperience might occasion." Robert Yates of New York who also took notes of the debates reported that: "When seated, he (General Washington) declared that as he never had been in such a situation, he felt himself embarrassed, that he hoped his errors, as they would be unintentional, would be excused." It is interesting to compare this modest speech with the equally deprecatory address made by Washington, twelve years before, in accepting the appointment as Commander-in-Chief of the Continental Army by the Continental Congress, June 16, 1775, when he concluded his speech of acceptance by saying: "But lest some unhappy event should happen unfavorable to my reputation, I beg it may be remembered by every gentleman in the room that I, this day, declare with the utmost sincerity that I do not think myself equal to the command I am honored with." [1]

It is to be remarked that Washington took no part in the discussions on the floor of the Convention, until the very last day, September 17. After the Committee of the Whole made its report on June 13, he was almost continually in the chair as presiding officer. Madison's *Notes* show, however, that he followed the discussions keenly, and his vote was recorded five times, when the Virginia delegation, without it, would have been evenly divided.[2] Like Franklin, he adopted an attitude of conciliation and a willingness to forego his own views on a particular subject if by so doing he would accom-

[1] Washington wrote to Gen. Henry Knox, May 31, 1787: "I was much against my wish placed in the chair."

[2] June 4, on the question for a single Executive; July 26, on the Resolution constituting the Executive; August 13, on the question of the right of the House to originate money bills; August 21, on the prohibition to tax exports; August 24, on the export tax; September 12, on the President's veto.

plish a larger end; and his influence was profound in the meetings of the delegates, at which their problems were discussed outside the Convention.

The *Herald*, May 30, described the organization of the Convention as follows; and its opinion that the work before it would be an "easy task" may be noted as a singularly poor prophecy : [1]

"On Friday last, the members of the Federal Convention chose his Excellency George Washington for their President and Mr. William Jackson for their secretary. It is said that the first step towards discharging the important duties of this National Council will be the appointment of a delegate from each State as a committee to receive communications from the other members and to arrange, digest and report a system for the subsequent discussion of the whole body. This plan is admirably adapted for the despatch of business as it cuts off a field for long and desultory debates upon first principles, and by collecting materials from every quarter to form a solid and comprehensive foundation leaves little besides the easy task of raising and adorning the superstructure to the collective labour of a popular assembly. When, indeed, we consider the critical situation of the country, the anxiety with which every good citizen regards this *dernier resorte* and the decisive effect it must have upon the peace and prosperity of America, though everything should certainly be given to prudence and deliberation, not a moment can be spared to useless forms or unprofitable controversy."

George Read of Delaware wrote to his co-delegate, John Dickinson, urging him to come on, Sunday evening :

[1] Reprinted in *New Hampshire Spy*, June 9; *Salem* (Mass.) *Mercury*, June 12; *Connecticut Courant*, June 13; *Independent Chronicle* (Boston), June 14; *Virginia Independent Chronicle*, June 13, 1787; and in many other newspapers.

The *Gazetteer* said, May 26: "Yesterday at the State House in this city seven States were fully represented in Convention. These forming a quorum, they proceeded to the choice of a President and his Excellency General Washington was unanimously elected to that important station." The *Packet* said, May 26: "Yesterday, a sufficient number of the Members of the Convention having met, they proceeded to business, when his Excellency George Washington, Esq., was chosen President."

"We make our quorum today. Two additional South Carolina delegates came in Allibone's Packet yesterday, and at New York, making four in the whole — but one from Maryland, yesterday — none as yet from Connecticut, New Hampshire or Rhode Island, tho the first of these three are hourly expected. You should be here at the first opening of the Budget. . . ."

It is to be noted that on this organization of the Convention, there were four States from the South with nineteen delegates present, and three from the North, with ten delegates. Massachusetts, Connecticut, and Maryland were first represented on the floor on May 28; Georgia, on May 31; New Hampshire, on July 23; and Rhode Island never appointed any delegates.

The States were represented by varying numbers of delegates. Thus, to constitute a quorum to represent it, Pennsylvania required four of its seven delegates; Delaware, three of its five; Virginia, three of its seven; North Carolina, three of its five; New Jersey, three of its five; Massachusetts, three of its four; South Carolina, two of its four; Georgia, two of its four; New Hampshire, two of its four; New York, two of its three; Maryland allowed one of its five to represent it; and Connecticut, one of its three. The result was that twenty-nine members present and acting might bind their States, when all twelve States were on the floor. There were never more than eleven States represented at any one time.[1]   And as the average attendance was little more than thirty (owing to members who were absent or who returned home from time to time) the Convention resembled a large Committee.[2]   Moreover,

[1] Massachusetts was absent from Convention on votes on five days (Aug. 22, 24, 27, Sept. 6, 12); New Jersey, on three days (July 31, Aug. 27, 28); Pennsylvania, on two days (June 30, Aug. 24); Delaware, on one day (June 30); North Carolina, on two days (Aug. 24, 27); Georgia, on two days (June 30, Aug. 27); New York after July 10.

[2] From May 28 to June 2, the hour of meeting of the Convention was 10 A.M.;

since a State delegation was often equally divided in opinion and hence not counted on either side upon a vote, a motion might prevail, as it frequently did, by less than a majority of the States on the floor.[1]

The most frequent speakers during the debates were G. Morris with 173 speeches; Wilson, 168; Madison, 161; Sherman, 138; Mason, 136; Gerry, 119.[2] Six of the delegates never made a speech during the Convention, prior to the last day (so far as appears from Madison's *Notes*) — Richard Bassett of Delaware, John Blair of Virginia, William Few of Georgia, Joseph Gilman of New Hampshire, Jared Ingersoll of Pennsylvania, and William Blount of North Carolina. It is interesting to note that, of the fifty-five delegates who attended at some time during the Convention, thirty-eight served on one or more of the Committees appointed to report on the various propositions debated.[3]

The chief source of information as to the debates in the Convention, as is well known, is the record kept by James Madison, which was interestingly described by

from June 4 to Aug. 18, it was 11 A.M., but without specified hour of adjournment. From Aug. 18 to Aug. 24, by special vote, the Convention sat each day from 10 A.M. to 4 P.M. After August 24, the hours were from 10 A.M. to 3 P.M. Washington in his diary speaks of "not less than five, for a large part of the time, six, and sometimes seven hours, sitting every day."

[1] On one hundred twenty-two motions, the votes of one or more of the States were evenly divided as follows: New Hampshire, on eleven motions; Massachusetts, fifteen; Connecticut, eight; New York, eight; New Jersey, one; Pennsylvania, twelve; Delaware, ten; Maryland, twenty-seven; Virginia, one; North Carolina, thirteen; South Carolina, four; Georgia, twelve. There were twenty-three occasions when, had there been no divided vote, the result of the vote might have been altered.

[2] *History of the People of the United States*, by John Bach McMaster, I, 421 note.

[3] Of the signers of the Constitution, Jacob Broom and Jonathan Dayton of New Jersey, Thomas Mifflin, Robert Morris, and Jared Ingersoll of Pennsylvania, Richard Bassett of Delaware, Daniel of St. Thomas Jenifer of Maryland, William Blount and Richard D. Spaight of North Carolina, and Washington, served on no Committee. Of the delegates who had left the Convention prior to the signing, the following had served on no Committee: Caleb Strong of Massachusetts; John Lansing of New York; William C. Houston of New Jersey; John F. Mercer of Maryland; James McClurg of Virginia; William Houstoun and William Pierce of Georgia.

him in a memorandum shortly before his death in 1836, in which he said : [1]

"The curiosity I had felt during my researches into the history of the most distinguished Confederacies, particularly those of antiquity, and the deficiency I found in the means of satisfying it, more especially in what related to the process, the principles, the reasons, and the anticipations, which prevailed in the formation of them, determined me to preserve as far as I could an exact account of what might pass in the Convention, whilst executing its trust, with the magnitude of which I was duly impressed, as I was with the gratification promised to future curiosity by an authentic exhibition of the objects, the opinions, and the reasonings from which the new system of government was to receive its peculiar structure and organization.   Nor was I unaware of the value of such a contribution to the fund of materials for the history of a Constitution on which would be staked the happiness of a people great even in its infancy, and possibly the cause of liberty throughout the world.   In pursuance of the task I had assumed, I chose a seat in front of the presiding member, with the other members on my right and left hands.   In this favorable position for hearing all that passed I noted, in terms legible and in abbreviations and marks intelligible to myself, what was read from the Chair or spoken by the members ; and losing not a moment unnecessarily between the adjournment and reassembling of the Convention, I was enabled to write out my daily notes during the session or within a few finishing days after its close. . . .   In the labour and correctness of doing this, I was not a little aided by practice and by a familiarity with the style and the train of observation and reasoning which characterized the principal speakers.   It happened also that I was not absent a single day, nor more than a casual fraction of an hour in any day, so that I could not have lost a single speech, unless a very short one. . . .   Of the ability and intelligence of those who composed the Convention, the debates and proceed-

[1] *Preface to Debates in the Convention.   A Sketch Never Finished nor Applied,* by James Madison.

ings may be a test; as the character of the work which was the offspring of their deliberations must be tested by the experience of the future, added to that of the nearly half century which has passed."

Madison's *Notes* were not published until the year 1840, and up to that date the chief information as to the Constitution came from notes kept by Robert Yates of New York (between May 25 and July 10, 1787), which were published in 1822. The minutes for the official Journal, never reduced to formal shape by the Secretary, William Jackson, were published for the first time, in 1819, by the Department of State. Since 1894, scattered notes by other delegates — Rufus King, James McHenry, William Paterson, Alexander Hamilton, and William Pierce — have come to light and have been published.[1] It is from these sources that our knowledge of the formation of the Constitution is derived.

SATURDAY, MAY 26, 1787

The Convention did not sit this day; and Washington noted:

"Returned all my visits this forenoon (where I could get an account of the lodgings of those to whom I was indebted for them), dined with a club at the City Tavern, and spent the evening at my quarters writing letters."

SUNDAY, MAY 27, 1787

In view of the provisions for freedom of religion which were to be embodied in the Constitution, the

[1] See Part Three, Chapter Two, *infra*. Max Farrand states in his *Records of the Federal Convention* that notes were kept also by Charles Pinckney, George Mason, Elbridge Gerry, and by another delegate (referred to by Wilson and by G. Morris).

Gouverneur Morris wrote to Timothy Pickering, Dec. 22, 1814: "While I sat in the Convention, my mind was too much occupied by the interests of our Country, to keep notes of what we had done. Some gentlemen, I was told, passed their evenings in transcribing speeches from shorthand minutes of the day. They can speak positively on matters of which I have little recollection. My facilities were on the stretch to forward the business, remove the impediments, obviate objections and reconcile jarring opinions." *Pickering Papers MSS.*, in *Mass. Hist. Soc.*, **XXX**, 338. See also *Life of Gouverneur Morris* (1832), by Jared Sparks, I, 282.

following entry in Washington's diary is of interest: "Went to the Romish Church to high mass." [1] The newspapers stated that Washington accompanied by a number of respectable members of the protestant and dissenting churches attended divine service at the Catholick Chapel. "The anthems and other solemn pieces of music performed on this occasion were admirably adapted to diffuse a spirit of devotion throughout a crowded congregation and to give effect to an excellent sermon delivered by the Rev. Mr. Beeston." [2] On the previous Sunday, the rest of the Virginia delegation had attended a similar service, as described by George Mason in a letter to his son: [3] "The Governor of Virginia, with all the Virginia delegates, except the General, attended the Roman Catholick Chapel today, more out of compliment than religion, and more out of curiosity than compliment. There was a numerous congregation; but an indifferent preacher, I believe a foreigner. The composition of his sermon was loose and trivial, his delivery and pronunciation ungraceful and faulty. Altho I have been in a Roman Catholic Chapel before, I was struck with the solemnity of the apparatus and could not help remarking how much everything was calculated to warm the imagination and captivate the senses. No wonder that this should be the popular religion of Europe! The church music was exceedingly fine, but while I was pleased with the air of solemnity so generally diffused thro the Church, I was somewhat disgusted with the frequent tinckling of a little bell; which put me in mind of the drawing up the curtain for a puppet show.

---

[1] St. Mary's Church, on Fourth Street, above Spruce.

[2] Reprinted in *Massachusetts Centinel*, June 9; *New Hampshire Spy*, June 12, 1787, and in papers in other States.

[3] George Mason to George Mason, Jr., May 20, 1787. Although this letter has been printed by Bancroft, Farrand, and others, the portion above quoted has hitherto been omitted. — See original letter in Library of Congress.

I wonder they have not substituted some more solemn and deep toned instrument." Mason wrote again to his son, this day stating that he was already tired of the social life in Philadelphia: "It is impossible to judge how long we shall be detained here, but from present appearance I fear until July, if not later. I begin to grow heartily tired of the etiquette and nonsense so fashionable in this city. It would take me some months to make myself master of them, and that it should require months to learn what is not worth remembering as many minutes, is to me so discouraging a circumstance as determines me to give myself no manner of trouble about them."

Madison wrote to James Madison, Sr., this day, that: "We have been here for some time, suffering and duly disappointed from the failure of the deputies to assemble. . . . It is impossible to form a judgment of the result of this experiment. Every reflecting man becomes daily more alarmed at our situation. The unwise and wicked proceedings of the Government of some States and the unruly temper of the people of others must, if persevered in, soon produce some new scenes among us." To Edmund Pendleton of Virginia, Madison wrote that: "A few days will now furnish some data in calculating the probable result of the meeting. In general, the members seem to accord in viewing our situation as peculiarly critical and in being averse to temporising expedients. I wish they may as readily agree when particulars are brought forward."

Edmund Randolph wrote to Lieutenant Governor Beverly Randolph:[1] "Seven States met on Friday, appointed a committee to prepare rules and adjourned till Monday. In four or five days we shall probably have every State represented, except Rhode Island, which has peremptorily refused to appoint deputies,

[1] *Calendar of Virginia State Papers*, IV, 290.

and New Hampshire, of which we can hear nothing
certain but her friendly temper towards the Union.
I ought, however, to add, that a respectable minority in
Rhode Island are solicitous that their State should
participate in the Convention."

MONDAY, MAY 28, 1787

IN CONVENTION

On this day, more delegates appeared on the floor of
the Convention — Nathaniel Gorham and Caleb
Strong from Massachusetts; Oliver Ellsworth from
Connecticut; Gunning Bedford from Delaware; and
James McHenry from Maryland. Benjamin Franklin,
George Clymer, Thomas Mifflin, and Jared Ingersoll
from Pennsylvania, who were not present on May 25,
also took their seats.

The Committee consisting of George Wythe, Alexander Hamilton, and Charles Pinckney reported the
"Rules to be Observed as the Standing Orders of the
Convention", which were adopted. The most momentous of these was that seven States should be a
quorum, and that "all questions should be decided by
a majority of the States which shall be fully represented." As to this rule, Madison's note is instructive
for its disclosure that, even before the Convention met,
a division between the large and the small States had
arisen — the division which later nearly wrecked the
Convention:

"Previous to the arrival of a majority of the States, the
rule by which they ought to vote in the Convention had been
made a subject of conversation among the members present.
It was pressed by Gouverneur Morris and favored by Robert Morris and others from Pennsylvania, that the large
States should unite in firmly refusing to the small States an
equal vote, as unreasonable, and as enabling the small States

to negative every good system of Government, which must, in the nature of things, be founded on a violation of that equality. The members from Virginia, conceiving that such an attempt might beget fatal altercations between the large and small States, and that it would be easier to prevail on the latter, in the course of the deliberations, to give up their equality for the sake of an effective Government, than on taking the field of discussion to disarm themselves of the right and thereby throw themselves on the mercy of the large States, discountenanced and stifled the project.''

A very necessary addition to the rules was suggested by Richard Dobbs Spaight of North Carolina, ''to provide that, on the one hand, the house may not be precluded by a vote upon any question from revising the subject matter of it, when they see cause; nor, on the other hand, be led too hastily to rescind a decision which was the result of mature discussion.'' The vital importance of this proposal may be seen when one notes the numerous instances during the progress of the Convention, when propositions decided upon and votes taken were rescinded and changed, as men's views altered and modified. Another important addition was suggested by Pierce Butler of South Carolina, ''that the House provide . . . against licentious publications of their proceedings.''

At the end of this day, a letter was received (and placed on file) from citizens of Rhode Island, deploring the failure of that State to send delegates to the Convention, owing to the nonconcurrence of the upper House of the Legislature with the vote of the lower House. They stated that they believed that ''the well informed throughout the State'' were in favor of giving to Congress full power over commerce: and they expressed the hope that the absence of Rhode Island would not result in action unfavorable to the ''commercial interest'' of that State, and that the Convention would make such provisions "as have a tendency to strengthen the Union, promote commerce, increase the power, and establish the credit of the United States." It was natural that there should be apprehensions lest Rhode Island's interests might suffer at the hands of the delegates; for there had been much resentment throughout the country at the attitude of that State, by reason of its refusal to grant to Congress power over imports and of its iniquitous paper money legislation. At the beginning of this very month of May, the following letter had appeared in a Boston newspaper (widely copied) from "a gentleman in the Southern States to his friend in Newport", saying: [1]

"The distracted state you are in is sufficient to wean and drive every good citizen from his native country. Matters have come to such an alarming crisis that the Confederation must take notice of you, and it seems the opinion of many here that when the Convention meets in Philadelphia, measures will be taken to reduce you to order and good govern-

[1] *American Herald*, May 7, 1787; *Massachusetts Centinel*, April 4, 1787; Rhode Island was frequently referred to in the newspapers as "Rogue Island." See *New York Morning Post*, April 26, 1787, "The Chronicles of Rogue Island," Chap. I, by Chronologist; *New York Daily Advertiser*, April 9, 1787, as to a letter from the delegates in Congress from Rhode Island to the Governor complaining of publication in the *Advertiser* of "Quintessence of Villainy or Proceedings of the Legislature of Rhode Island." For Rhode Island items, see *Pennsylvania Journal*, April 18, May 2; *Freeman's Journal*, April 4, 18; *Pennsylvania Gazette*, April 4, 18, 1787. James M. Varnum wrote to Washington from Rhode Island, June 18, 1787: "Permit me, sir, to observe that the measures of our present Legislature do not exhibit the real character of the State. They are equally reprobated and abhorred by gentlemen of the learned professions, by the whole mercantile body, and by most of the respectable farmers and mechanicks. The majority of the Administration is composed of a licentious number of men, destitute of education, and many of them void of principle. From anarchy and confusion, they derive their temporary consequence. . . . With these are associated the disaffected of every description, particularly those who were unfriendly during the war. Their paper money system, founded in oppression and fraud, they are determined to support at every hazard." *Washington Papers MSS* in Library of Congress. David Daggett of Connecticut, in an oration at New Haven, July 4, 1787, said: "Rhode Island has acted a part which would cause the savages of the wilderness to blush. Fraud and injustice there stalk openly. . . . That little State is an unruly member of the political body, and is a reproach and byeword among all her acquaintances."

ment, or strike your State out of the Union, and annex you
to others; for as your Legislature now conducts, they are
dangerous to the community at large and ruinous to every
honest and respectable character in the State; the clamor
is loud against your State and will daily increase."

And a writer in another Boston paper said that
Rhode Island had refused to coöperate in the Convention but that "from an antifederal disposition,
nothing better could have been expected":

"To that State, it is owing that the Continental impost
has not taken place; to her may be charged the poverty of
the soldiers of the late army; the heavy taxes of our citizens,
and the embarrassed state of the public funds. It is presumed, however, that her dissent will nevermore be permitted to defeat any federal measure; rather let her be
dropped out of the Union, or apportioned to the different
States which surround her, nor will the American constella-
tion lose one gem thereby. The State of Vermont shines
with far superior lustre and would much more than compensate the loss."

OUT OF CONVENTION

Washington noted:

"Met in Convention at 10 o'clock. Two States more,
viz. Massachusetts and Connecticut (made nine on the floor)
were on the floor today.

Established Rules agreeably to the plan brought in by the
Committee for the government of the Convention and
adjourned (about 2 o'clock). No communications without
doors.

Dined at home and drank tea in a large circle at [Tench]
Francis's."

CHAPTER TWO

THE NATIONAL LEGISLATURE

TUESDAY, MAY 29, 1787

IN CONVENTION

Two further members appeared on this day — John Dickinson of Delaware and Elbridge Gerry of Massachusetts. Two important new rules were adopted. One, following Spaight's suggestion, was as follows:

"That a motion to reconsider a matter which has been determined by a majority, may be made with leave unanimously given, on the same day on which the vote passed; but otherwise not without one day's previous notice, in which last case, if the House agree to the reconsideration, some future day shall be assigned for that purpose."

The other, of vast consequence, was the Secrecy Rule:

"That no copy be taken of any entry on the journal during the sitting of the House, without leave of the House. . . . That nothing spoken in the House be printed, or otherwise published or communicated without leave."

As to the value and necessity of this latter rule, most of the delegates, so far as appears, were in absolute accord. George Mason had written to his son, May 27, two days before the rule was adopted that: "It is expected our doors will be shut, and communications upon the business of the Convention be forbidden during its sitting. This, I think, myself, a proper precaution to prevent mistakes and misrepresentation until the business shall have been completed, when the whole may have a very different complexion from that in which the several crude and indigested parts might, in their first shape, appear if submitted to the public eye." [1]

James Madison wrote to Jefferson that: "It was thought expedient, in order to secure unbiassed discussion within doors and to prevent misconceptions and misconstructions without, to establish some rules of caution, which will for no short time restrain even a confidential communication of our proceeding." To James Monroe, he wrote: "One of the earliest rules of the Convention restrained the members from any disclosure whatever of its proceedings, a restraint which will not probably be removed for some time. I think the rule was a prudent one, not only as it will effectually secure the requisite freedom of discussion, but as it will save both the Convention and the community from a thousand erroneous and perhaps mischievous reports." To Jefferson, Madison wrote again that "the public mind is very impatient for the event, and various reports are circulating which tend to inflame curiosity. I do not learn, however, that any discontent is expressed at the concealment." [2] Many years later, the reason for the rule was stated by Madison in the course of a visit paid to him by Jared Sparks, in 1830: "Opinions were so various and at first so crude that it

---

[1] On June 1, Mason wrote to his son that: "All communications of the proceedings are forbidden during the sitting of the Convention. This, I think, was a necessary precaution to prevent misrepresentations or mistakes, there being a material difference between the appearance of a subject in its first crude and indigested shape, and after it shall have been properly matured and arranged."

[2] Madison to Jefferson, June 6, July 18, 1787; Madison to Monroe, June 10, 1787.

was necessary they should be long debated before any
uniform system of opinion could be formed. Meantime, the minds of the members were changing and
much was to be gained by a yielding and accommodating spirit. Had the members committed themselves
publicly at first, they would have afterwards supposed
consistency required them to maintain their ground,
whereas by secret discussion, no man felt himself
obliged to retain his opinions any longer than he was
satisfied of their propriety and truth and was open to
argument." And added Sparks: "Mr. Madison thinks
no Constitution would ever have been adopted by the
Convention, if the debates had been public." [1] Alexander Martin, a delegate from North Carolina, wrote to
Governor Caswell that: "This caution was thought
prudent, lest unfavourable representations might be
made by imprudent printers of the many crude matters
and things daily uttered and produced in this body,
which are unavoidable and which in their unfinished
state might make an undue impression on the
too credulous and unthinking mobility." Alexander
Hamilton wrote later: [2]

"It is a matter generally understood, that the deliberations of the Convention, which were carried on in private,

[1] *Life and Writings of Jared Sparks* (1893) by Herbert B. Adams, I, 560, Journal
entry of April 19, 1830. Jared Sparks himself, writing in the *North American Review*,
XXV, 251, in 1827, before the above interview which he had with Madison, and
before the publication of Madison's *Notes of Debates*, expressed a contrary view of
the Secrecy Rule: "On many accounts, it is deeply to be regretted that the debates
of the grand Convention at Philadelphia have not been preserved. The advantage
which might have been derived from the arguments of the members were then lost
to the public. The Journal of Proceedings, as recently published, is meagre beyond
description, and hardly fills a blank in history. Yates' volume of the proceedings
and debates of the Convention, together with Luther Martin's speech, supplies the
deficiency but very imperfectly. Those gentlemen were warm opposers of the Constitution and wrote and spoke as partisans. The expediency of a secret session
of that body is more than problematical at this day. . . . Had the deliberations
been public and reported daily in the newspapers, we apprehend no evil, but much
good, would have resulted."
[2] *Works of Alexander Hamilton* (Lodge's ed.), VII, letter of "Amicus" in *Gazette
of the United States*, Sept. 11, 1792.

were to remain undisturbed — and every prudent man must be convinced of the propriety both of the one and the other. Had the deliberations been open while going on, the clamors of faction would have prevented any satisfactory result; had they been afterwards disclosed, much food would have been afforded to inflammatory declamation. Propositions made without due reflection, and perhaps abandoned by the proposers themselves on more mature reflection, would have been handles for a profusion of ill-natured accusation. Every infallible declaimer, taking his own ideas as the perfect standard, would have railed without measure or mercy at every member of the Convention who had gone a single line beyond his standard."

Edmund Carrington, a Member of Congress from Virginia, wrote to Madison, June 13, from New York, as to the propriety of the prohibition : "Having matured your opinions and given them a collective form, they will be fairly presented to the public and stand their own advocates; but caught by detachments and while indeed immature, they would be actually the victims of ignorance and misrepresentations."

On the other hand, Jefferson, who was in Paris, and who could not understand the difficulties of the situation in the Convention, wrote to Adams in London (August 30), strongly attacking this rule and saying: "I am sorry they began their deliberations by so abominable a precedent as that of tying up the tongues of their members. Nothing can justify this example but the innocence of their intentions, and ignorance of the value of public discussions." And Luther Martin, who throughout the Convention was opposed to the whole plan of the Constitution, wrote, in January, 1788, to the Maryland Legislature, the following criticism of the Secrecy Rule : [1]

---

[1] *The Genuine Information, delivered to the Legislature of the State of Maryland,* Jan. 27, 1788, by Luther Martin, *Elliot's Debates,* I, 344.

Patrick Henry in the Virginia State Convention in 1788 said : "I believe it would

"So far did this rule extend that we were thereby prevented from corresponding with gentlemen in the different States upon the subjects under our discussion — a circumstance, sir, which I confess I greatly regretted. I had no idea that all the wisdom, integrity and virtue of this State, or of the others, were centred in the Convention. I wished to have corresponded freely and confidentially with eminent characters in my own and other States — not implicitly to be dictated to by them, but to give their sentiments due weight and consideration. So extremely solicitous were they that their proceedings should not transpire, that their members were prohibited even from taking copies of resolutions on which the Convention were deliberating, or extracts of any kind from the Journals, without formally moving for, and obtaining permission, by a vote of the Convention for that purpose."

The newspapers during the progress of the Convention made frequent comment on the secrecy of the proceedings. "Such circumspection and secrecy mark the proceedings . . . that the members find it difficult to acquire the habits of communication even among themselves, and are so cautious in defeating the curiosity of the public that all debate is suspended on the entrance of their own officers. . . . The anxiety of the people must be necessarily increased by every appearance of mystery in conducting this important business." So wrote the press in June.[1] The New York papers, in August, said that: "The profound secrecy hitherto observed by the Convention, we cannot help considering as a happy omen, as it demonstrates that the spirit of party on any great and essential point cannot have arisen to any height."[2] At the conclusion of the Convention, the press wrote of "the

have given more general satisfaction if the proceedings of the Convention had not been concealed from the public eye." *Elliot's Debates*, II, 171.

[1] See *New York Journal*, June 7; *Boston Gazette*, June 11; *Virginia Independent Chronicle*, June 20, 1787.

[2] *New York Daily Advertiser*, Aug. 14, 1787; *Pennsylvania Packet*, Aug. 22, 1787.

profound secrecy being observed by the members who composed it, which at least has done honor to their fidelity, as we believe that scarcely another example can be advanced of the same caution among so large a number of persons." [1]

The strictness with which the Convention observed the Secrecy Rule is shown by an anecdote related by Major William Pierce, a delegate from Georgia. "Early in the sessions, one of the delegates dropped a copy of the propositions which were before the Convention for consideration, and it was picked up by another of the delegates and handed to General Washington. After the debates of the day were over, just before putting the question of adjournment, Washington arose from his seat and reprimanded the member for his carelessness. 'I must entreat gentlemen to be more careful, lest our transactions get into the newspapers, and disturb the public repose by premature speculations. I know not whose paper it is, but there it is (throwing it down on the table), let him who owns it take it.' At the same time, he bowed, picked up his hat, and quitted the room with a dignity so severe that every person seemed alarmed. . . . It is something remarkable that no person ever owned the paper."

Having settled upon its rules of proceeding, the Convention was ready for business. Thereupon, Governor Edmund Randolph of Virginia arose. It was natural that the first move should come from Virginia; for it was Virginia which first submitted in the Continental Congress of 1776 the motion which led to the Declaration of Independence; it was Virginia which first suggested the Annapolis Convention of 1786; and it was Virginia which had first elected delegates to this Convention. In opening the business before them, Randolph "expressed his regret that it should fall to

[1] See *Pennsylvania Journal*, Oct. 6, 1787.

him rather than those who were of longer standing in life and political experience to open the great subject of their mission; but as the Convention had originated from Virginia, and his colleagues supposed that some proposition was expected from them, they had imposed this task on him." He then described the defects of the existing Confederation. "The framers of it," said he, "were wise and great men; but human rights were the chief knowledge of the times when it was framed so far as they applied to oppose Great Britain. Requisitions for men and money had never offered their form to our Assemblies. None of these vices that have since discovered themselves were apprehended. Its defects, therefore, (are) no reflexion on its contrivers." [1] He then set forth his ideas as to the remedy for the existing evils, and submitted a Plan for a new Government, embodied in fifteen resolutions.[2] And he concluded "with an exhortation not to suffer the present opportunity of establishing peace, harmony, happiness and liberty in the United States to pass away unimproved."

The genesis of this Plan (probably drafted by Madison) was described by Madison in a letter written towards the end of his life, as follows: [3]

[1] As reported in James McHenry's *Notes of Debates*, but not in Madison's.

[2] J. F. Jameson in *Studies in the History of the Federal Convention of 1787* in *Amer. Hist. Ass. Report* (1902), I, 103, was the first historian to point out that "there exist four different texts of these Randolph resolutions, and what is more remarkable, it can (in the view of the present writer) be proved that no one of the four is the exact text of the original series which Governor Randolph laid before the Convention. . . . The original text in Randolph's handwriting, if such there were, is nowhere said now to exist." These four texts are (1) that which Madison gives (printed in the *Documentary History of the Constitution* and in Hunt's *Writings of James Madison*, III, and in Gilpin's *The Madison Papers*, and in *Elliot's Debates*, V); (2) that printed with the official Journal of the Convention in 1819 under authority of the Secretary of State, and in Yates' *Secret Proceedings and Debates;* (3) that derived from manuscript deposited with the Department of State by Gen. Joseph Bloomfield, executor of David Brearley and printed in *Documentary History*, I, 329; (4) that found among the manuscripts of William Paterson. These were all reprinted with explanatory notes in *House Doc. No. 398, 69th Congress, 1st Sess.*, entitled *Documents Illustrative of the Formation of the Union of the American States.*

[3] *Writings of James Madison* (Hunt's ed.), IX, 502, Madison to John Tyler, 1833.

"The Resolutions proposed by him (Edmund Randolph) were the result of a consultation among the deputies, the whole number, seven, being present. The part which Virginia has borne in bringing about the Convention suggested the idea that some such initiative step might be expected from their deputation; and Mr. Randolph was designated for that task. It was perfectly understood that the propositions committed no one to their precise tenor or form; and that the members of the deputation would be as free in discussing and shaping them as the other members of the Convention. Mr. R. was made the organ on the occasion, being then the Governor of the State, of distinguished talents, and in the habit of public speaking. General Washington, though at the head of the list, was, for obvious reasons, disinclined to take the lead. It was foreseen that he would be immediately called to the presiding station. That the Convention understood the entire Resolutions of Mr. R. to be a mere sketch, in which omitted details were to be supplied and the general terms and phrases to be reduced to their proper details, is demonstrated by the use made of them in the Convention."

Since the Resolutions comprising this Virginia Plan will be described in detail as they were taken up by the Convention, it is not necessary to give here more than a short summary. They provided for a National Legislature of two branches, one to be elected by the people, the other by the first branch; the Legislature to have broad power to legislate wherever the States were incompetent or wherever the National harmony might otherwise be interrupted, also to have the power of negativing State laws which it regarded as contravening the Constitution. In the Legislature, the States were not to be represented equally, but according to number of free inhabitants or to amount of property. A National Executive and a National Judiciary were provided for. By omission of any provision for the necessity of action by the States after enactment of any law by the National Legislature, it was implied that the new Government should operate directly upon the individual citizens of the States. The problem had been "how to arrange a National system of Government of sufficient strength to operate in despite of State opposition, and yet not strong enough to break down State authority." [1]   The solution presented constituted a radical change, indeed, from the previous Articles of Confederation. The delegates, evidently unprepared to discuss such a plan, voted now that on the next day the Convention should go into Committee of the Whole, "to take into consideration the state of the American Union", [2] and that Randolph's Resolutions be referred to the Committee. Before adjournment, however, Charles Pinckney of South Carolina, one of the youngest of the delegates, submitted another draft for a Constitution, which he read, stating that "he had reduced his ideas of a new Government to a system", and "confessed that it was grounded on the same principles" as Randolph's. [3] This draft was also referred to the Committee.

Though Pinckney was one of the youngest men in the Convention, being only twenty-nine, his extreme ability

[1] Gouverneur Morris to W. H. Wells, Feb. 24, 1815.

[2] As reported in McHenry's *Notes*. Madison does not report it, but McHenry notes that: "It was observed by Mr. Hamilton, before adjourning, that it struck him as a necessary and preliminary inquiry to the propositions from Virginia, whether the United States were susceptible of one government, or required a separate existence connected only by leagues offensive and defensive and treaties of commerce."

[3] J. F. Jameson in *Amer. Hist. Ass. Report* (1902), I, 120, quotes a writer in *Debow's Mag.*, XXXIV, 63: "This draft was made in Charleston before the writer thereof had any opportunity of conference with his co-workers, and carried with him to the Convention." Pinckney himself said in a speech in the House, Feb. 13, 1821: "I was the only member of that body that ever submitted the plan of a Constitution completely drawn in articles and sections."

Madison himself did not take a copy of the draft nor did Pinckney furnish him one, as he did a copy of his speech which he later delivered in the Convention and which is printed as a part of the debates (session of Monday, June 25). Many years later, in 1818, when John Quincy Adams, then Secretary of State, was preparing the Journal of the Convention for publication, he wrote to Pinckney, requesting a copy of his plan, and in compliance with this request, Pinckney sent him what had already been recognized both in his own State and in Congress, where, in the preceding August, he had been Chairman of the Sub-Committee which reported a draft of amendments to the Articles of Confederation. A writer in a New York paper now made the following striking comment on him : [1]

"Great expectations are justly formed from the well-known abilities of several gentlemen from the Southern States now sitting in Convention, who have made civil government and the rights of mankind their peculiar study and who, it is well known, have brought with them plans and systems for a permanent Confederation, which, when promulgated, will afford ample satisfaction and pleasure to all wise and able statesmen, throughout the country.   In a note to Comte Chastellux, *Travels through America*, the translator of said *Travels* says : 'My friend, Mr. Charles Pinckney (now Doctor Pinckney, having been made Doctor of Laws by the University of Princeton) (who was my companion to see the famous town of Bethlehem), is a young gentleman, at present in Congress for South Carolina, and who, from the intimate knowledge I have of his excellent education, and strong talents, will, I venture to predict, whenever he pleases to exert them, stand forth among the most eminent citizens of the new Confederation of Republics.   It is my boast and pride to have coöperated with him, when he was only at the

purported to be the draft, but which appears to have been a copy of the report of the Committee of Detail of August 6, 1787, with certain alterations and additions. The alleged draft and Pinckney's letter transmitting it were written upon paper bearing the water-mark, "Russel & Co., 1797."

The Pinckney draft was not debated ; it was neither used in the Committee of the Whole nor in the Convention.   It was, however, referred to the Committee of Detail, which appears to have made use of it, as extracts from it have been identified by J. Franklin Jameson and an outline of it discovered by Andrew C. McLaughlin, among the papers and in the handwriting of James Wilson, deposited with the Pennsylvania Historical Society.   See *Amer. Hist. Ass. Report* (1902), I, 128, 132, and *Amer. Hist. Rev.* (1904), IX, 735.   See *Debates of the Federal Convention of 1787* (1920), edited by Gaillard Hunt and James Brown Scott, pp. 26, note, 595–598. See also a pamphlet published by Pinckney in New York in October, 1787, entitled *Observations on the Plan of Government submitted to the Federal Convention in Philadelphia on the 28th of May, 1787 . . . delivered at different times in the course of their discussions,* and see Madison to Washington, Oct. 14, 28, 1787.

[1] *New York Daily Advertiser,* May 31, 1787.

age of twenty, in the defence of the true principles of liberty, and to have seen productions from his pen, which in point of composition and argument would have done honor to the head and heart of the most experienced and most virtuous politician.'"

OUT OF CONVENTION

No intimation as to any of these proceedings of the Convention appeared in the newspapers, the *Gazetteer* simply saying (May 30): "Ten States, we learn, were yesterday represented in Convention."

Washington noted:[1]

"Attended Convention, and dined at home. After which accompanied Mrs. Morris to the benefit concert of a Mr. Juhan (at the City Tavern)."

General Henry Knox wrote from New York to General Washington, this day:

"Mr. Pierce and Mr. Houston from Georgia set off from this place for Philadelphia yesterday. Mr. Sherman and Doctor Johnson will be in Philadelphia in the course of a week. I have not heard anything from New Hampshire but I am persuaded, from circumstances, that the delegates from that State will be with you by the 10th of June. I am indeed happy that the Convention will be so full as to feel a confidence that they represent the great majority of the people of the United States. The grumblings in Massachusetts still continue. . . . Events are fast ripening to birth, anarchy threatening. A few hours being sprung we shall find ourselves without system or government. So impressed is my mind with the evils about to happen, which will naturally arise from the construction and imbecilities of the State and General Constitutions of this country, that I have no hope of a free government but from the Convention. If

---

[1] The programme of this Concert (admission 7 sh. 6 d.) was as follows: "Act I New Overture, Reinagle; Concerto Flute, Brown; Song, Sarto; Overture, Haydn. Act II, Sonata Piano Forte — Mr. Juhan, Haydn and Reinagle; Concerto Violoncello, Capron; Solo Violin, Juhan; The Grand Overture, Martini." See *Pennsylvania Journal*, May 23, 1787.

that fails us, we shall find ourselves afloat on an ocean of uncertainty — uncertain as to the shore on which we shall land, but most certain as to the storms we shall have to encounter."

That there were statesmen in Virginia who had no confidence that the Convention would have any favorable results is seen from a letter from William Grayson to James Madison, written from Congress in New York, this day:

"What will be the result of their meeting I cannot with any certainty determine, but I hardly think much good can come of it; the people of America don't appear to me to be ripe for any great innovations and it seems they are ultimately to ratify or reject; the weight of General Washington as you justly observe is very great in America, but I hardly think it is sufficient to induce the people to pay money or part with power. The delegates from the Eastward are for a very strong Government, and wish to prostrate all the State Legislatures and form a general system out of the whole; but I don't learn that the people are with them. On the contrary, in Massachusetts, they think that Government too strong and are about rebelling again, for the purpose of making it more democratical. In Connecticut, they have rejected the requisition for the present year decidedly, and no man there would be elected to the office of a constable if he was to declare that he meant to pay a copper towards the domestic debt; Rhode Island has refused to send members — the cry there is for a good government after they have paid their debts, in depreciated paper: — first demolish the Philistines, *i.e.*, their creditors and then for *propriety*. New Hampshire has not paid a shilling since peace and does not ever mean to pay one to all eternity; if it was attempted to tax the people for the domestic debt, 500 Shays would arise in a fortnight. In N. York, they pay well because they can do it by plundering N. Jersey and Connecticut. Jersey will go great lengths, from motives of revenge and interest; Pennsylvany will join, provided you let the sessions of the Executive of

America be fixed in Philada. and give her other advantages in trade to compensate for the loss of State power. I shall make no observations on the Southern States, but I think they will be, perhaps from different motives, as little disposed to part with efficient power as any in the Union."

WEDNESDAY, MAY 30, 1787

IN CONVENTION

A National Government

The Convention resolved itself for the first time into a Committee of the Whole, and the President (Washington) leaving the Chair, Nathaniel Gorham of Massachusetts (who had been President of the Congress of the Confederation in 1786 to 1787) was chosen by ballot as Chairman of the Committee.

The first step made in this first meeting of the Committee went to the root of the whole matter before the Convention; for Randolph, as a substitute for the first of his Resolutions, moved that the Convention at its very outset should commit itself to the following basic proposition: "That a National Government ought to be established consisting of a supreme Legislative, Executive and Judiciary." Complete silence followed, as the delegates began to realize the far-reaching effect of this proposal. Then Pierce Butler of South Carolina stated that he wished Randolph "to show that the existence of the States cannot be preserved by any other mode than a National Government." [1] Gerry of Massachusetts, Read of Delaware, and General Pinckney of South Carolina were also shy of the proposal. After considerable discussion, however, Randolph's Resolution was voted — Connecticut alone opposing, and New York being divided. It was the word "National" which alarmed and confused the delegates;

[1] As reported in McHenry's *Notes*, which are fuller for this day than Madison's.

for many feared that this term implied that the Nation should absorb and destroy the States. We of today are so accustomed to using the terms "National" and "Federal" as entirely interchangeable, both signifying simply the "Government of the United States", that it is difficult to realize the fears awakened in 1787, lest a "National Government" should mean a "consolidated" Government — one with unlimited powers. Such, however, was not the intent. In using the word "National", as contradistinguished from "Federal", Randolph was endeavoring to express, not the extent of power to be possessed by the new Government, but its mode of operation. And, as George Mason of the Virginia delegation later explained it: "Under the existing Confederacy, Congress represents the States, not the people of the States; their acts operate on the States, not on the individuals. The case will be changed in the new plan of Government." "National" implied a Government which should "directly operate on individuals and possess compulsive power on the people of the United States" — "Federal" implying a Government of compact, resting for enforcement of its acts "on the good faith of the parties." [1] "The term was used," wrote Madison later, "not in contradistinction to a limited, but to a Federal Government. As the latter operated within the extent of its authority through requisitions on the Confederated States, and rested on the sanction of State Legislatures, the Government to take its place was to operate within the extent of its powers directly and coercively on individuals, and to receive the higher sanction of the people of the States. And there being no technical or appropriate denomination applicable to the new and unique system, the term 'National' was used, with a confidence that it

[1] See speeches of George Mason, May 30, June 6; Gouverneur Morris, May 30; Rufus King, June 1 (as reported in McHenry's *Notes*).

would not be taken in a wrong sense." [1] That the Convention should at once abandon the form of Government contained in the Articles of Confederation and adopt an entirely new scheme was, indeed, a radical proposal. William Paterson of New Jersey was of the opinion that "the idea of a National Government, as contradistinguished from a Federal one, never entered into the mind" of any State in sending delegates; and Luther Martin of Maryland later said: "When I took my seat in the Convention, I found them attempting to bring forward a system which, I am sure, never had entered into the contemplation of those I had the honor to represent." [2] Richard Henry Lee wrote, after the Convention adjourned: "Had the idea of a total change [from the Confederation] been started, probably no State would have appointed members to the Convention. . . . Probably not one man in ten thousand in the United States had an idea that the old ship was to be destroyed." On the other hand, Charles Pinckney was right in saying to the South Carolina State Convention that the promoters of the Convention — those "who had seriously contemplated the subject", had been from the outset "fully convinced that a total change of system was necessary. . . . They also thought that the public mind was fully prepared for the change. . . . The necessity of having

[1] *Writings of James Madison* (Hunt's ed.), X, Madison to Robert S. Garnett, Feb. 11, 1824; Madison to Andrew Stevenson, March 25, 1826; Madison to Thomas Cooper, Dec. 26, 1826.

[2] Paterson in the Convention, June 9; *The Genuine Information* (1788) by Luther Martin, *Elliot's Debates*, I, 388; *Pamphlets on the Constitution* (1888), "Letters of a Federal Farmer," October, 1787, by Richard Henry Lee; Pinckney in the South Carolina State Convention in 1788, *Elliot's Debates*, IV, 254–256. Melancthon Smith of New York wrote in 1788: "Previous to the meeting of the Convention, the subject of a new form of Government had been little thought of and scarcely written upon at all." But this statement was not supported by the facts. He continued: "The idea of a Government similar to [the Constitution] never entered the minds of the Legislature, who appointed the Convention, and of but very few of the members who composed it, until they had assembled and heard it proposed in that body." *Pamphlets, supra.*

a Government which should at once operate upon the people and not upon the States was conceived to be indispensable by every delegation present, however they may have differed with respect to the quantum of power." The form of Government now offered — the dual system combining States and a Nation in one working whole — was new in history. Never before had there existed a Federal form of Republic in which the States should remain as sovereigns acting with limited powers upon their own citizens, and in which a central Government of the States should have Executive, Legislative, and Judiciary authority to enforce its own limited sovereign powers upon the citizens of the States. John Lansing of New York was correct when he said in his State Convention: "I know not that history furnishes an example of a confederated Republic coercing the States composing it, by the mild influence of laws operating on the individuals of those States. This, therefore, I suppose to be a new experiment in politics." [1] It is to be noted, however, that while such a separate central Government having independent Executive, Legislative, and Judicial Departments empowered to act directly upon the people was, in fact, a new experiment, it had been discussed for several years by the leaders of thought in the various States, both in letters and in print.[2]

It is difficult today for us, who are so familiar with our system of Government, to reproduce the frame of mind of the men of 1787, who were accustomed to obeying only the orders, and complying with the regulations, of a State Government, and who found it impossible to conceive how they could obey both a

---

[1] *Elliot's Debates*, II, 219.

[2] Madison wrote to William A. Duer, June 5, 1835: "The moment, indeed, a real Constitution was looked for as a substitute for the Confederacy, the distribution of the Government into the usual departments became a matter of course with all who speculated on the prospective changes."

National and a State Government, each acting within its own sphere of authority. Yet, when Pelatiah Webster, in his pamphlet published in 1783, suggested that the powers of sovereignty could be distributed between a National Government and the State Governments, the idea was so entirely novel, that his proposition that the supreme authority should operate directly on the individual citizen aroused the ire of one who signed himself "A Connecticut Farmer", and who "thought it an 'outrage that a member of the General Assembly of Connecticut might be dragged down to Congress' and subjected to fine, imprisonment, and possibly corporal punishment." [1]

Much of the opposition which arose in the Convention, and later in the State Conventions, to this National form of Government was based on the mistaken belief that the intent of its framers was ultimately to consolidate all power in the central Government and to abolish or destroy the power of the States. It is important to note, therefore, that the Nationalists in the Convention, the ardent advocates of the Constitution, were equally warm in their insistence upon the necessity of preserving the State Governments with all their powers intact, except so far as the relinquishment of certain powers was necessary for National purposes. Thus, Randolph, himself, stated that his plan "only meant to give the National Government power to defend and protect itself — to take, therefore, from the respective Legislatures of States no more sovereignty than is competent to this end." James Wilson said that by a "National Government, he did not mean one that would swallow up the State Governments. . . . He was tenacious of pre-

---

[1] See *Remarks on a Pamphlet entitled: A Dissertation on the Political Union . . . by a Citizen of Philadelphia, with some Brief Observations . . . by a Connecticut Farmer* (1784); *History of the United States* (1912), by Edward Channing, III, 479.

serving the latter. . . . They were absolutely necessary for certain purposes which the former could not reach." And throughout the Convention, it was made clear by the most vigorous Nationalists that they regarded the preservation of the powers of the States, in their legitimate sphere and wherever they could not impair the National sovereignty, as of as great importance as the establishment of the National powers; for, as Charles Pinckney said: "No position appears to me more true than this: that the General Government cannot effectually exist without reserving to the States the possession of their local rights. They are the instruments upon which the Union must frequently depend for the support and execution of their powers, however immediately operating upon the people, and not upon the States." [1]

OUT OF CONVENTION

Washington noted;

"Attended Convention. Dined with Mr. (John) Vaughan. Drank tea, and spent the evening at a Wednesday evening's party at Mr. and Mrs. [John] Lawrence's."

The *Gazetteer*, the *Gazette* and the *Journal* printed a two-column letter signed "Harrington" addressed "To the Freemen of the United States." Portions of this striking argument in favor of a new Constitution were printed in many papers through the country and must have had a powerful influence.[2] The writer first said that he was "a citizen of Pennsylvania in a retired situation who holds and wishes for no share in the power or offices of his country and who often addressed you in the years 1774 and 1775 upon the interesting

[1] Randolph, May 29; Wilson, June 19; Charles Pinckney, June 25.
[2] See *New York Independent Journal*, June 2; *Massachusetts Centinel*, June 9; *New Hampshire Spy*, June 9, 12; *Connecticut Courant*, June 11; *Salem Mercury*, June 12; *Virginia Independent Chronicle*, June 13; *Independent Chronicle* (Boston), June 14, 1787; *American Museum* (June, 1787), I.

subject of the liberties of America." He then concisely recited the necessity for a new form of Government:

". . . We must either form an efficient Government for
ourselves, suited in every respect to our exigencies and interests, or we must submit to have one imposed upon us by
accident or usurpation. . . . A foederal Shays may be more
successful than the Shays of Massachusetts Bay — or a
body of men may arise who may form themselves into an
order of hereditary nobility and by surprise or stratagem
prostrate our liberties at their feet. This view of our situation is indeed truly alarming. We are upon the brink of a
precipice. . . . America has it in her power to adopt a
government which shall secure to her all benefits of monarchy without parting with any of the privileges of a republic. She may divide her Legislature into two or three
branches. She may unite perfect freedom and wisdom together and may confer upon a supreme magistrate such a
portion of executive power as will enable him to exhibit a
representation of majesty, such as never was seen before,
for it will be the majesty of a free people. To preserve a
sense of his obligations to every citizen of the republic, he may
be elected annually and made eligible for seven years, or for
life. The more we abridge the States of their sovereignty
and the more supreme power we concenter in an Assembly
of the States (for by this new name let us call our Federal
Government) the more safety, liberty, and prosperity will be
enjoyed by each of the States. The ambition of the poor
and the avarice of the rich demagogue can never be restrained upon the narrow scale of a State Government. In
an Assembly of the States, they will check each other. In
this extensive reservoir of power, it will be impossible for
them to excite storms of sedition or oppression. . . . Let
the States who are jealous of each other's competitions and
encroachments, whether in commerce or territory, or who
have suffered under aristocratic or democratic juntos, come
forward and first throw their sovereignty at the feet of the
Convention. It is there only that they can doom their dis-

putes, their unjust tender commutation laws — their paper money — their oppressive taxes upon land and their partial systems of finance — to destruction."

He then depicted the various classes of people whose interests would be protected. As to the public creditor, the soldier, and the citizen, "it is from the united power and resources of America only that they can expect permanent and substantial justice." Citizens of Western America could "fly to a foederal power for protection." "The farmer who groans beneath the weight of direct taxation" could "seek relief from a government whose extensive jurisdiction will enable it to extract the resources of our country by means of imposts and customs." The merchant could obtain "a general system of commercial regulation." The manufacturer and mechanic could find only in a general Assembly of States "power to encourage such arts and manufactures as are essential to the prosperity of our country." He then asked the people, in order "to beget confidence in and an attachment to a new Foederal Government" to attend "to the characters of the men who are met to form it." And he described them as follows:

"Many of them were members of the first Congress that sat in Philadelphia in the year 1774. Many of them were part of that band of patriots who, with halters round their necks, signed the Declaration of Independence on the Fourth of July 1776. Many of them were distinguished in the field and some of them bear marks of the wounds they received in our late contest for liberty.

Perhaps no age or country ever saw more wisdom, patriotism, and probity united in a single assembly than we now behold in a Convention of the States.

Who can read or hear that the immortal Washington has again quitted his beloved retirement and obeyed the voice of God and his country by accepting the chair of this illustrious body of patriots and heroes, and doubt of the safety and blessings of the government we are to receive from their hands? Or who can hear of Franklin, Dickinson, Rutledge, Morris, Livingston, Randolph, Sherman, Gerry, Mifflin, Clymer, Pinckney, Read — and many others that might be mentioned whose names are synonymous with Liberty and Fame and not long to receive from them the precious ark that is to preserve and transmit to posterity the freedom of America?

Under the present weak, imperfect and distracted government of Congress — anarchy, poverty, infamy and slavery await the United States.

Under such a government as will probably be formed by the present Convention, America may yet enjoy peace, safety, liberty and glory."

On this same day, Lafayette was writing to Jay, as to the Convention:

"May the Convention be the happy epocha of Federal, energetic, patriotic measures! May the friends of America rejoice! May her enemies be humbled, and her censors silenced at the news of her noble exertions in the continuance of those principles which have placed her so high in the annals of history and among the nations of the earth."

William R. Davie, one of the delegates from North Carolina, wrote, this day, from Philadelphia, to James Iredell: [1]

"After a very fatiguing and rapid journey, I arrived here on the 22d. The gentlemen of the Convention had been waiting from day to day for the presence of seven States; on the 25th the members from New Jersey attended, and Gen. Washington was chosen President. Yesterday more States were represented, and the great business of the meeting was brought forward by Virginia, with whom the proposition for a Convention had originated. As no progress can yet be expected in a business so weighty, and at the same time so complicated, you will not look for any news from this

---

[1] *Life and Correspondence of James Iredell* (1858), by Griffith J. McRee, II, 161.

quarter. Be so good as to favor me, by the next post, with your opinion how far the introduction of Judicial and Executive powers, derived from Congress, would be politic or practicable in the States. And whether absolute or limited powers for the regulation of trade, both as to exports and imports, etc., I shall trouble you frequently; and I shall expect your opinion without reserve."

And Washington was writing to Jefferson in Paris:[1]

"Having since been appointed by my native State to attend the National Convention, and having been pressed to a compliance in a manner which it hardly becomes me to describe, I have, in a measure, been obliged to sacrifice my own sentiments, and to be present in Philadelphia. . . .

The business of this Convention is as yet too much in embryo to form any opinion of the conclusion. Much is expected from it by some; not much by others; and nothing by a few. That something is necessary none will deny; for the situation of the General Government, if it can be called a Government, is shaken to its foundation, and liable to be overturned by every blast. In a word, it is at an end; and, unless a remedy is soon applied, anarchy and confusion will inevitably ensue."

During the preceding spring, a book by John Adams (then Minister to Great Britain) had been published in Boston and New York, entitled *A Defense of the Constitutions of Government of the United States of America,* the leading theses of which were — a defense of the necessity of maintenance in a free republic of the independence of the three branches of government (the Executive, the Legislative, and the Judicial), and a strong argument for a Legislature consisting of two houses in order to preserve the necessary system of checks and balances. The subject, though now trite, was at that date not fully developed in political writings.

[1] The phraseology of this letter varies in different transcripts — cf. *Doc. Hist.,* IV, 172.

Consequently, Adams' book, appearing as it did just at a time when theories of government were the subject of general discussions, had a profound influence which can be traced in the letters and newspapers and debates of the period, through phrases literally quoted.[1] Its effect upon the delegates in the Convention was clearly marked; and Henry Knox, writing this day from New York to Mrs. Mercy Warren in Massachusetts, referred interestingly to this work in connection with the need for a strong National Government: [2]

"Our respectable and enlightened friend, Mr. Adams' book will be the surest basis of his reputation. . . . It should have been entitled 'The Soul of a Free Government.' But still it will be the means of great good. It is a word spoken in season. He clearly points out one of the capital causes of our misery and prostrate character — the will, the caprice, the headlong conduct of a Government without strong checks by different branches, or a division of power by a balance. . . . In addition to these local evils (paper money, ex post facto laws, etc.) all National character and interests are lost by the monstrous system of State Governments. . . . Granted, says candor, but the remedy? Pardon me, the Convention is sitting — and shall one of the Cincinnati presume to give his opinion? I confess, however, that my only hope of human assistance is founded on the Convention. Should they possess the hardihood to be unpopular and propose an efficient National Government, free from the entanglements of the present defective State sys-

---

1 William R. Davie wrote to James Iredell, May 30, 1787: "Among the late publications of particular merit, a performance of Mr. J. Adams, the American Minister at the British Court, now signally engages the attention of the public." The *Massachusetts Centinel*, June 16, 1787, quoted a Philadelphia paper, containing a letter from "Sydney" as to the opportune publication of Adams' book: "An excellent work. . . . It is to be hoped every freeman in the United States will furnish himself with a copy of this invaluable book. It is more essentially the duty of every person concerned in any way in the government of our country to read and study it." See also articles on Adams' book in *New York Journal*, May 3, *New York Daily Advertiser*, May 9, *Freeman's Journal*, May 16, 1787; and in many other newspapers.

2 *Mass. Hist. Soc. Coll.* (1925), LXXIII, *Warren-Adams Letters*, II, 294.

tems, we may yet be a happy and great Nation. But I have no expectations, if their propositions should be truly wise, that they will be immediately accepted. I should rather suppose that they would be ridiculed, in the same way as was the ark of old while building by Noah. . . . If the Convention should propose to erect a temple to liberty, on the solid and durable foundation of law and justice, all men of principle in the first instance will embrace the proposal. Demagogues and vicious characters will oppose for a while. But reason will at length triumph. But should the Convention be desirous of acquiring present popularity; should they possess local and not general views; should they propose a patchwork to the present wretchedly defective thing called the Confederation, look out, ye patriots, supplicate Heaven, for you will have need of its protection. . . . I wish at present to try the experiment of a strong *National Republic*. The State Governments should be deprived of the power of injuring themselves or their Nation. . . . This Government should possess every power necessary for National purposes which would leave the State Governments but very little. But every power should be defined with accuracy and checked according to the highest wisdom."

Franklin had already written to Adams, May 18, that his "work is in such request here, that it is already put to press, and a numerous edition will speedily be abroad." And Dr. Benjamin Rush wrote to Richard Price in London, June 2, that: "Mr. Adams' book has diffused such excellent principles among us, that there is little doubt of our adopting a vigorous and compounded Federal Legislature. Our illustrious Minister in this gift to his country has done us more service than if he had obtained alliances for us with all the nations of Europe." [1]

---

[1] Other letters written by statesmen of the time describe the great impression made by Adams' book. See Appendix C, Madison to Jefferson, June 6; Jay to Adams, July 4, 28; Richard Henry Lee to Adams, Sept. 3; Jefferson to Adams, Sept. 28, 1787.

THURSDAY, MAY 31, 1787

IN CONVENTION

A Legislature of Two Branches

On this day, the arrival of Major William Pierce and William Houstoun of Georgia gave that State a representation — the eleventh State to appear.

The Committee took up and agreed to Randolph's second Resolution, without debate (Pennsylvania alone dissenting), viz. : "That the National Legislature ought to consist of two branches." [1] While this provision was in accord with the Constitutions of eleven of the States, nevertheless, a Legislature of only one branch existed in Georgia and Pennsylvania, and in the Congress under the Articles of Confederation.   Moreover, the existence of a second branch of the Legislature — the Senate — had been, in Massachusetts, one of the chief grievances of those who sympathized with the movement which took outward shape in the Shays Rebellion, only six months prior ; for it was regarded as the representative of property.   In many of the other States also, since the property qualification for members of the Senate was greater than for members of the lower House, and the property qualification required of the electors of the Senate was greater than those of the electors of the other branch, the State Senates were regarded as representative of the property interests.   Under these conditions, it would not have been unnatural if there should have been considerable discussion over the adoption of a two-branch Legislature.   On this date, however, there was no difference of opinion on the subject.   Later in the Convention (on June 16), John Lansing of New York raised the

[1] Madison stated that the vote of Pennsylvania was "given probably from complaisance to Doctor Franklin, who was understood to be partial to a single House of Legislation."

point that the only object of having two branches was
that one should serve as a check, but, said he, in a Congress, "the delegations of the different States are checks
on each other." To this, James Wilson replied that
"in a single House, there is no check but the inadequate
one of the virtue and good sense of those who compose it." Roger Sherman of Connecticut (on June 20)
also stated that he saw no necessity for two branches,
and that the complaints of the Congress of the Confederation had not been of the unwisdom of its acts,
but the insufficiency of its powers. To these statements, George Mason of Virginia replied with finality,
that while "the mind of the people of America . . .
was unsettled as to some points . . . in two points he
was sure it was settled, in an attachment to republican
government — in an attachment to more than one
branch in the Legislature." Undoubtedly, also, many
of the delegates had been strongly impressed by the
forceful argument against a one-house Legislature,
which had been made by John Adams in his book, then
recently published.[1] When this Resolution adopted by
the Committee of the Whole came up for vote in the
Convention, on June 21, seven States voted aye (after
striking out the word "National"), with New York,
New Jersey, and Delaware voting no, and Maryland
divided.

Election by the People

The next of the Randolph Resolutions to be considered on this May 31, was another crucial one : "That
the members of the first branch of the National Legislature ought to be elected by the people of the several States." Here was presented the great question

---

[1] For an illuminating discussion of the bicameral (or two House) system in a
Legislature, see *Commentaries of the Constitution* (1895), by Roger Foster, I, 461
et seq., and works cited; see also *The Living Constitution* (1927), by Howard Lee
McBain, 162–169.

whether the new Government was to come from the people or from the State Legislatures. The line of cleavage among the delegates, developed thus early in the Convention, was striking. For it appeared then, and on many later occasions, that the most vigorous advocates of a National Government — James Wilson, James Madison, Rufus King, and Gouverneur Morris — were heartily in favor of popular election and trusted the action of the people; while, in general, the opponents of the National form of Government, as well as those who later opposed the Constitution (like Elbridge Gerry of Massachusetts), distrusted the people and wished all powers to be derived from the State Legislatures. Those who, in 1788, charged the proponents of the Constitution with favoring aristocracy, and those who now contend that the Constitution was chiefly framed in the interests of property, overlook the fact that belief in the people was a cardinal feature of those who were most prominent in framing the Constitution. This will be shown even more strikingly in the debates on the election of the Executive.

Eloquent arguments for popular election were made on this day. George Mason of Virginia said that the House "was to be the grand depository of the democratic principles of the Government. . . . It ought to know and sympathize with every part of the whole Republic. . . . We ought to attend to the rights of every class of the people. He had often wondered at the indifference of the superior classes of society to this dictate of humanity and policy; considering that, however affluent their circumstances or elevated their situations might be, the course of a few years not only might but certainly would distribute their posterity through the lowest classes of society. Every selfish motive, therefore, every family attachment ought to recommend such a system of policy as would provide no less carefully for the rights and happiness of the lowest than of the highest orders of citizens." Madison said that he "considered the popular election as essential to every plan of free government. . . . The great fabric to be raised would be more stable and durable, if it should rest on the solid foundation of the people themselves, than if it should stand merely on the pillars of the Legislatures." Wilson wished to give the "Federal pyramid . . . as broad a basis as possible." On the other hand, Roger Sherman of Connecticut favored election of the House by the State Legislatures, saying that: "The people immediately should have as little to do as may be about the Government. They want information and are constantly liable to be misled." Gerry of Massachusetts also objected to popular election, saying that "the evils we experience flow from the excess of democracy", and that though he was still republican, he "had been taught by experience the danger of the levelling spirit."

The Committee, on this May 31, voted for election of the first branch of the Legislature by the people, by a vote of six States to two, New Jersey and South Carolina voting no, and Connecticut and Delaware being divided.[1] Later, on June 6, the vote as to popular election of the first branch was reconsidered, and the subject was again debated. Charles Pinckney of South Carolina contended that "the people were less fit judges in such a case"; and his colleague, General Pinckney, denied that choice by the people "would be a better guard against bad measures than by the Legislatures. . . . The latter had some sense of character and were restrained by that consideration."

[1] The Convention discussed also, on this day, the manner in which the second branch of the Legislature should be chosen, but could arrive at no conclusion. (See June 7.)

Sherman again thought that "the right of participating in the National Government would be sufficiently secured to the people by their election of the State Legislatures", and that the latter ought to choose members of the National Legislature. The weight of the argument, however, was enormously with those who insisted on a popular basis for the new Government. Wilson said that: "He wished for vigor in the Government, but he wished that vigorous authority to flow immediately from the legitimate source of all authority. The Government ought to possess not only, first, the force, but secondly, the mind or sense of the people at large. The Legislature ought to be the most exact transcript of the whole society. Representation is made necessary only because it is impossible for the people to act collectively." Mason said that in the new Government, the people and not the States will be represented. "They ought, therefore, to choose the Representatives. The requisites in actual representation are that the Representatives should sympathize with their constituents, should think as they think and feel as they feel, and that for these purposes should even be residents among them." Madison stated that he considered "an election of one branch, at least, of the Legislature by the people immediately, as a clear principle of free government." Pinckney's motion was defeated, only Connecticut, New Jersey, and South Carolina voting for it.

When this vote of the Committee of the Whole came before the Convention for final action, on June 21, General Pinckney, seconded by Luther Martin of Maryland, moved that the first branch, instead of being elected by the people, be chosen "in such manner as the Legislature of each State should direct." Mason again opposed, urging that "whatever inconveniency may attend the democratic principle, it must actuate one part of the Government; it is the only security for the rights of the people." Wilson said that he considered popular election "not only as the corner stone but as the foundation of the fabric." No one supported General Pinckney, except his colleague, Rutledge; and the motion was lost by a vote of 6 States to 4, with Maryland divided. Thereupon, with only the dissenting vote of New Jersey and with Maryland divided, nine States voted that the first branch of the Legislature be elected by the people.

This was the first great victory for popular and liberal Government under the new Constitution. "They (the Representatives) are of the People and return again to mix with the People, having no more durable pre-eminence than the different grains in an hourglass; such an Assembly cannot easily become dangerous to liberty; they are the servants of the People, sent together to do the People's business," so wrote Franklin in picturesque language.[1]

The Powers of the Legislature

The third crucial Resolution proposed by Randolph was next considered on this May 31 — that establishing the powers of the National Legislature, as follows: "To enjoy the Legislative rights vested in Congress by the Confederation, and moreover to legislate in all cases to which the separate States are incompetent or in which the harmony of the United States may be interrupted by the exercise of individual legislation." The lack of power possessed by the Congress of the Confederation was one of the great evils of the old system. But in suggesting additional powers, few statesmen hitherto had ever dreamed of vesting Congress with such a breadth of authority as was given by this Resolution. It is true that, as Madison wrote

[1] Franklin to Whatley, May 23, 1788.

later, the entire Resolutions were presented as a "mere sketch in which omitted details were to be supplied, and the general terms and phrases to be reduced to the proper details." [1] Nevertheless, in view of the unrestricted language used, it is small wonder that Pierce Butler of South Carolina, who had, on the day before, said that he was "willing to go great lengths", now expressed his fear that "we were running into an extreme in taking away the powers of the States", or that his colleagues, Rutledge and Charles Pinckney, "objected to the vagueness of the term 'incompetent' and desired before voting to see an exact enumeration of the powers comprehended by this definition." Though Randolph, in answer, "disdained any intention to give indefinite powers to the National Legislature", Madison, on the other hand, stated that "he had brought with him into the Convention a strong bias in favor of an enumeration and definition of the powers necessary to be exercised by the National Legislature; but had also brought doubts concerning its practicability. His wishes remained unaltered; but his doubts had become stronger. What his opinion might ultimately be, he could not tell. But he should shrink from nothing which should be found essential to such a form of Government as would provide for the safety, liberty, and happiness of the community." It is probable that the Committee did not grasp the full extent of its action at this time, for, without any further debate, it accepted the Resolution, with no dissenting vote and with Connecticut divided.

Power to Negative State Laws

The Committee then proceeded to consider the extraordinary proposal, made in Randolph's sixth

[1] Madison to John Tyler, 1833. *Writings of James Madison* (Hunt's ed.), IX, 502.

Resolution, to give Congress authority to negative all laws passed by the States "contravening in its opinion the Articles of Union", in other words, power to reject any State statute which in its opinion should contravene any of the extremely broad objects as to which Congress, at that stage of the Convention, was authorized to legislate. It is a remarkable fact that, on this May 31, the Convention (all the States except Maryland being then represented) was willing to grant to Congress such an extreme authority over State laws, and even more remarkable that it did so "without debate or dissent" (after adding to the Resolution a further power to negative State laws contravening National treaties).[1]

To understand this action, one must appreciate with what grave apprehension the unwise and unjust legislation of the States had been regarded, and to what an extent it had been a factor in bringing about the Convention.[2] As early as 1783, George Mason of Virginia had written : [3]

"A strict adherence to the distinctions between right and wrong for the future is absolutely necessary to restore that confidence and reverence in the people for the Legislature which a contrary conduct has so greatly impaired, and without which their laws must ever remain little better than a dead letter. Frequent interferences with private property and contracts, retrospective laws destructive of all public

[1] See the further debates on this power to negative State laws, on June 8 and July 17, 1787, *infra*, pp. 316–324.

[2] See Madison, June 6, 7, 8, 9, July 17, 21, 25; G. Morris, July 21, Aug. 15; Mercer, Sept. 8; Dickinson, Aug. 14, 1787. Madison wrote to Jefferson, October, 1787 : "The mutability of the laws of the States is found to be a serious evil. The injustice of them has been so frequent and so flagrant as to alarm the most steadfast friends of Republicanism. I am persuaded I do not err in saying that the evils issuing from these sources contributed more to that uneasiness which produced the Convention and prepared the public mind for a general reform than those which accrued to our National character and interest from the inadequacy of the Confederation to its immediate objects."

[3] Mason to William Cabell, *Life and Times of James Madison* (1859), by William Cabell Rives, II, 225.

faith as well as confidence between man and man, and flagrant violations of the Constitution, must disgust the best
and wisest part of the community, occasion a depravity of
manners, bring the Legislature into contempt, and finally
produce anarchy and public convulsion."

And early in the Convention, Madison had said that
effectual provision "for the security of private rights
and the steady dispensation of justice" was essential,
"since interferences with these, perhaps more than
anything else, produced this Convention." And again,
he referred to the trespasses of the States on each other,
giving preference to their own citizens, and to aggressions on the rights of other States by emissions of paper
money and kindred measures; also to the retaliating
Acts passed by the States, as a "threatened danger not
to the harmony only, but the tranquillity of the Union."
Again, he said that: "Experience in all the States had
evinced a powerful tendency in the Legislature to
absorb all power into its vortex. This was the real
source of danger to the American Constitution." John
F. Mercer of Maryland said: "What led to the
appointment of this Convention? The corruption
and mutability of the Legislative Councils of the States.
If the plan does not remedy these, it will not recommend
itself." Gouverneur Morris of Pennsylvania also constantly expressed his opinion that "the public liberty
was in greater danger from Legislative usurpations than
from any other source"; and that Legislative instability and Legislative tyranny were the great dangers
to be apprehended. And John Dickinson of Delaware
said that "all were convinced of the necessity of making
the General Government independent of the prejudices,
passions, and improper views of the State Legislatures."
These views pervaded the Convention and influenced
much of its action. Nearly all the delegates agreed
that a curb on State legislation must be provided in the

new Constitution, but the difficult question was: how shall it be applied? By the Legislature, in the shape of preventive action or corrective statutes; by the Executive, in the shape of force; or by the Judiciary, in the shape of Court decisions, in cases involving State laws? The Convention began by adopting the first method. The idea was apparently original with Madison, and had never been "suggested or conceived among the people." "No speculative projector, and there are enough of that character among us in politics, as well as in other things, has in any pamphlet or newspaper thrown out the idea," said Elbridge Gerry.[1] As early, however, as March 19, 1787, Madison had written to Jefferson that, in addition to the positive powers of legislation to be vested in Congress, it would be necessary "to arm the Federal head with a negative *in all cases whatsoever* on the local Legislatures":

"Without this defensive power, experience and reflection have satisfied me that however ample the Federal powers may be made, or however clearly their boundaries may be delineated on paper, they will be easily and continually baffled by the Legislative authorities of the States. The effect of this provision would be not only to guard the National rights and interests against invasion, but also to restrain the States from thwarting and molesting each other and even from oppressing the minority in themselves by paper money and other unrighteous measures which favor the interests of the majority."

To Randolph, he had written, April 8, suggesting that the power to negative be vested in the Senate; and to Washington, he had written, April 16, that a power to negative *in all cases whatsoever* appeared to him "absolutely necessary and the least possible encroachment on the State jurisdiction. Without this defensive power, every positive power that can be given on paper

[1] Speech of Gerry, in Convention, June 8, 1787.

will be evaded and defeated." Madison, at the time, seems not to have thought of the means of controlling State legislation which was later adopted by the Convention, namely specific restraints on State legislation and enforcement of these restraints by the National Judiciary. It is a striking fact, which has not been emphasized by historians, that the first suggestion that the proper method of curbing State laws violative of the Constitution lay in the Judiciary, came from Thomas Jefferson. Replying to Madison's letter, June 20, 1787, he wrote : [1]

"The negative proposed to be given them on all the acts of the several Legislatures is now for the first time suggested to my mind. Prima facie I do not like it. It fails in an essential character, that the hole and the patch should be commensurate; but this proposes to mend a small hole by covering the whole garment. Not more than 1 out of 100 State acts concern the Confederacy. This proposition then, in order to give them 1 degree of power which they ought to have, gives them 99 more which they ought not to have, upon a presumption that they will not exercise the 99. But upon every act there will be a preliminary question : Does this act concern the Confederacy? And was there ever a proposition so plain as to pass Congress without a debate? Their decisions are almost always wise, they are like pure metal. But you know of how much dross this is the result. Would not an appeal from the State Judicatures to a Federal Court, in all cases where the Act of Confederation controuled

[1] This letter was probably not received by Madison until August, as it took six to eight weeks for letters to arrive from Paris. See also esp. Jefferson to Madison, March 15, 1789 (replying to Madison's letters of Oct. 17, Dec. 8, 12, 1788), in which Jefferson favored judicial review of legislation: "In the argument in favor of a declaration of rights, you omit one which has great weight with me — the legal check which it puts into the hands of the Judiciary. . . ."

It is to be noted that Richard Henry Lee wrote to George Mason, May 12, 1787: "Do you not think, sir, that it ought to be declared by the new system, that any State act of legislation that shall contravene or oppose the authorized acts of Congress, or interfere with the expressed rights of that body shall be ipso facto void, and of no force whatsoever." *Letters of Richard Henry Lee* (ed. by J. C. Ballagh, 1914), II.

the question, be as effectual a remedy, and exactly commensurate to the defect? A British creditor, e.g., sues for his debt in Virginia; the defendant pleads an act of the State excluding him from their Courts; the plaintiff urges the Confederation and the treaty made under that, as controuling the State law; the Judges are weak enough to decide according to the views of their Legislature; an appeal to a Federal Court sets all to rights. It will be said that this Court may encroach on the jurisdiction of the State Courts. It may, but there will be a power, to wit Congress, to watch and restrain them. But place the same authority in Congress itself, and there will be no power above them to perform the same office. They will restrain within due bounds a jurisdiction exercised by others much more rigorously than if exercised by themselves.''

It is possible that the idea of judicial enforcement of restraints on State legislation may also have been fostered by the publication, just as the Convention met, of a pamphlet entitled "Fragments on the Confederation of the American States", in which it was proposed that "in order to prevent an oppressive exercise of the powers deposited with Congress, a jurisdiction should be established to interpose and determine between the individual States and the Federal body upon all disputed points, and being stiled The Equalizing Court, should be constituted and conducted in the following manner." [1] This scheme, as widely reprinted in the newspapers, provided for the division of the States into three equal sections, and for the nomination by the Legislature of each State of one candidate "skilled in economics and jurisprudence", — Congress to draw by lot one Judge for each section. "It should be the duty of this Court to hear and determine on all appeals made by Congress against a State or by a State against Con-

---

[1] See *Pennsylvania Gazette*, June 6, 1787. This pamphlet was published by Thomas Dobson on 2d St., near Chestnut, price 6 d.

gress, whose determination shall be final and binding
upon the parties." Madison's insistence on the necessity of a curb on State Legislatures was due to the
underlying theory that there were individual rights,
based on conscience and natural justice, which not even
the majority in a government should have power to
violate — that a Constitution must provide restraints
on the majority and protection to the minority. "In
all cases where a majority are united by a common
interest or passion, the rights of the minority are in
danger", he said; and he pointed out that this was
true, whether the majority was formed on a basis of
property or lack of property, or of religion, of race, of
class or of politics.[1] Since oppressive use of power by
a strong faction could more easily prevail in a small
than in a large community, he considered the rights of
minorities to be safer in the hands of a National Legislature elected by the people with power to restrain the
State Legislatures. It is interesting to note that
Madison's theory was in reality that on which the
Fourteenth Amendment was later based — providing
a National guaranty that the States should not deprive

---

[1] Madison, June 6. Mason said, Aug. 13: "Notwithstanding the superiority
of the Republican form over every other, it had its evils. The chief ones were the
danger of the majority oppressing the minority. . . ." See also Mason, Aug.
21, 29.

Madison wrote to Jefferson, Oct. 14, 1787: "If then there must be different
interests and parties in society, and a majority when united by a common interest
or passion cannot be restrained from oppressing the minority, what remedy can be
found in a Republican Government where the majority must ultimately decide,
but that of giving such an extent to its sphere that no common interest or passion
will be likely to unite a majority of the whole number in an unjust pursuit. . . .
The same security seems requisite for the civil as for the religious rights of individuals. If the same sect form a majority and have the power, other sects will be
sure to be depressed. . . . The great desideratum in Government is, so to modify
the sovereignty as that it may be sufficiently neutral between different parts of the
Society to controul one part from invading the rights of another, and at the same
time sufficiently controuled itself from setting up an interest adverse to that of the
entire Society. . . . In the extended Republic of the United States, the General
Government would hold a pretty even balance between the parties of particular
States, and be at the same time sufficiently restrained by its dependence on the
community from betraying its general interest."

persons of their life, liberty, or property without due process or deny the equal protection of the laws. In Rufus King's *Notes*, under date of June 4, Madison's view as to minority protection was well summarized, in connection with the proposal to give to the Executive, joined with the Judiciary, the power to negative laws: "A check on the Legislature is necessary. Experience proves it to be so, and teaches us what has been thought a calumny on a Republican Government is nevertheless true — in all countries are diversities of interest, the rich and the poor, the debtor and creditor, the followers of different demagogues, the diversity of religious sects. The effects of these divisions in ancient Governments are well known, and the like causes will now produce like effects. We must, therefore, introduce in our system provisions against the measures of an interested majority — a check is not only necessary to protect the Executive power, but the minority in the Legislature."

Power to Enforce

The last of the crucial Resolutions to be discussed, this day, was that which gave the National Legislature power "to call forth the force of the Union against any member of the Union failing to fulfill its duty under the Articles thereof." One of the defects under the Articles of Confederation had been the lack of power in the Congress to compel any State to comply with the provisions of the Articles, or with any requisition for troops needed in the National defence or for money to pay the National debts. This proposal was designed to supply the deficiency. But Madison now stated, that the more he reflected on the use of force, "the more he doubted the practicability, the justice, and the efficacy, when applied to people collectively, and not individually", and he moved to postpone the clause.

This was done, and it was never acted upon thereafter.[1]

OUT OF CONVENTION

Washington noted :

" The State of Georgia came on the floor of the Convention today (by the arrival of Maj. Pierce and Mr. Houstoun) which made a representation of ten States [eleven, in fact]. Dined at Mr. Francis's, and drank tea with Mrs. Meredith."

[1] Charles Pinckney, on June 8, said that "any Government for the United States formed on the supposed practicability of using force against the unconstitutional proceedings of the States would prove as visionary and fallacious as the Government of Congress." Randolph, himself, on June 16, said that coercion of States was "impracticable" and that "we must resort therefore to a National Legislation over individuals." Mason, on June 20, said that civil liberty and military execution were incompatible in a Government, and that any plan (like Paterson's) which could not be enforced without military coercion was impracticable. Finally on July 14, Madison said that "the practicability of making laws with coercive sanctions for the States as political bodies had been exploded on all hands."

CHAPTER THREE

The Executive, the Judiciary, and the Report of the Committee of the Whole

FRIDAY, JUNE 1, 1787

IN CONVENTION

The Executive

Having disposed of the Legislature and its powers, the Committee took up the subject of the Executive and his powers. Here they approached one of the most difficult of all their problems. Fear of a return of Executive authority like that exercised by the Royal Governors or by the King had been ever present in the States from the beginning of the Revolution. Such Executive functions as the Congress of the Confederation possessed had been performed by Committees of three, until the appointment in 1781 of single officials as Secretary of Foreign Affairs, Secretary at War, and Superintendent of Finance. And the somewhat auto-

cratic acts of Robert Morris in the latter office had
reawakened fear of an Executive in the minds of many,
especially of the older Revolutionary patriots, and had
led to the substitution of a Treasury Board. When,
therefore, James Wilson now made the bold proposal
that "a National Executive to consist of a single person
be instituted", there was "a considerable pause"
among the delegates; and Franklin, observing "that
it was a point of great importance", urged the delegates to "deliver their sentiments on it." John
Rutledge of South Carolina "animadverted on the
shyness of gentlemen on this and other subjects. He
said it looked as if they supposed themselves precluded
by having frankly disclosed their opinions from afterwards changing them, which he did not take to be at all
the case." Wilson, Charles Pinckney, and Rutledge
favored a single Executive. Roger Sherman of Connecticut presented the restricted view which was then
held of the position of an Executive in the Government; for, said he, as it was "nothing more than an
institution for carrying the will of the Legislature into
effect", the Executive should be appointed by the
Legislature and its number fixed by the same body.
James Wilson, while conceiving that the only powers
"strictly Executive were those of executing the laws
and appointing officers, not appertaining to and appointed by the Legislature", insisted that a single
magistrate would give "most energy and despatch to the
office." Madison thought that before choice be made
"between a unity and plurality in the Executive, the
extent of his authority ought to be first agreed upon."
Randolph favored an Executive of three persons
and strenuously opposed a single Executive, regarding
it "as the foetus of monarchy." George Mason of
Virginia concurred with his colleague, Randolph, and
advocated joining an Executive of three persons with

a Council of Revision (composed of members of the Judiciary), whereby "we shall increase the strength of the Executive in that particular circumstance in which it will most want strength — in the power of defending itself against the encroachments of the Legislature." He was inclined to think a strong Executive necessary, but "if strong and extensive powers are vested in the Executive, and that Executive consists only of one person, the Government will of course degenerate into a monarchy — a Government so contrary to the genius of the people that they will reject even the appearance of it." To allay State jealousies, he proposed that "one member of the Executive be chosen by the Northern States, one by the Middle, and one by the Southern." [1] James Wilson, on the other hand, argued that "all the thirteen States, though agreeing in scarce any other instance, agreed in placing a single magistrate at the head of the Government. The idea of three heads has taken place in none. . . . Among three equal members, he foresaw nothing but uncontrolled, continued, and violent animosities, which would not only interrupt the public administration, but diffuse their poison through the other branches of the Government, through the States, and at length through the people at large." The debate on the subject was concluded on Monday, June 4, when the Committee adopted the single Executive, by a vote of 7 States to 3 (Delaware, Maryland, and New York being opposed). When the Convention, on July 17, considered this part of the report of the Committee of the Whole, it was accepted with no dissenting vote. [2]

[1] Madison in his *Notes of Debates* gives an incomplete report of George Mason's speech and does not include the portion quoted above. The speech may be found in more complete form in the *George Mason Papers MSS.* in Library of Congress.

[2] It is to be noted that Hugh Williamson of North Carolina, on July 24, stated that "he had wished the Executive power to be lodged in three men taken from three districts into which the States should be divided. As the Executive is to have a kind of veto on the laws, and there is an essential difference of interests between

The importance of having a strong and independent Executive to counterbalance the Legislative Department was insisted upon throughout the Convention; for, as Hamilton pointed out, later, in *The Federalist* (No. 71):

"The tendency of the Legislative authority to absorb every other has been fully displayed and illustrated. . . . In governments purely republican, this tendency is almost irresistible. The representatives of the people in a popular assembly seem sometimes to fancy that they are the people themselves, and betray strong symptoms of impatience and disgust at the least sign of opposition from any other quarter, as if the exercise of its rights, by either the Executive or Judiciary, were a breach of their privileges and an outrage to their dignity. They often appear disposed to exert an imperious control over the other departments; and as they commonly have the people on their side, they always act with such momentum as to make it very difficult for the other members of the Government to maintain the balance of the Constitution."

Executive Powers

With reference to the powers to be vested in the Executive, it must be recalled that most of the early State Constitutions granted little authority to their Governor or other Executive. In many States, he was scarcely more than a military official, taking slight part in the political administration of the Government. In practically all the States, he shared his powers with a Privy Council; and in all the States, the powers which he was to exercise were specifically prescribed by the State Constitutions; for the people did not intend that any Governor should exercise the prerogatives exercised by the Crown in England, unless expressly

the Northern and Southern States, particularly in the carrying trade, the power will be dangerous, if the Executive is to be taken from part of the Union, to the part from which he is not taken. . . . Another objection against a single Magistrate is that he will be an elective King."

conferred on him. It is probable that Madison and Randolph in preparing the Virginia Plan had in mind the conception of Executive power which Thomas Jefferson had set forth in his Draft of a Fundamental Constitution for Virginia in 1783, as follows: [1]

"The Executive powers shall be exercised by a Governor, who shall be chosen by joint ballot of both Houses of Assembly. . . . By Executive powers, we mean no reference to those powers exercised under our former government by the Crown as of its prerogative, nor that these shall be the standard of what may or may not be deemed the rightful powers of the Governor. We give them these powers only, which are necessary to execute the laws (and administer the government), and which are not in their nature either Legislative or Judiciary. The application of this idea must be left to reason. We do, however, expressly deny him the prerogative powers of erecting courts, offices, boroughs, corporations, fairs, markets, ports, beacons, light-houses, and sea marks; of laying embargoes, of establishing precedence, of retaining within the State, or recalling to it any citizens thereof, and of making denizens, except so far as he may be authorized from time to time by the Legislature to exercise any other like powers."

In the Randolph Resolutions, the only express provision for power in the Executive was that "besides a general authority to execute the National laws, it ought to enjoy the Executive rights vested in Congress by the Confederation." No specific power was given to appoint officers. The State Constitutions, however, had made express provisions as to the appointive power. In some States, as in Georgia and New Jersey, the Governor had no power to appoint any civil officers whatever; in some States, he could appoint only certain civil officers, the Legislature appointing the others, as in Delaware, Virginia, Penn-

[1] *Writings of Thomas Jefferson* (Ford's ed.), IV, 155–156. Jefferson sent a copy of this draft to Madison in a letter of June 17, 1783.

sylvania, and South Carolina. In Massachusetts, New Hampshire, and New York, power of appointment was in the Governor and his Council. In practically all the States, however, appointments by the Governor could only be made by and with the consent of a Council chosen to assist and advise him. Madison now thought that the extent of Executive authority should be more clearly defined, and he moved, as a substitute, that the Executive have "power to carry into effect the National laws, to appoint to offices in cases not otherwise provided for, and to execute such other powers not Legislative or Judiciary in their nature as may from time to time be delegated by the National Legislature." Objections being raised to the last portion of his motion, Madison replied that he "did not know that the words were absolutely necessary, or even the preceding words 'to appoint to offices', etc., the whole being perhaps included in the first member of the proposition."[1] This was a most significant admission that the power to appoint to office might be included in, and implied from, the power to execute the laws. The Committee of the Whole, on motion of Charles Pinckney, voted to eliminate as unnecessary, the words "to execute such other powers", etc., contained in Madison's proposal. It, however, retained the power "to appoint to offices in cases not otherwise provided for." This left to the Executive the power to appoint all officers, except Judges who were (under the Randolph Resolution) to be appointed by the National Legislature (changed later, by vote of the Committee, to by the Senate).[2]

No express provision, whatever, was made as to any power of removal. But if Madison was correct in

[1] This statement by Madison has an interesting bearing upon the question of the Executive's power of removal which was recently decided in *Myers* v. *United States,* 272 U. S. 52 in 1926. It is singular that neither the Chief Justice nor the dissenting Justices in their opinions made any reference to Madison's suggestion.

[2] These powers of the President were accepted by the Convention, on July 26.

implying a power to appoint from a power to execute
the laws, clearly a power of removal might be deduced
from the same source.[1]

It is a remarkable fact that this power to appoint was
given to the Executive alone, without any requirement
of advice and consent of the Senate or of any other body.
For under the State Constitutions, the Executives had
no such independent authority, and their powers were
always subject to advice and consent of a Council.
That the Federal Convention, notwithstanding its
jealousy of Executive power and its fear of erecting
anything resembling monarchy, should, at this stage
have been willing to grant so broad and unprecedented
a power of appointment to the National Executive
alone, and without constituting any Council for him,
is a striking example of their desire to establish the
entire independence of the Executive branch of the
Government.[2]

OUT OF CONVENTION

Washington noted:

"Attending in Convention, and nothing being suffered to
transpire no minutes of the proceedings has been or will be
inserted in this diary.

Dined with Mr. John Penn, and spent the evening at a
superb entertainment at Bush-hill given by Mr. (William)
Hamilton (the owner of it) at which were more than one
hundred guests."

[1] Power of removal by the Executive, if it existed in the States, must have been
implied from the Executive's power to execute the laws; for in no State Constitution prior to 1787 was there any specific provision authorizing the Executive to
remove, except as follows: in Delaware, a provision was made for appointment by
the Executive and Privy Council " and all such officers shall be removed on conviction of misbehaviour at common law, or on impeachment, or upon the address of
the General Assembly"; in Maryland, the Governor "may also suspend or remove
any civil officer who has not a commission during good behaviour."   The Charter
of Rhode Island of 1663 which served as its State Constitution stated that certain
officers were "for any misdemeanour or default to be removable by the Governor,
Assistants and Company."

[2] For the subject of an Executive Council, see *infra* under date of September 7.

On this day, George Mason of Virginia wrote to his son, George Mason, Jr., his high opinion of the Convention:

"The idea I formerly mentioned to you, before the Convention met, of a great National Council, consisting of two branches of the Legislature, a Judiciary and an Executive, upon the principle of fair representation in the Legislature, with powers adapted to the great objects of the Union, and consequently a control in those instances on the State Legislatures, is still the prevalent one. Virginia has had the honor of presenting the outlines of the plan, upon which the Convention is proceeding; but so slowly that it is impossible to judge when the business will be finished, most probably not before August — *festina lente* may very well be called our motto. When I first came here, judging from casual conversations with gentlemen from the different States, I was very apprehensive that, soured and disgusted with the unexpected evils we had experienced from the democratic principles of our Governments, we should be apt to run into the opposite extreme, and in endeavoring to steer too far from Scylla, we might be drawn into the vortex of Charybdis, of which I still think there is some danger, though I have the pleasure to find in the Convention, many men of fine republican principles. America has certainly, upon this occasion, drawn forth her first characters; there are upon this Convention many gentlemen of the most respectable abilities, and so far as I can discover, of the purest intentions. The eyes of the United States are turned upon this assembly, and their expectations raised to a very anxious degree. May God grant, we may be able to gratify them, by establishing a wise and just Government. For my own part, I never before felt myself in such a situation; and declare I would not, upon pecuniary motives, serve in this Convention for a thousand pounds per day. The revolt from Great Britain and the formations of our new Governments at that time, were nothing compared to the great business now before us. There was then a certain degree of enthusiasm, which inspired and supported the mind; but to view through the calm, sedate medium of reason the influence which the establishment now proposed may have upon the happiness or misery of millions yet unborn, is an object of such magnitude, as absorbs, and in a manner suspends, the operations of the human understanding. . . . All communications of the proceedings are forbidden during the sitting of the Convention; this I think was a necessary precaution to prevent misrepresentations or mistakes; there being a material difference between the appearance of a subject in its first crude and undigested shape, and after it shall have been properly matured and arranged."

SATURDAY, JUNE 2, 1787

IN CONVENTION

Two of the subjects which gave rise to the greatest differences of opinion and the greatest variety of votes throughout the Convention were discussed on this day — the mode of election and term of office of the Executive. As these were debated later on, it will be more convenient to describe the attitude of the delegates in connection with a subsequent date (July 26).

OUT OF CONVENTION

Washington noted: [1]

"Major Jenifer coming in with sufficient powers for the purpose (authorizing one member to represent it) added another State (now eleven) gave a representation to Maryland; which brought all the States in the Union into Convention, except Rhode Island, which had refused to send delegates thereto. Dined at the City Tavern with the Club and spent the evening at my own quarters."

Dr. Benjamin Rush wrote, this day, to Richard Price in London: [2]

---

[1] James McHenry had arrived from Maryland, May 28, and left June 1. Jenifer now took his place as the sole representative of that State.

[2] *Mass. Hist. Soc. Proc., Second Series*, XVII, 367.

"I have set down with great pleasure to inform you that eleven States have this day been represented in the Convention now assembled in this city for the purpose of revising the Federal Constitution. A delegation is expected in a few days from the twelfth. Rhode Island is destined to all the distress and infamy that can arise from her total separation from the Confederacy. Her insignificance in point of numbers, strength, and character render this event of no consequence to the general interests of the Union. Dr. Franklin exhibits daily a spectacle of transcendant benevolence by attending the Convention punctually, and even taking part in its business and deliberations. He says 'it is the most august and respectable Assembly he ever was in in his life,' and adds, that he thinks 'they will soon finish their business, as there are no prejudices to oppose, nor errors to refute in any of the body.' Mr. Dickinson (who is one of them) informs me that they are all *united* in their object and he expects they will be equally united in the means of attaining them. . . . You must not be surprised if you should hear of our new system of Government meeting with some opposition. There are in all our States little characters whom a great and respectable Government will sink into insignificance. These men will excite factions among us, but they will be of a temporary duration. Time, necessity, and the gradual operation of reason will carry it down, and if these fail, *force* will not be wanting to carry it into execution, for not only all the wealth, but all the military men of our country (associated with the Society of the Cincinnati) are in favor of a wise and efficient Government. The order of nature is the same in the political as it is in the natural world — good is derived chiefly from evil. We are travelling fast into order and National happiness. The same enthusiasm now pervades all classes in favor of *Government* that actuated us in favor of *liberty* in the years 1774 and 1775, with this difference, that we are more *united* in the former than we were in the latter pursuit. When our enemies triumph in our mistakes and follies, tell them that we are *men*, that we walk upon two legs, that we possess reason, passions, and senses, and that under these circumstances, it is as absurd to expect the ordinary times of the rising and setting of the sun will be altered, so as to suppose we shall not *finally* compose and adopt a suitable form of Government and be happy in the blessings which are usually connected with it."

The secrecy of the Convention was commented on in a Philadelphia despatch published in many newspapers: [1]

"Such circumspection and secrecy mark the proceedings of the Federal Convention that the members find it difficult to acquire the habits of communication even among themselves; and are so cautious in defeating the curiosity of the publick that all debate is suspended on the entrance of their own inferior officers. Though we readily admit the propriety of excluding an indiscriminate attendance on the discussion of this deliberative council, it is hoped that the privacy of this transaction will be an additional motive for despatch, as the anxiety of the people must be necessarily increased by every appearance of mystery in conducting this important business."

A New York despatch quoted in the Philadelphia press at this time said:

"It is most undoubted that the several States have delegated their wisdom to this august body. . . . If so, what have we now to do, but hope for the chiefest good, as politically accountable beings — a pure and adequate, *republican*, Federal Constitution. No pains shall be spared to procure the debates and resolutions of the Convention for the inspection of the public as soon as any of them transpire."

SUNDAY, JUNE 3, 1787

Washington noted:

"Dined at Mr. Clymer's and drank tea there also."

---

[1] See *New York Journal*, June 7; *Boston Gazette*, June 11; *Salem Mercury*, June 12; *Virginia Independent Chronicle*, June 20, 1787.

On this day, Nathaniel Gorham, one of the Massachusetts delegates, wrote to Nathan Dane, a Member of Congress from Massachusetts: [1]

"We have now eleven States and have been every day last week in a Committee of the Whole, in which to sound the sentiment of each other. Several propositions relative to a General Government have been submitted. The business was opened by Govr. Randolph of Virginia in an able manner, and I think there is a prospect that the Convention will agree in a pretty good plan. It is not easy to meet with any Boston newspapers here. I will therefore thank you to inclose to me those that you get, after you have read them. I do not know that I am at liberty to mention in any manner what the Convention has done; but to you in confidence I can say that they have agreed, I believe, unanimously, that there ought to be a National Legislative, Executive, and Judiciary."

Jeremiah Wadsworth of Connecticut wrote, this day, to Rufus King, another Massachusetts delegate, an interesting comment on the delegates chosen by Connecticut (the last of whom, Dr. William S. Johnson, had only the day before) arrived in Philadelphia: [2]

"I am satisfied with the appointments — except Sherman, who, I am told, is disposed to patch up the old scheme of Government. This was not my opinion of him, when we chose him; he is cunning as the Devil, and if you attack him, you ought to know him well; he is not easily managed, but if he suspects you are trying to take him in, you may as well catch an eel by the tail. Our Genl. Assembly will finish this week without making paper money or Tender Act. Our unfederal

---

[1] *Nathan Dane Papers MSS.* in Library of Congress.

[2] The *Independent Gazetteer* of May 19 noted the choice of delegates by the Connecticut Legislature on May 10, 1787, "after a debate of two hours." Johnson, Ellsworth, and Erastus Wolcott were chosen. Sherman was later appointed in place of Wolcott.

William Grayson, a Member of Congress from Virginia, wrote, June 3, from New York to General Washington introducing Dr. Johnson "a gentleman of great abilities and worth and who has been lately appointed one of the Convention. I am very happy to hear you have recovered your health." *Washington Papers MSS.*

party will lose ground. I am persuaded a good Government is wished for by the majority of our House of Assembly — but whether the people at large will be prepared to receive such an one as you and I wish, is uncertain; but I hope the Convention will be united in something that is not so totally unfit for our purposes as the present system, for I consider that at an end."

MONDAY, JUNE 4, 1787

IN CONVENTION

The Veto Power

Having agreed to a single Executive, and having agreed to vest in the Executive two powers, viz.: to execute the laws and to appoint all officers except Judges, the Committee now took up Randolph's Resolutions which gave to the Executive (in conjunction with the Judiciary) power to negative or veto Acts of the National Legislature, subject, however, to repassage. Elbridge Gerry of Massachusetts now proposed as a substitute, and in order to eliminate the Judiciary from any participation in the function, that "the National Executive shall have a right to negative any Legislative act, which shall not be afterwards passed by   parts of each branch of the National Legislature." This proposed power of veto was an extraordinary circumstance; for no power of the Royal Governors had been more unpopular, and in framing their own Constitutions, only three States — Massachusetts, South Carolina, and New York — had seen fit to grant such a veto power to their Governors. In eight States, the Legislature alone was concerned in enacting statutes.[1] The alarm felt by many of the delegates at the unjust and improper laws which such uncurbed State Legislature had been passing accounted for their willingness to accept the veto. "It was an

[1] See *A Short History of the Veto*, *Elliot's Debates*, IV, 620–626.

important principle, in this, and in the State Constitutions, to check Legislative injustice and incroachments," said Madison. "The experience of the States had demonstrated that their checks are insufficient." [1] James Wilson and Alexander Hamilton went so far as to advocate giving to the Executive an absolute veto, not subject to be overridden by any vote of the Legislature, Wilson saying that: "He believed as others did that this power would seldom be used. The Legislature would know that such a power existed and would refrain from such laws as it would be sure to defeat. Its silent operation would, therefore, preserve harmony and prevent mischief." But Franklin, Sherman, Pierce Butler of South Carolina, and Mason were opposed to any absolute veto; for if it be given, said Mason, "we are not indeed constituting a British Government, but a more dangerous monarchy, an elective one." Gunning Bedford of Delaware opposed any form of veto, saying: "The representatives of the people were the best judges of what was for their interest and ought to be under no external control whatever. The two branches would produce a sufficient control within the Legislature itself." The proposal for an absolute veto was defeated, as was a substitute motion, made by Butler and seconded by Franklin, that the Executive have power to suspend an act of the Legislature for a specified time. Thereupon, Gerry's motion that the Executive be given a revisionary check on the laws unless overruled by two-thirds of each branch of the Legislature (as provided in the Massachusetts State Constitution), was accepted by a vote of eight States to two (Connecticut and Maryland alone dissenting).

In Randolph's original Resolution, there was a provision for joining the Judiciary with the Executive

[1] Madison, Sept. 12, 1787.

in this power to reject Acts of the National Legislature. The grant to the Judiciary of such a function was now defeated on this day, and three renewals of this proposal on June 6, July 21, and August 15, were likewise defeated (as discussed *infra* under date of July 18).[1] The general opinion of the delegates was that it was improper to join the Judges in this veto power, since the question of the constitutionality of an Act of Congress might come up before them later in their judicial capacity, and they ought not to be given opportunity to pass twice on such an Act, once in a Legislative or Executive capacity, and once Judicially. Moreover, this veto power was to be exercised not only in case of unconstitutional laws, but in case of laws felt to be oppressive or unwise, and as to objections based on such latter grounds, the Judges were not qualified to act. The vote of the Committee granting the veto power to the Executive subject to overruling by a two-thirds vote of Congress was accepted by the Convention on July 18, without dissent.

OUT OF CONVENTION

Washington noted :

"Attended Convention. Representation as on Saturday. Reviewed (at the importunity of Genl. Mifflin and the officers) the Light Infantry, Cavalry and part of the artillery of the City. Dined with Genl. Mifflin and drank tea with Miss Cadwallader."

In the newspapers, the review was thus described : [2]

"On Monday afternoon, the Light Infantry of the respective battalions of Philadelphia militia, the City Light

---

[1] Jefferson, writing to Francis Hopkinson, as late as March 13, 1789, said that he approved of "the qualified negative on laws given to the Executive which, moreover, I should have liked better if associated with the Judiciary also, as in New York."

[2] *Pennsylvania Journal,* June 9; *Pennsylvania Herald,* June 9; *Freeman's Journal,* June 6; *New York Journal,* June 14, 1787. Hector Jean de Crèvecœur

Dragoons and a detachment of the Artillery in full uniform
and well accoutred, under the orders of Col. Read and Col.
Mentzes, inspector of the militia were reviewed on the commons near this city by his Excellency General Washington,
Generals Mifflin and Pinckney and several members of the
Convention. The usual maneuvres were performed with
alertness and regularity, much to the satisfaction of the
Generals, as well as to a vast concourse of respectable inhabitants who assembled on that occasion. In the evening, the
troops marched into the city in great order and were dismissed before his Excellency's Quarters, at the House of the
Honorable Robert Morris, Esq., in Market Street."

It would appear, however, from the evidence of others
that the success of the review was greatly impeded by
the pressure of the populace to see Washington. "Such
is the veneration and love which the presence of this
great man inspires that it was not possible for him to
review the fine militia of Philadelphia, as he had been
asked, so great was the crowd which unceasingly surrounded him and wished to see and talk with him. It
is upon tender and profound attachment that people
found their hope that the plans which the Convention
shall propose will be unanimously approved and
ratified by the States"—so wrote Jean de Crèvecœur,
the French traveller. And the *Herald* said that while
"the business of the day was conducted greatly to the
satisfaction of this judge of military merit, it is to be
regretted that the desire of the populace to gaze upon
their beloved General rendered his situation in some
degree, uncommodious and impaired the effect of the

to Duc de Rochefoucauld, *Copies of Crèvecœur Letters MSS* in Library of Congress.
    The diary of Jacob Hiltzheimer, quoted in *Washington, After the Revolution*
(1898), by William Spohn Baker said: "In the evening, my wife and I went to
Market Street gate to see that great and good man, General Washington. We
had a full view of him and Major Jackson who walked with him, but the number of
people who followed him on all sides was astonishing. He had been out on the
field to review Captain Samuel Miles, with his Troop of Horse, the light infantry
and artillery."

maneuvres. This inconveniency, however, can require but little excuse when we consider the motives that produced it and find the natural curiosity of the people sanctified by veneration and gratitude."

TUESDAY, JUNE 5, 1787

IN CONVENTION

The subjects of the Judiciary and of Ratification of the new Constitution were settled by the Committee in a preliminary way (as to which, see discussion under dates of July 18 and July 23).

OUT OF CONVENTION

Washington noted : [1]

"Dined at Mr. Morris's with a large company and spent the evening there. Attended in Convention the usual hours."

The *Gazetteer* reprinted an article from a New York paper on the need of the women to work for the Constitution : [2]

" . . . It is the duty of the American ladies in a particular manner to interest themselves in the success of the measures that are now pursuing by the Federal Convention for the happiness of America. They can retain their rank as rational beings only in a free government. In a monarchy (to which the present anarchy in America, if not restrained must soon lead us) they will be considered as valuable members of society only as they are capable of being mothers for soldiers who are the pillars of crowned heads. It is in their power, by their influence over their husbands, brothers and sons, to draw them from those dreams of liberty under a simple democratical form of government, which are so unfriendly to that order and decency of which nature has

---

[1] On succeeding days, when no entry is made in this book from Washington's diary, it is to be assumed that he merely recorded attendance in Convention, drinking tea and dining at Mr. Morris'.

[2] See also *Salem Mercury*, June 19, 1787.

made them such amiable examples. . . . As the miseries of slavery will fall with particular weight upon them, they are certainly deeply interested in the establishment of such a government as will preserve our liberties, and thereby preserve the rank, the happiness, the influence, and the character in society for which God intended them."

WEDNESDAY, JUNE 6, 1787

IN CONVENTION

On this day, as before noted, the Committee voted for election of the first branch of the Legislature by the people, and for a second time refused to join the Judges with the President in power to veto legislation.

OUT OF CONVENTION

Washington noted:

"In Convention as usual. Dined at the President's (Doctor Franklin) and drank tea there. After which retired to my lodgings and wrote letters for France."

Dr. William Samuel Johnson in a diary containing brief items (chiefly as to the weather), which he kept throughout the Convention noted: [1]

"Very Rainy. In Convention. Dined Dr. Franklin's."

The *Journal* reprinted a New York article on the necessity of free discussion of the Constitution by the newspapers: [2]

"It is not more essential to freedom, says a correspondent, that the press should be unrestrained in its production than that the circulation of its productions should be uninterrupted and universal. The strong, invidious distinction

---

[1] See *Records of the Federal Convention* (1911), by Max Farrand, III, 552–554. The first two entries in this diary are as follows: "June 1. Rain and fair. Came to Philadelphia at 7 o'clock and lodged at Dickenson's."

"June 2. Made visits. Took a seat in Convention. . . . In evening, took lodgings at City Tavern."

[2] See also *Pennsylvania Packet*, June 6; *Virginia Independent Chronicle*, June 20, 1787.

which different habits, manners and pursuits will naturally create between the Eastern and Southern inhabitants of so extensive an empire can be only counteracted by the freeest communication of the opinions and politics, and at this awful moment when a Council is convened, it may be justly said, to decide the fate of the Confederation, would it not be dangerous and impolitic to divert or destroy that great channel which serves at once to gratify the curiosity and collect the voice of the people? The Grand Convention will certainly be of the highest importance to the political existence and welfare of the United States. To revise the Confederation and to fall upon a system of commercial regulations which upon the whole may tend to the revival and establishment of our credit and the encouragement of our trade and manufactures are objects of such magnitude as require the united wisdom of the continent — and from the respectable names of the gentlemen deputed to this arduous business we have reason to be assured the greatest exertions will be made and the best measures adopted to render the Constitution of the Foederal Government adequate to the exigencies of the Union."

Edmund Randolph wrote this day to Lieutenant Governor Beverly Randolph that "the prospect of a very long sojournment here has determined me to bring up my family." He then added a statement which conditions in the Convention hardly seemed to warrant: "We have every reason to expect harmony in the Convention, altho the currents of opinion are various. But no man can yet divine in what form our efforts against the American crisis will appear to the public eyes. It will not be settled in its principles for perhaps some weeks hence." [1] Arthur Lee, then a Member of Congress, wrote from New York, this day, to John Rutledge that the representation of the United States in Convention was "much more complete than was expected", but that in New York, "hitherto

[1] *Calendar of Virginia State Papers*, IV, 293.

nothing has transpired touching their deliberations." [1]
Madison wrote, this day, to William Short that all
hopes were centered on the Convention:

"The Convention has been formed about 12 days. It
contains in several instances the most respectable characters
in the U. S., and in general may be said to be the best contribution of talents the States could make for the occasion.
What the result of the experiment may be is among the
arcana of futurity. Our affairs are considered on all hands
as at a most serious crisis. No hope is entertained from the
existing Confederacy. And the eyes and hopes of all are
turned towards this new Assembly. The result, therefore,
whatever it may be, must have a material influence on our
destiny, and on that of the cause of republican liberty. The
personal characters of the members promise much. The
spirit which they bring with them seems in general equally
promising. But the labor is great indeed, whether we consider the real or imaginary difficulties within doors or without doors."

To Jefferson in Paris, Madison wrote that: "The
names of the members will satisfy you that the States
have been serious in this business. The attendance of
General Washington is a proof of the light in which he regards it. The whole community is big with expectation;
and there can be no doubt that the result will in some
way or other have a powerful effect on our destiny."

Washington wrote to La Fayette:

". . . You will, I dare say, be surprised, my dear Marquis,
to receive a letter from me at this place. You will probably
be more so when you hear that I am again brought, contrary
to my public declamation and intention, on a public theatre.
Such is the vicissitude of human affairs, and such the frailty
of human nature, that no man, I conceive, can well answer
for the resolution he enters into. The pressure of the public
voice was so loud, I could not resist the call to a Convention
of the States which is to determine whether we are to have a

---

[1] *Life of Arthur Lee* (1829), by R. H. Lee.

Government of respectability under which life, liberty and property will be secured to us, or are to submit to one which may be the result of chance or the moment, springing perhaps from anarchy and confusion, and dictated perhaps by some aspiring demagogue who will not consult the interest of his country so much as his own ambitious views. What may be the result of the present deliberation is more than I am able, at present, if I was at liberty, to inform you, and therefore I will make this letter short. . . ."

THURSDAY, JUNE 7, 1787

IN CONVENTION

Election of the Senate by State Legislatures

The small States, having lost their fight against popular election of the first branch of the Legislature, now made a stand for election of the second branch, the Senate, by the State Legislatures.

In considering the place of the Senate in the scheme of the new Government, it is important to bear in mind a fact which is often overlooked — namely, that the original idea of a Senate was *not* that this branch should represent the States, while the House represented the people. That function of the Senate was occasioned by the Great Compromise by which the States secured equality of representation in one branch of the Legislature. Nor was the Senate established to be a body peculiarly representing property, as was the case with the State Senates, under the various State Constitutions which required high property qualifications for Senators and for those who voted for them; for though Madison, Gerry, Mason, and a few others thought that the Senate should represent wealth, the Convention expressly refused to adopt this idea, and voted against any property qualification.[1]

[1] See August 10, 1787. Gerry, on June 7, favored election of the Senate by the State Legislatures in order to protect the "commercial and monied interest" against

The actual theory on which the Senate was established was that there might be a body which should act as a check or curb on the House. It was expressed in homely fashion in the anecdote of the conversation between Jefferson and Washington when breakfasting together on the former's return from France. In answer to Jefferson's inquiry why a Senate was agreed to, Washington asked: "Why did you pour that coffee into your saucer?" "To cool it," replied Jefferson. "Even so," said Washington, "we pour legislation into the Senatorial saucer to cool it." [1] This was the theory which John Adams had urged, eleven years prior, when the States were about to form their own Constitutions in 1776, and which he had set forth in great detail in his book published in the spring of 1787. The statements made by delegates throughout the Convention show very clearly their views as to this function of the Senate.[2] Thus, Edmund Randolph said at the outset that the Senate should be smaller than the House, and "so small as to be exempt from the passionate proceedings to which numerous assemblies are liable"; that the origin of evils under which the United States labored were to be found "in the turbulence and follies of democracy", and that a good Senate seemed most likely to answer the purpose of a "check against this tendency of our Governments." And again, Randolph said that the object of the Senate was "to controul the democratic branch"; also

the people at large, whom he described as "chiefly composed of the landed interests." Madison said that "the Senate should come from and represent the wealth of the Nation." (See King's *Notes*.) Mason, on June 26, said that "one important object in constituting the Senate was to secure the rights of property." Baldwin, on June 29, said that he thought the Senate "ought to be the representation of property, and that in forming it, therefore, some reference ought to be had to the relative wealth of their constituents and to the principles on which the Senate of Massachusetts was constituted."

[1] *Farrand*, III, 359.

[2] Randolph, May 31, June 12; Madison, June 7, 27; Ellsworth, June 25; Mason, June 26; G. Morris, July 2, 19; C. Pinckney, Aug. 14; Carroll, Aug. 14; Gorham, Aug. 24, 1787.

that "a firmness and independence may be the more necessary in this branch, as it ought to guard the Constitution against encroachments of the Executive who will be apt to form combinations with the demagogues of the popular branch." Madison said that "the use of the Senate is to consist in its proceeding with more coolness, with more system, and with more wisdom than the popular branch"; and again, he said that its purpose was to give "stability" to the Government; and again, he said that, as one of the ends of Government was "to protect the people against the transient impressions in which they themselves might be led . . . an obvious precaution against this danger would be to divide the trust between different bodies of men who might watch and check each other." The Government, he said, should be so constituted "as that one of its branches might have an opportunity of acquiring competent knowledge of the public interests"; and, as a numerous body of Representatives "were liable to err also from fickleness and passion, a necessary fence against this danger would be to select a portion of enlightened citizens whose limited number and firmness might seasonably interpose against impetuous councils. . . . One great end of the institution was that, being a firm, wise and impartial body, it might give . . . stability to the General Government." Ellsworth of Connecticut, one of the leaders in the Great Compromise, said that "wisdom was one of the characteristics which it was in contemplation to give the second branch." G. Morris said: "What is this object? To check the precipitation, changeableness and excesses of the first branch." And again, he said that it was intended as "a check on the abuse of lawful powers" by the House. Charles Pinckney of South Carolina said that: "The Senate might be supposed to contain the fittest men. He hoped to see that body become a school of public Ministers, a nursery of statesmen." Carroll of Maryland, replying to his colleague, Martin, who said that "the Senate is to represent the States," stated: "The Senate was to represent and manage the affairs of the whole, and not to be the advocates of State interests." And, said Gorham: "It was wrong to be considering at every turn whom the Senate would represent. The public good was the true object to be kept in view."

In this debate on June 7, there was comparatively little opposition to election of the Senate by the State Legislatures. The Convention evidently considered it reasonable to make this concession to the adherents of State Sovereignty, especially since the crucial question of the proportion in which the States should be represented in the Senate was not involved in this vote. Hence, though Madison and Wilson continued to the end to argue in favor of founding the whole Government directly on the people, in both branches of the Legislative Department, as well as in the Executive, the motion for election of a Senate by State Legislatures (made by Dickinson of Delaware and Sherman of Connecticut) was carried, by a unanimous vote. When the Convention considered this vote of the Committee of the Whole, on June 25, it adopted it after some debate by a vote of 9 States to 2 (Virginia and Pennsylvania, led by Madison and Wilson, dissenting).

OUT OF CONVENTION

Washington noted:[1]

"Attended Convention as usual. Dined with a Club of Convention members at the Indian Queen. Drank tea and spent the evening at my lodgings."

[1] The Indian Queen Tavern, at which many of the delegates boarded, was on Fourth St., above Chestnut Street. It was later known as the Francis Hotel. Dr.

Joseph Jones wrote to Madison from Richmond, referring to the prospect of enhancement of value of Continental securities, through the adoption of an adequate form of government, and also to the fact that the State Governments were purchasing such securities : [1]

"I entertain hopes, from the disposition of the members convened, that harmony will prevail and such improvements of the Foederal system adopted as will afford us a prospect of peace and happiness. I am, however, strongly impressed with fears that your labours in Convention, though wisely conducted and concluded, will, in the end, be frustrated by some of the States, under the influence of interests operating for particular rather than general welfare. Be this as it may, I cannot doubt but the meeting in Philadelphia will (composed as it is of the best and wisest persons in the Union) establish some plan that will be generally approved. . . . A letter from Mr. A. Lee which the Governor has sent us intimates the propriety of proceeding without delay (if the Executive have any money at their command) to purchase up Continental securities which are now low, but which he seems to think will (if the Convention do anything that will probably meet the approbation of the States, and the sales of the lands by Congress take place) rapidly rise in value. He says also that other States are doing this while it is to be effected on easy terms. I wish for information as to the fact, and your sentiments so far as you conjecture respecting the rise of the value of these papers."

Johnson recorded in his diary, this day: "June 7. Showery. In Convention. Dined Mr. Clymer's."

On the next day, June 8, Jacob Hiltzheimer recorded in his diary: "In the morning, I called on General Pinckney from South Carolina and showed him two bay geldings, now in his carriage, six years old. . . . The General agreed to take them, price 55 pounds each."

[1] *Letters of Joseph Jones, 1777–1787* (1889). As to these letters, see Worthington C. Ford, in *Mass. Hist. Soc. Proc., Second Series* (1901), XV, 116 et seq.

FRIDAY, JUNE 8, 1787

IN CONVENTION

On this day, the power of the National Legislature to negative State laws was again debated (as discussed under a subsequent date, July 17).

OUT OF CONVENTION

On this day, the *Herald* published a purported action of the Convention as to Rhode Island; but the story was absolutely untrue:

"We are informed that the Federal Convention, among other things, has resolved that Rhode Island should be considered as having virtually withdrawn herself from the Union, and that the right of emitting paper money by the States jointly or severally ought to be abrogated. It is proposed in the first case that for the proportion of the federal debt now due from Rhode Island, she shall be held, and if gentler means will not avail she shall be compelled to be responsible, but upon no account shall she be restored to her station in the Union. And in the other case, it is proposed to establish a mint for the receipt of bullion, from which the States are to draw coin in proportion to their respective contributions."

That no credit should be given to reports like the above was urged in a letter published a fortnight later: [1]

"It is a fact of public notoriety that the Members of the Convention ever since a quorum has been formed have observed the greatest secrecy in all their transactions. Nothing whatever of a public nature has been officially communicated or transpired. Very little credit can therefore be given to what has hitherto appeared in the newspapers as to their resolves that Rhode Island should be considered as having withdrawn herself from the Union and shall upon no account be restored to her station again, and for her pro-

[1] Philadelphia despatch dated June 22, in *Connecticut Courant*, July 2, 1787; see also *New York Daily Advertiser*, June 27, *New York Packet*, June 15, *New Jersey Journal*, June 13, 1787.

portion of the federal debt, if gentler means will not avail, she shall be compelled to be responsible — the abrogation of paper emissions and the establishment of a mint for the receipt of bullion, etc. The mere idle reports of busy bodies and the absurd foolish suggestions of idle pretenders are not to be viewed and considered as the real and regular proceedings of the Convention."

Gen. Henry Knox of Massachusetts wrote, this day, to Rufus King that: "It is the Convention to whom the thinking part of the community are looking up for a good form [of government]. God grant that they may not be disappointed."

SATURDAY, JUNE 9, 1787

IN CONVENTION

On this day, the Committee for a second time struggled with the question how the National Executive should be chosen, but came to no final conclusion. There then loomed up a dangerous subject which, it was early foreseen, might be the rock on which the Convention might split. On the first day of debate, May 30, Madison, seconded by Gouverneur Morris, had moved: "That the equality of suffrage established by the Articles of Confederation ought not to prevail in the National Legislature and that an equitable ratio of representation ought to be substituted." This had raised the question whether the old equality of suffrage of the States which prevailed in the Congress of the Confederation should be continued or be abandoned. The Committee of the Whole had not been ready to struggle with so fundamental a subject. On this June 9, it could no longer be avoided. Paterson of New Jersey said that the Resolution for a proportional representation struck at the very existence of the lesser States; he pointed out that it would place the control of the new Government

entirely in the hands of the three large States —
Virginia, Massachusetts, and Pennsylvania; and he
concluded by saying hotly: "New Jersey will never
confederate on the plan before the Committee. She
would be swallowed up. He had rather submit to a
monarch, to a despot, than to such a fate. He would
not only oppose the plan here, but on his return home
do everything within his power to defeat it there."
To this, Wilson then retorted: "Shall New Jersey
have the same right or influence in the councils of the
Nation with Pennsylvania? I say no. It is unjust—I
never will confederate on this plan. The gentleman
from New Jersey is candid in declaring his opinions.
I commend him for it. I am equally so, I say again
I never will confederate on his principle. If no State
will part with any of its sovereignty, it is vain to talk
of a National Government." [1]   At the end of this heated
discussion, Paterson wisely moved to postpone the
decision. Luckily, a Sunday was to intervene, during
which the delegates had an opportunity to cool off.
It is apparent that all appreciated the fact that a crisis
had arrived, and that the considered thought of this
Sunday might determine whether the Convention was
to continue or to break upon this rock.[2]

OUT OF CONVENTION

Washington noted:

"At Convention. Dined with the Club at the City Tavern. Drank tea and set till 10 o'clock at Mr. Powell's."

---

[1] Robert Yates in his *Notes* reported Wilson, as above quoted, and Paterson, as
follows: "I will never consent to the present system and I shall make all the interest against it in the State which I represent that I can. Myself or my State will
never submit to tyranny or despotism."

[2] Francis N. Thorpe, in his *Constitutional History of the United States* (1901), I,
353, says: "No day of the long summer session was filled with more anxiety than
the following Sunday, the tenth of June, for it was uncertain whether the members
had not met in vain. The great question of representation was to come up on Monday and the discussion had already become threatening."

"The plans for reform which have been communicated to me since (April 10) make it possible to inform you more fully as to the changes which the delegates propose to introduce. . . . It is rare that one is a spectator at a political movement more important than this and it is difficult to enclose in a few pages the plan which must settle the happiness, the power and the future energy of a new born empire."

Otto then proceeded to set forth in considerable detail the plan to be adopted by the Convention, as he understood it. In general, the information given by him was a surprisingly accurate description of the work of the Convention up to this date, though there were some inaccuracies in his statement. The most striking part of his letter, however, is his description of the political division of opinion over the Constitution in this country:

"The delegates who have communicated to me these different plans are determined to support them with vigor in the Convention. I will not repeat here the doubts which I have expressed elsewhere as to their success; but it is my duty to submit to you my opinion as to another class of men whose party will be equally strong and perhaps more obstinate in the Convention. These men observe that, in the actual situation of affairs, it is impossible to unite under a single head all the members of the Confederation. Their political interests, their commercial views, their customs, and their laws are so divergent that there is not a resolve of Congress which is equally useful and popular in the South and in the North. Their jealousy seems to be an unsurmountable obstacle. . . . The inhabitants of the North are fishers and sailors; those of the Central States, farmers; those of the South, planters."

Accordingly, he said, these men urged a division of the country into three sections: a Confederation of the North — New Hampshire, Massachusetts, Rhode Island, Connecticut, Vermont, and New York to the

should be according to the respective number of free inhabitants of the States, and that in the second branch (the Senate) each State should have one vote. The delegates from the larger States, however, were still insistent that the old inequitable system of equal representation should be completely abolished. As a first step, King and Wilson now moved that in the first branch the right of suffrage should *not* be that which prevailed under the Confederation.[1]

It was at this point that Doctor Franklin made one of the characteristic speeches (read for him by Wilson) which proved his inestimable value in the Convention.[2] This old man of eighty-one years, who had behind him a long life of useful, patriotic achievement, and of vast experience with human nature and mankind, possessed the entire confidence of the delegates. Hence, after the excited talk which took place on the previous Saturday, the following wise words of the Doctor came like a cooling breeze into the Convention:

"It has given me great pleasure to observe that till this point, the proportion of representation, came before us, our debates were carried on with great coolness and temper. If anything of a contrary kind has, on this occasion, appeared, I hope it will not be repeated; for we are sent here to *con-*

[1] Sherman had already, as early as 1776, suggested a dual system of legislation, partly by States and partly by proportional representation; see *Roger Sherman in the Federal Constitution*, by L. H. Boutell, *Amer. Hist. Ass. Report* (1893), p. 231; *Works of John Adams*, II, 499; *The Constitutional History of the United States* (1901), by Francis N. Thorpe, I, 393.

Bancroft states that Sherman had prepared a series of propositions (termed by Bancroft the "Connecticut Plan") in nine sections, for presentation to the Convention; but this is undoubtedly a mistake, as the document referred to by Bancroft was prepared prior to 1784 as a plan for amendments of the Articles of Confederation when Sherman was in Congress. As to this, see *A Bancroftian Invention*, by Hannis Taylor, *Yale Law Journal* (1908), XVIII; and *The Origin and Growth of the American Constitution* (1911), by Hannis Taylor.

[2] Madison wrote to J. K. Paulding, in 1831: "Of Franklin, I had no personal knowledge till we served together in the Federal Convention of 1787, and the part he took there has found its way to the public, with the exception of a few anecdotes which belong to the unveiled part of the proceedings of that Assembly. He has written his own life, and no man had a finer one to write or a better title to be himself the writer." *Writings of James Madison* (Hunt's ed.), IX, 431.

sult, not to *contend* with each other; and declarations of a fixed opinion, and of determined resolutions never to change it, neither enlighten nor convince us. Positiveness, and warmth on one side naturally beget their like on the other; and tend to create and augment discord and division in a great concern, wherein harmony and union are extremely necessary to give weight to our councils, and render them effectual in promoting and securing the common good."

He, therefore, entered into a long discussion of a compromise, so impracticable in form as to warrant the suspicion that it was put forward simply to distract the minds of the delegates. At the end of his speech, however, the Convention voted against equality of the States in the suffrage in the first branch of the Legislature. On this vote, Connecticut cast its ballots with the large States, in compliance with Sherman's suggestion of a compromise.

Wilson then took a tactful step which assured the continued adherence of the Southern States to proportional representation; for, as a recognition of the fact that these States should be allowed to count their slaves to a certain extent in ascertaining their respective populations, he moved that the rule of suffrage to be adopted should be that proposed by the Congress of the Confederation, April 18, 1783, namely, in proportion to the whole number of white and other free citizens and three fifths of all others except Indians not paying taxes. The Committee accepted this proposal, New Jersey and Delaware alone dissenting. The vote of Delaware, by necessity, was in the negative; for the credentials of the delegates from that State authorized them to join in "devising, deliberating on, and discussing such alteration and further provision as may be necessary to render the Federal Constitution adequate to the exigencies of the Union", but with the express proviso that "such alterations or further provisions or

"The Convention is proceeding in their arduous undertaking, with eleven States, under an injunction of secrecy. New Hampshire has elected members who are soon expected. The object of this meeting is very important in my mind. Unless a system of government is adopted by compact, force, I expect, will plant the standard; for such an anarchy as now exists cannot last long. Gentlemen seem to be impressed with the necessity of establishing some efficient system and I hope it will secure us against domestic as well as foreign invasions."

TUESDAY, JUNE 12, 1787

IN CONVENTION

On this day, the Committee of the Whole acted upon the Randolph Resolutions, providing for method of ratification of the new system, and for the term, qualifications, and eligibility to office of members of the Legislature — all of which will be considered later. (See August 10, September 3.)

OUT OF CONVENTION

Washington noted:

"Dined and drank tea at Mr. Morris's.   Went afterwards to a concert at the City Tavern."

William Grayson wrote from New York to Edmund Randolph, as to the conditions in Congress: [1]

"Many of the Members of Congress are now attending at the Convention, and some of the States have not sent delegates either to the one or the other. It is much to be lamented that the desire of dismembering States prevails in so great a degree among the citizens of the Union. If a doctrine of this sort is allowed, it will go directly to the destruction of all government; for if the right exists in the first instance, it may be carried so far as to reduce a State to the size of a county or parish. It was a great misfortune that the principle was not attacked in the instance of Vermont.

[1] *Catalogue of Washington-Madison Papers, in Estate of James C. McGuire.*

They might have been crushed in the beginning, but they have been permitted in quietness to grow powerful and to furnish a fatal example to the Union. There can be no doubt but the United States are bound to guaranty the limits of every State in the Confederation. . . ."

WEDNESDAY, JUNE 13, 1787

IN CONVENTION

On this day, the Committee of the Whole took up the subject of the Judicial branch of the new Government, and agreed to appointment of the Judges of the Supreme Court by the Senate, and to the general jurisdiction which the National Courts should exercise (as discussed under date of July 18). Having completed its consideration of Randolph's original fifteen Resolutions, with remarkably little dissension, except over the appointment of the Executive and the equal representation of the States, the Committee had now agreed upon a complete outline of a Federal Republic, differing essentially from the Confederation of States then in existence; [1] and this outline, contained in nineteen Resolutions, it reported to the Convention itself. Action upon the Committee's Report was postponed until the next day, in order to "give an opportunity for other plans to be proposed."

OUT OF CONVENTION

Washington noted:

"In Convention. Dined at Mr. Clymer's and drank tea there. Spent the evening at Mr. Bingham's."

---

[1] On June 16, the *Massachusetts Centinel* said: "On the subject of the Grand Convention — Essential alterations in our Federal Constitutions, experience, powerful experience has convinced us are wanting; and apprehensive that these wants if left to themselves may operate with violence, prudent Legislatures have been sensible of the propriety of curing by anticipation. Accordingly, we are informed that the authority granted to their delegates by some States are very extensive, by others even general, and by all much enlarged."

Dr. William Samuel Johnson recorded in his diary:

" Hot.   In Convention.   Dined Ingersoll's."

Edward Carrington of Virginia wrote, this day, from New York to Madison, emphasizing the necessity that the Federal Government be given power to negative State laws.   This was the favorite Virginia plan, and was fought for in the Convention by Madison, with great vigor:

"The public mind is now on the point of a favorable turn to the objects of your meeting, and being fairly met with the result, will, I am persuaded, eventually embrace it.   Being calculated for the permanent fitness, and not the momentary habits of the country, it may at first be viewed with hesitation; but derived and patronized as it will be, its influence must extend into an adoption, as the present fabric gives way.   The work once well done will be done forever, but patched up in accommodation to the whim of the day, it will soon require the hand of the cobbler again. . . .   Constitute a Federal Government, invigorate and check it well; give it then independent power over the trade, the revenues and forces of the Nation, and all things that involve any relationships to foreign powers; give it also the revisal of all State acts.   Unless it possesses a complete control over the State Governments, the constant effort will be to resume the delegated powers; nor do I see what inducement the Federal sovereignty can have to negative an innocent act of a State.   Constitute it in such shape that, its first principles being preserved, it will be a good republic.   I wish to see that system have a fair experiment.   But let the liability to encroachments be rather from the Federal than the State governments.   In the first case, we shall insensibly glide into monarchy; in the latter nothing but anarchy can be the consequence.   Some gentlemen think of a total surrender of the State sovereignties.   I see not the necessity of that measure for giving us National stability or consequence.   The negative of the Federal sovereignty will effectually prevent the existence of any licentious or inconsiderate act."

The general situation of the country in its relation to the Convention was described, this day, in the *Massachusetts Centinel*, as follows:

"As a Nation, these States are now arrived at a crisis truly alarming, perhaps more so than at any period during the war — as *then* they were united and were *all* opposed to an enemy from without — but now the destruction and calamities which threaten us spring up from among ourselves and by dividing will conquer us. While in the States individually, local and selfish principles predominate, the Confederated States in Congress assembled have not the power to apply to effect any remedy, however salutary, to cure our National disorder. But while there is hope, we must not distrust Providence, and we have this hope in the Grand Federal Convention. Ye men of America, banish from your bosoms those daemons, suspicion and distrust, which have so long been working your destruction. Be assured, the men whom ye have delegated to work out, if possible, your National salvation are the men in whom ye may confide — their extensive knowledge, known abilities, and approved patriotism warrant it — their determinations must be just, and if ye wish well to your country, ye will place such confidence in them as to sanction with your approbation, the measures they may recommend, notwithstanding they may in some small points militate against your ideas of right. Consider, they have at their head a Washington, to describe the amiableness of whose character would be unnecessary."

The economic situation in Philadelphia was thus described in the *Gazette:*

"It is remarkable that the cry of scarcity and poverty encreases with the appearance of expence and luxury in the mode of living pursued by the inhabitants of this city. The costliness of the furniture, the profusion of the table, the elegance of the equipage and the refinements of dress, must, to the observation of a stranger, bespeak affluence and prosperity; while the tenor of conversation, the accumulation of debts and the unpunctuality of payments would, indeed, indicate a real want and actual insolvency. There is scarce a street too that does not present us with some improvements in building, at the very moment that hundreds of houses are untenanted; and while crowds are daily retiring to the distant districts of the Continent, we find the city rapidly extending its western boundaries. Would it not add to the happiness of Pennsylvania were her citizens to profess less poverty and to practise more economy?"

THURSDAY, JUNE 14, 1787

IN CONVENTION

The form of government thus far adopted by the Committee of the Whole was so strongly National and so divergent from previous plans that many of the members, especially of those from the smaller States, were aghast. Their views of the situation at this stage of the Convention were strikingly set forth later by Luther Martin of Maryland.[1] It was proposed, said he, that the Senate should have twenty-eight members, of which Virginia, Pennsylvania, and Massachusetts were to have thirteen. "Having this inequality in each branch of the Legislature, it must be evident that they would make what laws they pleased, however injurious or disagreeable to the other States; and that they would always prevent the other States from making any laws, however necessary and proper, if not agreeable to the views of these three States." Martin pointed out, moreover, that as the Executive was to be elected by the Legislature, and the Judges by the Senate, and as the Legislature was to have a negative on all State laws which it deemed not in harmony with the Union, these three States might control the whole system of Government; "a system of slavery which bound hand and foot ten States in the Union and placed them at the mercy of the other three and under

[1] *The Genuine Information* (1788), by Luther Martin, *Elliot's Debates*, I.

the most abject and servile subjection to them."
Since Virginia, Pennsylvania, and Massachusetts had
then a population of about 1,350,000 as against a
population of about 1,750,000 in the other ten States,
there were some grounds for this apprehension.[1] Martin then pointed out that General Washington, during
the sessions of the Committee of the Whole, was on the
floor, "in the same situation with the other members
of the Convention at large, to oppose any system he
thought injurious or to propose any alterations or
amendments he thought beneficial", and that both
Washington and Franklin "appeared cordially to
approve and give their hearty concurrence" to the
proposals of the Committee. The delegates who opposed such a system of Government had considerable
reason to feel grave at the trend of the Convention;
and accordingly, William Paterson, of New Jersey, on
this day, asked for an adjournment, so that they might
"contemplate the plan reported" and "digest one
purely Federal and contradistinguished from the
reported plan." The situation was complicated, for
the opposition arose on two distinct grounds. Some
members of the New Jersey, Connecticut, New York
delegations and Luther Martin of Maryland were
against any departure from the principle of the Con-

[1] It may be noted that according to the *Pennsylvania Packet*, Dec. 11, 1786, the
populations of the States were then estimated as follows: New Hampshire, 150,000;
Massachusetts, 400,000; Rhode Island, 59,670; Connecticut, 192,000; New York,
250,000; New Jersey, 150,000; Pennsylvania, 300,000; Delaware, 50,000; Maryland, 320,000; Virginia, 650,000; North Carolina, 300,000; South Carolina,
225,000; Georgia, 56,000. By the first census in 1790 of the free white population
of 3,100,000, Massachusetts had 469,000; New York, 314,000; Pennsylvania,
424,000; Virginia, 503,000 — a total of 1,710,000, leaving 1,390,000 to the other
nine States. These four States in 1790 had fifty-six members of the House, while
the other nine had forty-seven. It is interesting to note that the whole territory
included in the thirteen States was about 500,000 square miles; of this, Virginia
(including the Kentucky district) held 103,000; North Carolina (including the
Tennessee district) held 84,000; and Georgia (including the Alabama and Mississippi districts) held 153,000 — a total of 340,000 in these three States, and the
other ten States held 167,000 square miles; in addition, the Northwest Territory
(comprising the districts of Ohio, Indiana, and Illinois) held 134,000 square miles.

federation, wishing merely to add a few new powers to Congress rather than to substitute a National Government; others of New Jersey and Delaware were opposed to any new Government unless it should embody the principle of equality of representation of the States. As John Dickinson of Delaware said to Madison: "You see the consequence of pushing things too far. Some of the members from the small States wish for two branches in the General Legislature and are friends to a good National Government; but we would sooner submit to a foreign power than submit to be deprived of an equality of suffrage in both branches of the Legislature, and thereby be thrown under the domination of the large States."[1] Accordingly, the Convention adjourned "that leisure might be given for the purpose."

OUT OF CONVENTION

Washington noted:

"Dined at Major [Thomas Lloyd] Moore's (after being in Convention) and spent the evening at my lodgings."

The North Carolina delegates wrote, this day, to Governor Caswell:

"Though we sit from day to day, Saturdays included, it is not possible for us to determine when the business before us can be finished. A very large field presents to our view without a single straight or eligible road that has been trodden by the feet of Nations. An Union of Sovereign States, preserving their civil liberties and connected together by

---

[1] Dickinson, then fifty-five years of age, was "one of the most active members of the Convention and took part in the discussion of a great variety of subjects — a fact which is a little remarkable, for his health during the session was more than usually feeble." *Life and Times of John Dickinson* (1891), by Charles J. Stillé, 258. Dickinson himself wrote to Benjamin Rush, a year later, Aug. 4, 1788: "It is impossible for me to engage again in the duties of public life. I believe there is not a man upon earth besides myself who can form any idea of the distresses, from weakness of body, that I have undergone by endeavoring to sustain a public character with some decency, while laboring under such infirmities." *Ibid.*, 279.

such tyes as to preserve permanent and effective Governments, is a system not described, it is a circumstance that has not occurred in the history of men; if we shall be so fortunate as to find this in descript, our time will have been well spent. Several Members of the Convention have their wives here and other gentlemen have sent for theirs. This seems to promise a summer's campaign. Such of us as can remain here from the inevitable avocation of private business, are resolved to continue whilst there is any prospect of being able to serve the State and Union. . . ."

CHAPTER FOUR

THE SMALL VERSUS THE LARGE STATES

FRIDAY, JUNE 15, 1787

IN CONVENTION

The Paterson Plan

On this day, William Paterson laid before the Convention a Plan which had been prepared as a substitute for Randolph's Virginia Plan. Its authorship is not known, but probably Roger Sherman, Luther Martin, and Paterson took the leading part in drafting it.[1] The very first section stated its theory: "That

---

[1] Bancroft states (II, 40, note) that informants of the English Government named Governor William Livingston of New Jersey as the author of this Plan. It may be remembered, says Bancroft (II, 143), that Ellsworth, Paterson and Luther Martin were fellow students at Princeton, Paterson in the Class of 1763, and the other two in the Class of 1766. It may also be noted that six other delegates were

the Articles of Confederation ought to be so revised, corrected and enlarged as to render the federal Constitution adequate to the exigencies of Government and the preservation of the Union." It provided for grant of additional powers to Congress, including power to levy import duties and stamp taxes, "to be applied to such federal purposes as they shall deem proper and expedient"; if requisitions made by Congress upon the States were not complied with, Congress might pass acts to direct the collection thereof; but none of the powers of Congress were to be exercised except with the assent of a specified number of States. The only other substantial changes in the Articles of Confederation were a provision for an Executive to consist of several persons elected by Congress and removable by Congress on application of a majority of the State Governors, and for a Judiciary appointed by the Executive.[1]

It is probably true, as Farrand says, that "it would seem as if the New Jersey Plan more nearly represented what most of the delegates supposed that they were sent to do," and if presented earlier, on May 29, when the Virginia Plan was offered, it might have been adopted. "But in the course of the two weeks discussion, many of the delegates had become accustomed to what might well have appeared to them at the outset as somewhat radical ideas."[2]

One point must be emphasized. Those who opposed the Virginia Plan based their opposition on political

Princeton graduates — Alexander S. Martin, of the Class of 1756; William C. Houston, '68; Gunning Bedford, '71; James Madison, '71; Jonathan Dayton, '76; and William R. Davie, '76.

[1] J. F. Jameson pointed out in *Amer. Hist. Ass. Report* (1902), I, 133, that there are four different texts of these Paterson Resolutions: (1) that given by Madison and printed in *Documentary History, Elliot's Debates*, V, *Hunt's Writings of Madison*, III, and Gilpin's *The Madison Papers;* (2) that printed in the Journal of the Convention, in 1819, derived from manuscript deposited by Gen. Joseph Bloomfield, Executor of David Brearley; (3) that printed in *Maryland Gazette*, Feb. 15, 1788, and Carey's *American Museum*, III, 362; (4) that printed from notes by King in *Life and Correspondence of Rufus King*, I, 600.

[2] *The Framing of the Constitution* (1913), by Max Farrand.

grounds and not on economic grounds. They were not opposed to it because it favored the interests of property, but because it trespassed on the political rights of the States. And later, the leading opponents of the Constitution — like Robert Yates, Elbridge Gerry, Luther Martin, Patrick Henry, George Mason, and Richard Henry Lee — were afraid of the principles of the Virginia Plan as finally embodied in the Constitution, not because of the protection it gave to property interests, but because they feared it as a possible engine of a consolidated Government, encroaching on or abolishing the powers and rights of the States.

SATURDAY, JUNE 16, 1787

IN CONVENTION

On this day, in the Convention sitting as a Committee of the Whole, the battle was directly joined between the advocates of the Randolph or Virginia Plan and those of the Paterson or New Jersey Plan. Against the latter, Wilson made one of the strongest speeches of the Convention, comparing it with the Virginia Plan, point by point, and setting forth the defects in the theory of the Congress under the Confederation — a single house Legislature elected by the States. Randolph also forcibly showed the necessity of establishing a National form of Government which should legislate for and act upon individuals. In behalf of the New Jersey Plan, Paterson and John Lansing of New York argued at length. The latter said that "New York would never have concurred in sending delegates to the Convention if she had supposed the deliberations were to turn on a consolidation of the States and a National Government"; and he expressed his opinion that the States would never ratify. "The scheme is itself totally novel. There is no parallel to it to be found."

Paterson preferred his Plan, "because it accorded, first with the powers of the Convention, and second with the sentiments of the people." He urged that "our object is not such a Government as may be best in itself, but such a one as our constituents have authorized us to prepare and as they will approve." Paterson thus expressed a point of view which differed radically from that of the advocates of a new Constitution. They were not concerned about the authority from their "constituents." They desired to form a Government such as "may be best in itself." This idea they expressed throughout the Convention. Randolph said now that he "was not scrupulous on the point of power. When the salvation of the Republic was at stake, it would be treason to our trust not to propose what we found necessary." And Hamilton undoubtedly presented the views of the bulk of the delegates, when he said (two days later): "We owed it to our Country to do, on this emergency, whatever we should deem essential to its happiness. The States sent us here to provide for the exigencies of the Union. To rely on and propose any plan not adequate to these exigencies, merely because it was not clearly within our powers, would be to sacrifice the means to the end. . . . The great question is, what provisions shall we make for the happiness of our country?"

The precise powers which the delegates possessed, in attending the Convention, were as follows: The Articles of Confederation had provided that they should "be inviolably observed by every State, and the Union shall be perpetual; nor shall any alteration at any time hereafter be made in them, unless such alteration be agreed to in a Congress of the United States, and be afterwards confirmed by the Legislature of every State." In accordance with this Article, the credentials of the delegates from every State (except New Jersey)

had expressly provided that any Act determined upon
by the Convention should be reported to Congress and
when agreed to therein, be duly confirmed by the
several States.[1] The purposes for which the delegates
were to meet were expressed in their credentials in
every State, as, in substance, "to render the Federal
Constitution adequate to the exigencies of Government
and the preservation of the Union." Under this broad
power, it is clear that (except in New Jersey and
Delaware) there was no limitation whatever upon the
kind of amendment or change in the Articles of Confederation which the delegates might adopt, provided
they reported it to Congress for acceptance and to the
States for unanimous confirmation.[2] The delegates did
not, in fact, exceed their powers, until the crucial day
(August 31) when they decided, without requiring the
acceptance by Congress, to submit their work directly
to Conventions of the People in the respective States.
This was a revolutionary step. When the delegates
took that action, they threw off entirely the restrictions
of their credentials, and acted solely on their own
authority.

OUT OF CONVENTION

Washington noted:

"In Convention. Dined with the Club at the City Tavern, and drank tea at Doctor [William] Shippen's with Mrs.
Livingston's party."

[1] New Jersey had empowered its delegates "to meet . . . for the purpose of
taking into consideration the state of the Union as to trade and other important
objects, and of devising such other provisions as shall appear to be necessary to
render the Constitution of the Federal Government adequate to the exigencies
thereof."

[2] The only restrictions upon the power of the delegates to amend were those contained in the credentials from Connecticut which provided that the delegates were
"to confer . . . and discuss upon such alterations and provisions *agreeable to the
general principles of Republican Government*, as they shall think proper to render the
Federal Constitution adequate to the exigencies of Government and the preservation of the Union"; and those contained in the credentials from Delaware which
contained a proviso that "such alterations or further provisions do not extend to

Rufus King wrote, this day, to Nathan Dane in New York : [1]

"I think that I informed you that by an early order of the Convention, the members are restrained from communicating anything done in Convention during the time of their session. The object was the prevention of partial representations, and also the additional consideration of leaving the Report of the Convention to stand or fall on its own merits. I am, therefore, prevented from writing to you with that freedom which otherwise I should do, as well for your information of the proceedings of the Convention, as to obtain your sentiments on points of consequence which must here receive their discussion. . . . We hear nothing from New Hampshire, not even who is President."

The *Journal* printed fifty-two names as "an exact list of the Members of the Convention." The *Gazetteer* stated that :

"By the present very respectable delegation in Convention, eleven States are represented. The Delegates from the State of New Hampshire, though appointed, have not yet made their appearance. Rhode Island is the only State in the Union that has refused to take a seat at this honorable board of counsellors. A very short period will unfold whether this refusal will redound to her honour or disgrace."

The *Gazetteer* also gave currency to the statement that great unanimity prevailed in the Convention : [2]

"We hear that the greatest unanimity subsists in the Councils of the Federal Convention. It is to be hoped, says a correspondent, the United States will discover as much wisdom in receiving from them a suitable form of government to preserve the liberties of the people, as they did fortitude

that part of the Fifth Article of the Confederation . . . which declares that 'in determining questions in the United States in Congress assembled, each State shall have one vote.' "

[1] *Nathan Dane Papers MSS.*

[2] This statement was reproduced widely in the newspapers and gave a wrong impression to the country; see *Boston Gazette,* July 2; *Connecticut Courant,* June 25, 1787.

in defending them against the arbitrary and wicked attempts of Great Britain. Nothing but Union and a vigorous Continental Government can save us from destruction."

This report was so far from the truth as to be almost humorous. It has been suggested that it may have been disseminated by delegates who feared that if the actual state of the Convention should be known, the country might despair. A more accurate picture of the conditions appeared a few days later in newspapers of Boston : [1]

"Though the particular arguments, debates, and decisions that take place in the Federal Convention are considered as matters of secrecy, we understand, in general, that there exists a very great diversity of opinion among the members and that there has been already a wonderful display of wisdom, eloquence, and patriotism. Some schemes, it is said, have been projected which preserve the form, but effectually destroy the spirit of a democracy; and others, more bold, which regarding only the necessity of a strong Executive power, have openly rejected even the appearance of a popular Constitution. From the plans of this last description, there is little reason to apprehend danger, for the people will hardly be induced to make a voluntary surrender of their rights, but they may be deceived by the flattery of outward show into a passive and destructive acquiescence."

One of the few pessimistic letters as to the possibility of accomplishment of results by the Convention was written, this day, by Stephen Higginson, a former Member of Congress from Massachusetts, to Nathan Dane.

"My expectations from the Convention are not great, though it must be admitted we shall probably never have more wisdom and political knowledge again collected, than they possess. They may draw the great outlines of a Government for the Union, much more respectable and efficient

---

[1] *Massachusetts Centinel*, June 20; *Independent Chronicle*, June 21, 1787.

in its principles and structure than the present. They may harmonize well, and be themselves convinced that such a system is necessary to our safety and happiness as a nation. They may at their return to their respective States be diffusing the principles and reasons which satisfied themselves and by degrees may in that way be preparing the public mind for its reception. But much time will be necessary to extend these impressions and much must be our suffering from the obvious weakness of the present system before competent powers will be delegated by the States. Sad experience alone will fully satisfy the body of this people that the sovereignty of the several States must in a degree be transferred to the Union and the people at large not so violently opposed to every degree of implicit obedience."

SUNDAY, JUNE 17, 1787

Washington noted : [1]

"Went to Church. Heard Bishop [William] White preach, and see him ordain two gentlemen (into the order of) Deacons. After which rid 8 miles into the Country and dined with Mr. Jno. Ross in Chester County. Returned (to town again about dusk) in the afternoon."

MONDAY, JUNE 18, 1787

IN CONVENTION

Hamilton's Speech

On this day, Alexander Hamilton of New York, who (as Madison states) "had been hitherto silent on the business before the Convention, partly from respect to others whose superior abilities, age and experience rendered him unwilling to bring forward ideas dissimilar to theirs, and partly from his delicate situation with respect to his own State, to whose sentiments

[1] Jacob Hiltzheimer recorded in his Diary: "Went twice to church. Mr. Robert Morris went with General Washington in the General's carriage to dine at Mr. John Ross's country house over Schuylkill."

as expressed by his colleagues he could by no means accede ", came forward with a speech of great length, which must have surprised and disturbed the Convention. He began by saying that: "The crisis which now marked our affairs was too serious to permit any scruples whatever to prevail over the duty imposed on every man to contribute his efforts for the public safety and happiness." He then proceeded to state that he was unfriendly to both Plans and particularly to that from New Jersey. He, like Randolph, pointed out the essential defects in the existing Federal system; but, unlike Randolph, he believed the Virginia Plan did not provide for a sufficiently strong Government. He stated his belief that "the British Government was the best in the world and that he doubted much whether anything short of it would do in America." He concluded with submitting a sketch of a plan, which, he admitted, "went beyond the ideas of most members", but which embodied principles necessary to check and control the existing evils. This sketch provided, amongst other things, for a Senate and an Executive, both elected to serve during good behavior, and for the appointment of State Governors by the General Government. Such provisions alone would have made it impossible of acceptance. Hence, it is not singular that this Hamilton sketch was neither referred to any Committee, nor taken up by the Convention for action in any way.[1] "The gentleman from New York is praised by all, but supported by no gentleman," observed Dr. William Samuel Johnson.[2] In this connection, Thomas H. Benton later reported a striking conversation with Rufus King in the Senate, in 1824:[3]

[1] Towards the close of the Convention, Hamilton handed to Madison a draft of a proposed Constitution (elaborated from his sketch), but it was not actually submitted to the Convention. See *infra*, p. 824, Hamilton to Pickering, Sept. 18, 1803.

[2] As reported in King's *Notes*.

[3] *Thirty Years' View* (1854), by Thomas H. Benton, I, 58.

"He said some things to me which I think ought to be remembered by future generations, to enable them to appreciate justly those founders of our Government, who were in favor of a stronger organization than was adopted. He said : 'You young men who have been born since the Revolution look with horror upon the name of a King and upon all propositions for a strong Government. It was not so with us. We were born the subjects of a King and were accustomed to subscribe ourselves, his Majesty's most faithful subjects, and we began the quarrel which ended in the Revolution not against the King but against his Parliament; and in making the new Government many propositions were submitted which would not bear discussion and ought not to be quoted against their authors, being offered for consideration and to bring out opinions, and which, though behind the opinions of this day, were in advance of that day.' "

And added Benton :

"These things were said chiefly in relation to General Hamilton who had submitted propositions stronger than those adopted, but nothing like those which party spirit attributed to him. I heard these words of [King] I hope with profit; and commit them, in the same hope, to after generations."

OUT OF CONVENTION

Washington noted :

"Attended the Convention. Dined at the Quarterly Meeting of the Sons of St. Patrick, held at the City tavn. Drank tea at Doctr. Shippen's with (the party of) Mrs. Livingston."

A Philadelphia despatch of this date in the Boston papers and elsewhere said : [1]

"They have a great work amid many difficulties before them. To form a generous plan of power for thirteen States certainly requires the most consummate wisdom, and from

[1] *American Herald*, June 25; *Independent Chronicle*, June 28, 1787.

the unanimity and spirit which have heretofore pervaded the Continent, we may have reason to expect that we shall keep the chain of friendship bright, and unite as citizens of one respectable and mighty empire. The same hands that laid the foundation of the temple of liberty are again employed in this arduous task; may they be enabled to finish the fabrick and bring forth the headstone with triumphant shoutings."

Nathaniel Gorham of Massachusetts, who had been serving as Chairman of the Committee of the Whole, wrote this day to Theophilus Parsons an extremely interesting description of the conditions then prevailing in the Convention — a letter somewhat violative, however, of the Secrecy Rule: [1]

"The present Federal Government seems near its exit; and whether we shall in the Convention be able to agree upon mending it, or forming and recommending a new one, is not certain. All agree, however, that much greater powers are necessary to be given under some form or other. But the large States think the representation ought to be made in proportion to the magnitude of the States, and consequently more like a National Government, while the small States are for adhering to the present mode. We have hitherto considered the subject with great calmness and temper; and there are numbers of very able men in this body who all appear thoroughly alarmed with the present prospect. I do not know that I am at liberty to write anything on this subject. I shall, therefore, only observe further that all agree the Legislative and Executive ought to be separate and that there should be a National Judiciary. I beg you not to mention having heard anything from me on the subject, except to your brother to whom I should have written, but I am quite overcome with the heat of the weather."

Theodore Sedgwick of Massachusetts, who had been lukewarm as to the desirability of a Convention, and

---

[1] *Memoir of Theophilus Parsons* (1859), by Theophilus Parsons.

who, highly conservative, had been much disturbed by the Shays Rebellion, wrote to Rufus King, this day:

"I am happy to be informed that the characters composing the Convention give us a prospect of deriving advantage from their deliberations. Much is to be done. Every man of observations is convinced that the end of government, security, cannot be attained by the exercise of principles founded on democratic equality. A war is now actually levied on the virtue, property, and distinctions in the community, and however there may be an appearance of a temporary cessation, yet the flame will again and again break out."

This letter is of interest as being one of few instances, in all the correspondence which has hitherto come to light, of the expression of a sentiment which gave justification to the charge made subsequently by opponents of the Constitution, that its upholders were imbued with a desire for aristocratic government.

TUESDAY, JUNE 19, 1787

IN CONVENTION

Most of this day was occupied by a long, masterly, brilliant, and convincing speech by Madison, concluding the debate. He examined Paterson's Plan, point by point, arguing successively that its provisions could neither prevent those violations by the States of the law of nations and of treaties "which if not prevented must involve us in the calamities of foreign wars"; nor "prevent encroachments on the Federal authority"; nor "trespasses of the States on each other", such as the aggressions caused by emission of paper money, retaliatory statutes, etc., which "threatened danger not to the harmony only, but the tranquillity of the Union"; nor would it "secure the internal tranquillity of the States themselves" or "good internal legislation and administration to the particular States themselves"; nor would it "secure the Union against the influence of foreign powers over its members."

At the conclusion of Madison's speech, a vote was taken on the plain proposition whether the Randolph Resolutions "should be adhered to as preferable to those of Mr. Paterson." Seven States favored such adherence, while New York, New Jersey, and Delaware voted no, and Maryland was divided.

It is to be remarked that in all the votes thus far, the State of Georgia, with less than sixty thousand inhabitants, voted with the large States. This was due to the fact that, as her area exceeded that of Virginia and North Carolina, and was only fourteen thousand square miles less than all the other ten States together, Georgia expected in the near future to develop into one of the most important and populous States in the Union.[1]

The Committee of the Whole then dissolved, and Randolph's nineteen Resolutions were again reported to the Convention.

OUT OF CONVENTION

Washington noted:

"Dined (after leaving Convention) in a family way at Mr. Morris's, and spent the evening there in a very large company."

William R. Davie, a delegate from North Carolina, wrote to Governor Caswell that: "We move slowly in our business. It is indeed a work of great delicacy and difficulty, impeded every step by jealousies and interest."[2] Nathan Dane, on this day, wrote from

---

[1] General Nathanael Greene wrote to Charles Thomson, from Georgia, April 24, 1786: "I hope the politicks of this State will please you better than they have done. The people begin to grow more enlightened and a more liberal policy to prevail. . . . The State has been of little importance to the Union, but its great increase of tracts and population will soon place it among the first in the Confederation. If you can keep the ship afloat a few years, the navigation will be less difficult." *Charles Thomson Papers MSS*, in Library of Congress.

[2] *North Carolina Records*, XX, 725.

New York to Rufus King, intimating that Major William Pierce of Georgia (who, though a delegate, was then in New York attending Congress) had somewhat infringed the Secrecy Rule:

"I fully agree to the propriety of the Convention order restraining its members from communicating its doing, tho' I feel a strong desire and curiosity to know how it proceeds. I think the public never ought to see anything but the final report of the Convention — the digested result only of their deliberations and enquiries. Whether the plans of the Southern, Eastern or Middle States succeed, never, in my opinion, ought to be known. A few reflections on the subject lead me to doubt whether one of your members, Mr. P. who two or three days since came to this city, fully understood the true meaning, and full and just extent of the order not to communicate."

WEDNESDAY, JUNE 20, 1787

IN CONVENTION

As the Nationalist party in the Convention had apparently secured a great triumph in the vote to adhere to the Virginia Plan for the new Government, its leaders evidently believed that they could afford to make minor concessions. Accordingly, on this day, they adopted a suggestion made by Ellsworth, seconded by Gorham, that the word "National" be dropped wherever used, and the words "of the United States" be substituted. This was, of course, a mere verbal modification, as the system still remained National in its scope; and all parties so understood. Speeches in opposition to the whole system were made by Lansing, Luther Martin, and Sherman. In the course of this debate, however, Sherman again outlined the compromise on which the future success of the Convention was to be built. "If the difficulty on the subject of representation cannot be otherwise got over," he said that "he would agree to have two branches, and a proportional representation in one of them, provided each State had an equal voice in the other." And Mason made a sage and conciliatory speech which calmed the debate, saying: "Though some have expressed much warmth on this and former occasions, I can excuse it, as the result of sudden passion, and hope that although we differ in some particular points, if we mean the good of the whole, our good sense, upon reflection, will prevent us from spreading our discontents further." [1]

OUT OF CONVENTION

Washington noted:

"Attended Convention. Dined at Mr. [Samuel] Meredith's and drank tea there."

The *Herald* well characterized the work of the Convention by saying that: [2]

"Whatever measure may be recommended by the Federal Convention, whether an addition to the old Constitution or the adoption of a new, it will in effect be a revolution in Government, accomplished by reasoning and deliberation; an event that has never occurred since the formation of society and which will be strongly characteristic of the philosophic and tolerant spirit of the age."

The *Gazette* voiced a theory, which later was widely shared by adherents of the Constitution, that opposition to that instrument proceeded largely from persons holding office in the States: [3]

[1] As reported in Yates' *Notes*, but not by Madison.

[2] See *Pennsylvania Journal*, June 23, 1787. This article was widely republished — see *New York Journal*, June 28; *Independent Chronicle*, July 19; *Boston Gazette*, July 23, 1787.

[3] See also *Massachusetts Centinel*, June 27, 1787: "The Grand National Convention now sitting at Philadelphia, it is said, is the most respectable body of men ever convened in the Western World." On June 30, this paper said: "The principal difficulty (says a correspondent) in the way of necessary alterations in our Government will arise from the officers of Government. Their interests, it is

"It is agreed, says a correspondent, that our Convention are framing a wise and free Government for us. This Government will be opposed only by our civil officers who are afraid of new arrangements taking place, which will jostle them out of office. . . . In the meantime, the people are desired to beware of all essays and paragraphs that are opposed to a reform in our Government, for they all must and will come from civil officers or persons connected with them."

Jefferson in Paris wrote to Madison, this day:

"The idea of separating the Executive business of the Confederacy from Congress, as the Judiciary is already in some degree, is just and necessary. . . . The negative proposed to be given them on all the acts of the several Legislatures is now for the first time suggested to my mind. *Prima facie* I do not like it. . . . Would not an appeal from the State Judicatures to a Federal Court, in all cases where the Act of Confederation controuled the question, be as effectual a remedy, and exactly commensurate to the defect?"

Nathan Dane wrote from Congress in New York to Nathaniel Gorham, a curious description of the harmful effect which the Convention was having upon the people's attitude towards Congress:[1]

"I wish the officers of Congress and members not engaged in the Convention would return to New York. I do not know how it may be in the Southern States, but, I assume, the present state of Congress has a very disagreeable effect

imagined, will be affected by the alteration. . . . But it is to be hoped the people will neither be influenced by such men or their contentions, in the adoption of a new Federal Government." And see *Boston Gazette*, July 9, 1787.

[1] *Mass. Hist. Soc. Proc.* (1925), LIX, 95. Dane had written to Governor John Hancock, May 31, 1787: "I beg leave to inform your Excellency that Mr. Gorham and Mr. King are attending the Federal Convention now setting at Philadelphia, and that there has not been a representation of Massachusetts in Congress since the 23d instant. It is generally thought probable that the Convention will continue setting for some months and it seems to be uncertain whether either of those gentlemen can attend Congress while the Convention shall be setting. . . . Several of the members of Congress are attending the Convention, and only four States, at present, are represented in Congress, and it appears highly probable that Congress will not be in a situation to do much business till its members shall return from the Convention." See *Massachusetts State Archives, Letters 1786–1787*, p. 67.

in the Eastern States. The people hear of a Convention in Philadelphia, and that Congress is done sitting, etc. Many of them are told, it seems, that Congress will never meet again. Dr. (Samuel) Holten says he saw several sober men who had got an idea that the people were to be called on to take arms to carry into effect immediately the report of the Convention, etc. I see no help for men's being so absurd and distracted; but those things have a pernicious effect on the industry, peace and habits of the people."

Dane also thought that too many rumors were being published in the newspapers as to the Convention:

"Are not the printers imprudent to publish so many contradictory pieces about the proceedings of your body, which must be mere conjecture? You know many people believe all they see in the newspapers, without the least examination. . . ."

THURSDAY, JUNE 21, 1787

IN CONVENTION

The Convention proceeded to consider and vote the Randolph Resolutions voted by the Committee of the Whole with reference to the election of the National Legislature (as discussed *infra*).

OUT OF CONVENTION

Washington noted:

" Attended Convention. Dined at Mr. Prager's, and spent the evening in my chamber."

FRIDAY, JUNE 22, 1787

IN CONVENTION

The Convention continued to consider and vote the Randolph Resolutions with reference to the National Legislature, voted by the Committee of the Whole (as discussed *infra*).[1]

[1] The debates on this day can be studied best in Yates' *Notes*, which are fuller than Madison's.

OUT OF CONVENTION

Washington noted:

"Dined (in a family way) at Mr. Morris's and drank tea with Mr. Francis Hopkinson."

SATURDAY, JUNE 23, 1787

IN CONVENTION

The Convention continued to consider and vote upon the Randolph Resolutions, with reference to the National Legislature, voted by the Committee of the Whole (as discussed *infra*).[1]

OUT OF CONVENTION

Washington noted:

"In Convention. Dined at Doctr. Ruston's and drank tea at Mr. Morris's."

Apparently, Washington did not attend, on this Saturday, an entertainment given for the benefit of Americans held in captivity by Algerine pirates which was advertised to be given in the "cool and commodious Operahouse" at Southwark:[2]

"For the relief of our fellow citizens enslaved at Algiers on Monday next — a Concert, Vocal and Instrumental, in the first part of which will be introduced 'The Grateful War or The Pupil in Love', and in the second part will be presented the musical entertainment of 'The Poor Soldier.' . . . A

[1] The debates on this day can be studied best in Yates' *Notes*, which are fuller than Madison's.

[2] *Pennsylvania Herald*, June 23, 1787. That the attendance did not fulfil expectations appears from a letter in a subsequent issue of the *Herald* (June 27): "I was at the opera on Monday night and very sorry to see so thin a house for such a desirable purpose; many people, I have been informed, were prevented going at this hot season for fear of being overheated. This, I own, weighed some time with me — but humanity prevailed. I was not a little surprised at the neat and elegant manner in which the managers have fitted up the building; which, from the methods taken of ventilating, it is certainly the coolest in Philadelphia." The editor adds that: "The benevolent intention of the managers in favor of our brethren at Algiers has perhaps been frustrated by the inattention of the citizens to the object of the performance."

poetical address composed for the occasion will be delivered at the opening of the entertainment. And the whole will conclude with an elegant Vaud-ville."

The *Gazetteer* published a New Jersey letter as to the public expectations of the Convention : [1]

"We expect something great will be recommended by the Convention now sitting in your city. They can recommend. Congress can do the same. But if for the better, will all the States adopt the measures so recommended? I fear not, but wish for the best. Until one Supreme Head is fixed upon a permanent foundation, with power sufficient to regulate trade over the whole Union and can command cash to pay the foreign debt, regulate peace, war, etc., we shall not thrive. I have no notion that any individual should chuse a law to suit himself. This is the idea that many have of liberty and independence; but it is a very false one. If the United States and individual States were honest, they might enact laws to make their citizens and subjects so. But really we cannot expect to see people honest and punctual, when they see the Legislatures so far from it themselves. A general reformation (of all things) at this time is most necessary, or we must sink."

And the *Packet* printed a letter from Philadelphia to Baltimore on the same subject :

"I know you are waiting with anxious expectation to be informed of the proceedings of the Grand Convention. Nothing as yet has transpired. All that we know is that a Committee is appointed to collect materials and to form a report for the discussion of this respectable body."

SUNDAY, JUNE 24, 1787

Washington noted :

"Dined at Mr. Morris' and spent the evening at Mr. Meredith's (in drinking tea only)."

[1] See also *Pennsylvania Gazette*, June 27; *Independent Chronicle* (Boston), July 12, 1787.

MONDAY, JUNE 25, 1787

IN CONVENTION

Charles Pinckney's Speech

This day was made memorable by a speech of one of the youngest of the delegates, Charles Pinckney of South Carolina. With the exception of those by Madison and Wilson, no such powerful, eloquent, and brilliant contribution had been made. Into the debates which had so largely turned on devotion to the States, Pinckney now breathed a spirit of Americanism. He pointed out the peculiarly favorable situation of this country, provided it should have an adequate system of Government — a country in which "every member of the society almost will enjoy an equal power of arriving at the supreme office, and consequently of directing the strength and sentiments of the whole community" — a country "in which the whole community will enjoy in the fullest sense that kind of political liberty which consists in the power the members of the States reserve to themselves of arriving at the public offices, or at least of having votes in the nomination of those who fill them", — "a new extensive country containing within itself the materials of forming a Government capable of extending to its citizens all the blessings of civil and religious liberty, capable of making them happy at home." This, said he, was "the great end of a Republican form of Government." In such a country, though there might be three classes of men — the professional, the commercial, and the landed (or "owners and cultivators of the soil"), there is, after all, "but one great and equal body of citizens among whom there are no distinctions of rank and very few or none of fortune." This speech has been well described as follows : [1]

[1] *Constitutional History of the United States* (1901), by Francis N. Thorpe, I, 404–405.

"Hitherto, whenever a delegate had thought it necessary to support an opinion by historical examples, he had referred to the republics and confederacies of earlier times, or to the British government. Pinckney brought the mind of the Convention back to America and emphasized the unique situation of its people. He would not break with the past, yet would found a Government adapted to the wants of a new country and a new Nation. . . . To them [the delegates], there was no American history in the sense in which these words are now understood. The Government they were forming would be an experiment, and the people were yet to prove it administrable. Pinckney's speech was, therefore, the more remarkable because of its American tone. . . . It raised their minds to a clearer concept of the unique situation of the American people, and to the conclusion that a Government should be formed adapted to such a country as ours. Hamilton not only believed that the British Constitution was the best in existence, but he wished it copied as closely as possible in America. Pinckney acknowledged its excellence, but showed with larger wisdom that it was not adapted to the American people. From the time Pinckney spoke, and only a fragment of his speech is preserved, the members must have been persuaded, if any were yet in doubt, that the Constitution which they were making must be American in character."

OUT OF CONVENTION

Washington noted :

"Attended Convention. Dined at Mr. Morris's, drank tea there, and spent the evening in my chamber."

Robert Morris wrote to his sons (Robert and Thomas), then in Leipsic : [1]

"General Washington is now our guest, having taken up his abode at my house during the time he is to remain in this city. He is President of a Convention of Delegates from the thirteen States of America, who have met here for the pur-

---

[1] *Maria White — Mrs. Robert Morris* (1878), by Charles Henry Hart.

pose of revising, amending, and altering the Federal Government. There are gentlemen of great abilities employed in this Convention, many of whom were in the First Congress, and several that were concerned in forming the Articles of Confederation now about to be altered and amended. You, my children, ought to pray for a successful issue to their labours, as the result is to be a form of Government under which you are to live, and in the administration of which you may hereafter probably have a share, provided you qualify yourselves by application to your studies. The law of Nations, a knowledge of the Germanic system and the Constitutions of the several Governments in Europe, and an intimate acquaintance with ancient and modern history are essentially necessary to entitle you to participate in the honor of serving a free People in the administration of this Government."

TUESDAY, JUNE 26, 1787

IN CONVENTION

Terms of Office of Members of the Legislature

On this day, the question of the terms of office for members of the National Legislature was finally determined. This subject had been discussed in the Committee of the Whole, on June 12. For members of the first branch, there had been great insistence on annual elections. In Colonial times, the annual session of the popular Assembly had been the only check which the people had had on the Royal Governors; [1] and though this reason for such frequent elections had now disappeared, the tradition still persisted. Moreover, the history of the English Parliament and the extension of its term from two to seven years by the Septennial Act of 1716 in order to defeat the will of the people, had impressed upon the delegates the importance of limiting the duration of the terms

---

[1] See also *The Federalist*, No. 51.

of the Legislature. Elbridge Gerry of Massachusetts said that "he considered annual elections as the only defence of the people against tyranny." Madison, on the other hand, believed that at least three years would be required for Representatives to gain a knowledge of the needs and interests of the other States; and his arguments prevailed. Accordingly, the Committee voted for triennial elections. For Senators, a seven year term was voted. Richard D. Spaight of North Carolina, Randolph, and Madison urged this long term on the ground that the object of the Senate was to give stability to the Government and to check excesses in the first branch of the National Legislature, though the New England States again favored a shorter term. When the Convention debated the Committee's report, on June 21, the delegates changed their minds with reference to members of the first branch, and voted for biennial elections instead of triennial, as a compromise with those who still urged annual. "The people were attached to frequency of elections," said Randolph. "The Representatives ought to return home and mix with the people. By remaining at the seat of Government they would acquire the habits of the place which might differ from those of their constituents," said Roger Sherman. On the other hand, Hamilton said that "frequency of elections tended to make the people listless to them, and to facilitate the success of little cabals. This evil was complained of in all the States."

The length of the term of office for Senators was taken up by the Convention, on June 25. The term of the Senate in Maryland was five years; in New York and Virginia, four years; in Delaware, three years; and in South Carolina, two years. Gorham of Massachusetts urged that the seven year term be cut down to four years, and that one quarter of the Senate be elected each year. General Pinckney concurred. Randolph supported the idea of division of Senators into classes and of rotation as "favorable to the wisdom and stability of the corps, which might possibly be always sitting and aiding the Executive." Such a system of rotation prevailed in the Senates under the State Constitutions of New York, Virginia, and Delaware. Hugh Williamson of North Carolina wisely suggested a term of six years as more convenient for rotation than seven. On this June 26, Gorham moved a six year term, and that the rotation be triennial. George Read of Delaware moved a nine year term, one third going out triennially (though Read and Robert Morris really agreed with Hamilton in preferring a Senate elected "during good behaviour"). Charles Pinckney opposed six years, fearing that the members will "be too long separated from their constituents, and will imbibe attachments different from that of the State." [1] Madison made an eloquent speech, urging the Convention to consider the ends to be served by a Senate, and arguing that considerable duration should be given to that branch, which, "respectable for its wisdom and virtue", might be a check to attempts of majorities to oppress minorities. Wilson concurred. On the other side, Sherman and Gerry still stood out for frequent elections. The nine year term was then defeated; and the Convention adopted Williamson's and Gorham's proposal of a six year term, one third to go out biennially.

OUT OF CONVENTION

Washington noted:

"Attended Convention. Partook of a family dinner with Govr. Randolph and made one of a party to drink tea at Gray's Ferry."

[1] As reported in Yates' *Notes*.

A letter from a gentleman in Virginia in the *Gazetteer* commented on the value of the Convention's plan for a Congress with two branches :[1]

"It is not owing to a want of knowledge, if the present respectable Convention fail to establish an energetic Government which will diffuse equal advantages to the remotest corner of the United States. It will be owing to the narrow minds or selfish views of little politicians, perhaps corrupted by the influence of a foreign power, who hates to see the United States rise into importance and respect among the nations of the earth. It is thought that the persons who opposed the impost and labored for emissions of paper were ignorant of or inimical to the interest of America. The idea of having the supreme Federal power divided into two or more branches meets with universal approbation — it will be a check on the intriguing spirit of the members of one House, and will be the means of bringing the deliberations of the supreme power to greater maturity — it will be a guard against precipitancy and temerity of council. The advantage of two branches has been conspicuous lately in Maryland — the firmness of their Senate saved their country from perdition. I reprobate the idea of a division of the States into three or four republics. The greatest enemy of America could have suggested nothing worse or more destructive. . . . You tell me that you suspect a combination against the Federal Government in Rhode Island and New York. The majority of the House of Delegates of Rhode Island have lost all character and even shame itself. Yet you see there are honest men in that State. The Judges behaved handsomely in the affair of the Tender Law, and the minority have sent some gentlemen to the Convention, who no doubt will meet with all the attention they can expect. . . . Such is the present temper of the Americans and the resentment for the contempt they have so universally incurred on account of the weakness of government is so great, that I believe, upon my honour,

---

[1] See also *Pennsylvania Gazette*, June 27; *Virginia Independent Chronicle*, July 4; *Massachusetts Centinel*, July 7; *Salem Mercury*, July 10, 1787.

the Supreme Federal Power, after an adequate government
is determined upon, may command the service of 20,000
volunteers for a year without pay to execute these orders
and fix Government upon a firm and permanent basis."

It is interesting to note the reference in this letter to
the action of the Judges in Rhode Island.   The decision
of the Court in *Trevett* v. *Weeden*, in the fall of 1786,
holding the paper money statute of that State unconstitutional on the ground that it failed to provide a jury
trial had been given wide publicity in the newspapers
of all the States.[1] Advertisements of a pamphlet
containing an account of the case had appeared in the
Pennsylvania Packet, in the opening weeks of the Convention.[2] The delegates had already discussed this
power of Courts to hold statutes unconstitutional on
two occasions during this month of June, and were
about to discuss it again in the debates over the Judiciary in July.[3]

WEDNESDAY, JUNE 27, 1787

IN CONVENTION

Luther Martin's Speech

The Convention, having on previous days disposed of
those details relating to the National Legislature which

[1] A letter from Providence on this subject was widely republished, stating that:
"The happiness of individuals as well as the public safety depends more on the
Superior Court than many people apprehended.   They are a shield, nay a bulwark
to their fellow citizens against all kinds of injustice and oppression.   It is not only
their duty to controul and restrain all inferior Courts; but to discern the bound-
aries of the power both of State and Federal legislation."   See *Pennsylvania Packet*,
Jan. 10, 1787; *Pennsylvania Journal*, May 2, 1787; *Independent Gazetteer*, Jan. 12,
May 3, 1787; see also *New Hampshire Spy*, Feb. 16, 1787.

[2] See *Pennsylvania Packet*, April 25, May 2, 9, 16, 23, 1787: "Just come to hand
and to be had of J. Dodson, Bookseller, Second Street, and J. Cruikshank, Market
Street, Price 2 sh. 6 d.   *The Case, Trevett against Weeden*, on information and
complaint for refusing paper bills in payment for butcher's meat, etc.   Tried before
the honorable Superior Court in the County of Newport, Rhode Island, Also The
Case of the Judges of said Court before the General Assembly, on citation for dis-
missing said complaint.   By James M. Varnum, Esq., Counsellor at Law, etc."

[3] James Madison, in his speech in the Convention, July 17, 1787, referred to the
case of *Trevett* v. *Weeden*.

gave rise to less contention — term of office, qualifications, re-eligibility to election, etc., now came face to
face with the crucial question: What should be the
rules of suffrage in the two branches, or, in other words,
should they be chosen in proportion to the respective
populations of the States; or should each State be
equally represented? On June 11, the Committee of
the Whole had voted that the former system should
apply to both Houses; but with regard to the Senate,
the vote was close, six States to five, — Connecticut,
New Jersey, Delaware, and Maryland, together with
New York, voting for equality. "It is apparent," says
Farrand, "that this is nearly the same division which
had manifested itself in the old Congress, notably in
connection with the adoption of the Confederation, and
the negotiations over the treaty of peace." [1] It has
been customary for historians to depict this as a struggle
between the larger and the smaller States, yet New
York, of course, can hardly be classed as a smaller
State. It would be more accurate to say that it was
a struggle between the South, aided by Pennsylvania
and Massachusetts, and the rest of the Union.

The question as to the rule of suffrage was presented,
on this day, with reference solely to the first branch of
the Legislature; and as to this most of the delegates
had practically made up their minds, and were ready
to vote. With the Convention impatient to meet the
issue, "Luther Martin of Maryland chose this most
inopportune time and in a spell of hot weather, too, to
deliver a lengthy harangue." He spoke for three hours,
until exhausted by the "heat of the season" and then
continued on the next day. Of this speech, Ellsworth
wrote later that "it might have continued two months,
but for those marks of fatigue and disgust you saw
strongly expressed on whichever side of the House you

[1] *The Framing of the Constitution* (1913), by Max Farrand, pp. 81–82.

turned your mortified eyes." [1] Yates stated that Martin's arguments "were too diffuse and in many instances desultory", so that it was not possible "to trace him through the whole, or to methodize his ideas into a systematic or argumentative arrangement." Even the moderate and courteous Madison reported that Martin spoke "with much diffuseness and considerable vehemence." The theme of this fatiguing speech was, that "the General Government was meant merely to preserve the State Governments and not to govern individuals, and that its powers should be kept within narrow limits"; that justice and freedom, as well as policy, demanded that States, equally sovereign and free, should retain an equal vote. As Martin was one of the chief upholders of State Sovereignty, it is evident that the advocates of that cause in the Convention were far inferior to the Nationalists in debating ability.

OUT OF CONVENTION

On this day, William Samuel Johnson, one of the Connecticut delegates, wrote to his son as to the great diversity of sentiment in the Convention:

"We have delegates from eleven States actually assembled consisting of many of the most able men in America. . . .

---

[1] See letter of "The Landholder" in *Maryland Journal*, Feb. 29, 1788, in which he referred to: "A sarcastic reply from the pleasant Mr. Gerry, in which he admired the strength of your lungs and profound knowledge in the first principles of government; mixing and illustrating his little remarks with a profusion of those 'hems' that never fail to lengthen out and enliven his oratory. This reply (from your intimate acquaintance), the match being so equal and the contrast so comic, had the happy effect to put the House in good humour and leave you a prey to the most humiliating reflections. But this did not teach you to bound your speeches by the lines of moderation; for the very next day you exhibited without a blush another specimen of eternal volubility. . . . You cannot have forgotten that by such ignorance in politics and contradictory opinions you exhausted the politeness of the Convention, which at length prepared to slumber when you rose to speak; nor can you have forgotten you were only twice appointed a member of a Committee or that these appointments were made merely to avoid your endless garrulity, and if possible to lead you to reason, by the easy road of familiar conversation."

Gerry in the *New York Journal*, April 30, 1788, denied that he ever made any reply to Martin, as charged by Ellsworth. And see Martin's reply in *Maryland Journal*, March 18, 1788,

It is agreed that for the present our deliberations shall be kept secret, so that I can only tell you that much information and eloquence has been displayed in the introductory speeches, and that we have hitherto preserved great temperance, candor, and moderation in debate, and evinced much solicitude for the public weal. Yet, as was to be expected, there is great diversity of sentiment, which renders it impossible to determine what will be the result of our deliberations."

For the second time in two consecutive days, the attention of the delegates was directed to references in the newspapers to the subject of the power of the Courts to declare statutes invalid; for the *Packet*, this day, published a despatch from Newbern, North Carolina, announcing the decision of the Supreme Court of that State in *Bayard* v. *Singleton*, a case involving the constitutionality of a State law which abolished jury trial in certain classes of cases, in which the Judges held the law invalid.[1]

---

[1] "May 30: Yesterday was agitated the celebrated question whether the suits brought for the recovery of confiscated property should be dismissed, according to the Act of Assembly commonly called the Quieting Act, when the Court gave their opinion in the negative."

It is to be noted that the *Maryland Gazette* of July 3, and the *Virginia Independent Chronicle* of July 4, published a long detailed description of this case and its decision. So that, before the middle of July, all the North Carolina, Maryland, and Virginia members of the Convention must undoubtedly have been made familiar with the Court's action.

See also *Exchange Advertiser* (Boston), July 27, 1786, quoting as a despatch from Princeton, N. J., July 6, an "extract of a letter from a gentleman in Newbern (North Carolina) to his father here, dated June 9, 1786," as follows: "Our Superior Court has lately risen here. Among the causes which came before the Court, there was one which excited great agitation among the people. At the last session of Assembly an act was passed directing that purchasers from commissioners at the sales of confiscated property under the confiscation laws should not be liable to suits at law for that property, and that all suits already brought by persons whose property was confiscated or their representatives should be dismissed on motion. Under this law, a motion was made for the dismission of a suit brought by Bayard and wife of New York for the best house with wharves, etc., in this town, formerly the property of a Mr. Connel who in seventy-seven had conveyed this property to his daughter, now Mrs. Bayard. The Judges who have taken it into their heads that they have a right to determine that an Act of Assembly is no law and not to be obeyed as such, when in their opinion unconstitutional, did not dismiss the suits; indeed they would give no opinion immediately, but evidently showed their disinclination to the laws having any operation. This threw the people into a

On this day, the *Gazetteer* published a highly favorable description of the delegates to the Convention, which was copied in the papers in many States: [1]

"The present Federal Convention, says a correspondent, is happily composed of men who are qualified from education, experience, and profession for the great business assigned to them. The principles, the administrative or executive duties of government, will be pointed out by those gentlemen who have filled or now fill the offices of first Magistrate in several of the States — while the commercial interests of America will be faithfully represented and explained by the mercantile part of the Convention. These gentlemen are assembled at a most fortunate period — in the midst of peace — with leisure to explore the perfections or defects of all the governments that ever existed, with passions uncontrouled by the resentments and prejudices kindled by the late war — and with a variety of experiments before them of the feebleness, tyranny, and licentiousness of our American forms of government. Under such circumstances, it will not be difficult for them to frame a Federal Constitution that will suit our country."

THURSDAY, JUNE 28, 1787

IN CONVENTION

On this day, seventeen days after the Committee of the Whole had voted against equal representation for the States in the National Legislature, the direct issue was precipitated by a motion made by Lansing of New York, seconded by Jonathan Dayton of New Jersey, to reverse the action of the Committee. Madison and Wilson again reiterated the arguments against such a return to the system which had proved so unsatisfactory under the Articles of Confederation; and they

great ferment, and thirty or forty defendants similarly circumstanced determined to go into Court in a body and demand a dismission of their suits. The Court, finding the disposition of the people, thought proper to soften a good deal what they had said, but deferred giving their opinion till the succeeding Court."

[1] *Pennsylvania Packet,* June 28; *Connecticut Courant,* July 9, 1787.

again tried to allay the dread by the small States of a possible combination against them of the large States. Virginia, Massachusetts, and Pennsylvania, said Madison, had no common interests, either in point of manners, religion, or staple productions, their staples being respectively tobacco, fish, and flour; and hence they had no motive for combining. It was evident, however, that the delegates from the small States were not to be moved by argument.

It was at this juncture that Doctor Franklin made his famous speech suggesting that the sessions be opened with prayer. "The small progress we have made after four or five weeks' close attendance, and continual reasonings with each other," said he, "our different sentiments on almost every question . . . is, methinks, a melancholy proof of the imperfection of human understanding." And he continued:

"In this situation of this Assembly, groping, as it were, in the dark to find political truth, and scarce able to distinguish it when presented to us, how has it happened, that we have not hitherto once thought of humbly applying to the Father of lights to illuminate our understandings? . . . I have lived, sir, a long time, and the longer I live, the more convincing proofs I see of this truth — *that God governs in the affairs of men.* And if a sparrow cannot fall to the ground without his notice, is it probable that an empire can rise without his aid? . . . I also believe that without his concurring aid we shall succeed in this political building no better than the builders of Babel. We shall be divided by our little, partial, local interests; our projects will be confounded, and we ourselves shall become a reproach and bye word down to future ages. And what is worse, mankind may hereafter, from this unfortunate instance, despair of establishing Governments by human wisdom and leave it to chance, war and conquest."

Franklin's motion that prayers be offered every morning in the Convention was seconded by Sherman.

Thirty-eight years later, Jonathan Dayton, the youngest member of the Convention, wrote a letter giving his recollection of this episode : [1]

"The Doctor sat down, and never did I behold a countenance at once so dignified and delighted as was that of Washington, at the close of this address. Nor were the members of the Convention generally less affected. The words of the venerable Franklin fell upon our ears with a weight and authority even greater than we may suppose an oracle to have had in a Roman Senate. A silent admiration superseded, for a moment, the expression of that assent and approbation which was strongly marked on almost every countenance."

Although Dayton stated in his letter that the motion was carried, such was not the fact. Opposition arose on various grounds — lack of funds to pay chaplains, dislike of offending the Quaker usage, fear lest the public might be led to believe that dissensions made the step necessary. Accordingly, as Franklin himself recorded, "the Convention, except three or four persons, thought prayers unnecessary", and no action was taken on his motion.[2]

[1] See letter of Jonathan Dayton to William Steele, written in Sept., 1825, and printed in the *National Intelligencer*, Aug. 26, 1826, reprinted in *Farrand*, III, 46, and the *Constitution of the United States* (1924), by James M. Beck, pp. 125 *et seq.* The letter incorrectly states that the episode occurred after the vote had been taken as to the Senate and is also evidently erroneous in other details.

[2] Madison wrote to T. S. Grimke, Jan. 6, 1834, that Dayton's letter was inaccurate in many points: "You wish to be informed of the errors in your pamphlet alluded to in my last. The first related to the proposition of Doctor Franklin in favor of a religious service in the Federal Convention. The proposition was received and treated with the respect due to it; but the lapse of time which had preceded, with considerations growing out of it, had the effect of limiting what was done, to a reference of the proposition to a highly respectable Committee. This issue of it may be traced in the printed Journal. The Quaker usage, never discontinued in the State, and the place where the Convention held its sittings, might not have been without an influence, as might also the discord of religious opinions within the Convention, as well as among the clergy of the spot. The error into which you had fallen may have been confirmed by a communication in the *National Intelligencer* some years ago, said to have been received through a respectable channel from a member of the Convention. That the communication was erroneous is certain; whether from misapprehension or misrecollection, uncertain."

Madison wrote to Jared Sparks, April 8, 1831: "It was during that period of

Dayton, in the letter giving his recollections, described another interesting suggestion for an adjournment of the Convention for three days, which, he states, was made by Franklin on this day. As Madison makes no mention of it, Dayton probably confused it with action on a later day; but as described by him, it is so entirely in Franklin's wise and conciliatory vein, that it must have occurred at some point in the Convention. In support of his motion, said Dayton, Franklin said: "And I would earnestly recommend to the members of this Convention that they spend the time of this recess, not in associating with their own party and devising new arguments to fortify themselves in their old opinions, but that they mix with members of opposite sentiments, lend a patient ear to their reasonings, and candidly allow them all the weight to which they may be entitled; and when we assemble again, I hope it will be with a determination to form a Constitution, if not such an one as we can individually and in all respects approve, yet the best which, under the existing circumstances, can be obtained." Here, said Dayton, "the countenance of Washington brightened and a cheering ray seemed to break in upon the gloom which had recently covered our political horizon."

William Few, one of the delegates from Georgia, many years later, gave his impressions of this critical stage of the Convention: [1]

"The modification of the State Rights, the different interests and diversity of opinions seemed for sometime to present obstacles that could not be surmounted. After about three weeks deliberation and debating, the Convention had serious thoughts of adjourning without doing anything. All human efforts seemed to fail. Doctor Franklin proposed

gloom that Dr. Franklin made the proposition for a religious service in the Convention, an account of which was so erroneously given, with every semblance of authenticity, through the *National Intelligencer*, several years ago."

[1] *Autobiography of William Few*, written about 1816, *Farrand*, III, 423.

to appoint a chaplain and implore Divine assistance, but his motion did not prevail. It was an awful and critical moment. If the Convention had then adjourned, the dissolution of the Union of the States seemed inevitable. This consideration, no doubt, had its weight in reconciling clashing opinions and interests. It was believed to be of the utmost importance to concede to different opinions so far as to endeavor to meet opposition on middle ground and to form a Constitution that might preserve the Union of the States. On that principle of accommodations, the business progressed, and after about three months labor, a plan of Constitution was formed on principles which did not altogether please anybody, but it was agreed to be the most expedient that could be devised and agreed to."

OUT OF CONVENTION

Washington noted:

"Attended Convention. Dined at Mr. Morris's in a large company (the news of his Bills being protested, arriving last night a little malapropos). Drank tea there and spent the evening in my chamber."

The sentiment of the people in Virginia may be seen from a letter of this date from Chesterfield, Virginia (quoted from a Virginia paper), which stated that "all persons impatiently wait the result of the deliberations of the collective wisdom of our vast Continent now convened at Philadelphia. In the rectitude of the measures essential to our future well-being, by them finally recommended to be pursued, from the tried integrity of most of the characters of which this august body is composed, and crowned with the approbation of our still immutable Washington, I doubt not but we may most cheerfully repose the most implicit confidence." [1]

[1] Reprinted in *Pennsylvania Packet*, Aug. 18, 1787.

not venture to speculate in indents or any other Continental securities. Had we the power and the means to follow a certain gentleman's advice, the adoption of his plan would, with me at least, require other authority to support it."

SATURDAY, JUNE 30, 1787

IN CONVENTION

At the opening of the session, Judge Brearley of New Jersey, moved that the President of the Convention write to Governor Sullivan of New Hampshire, urging the attendance of the delegates from that State. Rutledge, King, and Wilson were opposed (although it is to be noted that General Knox, an ardent supporter of the new Constitution, had already entreated Governor Sullivan to expedite his delegates). The motion was defeated.

The debate now continued on Ellsworth's motion; and the delegates from the large States and strong Nationalists, encouraged by the previous day's vote, seemed inclined to press their advantage — Wilson, Madison, and King bearing the brunt of the attack. "Can we forget for whom we are forming a Government?" asked Wilson. "Is it for men, or for the imaginary beings called States." A Government, said he, founded on a principle by which a number of States containing a minority of the people could control those containing a majority, "can be neither solid nor lasting." King said that the reform would be "nugatory and nominal only, if we should make another Congress of the proposed Senate." Convinced of the obstinacy of the small States, he considered, despairingly, that we were already cut asunder, sacrificed to the "phantom of State Sovereignty." He conceived this to be "the last opportunity of providing for its (America's) liberty and happiness"; and he was amazed that "when a just Government founded on a fair representation of the people of America was within our reach, we should renounce the blessing from an attachment to the ideal freedom and importance of *States*." Madison now laid his finger on the real and essential dividing line between the parties in the Convention. He stated that there was no reason for the small States to fear a combination against them of the large States from the North and from the South; because "the States were divided into different interests, not by their difference of size, but by other circumstances; the most material of which resulted partly from climate, but principally from the effects of having or not having slaves. These two causes concurred in forming the great division of interests in the United States. It did not lie between the large and small States; it lay between the Northern and Southern." [1]   On the basis of such a line of division, Madison suggested as a compromise that in the Senate, the Southern States might count the whole number of their slaves in determining the population to be represented; and in the House, the population should be regarded as including only three fifths of the slaves. Franklin also proposed a compromise of a somewhat impractical nature, but accompanied his suggestion with these shrewd words: "When a broad table is to be made, and the edges of planks do not fit, the artist takes a little from both, and makes a good joint. In like manner, here, both sides must part with some of their demands, in order that they may join in some accommodating proposition." In spite of these conciliatory suggestions, the delegates from the small States became more insistent and more violent in their language, in adhering to their own view —all excepting Ellsworth, who said that his State was "entirely

[1] Opinions were expressed to the same effect as to the real division being between the Northern and Southern States, by Charles Pinckney, June 26, July 2; Rufus King, July 10; G. Morris, July 13; George Mason, July 23; General Charles C. Pinckney, July 24.

puts it out of my power to give you any particular information upon the subject. *Festina lente* seems hitherto to
have been our maxim. Things, however, are now drawing
to that point on which some of the fundamental principles
must be decided, and two or three days will probably enable
us to judge — which at present is very doubtful — whether
any sound and effectual system can be established or
not. If it cannot, I presume we shall not continue here
much longer; if it can, we shall probably be detained till
September.

I feel myself disagreeably circumstanced in being the only
member of the Assembly, in the Virginia delegation, and,
consequently, if any system shall be recommended by the
Convention, that the whole weight of explanation must fall
upon me."

SUNDAY, JULY 1, 1787

Washington noted simply that he "dined and spent
the evening at home"; and in view of the tense
situation which prevailed in the Convention on the
preceding day, and of the fact that on the next day
the vote was to be taken on the critical question as to
equality of representation in the Senate, it is not surprising that, on this day, he wrote to David Stuart his
views, in a not very hopeful mood as to the situation:

"Happy indeed would it be, if the Convention shall be
able to recommend such a firm and permanent Government
for this Union, that all who live under it may be secure in
their lives, liberty, and property; and thrice happy would
it be, if such a recommendation should obtain. Everybody
wishes, everybody expects something from the Convention;
but what will be the final result of its deliberation the book
of fate must disclose. Persuaded I am, that the primary
cause of all our disorders lies in the different State Governments, and in the tenacity of that power which pervades
the whole of their systems. Whilst independent sovereignty
is so ardently contended for, whilst the local views of each

State, and separate interests by which they are too much governed, will not yield to a more enlarged scale of politics, incompatibility in the laws of different States, and disrespect to those of the General Government, must render the situation of this great country weak, inefficient, and disgraceful. It has already done so, almost to the final dissolution of it. Weak at home and disregarded abroad is our present condition, and contemptible enough it is. . . . I have had no wish more ardent, through the whole progress of this business, than that of knowing what kind of Government is best calculated for us to live under. No doubt there will be a diversity of sentiments on this important subject; and, to inform the judgment, it is necessary to hear all arguments that can be advanced. To please all is impossible, and to attempt it would be vain. The only way, therefore, is, under all the views in which it can be placed, and with a due consideration to circumstances, habits, etc., etc., to form such a Government as will bear the scrutinizing eye of criticism, and trust it to the good sense and patriotism of the people to carry it into effect. Demagogues, men who are unwilling to lose any of their State consequence, and interested characters in each, will oppose any General Government. But let these be regarded rightly, and justice, it is to be hoped, will at length prevail."

MONDAY, JULY 2, 1787

IN CONVENTION

Immediately after its assembling this day, the Convention faced the crucial question — Ellsworth's motion for equality of representation in the Senate. To the despair of some and the relief of many others, no decision was reached; for the vote resulted in a tie — five States voting on each side — Connecticut, New York, New Jersey, Delaware, and Maryland favoring the motion; while Massachusetts, Pennsylvania, Virginia, North Carolina, and South Carolina were opposed, and Georgia was equally divided. The absence of two men changed the fate of the Constitution and the whole future history of the country. William Pierce of Georgia had gone to New York to attend Congress (and incidentally to fight a duel).[1] Daniel of St. Thomas Jenifer of Maryland was late in taking his seat that morning. Both of these men were opposed to equality of representation. Had Pierce been present, the vote of Georgia would not have been equally divided and would have been cast with the large States. Had Jenifer been more prompt in his attendance, the vote of Maryland (actually cast by Luther Martin with the small States) would have been divided, and the large States would have prevailed on the motion.[2] On such slight chance circumstances did this crisis depend.

[1] Alexander Hamilton was to serve as second to Pierce's adversary in the duel; see Hamilton to Pierce, July, 1787; Hamilton to Auldjo, July 26, 1787; *Writings of Alexander Hamilton* (Lodge's ed., 1904), IX, 419, 420, 421.

[2] Interesting explanations of this situation have been given. Luther Martin, in his letter to the Maryland Legislature, described the vote as follows: "Georgia had only two representatives on the floor, one of whom (not, I believe, because he was against the measure, but from a conviction that we would go home and thereby dissolve the Convention before we would give up the question) voted also in the negative by which that State was divided. On this question, Mr. Martin was the only delegate for Maryland present, which circumstance secured the State a negative. Immediately after the question had been taken and the President had declared the votes, Mr. Jenifer came into the Convention; when Mr. King of Massachusetts, valuing himself on Mr. Jenifer to divide the State of Maryland on this question as he had on the former, requested of the President that the question might be put again. However, the motion was too extraordinary in its nature to meet with success." *Elliot's Debates*, I, 356.

Max Farrand in *The Framing of the Constitution* (1913), p. 96, says: "The vote was a tie — five States to five. This unexpected result was achieved through a combination of two circumstances. Jenifer of Maryland was absent, thus enabling Luther Martin to cast the vote of that State in the affirmative; and Abraham Baldwin by changing his vote to the affirmative (in favor of equality of representation) divided the vote of Georgia. . . . Baldwin was a former Connecticut man and so was doubtless in friendly understanding with the attitude of the delegates of that State."

William Garrott Brown in *The Life of Oliver Ellsworth* (1905), p. 144, says: "It was Georgia that had changed. Her vote, hitherto regularly given to the majority, was this time divided. It was, in fact, one man only that had changed, and that man was Abraham Baldwin, a native of Connecticut, a graduate and sometime tutor of Yale, and but recently become a citizen of the State which he now sat for. The facts countenance a conjecture that the personal influence of the three leading men of his native State may have helped to turn him; but he may also have felt, as Georgia was the last State to vote and had but two representatives, that he and his colleague had to decide whether the Convention should continue in existence."

The Convention had reached an entire impasse. Charles Pinckney and General Charles C. Pinckney now expressed their desire for an agreement, and the latter proposed that a Committee consisting of a member from each State be appointed to devise and report for some compromise. His suggestion was strongly supported. Gouverneur Morris, who had been absent since May 30, and who had just returned from New York, now took occasion to interpolate an elaborate and not very pertinent speech, expounding his theories as to the necessity of life tenure in the Senate, in order to establish the independence of that body.[1] The striking feature of this speech, however,

[1] An interesting illustration of the danger of trusting to oral tradition occurs in the *Life of Gouverneur Morris,* by Jared Sparks. In writing this book, before Madison's *Notes of Debates* had been published, and while the only knowledge of the Convention was to be obtained from the Journal and from Yates' *Notes,* Sparks asked Madison whether the following anecdote then current, as to Morris, was correct: "While the Convention was sitting, Mr. Morris was absent for several days. On his return to Philadelphia, he called at the house of Robert Morris, where he found General Washington, who, as well as Robert Morris, was much dejected at what they regarded the deplorable state of things in the Convention. Debates had run high, conflicting opinions were obstinately adhered to, animosities were kindling, some of the members were threatening to go home, and, at this alarming crisis, a dissolution of the Convention was hourly to be apprehended. Instructed in these particulars, Gouverneur Morris went into the Convention on the day following, and spoke with such eloquence and power, on the necessity of union, of partial sacrifices, and temperate discussion, that he contributed much to work a change in the feeling of the members, which was the means of restoring harmony and ultimately of attaining the objects of the Convention. It is added that, as his absence had prevented his partaking of the warmth which had been excited by the previous discussions, his counsel and coolness had the greater effect." In reply, Madison wrote to Sparks, April 8, 1831: "It is certain that the return of Mr. Morris to the Convention was at a critical stage of its proceedings. . . . Great zeal and pertinacity had been shown on both sides, and an equal division of votes on the question had been reiterated and prolonged, till it had become not only distressing but seriously alarming. . . . This crisis was not over when Mr. Morris is said to have had an interview and conversation with General Washington and Mr. Robert Morris, such as may well have occurred. But it appears that on the day of his re-entering the Convention, a proposition had been made from another quarter to refer the knotty question to a Committee, with a view to compromise, the indications being that sundry members from the larger States were relaxing in their opposition. . . . Mr. Morris . . . combated the compromise throughout. The tradition is, however, correct, that on the day of his resuming his seat, he entered with anxious feelings into the debate, and in one of his speeches painted the consequences of an abortive result to the Convention, in all the deep colors suited to the occasion. But it is not believed that any material influence on the turn which things took could be ascribed to his efforts; for besides the mingling with them of some of his most disrelished ideas,

to be particularly noted, was that he stated his "fears of the influence of the rich" whose "schemes will be favored by the extent of the country. The people in such distant parts cannot communicate and act in concert. They will be the dupes of those who have more knowledge and intercourse. The only security against encroachments will be a select and sagacious body of men instituted to watch against them on all sides." Randolph favored a Committee, though, said he, "considering the warmth exhibited in debate on Saturday, I have, I confess, no great hopes that any good will arise from it." Caleb Strong of Massachusetts, Sherman of Connecticut, and Lansing of New York thought that a Committee might be useful, and Williamson of North Carolina said that "if we do not concede on both sides, our business will soon be at an end." Gerry of Massachusetts said that: "Something must be done, or we shall disappoint not only America, but the whole world. . . . We must make concessions on both sides. Without these, the Constitutions of the several States would never have been formed."

The only leaders who held out to the end against any compromise on this question were Wilson and Madison; but the Convention, with only Pennsylvania dissenting, voted to elect by ballot such a Committee, and the following were chosen: from the large States, Gerry, Franklin, Mason, Davie, and Rutledge; from the small States, Ellsworth, Yates, Paterson, Bedford, and Martin; from Georgia, Baldwin (who had voted for the Ellsworth amendment on this day, when Georgia divided its vote). To give this Committee time to consider, the Convention adjourned over the ensuing holiday, until Thursday, July 5.

the topics of his eloquent appeals to the members had been exhausted during his absence and their minds were too much made up to be susceptible of new impressions."

OUT OF CONVENTION

Washington noted:

"Attended Convention. Dined with some of the Members of Convention at the Indian Queen. Drank tea at Mr. Bingham's, and walked afterwards in the State House Yard. Set this morning for Mr. Pine who wanted to correct his portrait of me [painted in 1785]."

The *American Herald* in Boston, on this day, urged acceptance of any plan which might "be recommended by the united wisdom of the Convention":

"Many have been handed out already by the imagination of writers. In our humble opinion no government can be entirely safe for the liberty of the subject unless the three distinct powers are lodged in separate hands. We ought, however, to submit this matter to that great council with the most respectful confidence. It would be better to embrace almost any expedient rather than to remain as we are. . . . It is wished the people may be awakened to the necessity of the measure and be on their guard against these pretended friends but real enemies who may perhaps approach them with the mask of gravity and popular zeal and enkindle jealousy and faction to the ruin of our fairest prospects."

TUESDAY, JULY 3, 1787

The Convention did not sit on this day. Washington noted: [1]

"Sat before the meeting of the Convention for Mr. [Charles Willson] Peale, who wanted my picture to make a print or Mezzatinto by. Dined at Mr. Morris's and

---

[1] In the *Massachusetts Centinel*, Sept. 29, 1787, the following advertisement appeared: "A mezzatinto print of his Excellency General Washington by Charles Willson Peale of this city, from a portrait which he painted since the sitting of the Convention is now compleated. The likeness is esteemed the best that has been executed in a print. . . . The price of these prints in a neat oval frame (the inner frame gilt) is two dollars each, or one dollar for the print only; and a large allowance will be made to those who purchase to sell again. Apply to Charles W. Peale at the corner of Third and Lombard Streets, Phil." Carpenter's Hall was located at Fourth and Chestnut Streets.

drank tea at Mr. Powell's. After which, in company with him, I attended the Agricultural Society at Carpenter's Hall."

Jacob Hiltzheimer wrote in his diary:

"Before breakfast went with my daughter, Hannah, to the meadows, where I found three men mowing the five acre piece. On returning, we met his Excellency General Washington taking a ride on horseback, only his coachman, Giles, with him."

Richard Dobbs Spaight, a delegate from North Carolina, wrote this day to James Iredell that: "The Convention has made, as yet, but little progress in the business they have met on; and it is a matter of uncertainty when they will finish. Secrecy being enjoined, I can make no communications on that head." [1]

[1] McRee's *Iredell*, II.

CHAPTER FIVE

THE GREAT COMPROMISE

WEDNESDAY, JULY 4, 1787

The Convention did not sit on this holiday; but the members took part in the celebration of Independence Day, which was marked by military maneuvres, dinners, and speeches.

Washington noted:

"Visited Dr. Chovet's Anatomical figures, and (the Convention having adjourned for the purpose) went to hear (at the Calvinist Church) an Oration on the Anniversary of Independence delivered by a Mr. Mitchell, a student of law. After which I dined with the State Society of Cincinnati at Epple's Tavern, and drank tea at Mr. Powell's."

The celebration was described by the *Herald*, the next day, stating that: the Society of the Cincinnati (of which he, Washington, had just been elected President General, and of which General Arthur St. Clair was local President, and Chief Justice Thomas

McKane was Vice President) "met at the State-House, marched in procession, with accompanyments of music from martial instruments and ringing of bells, to the new German Lutheran Church in Race Street, where an oration well adapted to the occasion was delivered to a very numerous and crowded auditory by James Campbell, Esq.[1] Entertainments were prepared at the City Tavern, at Eppel's, Gray's Ferry, Fishhouse, Wigwam, Geiffe's and Lilliput on the Jersey Shore, etc., where different parties from this city and Jersey met with mutual congratulations, and spent the remainder of the day with liberality and good humor which always mark and characterize the Sons of Freedom on this glorious festival."[2]

The subject of the oration by James Campbell was "The Advantages which have resulted to Mankind from the Independence of America."[3] Addressing himself particularly to Members of the Convention, he said:

"Illustrious Senate! to you your country looks with anxious expectation, on your decisions she rests, convinced that men who cut the cords of foreign legislation are competent to framing a system of Government which will embrace all interests, call forth our resources, and establish our credit. But in every plan for improvement or reformation, may an attachment to the principles of our present Government be the characteristic of an American, and

[1] It may be noted that Washington apparently mistook the name of the orator, in recording it in his diary.

[2] The *Gazette* described the day, as follows: "Early in the morning, the Light Horse Artillery Light Infantry, together with Col. Willis' battallion of Militia, assembled on the Commons; and after performing various evolutions, etc. fired a feu de joie. The train of artillery fired the salute of the United States, with three times thirteen rounds. The officers of the Militia and the corps in uniform then attended the State Society of Cincinnati, who met at the State House and marched in procession, with accompaniments of music from martial instruments and ringing of bells to the New Reformed Calvinist Church in Race Street. . . ."

[3] *An Oration Delivered at the Reformed Calvinist Church in Philadelphia, by James Campbell, Esq., to which is prefixed an Introductory Prayer by Rev. William Rogers* (1787).

may every proposition to add kingly power to our Federal system be regarded as treason to the liberties of our country."

He noted as one of the advantages, the development of the science of Government as shown "in the wisdom and energy of many of our Constitutions, and witness the literary productions of those illustrious civilians, Jefferson and Adams, whose works are not only calculated to instruct their countrymen but to enlighten Europe and posterity in the great science of social and political happiness." But, since "our Constitutions were made upon the spur of the occasion, with a bayonet at our breasts, and in the infancy of our knowledge of Government and its principles," it might be admitted that they were not perfect or entirely "accommodated to the temper of our citizens." Yet, said he:

"How fallen would be the character we have acquired in the establishment of our liberties, if we discover inability to form a suitable Government to preserve them! Is the science of Government so difficult that we have not men among us capable of unfolding its mysteries and binding our States together by mutual interests and obligations? . . . Methinks, I already see the stately fabric of a free and vigorous Government rising out of the wisdom of the Foederal Convention. I behold order and contentment pervading every part of the United States, our forests falling before the hand of labour, our fields doubling their encrease from the effects of well directed industry, our villages enlivened by useful manufactures, and our cities thriving under foreign and domestic commerce. I behold millions of freemen covering the shores of our rivers and lakes with all the arts and enjoyment of civilized life, and on the Anniversary of the Day, 1887, shouting forth the praises of the heroes and patriots who, in 1776, secured and extended to them all their happiness."

Comment was made later by the *Herald* (July 14) that the blessings brought about by the Declaration of Independence must be perpetuated by the Convention : [1]

"When we look forward to the happiness, the power and the dignity which the event of that great day ought to communicate to our posterity, it becomes us, in the pride of our honest triumphs, to promote the means for perpetuating the blessings we enjoy and to expect with zeal and confidence from the Federal Convention a system of Government adequate to the security and preservation of those rights which were promulgated by the ever memorable Declaration of Independency."

The same sentiments were eloquently voiced by Dr. Benjamin Rush in an address made by him in Philadelphia, this day, in which he said : [2]

"There is nothing more common than to confound the terms of American Revolution with those of the late American War. The American War is over; but this is far from being the case with the American Revolution. On the contrary, nothing but the first act of the great drama is closed. It remains yet to establish and perfect our new forms of Government; and to prepare the principles, morals and manners of our citizens for these forms of Government after they are established and brought to perfection. The Confederation,

---

[1] It may be noted that at the celebration of the day by the Society of the Cincinnati, in Trenton, New Jersey, one of the toasts was: "The Grand Convention — may they form a Constitution for an eternal Republic." The *Massachusetts Centinel*, July 14, 1787, quoted another toast: "The Federal Convention — may the result of their meeting be as glorious as its members are illustrious"; and the *Pennsylvania Gazette*, July 18, a toast at Lancaster: "The members of the present Convention — may they do as much towards the support of our independence as their virtuous President did towards its establishment."

[2] *Principles and Acts of the Revolution* (1822), by Hezekiah Niles. The *Pennsylvania Gazette*, May 30, and the *New York Daily Advertiser*, June 4, 1787, published the following suggestions for ensuing celebrations of Independence Day: "As the day for celebrating the anniversary of independence is approaching, a correspondent proposes that added to the usual mode of celebrating it, a suitable person should be pitched upon in the different villages, counties or townships, to introduce the entertainment of the day with an oration upon some subject connected with the liberty of the Government of the United States. When a clergyman can be had, delivery of a prayer suited to the day should precede the delivery of the oration. By these means, rational entertainment and useful knowledge may be blended with the pleasures of the table, and the history of important events and illustrious characters may be conveyed in an easy and agreeable manner to posterity."

together with most of our State Constitutions, were formed under very unfavorable circumstances. We had just emerged from a corrupted monarchy. Although we understood perfectly the principles of liberty, yet most of us were ignorant of the forms and combinations of power in republic. . . . In our opposition to monarchy, we forgot that the temple of tyranny has two doors. We bolted one of them by proper restraints; but we left the other open, by neglecting to guard against the effects of our own ignorance and licentiousness."

On this Fourth of July, John Jay was writing from New York to John Adams in London, as to the Convention:

"The public attention is turned to the Convention. Their proceedings are kept secret, and it is uncertain how long they will continue to sit. It is, nevertheless, probable that the importance and variety of objects that must engage their attention will detain them longer than many may expect. It is much to be wished that the result of their deliberations may place the United States in a better situation; for if their measures should either be inadequate or rejected, the duration of the Union will become problematical. For my own part, I am convinced that a National Government, as strong as may be compatible with liberty, is necessary to give us National security and respectability. Your book gives us many useful lessons; for, although I cannot subscribe to your chapter on Congress, yet I consider the work as a valuable one, and one that will tend greatly to recommend and establish those principles of government on which alone the United States can erect any political structure worth the trouble of erecting."

THURSDAY, JULY 5, 1787

IN CONVENTION

Report of the Compromise

On this day, Elbridge Gerry brought into the Convention the Report of the Committee appointed on July 2. As hoped for, it contained the grounds of a compromise, founded on a motion made in the Committee by Doctor Franklin, who, as usual, took this opportunity to employ his conciliatory methods. It recommended three propositions — (*a*) that in the first branch of the Legislature, there should be one Representative for every 40,000 inhabitants; (*b*) that this first branch should have the power to originate all bills for raising or appropriating money and for fixing salaries, not to be altered or amended by the second branch; (*c*) that in the second branch, each State should have an equal vote.

As Madison states, this compromise was regarded as a victory by the smaller States. Before taking up the specific proposals, the leading delegates gave energetic expression to their general views of the situation. Ellsworth, Gerry, and Mason — one from a small State and two from the large States — urged acceptance of the compromise, though each had objections to parts of it. Unless a compromise should take place, they said, a secession would occur; and if "we do not come to some agreement among ourselves, some foreign sword will probably do the work for us." "Accommodation is the object," said Mason, and though "it could not be more inconvenient to any gentleman to remain absent from his private affairs than it was for him, he would bury his bones in this city rather than expose his country to the consequences of a dissolution of this Convention without anything being done." Paterson, however, thought that the Report yielded too much to the large States and stated his intention to vote against it. The three great Nationalists — Wilson, Madison, and G. Morris — also opposed the Compromise Report. Madison stated that if he must have the option between justice and gratifying the majority of the people, or conciliating the smaller States, he must choose the former. "It was in vain to purchase concord in the Convention on terms which would perpetuate discord among their constituents. The Convention ought to pursue a plan which would bear the test of examination and which would be espoused and supported by the enlightened and impartial part of America." He did not believe that Delaware and other smaller States would bid defiance to the rest of the Union. Wilson said that he "was not deficient in a conciliating temper, but firmness was sometimes a duty of higher obligation." G. Morris also thought the whole theory of the Compromise Report to be wrong. He said that: "He came here as a Representative of America; he flattered himself that he came here in some degree as a Representative of the whole human race; for the whole human race will be affected by the proceedings of this Convention. He wished gentlemen to extend their views beyond the present moment of time, beyond the various limits of peace, from which they derive their political origin." We are not here, he said, "to truck and bargain for our particular States. . . . State attachments and State importance have been the bane of this country. . . . He wished our ideas to be enlarged to the true interest of man, instead of being circumscribed within the narrow compass of a particular spot." These views he repeated, later, saying that: "It had been early said by Mr. Gerry that the new Government would be partly National, partly Federal; that it ought in the first quality to protect individuals; in the second, the State. But in what quality was it to protect the aggregate interests of the whole? Among the many provisions which had been urged, he had seen none for supporting the dignity and splendor of the American empire. It had been one of our greatest misfortunes that the great views of the

Nation had been sacrificed constantly to local views."
And again, he said, that though "the States had many
Representatives on the floor . . . he feared few were
to be deemed the Representatives of America." [1]

OUT OF CONVENTION

Washington noted:

"Attended Convention. Dined at Mr. Morris's and
drank tea there, spent the evening also."

Nathan Dane wrote, this day, from New York to
Rufus King of Massachusetts:

"I am very sorry to hear you say that it is uncertain what
will be the result of the Convention, because I infer there
must be a great diversity of sentiments among the members.
The Convention must do something. Its meeting has all
those effects which we and those who did not fully discern
the propriety of the measure apprehended. You know the
general opinion is, that our Federal Constitution must be
mended; and if the Convention do not agree at least in some
amendments, a universal despair of our keeping together
will take place. It seems to be agreed here that the Virginia plan was admitted to come upon the floor of investigation by way of experiment and with a few yieldings on this
point, and that it keeps its ground at present. The contents
of this plan was known to some, I believe, before the Convention met. Perhaps the public mind will be prepared in
a few years to receive this new system."

FRIDAY, JULY 6, 1787

IN CONVENTION

Power to Originate Money Bills

The Convention, at the outset, referred to a Special
Committee that part of the Report of the Compromise
Committee, which fixed the ratio of votes in the
House at one member for every 40,000 inhabitants.

[1] Gouverneur Morris, July 7, 10, 1787.

It then proceeded to consider the second portion of the
proposed compromise, giving to the House the exclusive right to originate bills for raising or appropriating money. A curious mixture of views appeared
with reference to this. The proposal had apparently
originated with Gerry. As early as June 13, he had
moved to restrain the Senatorial branch from originating money bills, saying that: "The other branch
was more immediately the representative of the people, and it was a maxim that the people ought to
hold the purse strings." Gerry's proposal was in
accord with the provisions of most of the State
Constitutions, viz., those of Delaware, Maryland,
Massachusetts, New Hampshire, New Jersey, South
Carolina, and Virginia, in which power to originate
money bills lay exclusively in the lower branch of the
Legislature (though Delaware, Massachusetts, and
New Hampshire allowed its Senate to alter or amend).
Hugh Williamson of North Carolina had favored the
proposal, as "it will oblige some member in the lower
branch to move, and people can then mark him."
Pierce Butler of South Carolina had said that he saw
no reason for such a discrimination; that though it
was borrowed from the British Constitution, there was
no analogy between the Senate and the House of
Lords; and he had then made two curious arguments
against it — prophecies, one of which was never ful-
filled, but the other of which showed foresight of a
practice which has been frequently indulged in by the
House. "If the Senate shall be degraded," he said,
"by any such discriminations, the best men would be
apt to decline serving in it, in favor of the other branch;"
and, he continued, "it will lead the latter into the
practice of tacking other clauses to money bills." King
and Madison had concurred in opposing, saying that
"as the Senate would be generally a more capable set

of men, it would be wrong to disable them " in this way ; and that the proposal if adopted must be extended to amending as well as to originating money bills. Sherman had said that as the Senate would bear their share of the taxes, they would also be representatives of the people ; and that the right of both branches to originate money bills had prevailed in Connecticut and had been found to be "safe and convenient." General Pinckney had said that Gerry's proposed system prevailed in South Carolina, "and has been a source of pernicious disputes between the two branches; moreover, it was evaded by the Senate's handing amendments, informally, to the House." Gerry's motion receiving little support had been rejected, only New York, Delaware, and Virginia voting for it. This action by the Convention had shown clearly that they regarded the new Senate which they were about to constitute, as a Legislative body of an entirely different nature from the Senates under the State Constitutions; for, unless this was so, it is unlikely that the Convention would have failed to follow the provisions of those Constitutions.

When the delegates, on this July 6, took up this part of the compromise, they appeared to be split into five distinct factions : (a) those delegates from the smaller States who opposed taking this power from the Senate in any event; (b) those from the smaller States who, though opposed, were willing to vote for it as a concession or compromise; (c) those from the larger States who regarded it as an essential right to be possessed by the House since that body as the immediate representatives of the people ought to have control of the people's money, and since the large States would probably have a majority in the House ; (d) those from the larger States who regarded the right as of no consequence and hence as constituting no concession whatever on the part of the smaller States; (*e*) those from the larger States who regarded the deprivation of the Senate of this right as fundamentally wrong in theory, and likely to be a dangerous source of dispute between the two branches.[1] The delegates comprising (*b*) and (*c*) were willing to vote for this provision; those comprising (*a*), (*d*), and (*e*) were opposed to it. This part of the compromise was debated on July 5; and it was the first to be adopted, on July 6, by a vote of five States to three (Pennsylvania, Virginia, and South Carolina voting against it, and Massachusetts, New York, and Georgia being divided). It was carried, therefore, by North Carolina voting with the smaller States of Connecticut, New Jersey, Delaware, and Maryland. Reconsideration of this vote was had on July 14, but on July 16, the whole compromise, including this provision as to money bills, was accepted (as hereafter described) by five States to four, with Massachusetts divided — North Carolina again joining with the smaller States.

OUT OF CONVENTION

Washington noted :

"Sat for Mr. Peale in the morning. Attended Convention. Dined at the City Tavern with some members of Convention, and spent the evening at my lodgings."

Dr. William Samuel Johnson noted, this day : "Hot. In Convention. Dined G. Washington." A Philadelphia despatch published in many other States said : [2]

"A correspondent remarks that the Convention now sitting seems quite novel in the history of governments, and stands remarkable and alone in political history. After establishments of governments in various parts of the Con-

---

[1] (*a*) Mercer (Aug. 8); Carroll (Aug. 13); (*b*) Bedford, Ellsworth, Gerry, Mason; (*c*) Williamson, Dr. Franklin; (*d*) Madison, Butler, Pinckney, General Pinckney; (*e*) G. Morris, Wilson, Rutledge (Aug. 13).

[2] See *Connecticut Courant*, July 16; *Salem Mercury*, July 17, 1787.

tinent, some of which have been forced upon the majority of the government, and after the existence of others which have not only been cheerfully submitted to but eagerly embraced by the people; it is still singular to see an authority, however great and respectable in itself, presiding tacitly over the Confederation of the States by voluntary election."

Joseph Jones wrote from Virginia to Madison relative to the vacancy left by the departure of George Wythe, from the Convention, and also said:

"It is supposed by some Dr. McClurg will soon retire. Should that be the case, and the other gentlemen remain, I am inclined to think from what formerly passed at the Board, they will be deemed a representation competent to the great objects for which they were appointed. If the Massachusetts Assembly should pursue such measures, as from the specimens you mention there is reason to fear they will, the example may probably prove contagious and spread into New Hampshire; whereby the Eastern politics will become formidable, and from the principles which appear to govern them and the number of adherents pernicious consequences are to be apprehended."

SATURDAY, JULY 7, 1787

IN CONVENTION

On this day, a preliminary vote was taken to the effect that the clause allowing each State one vote in the Senate should stand as a part of the Report. It was recognized, however, that this was not a final action. "This is the critical question," said Gerry, and while opposed to the provision as a separate question, "he had rather agree to it than have no accommodation." For, said he, "a Government short of a proper National plan, if generally acceptable, would be preferable to a proper one which, if it could be carried out at all, would operate on discontented States." G. Morris said, "he had no resolution unalterably fixed except to do what should finally appear to him right," but that he was opposed to the Report.[1]

OUT OF CONVENTION

Washington noted:

"Attended Convention. Dined at the Cold Spring with the Club at Springsbury. Returned in the evening and drank tea at Mr. Meredith's."

On this day, the *Packet* again repeated the ridiculously erroneous report that: "So great is the unanimity we hear that prevails in the Convention upon all great federal subjects, that it has been proposed to call the room in which they assemble Unanimity Hall." This statement, reprinted throughout the country, long deceived the people as to the situation in the Convention.[2] It is not improbable that it was intended to do so.

SUNDAY, JULY 8, 1787

Washington noted:

"About 12 o'clock rid to Doctor Logan's near Germantown, where I dined. Returned in the evening and drank tea at Mr. Morris's."

This visit paid to Dr. George Logan at his estate of Stenton was later described by his widow, in a striking picture of the human side of Washington. "His reputation as a skilful agriculturist procured for him the grateful favour of a visit from the 'Father of his Country', then in Philadelphia officiating as President of the Federal Convention. He came with his friend

---

[1] Madison wrote to Jared Sparks, April 8, 1831: "It is but due to Mr. Morris to remark that to the brilliancy of his genius, he added — what is too rare — a candid surrender of his opinions, when the lights of discussion satisfied him that they had been too hastily formed, and a readiness to aid in making the best of measures in which he had been overruled."

[2] See *Pennsylvania Gazette*, July 18; *Pennsylvania Herald*, July 21; *Pennsylvania Journal*, July 21; *New York Daily Advertiser*, July 23; *American Herald* (Boston), July 30; *Connecticut Courant*, July 30, 1787.

Daniel Jenifer, Esq. of Maryland, who had often before
been with us, and passed a day at Stenton in the most
social and friendly manner imaginable, delighted with
the fine grass land and beautiful experiments with
gypsum, some of which plainly showed initials and
words traced upon the sod of a far richer hue and thick-
ness than the surrounding grass, and other subjects of
rural economy which Dr. Logan then had to show. His
praise conferred distinction, nor did he make me less
happy by his pleasing attention to myself and his kind
notice of my children whom he caressed in the most
endearing manner, placing my little boy on his knee
and taking my infant in his arms with commendations
that made their way immediately to a mother's heart.
I had always looked up to General Washington, from
the first time that I ever heard his auspicious name, as
a rare and perfect pattern of the dignity to which man
might attain by living up to the laws of virtue and
honour, and now that I beheld the colossal greatness
at nearer view, I perceived it polished and adorned with
all the amenity and gentleness which delights and
endears in domestic society." [1]

Francis Hopkinson wrote this day from Philadelphia
to Jefferson that: "It will be very difficult to frame
such a system of Union and Government for America
as shall suit all opinions and reconcile clashing interests.
Their deliberations are kept inviolably secret, so that
they sit without censure or remark; but no sooner will
the chicken be hatched but everyone will be plucking
a feather." Dr. Hugh Williamson, a delegate from
North Carolina, wrote to James Iredell: "I think it
more than likely that we shall not leave this place
before the middle of August. The diverse and almost
opposite interests that are to be reconciled occasion

[1] *Memoirs of Dr. George Logan of Stenton* (1899), by Deborah Norris Logan,
p. 44.

us to progress very slowly. I fear that Davie will be obliged to leave us before our business is finished, which will be a heavy stroke to the delegation. We have occasion for his judgment, for I am inclined to think that the great exhibitions of political wisdom in our late Governor (Martin) while he sat at the helm of our State have so exhausted his fund that time must be required to enable him again to exert his abilities to the advantage of the Nation."

MONDAY, JULY 9, 1787
IN CONVENTION

The Convention had under discussion the first portion of the Compromise Report as to representation in the House.   The arrival of Daniel Carroll (the third delegate from Maryland), on this day, made it certain that the vote of the State of Maryland would be cast on the compromise proposal; hitherto, its vote had been divided, owing to the divergent views of Luther Martin and Jenifer.

OUT OF CONVENTION

Washington noted :

"Sat in the morning for Mr. Peale.   Attended Convention.   Dined at Mr. Morris's and accompanied Mrs. Morris to Doctr. [John] Redman's, 3 miles in the Country, where we drank tea and returned."

TUESDAY, JULY 10, 1787
IN CONVENTION

The Convention continued its discussion of the mode of representation in the House.

On this day, two of the three delegates from New York — Robert Yates and John Lansing — left the Convention and never returned.[1] In a letter to

[1] George Mason in a conversation with Jefferson, at Gunston Hall, Sept. 30, 1792, gave as the reason for their departure — the necessity that they should attend

Governor Clinton explaining their reasons for this action, they stated that they were convinced that the form of Government which the Convention was adopting was in excess of the powers vested in the delegates by the respective States and that it was impracticable to establish "a General Government pervading every part of the United States and extending essential benefits to all" — that such a Government, however guarded, "must unavoidably in a short time be productive of the destruction of the civil liberty of such citizens who could be effectively coerced by it." This defection of New York and its delegates was attributed by Madison to commercial reasons. Writing in 1833, he said that Yates and Lansing "were the Representatives of the dominant party in New York which was opposed to the Convention and the object of it, which was averse to any essential change in the Articles of Confederation, which had inflexibly refused to grant even a duty of 5 per cent. on imports for the urgent debt of the Revolution, which was availing itself of the peculiar situation of New York for taxing the consumption of her neighbors, and which foresaw that a primary aim of the Convention would be to transfer from the States to the Common Authorities the entire regulation of foreign commerce. Such were the feelings of the two Deputies that, on finding the Convention bent on radical reform of the Federal system, they left it in the midst of its discussions, and before the opinions and views of many of the members were drawn out to their final shape and practical application." [1]

Court in New York: "Yates and Lansing never voted *in one instance* with Hamilton, who was so much mortified at it that he went home. When the season for Courts came on, Yates a Judge and Lansing a lawyer went to attend the Courts. Then Hamilton returned." *Writings of Thomas Jefferson* (Ford's ed.), I, 238, "The Anas."

[1] *Writings of James Madison* (Hunt's ed.), IX, letter to John Tyler, 1833: see also Madison to Joseph Gales, Aug. 28, 1821: "Whatever may have been the personal worth of the two delegates . . . it cannot be unknown that they represented

OUT OF CONVENTION

Washington noted:

"Attended Convention. Dined at Mr. Morris's. Drank tea at Mr. Bingham's and went to the Play."

The play referred to was: "A Concert, in the first part of which will be introduced an Entertainment called the Detection or the Servants Hall in an Uproar, to which will be added a Comic Opera in two Acts called Love in a Camp or Patrick in Prussia, being the second part of the Poor Soldier, with the original Overture Accompaniments, etc., with entire new scenery, A View of the Camp at Grossentinz."[1]

the strong prejudices in New York against the object of the Convention, which was, among other things, to take from that State the important power over its commerce. . . ." And writing to Andrew Stevenson, March 25, 1826, he said: "Both Mr. Yates and Mr. (Luther) Martin brought to the Convention predispositions against its object, the one, from Maryland, representing the party of Mr. [Samuel] Chase opposed to Federal restraints on State legislation; the other, from New York, the party unwilling to lose the power over trade through which the State levied a tribute in the consumption of its neighbors. Both of them left the Convention long before it compleated its work, and appear to have reported in angry terms what they had observed with jaundiced eyes."

[1] Though under the Pennsylvania statutes, performance of theatrical plays was unlawful, such plays were, in fact, acted under the *nom de plume* of "concert." See advertisement in the *Pennsylvania Journal*, January 6, 1787, of a "Concert", at which "Lectures Moral and entertaining", were given, concluding with "A Grand pantomimical finale in two acts called Robinson Crusoe or Harlequin Friday. Concert at six. Vivat Respublica." The citizens of Philadelphia of that day, were even offered moving pictures. See an article in the *Pennsylvania Packet* of January 9, 1787, written by Charles Willson Peale (who during the Convention was about to paint General Washington's portrait) stating: "In Mr. Peale's first ideas of an exhibition of moving pictures, it was his intention to have occasionally added new pictures with figures moving by machinery, but the great labour and expense to produce effects in any tolerable degree imitating those wonderful and pleasing presentations which Dame Nature so frequently offers to our view, which to be made worthy the notice of an attentive observer, is such a labour as the present number of encouragers of the fine arts in this city will not support. This, from repeated trials, is a known fact, and Mr. Peale, in his present offers of entertainment to the Public, having thought it better to perfect what he had made than to attempt any new and difficult scene has considerably improved his six perspective views by new machinery. Mr. Peale takes this opportunity of thanking those Ladies and Gentlemen who have honored his exhibition with their company, and whose compassion for an artist's feelings have made them excuse the faults occasioned by accidents in a complicated machinery which have too frequently happened in the then promised representation. This, the last time of addressing the public on the subject of exhibitions, is partly to inform those who may yet desire to partake of the entertainment that Mr. Peale will only continue his Exhibitions of Moving Pictures with changeable effects for a short time, and then those pictures will be locked up, probably forever."

Nothing in his diary reveals any perturbation on Washington's part; but a letter written by him, this day, to Hamilton — an almost despairing letter — shows the seriousness of the situation in the Convention:

"I thank you for your communication of the 3d. When I refer you to the state of the counsels which prevailed at the period you left this city, and add that they are now, if possible, in a worse train than ever, you will find but little ground on which the hope of a good establishment can be formed. In a word, I almost despair of seeing a favorable issue to the proceedings of our Convention, and do therefore repent having had any agency in the business. The men who oppose a strong and energetic Government, are, in my opinion, narrow-minded politicians, or are under the influence of local views. The apprehension expressed by them, that the *people* will not accede to the form proposed, is the *ostensible*, not the *real* cause of opposition. But, admitting that the present sentiment is as they prognosticate, the proper question ought nevertheless to be: Is it or is it not the best form that such a country as this can adopt? If it be the best, recommend it, and it will assuredly obtain, maugre opposition. I am sorry you went away. I wish you were back. The crisis is equally important and alarming, and no opposition, under such circumstances, should discourage exertions till the signature is offered."

This letter was in answer to Hamilton's letter, written from New York, July 3, describing somewhat optimistically the attitude of men in New Jersey and New York towards the Convention:

"In my passage through the Jerseys and since my arrival here, I have taken particular pains to discover the public sentiment and I am more and more convinced that this is the critical opportunity for establishing the prosperity of this country on a solid foundation — I have conversed with men of information not only of this city but from different parts of the State; and they agree that there has been an astonish-

ing revolution for the better in the minds of the people.   The
prevailing apprehension among thinking men is, that the
Convention, from a fear of shocking the popular opinion, will
not go far enough.   They seem to be convinced that a strong,
well-mounted Government will better suit the popular palate
than one of a different complexion.   Men in office are indeed
taking all possible pains to give an unfavourable impression
of the Convention; but the current seems to be running
strongly the other way.   A plain but sensible man, in a conversation I had with him yesterday, expressed himself nearly
in this manner — The people begin to be convinced that
their 'excellent form of Government' as they have been used
to call it, will not answer their purpose; and that they must
substitute something not very remote from that which they
have lately quitted.   These appearances, though they will
not warrant a conclusion that the people are yet ripe for such
a plan as I advocate, yet serve to prove that there is no reason to despair of their adopting one equally energetic, if the
Convention should think proper to propose it.   They serve
to prove that we ought not to allow too much weight to
objections drawn from the supposed repugnancy of the
people to an efficient Constitution — I confess I am more and
more inclined to believe that former habits of thinking are
regaining their influence with more rapidity than is generally
imagined.   Not having compared ideas with you, Sir, I
cannot judge how far our sentiments agree; but as I persuade myself the genuineness of my representations will
receive credit with you, my anxiety for the event of the
deliberations of the Convention induces me to make this
communication of what appears to be the tendency of the
public mind. . . .   I own to you, Sir, that I am seriously and
deeply distressed at the aspect of the councils which prevailed when I left Philadelphia — I fear that we shall let
slip the golden opportunity of rescuing the American empire
from disunion, anarchy and misery — No motley or feeble
measure can answer the end or will finally receive the public
support.   Decision is true wisdom and will be not less rep-
utable to the Convention than salutary to the community.
   I shall of necessity remain here ten or twelve days; if I

have reason to believe that my attendance at Philadelphia will not be mere waste of time, I shall after that period rejoin the Convention."

William Blount wrote to Governor Caswell of North Carolina that he left New York for Philadelphia on June 18, and returned on July 4 :[1]

"I conceived it more for the benefit and honor of the State, in which opinion my colleagues in the Convention agreed, to return with Mr. Benj. Hawkins and represent the State in Congress than to continue in the Convention, especially as my colleagues in that body were generally unanimous and competent to the purposes of their mission."

WEDNESDAY, JULY 11, 1787

IN CONVENTION

The Convention continued its discussion of the mode of representation in the House.

THURSDAY, JULY 12, 1787

IN CONVENTION

The Convention continued its discussion of the mode of representation in the House.

FRIDAY, JULY 13, 1787

IN CONVENTION

Ratio of Representation in the House

Before making any final decision on the crucial part of the compromise — the equality of votes — the Convention entered into a long and excited debate on a subject which, strictly speaking, had not been referred to the Committee, but on which it had reported — namely, that in the House each State should have

[1] North Carolina State Archives, XX, 734.

one vote for every 40,000 inhabitants.[1] On this proposal, which in reality formed no part of the real compromise, a discussion took place of the greatest significance in character. In view of the contention made during recent years, that the Constitution was economic in its nature, framed chiefly in the interests of property and the privileged classes, it should be noted that, on at least three occasions, the direct issue was made in the Convention between property and non-property, and that each time the vote was against any privilege for property. One of those occasions occurred in this debate on the compromise, in the following manner. On July 5, Gouverneur Morris raised an objection to fixing the representation in the House on the basis of one member for every 40,000 inhabitants, as reported by the Committee, on the ground that "he thought property ought to be taken into the estimate as well as the number of inhabitants. Life and liberty were generally said to be of more value than property. An accurate view of the matter would nevertheless prove that property was the main object of Society." John Rutledge, General Pinckney, and Pierce Butler of South Carolina concurred. So did Rufus King and Elbridge Gerry of Massachusetts. The question was referred, on July 6, to a Committee,

---

[1] Gen. Charles C. Pinckney in the South Carolina State Convention of 1788 stated: "The numbers in the different States according to the most accurate accounts we could obtain were: New Hampshire, 102,000; Massachusetts, 360,000; Rhode Island, 58,000; Connecticut, 202,000; New York, 238,000; New Jersey, 138,000; Pennsylvania, 360,000; Delaware, 37,000; Maryland (including three fifths of 80,000 negroes), 218,000; Virginia (including three fifths of 280,000 negroes), 420,000; North Carolina (including three fifths of 60,000 negroes), 200,000; South Carolina (including three fifths of 80,000 negroes), 150,000; Georgia (including three fifths of 20,000 negroes), 90,000. Total population of the United States (including 520,000 negroes), 2,781,000."

It is to be noted that these figures differed greatly from the estimate of population which had appeared in the *Pennsylvania Packet*, Dec. 11, 1786, as follows: New Hampshire, 150,000; Massachusetts, 400,000; Rhode Island, 59,670; Connecticut, 192,000; New York, 250,000; New Jersey, 150,000; Pennsylvania, 300,000; Delaware, 50,000; Maryland, 320,000; Virginia, 650,000; North Carolina, 300,000; South Carolina, 225,000; Georgia, 56,000.

composed of G. Morris, Gorham, Randolph, Rutledge, and King. Three days later, the Committee reported, fixing the number of Representatives from each State, respectively, for the first meeting of the Legislature (with a total of fifty-six Representatives, changed later to sixty-five), and also providing that "as the present situation of the States may probably alter as well in point of wealth as in number of inhabitants", the Legislature should have power from time to time to increase the numbers; it also reported that, in case of admission of new States, the Legislature should "possess authority to regulate the number of Representatives upon the principles of wealth and number of inhabitants." The latter part of the Report was at first accepted without debate (on July 9). But on a proposal by Randolph (on July 10) that a census be taken to ascertain the alterations in population and wealth of all the States, at regular intervals, and that the Legislature arrange the representation accordingly, vigorous opposition arose to the allowance of wealth as a basis for representation. Wilson, Madison, Sherman, Dr. W. S. Johnson, and Gorham favored fixing numbers alone as the perpetual standard. "Wealth is an impracticable rule", said Wilson, and even if it were not, population is "a sufficiently accurate measure of wealth." Underlying the whole debate was the feeling by some of the Northern delegates that slaves, if regarded by the Southerners as property, ought not to receive any representation whatever.[1] Perceiving this opposition to a representation of their slaves under the guise of property, the Southern

[1] Paterson, on July 9, said that he could regard negro slaves in no light but as property, and that if slaves were not represented in the States as voters they should not be in the General Government. New Jersey would, therefore, vote against "wealth" as a basis for representation. Gen. Pinckney, on July 10, "dwelt on the superior wealth of the Southern States and insisted on its having its due weight in the Government."

States now sought a change in the entire basis of popular election of the House. It will be recalled that, a month prior, on June 11, it had been voted that representation of the States in the House should be proportionate to the whole number of whites, together with two thirds of all others (except non-taxpaying Indians). Butler and Pinckney, now on July 11, insisted that blacks be included in the representation equally with whites. Gerry, Gorham, Mason, and Williamson opposed and the proposal was defeated, only Delaware, South Carolina, and Georgia favoring it. Thereupon, those delegates who took the position that negroes, if regarded by the South as property, were entitled to no more representation than any other form of property, now moved to exclude the negroes from even the three fifths representation which had been previously agreed upon. And this motion was adopted by a vote of six to four (Connecticut, Virginia, North Carolina, and Georgia being in the minority).[1] This action, however, so aroused the South that Davie of North Carolina stated that "he was sure that North Carolina would never confederate on any terms that did not rate them (the negroes) at least as three fifths. If the Eastern States meant, therefore, to exclude them altogether, the business was at an end." To this, a reply was made by G. Morris that "he came here to form a compact for the good of America", and that it was vain for some States to insist on such a compact on matters that other States will never agree to. It was G. Morris himself, however, who now provided a bridge over the difficulties which had arisen. On July 12, he suggested that to the clause empowering the Legislature to vary the representation according

---

[1] It is to be noted that South Carolina delegates voted with the Northern States to exclude the three-fifths representation, *not* because they favored the proposal, but because they wished the whole number of negroes to be counted in establishing their population.

to the principles of wealth and numbers of inhabitants, there be added a proviso, which, as amended by him, read : "That direct taxation shall be in proportion to representation." The purpose of this provision was to lessen the inducement to the Southern States to seek to increase their representation; since, by so doing, they would proportionally increase their share of the tax burden. It is important to note, however, that Morris and some other delegates from the North were actuated quite as much by their fears of conditions which might arise in the West, as by their anxiety over the South. They apprehended that the Western States, by increasing more rapidly in population than in wealth, might acquire a majority in Congress and tax unduly the property of the East. Against such possibilities, Morris' motion formed a protection. The motion was accepted without debate; and thus there was introduced into the Constitution the principle which had been long fought for in the American Colonies — that taxation and representation should go together. The Convention now made it certain that "when Congress, and especially the House of Representatives (where it was specifically provided that all revenue bills must originate), voted a tax upon property, it should be with the consciousness and under the responsibility that in so doing, the tax voted would proportionally fall upon the immediate constituents of those who imposed it." [1]

The danger lest the South would seek to gain excessive representation for its slaves being now lessened, since such increase would result in proportionate increase of taxation upon it, Ellsworth thought it safe to renew the proposal to allow representation of three fifths of the slaves, and he suggested that "the rule of contribution

[1] Fuller, C. J., in *Pollock* v. *Farmers Loan and Trust Co.* (1895), 158 U. S. 429, 556, 557.

by direct taxation . . . shall be the number of white inhabitants and three fifths of every other description", until some other rule could be devised by the Legislature. Randolph agreed with him that some representation of the slaves ought to be granted, and that, "as it was perceived that the design was entertained by some of excluding slaves altogether, the Legislature ought not to be left at liberty." He wished a binding provision in the Constitution. He proposed, therefore, that a census be taken every ten years of all the inhabitants of the States according to the total whites and three fifths of the blacks ratio.[1] Wilson agreed to this, but suggested that it be phrased so as to provide that the Legislature of the United States should proportion direct taxation in accordance with such census and that representation of the States be proportioned according to direct taxation. The Convention adopted this motion; and thus it entirely reversed its action of the previous day excluding representation of three fifths of the slaves. Madison's *Notes* contain no hint of the real reasons which brought about this change. The account given by Rufus King of Massachusetts, many years later, probably explains the action. Speaking in the Senate, March, 1819, he said:[2]

"The present House of Representatives consists of one hundred eighty-one members which are apportioned among the States in a ratio of one Representative for every 35,000

[1] Hamilton wrote in *The Federalist*, No. 54: "In one respect, the establishment of a common measure for representation and taxation will have a very salutary effect. As the accuracy of the census to be obtained by the Congress will necessarily depend, in a considerable degree, on the disposition, if not the coöperation, of the States, it is of great importance that the States should feel as little bias as possible to swell or reduce the amount of their numbers. Were their share of representation alone to be governed by this rule, they would have an interest in exaggerating their inhabitants. Were the rule to decide their share of taxation alone, a contrary temptation would prevail. By extending the rule to both objects, the States will have opposite interests, which will controul and balance each other, and produce the requisite impartiality."

[2] *Life and Correspondence of Rufus King* (1900), VI, 697–700.

Federal numbers, which are ascertained by adding to the whole number of free persons three fifths of the slaves. . . . Thus, while 35,000 free persons are requisite to elect one Representative in a State where slavery is prohibited, 25,559 free persons in Virginia may and do elect a Representative — so that five free persons of Virginia have as much power in the choice of Representatives to Congress, and in the appointment of Presidential electors, as seven free persons in any of the States in which slavery does not exist. This inequality in the appointment of Representatives was not misunderstood at the adoption of the Constitution; but as no one anticipated the fact that the whole of the revenue of the United States would be derived from indirect taxes (which cannot be supposed to spread themselves over the several States according to the rule for the appointment of direct taxes), but it was believed that a part of the contribution to the common treasury would be apportioned among the States by the rule for the apportionment of Representatives — the States in which slavery is prohibited ultimately, though with reluctance, acquiesced in the disproportionate number of Representatives. . . . The concession was, at the time, believed to be a great one, and has proved to have been the greatest which was made to secure the adoption of the Constitution. . . . The departure from this principle (equality of rights) in the disproportionate power and influence allotted to the slave States, was a necessary sacrifice to the establishment of the Constitution."

Having decided on population as a basis for representation, it became necessary to change the vote passed on July 9 which allowed the Legislature, on admission of new States, to regulate the number of Representatives "upon the principle of their wealth and number of inhabitants." Accordingly, Randolph, on July 13, moved to strike out the word "wealth." On this motion, Wilson made a powerful speech, in which he said that he "could not agree that property was the sole or primary object of Government and society.

The cultivation and improvement of the human mind was the most noble object. With respect to this object, as well as to other personal rights, numbers were surely the natural and precise measure of representation. And with respect to property, they could not vary much from the precise measure." The word "wealth" was voted to be stricken out by nine States, Delaware being divided. And in this manner, the first attempt to give property special recognition under the Constitution was defeated.

This debate made plain a line of cleavage in the Convention which was to become even more apparent — the division between the Southern and Northern States. As early as June 30, James Madison had said that: "The States were divided into different interests, not by their difference of size, but by other circumstances, the most natural of which resulted partly from climate, but principally from the effects of their having or not having slaves. These two causes concurred in forming the great division of interests in the United States. It did not lie between the large and small States; it lay between the Northern and Southern." On July 14, he said: "It seemed now to be pretty well understood that the real difference of interests lay not between the large and small, but between the Northern and Southern States. The institution of slavery and its consequences formed the line of discrimination." Rufus King had also said, on July 13, that he was "fully convinced that the question concerning a difference of interests did not lie where it had hitherto been discussed, between the great and small States, but between the Southern and Eastern." George Mason of Virginia, on July 13, said that he had "always conceived that the difference of interest in the United States lay not between the large and small, but the Northern and Southern States." Charles Pinckney said, on July 2, that there was "a real distinction between the Northern and Southern, the latter having peculiar commercial interests."

When the debate over the question of equality of representation in the Senate first arose, the line of division had been clearly between the larger and the smaller States. But towards the end of the debate, this line had plainly shifted. There were delegates from the larger States sharing the views of G. Morris, who started out with violently opposing equality of representation, but who modified his views, when the Convention refused to adopt wealth as a basis of representation in the House and when it yielded to the Southern insistence that three fifths of the slaves should be counted as inhabitants. This move convinced him that "the Southern gentlemen will not be satisfied unless they see the way open to their gaining a majority in the public councils. The consequence of such a transfer of power from the maritime to the interior and landed interest will be such an oppression of commerce, that he shall be obliged to vote for the vicious principle of equality in the second branch in order to provide some defence for the Northern States against it." The result of the insistence by the South on protecting their slave property was to favor the acceptance of the compromise in the North, so as to increase the influence of the North in the Senate. In fact, this was an aspect of the compromise which Madison (who opposed it) regarded (July 14) as very serious, viz. — "the perpetuity it would give to the preponderance of the Northern against the Southern States."

The Decennial Census

In connection with this matter of elimination of wealth as a basis for representation, the provision for a change in the representation of the States at regular intervals should be especially noted; for the reasons then existing for the inclusion of this provision prevail today. It arose as follows. The Compromise Committee's Report of July 5 provided for a representation only of the States then in the Union — one member for every 40,000 inhabitants. Nothing was said about any change in the future. The Special Committee, which reported on July 9, fixed a specific number of Representatives for each State, and authorized the Legislature to increase the number from time to time. Such an authority left the Legislature entirely supreme. It was at once objected by Randolph that, "as the number was not to be changed till the National Legislature should please, a pretext would never be wanting to postpone alterations, and keep the power in the hands of those possessed of it." [1] He accordingly moved (July 10) "that a census be taken at regular intervals", and that the Legislature arrange the representation accordingly. Mason (July 11) supported this, saying that "from the nature of man, we may be sure that those who have power in their hands will not give it up while they can retain it." As the Southern States increased, they must have some guarantee of increase in their Representatives, and this provision must be inserted in the Constitution. Williamson insisted on "making it the duty of the Legislature to do what is right and not leaving it at liberty to do or not to do it." Randolph urged that the power was now vested in the North and "would not be voluntarily renounced, and that it was consequently the duty of the Convention to secure its

---

[1] It may be noted that the Special Committee fixed a House consisting of fifty-six Members. This was referred to another Committee which reported, July 10, advising a House of sixty-five members — the increases suggested being seven from the States North of the Potomac and two from the States South. The total from the Northern States (including Rhode Island) would be forty-two; from the South twenty-three. Even if Maryland with its six votes were to be included with the South, there was a strong majority in the North.

renunciation when justice might so require, by some Constitutional provision." He urged that it was "inadmissible that a larger and more populous district of America should hereafter have less representation than a smaller and less populous district. If a fair representation of the people be not secured, the injustice of the Government will shake it to its foundations." Sherman of Connecticut and Gorham of Massachusetts were of the opinion that "the periods and rules of revising the representation ought to be fixed by the Constitution." General Pinckney "foresaw that if the revision of the census was left to the discretion of the Legislature, it would never be carried into execution. The rule must be fixed and the execution of it enforced by the Constitution."

There was a two-fold fear of leaving to the Legislature the power of future alterations in the representation of the States; first, lest the majority in control at any particular time should not make any change in the numbers of representation which would affect that control; second, lest the Legislature might change the *basis* of representation and might eliminate or increase the representation of the slaves. Randolph's motion, therefore, after being amended, was adopted (as above described) providing for a decennial census of inhabitants and for an apportionment by the Legislature of the United States of both representation and direct taxation "accordingly." This provision was, in substance, included in the draft of the Constitution reported by the Committee of Detail on August 6.[1]   It was debated and accepted on August

[1] In this Report, the Committee of Detail reinserted the provision, allowing in the future one Representative for every 40,000 inhabitants. This, which had been the original proposal of the Compromise Committee of July 5, had entirely disappeared from the votes taken by the Convention subsequently. No such provision occurred in the resolutions submitted to the Committee of Detail on July 26. On August 8, Madison thought 1 for 40,000 would "render the number of Representatives excessive" if the Union should continue to increase. Gorham, on the

8, and August 21; and it appears in the final draft of the Constitution as Article One, section 2, clause three, as follows:

"Representatives and direct taxes shall be apportioned among the several States which may be included within this Union, according to their respective numbers, which shall be determined by adding to the whole number of free persons, including those bound to service for a term of years, and excluding Indians not taxed, three fifths of all other persons. The actual enumeration shall be made within three years after the first meeting of the Congress of the United States, and within every subsequent term of ten years, in such manner as they shall by law direct. . . ."

It will be noted that the only reason for establishing a census by the Constitution was to afford a basis for a decennial reapportionment of Representatives.[1] A failure of Congress to make an apportionment in accordance with this provision is a violation of the Constitution. Such a failure to comply with the

other hand, doubted that the Government would last so long as to produce this effect: "Can it be supposed that this vast country including the Western Territory will 150 years hence remain one Nation?" The provision was changed on motion of Sherman and Madison to read "not exceeding one for every 40,000."

On September 17, at the very end of the Convention, it was voted to change this to "not exceeding one for every 30,000."

[1]

Census	Date of Apportionment Act	States	Members	Ratio
	1789	13	65	30,000
1790	Apr. 14, 1792	15	105	33,000
1800	Jan. 14, 1802	16	141	33,000
1810	Dec. 21, 1811	17	181	35,000
1820	Mar. 7, 1822	24	213	40,000
1830	May 22, 1832	24	240	47,700
1840	June 25, 1842	26	223	70,680
1850	May 23, 1850	32	234	93,423
1860	May 23, 1860	34	243	127,381
1870	Feb. 2, 1872	37	293	131,425
1880	Feb. 25, 1882	38	325	151,911
1890	Feb. 7, 1891	44	356	173,901
1900	Jan. 16, 1901	45	386	194,182
1910	Aug. 8, 1911	46	433	211,877
1920	Not made up to May, 1928	48	435	

Constitution not only affects the representation of the respective States in Congress, but — what is far more important — affects the number of electoral votes which the States may respectively cast for President; for, under Article II, section 1 of the Constitution as finally drafted, a State's electoral vote depends upon "the whole number of Senators and Representatives to which the State may be entitled in the Congress." A failure by Congress to apportion the Representatives according to the respective State populations might, in a close Presidential campaign, materially affect the result of the election.[1]

OUT OF CONVENTION

In the debate which had been taking place on representation in the House considerable apprehension had been expressed, by G. Morris and some of the Eastern delegates, at the possible growth of the Western States, to the disadvantage of the Eastern. "If the Western people get the power into their hands, they will ruin the Atlantic interests", said Morris. "The back members are always most adverse to the best measures." And Gerry of Massachusetts said that "they will oppress commerce and draw our wealth into the Western Country. To guard against these consequences, he thought it necessary to limit the number of new States to be admitted into the Union, in such a manner that they should never be able to outnumber the Atlantic States." Madison, Mason, and Butler from the South, however, did not share these fears. "People are constantly swarming from the more to the less populous places — from Europe to America, from

[1] See speech of Clarence J. McLeod, *70th Cong., 1st Sess.*, May 24, 1928. As to differing methods for apportioning representation advocated by Jefferson and Webster, see *Story on the Constitution* (5th Ed.) II, 495–512. See also *The Federalist*, No. 78.

the Northern and Middle parts of the United States to the Southern and Western. They go where land is cheaper because their labour is dearer", said Madison with true insight. "The people and strength of America are evidently bearing southwardly and southwestwardly", said Butler.

It was a striking fact that on the very day when this discussion took place, Congress, sitting in New York, adopted the famous Ordinance for the Government of the Northwest Territory, which made provision for the admission of five new States as soon as each acquired a population practically equal to that of Delaware, *i.e.*, 60,000 inhabitants. This matter had been long pending. Jefferson had drafted, in 1784, a resolve for the government of the lands ceded by the States and by Great Britain to the United States, and had made the first suggestion that slavery be abolished in this whole territory — from Florida to the Northern boundary — a proposal which Congress had rejected. In 1786, a Committee headed by Monroe had drafted an ordinance, with no reference to slavery in it. A jealousy of the possible political power of new Western States impeded any action by Congress. In March, 1787, a meeting was held in Boston, by a number of military officers and other men who were willing to become pioneers, which formed The Ohio Company for making settlements north of the Ohio River. The Company, with Gen. Rufus Putnam, Winthrop Sargent, Rev. Manasseh Cutler of Massachusetts, and Gen. Samuel Holden Parsons of Connecticut as its leading forces, made an application to Congress for the purchase of lands adequate to their purposes, offering to purchase 1,500,000 acres for $1,000,000, payable in the United States certificates of debt (then worth, however, only eight cents in specie). Such a proposal, which might result in some reduction of the Continental indebtedness, was welcomed by Congress; and a new Committee was appointed, on July 9, to consider a new draft for an Ordinance for the government of this Western territory. On July 11, this Committee, consisting of Richard Henry Lee (who had just been spending a week in Philadelphia, conferring with the delegates to the Convention), Edward Carrington of Virginia, John Kean of South Carolina, Melancthon Smith of New York, and Nathan Dane of Massachusetts, reported an entirely new draft of an Ordinance, containing provisions for freedom of religious worship, a bill of rights, prohibition of slavery, and a clause making the significant provision that: "In the just preservation of rights and property, it is understood and declared that no law ought ever to be made or have force in the said territory that shall, in any manner whatever, interfere with or affect private contracts or engagements, bona fide and without fraud, previously formed." [1] The honor of framing this famous document has been ascribed to various persons — Nathan Dane, Richard Henry Lee, Manasseh Cutler, and Rufus King; and each is probably entitled to a share.[2] To Jefferson, however, is due the chief honor of having been the first to suggest exclusion of slavery from the whole of the Western and Southern lands belonging to the United States.

On this July 13, this Ordinance was passed in Congress, by the votes of Georgia, South Carolina, North Carolina, Virginia, Delaware, New Jersey, New York, and Massachusetts — all the States then present (Pennsylvania, Maryland, New Hampshire, Connecticut, and Rhode Island being absent). And,

---

[1] See *Bancroft*, II, Chapter VI; *Dr. Cutler and the Ordinance of 1787*, by William F. Poole, *North American Review* (1876), CXX; *History of the United States* (1912), by Edward Channing III, Chap. 17, esp. bibliography, p. 551; *History of the Constitution* (1858), by George Ticknor Curtis, II, 291 *et seq.*, 341 *et seq.*

[2] See *Channing*, III, 547, note.

the next day (July 14) Richard Henry Lee wrote to Francis Lightfoot Lee : [1]

"After some difficulty, we passed an Ordinance for establishing a temporary Government beyond the Ohio, as preparatory to the sale of that country.   And now we are considering an offer made to purchase 5 or 6 million of acres with public securities.   I hope we shall agree with the offer, but really the difficulty is so great to get anything done, that it is not easy for the plainest propositions to succeed.   We owe much money, the pressure of taxes is very great and much complained of.   We have now something to sell that will pay the debt and discharge the greatest part of the taxes, and altho this same thing is in a fair way of being soon wrested from us by the Sons of Violence, yet we have a thousand little difficulties that prevent us from selling.   I found the Convention at Philadelphia very busy and very secret.   It would seem, however, from variety of circumstances that we shall hear of a Government not unlike the British Constitution, that is, an Executive, with 2 branches composing a Federal Legislature and possessing adequate tone.   This departure from simple Democracy seems indispensably necessary if any Government at all is to exist in North America.   Indeed, the minds of men have been so hurt by the injustice, folly and wickedness of the State Legislatures and State Executives that people in general seem ready for anything.   I hope, however, that this tendency to extreme will be so controuled as to secure fully and completely the democratic influence acting within just bounds."

[1] *Letters of Richard Henry Lee* (ed. by J. C. Ballagh, 1914), II.   To General Washington, Lee wrote July 15: "An object of much consequence this, since the extinguishment of this part of the public debt would not only relieve us from a very heavy burthen but by demolishing the ocean of public securities, we should stop that mischievous deluge of speculation that now hurts our morals and extremely injures the public affairs."   In this letter Lee also said that the Ordinance was designed to provide "a strong-toned government" for the security of property "among uninformed and perhaps licentious people, as the greater part of those who go there are."   See also W. P. Cutler in *Mag. of Amer. Hist.*, XXII, 484.

Jefferson, writing to W. Carmichael, Dec. 11, 1787, said that: "The sale of our Western lands is immensely successful "; that 5,000,000 acres had been sold at private sale for $1.50 an acre in certificates and at public sale as high as $2.40 an acre; and that by these means and taxes the public debt (originally $28,000,000) had been reduced, by October 1, 1787, to $12,000,000.

While the Congress was debating this Ordinance, Rev. Manasseh Cutler, one of the agents of the Ohio Company, who had been conferring with the Members of Congress in New York, from July 5 to July 10, and who had suggested to the Southern Members many amendments, took a trip to Philadelphia. He recorded in his diary his impressions of the conditions there. As he was "second, perhaps, to no living American except Dr. Franklin, in scientific attainments", and as no other man has left any contemporaneous account of the place in which the Convention was then sitting, his diary entries are of extreme interest.[1] On his arrival on July 12, he went to the Indian Queen Tavern, located "not far from the centre of the city. It is kept in an elegant style, and consists of a large pile of buildings, with many spacious halls and numerous small apartments appropriated for lodging rooms."

"As soon as I had inquired of the barkeeper when I arrived last evening, if I could be furnished with lodgings, a livery servant was ordered immediately to attend me, who received my baggage from the hostler and conducted me to the apartment assigned by the barkeeper which was a rather small but a very handsome chamber (No. 9), furnished with a rich field bed, bureau, table with drawers, a large looking glass, neat chair and other furniture. Its front was east, and being in the third story, afforded a fine prospect towards the river and the Jersey Shore. The servant that attended me was a young, sprightly, well-built, black fellow, neatly dressed — blue coat, sleeves and cape red, and buff waistcoat and breeches, the bosom of his shirt ruffled and hair powdered. After he had brought up my baggage and properly deposited it in the chamber, he brought two of the latest London magazines and laid them on the table. I ordered him to call a barber, furnish me with a bowl of water for washing, and to have tea on the table by the time I was dressed."

[1] *Life, Journals and Correspondence of Manasseh Cutler* (1888), I, 253–271.

After these preliminaries, Cutler met many of the delegates to the Convention, which he described as follows:

"Being told while I was at tea, that a number of the members of the Continental Convention now convened in this city for the purpose of forming a Federal Constitution lodged in this house and that two of them were from Massachusetts, immediately after tea, I sent into their Hall (for they live by themselves) to Mr. Strong and requested to speak with him. Mr. Strong very politely introduced me to Mr. Gorham of Charlestown, Mass., Mr. Madison and Mr. Mason and his son of Virginia, Governor Martin, Hon. Hugh Williamson, of North Carolina, the Hon. John Rutledge and Charles Pinckney of So. Carolina, Mr. Hamilton of New York who lodges in the house, and to several other gentlemen who were spending the evening there. I spent the evening with these gentlemen very agreeably. . . . We sat until half after one. . . . Mr. Strong proposed going with me in the morning to Mr. Gerry's as early as I pleased, and so wished goodnight. I rose very early this morning, and the servant assigned me came into the chamber before I was dressed to know my commands. Mr. Strong was up as early as myself and we took a walk to Mr. Gerry's in Spruce Street, where we breakfasted. Few old bachelors, I believe, have been more fortunate in matrimony than Mr. Gerry. His lady is young, very handsome and exceedingly amiable. . . . They have been married about eighteen months and have a fine son about two months old of which they appear both to be extravagantly fond. Mr. Gerry has hired a house and lives in a family state. I was surprised to find how early ladies in Philadelphia can rise in the morning and to see them all breakfast at half past five, when in Boston they can hardly see a breakfast table at nine without falling into hysterics."

After visiting many points of interest in the city, on this July 13, Cutler described the State-House, and incidentally noted that the Federal Convention was sitting in a room upstairs: [1]

[1] See *infra*, p. 626.

"From Mr. Peale's we went to the State House. This is a noble building; the architecture is in a richer and grander style than any public building I have before seen. The first story is not an open walk as is usual in buildings of this kind. In the middle, however, is a very broad cross aisle, and a floor above supported by two rows of pillars. From this aisle is a broad opening to a large hall toward the west end, which opening is supported by arches and pillars. In this Hall, the Courts are held, and, as you pass the aisle, you have a full view of the Court. The Supreme Court are now sitting. This bench consists of only three Judges. Their robes are scarlet, the lawyers' black. The Chief Judge, Mr. McKean, was sitting with his hat on, which is the custom, but struck me as being very odd, and seemed to derogate from the dignity of a Judge. The hall east of the aisle is employed for public business. The Chamber over it is now occupied by the Continental Convention, which is now sitting, but sentries are planted without and within — to prevent any person from approaching near — who appear to be very alert in the performance of their duty. . . ."

It is to be noted that the "hall east of the aisle", thus referred to, was the room in which the Declaration of Independence was signed.[1] Cutler then proceeded to call upon Dr. Franklin and his account of his interview is of interest, not only for its description of the man, but for its reference to the narrow escape which Franklin had from breaking the secrecy rule of the Convention:

"Dr. Franklin lives in Market Street, between Second and Third Streets . . . but his house stands up a courtyard at some distance from the Street. We found him in his garden sitting upon a grass plat under a very large mulberry with several other gentlemen and two or three ladies. I saw a short, fat, trunched, old man in a plain Quaker dress, bald pate and short white locks, sitting without his hat under the

[1] Cutler, in his diary, describes a room in Carpenter's Hall in Philadelphia as that in which the Declaration of Independence was signed, and pictures it as filled with trophies of the War of the Revolution. It is singular that he should have been so misinformed on a visit only thirteen years after the signing.

tree; and as Mr. Gerry introduced me, rose from his chair, took me by the hand, expressed his joy to see me, welcomed me to the city and begged me to seat myself close to him. His voice was low but his countenance open, frank, and pleasing. . . . The Doctor showed me a curiosity which he had just received and with which he was much pleased. It was a snake with two heads preserved in a large vial. . . . The Doctor mentioned the situation of this snake, if it was travelling among bushes, and the head should choose to go on one side of the stem of a bush and the other head should prefer the other side, and that neither of the heads would consent to come back or give way to the other. He was then going to mention a humorous matter that had that day taken place in Convention, in consequence of his comparing the snake to America, for he seemed to forget that everything in Convention was to be kept a profound secret; but the secrecy of Convention matters was suggested to him, which stopped him and deprived me of the story he was going to tell. . . . Notwithstanding his age, his manners are perfectly easy and everything about him seems to diffuse an unrestrained freedom and happiness. He has an incessant vein of humor, accompanied with an uncommon vivacity which seems as natural and involuntary as his breathing. We took our leave at ten and I retired to my lodgings. The gentlemen who lodged in the house were just sitting down to supper; a sumptuous table was spread and the attendance in the style of noblemen. After supper, Mr. Strong came in and invited me into their Hall where we sat till twelve. Mentioning my engagement the next morning, Governor Martin, Mr. Mason, Mr. Strong and several of the other gentlemen wished to be of our party, but would have preferred an earlier hour than six, on account of retiring in season to attend the Convention."

SATURDAY, JULY 14, 1787

IN CONVENTION

Having disposed of three of the proposals by the Compromise Committee, the Convention had now

reached the critical moment. On this day, Luther
Martin, impatient over the long delays, "called for the
question on the whole report", stating that, while he
did not like it, "he was willing to make trial of the plan
rather than do nothing"; he would, however, let the
larger States separate and form two Confederacies
rather than abandon the principle of equality of
representation in the Senate. Dayton also said that
he would in no event yield this security to the States.
Though the debate as to the second branch of the
Legislature had lasted from June 25 to July 2, and
from July 5 to July 13, Wilson wanted more time to
discuss a point "of such critical importance." Sherman felt that as a great deal of time had been spent
on this conciliatory plan, it ought not now to be gone
over again. Gerry said that while the report was
"not altogether to his mind, he would agree to it as
it stood rather than throw it out altogether." Gerry's
colleague from Massachusetts, King, on the other hand,
announced that he "preferred the doing of nothing
to an allowance of an equal vote to all the States. It
would be better to submit to a little more confusion
and convulsion than to submit to such an evil"; and
he boldly and baldly proclaimed his belief that the
proposed Government would and should be "a General
and National Government over the people of America.
There never will be a case in which it will act as a Federal
Government on the States, and not on the individual
citizens." Caleb Strong differed from King, saying
that "if no accommodation takes place, the Union
itself must be soon dissolved", and that under such
circumstances he "was compelled to give his vote for
the report taken altogether." On the other side,
Madison and Wilson, unmoved by the arguments for
concession, still opposed the compromise as fundamentally wrong in principle. "There was not a single

case", said Wilson, "in which the General Government was not to operate on the people individually"; hence there was no occasion for the States to be represented, as *States*, in the Government; moreover, equality of State representation in the Senate would give a preponderance to the Northern States in perpetuity. Controverting this last argument, Gerry was afraid that the new States in the West might ultimately preponderate, to the injury of the East; and he wanted some provision made against this possibility. Sherman, with broader vision, replied that no discrimination should be made against new States. "We are providing for our posterity, for our children and our grandchildren who would be as likely to be citizens of new Western States as of the old States." A motion made by Charles Pinckney providing for a specific and unequal number of votes for each State respectively in the Senate was lost by vote of four States to six.[1] At the close of the discussion, the views of the two factions seemed as divergent as they had been a month before. But once more, for the third time, a Sunday intervened, giving opportunity for cool consideration.

OUT OF CONVENTION

Washington noted:

"In Convention. Dined at the Cold Spring, Springsbury, with the Club and went to the play in the afternoon."

This play at the Opera House was advertised as a "Concert" — "Spectaculum Vitae — an Opera called the Tempest or the Enchanted Island, altered from Shakespeare by Dryden, to conclude with a Grand Masque of Neptune and Amphytrite, with entire new scenery, the music composed by Dr. Purcell."

---

[1] King in his *Notes*, July 15, states that this vote was lost by the vote of Massachusetts, "to my mortification", Gorham being absent and King voting aye. But his statement is erroneous, for the presence of Gorham would only have divided the vote of Massachusetts and the States would still have stood six to five in opposition.

Dr. Manasseh Cutler described, this day, in his diary a trip which he made to Bartram's famous botanical gardens and a breakfast at Gray's Tavern on the south side of the Schuylkill River "at the foot of the floating bridge" — in company with Caleb Strong, Alexander Martin, George Mason, Hugh Williamson, Madison, Rutledge, and Hamilton.[1]

SUNDAY, JULY 15, 1787

Washington noted :

"Dined at Mr. Morris's and remained at home all day."

One of the few statesmen of the day who advocated a general consolidation of the States into one Government was General Henry Knox, who wrote from New York, this day, to Rufus King the following extreme expression of this view :

"I am happy the Convention continue together, without agitating the idea of adjournment. If their attempts should prove inadequate to effect capital alterations, yet experience will be gained, which may serve important purposes on another occasion. . . . The State systems are the accursed things which will prevent our being a Nation. The democracy might be managed, nay it would remedy itself after being sufficiently fermented ; but the vile State Governments are sources of pollution which will contaminate the American name, perhaps for ages — machines that must produce ill, but cannot produce good. Smite them, in the name of God and the people."

[1] Cutler returned to New York on this day, after recording a description of Philadelphia in his diary, stating that it had 10,000 houses, and that "the State House, Hospital, and most of the other public buildings are magnificent, but it is singular that there are only two steeples in the city, while there are upwards of twenty houses for public worship."

MONDAY, JULY 16, 1787

IN CONVENTION

Adoption of the Great Compromise

As soon as the Convention met, the final vote was taken on the compromise, and it was carried by the votes of five States to four — Connecticut, New Jersey, Delaware, Virginia, and North Carolina voting aye, and Pennsylvania, Maryland, South Carolina, and Georgia voting no, Massachusetts being divided (Gerry and Strong voting aye and King and Gorham, no). And so, by this close vote, and only by reason of the division in the Massachusetts delegation, this Great Compromise was adopted. Had it failed, the Convention itself would have failed; for it is certain that the delegates of the small States would not have remained longer. Luther Martin very truly said, later, in his message to the Maryland Legislature, that for the past fortnight "we were on the verge of dissolution, scarce held together by the strength of a hair, though the public papers were announcing our extreme unanimity."

The acceptance of the compromise was not only essential to the continuance of the Convention; but it also had the important effect of converting the representatives from Connecticut, New Jersey, and Delaware into ardent supporters of the new Government. As George Bancroft wrote (in 1882): "From the day when every doubt of the right of the smaller States to an equal vote in the Senate was quieted, they — so I received it from the lips of Madison, and so it appears from the records — exceeded all others in zeal for granting powers to the General Government. Ellsworth became one of its strongest pillars."[1] It is particularly to be noted that this whole contest was

[1] *Bancroft*, II, 88.

not one over the degree of power to be granted to the new Government, but on the degree of representation of the States.[1]

Moreover, the acceptance of the compromise by the Convention was not only a victory for the smaller States; but it was a deserved victory. Writers on the Constitution have been prone to regard the leaders of these States as a somewhat fractious minority, to pacify whom the Nationalists were forced to yield their more valid principle of proportional representation. But the fact is that the small States were entirely right in believing that no such form of Government as the Nationalists, at that stage in the Convention, were supporting would ever be accepted by the people of the States — a Government in which the National Legislature was practically supreme, having power to elect the Executive and the Judiciary, and to negative all State laws which it deemed to infringe on its own broad and practically unlimited National powers. Students of the Constitution often forget now that at the time of the compromise the form of Government proposed was radically different from that which was finally adopted. The degree of the change marked the wisdom of the delegates in modifying their views after repeated discussions of the effects of their proposals upon the varying needs and conditions of the different States and of the country at large.

After the compromise was adopted, Randolph moved that the Convention adjourn temporarily, "that the large States might consider the steps proper to be taken in the present solemn crisis of the business,

---

[1] Madison wrote to Martin Van Buren, May 13, 1828: "The threatening contest in the Convention of 1787 did not . . . turn on the degree of power to be granted to the Federal Government, but on the rule by which the States should be represented and vote in the Government. . . . The contests and compromises turning on the grants of power, tho very important in some instances, were knots of a less Gordian character."

and that the small States might also deliberate on the means of conciliation." He stated that he had come prepared to offer another scheme of adjustment, but that the vote taken rendered it useless. His proposed plan (which he had already communicated to Madison on July 10) was of great interest and has received less attention than it deserves — in view of its very broad suggestions as to the functions of the Judiciary. It proposed, first, that in the Senate, each State have one vote on all legislation on thirteen specified subjects — these subjects being substantially those over which Congress was later granted power, in the Report of the Committee of Detail of August 6, — and that on all other subjects of legislation, the right of suffrage in the Senate should be by an equitable and proportionate representation; second, that on some subjects a greater vote than a majority be required; third, that the National Judiciary on appeal from a State should have power to adjudge void any negative of a State law by Congress which the Judiciary should regard as contrary to the powers granted by the Constitution; fourth, that: "Any individual conceiving himself injured or oppressed by the partiality or injustice of a law of any particular State may resort to the National Judiciary, who may adjudge such law to be void, if found contrary to the principles of equity and justice."[1] It was this last proposal which was the most extraordinary; for it would have allowed the National Courts not only to hold void any State law found to be in conflict with the Constitution, but also any law found to be "contrary to the principles of equity and justice." No such a radical extension of judicial power had ever been suggested; nor has such a proposal been made since.

Paterson of New Jersey, who was not at all satisfied with the actual compromise, now stated that he was

[1] See text of the proposal in *Documentary History of the Constitution*, V, 437.

willing to adjourn *sine die*, "with all his heart." General Pinckney was hotly opposed to such a suggestion; Randolph said that he had never entertained such an idea; and Broom thought that "it would be fatal." Finally, it was agreed to adjourn to the next day.

OUT OF CONVENTION

Washington noted:

" In Convention. Dined at Mr. Morris's, and drank tea (at Mr. Powell's) with Mrs. Powell."

CHAPTER SIX

COMPLETION OF THE PLAN

TUESDAY, JULY 17, 1787

IN CONVENTION

Before the Convention met on this morning, there was a conference of a number of the delegates from the larger States to consider the situation. It was found that they were sharply divided, some being unwilling to risk a failure of the Convention by inflexibly opposing the equality of votes, others believing that, as they had a majority of votes in the Convention, they should propose such system as seemed best to them, regardless of the minority, others being inclined to yield. Nothing was done; and as Madison records, "it is probable that the result of this consultation satisfied the smaller States that they had nothing to apprehend from a union of the larger in any plan whatever against the equality of votes in the Senate."

Powers of the National Legislature

At the end of the preceding day, the Convention considered briefly what powers should be vested in the

Legislature. Many of the delegates had wished to fix the powers, before they voted on the question of how the Legislature should be constituted, but it had been otherwise decided. Now, the very broad provision adopted by the Committee of the Whole was taken up, as follows: "To enjoy the Legislative rights vested in Congress by the Confederation, and moreover to legislate in all cases to which the separate States are incompetent or in which the harmony of the United States may be interrupted by the exercise of individual legislation." Butler thought the term "incompetent" required some explanation,[1] and he stated that "the vagueness of the terms rendered it impossible for any precise judgment to be formed." To this, Gorham replied that: "the vagueness of the terms constitutes the propriety of them. We are now establishing general principles, to be extended hereafter into details which will be precise and explicit." The Convention, by an equally divided vote, refused to recommit the subject "to the end that a specification of the powers comprised in the general terms might be reported." On July 17, Sherman, alarmed at the possible encroachments on States' Rights involved in these powers, proposed that the following change be made:

"To make laws binding on the people of the United States in all cases which may concern the common interests of the Union; but not to interfere with the Government of the individual States in any matters of internal police which respect the Government of such States only, and wherein the general welfare of the United States is not concerned."

Wilson, one of the extreme Nationalists, favored this motion. That he should do so, was not surprising,

[1] The word "incompetent" was a somewhat singular term; and it is possible that it was taken from Pelatiah Webster's famous pamphlet of Feb. 16, 1783, containing a project for a new Constitution, in which he said: "I propose further that the powers of Congress . . . shall be restricted to such matters of general authority and utility to all the States as cannot come within the jurisdiction of any particular State or to which the authority of any particular State is not *competent*."

since, had it been adopted in the final draft of the
Constitution, Congress could have exercised the broad-
est possible powers for the "general welfare." In
view of the controversy which, later in our history,
developed over the meaning of the general welfare
clause in the taxing-power section of the Constitution
as finally drafted, it is interesting to note this occurrence
of the phrase "general welfare" thus early in the
Convention. G. Morris expressed his opposition to
Sherman's motion, on the sensible ground that there
were cases in which "the internal police, as it would
be called and understood by the States", ought to be
infringed and legislated upon by the National Government, notably to prevent paper money. The motion
was defeated by the decisive vote of eight States to two,
only Connecticut and Maryland voting for it. Gunning
Bedford of Delaware, seconded by G. Morris, then
moved that the powers of Congress be altered so as to
read:

"To enjoy the Legislative rights vested in Congress by the
Confederation, and moreover to legislate in all cases for the
general interests of the Union, and also in those to which
the States are separately incompetent, or in which the harmony of the United States may be interrupted by the exercise of individual legislation."

This gave to Congress even more extensive power
than Sherman had proposed. It is slight wonder that
Randolph himself exclaimed: "This is a formidable
idea indeed. It involves the power of violating all the
laws and Constitutions of the States and of inter-
meddling with their police." Despite these facts, the
Convention voted this broad power, by a vote of six
States to four, Connecticut, Virginia, South Carolina,
and Georgia voting against it. It is interesting to note
that the small States of New Jersey, Delaware, and
Maryland, which had hitherto been, in general, antago-

nistic to the Randolph or Virginia Plan of Government, now voted for the grant of this broad power to Congress. Having won their contention as to equality of votes in the Senate, they were now willing to join hands with their opponents in making the Congress an adequate body.

Negative on State Laws

One special power vested in Congress by the vote of the Committee of the Whole now failed to meet the approval of the Convention, namely, the power to negative State laws "contravening in its opinion the Articles of Union." This power, accepted by the Committee on May 31, had been given further consideration, when, on June 8, Charles Pinckney had moved to vest even broader power in Congress by authorizing it to negative *all* State laws "which they should judge to be improper." Madison had seconded this, saying that such a power was "absolutely necessary to a perfect system. Experience had evinced a constant tendency in the States to encroach on the Federal authority, to violate National treaties, to infringe the rights and interests of each other, to oppress the weaker party within their respective jurisdiction." The alternative to such a power to negative was the use of force against State Governments, a "visionary and fallacious" suggestion, he said. Wilson said that "unless the General Government can check the State laws, the Nation may be involved in tumult and confusion"; [1] that those States should, like individuals, submit to some control. "We are now one nation of brethren. We must bury our local interests and distinctions." Williamson, on the other hand, was "against giving a power that might restrain the States from regulating their internal police." Gerry was

[1] As reported in King's *Notes*.

strongly opposed, saying that such a power might "enslave the States." Gunning Bedford of Delaware, Sherman, and Butler were also opposed. The proposal had been killed by a vote of seven to three, only Massachusetts, Pennsylvania, and Virginia voting for it, with Delaware divided.

The more limited power to negative had been discussed, on June 16, by John Lansing of New York, who said that: "The States will never feel a sufficient confidence in a General Government to give it a negative on their laws. The scheme is itself entirely novel. There is no parallel to it to be found." Again, on June 20, Lansing had said that "such a negative would be more injurious than that of Great Britain heretofore was." Luther Martin of Maryland had said that "the States, particularly the smaller, would never allow a negative to be exercised over their laws." On the other hand, Wilson had said (June 16) that such a negative was preferable to the proposal for coercion on the States, contained in Paterson's New Jersey Plan. Mason, on June 20, had pointed out also that Paterson's Plan "could not be enforced without military coercion."

Randolph, in the compromise which he had prepared to offer to the smaller States, had suggested the following modification of this power to negative:

"4. That altho every negative given to the law of a particular State shall prevent its operation, any State may appeal to the National Judiciary against a negative; and that such negative, if adjudged to be contrary to the powers granted by the Articles of the Union, shall be void.

5. That any individual conceiving himself injured or oppressed by the partiality or injustice of a law of any particular State may resort to the National Judiciary, who may adjudge such law to be void, if found contrary to the principles of equity and justice."

and became one of the fundamental provisions of the Constitution. It not only declared the supremacy of the United States over the States, but made it the duty of the Judiciary to enforce this supremacy.[1] That it was Martin's understanding and intent that the State Judges must hold invalid and unconstitutional any State law passed in contravention of the Federal laws or treaties is clear; for he was familiar with the fact that already in the various States the Judges were holding void State laws which infringed State Constitutions; and, only four days later (on July 21), he opposed the association of the Federal Judges with the President in a power of veto, because, he said: "As to the constitutionality of laws, that point will come before the Judges in their proper official character. In this character, they have a negative on the laws. Join them with the Executive in the revision and they will have a double negative." And in his letter to the Maryland Legislature, later, Martin pointed out specifically that the Judges would determine whether laws of the State or of Congress and actions of the President and other officers were or were not violative of the Constitution.[2] But Martin did not intend or foresee the potent and far-reaching effect which his motion, by reason of amendments made to it later, would have in establishing the supremacy of the

---

[1] As Madison wrote to William C. Rives, Oct. 21, 1833: "It must be kept in mind that the radical defect of the old Confederation lay in the power of the State to comply with, to disregard, or to counteract the authorized requisitions and regulations of Congress; that a radical cure for this fatal defect was the essential object for which the reform was instituted; that all the friends of the reform looked for such a cure; that there could, therefore, be no question but as to the mode of effecting it. . . . In every proceeding of the Convention where the question of paramountship in the laws of the Union could be involved, the necessity of it appears to have been taken for granted."

[2] *The Genuine Information*, by Luther Martin, *Elliot's Debates*, I, 380: "Whether, therefore, any laws or regulations of the Congress, any acts of its President or other officers, are contrary to, or not warranted by the Constitution, rests only with the Judges, who are appointed by Congress, to determine, by whose determination every State must be bound."

Constitution. When the Committee of Detail drafted its Report, on August 6, putting into more systematic form the various Resolutions adopted up to that time, it compressed Martin's proposal and made two vital changes in it, as follows:

"The Acts of the Legislature of the United States made in pursuance of this Constitution, and all treaties made under the authority of the United States, shall be the supreme law of the several States, and of their citizens and inhabitants; and the Judges in the several States shall be bound thereby in their decisions; anything in the Constitutions or laws of the several States to the contrary notwithstanding."

The first of the changes made was that the Federal laws were to be supreme over State Constitutions as well as over State laws — a provision which Martin never intended and to which infringement on State Sovereignty he was violently opposed.[1] The second change was that a duty was imposed on "the Judges *in* the several States", instead of "the Judiciaries *of* the respective States." On August 23, the Convention further amended this Article (on motion of John Rutledge) by providing that: "*This Constitution and the laws of the United States made in pursuance thereof* . . . shall be the supreme law of the several States." When the Committee on Style reported the

[1] Martin later wrote: "When this clause was introduced, it was not established that Continental Courts should be appointed for trial of all questions arising on treaties and on the laws of the General Government and it was my wish and hope that every question of that kind would have been determined in the first instance in the Courts of the respective States; had this been the case, the propriety and the necessity that treaties duly made and ratified, and the laws of the General Government, should be binding on the State Judiciaries which were to decide upon them must be evident to every capacity; while at the same time, if such treaties or laws were inconsistent with our Constitution and bill of rights, the Judiciaries of this State would be bound to reject the first and abide by the last, since in the form I introduced the clause, notwithstanding treaties and the laws of the General Government were intended to be superior to the laws of our State Governments, where they should be opposed to each other, yet that they were not proposed nor meant to be superior to our Constitution and bill of rights." See letter of Martin in *Maryland Journal*, March 21, 1788; *Essays on the Constitution* (1892), by Paul Leicester Ford, 360–371.

final draft of the Constitution on September 12, this Article became Article VI (as it now appears in the Constitution);

"This Constitution and the laws of the United States which shall be made in pursuance thereof; and all treaties made, or which shall be made, under the authority of the United States, shall be the supreme law of the land; and the Judges in every State shall be bound thereby, anything in the Constitution or laws of any State to the contrary notwithstanding."

In this final draft, the phrase previously adopted "the supreme law of the several States" became "the supreme law of the land"; and "the Judges in the several States" became "the Judges in every State." And it is under this Article, as proposed originally by Luther Martin to guard against conflicts between State statutes and Federal laws, and as amended by motion of John Rutledge, that the Judges of every Court (State, inferior Federal, and Supreme) must uphold the supremacy of the Federal Constitution, whether against Acts of Congress or against State laws which may be held to infringe it.

Charles Pinckney (on August 23), apparently disbelieving in the efficacy of Martin's original Resolution, again made an effort to vest in Congress power, by a two-thirds vote, to negative all State laws "interfering in the opinion of the Legislature with the general interests and harmony of the Union." This was an even broader proposal than that which had been rejected on July 17. Madison and Langdon of New Hampshire favored the proposal, but Sherman, Mason, Williamson, Gouverneur Morris, and Ellsworth were opposed; and Rutledge said that: "If nothing else, this alone would damn and ought to damn the Constitution. Will any State ever agree to be bound hand and foot in this manner?" After a vote of six States to five rejecting commitment of his motion, Pinckney withdrew it, evidently satisfied that it could not be carried. It is to be noted that Madison never became reconciled to the rejection of this power to negative, although he recognized that the power vested in the Supreme Court to pass upon the constitutionality of State laws would cure many of the evils which he feared in State legislation. On August 28, while favoring a prohibition on the States to coin money or issue bills of credit, he stated that "he conceived, however, that a negative on the State laws could alone secure the effect. Evasions might and would be devised by the ingenuity of the Legislature." Madison, however, realized that such restrictions on the States would to some extent be enforced by the Supreme Court in holding State laws unconstitutional; for, on September 12, when the question was debated whether the States might not evade the prohibition against export duties by enacting inspection duties, and when it was asked: "How was redress to be obtained in case duties should be laid beyond the purpose expressed?" Madison replied: "There will be the same authority as in other cases. The jurisdiction of the Supreme Court must be the source of redress." This, he said, was the only provision "made by the plan against injurious acts of the States. His own opinion was, that this was insufficient. A negative on the State laws alone could meet all the shapes which these could assume; but this had been overruled." [1]

[1] Other Virginians also continued to urge the power to negative. James Monroe wrote to Jefferson, July 27, 1787 (*Farrand*, III, 65): "I have heard from Becly tho' not from himself (who accompanied the Governor up, on expectation of being appointed clerk) they had agreed giving the United States a negative upon the laws of the several States. This I should think proper — it will, if the body is well organized, be the best way of introducing uniformity in their proceedings that can be devised, of a negative kind or by a power to operate indirectly; but a few months will give in the result, be it what it may." James McClurg wrote to Madison, Aug. 22, 1787 (*Doc. Hist.*, IV, 264): "I have still some hope that I shall hear from you of the reinstatement of the Negative — as it is certainly the only means by which the

And writing to Jefferson, October 24, 1787, he said:

"It may be said that the Judicial authority under our new system will keep the States within their proper limits and supply the place of a negative on their laws. The answer is that it is more convenient to prevent the passage of a law than to declare it void, after it is passed; that this will be particularly the case, where the law aggrieves individuals who may be unable to support an appeal against a State to the Supreme Judiciary, that a State which would violate the Legislative rights of the Union would not be very ready to obey a Judicial decree in support of them, and that a recurrence to force, which in the event of disobedience would be necessary, is an evil which the new Constitution meant to exclude as far as possible.

2. A constitutional negative on the laws of the States seems equally necessary to secure individuals against encroachments on their rights. The mutability of the laws of the States is found to be a serious evil. The injustice of them has been so frequent and so flagrant as to alarm the most stedfast friends of Republicanism. I am persuaded I do not err in saying that the evils issuing from these sources contributed more to that uneasiness which produced the Convention and prepared the public mind for a general reform, than those which accrued to our National character and interest from the inadequacy of the Confederation to its immediate objects. A reform, therefore, which does not make provision for private rights must be materially defective. The restraints against paper emissions and violations of contracts are not sufficient. Supposing them to be effectual as far as they go, they are short of the mark. Injustice may be effected by such an infinitude of Legislative expedients that where the disposition exists, it can only be controuled by some provision which reaches all cases whatsoever. The partial provision made, supposes the disposition which will evade it."

several Legislatures can be restrained from disturbing the order and harmony of the whole and the Government rendered properly national and one. I should suppose that some of its former opponents must, by this time, have seen the necessity of advocating it, if they wish to support their own principles."

Powers of the Executive

The Convention, on this July 17, voted to adopt the proposal made by the Committee of the Whole that there should be an Executive consisting of a single person, to be chosen by the National Legislature. It further voted to vest in him two powers — "to carry into execution the National laws", and "to appoint to offices in cases not otherwise provided for"; and, four days later (on July 21), it vested in him the power to veto (as previously discussed).

OUT OF CONVENTION

Washington noted:

"In Convention. Dined at Mrs. House's and made an excursion with a party for Tea to Gray's Ferry."

In the diary of Jacob Hiltzheimer, it is said: [1]

"In the afternoon went with my wife, Matthew Clarkson and Mr. and Mrs. Barge to Gray's Ferry, where we saw the great improvements made in the garden, summer house and walks in the woods. General Washington and a number of other gentlemen of the present Convention came down to spend the afternoon."

WEDNESDAY, JULY 18, 1787

IN CONVENTION

The Judiciary

On this day, the Convention agreed upon the provisions for the Judiciary branch of the Government. There had been little discussion over this subject in the Committee of the Whole. The proposal for one Supreme Tribunal had been accepted without debate, on June 4; but the proposal that there should be inferior tribunals had occasioned some controversy.

---

[1] *Washington After the Revolution* (1898), by William Spohn Baker. Manasseh Cutler visited the Gray's Ferry garden, July 14.

Rutledge of South Carolina, on June 5, had argued that "the State tribunals might and ought to be left in all cases to decide in the first instance, the right of appeal to the Supreme National Tribunal being sufficient to secure the National rights and uniformity of judgments" and that any other provision would make "an unnecessary encroachment on the jurisdiction of the States and create unnecessary obstacles to their adoption of the new system." Butler of South Carolina had stated that: "The people will not bear such innovations. The States will revolt at such encroachments." In view of the hot contentions made in later years by the Southern States, that the 25th Section of the Judiciary Act of 1789, which provided for appeals to the Supreme Court from the State Courts by writ of error, was utterly unconstitutional, it is curious to note that, in the Convention, these two South Carolina delegates were arguing for a vastly broader power of the Supreme Court over State Courts than was later vested by Congress. Sherman of Connecticut, agreeing with Rutledge and Butler, had deplored an expensive new system of Courts when the existing State Courts would answer the same purpose. In reply to Rutledge, Madison had pointed out unless there should be National inferior tribunals "dispersed throughout the Republic, with final jurisdiction in many cases, appeals would be multiplied to a most oppressive degree." He contended that such tribunals would be necessary to counteract local State prejudices, and that "an effective Judiciary establishment commensurate to the Legislative authority was essential." King, Wilson, and Dickinson had concurred with him. Finally, the matter had been compromised, on motion of Madison and Wilson, by providing that "the National Legislature be empowered to institute inferior tribunals", thus leaving it to the discretion of the

Legislature to say whether or not any such tribunals should be constituted; and thus it came about that the National inferior Courts are now established by Congress and not by the Constitution itself. When this proposal of the Committee of the Whole was considered by the Convention, on this July 18, it again met with opposition. Butler said that "he could see no necessity for such tribunals, since the State tribunals might do the business." Luther Martin said that "they will create jealousies and oppositions in the State tribunals, with the jurisdiction of which they will interfere." On the other hand, Randolph observed "that the Courts of the States cannot be trusted with the administration of the National laws. The objects of jurisdiction are such as will often place the general and local policy at variance." Gorham, G. Morris, and Mason agreed with him. Sherman was willing to leave the matter to the National Legislature, but he "wished them to make use of the State tribunals whenever it could be done, with safety to the general interest." The Convention then adopted the Committee's proposal, with no State dissenting.

The second subject of discussion as to the Judiciary, in the Committee of the Whole, had been the method of appointment of the Judges. Randolph's Resolution of May 29 provided for appointment by the National Legislature. This followed the practice under most of the State Constitutions; for only in Massachusetts, New Hampshire, and New York were the Governors empowered to appoint the Judges, and even in those States the Governor's appointing power was shared with his Council. When the Committee debated this, on June 5, Wilson favored appointment by the Executive, stating that "experience showed the impropriety of such appointments by numerous bodies", and that "intrigue, partiality and concealment were the necessary consequences." Rutledge, on the other hand, was against granting so great a power to any single person. Franklin opposed both methods. Madison favored choice by the Senate. The subject was postponed until June 13, when Madison, again contending that a whole Legislature was incompetent to pass upon the requisite qualifications for Judges, moved that appointment be made by the Senate, which, "as a less numerous and more select body, would be more competent." This was voted by the Committee. When the subject was considered by the Convention, on this July 18, Gorham moved that the Judges be nominated and appointed "by the Executive and by and with the advice and consent of the Senate." The motion was lost by an evenly divided vote. Madison then modified his previous motion for choice by the Senate, so that "the Judges should be nominated by the Executive, and such nomination should become an appointment if not disagreed to within   days by two thirds vote of the Senate." This proposal was debated on July 21, when Madison explained the reasons for his change of mind. As the Senate was now to be composed of equal votes from each State, if it should alone have the power of appointment, the Judges might be appointed by a minority of the people though by a majority of the States, and the appointments might be thrown entirely into the hands of the Northern States, and "a perpetual ground of jealousy and discontent would be furnished to the Southern States." The Executive, however, as a National officer, would represent the whole people. Randolph agreed with Madison, stating that appointments by the Legislatures "have generally resulted from cabal, from personal regard or some other consideration than a title derived from proper qualifications." Ellsworth, Gerry, and Mason were, however, opposed to augmenting the power of the Executive.

Madison's motion was defeated, and the Convention voted for appointment of Judges by the Senate.

The third question relating to the Judiciary taken up by the Convention on this July 18, was: What should be the jurisdiction of this National Judiciary? Randolph's original Resolution of May 29 had provided for original jurisdiction in the inferior National Tribunals and appellate jurisdiction for the Supreme Tribunal in the following class of cases: (a) "all piracies and felonies on the high seas; (b) captures from an enemy; (c) cases in which foreigners or citizens of other States applying to such jurisdiction may be interested; (d) or which respect the National revenue; (e) impeachments of any National officers; (f) questions which may involve the National peace and harmony." Pinckney's Plan provided for a Supreme Federal Court with appellate jurisdiction from the State Courts: (a) "in all causes wherein questions shall arise on the construction of treaties made by the United States; (b) or on the law of nations; (c) or on the regulations of the United States concerning trade and revenue; (d) or wherein the United States shall be a party." His plan also provided for Federal Admiralty Courts in each State "for all maritime causes which may arise therein respectively." [1] Paterson's Plan had provided for a Supreme Tribunal

[1] In the Report to Congress made on August 7, 1786, by a sub-committee, and drafted by Charles Pinckney, a suggested amendment of the Articles of Confederation provided for a Federal Judicial Court of seven Judges (to be appointed — one from New Hampshire, Rhode Island and Connecticut; one from Massachusetts; and one from New York and New Jersey; one from Pennsylvania, one from Delaware and Maryland, one from Virginia and one from North Carolina, South Carolina, and Georgia). It was to have power to try all crimes, offences and misbehavior in office by all officers appointed by Congress. It was also to have appellate jurisdiction from State Courts "in all causes wherein questions shall arise on the meaning and construction of treaties entered into by the United States with any foreign power, or on the law of nations, or wherein any question shall arise respecting any regulations that may hereafter be made by Congress relative to trade and commerce, or the collection of Federal revenues, pursuant to powers that shall be vested in that body, or wherein questions of importance may arise, and the United States shall be a party."

(with no inferior National Courts) which should have original jurisdiction only over impeachments of Federal officers, but which should have appellate jurisdiction (on appeal from the State Courts) in the following cases: (*a*) "touching the rights of Ambassadors; (*b*) in all cases of captures from an enemy; (*c*) in all cases of piracies and felonies on the high seas; (*d*) in all cases in which foreigners may be interested; (*e*) in the construction of any treaty or treaties; (*f*) or which may arise on any of the acts for regulation of trade or the collection of the Federal revenue."

When the Committee of the Whole had considered Randolph's proposal for the first time on June 12, it struck out the jurisdiction over "piracies and felonies on the high seas" and over "captures from an enemy"; and it voted to give jurisdiction in "cases in which foreigners or citizens of two distinct States of the Union" may be interested. On June 13, Randolph had stated that he "observed the difficulty in establishing the powers of the Judiciary"; and said that the object at present was merely "to establish this principle, to wit, the security of foreigners where treaties are in their favor, and to preserve the harmony of States and that of the citizens thereof. This being once established, it will be the business of a subcommittee to detail it." [1] He accordingly had moved that a broad outline alone should be made, as follows: "That the jurisdiction of the National Judiciary shall extend to cases which respect the collection of the National revenue; impeachments of any National officers and questions which involve the National peace and harmony." This had been adopted. Such an extraordinarily broad jurisdiction was far more radical than that which the Convention finally adopted or than now appears in the Constitution. On this July

[1] As reported in Yates' *Notes*.

18, however, the jurisdiction was broadened still further, on motion of Madison, so as to read: "That the jurisdiction of the National Judiciary shall extend to cases under laws passed by the General Legislature; and to such other questions as involve the National peace and harmony." The Convention voted for this, without dissent. And so it settled the jurisdiction of the Courts, *i.e.*, the subjects over which their judicial power should extend. It is to be noted, however, that as Madison wrote later: "By questions involving the National peace and harmony, no one can suppose more was meant than might be *specified* by the Convention, as proper to be referred to the Judiciary either by the Constitution or the Constitutional authority of the Legislature. . . . That the Convention understood the entire Resolutions of Mr. Randolph to be a mere sketch in which omitted details were to be supplied and the general terms and phrases to be reduced to their proper details is demonstrated by the use made of them in the Convention. . . . Candour discovers no ground for the charge that the Resolutions contemplated a Government materially different from, or more National than, that in which they terminated. . . . The plan expressly aimed at a specification, and, of course, a limitation of the powers." [1]

Opponents of the Court's power to pass on the constitutionality of Acts of Congress frequently ask: Why did not the framers of the Constitution expressly provide for such a power, if they intended the Court to possess it? The answer is, that the framers made no provision whatever as to the powers of the Court — neither for this power nor for any other function or power exercised by the Court. It is always important to bear in mind that there is a vital distinction between a Court's jurisdiction and a Court's power. Judicial

---

[1] *Writings of James Madison* (Hunt's ed.), IX, Madison to John Tyler, 1833.

power comprises the functions exercised by a Court after it has obtained jurisdiction. Having fixed the Court's jurisdiction, the delegates assumed that the Court, having obtained jurisdiction, would exercise all functions and powers which Courts were at that time in the judicial habit of exercising. One power which the State Courts were at this time exercising was that of holding State laws to be void if they infringed the written State Constitutions. The attention of the delegates had already been called to this exercise of power, in previous debates in the Convention. As early as June 4, Randolph's Resolution for a Council of Revision composed of the Executive and a number of the National Judiciary, with power to veto any Act of Congress, had occasioned vigorous debate; for many delegates were opposed to the joining of the Judiciary in this veto function. Elbridge Gerry said that Judges ought not to decide on the policy of public measures: "They will have a sufficient check against encroachments on their own department by their exposition of laws which involved a power of deciding on their constitutionality. In some States, the Judges had actually set aside laws as being against the Constitution. This was done, too, with general approbation." Rufus King stated that he "was of opinion that the Judicial ought not to join it in negative of a law, because the Judges will have the expounding of those laws when they come before them; and they will no doubt stop the operation of such as shall appear repugnant to the Constitution." [1]

The Committee had voted to exclude the Judiciary from exercising this power of veto with the Executive. On June 6, the question had again been presented, Wilson favoring the proposition. Madison also favored it on several grounds, one of which was that "it would

[1] As reported in William Pierce's *Notes*.

enable the Judiciary Department the better to defend
itself against Legislative encroachments." King,
Gerry, Charles Pinckney, and Dickinson were opposed,
as it "involved an improper mixture of powers." The
proposal was again voted down. On July 21 (three
days after the jurisdiction of the National Judiciary
had been established by the Convention) a third
attempt was made by Wilson to join the Judiciary with
the President in vetoing laws passed by Congress.
He wished their power of veto to extend not only to
unconstitutional laws but to unwise laws, for, said he:
"It had been said that the Judges as expositors of the
laws would have an opportunity of defending their
constitutional rights. There was weight in this observation, but this power of the Judges did not go far
enough. Laws may be unjust, may be unwise, may be
dangerous, may be destructive; and yet may not be
so unconstitutional as to justify the Judges in refusing
to give them effect." Ellsworth, Mason, and Madison
favored Wilson's proposal. On the other hand, it was
pointed out by several delegates that these laws might
come up before the Courts in their judicial capacity,
which would thus have a double chance of passing upon
them — an undesirable situation. Gerry, Gorham, and
Strong of Massachusetts stated that "it was making
the expositors of the laws, the Legislators, which ought
never to be done. . . . The power of making laws
ought to be kept distinct from that of expounding the
laws." Luther Martin said: "As to the constitutionality of laws, that point will come before the Judges
in their proper official character. In this character,
they have a negative on the laws. Join them with the
Executive in the revision and they will have a double
negative." Rutledge said that "the Judges ought
never to give their opinion on a law till it comes before
them." Madison himself admitted (July 23) that:

"A law violating a Constitution established by the people themselves would be considered by the Judges as null and void." But Madison, Wilson, G. Morris, and Mason, however, were afraid that the Legislature would be too powerful, unless this veto power in both Executive and Judiciary should be conferred in addition to the power of the Judges to declare a law null and void. Mason admitted that in their judicial capacity, the Judges "could declare an unconstitutional law void"; but, he said, there were "unjust, oppressive, or pernicious" laws which did not come plainly under the description of unconstitutional laws, and he wished the Judges to be empowered to aid "in preventing every improper law."[1] The proposal, however, was voted down for a third time. The proposal was renewed again, on August 15, by Madison, seconded by Wilson. Charles Pinckney then "opposed the interference of the Judges in the Legislative business; it will involve them in parties, and give a previous tincture to their opinions." In this debate, there occurred the only reported instance in which any delegates opposed the exercise of the power to hold statutes void, and even these delegates did not deny the *existence* of the power. John F. Mercer of Maryland (who only attended the Convention from August 6 to August 17) said that "he disapproved of the doctrine that the Judges as expositors of the law should have authority to declare a law void. He thought laws ought to be well and cautiously made, and then to be uncontrollable." John Dickinson of Delaware said that he was "strongly impressed with the remark of Mr. Mercer, as to the power of the Judges to set aside the law. He thought no such power ought to exist. He was at the same

---

[1] The New York Constitution provided for a Council of Revision, composed of Governor and Judges, since "laws inconsistent with the spirit of their Constitution or with the public good may be legally and unadvisedly passed."

time at a loss what expedient to substitute." The proposal to join the Judges with the President in a power to veto the laws was defeated for a fourth time.[1]

It thus appears that while many delegates expressly admitted the existence of the power of the Courts to hold Acts of Congress void, no delegates denied its existence, though two disapproved of both the existence and the exercise of power.   There is one plain reason why the subject was not more fully discussed, which has not been adverted to by legal writers — and that is, that the form in which the Constitution was drafted at the time of the debates on June 4, June 6, and July 21 made it practically impossible that any case could arise in which an Act of Congress would be likely to be held unconstitutional.   It will be noted that, on these dates, the powers of Congress were not specifically limited, as in the Constitution when finally adopted; but that Congress was empowered "to legislate in all cases for the general interests of the Union and also in those to which the States are separately incompetent, or in which the harmony of the United States may be interrupted by the exercise of individual legislation." Now, it is evident under such a broad grant of power, the discretion of Congress was practically unlimited. Certainly, no Court would ever hold that any specific act of legislation was *not* "for the general interests of the Union", or was *not* one "in which the States are separately incompetent", or was *not* one "in which the harmony of the United States may be interrupted" — if Congress should have expressly determined to the contrary, by passing the statute.   Hence, at that time,

[1] Madison, as late as 1817, thought that a qualified negative on Legislative bills by the Judiciary would have been better than the power of judicial review of statutes involved, in litigated cases.   Writing to Monroe, Dec. 27, 1817, he said: "Such a controul, restricted to Constitutional points, besides giving greater stability and system to the rules of expounding the instrument would have precluded the question of a Judiciary annulment of Legislative Acts."

it was almost impossible to conceive of a case arising, in which, as a matter of fact, a Court would be in position to hold an Act of Congress void. Substantially, the only case likely to arise, in which it could take such action, would be some case in which Congress had passed a law infringing the Judicial powers of the Courts or the Executive powers of the President. And it was perhaps for this reason that delegates referred, several times, to the exercise of the power by the Courts to prevent encroachment by the Legislature upon the Judiciary Department. When, however, in the later drafts of the Constitution adopted after August 6, the powers of Congress were specifically set forth and limited, then it was evident to everyone that these limitations were entirely useless and of no effect, unless a power lay somewhere to enforce them; and the only power to enforce restraints or restrictions contained in a written Constitution is the Judicial power. If it did not exist there, it existed nowhere. Either the Constitution must be supreme, or Congress must be supreme. Both could not be. And the last thing that the delegates wanted or favored was a Congress with supreme and unlimited power.

OUT OF CONVENTION

Washington noted:

" In Convention. Dined at Mr. (James) Milligan's and drank tea at Mr. Meredith's."

THURSDAY, JULY 19, 1787

IN CONVENTION

After finally disposing of the subject of the Judiciary, the delegates again grappled, without success, with the method of appointment of the Executive, his term of office and eligibility to re-election — subjects over which they had long and repeatedly struggled on June 1 and 2, and July 9 and 17.   (See discussion under date of July 26.)

OUT OF CONVENTION

Washington noted:

"Dined (after coming out of Convention) at Mr. John Penn, the younger's.   Drank tea and spent the evening at my lodging."

On this day, the newspapers carried a despatch from Portsmouth, New Hampshire, to the effect that: "The General Court during their late session repealed the ten pound act, and thereby justified the conduct of the Justices of the Inferior Court who have uniformly opposed it as unconstitutional and unjust." [1]   Thus, there was brought to the attention of the delegates, for the fourth time since they began their sessions, an instance of cases in which the State Courts had held statutes invalid.   It is an interesting fact that this New Hampshire case should have been published on the very day when the Convention was discussing the subject of the National Judiciary.

Madison wrote, this day, to Jefferson a letter expressing more confidence than he had hitherto shown in the ultimate result:

"The Convention continue to sit, and have been closely employed since the commencement of the session.   I am still under the mortification of being restrained from disclosing any part of their proceedings.   As soon as I am at liberty, I will endeavor to make amends for my silence; and if I ever have the pleasure of seeing you, shall be able to give you pretty full gratification.   I have taken lengthy notes of every thing that has yet passed, and mean to go on

---

[1] *Independent Gazetteer*, July 18; *Pennsylvania Packet*, July 19; *New York Daily Advertiser*, July 14; *New York Journal*, July 19, 1787.   See also letter of "Watchman" in *New Hampshire Spy*, June 30, 1787; *Life of William Plumer*, (1857) by William Plumer, Jr., p. 59.

with the drudgery, if no indisposition obliges me to discontinue it. It is not possible to form any judgment of the future duration of the session. I am led by sundry circumstances to guess that the public mind is very impatient for the event, and various reports are circulating which tend to inflame curiosity. I do not learn, however, that any discontent is expressed at the concealment; and have little doubt that the people will be as ready to receive, as we shall be able to propose, a Government that will secure their liberties and happiness."

FRIDAY, JULY 20, 1787

IN CONVENTION

The debate over the method of election of the Executive continued. The subject of impeachment was also considered. (See discussion under date of September 8.)

OUT OF CONVENTION

Washington noted:

"In Convention. Dined at home and drank tea at Mr. [George] Clymer's."

SATURDAY, JULY 21, 1787

IN CONVENTION

The day was chiefly spent in debate over the proposal to join the Judiciary with the President in a power to veto. It was defeated for the third time, and the Executive alone was vested with the qualified veto power, subject to overruling by two thirds of each branch of the Legislature (as discussed *supra*, June 4).

OUT OF CONVENTION

Washington noted:

"In Convention. Dined at the Cold Spring, Springsbury, with the Club of Gentlm. and Ladies. Went to the Play in the afternoon afterwards."

The play at the Opera House was "A Concert", at which was recited, "A Moral Poem called The Crusade or the Generous Sultan, by Mr. James Thompson, Author of The Seasons, with the original Epilogue to Edward and Eleonora." [1]

On this day, the Philadelphia papers for the first time took notice of the vigorous opposition to the new Constitution which had sprung up in New York, under the leadership of Governor George Clinton, who represented the extremest devotion to State Sovereignty. This "idol" was now attacked in the *Herald* as follows : [2]

"In the beginning of the late war, the citizens of America looked up to a Foederal Government only for safety and protection; they were then powerful and successful at home and abroad. As soon as they set up the idol of State Sovereignty, they forgot the rock from which they derived their freedom and independence, and confined their allegiance and affections only to the State Governments; and hence the distress, confusion, debts and disgrace of the United States. Calamities have at last opened their eyes and they again turn to a Foederal Government for safety and protection. May the enemies of the new Confederation, whether in Rhode Island or elsewhere, whether secret or open, meet with the fate of the disaffected in the late War."

Very little opposition to the Convention in its early days had appeared in New York, while, on the other hand, the newspapers had printed many articles in its

---

[1] It is interesting to note that there was advertised at the Opera House, on July 19, a "Concert", consisting of "A Serious and Moral Lecture on the Vice of Gaming."

On July 25, the Opera House announced a "Concert, between the parts of which will be introduced a Moral and instructive Tale called Filial Piety, exemplified in the history of the Prince of Denmark . . . to which will be added a Comic Opera called Lethe or Aesop in the Shades. Doors open at 7, curtain drawn up precisely at 8. Ladies and Gentlemen are requested to send their servant in time to keep their boxes."

[2] Quoted in *Pennsylvania Packet*, June 26; *Pennsylvania Gazette*, June 27; *Independent Chronicle*, July 4; *Massachusetts Centinel*, July 7; *Salem Mercury*, July 10, 1787.

favor.[1] As early as May 24, a letter addressed "to the (Political) Free-thinkers of America", stated that reforms in the old Confederation were clearly necessary; that the object to be obtained was not a Government necessarily perfect for all time, but "a Government equal to the exigencies of the country and made capable of anticipating the important changes which await it"; and that the Convention of States now sitting was "created from fear and suffering." On May 26, it was stated that "a strong and efficient Executive power must be somewhere established." On June 18, a correspondent in several of the papers said:

"It is remarkable that those very men who have not only ransacked their brain for arguments, but every political publication for authorities, to support their favorite measure of withholding the necessary powers from the Union should all at once be fairly silenced. We see or read no more of their elaborate pieces, with long and uninteresting quotations from musty authors. Are they conscious of their errors? Or does the wisdom and dignity of that respectable group of characters now sitting in Convention at Philadelphia for the express purpose of strengthening the Confederacy strike them with awe, or make them apprehensive that their sinister policy will be crushed?"

Another correspondent wrote (June 26) that:[2]

"The principal difficulty in the way of necessary alterations in our Government will arise from the officers of Government. Their interest, it is imagined, will be affected by the alterations. . . . But it is to be hoped the people will neither be influenced by such men nor their connections in the adoption of a Foederal Government."

---

[1] See *New York Daily Advertiser*, May 24; *New York Independent Journal*, May 26. The New York papers contained many plans for the new Government; see "West Chester Farmer" and "Sketch of a Federal Government" in *New York Daily Advertiser*, June 8, 11, 1787.

[2] Quoted in *Pennsylvania Journal*, June 30, 1787.

After July 10, however, when Yates and Lansing left the Convention and returned to New York, with a report to the Governor that it was violating its instructions and planning a despotic Government, Clinton was encouraged to renew the opposition which he had raised at the time when the New York delegates were originally named.   Widespread rumors of projects of the Convention hostile to the liberties of the people began to be spread.   Sarcastic and antagonistic articles appeared, of which the following is a sample : [1]

"The Convention should respect the limits of every individual; and it is my advice that they would prevent any individual from issuing a paper medium, by an express clause in the new Government which is to combine all the jarring interests of the States without an army or resources.   If our notables, or notable attornies and politicians, who are called the wisdom of the western world, and who have convened for the purpose of mending a rotten silk stocking or cementing a rope of sand, would establish a tribunal of inquiry into the speculations of financiers and contractors, and force them to disgorge the contents of their voracious maws, they would give the world better specimens of their political wisdom, than exhibiting to Europe a laughable realization of Cervantes' fiction of Governor Sancho, by forming speculative systems which look beautiful and perfect in the recess of the State House, but vanish when exposed to the touch of the people.   They might preserve for one year more that *dignity* which is always in the mouths of those political *upstarts* who have no real claim to publick or private respect."

To counteract these influences, there now appeared in the *New York Daily Advertiser*, a long letter in the nature of a personal attack on Clinton and a defence of the need of a Convention.   It stated that:

[1] Quoted in *Massachusetts Centinel*, July 21, 1787, from a New York paper of July 6.

"It is currently reported and believed that his Excellency, Governor Clinton, had, in public company, without reserve, reprobated the appointment of the Convention and predicted a mischievous issue of that measure. His observations are said to be to the effect : that the appointment of a Convention is calculated to impress the people with an idea of evils which do not exist; therefore, that to all probability the result of their deliberations, whatever it might be, would only serve to throw the community into confusion."

And it criticised Clinton's attitude as "unwarrantable and culpable", arousing grave doubts as to whether he was working for the public good, or was seeking dangerously after personal power.[1] This letter, though published anonymously, was admitted, two months later, to be written by Alexander Hamilton. It was followed in the same paper, July 26, by a letter from "An Admirer of Anti-Federal Men", urging the people to have "confidence in those illustrious characters" convened at Philadelphia, and saying that "the conduct of several leading men among us has of late given the friends of liberty much uneasiness." From this time on, the opposition to the Constitution was stronger in New York than in any other State.

SUNDAY, JULY 22, 1787

Washington noted :

"Left town by 5 o'clock A. M. Breakfasted at Genl. Mifflin's. Rode up with him and others to the Spring Mills and returned to Genl. Mifflin's to Dinner, after which proceeded to the City."

General Mifflin's country home was east of the Falls of the Schuylkill, and the object of the trip was to

---

[1] See *Pennsylvania Packet*, Aug. 3; *Massachusetts Centinel*, Aug. 11, 1787, and other papers; *New York Journal*, Sept. 6; *New York Daily Advertiser*, Sept. 10, 15, 1787. See *The Ratification of Federal Constitution by the State of New York* (1921) by Clarence E. Vernier. For an attack on Clinton by the Federalists, see *New York Daily Advertiser*, June 23, 1787.

inspect the vineyards and apiary of Peter Legaux. The latter in his manuscript diary wrote; [1]

"This day Gen. Washington, Gen. Mifflin and four others of the Convention did us the honor of paying us a visit in order to see our vineyards and bee houses. In this they found a great delight, asked a number of questions, and testified their highest approbation with my manner of managing bees, which gave me a great deal of pleasure."

Franklin wrote this day to Captain John Paul Jones, who was then in Europe, that "the Convention goes on well and that there is hope of great good to result from their counsels."

Dr. Hugh Williamson wrote to James Iredell:

"After much labor the Convention have nearly agreed on the principles and outlines of a system which we hope may fairly be called an amendment of the Federal Government. This system we expect will, in three or four days, be referred to a small committee to be properly dressed; and if we like it, when clothed and equipped, we shall submit it to Congress, and advise them to recommend it to the hospitable reception of the States. I expect that some time in September we may put the last hand to this work."

Richard Henry Lee, a Member of Congress from Virginia (and later one of the leaders in opposing the adoption of the Constitution), wrote from New York to Francis Lightfoot Lee that he had spent the week before July 10 in Philadelphia, where "the Federal Convention is proceeding slowly, but I hope surely, in a practical improvement of our Federal Constitution":

"Experience seems to have proved that our Governments have not tone enough for the unruly passions of men, and so far as I can judge, the general wish is for a balanced Government, where the powers shall be placed independently, as in England; and of duration somewhat longer than the present. . . . I suppose it will be recom-

[1] *Washington After the Revolution* (1898), by William Spohn Baker.

mended to the States to call Conventions for the special purpose of approving the new system, that it may rest on the broad base of the people's choice, rather than on the more feeble opinion of the ordinary Legislatures."

MONDAY, JULY 23, 1787

IN CONVENTION

On this day, the twelfth State appeared on the floor of the Convention, when — two months after its assembly — John Langdon and Nicholas Gilman of New Hampshire took their seats. Of their arrival, Gilman wrote to Joseph Gilman (July 31) that "notwithstanding we are so late in the day, it is a circumstance in this critical state of affairs that seems highly pleasing to the Convention." [1] Had they appeared earlier, during the great contest which led up to the Compromise of July 16, the whole course of history might have been changed. Although the leaders of the small States' party evidently expected New Hampshire to line up with them, it is probable, in view of the extremely National sentiments which Langdon and Gilman expressed later, that they would have allied themselves with the Virginia side, in which case the Compromise might not have succeeded. Their absence, therefore, was probably a fortunate occurrence.

Per Capita Voting

Up to this point, the Convention, in debating the State equality of votes in the Senate, had apparently contemplated that the delegates of each State should

---

[1] *Freemen's Journal*, July 23, 1787, published the following despatch from Hartford, Connecticut, of July 16: "Saturday last passed through this city on their way to Philadelphia, the honorable John Langdon, Esq., late president of New Hampshire, and Colonel Gardner, delegate from that State to the Federal Convention. 'The prayers of the good (says a New Hampshire paper) will follow this disinterested patriot (Mr. Langdon) who, when the public treasury was incapable of furnishing supplies, generously offered to bear the expenses of himself and colleague on this important mission.' "

cast their votes as a unit — the vote thus being taken by States, as in the Congress of the Confederation. The first suggestion to the contrary was made by Gerry. On July 14, he proposed that "the States should vote per capita, which, he said, would prevent the delays and inconveniences that had been experienced in Congress and would give a National aspect and spirit to the management of business." Though the delegates from the smaller States undoubtedly believed that the Senators from a State would always vote alike, Gerry's suggestion was a radical alteration of the equality system; for it made it possible at least that, by division of its Senatorial vote, a State might lose its position of equality. In spite of this fact, Sherman said that he had no objection to the Senators voting per capita. Gerry's proposal was not acted on until after the Great Compromise had been settled. Then, on July 23, G. Morris and King (neither of whom had favored equality of votes) moved that the representation in the Senate "consist of three members from each State, who shall vote per capita." Williamson concurred. Ellsworth said that he "had always approved of voting in that mode." With far more consistency and insight, Luther Martin, perceiving how this would derogate from the equality theory, announced his opposition to per capita voting, "as departing from the idea of the States being represented" in the Senate. His colleague, Carroll, said, wisely, that though he "was not struck with any particular objection against the mode, he did not wish so hastily to make so material an innovation." No further consideration was given to this very vital change. The discussion then turned on the number of Senators for each State. Gorham preferred two rather than three, as "a small number was most convenient for deciding on peace and war which he expected would be vested" in the Senate.   Mason also thought that three Senators would make the Senate too numerous.   Williamson argued that "if the number be too great, the distant States will not be on an equal footing with the nearer States as the latter can more easily send and support their ablest citizen."

The Convention voted (with Maryland alone dissenting) that the Senate should consist of two members from each State who should vote per capita.   In this manner, and with very slight debate, this important question was settled.

On August 9, a proposal by Randolph, Mason, and Strong was made to postpone action on the last sentence until it should be seen whether the Convention was going to adhere to that part of the Great Compromise which gave to the House the origination of money bills — Randolph stating that unless the whole Compromise was accepted, he should propose to vary the representation in the Senate.   The motion to postpone was defeated, and the plan of one vote for each Senator was accepted by the Convention.

Mode of Ratification of the Constitution

Having settled most of the general outlines of the new Government (except the method of the election of President), the Convention took up this day the question :   How shall the new Constitution be adopted ?

Randolph's Resolutions of May 29 provided that :

"The amendments which shall be offered to the Confederation by the Convention ought at a proper time or times, after the approbation of Congress, to be submitted to an assembly or assemblies of Representatives recommended by the several Legislatures; to be expressly chosen by the people, to consider and decide thereon."

This proposal at once raised the fundamental question whether the new Constitution was to come from the people or from the States; whether it was to be adopted by vote of the people either directly or through their representatives assembled in State Conventions, or whether it was to be adopted by the States acting through their Legislatures. It must be remembered that of the States which adopted Constitutions between 1776 and 1784, only two — New Hampshire and Massachusetts — had framed their Constitutions by Conventions especially chosen for that purpose and distinct from the Legislative body, and only in these two States were the Constitutions so framed submitted to the people themselves for adoption. In Pennsylvania, New Jersey, Delaware, Maryland, North Carolina, and Georgia, the Constitutions were framed and adopted by bodies specially chosen for that purpose but which also acted as the Legislatures. In Virginia, South Carolina, and New York, the Legislatures framed and enacted the Constitutions, without special authority from the people. In no one of the States, other than New Hampshire and Massachusetts, did the people themselves act on the Constitution so adopted.[1] The Articles of Confederation themselves had been ratified by the people in a few of the Eastern States, but in the Southern States and elsewhere, they had been ratified by the Legislatures.[2]

The line of cleavage between those delegates who wanted the new Government to rest on a popular basis and those who wished it to rest on the State Legislatures had become apparent, on the very first day (June 5) when the Committee of the Whole considered this particular Randolph Resolution.[3] Madison stated that

[1] *The First State Constitutional Conventions 1776–1783*, by W. F. Dodd, *Amer. Pol. Sci. Rev.* (1908), II; *Constitutional History of the American People* (1898), by Francis N. Thorpe, I, Chap. 4; *Constitutional Conventions* (4th ed. 1887), by John A. Jameson.

[2] See statements by Gerry and King, June 5; Ellsworth, July 23.

[3] It is interesting to note that this Resolution, when it was debated, was described as one "for recommending Conventions under appointment of the people to

"he thought it indispensable that the new Constitution should be ratified in the most unexceptionable form and by the supreme authority of the people themselves." Wilson took the same view. Rufus King concurred, but on the ground that it would be easier to secure adoption by Conventions than by Legislatures, since the latter "being to lose power will be most likely to raise objections." On the other hand, Sherman of Connecticut, a sturdy upholder of State Sovereignty, wished for ratification by the State Legislatures; and Gerry of Massachusetts (who later refused to sign the Constitution) was afraid of referring the new system to the people, saying, as to the Eastern States, "the people in that quarter have at this time the wildest ideas of Government in the world." Ellsworth of Connecticut also stated (June 20) that "he did not like these Conventions. They were better fitted to pull down than to build up Constitutions."[1] Luther Martin of Maryland, another States' Rights adherent, also opposed Conventions in the States (June 20). When the Convention took up this subject, on this July 23, Ellsworth at once moved that the new plan be referred to the State Legislatures for ratification, arguing that the Legislatures were more likely to ratify than the people, since "the prevailing wish of the people in the Eastern States is to get rid of the public debt", whereas "the idea of strengthening the National Government carries with it that of strengthening the public debt." He stated further that: "A new set of ideas seemed to have crept in since the Articles of Confederation were

ratify the new Constitution." Somewhere between May 29 and June 5, the phrase "the amendments which shall be offered to the Confederation by the Convention" had become the phrase "the new Constitution", a very significant change.

[1] One reason why the Connecticut delegates disliked ratification by Conventions was that, in that State, a Convention had assembled at Middletown in December, 1783, which had violently opposed the votes of Congress as to commutation of pay for officers of the Continental army — and other subjects, and the action of this Convention had caused considerable disturbance in other States.

established. Conventions of the people or with power derived expressly from the people were not then thought of. The Legislatures were considered as competent." Gerry also argued that: "Great confusion would result from a recurrence to the people. They would never agree on anything." Ellsworth's "new set of ideas", however, could hardly be said to have been new; for they had been expressed in the Virginia Bill of Rights of June 12, 1776, as drafted by George Mason:

"That all power is vested in, and consequently derived from the people, that magistrates are their trustees and servants and at all times amenable to them. That Government is, or ought to be instituted for the common benefit, protection and security of the people, nation or community . . . and that when any Government shall be found inadequate or contrary to these purposes, a majority of the community hath an indubitable, inalienable and indefeasible right to reform, alter, or abolish it, in such manner as shall be judged most conclusive to the public weal."

And they had been reëchoed by Jefferson in the Declaration of Independence. Powerful arguments in behalf of action by the people were made by Mason, Randolph, and Madison of Virginia, King and Gorham of Massachusetts, Wilson of North Carolina, and G. Morris of Pennsylvania. Mason urged that resort must be had "to the people with whom all power remains that has not been given up in the Constitutions derived from them. It was of great moment that this doctrine should be cherished as the basis of free Government." In these words, he set forth the fundamental principle of the Constitution. Randolph, Williamson, King, and Gorham argued that members of the Legislatures, being about to lose power, would not discuss the subject candidly; and it was pointed out that in some States "many of the ablest men are excluded from the

qualifications (in some States larger for Senators than for Representatives). On the other hand, in all the States, whoever was qualified to vote for State Representative could vote for members of a Convention; and in Massachusetts and some other States, every freeman of a town (irrespective of possession of property) could vote for a member of a Convention. Moreover, members of Conventions themselves were not obliged to possess any property qualifications. Hence, the vote by which the Federal Convention referred ratification to the people was a democratic vote, and not in the interests of property.[1]

OUT OF CONVENTION

Joseph Jones wrote from Virginia, this day, to Madison:

"Are we likely to have a happy issue of your meeting or will it pass over without any effect? Finding you still continue together, our hopes are not lost; my fears, however, I must confess, are rather increased than diminished by the protraction of your session, taking it for granted many and great difficulties have been encountered, as there were many and great to remove before a good system could be established."

---

[1] When the Constitution was actually submitted to the State Conventions for ratification in 1787–1788, the State Legislatures voted in Massachusetts, Pennsylvania, Delaware, Maryland, North Carolina, South Carolina, and Georgia that persons qualified to vote for members of the lower House of the Legislature might vote for members of the Convention; in New York, the straight principle of manhood suffrage was adopted in the election of delegates to the ratifying Convention; in Connecticut, those "qualified by law to vote in the town meetings" could vote for members of the Convention; in New Hampshire, the duly qualified voters for members of the lower House, together with certain additional classes. See *An Economic Interpretation of the Constitution* (1913), by Charles A. Beard, 240–242.

In Virginia, the Assembly voted, Oct. 25, 1787: "Resolved that every citizen being a freeholder in this Commonwealth be eligible to a seat in the Convention, and that the people, therefore, be not restrained in their choice of Delegates by any of those legal or constitutional restrictions which confine them in their choice of Members of the Legislature."

TUESDAY, JULY 24, 1787

IN CONVENTION

Though the delegates were still struggling with the question of the mode of election of the President, yet, as all the other subjects comprised in Randolph's original Resolutions of May 29 had now been acted upon, the Convention, this day, appointed a Committee, consisting of John Rutledge of South Carolina, Edmund Randolph of Virginia, Nathaniel Gorham of Massachusetts, Oliver Ellsworth of Connecticut, and James Wilson of Pennsylvania — a well-balanced group of two representatives of the Southern, two of the Northern, and one of the Middle States (known later as the Committee of Detail) — "to report a Constitution conformable to the Resolutions passed by the Convention." To this Committee, there were referred all the proposals thus far adopted, as well as the plans for a government submitted by Charles Pinckney on May 29, and by William Paterson on June 15.

OUT OF CONVENTION

John Jay wrote, this day, to Jefferson in Paris [1] that:

"The Convention is sitting, but their proceedings are secret. Our Indian affairs in the West still give us uneasiness, and so I fear they will continue to do, for reasons you will not be at a loss to conjecture. Our affairs in general will admit of much melioration, and they will afford the Convention ample field for the display of their patriotism and talents."

WEDNESDAY, JULY 25, 1787

IN CONVENTION

The delegates continued to struggle with the question of the Executive.

[1] *Diplomatic Correspondence of the United States,* **II,** 43.

On this day, the Secrecy Rule was so rigidly applied that a motion that the members of the Convention might take copies of the Resolutions which had been agreed to was defeated; although it was voted that copies of the proceedings should be furnished to the Committee of Detail. So extreme an application of the Rule was severely commented on, later, by Luther Martin, in his Report to the Maryland Legislature, in which he stated: [1]

"I moved for liberty to be given to the different members to take correct copies of the propositions to which the Convention had then agreed, in order that during the recess of the Convention, we might have an opportunity of considering them, and if it should be thought that any alterations or amendments were necessary, that we might be prepared, against the Convention met, to bring them forward for discussion. But the same spirit which caused our doors to be shut, our proceedings to be kept secret, our Journals to be locked up, and every avenue, as far as possible, to be shut to public information, prevailed also in this case, and the proposal, so reasonable and necessary, was rejected by a majority of the Convention; thereby precluding even the members themselves from the necessary means of information and deliberation on the important business in which they were engaged."

OUT OF CONVENTION

John Jay wrote from New York, this day, to General Washington:

"Permit me to hint whether it would not be wise and reasonable to provide a strong check to the admission of foreigners into the administration of our National Government, and to declare expressly that the command in chief

[1] Martin wrote in *Maryland Journal*, March 7, 1788, that: "We were permitted to read them (the Journals), although we were not always permitted to copy them. . . . The business of the Committees were not of a secret nature, nor were they conducted in a secret manner, I mean as to Members of the Convention. . . . I am satisfied that there was no Committee while I was there of whose proceedings I was not informed."

of the American Army shall not be given to, nor devolve on, any but a natural born citizen."

The necessity of forming a strong Government which might suppress the serious combination of the Indian tribes (fostered, it was hinted, by Great Britain), and the difficulty of dealing with such a matter by a Government having no Executive, were impressed upon Madison, in a letter written by Edward Carrington from Congress in New York:

"We are trying to do something with our Western Territory to make it useful to the purposes for which the United States was vested with it. You have seen in the papers the scheme for the temporary as well as perpetual government of it. A practical measure for the sale of it, or rather by means of it to redeem the domestic debt, remains still to be agreed upon, and I fear the difficulties which have always stood in the way of this great object are not yet to be surmounted. Col. Lee joins Grayson and myself with great zeal, but what will be the issue of our efforts, I know not. Indian affairs wear an hostile aspect, and money must in all probability be expended on treaties with them. A general Confederacy is formed of all the nations and tribes, from the Six Nations inclusive to the Mississippi, under the immediate influence of Brandt — a general Council has been held, in form, near Detroit as long ago as last December, in which have been considered as grievances, our surveying over the Ohio, the cessions being made by only parts of the tribes having rights in the ceded tracts. Of these injuries or grievances, they have sent an united representation to Congress requesting that a General Treaty may be held — perhaps this business may be directed by an authority higher than Brandt, and should our titles to the land be compleat, it will still be better to spend a little money in Treating rather than expend a great deal in War, which, from the generality of the confederacy, is seriously to be apprehended. This subject is now under consideration. As to the hostilities upon Kentucky the

Superintendent of Indian Affairs or, in case of his inability
to go, Col. Josiah Harmon is ordered to proceed immediately to some convenient place for holding a treaty with
the hostile tribes and by that means restore peace between
them and our people if practicable. In the meantime, Col.
Harmon is so to post the Federal troops as to provide the
best defence for the country and to call for such aids of
militia as he shall find necessary. Should the treaty not
succeed, report is to be made to Congress for their further
orders as to offensive operations. The state of the general
Confederacy requires some care in the direction of this
business."

And the necessity of an Executive was also commented upon in a letter from Baltimore of July 17,
published in the *Gazette*:

"We are all anxious to hear what the Fœderal Convention are doing, and from their silence and secrecy are
in hopes something will be done of future advantage to
America. I pray not only that a reform of our Confederation may take place, but the defects of our Statical
Government pointed out and amendments recommended,
so that we may be as much in unison with each other as is
compatible with our local situation and different habits of
thinking. . . . I am in hopes that Mr. Adams' defence
(as it is generally termed) but what I call his condemnation
of our Constitutions will have a good effect in impressing
the necessity of supplemental checks on our Legislatures,
and of cloathing an Executive with additional power and
respectability, so as to be adequate to every exigency."

The *Herald* and the *Journal* sanguinely announced,
this day, that the Convention would only last a month
longer:

"We are informed that the Federal Convention will
continue their deliberations about a month longer; and
that there will then be presented to the public a scheme
of Continental Government adapted to the circumstances

and habits of the people without regard to the fine spun systems of elementary writers."

THURSDAY, JULY 26, 1787

IN CONVENTION

Election of Executive

On this day, after a debate occupying the better part of eight days (June 1, 2, 9, July 19, 20, 24, 25, 26), the delegates finally arrived at an agreement on the subject of the manner of election and term of office of the Executive — that he should be chosen by the National Legislature, for a term of seven years, and to be ineligible to re-election. (They had already agreed that he was to be subject to impeachment and to have power to appoint all officers except Judges, and to carry into execution the National laws.) In arriving at this conclusion, however, they had shown every variety of vacillation, having voted, in turn, both for and against many other proposals. The problems were: how to make the Executive independent of the Legislature, and yet not too independent — how to give him effective power and yet keep him responsible to the people? The sinuous and perplexing course of their proceedings was as follows. On June 1 and 2, the method of election proposed by Randolph's Resolutions of May 29, namely, by the National Legislature, had been adopted, only Pennsylvania and Maryland being opposed. James Wilson of Pennsylvania, however, an ardent advocate of the Constitution, had stated that while he was "apprehensive that it might appear chimerical", he was, "in theory at least, for an election by the people." The remark was significant; for at that time popular election of State Executives prevailed under the written Constitutions of only three States — New Hampshire, Massachusetts, and New

York. Accordingly, he proposed choice of Executive by electors chosen by the people. Elbridge Gerry of Massachusetts was also opposed to Legislative election as promotive of constant intrigues for Executive favor; but he thought the "community was not yet ripe for stripping the States of their powers" and vesting them in the people; moreover, he thought the people were "too little informed of personal characters" to choose electors. Wilson's proposal was defeated. The term for the Executive was fixed at seven years, and he was made ineligible for re-election. A week later, Gerry moved that the National Executive be elected by the Executives of the States, urging again that the method already adopted "would give birth to both corruption between the Executive and Legislature previous to election and to partiality in the Executive afterwards to the friends who promoted him." After an earnest speech in opposition by Randolph, the motion had been defeated. On July 17, the subject was again heatedly debated. The most earnest advocates of the new Constitution were equally earnest for election by the people, their view being, as Wilson said, that otherwise the Executive "would be too dependent to stand as the mediator between the intrigues and sinister views of the Representatives and the general liberties and interests of the people." George Mason, Charles Pinckney, and Hugh Williamson, on the other hand, urged that "the extent of the country renders it impossible that the people can have the requisite capacity to judge of the respective pretensions of the candidates" and that the people would be "led by a few active and designing men." These views prevailed, and a motion for election by the people secured the vote of only one State (Pennsylvania). A motion by Luther Martin for choice by electors appointed by the State Legislatures was also defeated.

The Convention then, however, proceeded to reverse its previous action as to ineligibility to re-election. Houston, Sherman, and G. Morris now urged that this provision "tended to destroy the great motive to good behaviour, the hope of being rewarded by a reappointment. It was saying to him, make hay while the sun shines"; and the delegates now voted that the Executive should be re-eligible. This brought forth a motion by James McClurg that the Executive be given a term during good behaviour, since a seven-year term with re-eligibility would make him dependent forever on the Legislature. Mason considered that an Executive during good behaviour "is a softer name only for an Executive for life and that the next would be an easy step to an hereditary monarchy." Madison said that he could not be "thought to favor any step towards monarchy; the real object with him was to prevent its introduction." He pointed out that the danger which was turning the people towards a revolution against Republican government was the instability and encroachment of the Legislatures, and that: "Experience had proved a tendency in our Government to throw all power into the Legislative vortex. The Executives of the States are in general little more than cyphers, the Legislatures omnipotent." Hence, it was absolutely necessary to adopt some expedient, either by method of election or length of term, which would make the Executive and the Legislative independent of each other. G. Morris also said that he was "as little a friend to monarchy as any gentleman", but that "the way to keep out a monarchical Government was to establish such a Republican Government as would make the people happy and prevent a desire of change." McClurg's motion, however, was defeated; and so was a motion to strike out the seven-year term already voted. On July 19, Luther Martin moved to reinstate ineligibility. Randolph concurred, thinking the Executive should "not be left under a temptation to court a reappointment. If he should be reappointable by the Legislature, he will be no check on it." G. Morris stated that the Executive "ought to be so constituted as to be the great protector of the mass of the people"; but if he was to be both appointed by and impeachable by the Legislature, "it will hold him in such dependence that he will be no check on the Legislature, will not be a firm guardian of the people and of the public interest. He will be the tool of a faction." He accordingly favored either not making the Executive impeachable, or else allowing his election by the people. King of Massachusetts was opposed to the ineligibility and "much disposed to think that in such cases the people at large would chuse wisely." Paterson, Madison, and Gerry were inclined to choice of the Executive by electors (Gerry favoring electors appointed by the State Executives), Madison still retained his belief, however, that choice by "the people at large" was the fittest. Wilson of Pennsylvania stated that "it seems to be the unanimous sense that the Executive should not be appointed by the Legislature unless he be rendered ineligible a second time; he perceived with pleasure that the idea was gaining ground of an election mediately or immediately by the people." Ellsworth of Connecticut now moved for choice by electors appointed by the State Legislatures, and this was adopted.[1] At the same time, it was voted that the term be changed from seven years to six; and Luther Martin's attempt to reimpose ineligibility to re-election was defeated.[2] On July 20, the Con-

[1] This same motion made by Luther Martin, on July 17, had then been defeated. A similar motion again made on July 25, by Butler, was defeated.

[2] Notice the reasons given a shorter term. Ellsworth said: "If the elections be too frequent, the Executive will not be firm enough. There must be duties which will make him unpopular for the moment. There will be *antis* as well as *ins*. His administration, therefore, will be attacked and misrepresented."

vention adopted the ratio for electors suggested by
Gerry, which gave Pennsylvania, Virginia, and Mas-
sachusetts three each; Connecticut, New York, New
Jersey, Maryland, North Carolina, and South Carolina
two each; and New Hampshire, Rhode Island, and
Delaware, one each. Three days later, on July 24, the
Convention reversed its whole action on this subject;
and on motion of Houston of New Jersey, supported by
Williamson of North Carolina and Strong of Massachusetts, again voted for choice of Executive by the
National Legislature. This reversal necessitated reconsideration of the vote as to re-eligibility and as to
term of office. Various suggestions were now made
for an eight, eleven, fifteen, and twenty year term, but
no votes were taken. "The difficulties and perplex-
ities" which accompanied choice by the Legislature
were now again impressed upon the Convention by
Wilson, who said that he "remained unshaken" that
"we ought to resort to the people", but he suggested
a compromise that election be made by fifteen of the
Legislature drawn by lot. G. Morris stated that ";of
all possible modes of appointment that by the Legislature is the worst. If the Legislature is to appoint
and to impeach or to influence the impeachment, the
Executive will be the mere creature of it." He thought
that Wilson's suggestion "deserved consideration. It
would be better that chance should decide, than
intrigue." King and Gerry thought we ought to be
governed "by reason and not by chance", and Gerry
urged that, as "we seem to be entirely at a loss on this
head", the whole subject be referred to the Committee
of Detail.

On July 25, various new proposals were made.
Ellsworth suggested that only in case of a candidacy
for re-election should the choice be by electors. Gerry
suggested choice by the State Executives with the

concurrence of their Councils. Pinckney suggested that choice by the Legislature be qualified by the proviso that no person be eligible for more than six years in any twelve. Butler suggested choice by electors chosen by the State Legislatures. All these proposals were defeated. G. Morris and Madison reiterated insistently the reasons in favor of popular election — first, to avoid intrigues with Legislative factions by candidates for appointment; second, to avoid the temptation to foreign powers to influence the National Legislature, it being "an object of great moment with such powers to have at the head of our Government a man attached to their respective politics and interests." Williamson of North Carolina and Butler of South Carolina agreed that "the two great evils to be avoided are cabal at home and influence from abroad." Mason, though agreeing that the danger of foreign influence was the most serious objection that had been urged, nevertheless favored appointment by the Legislature. Ellsworth concurred, fearing lest election by the people would always result in choice of the Executive by the largest States. Gerry thought popular election to be "radically vicious." "The ignorance of the people," he said, "would put it in the power of some one set of men dispersed through the Union and acting in concert to delude them in any appointment"; and he feared that in this way the Society of the Cincinnati might control elections (in which opinion Mason concurred, though both professed great respect for the members of that military Society).

Gouverneur Morris now renewed the objection which he had continually raised to the attempts made by Gerry and L. Martin to reinstate a provision against re-election. Ellsworth also (July 24) thought the Executive should be re-elected "if his conduct proved him worthy of it. And he will be more likely to render

himself worthy of it if he be rewardable with it." The
theory of rotation in office, however, and consequent
opposition to re-elections had long been cardinal
doctrines with the statesmen of the Revolution. The
Articles of Confederation had contained a provision
that no member of Congress should be allowed to serve
more than three years in a period of six. In 1782, a
Committee of Congress (consisting of Hamilton, Madison, and T. Fitzsimmons) had reported that: "The
truth is, the security intended to the general liberty
in the Confederation consists in the frequent election
and in the rotation of the members of Congress, by
which there is a constant and effectual check upon
them. This is the security which the people in every
State enjoy against the usurpations of their internal
government, and it is the true source of security in a
representative republic." [1] On the other hand, G.
Morris now argued that under this doctrine of rotation,
there was formed "a political school in which we were
always governed by scholars and not by the masters",
and that to adopt a rotation "produces instability of
councils." In reply to these arguments, Mason maintained that: "Having for his primary object, for the
pole-star of his political conduct, the preservation of
the rights of the people, he held it as an essential point,
as the very palladium of civil liberty, that the great
officers of State and particularly the Executive, should
at fixed periods return to that mass from which they
were at first taken, in order that they may feel and
respect those rights and interests which are again to be
personally valuable to them." [2] This view was shared

---

[1] *Journals of the Continental Congress*, Dec. 16, 1782.

[2] Mason, in the Virginia State Convention in 1788, stated, in opposition to the
Constitution: "The great fundamental principles of republicanism is here sapped.
The President is elected without rotation. . . . The President will be elected time
after time; he will be continued in office for life. . . . Nothing is so essential to the
preservation of a republican government as a periodical rotation. Nothing so
strongly impels a man to regard the interest of his constituents as the certainty of

by Dr. Franklin, who said that "in free Governments, the rulers are the servants, and the people their superiors and sovereigns. For the former, therefore, to return among the latter was not to degrade but to promote them."

With the expression of these views, the great debate was closed; and on this July 26, on motion of Mason, the Convention (having already voted for election by the Legislature) proceeded again to reverse itself as to the term and eligibility, by voting that the Executive should be appointed for seven years and be ineligible a second time. And thus the subject was left precisely as recommended by Randolph in his original Resolution.[1]

It is important to note that, in almost all the votes a long term with no re-election was favored, if the choice of Executive was to be by the Legislature; and a short

returning to the general mass of the people, from whence he was taken, where he must participate their burdens. . . . I should be contented that he might be elected for eight years; but I would wish him to be capable of holding the office only eight out of twelve or sixteen years." In reply to Mason, Edmund Randolph said: "That which has produced my opinion against the limitation of his eligibility is this — that it renders him more independent in his place, and more solicitous of promoting the interest of his constituents; for unless you put it in his power to be re-elected, instead of being attentive to their interests, he will lean to the augmentation of his private emoluments." *Elliot's Debates*, III, 484–485.

That Washington was not particularly favorable to the theory of rotation may be inferred from an account written of George Lux of Baltimore, by Alexander Graydon in his *Memoirs of a Life Chiefly Spent in Pennsylvania* (1811): "Among his guests, he was once honored with the company of Mrs. Macaulay, the historian, whom, at his request (as he informed me) he accompanied to Mount Vernon on a visit to General Washington, where they stayed some days. While in conversation one day at dinner, the lady, in a high, republican strain, took occasion to expatiate on the vast advantages of rotation in office. This was in the manner of appeal to her host, of whose approbation she seemed to be secure; but as the General was rather a practical or accidental, rather than a republican by preference — I will not say a republican *malgré lui* — he could only carry his politeness so far as not absolutely to dissent from the opinion, and there was, of course, no commingled flow of soul upon the occasion."

[1] Six States (New Hampshire, Connecticut, New Jersey, North Carolina, South Carolina, and Georgia) voted for the final resolution; three (Pennsylvania, Delaware, and Maryland) against it; Massachusetts was not on the floor; and Virginia was divided by the temporary absence of Randolph from the room, Madison and Washington voting against the resolution as they were opposed to election by the Legislature.

term with possibility of re-election, if the choice was to be otherwise than by the Legislature. In other words, the views of most of the delegates as to length of term and as to re-election were dependent on the *mode* of election. This fact is generally overlooked in debates at the present day over the third-term question and over the proposed Constitutional amendment for a Presidential term of office of seven years; and votes of the Federal Convention are quoted as if they represented an absolute expression of opinion of views as to the proper term of the Presidential office, whereas, in fact, they should be considered as expressing views of such a term only in its relation to the specific mode of election which was being concurrently voted.

During the course of this long debate, three proposals were made (but not voted upon), which contained the germs of the method of Presidential election finally adopted in the closing sessions of the Convention. Williamson of North Carolina (on July 25) suggested that in a popular election, each voter should vote for three candidates (one of whom, he thought, would be probably from the voter's own State); Morris then suggested that each voter vote for two persons, one of whom *should not be* of his own State; Dickinson of Delaware suggested that the people of each State should elect one of their citizens, and that the National Legislature or electors choose from these candidates; Wilson (on July 17) suggested that the people vote, but that in case no candidate obtained a majority, then the National Legislature should choose. From these various suggestions, there was finally reported (on September 4) the plan of State electors, who should vote for two candidates (one of whom should not be from the elector's own State), and choice by the Legislature, if no candidate should secure a majority of the electoral vote (see *infra* p. 623).

With its action on the subject of the Executive, the Convention on this July 26 had now completed its consideration of the Randolph Resolutions, and accordingly, it adjourned until August 6, in order that the Committee might have time to prepare and report a draft of a Constitution.[1]

OUT OF CONVENTION

Washington noted (erroneously under date of July 27):

"In Convention, which adjourned this day, to meet again on Monday, the 6th of August, that a Committee which had been appointed (consisting of 5 members) might have time to arrange, and draw into method and form the several matters which had been agreed to by the Convention as a Constitution for the United States. Dined at Mr. Morris's and drank tea at Mr. Powell's."

The news of the adjournment was announced in the newspapers as follows: [2]

"The Federal Convention having resolved upon the measures necessary to discharge their important trust adjourned in order to give a committee, appointed for the purpose, time to arrange and systematize the materials which that honorable body have collected. The public curiosity will soon be gratified; and it is hoped, from the universal confidence reposed in this delegation, that the minds of the people throughout the United States are prepared to receive with respect and to try with a fortitude and perseverance the plan which will be offered to them by men distinguished for their wisdom and patriotism."

[1] Before adjourning, the Convention decided, on motion of Mason, to direct the Committee of Detail to consider the subject of property and citizenship qualifications for members of the Legislature. Mason also wanted the Committee to report a provision that the seat of the General Government should not be fixed at any State Capital; but he did not press his idea, not wishing "to excite any hostile passions against the system."

[2] *Pennsylvania Herald*, July 28; *Pennsylvania Packet*, July 31; *Freeman's Journal*, Aug. 1; *Pennsylvania Journal*, Aug. 1; *Connecticut Courant*, Aug. 6; *Virginia Independent Chronicle*, Aug. 8; *Independent Chronicle* (Boston), Aug. 9; *New York Daily Advertiser*, Aug. 14, 1787.

Governor Caswell of North Carolina wrote to Richard D. Spaight, one of the delegates : [1]

"From the hint you threw out in your first letter, I am induced to think that the plan of a National Parliament and Supreme Executive with adequate powers to the Government of the Union will be more suitable to our situation and circumstances than any other; but I should wish also an independent Judicial department to decide any contest that may happen between the United States and individual States, and between one State and another; this, however, is only a hint, you may not see the necessity of it as forcibly as I do."

[1] *North Carolina State Records*, **XX, 752.**

CHAPTER SEVEN

THE PREAMBLE AND CONGRESS

FRIDAY, JULY 27, 1787

Beginning with this day, the Convention took a recess, for a period of ten days, not assembling again until Monday, August 6.

Jacob Hiltzheimer wrote, this day, in his diary:

" Gave the Hon. General Pinckney of South Carolina, and a member of the present Convention, a list of the best public houses on the road to Bethlehem, where he is going to visit for a few days, as the Convention had adjourned for ten days."

James Monroe wrote, this day, to Jefferson in Paris:

"The affairs of the Federal Government are, I believe, in the utmost confusion. The Convention is an expedient that will produce a decisive effect. It will either recover us from our present embarrassments, or complete our ruin; for I do suspect that, if what they recommend should be rejected, this would be the case. But I trust that the presence of Gen. Washington will have great weight in the body itself, so as to overawe and keep under the demon of party, and that the signature of his name to whatever act shall be the result of their deliberations will secure its passage thro the Union. I have heard from Beckley, tho' not from himself (who accompanied the Governor up, in expectation of being appointed clerk), they had agreed upon giving the United States a negative upon the laws of the several States, if it can be done consistently with the Constitution of the several States. Indeed, it might be well to revise them all and incorporate the Federal Constitution in each. This I should think proper. It will, if the body is well organized, be the best way of introducing uniformity in their proceedings that can be devised of a negative kind, or by a power to operate indirectly. But a few months will give us the result, be it what it may."

On this day also, Alexander Martin, a delegate from North Carolina, wrote to Governor Caswell, describing the need for the Secrecy Rule and emphasizing the difficulty of the task of the Convention:

"You may think I have been remiss in making you communications from the Federal Convention, which you had a right to expect from my engagements to you in my last letter from Carolina. But when you are informed that the members of that body are under an injunction of secrecy till their deliberations are moulded firm for the public eye, you will readily, I flatter myself, excuse me. This caution was thought prudent, lest unfavorable representations might be made by imprudent printers of the many crude matters and things daily uttered and produced in this body, which are unavoidable, and which in their unfinished state might make an undue impression on the too credulous and unthinking mobility. How long before the business of

Convention will be finished is very uncertain, perhaps not before September if then. Believe me, Sir, it is no small task to bring to a conclusion the great objects of a United Government viewed in different points by thirteen Independent Sovereignties; United America must have one general interest to be a Nation; at the same time preserving the particular interest of the individual States. However, Sir, as soon as I am at liberty to make communications, Your Excellency shall have the earliest information."

Hector Jean de Crèvecœur, the noted Frenchman, author of "Letters of an American Farmer", who was visiting this country for a second time, wrote to the Duc de Rochefoucauld from New York, this day, an interesting picture of conditions as he now saw them: [1]

"The space of two years has necessarily brought three great changes in the political complexion of this Continent. The weakness of all these separate Governments and their independence of each other, the diversity of their interests, the nullity of the Confederation, the hostility of the Spaniards on the Mississippi which they have wholly closed to navigation by Americans, the tremendous increase of new population upon the Ohio, the particular care with which the British increase their forces in Canada, the Federal Convention now sitting in Philadelphia, presided over by General Washington and composed of the most enlightened men of the Continent — these are the prominent features of the new picture which North America now presents and which deserves to be carefully followed. The insufficiency of all these democracies, the little uniformity which these States have observed in their laws as to commerce, the lessening of their dignity and their National credit, the fear of more universal dangers and perhaps of a separation — such are the reasons which have struck the best minds from North to South, and have determined them, as a last resource, to form what they call a Federal Convention. Thus far the most profound secrecy

[1] *Copies of Jean de Crèvecœur Letters MSS.* in Library of Congress.

has been observed by all the members who compose it. It has been very astonishing to see that General Washington, who had sworn to pass the rest of his days in obscurity as a private citizen, has been persuaded to expose his reputation to the dangers, perhaps, of a second Revolution; but he has undoubtedly thought that he must yield once more to the call of his country. Such is the veneration and love which the presence of this great man inspired that it was not possible for him to review the fine militia of Philadelphia . . ., as he had been asked, so great was the crowd which increasingly surrounded him and wished to see and talk with him. It is upon tender and profound attachment that people found their hope that the plans which the Convention shall propose will be unanimously approved and ratified by the States. I fear, nevertheless, that this will not happen without some moves in opposition."

SATURDAY, JULY 28, 1787

Washington noted:

"Dined at the Cold Spring Club with the Club at Springsbury. Drank tea there, returned to Mr. Morris's and spent the evening there."

He apparently did not attend the play, which was elaborately advertised at the Opera House as:

"A Concert and Comic Opera (never performed here) in three Acts called Selima and Azor or the Powers of Enchantment . . . to which will be added The Modern Lovers or Generosity Rewarded. The Managers respectfully inform the Public that the above Opera contains more Capital Songs than any Musical Entertainment that has appeared on this side of the Atlantic, and as they have spared no expense in the Scenery and Decorations, they trust it will be worthy the attention of a judicious Community."

Madison wrote, this day, to James Madison, Sr.:

"I am sorry that I cannot gratify your wish to be informed of the proceedings of the Convention. An order of secrecy leaves me at liberty merely to tell you that nothing definitive is yet done, that the session will probably continue for some time yet, that an adjournment took place on Thursday last until Monday week, and that a Committee is to be at work in the meantime."

SUNDAY, JULY 29, 1787

Washington noted : [1]

"Dined and spent the whole day at Mr. Morris's, principally in writing letters."

MONDAY, JULY 30, 1787

Washington spent his time during the ten days' adjournment of the Convention on fishing trips with Gouverneur Morris and Mr. and Mrs. Robert Morris. He noted this day : [2]

"In company with Mr. Govr. Morris and in his Phaeton with my horses, went up to one Jane Moore's in whose house we lodged in the vicinity of Valley Forge to get Trout."

On this day, the *Connecticut Courant* reported the arrival from Philadelphia on July 22, of Roger Sherman, a delegate from Connecticut, and it repeated the report as to unanimity, saying : "No particular intelligence respecting the proceedings of that illustrious assembly is communicated. We only learn, in general, that a happy and auspicious unanimity prevails in their councils, and that they will probably finish the important business entrusted to them by the beginning of September." On the same day, the *Boston Gazette*

[1] James M. Beck in *The Constitution of the United States* (1925), p. 77, says : "A letter by Mrs. Morris gives us a passing glimpse of the silent soldier as he worked with his colleagues. She tells us that he would come into the house so quietly that they would be wholly unaware of the fact until they discovered it by accident. He would go to his room and remain for hours, and they would find him there absorbed in his papers or sitting in silent meditation."

[2] *Pennsylvania Packet*, Aug. 1, 1787, said : "His Excellency, General Washington set out for Moore Hall, in order to visit his old quarters at the Valley Forge in this State."

stated that: "Nothing authentick has yet transpired from the honorable Federal Convention. It is said, however, that they are out on Committees. It is not doubted that when these Committees report, some important resolutions, resolutions which may be big with the fate of America, will be adopted and made publick." [1]

TUESDAY, JULY 31, 1787

Washington noted this day:

"Whilst Mr. Morris was fishing, I rid over the whole old Cantonment of the American Army of the Winter 1777 and 8, visited all the Works wch. were in Ruins; and the Incampments in woods where the grounds had not been cultivated. On my return back to Mrs. Moore's, observing some Farmers at Work, and entering into Conversation with them, I received the following information with respect to the mode of cultivating Buckwheat, and the application of the grain. . . . On my return to Mrs. Moore's, I found Mr. Robt. Morris and his lady there. Spent the day there fishing, etc., and lodged at the same place."

John Jay wrote this day from New York to John Adams that "It seems that the Convention at Philadelphia have agreed on the leading principles or great outlines of their plan, and appointed a committee to put it into form; but we know not what it is, and I believe it is best that we should not." Nicholas Gilman of New Hampshire wrote this day to Joseph Gilman as to the "critical state of affairs", and it appeared that he did not realize the binding force of the Secrecy Rule, for he said:

"Much has been done (though nothing conclusively) and much remains to do. A great diversity of sentiment must be expected on this great occasion; feeble minds

---

[1] Published also in *Connecticut Courant*, July 23; *Independent Chronicle*, July 26, 1787.

are for feeble measures and some for patching the old garment with here and there a shred of new stuff; while vigorous minds and warm constitutions advocate a high toned Monarchy — This is perhaps a necessary contrast, as 'all nature's difference keeps all nature's peace.' It is probable the conclusion will be on a medium between the two extremes.

A secrecy is not otherwise enjoined than as prudence may dictate to each individual — in a letter to my brother John, of the 28th instant, I gave him (for the satisfaction of two or three who will not make it public) a hint respecting the general principles of the plan of National Government, that will probably be handed out — which will not be submitted to the Legislatures but after the approbation of Congress to an assembly or assemblies of Representatives recommended by the several Legislatures, to be expressly chosen by the people to consider and decide thereon.

Great wisdom and prudence, as well as liberality of sentiment and a readiness to surrender natural rights and privileges for the good of the Nation, appears in the Southern delegates in general; and I most devoutly wish that the same spirit may pervade the whole Country, that the people, by absurdly endeavoring to retain all their natural rights, may not be involved in calamitous factions which would end but with the loss of all. . . . I think the business of the Convention will not be completed until the first of September."

William White, Bishop of Pennsylvania, wrote to Dr. Richard Price in London : [1]

"The interest you take, sir, in the civil happiness of America will doubtless make you anxious to hear of the event of the Convention now sitting for the improvement of our Federal Government. As they observe secrecy in their measures, I have cautiously avoided every thing which might look like a prying into their system. This much, however, I find, that gentlemen among them whom

[1] *Price Papers* in *Mass. Hist. Soc. Proc.*, 2d *Series* (1903), XVII.

I consider as possessed of great and enlightened minds entertain agreeable prospects of the occasion. It is now known that they have settled the principles of the plan which they are to propose, as the body have lately adjourned for a short time, leaving a Committee to digest and arrange the business."

WEDNESDAY, AUGUST 1, 1787

Washington noted:

"About 11 o'clock after it had ceased raining, we all set out for the City and dined at Mr. Morris's."

Pierce Butler, a delegate from South Carolina, wrote from New York to his son, Weedon Butler:

"As I declined the honorary fellow citizens offered me of the Chief Magistracy, I could not refuse the last appointment of acting as one of their Commissioners to the Convention to be held at Philadelphia. No doubt you have heard of the purport of the meeting — to form a stronger Constitution on strict Foederal principles for the government of the whole. I hope we may succeed. Our country expects much of us. We have sat every day since the 25th of May till last Saturday, when we adjourned for one week. Having placed my family here, Philadelphia not being so healthy, I embraced the opportunity of visiting them."

James Madison, Sr., wrote this day from Virginia to James Madison, Jr., suggesting a possible means of evasion of the Secrecy Rule:

"We are here, and I believe everywhere, all impatience to know something of your Conventional deliberations. If you cannot tell us what you are doing, you might at least give us some information of what you are not doing. This would afford us a clue for political conjecture, and perhaps be sufficient to satisfy present impatience. I hope you have already discovered the means of preserving the American Empire united, and that the scheme of a disunion has been found pregnant with the great evils. . . . We can only hope . . . that your exertions will be commensurate to the great expectations which have been formed."

William Short wrote from Paris, this day, to Madison: [1]

"We are happy, sir, in being of a country where the rights of man are considered the gift of heaven and not the grant of a crowned head. But we should be still more happy if our countrymen knew how to estimate such a situation. The result of the deliberations of the Convention and the spirit with which they may be received in the different States will show whether we know how to make small sacrifices, where necessary to secure general happiness. I confess to you, sir, that past experiences makes me fear to look forward to the event of the trial now making. A want of certainty of its doing good, and a certainty of its doing much harm if it does not, makes me regard with anxiety the dubious event. The representation, however, is such an one as must affect whatever can be affected by such a Convention. You may be sure, sir, I am happy to see that Virginia has furnished her full quota of virtue and talents on this occasion. I am sorry that the Socrates of our State should have been obliged to withdraw his aid on account of the indisposition of a part of his family."

The *Massachusetts Centinel* published a letter from Philadelphia, describing the attitude of that city towards the Convention:

"The Federal Convention have acquired a large share of the confidence of this city; and there is little doubt of our taking the lead in adopting such a Government as they shall recommend. General Washington presides in the Convention with his usual dignity. The venerable Dr. Franklin attends it daily and is contributing his experience

---

[1] *Madison Papers MSS.*, in Library of Congress. The "Socrates" referred to in this letter was George Wythe, then sixty-one years of age, and he had left the Convention, June 5, owing to the serious illness of his wife at home in Virginia.

and knowledge to assist his country in her present crisis. Mr. Dickinson, it is said, has turned his thoughts for some time past to the business of the Convention and intends to offer them to his country. From the characters of the gentlemen who compose this illustrious Assembly, from the increase of our National difficulties, and above all, from the growing disposition our citizens everywhere discover to improve our Foederal Government, I have not a doubt but that America will in a few years realize all the happiness for which she has contended."

The *Gazette* published an interesting comment on taxation — a subject with which the Convention was soon to deal:

"To encourage agriculture, it is to be hoped that the present mode of taxing lands so heavily will be laid aside — otherwise, instead of seeing our merchants, shopkeepers, lawyers and doctors retreat to farms, we shall soon see our farmers retreat to Kentucky, or to the shores of the South Sea, in order to enjoy the fruits of their industry. An efficient Federal Government alone can relieve us from our oppressive State systems of taxation, and realize all our hopes and wishes of National glory and prosperity."

The *Herald* published a statement as to the alarming antagonism of Governor George Clinton and his adherents in New York to the work of the Convention:

"A gentleman from New York informs us that the antifoederal disposition of a great officer of that State has seriously alarmed the citizens, as every appearance of opposition to the important measures upon which the people have reposed their hopes created a painful anticipation of anarchy and division. At this critical moment, men who have an influence upon society should be cautious what opinions they entertain and what sentiments they deliver — yielding to the passions and exigencies of the country all dogmatic fondness for particular systems and arrangements."

THURSDAY, AUGUST 2, 1787

Washington noted :

" Dined, drank tea, and spent the evening at Mr. Morris's."

A letter written, this day, by Mrs. Mercy Warren, the historian of the American Revolution, to the English historian, Mrs. Catharine Macaulay, discloses in striking fashion the grave fears which those who later became Antifederalists felt lest the military class, the Society of the Cincinnati, and the favorers of aristocracy and monarchy, might exercise an undue influence in the determination of the principles of the new Government : [1]

"Every man of sense is convinced a strong, efficient Government is necessary ; but the old patriots wish to see a form established on the pure principles of Republicanism. An influential party in all the States, rendered so, some of them by office, others more by the accidental possession of property than real abilities, secretly wish for Aristocracy ; while the young, ardent spirits, coming forward in pursuit of honours, office, and emolument, cry out boldly for Monarchy. These, joined by the whole class of Cincinnati who are panting for nobility and with the eagle dangling at their breast assume distinctions that are yet new in this Country — these parties make a formidable body, ready to bow to the sceptre of a King, provided they may be the lordlings who in splendid idleness may riot on the hard earnings of the peasant and the mechanic. These plead the necessity of a standing army to suppress the murmurs of a few who yet cherish that spirit of freedom which only calls forth the exertions and leads to the best improvement of the human mind. America has fought for this boon and successfully obtained it by the sacrifice of her blood, and her treasures, her heroes, and her friends ; and Heaven forbid that it should be sported away by the blind fury of a licentious mob, or the subtile intrigues of those who had

[1] *Mercy Warren Papers MSS*, in possession of Winslow Warren, Dedham, Mass.

little share in her struggles, nor ever felt that energetic spirit which procured her emancipation and gave her a rank among the nations. . . . The Convention is yet sitting; and though some have a seat there who never participated in the distress of this country, yet it is adorned by others who acted an illustrious part in the late Revolution. The eyes of all Europe are upon them — and America in distress is stretching out her arms for relief, though she yet appears in so infantile a state in some respects, as scarcely to know what it is she needs, much less is she capable of pointing out at once the best means for her own security, freedom, and happiness. God grant that a system may be devised that will give energy to law and dignity to Government, without demolishing the work of their own hands, without leveling the fair fabric of a free, strong and National Republic, beneath the splendid roof of royal or aristocratic pageantry. You will doubtless be surprised when I tell you that Republicanism, the idol of some men, and Independence, the glory of all, are nearly dwindled into theory. The ideas of the first are defaced by a spirit of anarchy, and the latter almost annihilated by the views of private ambition and a rage for the accumulation of wealth by a kind of public gambling instead of private industry. . . . Yet, it must be a work of time to obliterate opinions, founded in reason, and formed by enthusiasm till they have been made a part of the religious creed of some of the patriots of 1775. The yoke cannot readily be made supple enough to be worn by those who would spurn the hand that should attempt to affix it, though under the display of the banarets of a standing army aided by the noble order of the Cincinnati. It is difficult to calculate the consequences of present appearances; the spirit of intrigue is matured in this country, even among the politicians of yesterday. A sample of this truth may be exhibited in the future establishments of America, and the systems of policy that may be adopted by the busy genius's now plodding over untrodden ground, and who are more engaged in the fabrication of a strong Government than attentive to the ease, freedom and equal rights of man."

FRIDAY, AUGUST 3, 1787

Washington noted:

"In company with Mr. Robert Morris and his Lady and Mr. Gouvr. Morris, I went up to Trenton on another Fishing party. Dined and Lodged at Colo. Sam Ogden's at the Trenton [Iron] Works. In the evening fished, not very successfully."

The *Packet* (August 4) said:

"His Excellency General Washington attentive to everything interesting to this country yesterday visited and examined the steel furnace belonging to Nancarrow and Matlack recently rebuilt in this city. It is much the largest and best constructed furnace in America, being charged with fourteen tons of iron, at that time converting into steel; and His Excellency was pleased to express his approbation of it. The encouragement given by the countenance of distinguished characters to manufacturers among us is of much greater importance to the public than many unthinking people are aware of."

Jefferson wrote, this day, from Paris, to Edmund Randolph, in the Convention:

"I am anxious to hear what you have done in your Federal Convention. I am in hopes at least you will persuade the States to commit their commercial arrangements to Congress, and to enable them to pay their debts, interest and capital. The coercive powers supposed to be wanting in the Federal head, I am of opinion they possess by the law of nature, which authorizes one party to an agreement to compel the other to performance. A delinquent State makes itself a party against the rest of the Confederacy."

SATURDAY, AUGUST 4, 1787

Washington noted: [1]

"In the morning and between breakfast and dinner, fished again with more success (for perch) yesterday. Dined

---

[1] At the Opera House there was performed a "Concert for the benefit of the poor and Comic Lecture in five Acts called The Generous American, concluding with a Comic Opera in two acts called The Padlock."

at Genl. [Philemon] Dickinson's on the east side of the River a little above Trenton and returned in the evening to Colo. Ogden's."

On this day, James McHenry, a delegate from Maryland, who had been absent from the Convention since June 1, returned to Philadelphia, and entered in notes kept by him of the Convention proceedings from this date: "The Committee of Convention ready to report. Their Report in the hands of Dunlop, the printer, to strike off copies for the members." That the delegates had obtained advance information as to the nature of this Report from the Committee of Detail and as to the broad powers which it proposed to vest in each of the three branches of the new Government is evident from a further note made by McHenry on this day, stating that he "proposed to Mr. D. Carroll, Mr. Jenifer, Mr. Mercer and Mr. Martin (his colleagues) to meet to confer on the Report and to prepare ourselves to act in unison," and that they met at Mr. Carroll's lodgings in the afternoon; that at this meeting Martin said that "he was against the system, that a compromise only had enabled its abetters to bring it into its present stage, that had Mr. Jenifer voted with him, things would have taken a different turn. Mr. Jenifer said he voted with him, till he saw it was in vain to oppose its progress." Then, wrote McHenry, "finding that we could come to no conclusion, I recommended meeting again tomorrow, for unless we could appear in the Convention with some degree of unanimity, it would be unnecessary to remain in it, sacrificing time and money, without being able to render any service. They agreed to meet tomorrow except Mr. Martin who said he was going to New York and would not be back till Monday following." As a final suggestion to his colleagues, McHenry urged that a motion be made by them to "postpone the Report, to try the affections of the House to an amendment of the Confederation, without altering the sovereignty of suffrage"; and if this motion should fail, "that the delegation would act unanimously in trying to perfect the system proposed by the Committee Report."

That the Maryland delegation should have considered that, at this late date in the Convention and after the adoption of the Compromise, it might still be possible to return to the old plan of merely amending the Confederation, is a sign that the victory of the Nationalists' theory was still not regarded as entirely secure.

Jefferson writing, this day, from Paris to Edward Carrington in Congress in New York, gave his views as to the form of new Government needed:

"I am happy to find that the States have come so generally into the scheme of the Federal Convention, from which I am sure we shall see wise propositions. I confess I do not go as far in the reforms thought necessary as some of my correspondents in America; but if the Convention should adopt such propositions I shall suppose them necessary. My general plan would be to make the States one as to everything connected with foreign nations, and several as to everything purely domestic. But with all the imperfections of our present Government, it is without comparison the best existing or that ever did exist. Its greatest defect is the imperfect manner in which matters of commerce have been provided for. It has been so often said, as to be generally believed, that Congress have no power by the Confederation to enforce anything, for e.g., contributions of money. It was not necessary to give them that power expressly; they have it by the law of nature. When two parties make a compact, there results to each a power of compelling the other to execute it. Compulsion was never so easy as in our case, where a single frigate would soon levy on the commerce of any State the deficiency of its contributions; nor more safe than in the

hands of Congress which has always shown that it would
wait, as it ought to do, to the last extremities before it would
execute any of its powers which are disagreeable. I think
it very material to separate in the hands of Congress the
Executive and Legislative powers, as the Judiciary already
are in some degree. This I hope will be done. The want
of it has been the source of more evil than we have experienced from any other cause."

Jefferson also wrote to Benjamin Hawkins:

"I look up with you to the Federal Convention for an
amendment of our Federal affairs. Yet I do not view
them in so disadvantageous a light at present as some do.
And above all things, I am astonished at some people's
considering a kingly Government as a refuge. . . . Send
them to Europe to see something of the trappings of monarchy, and I will undertake that every man shall go back
thoroughly cured. If all the evils which can arise among
us from the republican form of Government from this day
to the day of judgment could be put into a scale against
what this country suffers from its monarchical form in a
week or England in a month, the latter would preponderate."

SUNDAY, AUGUST 5, 1787

Washington noted:

"Dined at Colo. Ogden's early; and about 4 o'clock
set out for Philadelphia — halted an hour at Bristol, after
which in the company I came, I returned to Philadelphia,
at which we arrived abt. 9 o'clock."

Dr. James McClurg wrote from Virginia to Madison,
this day:

"I am much obliged to you for your communication of
the proceedings of the Convention since I left them; for I
feel that anxiety about the result which its importance
must give to every honest citizen. If I thought that my
return could contribute in the smallest degree to its improvement, nothing should keep me away. But as I know

the talents, knowledge and well established character of
our present delegates have justly inspired this country
with the most entire confidence in their determinations,
and that my vote could only operate to produce a division
and so destroy the vote of the State, I think that my attendance now would certainly be useless, perhaps injurious.
. . . The doctrine of three Confederacies, or great Republics has its advocates here. . . . The necessity of some
independent power to control the Assembly by a negative
seems now to be admitted by the most zealous Republicans. . . . I hope that our Representative, Marshall,
will be a powerful aid to Mason in the next Assembly. He
has observed the continual depravation of men's manners
under the corrupting influence of our Legislature; and is
convinced that nothing but the adoption of some efficient
plan from the Convention can prevent anarchy first, and
civil convulsions afterwards."

MONDAY, AUGUST 6, 1787

IN CONVENTION

Report of the Committee of Detail

On this day, John Rutledge, as Chairman of the
Committee of Detail, made its report of a draft of a
Constitution — a printed pamphlet of seven folio pages
with broad margins for notes by each delegate. While
based on the votes of the Convention adopting or
modifying Randolph's Virginia Plan of May 29, it
embodied many portions of the Articles of Confederation and of the Plans submitted by Paterson and by
Charles Pinckney, as well as many provisions from the
various State Constitutions which the Committee had
found applicable. One other source of the powers
which it was proposed to vest in the new Congress has
been somewhat overlooked by historians, namely, the
report made on August 22, 1781, by the Committee of
the Old Congress appointed "to prepare an exposition

of the Confederation, a plan for its complete execution, and supplemental articles."[1] This Committee, consisting of Edmund Randolph, Oliver Ellsworth, and James M. Varnum, had recommended that "the Confederation requires execution in the following manner"; and it is interesting to see how many of the recommendations were now embodied, six years later, in the Report of the Committee of Detail (of which Randolph and Ellsworth were members):

1. By adjusting the mode and proportions of the militia aid to be furnished to a sister State labouring under invasion.

2. By describing the privileges and immunities to which the citizens of one State are entitled in another.

3. By setting forth the conditions upon which a criminal is to be delivered up by one State upon the demand of the Executive of another.

4. By declaring the method of exemplifying records and the operation of the Acts and judicial proceedings of the Courts of one State contravening those of the States in which they are asserted. . . .

7. By specifying the privileges of delegates from arrests, imprisonments, questioning for free speech and debates in Congress. . . .

9. By one universal plan of equipping, training and governing the militia. . . .

11. By establishing rules for captures on land and the distribution of the sales.

12. By ascertaining the jurisdiction of Congress in territorial questions.

13. By erecting a mint.

14. By fixing a standard of weights and measures throughout the U. S.

15. By appointing a Committee for Indian Affairs.

16. By regulating the Postoffice.

17. By establishing a census of white inhabitants in each State.

[1] *Journals of the Continental Congress* (1912), XXI.

18. By publishing the Journal of Congress monthly.
. . .

21. By providing means of animadverting on delinquent States.

And the Committee of 1781 had urged the several States to grant the following additional powers to Congress (together with some others of less note) :

1. To lay embargoes in time of war without any limitation.

2. To prescribe rules for impressing property into the service of the U. S., during the present war.

3. To appoint the Collectors of and direct the mode of accounting for taxes imposed according to the requisitions of Congress.

4. To recognize the independence of and admit into the Federal Union any part of one or more of the U. S., with the consent of the dismembered State.

6. To distrain the property of a State delinquent in its assigned proportion of men and money.

7. To vary the rules of suffrage in Congress. . . .

There are now in existence (brought to light in recent years) several documents used by the members of the Committee of Detail in the performance of their work. The most important of them, consisting of nine folio pages in the small, fine handwriting of Edmund Randolph, undoubtedly represents the first and basic draft of the Constitution, with introductory and concluding explanations and occasional running comments in the text.[1] It has been well described by Farrand as follows : "This draft was subjected to extensive and occasionally to radical changes, some of which were made in the writing of Randolph, but others were by

---

[1] This draft was first discovered in the papers of George Mason, by Moncure D. Conway and described by him in his *Forgotten Chapters of History* in 1881. Conway erroneously thought that the draft was one prepared by Randolph before the meeting of the Convention. See also *The Framing of the Constitution* (1913), by Max Farrand.

the hand of Rutledge. The inference is that the draft was submitted to the Committee, and after discussion and criticism, the modifications agreed upon were inserted by the Chairman. As an indication that the document was one of a series, practically every item in it has been checked off with a pen. It is quite possible that James Wilson had been working independently at the same time, and in a similar way, but the next stage of which we have record shows documents in the handwriting of Wilson, presenting portions of the Randolph draft further developed, together with extracts carefully taken from the New Jersey plan and extracts from the plan of Charles Pinckney. These disjointed parts were then apparently worked over by Wilson and fitted together into a single harmonious document. This may have been done alone or with the assistance of the rest of the Committee. . . . The Wilson compilation represented a fairly advanced stage of the Committee's work. Certainly, it seems to have been satisfactory to the other members, for it was gone over by them not only for the purpose of making important changes, but to see that the phrasing of the various clauses accorded with what they wished to convey. As in the case of the Randolph draft, most of the changes made were in the handwriting of Rutledge, the Chairman. This represented the last step in the preparation of the Report, except that, as the document was to be printed, a fair copy was doubtless made before it was turned over to the printer."

These papers make it evident that the authorship of the final draft can be attributed to no single one member of the Committee. To Randolph must go the lion's share of the credit. Oliver Ellsworth also claimed his share.[1]

[1] Ellsworth is reported to have said to his son, in the closing years of his life, "that President Washington's influence while in the Convention, was not very

When the report was presented to the Convention, on this August 6, it was found to consist of a preamble and twenty-three articles, divided into forty-one sections.

The first matter of note in the Report was that the term "Legislature of the United States", contained hitherto in the votes of the Convention, became the "Congress"; the term "the first branch" became "the House of Representatives", and "the second branch" became "the Senate", thus following the provisions of most of the State Constitutions; for in all the States except Delaware and New Jersey, the upper House was called the Senate, and in Massachusetts, New Hampshire, Pennsylvania, Georgia, and South Carolina the lower branch was called the "House of Representatives" (in New Jersey, New York, and Delaware, it was called the "Assembly"; in Virginia and Maryland, the "House of Delegates"; and in North Carolina, the "House of Commons").

Three articles of the Report, containing twenty-four sections, provided for the qualifications of Members of the Congress and regulations of their Legislative proceedings — all of which were taken from similar provisions in the State Constitutions, principally from those of New York and Massachusetts.

The fundamental change introduced by the Report was in Article VII, in which, instead of vesting the Congress with the broad and indefinite authority, as voted by the Convention, viz.: "the Legislative rights vested in Congress by the Confederation", and moreover, power "to legislate in all cases for the general interests of the Union, and also in those to which the

great, at least not much as to the forming of the present Constitution — he said that he himself was one of the five men who drew up that Constitution." *Life of Oliver Ellsworth* (1905), by William Garrott Brown, p. 169. As to James Wilson, see *Pickering Papers MSS.*, in Mass. Hist. Soc. Library, letter of Pickering to John Lowell, Jan. 9, 1828, March 10, 1828.

States are separately incompetent, or in which the harmony of the United States may be interrupted by the exercise of individual legislation", the Committee now vested in Congress eighteen specific and limited powers, definitely set forth. At least seven of these powers were taken bodily from the old Articles of Confederation — to make war; to make rules concerning captures on land and water; build and equip fleets; coin money; establish the standard of weights and measures; establish post offices; borrow money and emit bills on the credit of the United States. From the Plan submitted by Charles Pinckney on May 29, the Committee took the following powers for Congress — "to regulate trade and levy imposts"; [1] and from Paterson's Plan of June 15, the Committee took the powers to levy import duties and stamp taxes, and "to pass acts for the regulation of trade and commerce as well with foreign nations as with each other." In addition, the Committee's Report vested in Congress the following powers, not before appearing in any plan submitted — "to lay and collect taxes, duties, imposts and excises"; "to establish an uniform rule of naturalization" throughout the Nation; "to regulate the value of foreign coin"; "to appoint a Treasurer by ballot"; "to subdue a rebellion in any State on the application of its Legislature"; "to raise armies"; "to call forth the aid of the militia in order to execute the laws of the Union, enforce treaties, suppress insurrections, and repel invasions." In this Article, there was one very significant and new feature. The Committee inserted six express prohibitions on Congressional power — the first as to the crime of treason; second, against export duties; third, against taxes or restrictions on migration

[1] The Pinckney Plan referred to in the text of this book throughout is the restoration of the plan by J. F. Jameson and A. C. McLaughlin and reprinted in *Debates in the Federal Convention of 1787* (ed. by Gaillard Hunt and James Brown Scott, 1920), pp. 596–598.

or importation of slaves; fourth, against capitation taxes unless in proportion to the census; fifth, against navigation acts unless passed by assent of two thirds of each House; sixth against grant of titles of nobility (the latter also appearing in the Articles of Confederation).

Having thus specified the powers granted and also those prohibited to Congress, the Report proceeded to set forth in Article IX powers granted exclusively to the Senate. In Article X, it set forth the powers of the Executive. Here again, it borrowed largely from the State Constitutions of New York and Massachusetts. It named the Chief Executive "The President" of the United States — that being the title given to the Chief Executive of the States of Pennsylvania, Delaware, New Jersey, and New Hampshire, as well as to the presiding officer of the Congress under the Articles of Confederation. In Article XI, relating to the Judiciary, the Committee again made an entire and radical change from the provisions voted theretofore by the Convention. Instead of the broad and almost unlimited jurisdiction voted, viz., to extend to "cases arising under laws passed by the General Legislature; and to such other questions as involved the National peace and harmony", the Committee now set forth eight specific subjects of jurisdiction, in three of which the Supreme Court was given original jurisdiction, and in all others appellate. Some of these subjects were taken from Pinckney's Plan of May 29, and some from Paterson's Plan of June 15; but some had not been mentioned in either of those Plans.

Still another radical change from the votes theretofore adopted by the Convention was made by the Committee, by inserting two Articles (XII and XIII) containing prohibitions on the powers of the States, including not only such restrictions as had appeared in the Articles of Confederation, but also new State prohibitions, viz., against coining money; grant of letters of marque and reprisal; emission of bills of credit or making anything but specie a tender in payment of debts; laying of imposts or duties on imports.

So radical a departure from the old Articles of Confederation as was embodied in this Report evidently amazed the delegates, and an attempt was made, unsuccessfully, to adjourn until Wednesday "in order to give leisure to examine the Report." [1]

OUT OF CONVENTION

Washington noted:

"Met according to adjournment in Convention, and received the Rept. of the Committee. Dined at Mr. Morris's and drank tea at Mr. Meredith's."

TUESDAY, AUGUST 7, 1787

IN CONVENTION

The Preamble

On this day, the Convention proceeded to take up the Report of the Committee of Detail, section by section. There was little occasion for debate over Article I, that "the stile of the Government shall be 'The United States of America.'" The name "United States of America" was, of course, that which appeared

[1] J. F. Jameson in *Studies in the History of the Federal Convention of 1787, Amer. Hist. Ass. Report* (1902), I, states that the Committee of Detail took from Paterson's Plan the proposals as to duties on exports, "regulation of trade and commerce as well with foreign nations as with each other"; uniform rules of naturalization, Executive power over the military, Federal Court power over cases involving Ambassadors, and the provision for return of fugitives from justice. And Jameson states that nineteen or twenty of the provisions contained in the Pinckney Plan which were not contained in the Virginia Plan Resolutions as adopted were to be found in the Report of the Committee of Detail — "Taken together they constitute a noteworthy contribution for the youngest delegate to have made. . . . As a maker of the Constitution, Charles Pinckney deserves to stand higher than he has stood of late years and . . . he would have a better chance of doing so, if in his old age he had not claimed so much."

in the Articles of Confederation, where it appeared as
"the stile of this Confederacy." In the final draft made
by the Committee of Style on September 12, this
provision disappeared as a separate Article and was
embodied in a new Preamble. There was also no
occasion for debate over Article II, that "the Government shall consist of supreme Legislative, Executive
and Judicial powers." For all the delegates had agreed
on this provision as a fundamental part of any new
Constitution, and even of any amendment of the old
Articles of Confederation. These Articles were at once
adopted, as well as Article III, that the Legislative
power should be vested in Congress "to consist of two
separate and distinct bodies of men, a House of Representatives and a Senate." This provision was one of
the fundamental concepts of the new form of Government and had been already thoroughly debated and
accepted, though some delegates still remained believers in a single-chamber Legislature.

The wording of the Preamble, though it was never
discussed by the Convention, deserves some attention.
Randolph's first draft of a Constitution submitted to
the Committee of Detail had opened with the following
suggestion :

"In the draught of a fundamental Constitution two things
deserve attention. 1. To insert essential principles only,
lest the operation of government should be clogged by
rendering those provisions permanent and unalterable
which ought to be accommodated to times and events.
2. to use simple and precise language, and general
propositions, according to the example of the Constitution of the several States."

Randolph had then proceeded to state his ideas of
what a Preamble should contain :

"A Preamble seems proper, not for the purpose of desig-
nating the ends of government and human politics. This

display of theory, however proper in the first formation of
State Governments, is unfit here; since we are not working on the natural rights of men not yet gathered into society, but upon those rights modified by society and inter-
woven with what we call the rights of States, nor yet is
it proper for the purpose of mutually pledging the faith
of the parties for the observance of the Articles. This
may be done more solemnly at the close of the draft as in
the Confederation. But the object of our Preamble ought
to be briefly, to declare that the present Foederal Government is insufficient to the general happiness, that the conviction of this fact gave birth to this Convention, and that
the only effectual mode which they can devise for curing
this insufficiency is the establishment of supreme Legislative, Executive and Judiciary. Let it be next declared
that the following are the Constitution and fundamentals
of Government for the United States."

The Preamble as finally drafted by the Committee
of Detail, was much simpler and shorter than Randolph proposed. It began, "We, the people of the
States of New Hampshire, Massachusetts, Rhode
Island", etc., and ended, "do ordain, declare, and
establish the following Constitution for the Government of Ourselves and our Posterity." [1]   This wording
should be contrasted with the Articles of Confederation,
which had begun with the words: "Articles of Confederation and perpetual Union between the States of
New Hampshire, Massachusetts Bay, Rhode Island", etc.

When, at the close of the Convention, the Committee of Style appointed to prepare a final draft of
the Constitution made its Report on September 12,
it entirely changed the phraseology of the Preamble.

[1] This phraseology was taken from the Preamble of the Constitution of Massachusetts of 1780, drafted by John Adams as follows: "We, the people of Massachusetts . . . do . . . ordain and establish the following . . . as the Constitution of
the Commonwealth of Massachusetts." See also the Pennsylvania Constitution
of 1776. The New York and Georgia Constitutions contained the words "ordain
and declare."

The words, "We, the people of the States of New Hampshire", etc., became, "We, the people of the United States." The final clause, "declare and establish the following Constitution for the Government of Ourselves and our Posterity", became "do ordain and establish this Constitution for the United States of America." Between these two clauses, there was then inserted a statement of the purpose of the Constitution, taken from the first Resolution of Randolph's Plan of May 29, as follows: "Resolved, that the Articles of Confederation ought to be so corrected and enlarged as to accomplish the objects proposed by their institution, namely, 'common defence, security of liberty, and general welfare'", — which in turn had been taken from Article III of the Articles of Confederation averring the purpose of that "league of States" to be "for their common defence, the security of their liberties and their mutual and general welfare." In the Report of the Committee of Style of September 12, this part of the Preamble became: "in order to form a more perfect union, to establish justice, insure domestic tranquillity, provide for the common defence, promote the general welfare, and secure the blessings of liberty to ourselves and our posterity."

In later years, an attempt was made to attribute great significance to the change made by the Committee of Style in substituting the phrase "We, the people of the United States", for the phrase, "We, the people of New Hampshire, Massachusetts, Rhode Island", etc. But this change was not intended by the Convention to be anything more than a matter of form. As the phrase was originally drafted, reciting the people of each of the thirteen States separately by name, it was then intended by the Convention that this new Constitution, before it should become effective, must be ratified by all the thirteen States, and that the requirement of the Articles of Confederation for unanimity of States on any Amendment should be complied with, this new Constitution being regarded in the light of such an amendment. But when, on August 31, the Convention decided that the new Government should go into operation upon ratification of the Constitution by nine out of the thirteen States, such action made it necessary to eliminate from the Preamble the names of the specific States; for it could not be known, at the date of the signing of the Preamble and the rest of the Constitution by the delegates, just which of the thirteen States would ratify. Hence, the language, "We, the people of the United States", was used, the meaning being, "We, the people of the States united", *i.e.*, the people of those States which should agree to unite, by ratifying the new Constitution. "No other intent was suggested or contemplated" by this change of language.[1] The idea that "We, the people of the United States" was intended to mean the people, as a whole, of the country known as the United States of America, irrespective of the States of which the people were citizens, was an idea which did not enter the heads of the delegates at the time. Such a theory was later developed by Daniel Webster in the great struggle for the maintenance of National Union, in the Nullification era of the 1830's. The change in phraseology, however, was seized on by opponents of the adoption of the Constitution in some of the State Conventions in 1788 — notably in that of Virginia, when Patrick Henry, at the very outset, exclaimed:

"That this is a consolidated Government is demonstrably clear, and the danger of such a Government is, to my mind,

---

[1] See esp. *Commentaries of the Constitution* (1895), by Roger Foster, I, 43, 94.

The phrase in the Preamble "the people of the United States" was intended to be synonymous with the phrase in Article I, section 2, of the Constitution as finally drafted: "The House of Representatives shall be composed of Members chosen every second year *by the People of the several States*."

very striking. I have the highest veneration for those gentlemen; but, sir, give me leave to demand: what right had
they to say, *We, the people?* Who authorized them to
speak the language: *We, the people,* instead of, *We, the
States?*"

And again, he referred to the framers of the Constitution as seeking to require the assent of the people
in their collective capacity, thus making a consolidated
Government.[1] His objection was completely answered
by Henry Lee, who said:

"If this were a consolidated Government, ought it not
to be ratified by a majority of the people as individuals,
and not as States? Suppose Virginia, Connecticut, Massachusetts, and Pennsylvania had ratified it, these four States,
being a majority of the people of America, would, by their
adoption, have made it binding on all the States, had this
been a consolidated Government. But it is only the Government of those seven States, who have adopted it. If
the honorable gentleman will attend to this, we shall hear
no more of consolidation."

And Madison authoritatively declared the real meaning
of the words:

"Who are parties to it? The people — but not the
people as composing one great body; but the people as
composing thirteen sovereignties. . . . Should all the
States accept it, it will be then a Government established
by the thirteen States of America, not through the inter-
vention of the Legislatures, but by the people at large."

OUT OF CONVENTION

Washington noted:

"In Convention. Dined at Mr. Morris's, drank tea
no where, and spent the evening (at home) there also."

---

[1] *Elliot's Debates,* III, Henry, p. 22; Lee, p. 180; Madison, p. 94. Edmund
Pendleton had said (p. 37): "Permit me to ask the gentleman who made the objection: Who but the people can delegate powers? Who but the people have a right
to form government?"

Renewed evidence appeared, this day, that the real line of division in the Convention was between the South and the North — between the shipping and commercial States who might be interested to impose restrictions on foreign imports and shipping, and the exporting States who desired unrestricted commerce. James McHenry of Maryland recorded in his *Notes* a description of a conference and discussion held by the delegation from that State at the lodgings of Daniel Carroll. At this meeting, Carroll and McHenry agreed "that the deputation should oppose a resolute face" to the section granting to the House the sole power to originate money bills, as it "gave to that branch an inordinate power in the Constitution which must end in its destruction," since without equal powers the House and Senate "were not an equal check upon each other." It was also "accorded that the deputation should in no event consent" to the clause as to navigation acts, since "the dearest interests of trade" might be placed under the control of four States. As to the clause giving Congress power to regulate commerce, "we almost shuddered at the fate of the commerce of Maryland, should we be unable to make any change in this extraordinary power. We agreed that our deputation ought never to assent to any article in its present form." The delegates also decided to oppose the mode of ratification of the Constitution by State Conventions, suggested by the Committee of Detail, on the ground that it violated the provision of the State Constitution. They also were apprehensive of the broad powers of taxation proposed to be vested in the new Government; for, said McHenry, "an increase of taxes, and a decrease in the objects of taxation as they respected the revenue for the State, would not prove very palatable to our people, who might think that the whole objects of taxation were hardly sufficient to discharge the State obligations. Mr. Mercer came in and said he would go with the deputation on the points in question. He would wish it to be understood, however, that he did not like the system, that it was weak — that he would produce a better one, since the Convention had undertaken to go radically to work, that perhaps he would not be supported by any one, but if he was not, he would go with the stream." It appeared that Jenifer of the delegation was the only enthusiastic supporter of the Constitution, as it then stood; and McHenry reports that when Luther Martin "said one day in company with Mr. Jenifer, speaking of the system before the Convention, 'I'll be hanged if ever the people of Maryland agree to it' — 'I advise you,' said Jenifer, 'to stay in Philadelphia, lest you should be hanged.'"

The *Gazetteer* published, this day, a letter "from a Gentleman in one of the most Southern States" evidencing the feelings towards the Convention : [1]

"The eyes of the whole continent are now cast on that respectable body, the Convention. The heart of every American, good or bad, must be interested in the result of their deliberations. It will either form a glorious epoch in the history of America, or by doing nothing, leave the disease to the violent remedy of curing itself. I hope Rhode Island is no bar to their proceedings. Whenever I think of that petty State, it brings to my recollection a saying of the Grand Signior respecting the small States of Holland that if they gave him as much trouble as they did the King of Spain he would send his men with shovels and pickaxes and throw them all into the sea. Do you

[1] Widely republished, see *Pennsylvania Journal*, Aug. 8; *Pennsylvania Gazette*, Aug. 8; *Freeman's Journal*, Aug. 8; *New York Daily Advertiser*, Aug. 11; *Connecticut Courant*, Aug. 20, 1787; and other papers.

The *Independent Gazetteer*, Aug. 6, 1787, had quoted similar sentiments from a letter of a "well-meaning, plain citizen" in the *New York Daily Advertiser* saying that "the wisdom of the continent is now, as it were, concentered in the present Convention met to deliberate on the best mode of consolidating our Federal Government."

think by such a measure the Union would suffer? I would send what few negroes I have, with all my heart, and furnish them with tools at my own expense."

The North Carolina Delegates wrote this day to Governor Caswell: [1]

"The Convention, having on the 26th of last month finished the outline of the Amendments proposed to the Federal system, the business was of course committed for detail, and we have the pleasure to inform your Excellency that the report was received on yesterday. From the progress which has already taken up near three months, we are induced to believe the result of our deliberations will shortly be presented to the United States in Congress, and as they are only to consider whether the system shall or shall not be recommended to the States, the business cannot remain long before them."

WEDNESDAY, AUGUST 8, 1787

IN CONVENTION

Qualifications for Voters

On this day the Convention settled the qualifications which should be required for voters in the election of Members of the House of Representatives. The Committee of Detail, in its Report, had provided that the qualifications of electors for the House of Representatives "shall be the same, from time to time, as those of the electors in the several States, of the most numerous branch of their own Legislatures." When taken up first, on August 7, considerable discussion arose over this very wise and far-sighted provision. It would have been impossible to devise any uniform qualifications for electors which would have satisfied all the States; for the provisions already existing in the State Constitutions were very diverse. Every State required

[1] *North Carolina Records*, XX, 733, the date being erroneously given on July 7, 1787.

a certain length of residence; Maryland and Virginia excluded free negroes; all the States required an elector to own a certain amount of property, except Pennsylvania, Georgia, and New Hampshire which allowed taxpayers to vote. The property qualifications varied greatly; some States required him to own freehold in a certain number of acres, or in land paying a certain income; New Jersey required ownership of fifty pounds of property of any kind.[1] Freehold in fifty acres was the maximum qualification as to land; and ownership of sixty pounds' worth of other property, the maximum as to personalty. It has been estimated that about one fifth of the adult white males possessed no vote.[2] But it should be noted, however, that the operation of a property qualification in those days was different from what it would be today. The population then comprised only the following classes: first, the farmers, frontiersmen, and planters who formed the greatest single class, but almost all of whom owned land, even if they had no other property; second, the craftsmen and mechanics who largely worked on their own business; third, the mercantile interest composed of shopkeepers and their clerks; fourth, the commercial interest, most of whom were shipowners or importers or exporters; fifth, the shipbuilding interest; sixth, apprentices, domestic servants, and farm laborers; seventh, the lawyers, doctors, and clergymen. There

[1] See table of qualifications of electors in *Constitutional History of the American People* (1898), by Francis N. Thorpe, I, 93, 96; and in *The History of the United States* (1912), by Edward Channing, III, 446.

[2] See *An Economic Interpretation of the Constitution* (1913), by Charles A. Beard, pp. 140–142: ". . . It is impossible to say just what proportion of the adult males twenty-one years of age was disfranchised by these qualifications. When it is remembered that only about three per cent. of the population dwelt in towns of over 8000 inhabitants in 1790, and that freeholders were widely distributed, especially in New England, it will become apparent that nothing like the same proportion was disfranchised as would be today under similar disqualifications. Dr. Jameson estimates that probably one fifth of the adult males were shut out in Massachusetts, and it would probably be safe to say that nowhere were more than one third of the adult males disfranchised by the property qualification."

were no manufacturing employees, no railroad or other
public utility employees, no municipal and State
employees. There were few farm laborers (other than
slaves) not owning lands. To many of those included
in the above seven categories, the small amount of
property required as a qualification for voting in most
of the States had not proved a serious burden. But
a proposal now made in the Convention for a qualification to vote for Members of Congress, would, if
adopted, have produced a considerable discrimination
and worked a grave injustice. G. Morris proposed
"to leave it to the State Legislatures to establish the
qualifications of the electors and elected, or to add a
clause giving to the National Legislature power to alter
the qualifications." To this, Ellsworth objected that
"if the (National) Legislature can alter the qualifications, they can disqualify three fourths or a greater
proportion of the electors — this would go far to create
aristocracy. The clause is safe as it is — the States
have staked their liberties on the qualifications which
we have proposed to confirm";[1] and said he, "the
States are the best judges of the circumstances and
temper of their people." Wilson also said that "it
would be difficult to form any uniform rule of
qualification for all the States." It was then suggested
by G. Morris to confine the electors to freeholders, *i.e.*,
to persons owning land. Dickinson also favored this
proposal, considering such a provision to be "a
necessary defence against the dangerous influence of
those multitudes without property with which our
country like all others will in time abound." G.
Morris was afraid that if the vote was given to people
with no property they would sell their vote to the rich
and thus increase the power of the rich, and, said
he, "the ignorant and the dependent can be as little

[1] As reported in King's *Notes*.

trusted with the public interest." On the other hand, Wilson, Ellsworth, Mason, Butler, and Gorham were opposed to confining the electors to freeholders. They pointed out that the people would not adopt the new Constitution if it should subject them to be disfranchised. "The people have been long accustomed to this right in various parts of America, and will never allow it to be changed," said Gorham. "We must consult their rooted prejudices if we expect their concurrence." Gorham also pointed out that a requirement of freehold would operate against mechanics and merchants. Mason said that "every one who is of full age and can give evidence of his common interest in the community should be an elector"; and Ellsworth said that "the rule should be that he who pays and is governed should be an elector; virtue and talents are not confined to the freeholders." [1] Madison thought that the right of suffrage was so fundamental a part of Republican Government that it ought to be regulated by the Constitution rather than be left to the Legislatures which might restrict it to freehold owners; [2] and he was inclined to favor different qualifications for voting for the two branches of the Legislature, so as to provide reasonable security for both persons and property, each being an essential object of Government. [3] Finally, Doctor Franklin, always liberal in spirit, said that: "It is of consequence that we should not depress the virtue and public spirit of our common people. . . . This class possess hardy virtues and

[1] As reported in King's *Notes*.

[2] Madison, previously, on July 26, had concurred with G. Morris in thinking that a qualification as to property was more suitable to be required of the electors than of the elected; but he realized the difficulty of establishing any uniform standard that would satisfy all the States.

[3] *The Debates in the Federal Convention of 1787*, ed. by Gaillard Hunt and James Brown Scott, Appendix, p. 619. Madison, later in life, modified his views and wrote that "it seems indispensable that the mass of citizens should not be without a voice in making the laws which they are to obey and in chusing the magistrates who are to administer them." *Ibid*, p. 623.

great integrity." [1] When the vote was taken, G. Morris' proposal to confine electors to freeholders was defeated; and the Committee's proposal was then adopted without dissent, on August 8, and thus the Convention declined to establish any special form of property as a necessary qualification of those who were to elect the Congress. It is fair to point out, however, that this rejection of possession of freehold as a qualification was not entirely the result of an opposition to property qualifications *per se;* for it was perceived by many that such action would exclude owners of other kinds of property (merchants and security holders) from voting and would subject their interests to attacks from the small farmers who were freeholders but who at the same time were the advocates of paper money and similar destructive forms of legislation. [2]

The result of the Convention's action, however, was to avoid discriminating for or against any particular class of property owner and to leave the whole matter of qualification of voters to regulation by each State for itself. If the States in whose Legislatures the small farm owners had a large representation were content to exclude other classes of men from the suffrage, the Convention was content to abide by their decision.

OUT OF CONVENTION

Washington noted:

"In Convention. Dined at the City Tavern and remained there till near ten o'clock."

---

[1] As reported in King's *Notes.*

[2] Charles A. Beard said in his *An Economic Interpretation of the Constitution,* p. 71: "While these qualifications operated to exclude a large portion of the adult males from participating in elections, the wide distribution of real property created an extensive electorate, and in most rural regions gave the Legislatures a broad popular basis. Far from rendering to personal property that defence which was necessary to the full realization of its rights, these qualifications for electors admitted to the suffrage its most dangerous antagonist, the small farmers and many of the debtors who were the most active in all attempts to depreciate personalty by legislation. Madison with his usual acumen saw the inadequacy of such defence and pointed out to the Convention that the really serious assaults on property (having in mind of course personalty) had come from the freeholders."

The *Herald* said that: "On Monday last, the Foederal Convention met after their short adjournment . . . and we are told that they are now debating by paragraphs the plan which is to be submitted for public consideration."

On this day, there appeared the first notice in the newspapers of any opposition to the work of the Convention in any State outside of New York. It now appeared that in Pennsylvania some leaders of the party known as the Constitutionalists — the party which favored its old State Constitution with its single Legislative chamber and lack of independent Executive or Judiciary — were preparing to attack the proposed new Federal Constitution as destructive of the powers of the State. The *Gazetteer* said:

"We hear that a certain party have lately had sundry meetings at the houses of George Bryan and Jonathan Bayard Smith and that a large collection of pamphlets have been circulated from these meetings through the State. It is said the design of these publications is to excite prejudices against the new Federal Government and thereby prevent its adoption by this State. It is to be hoped this pampered official family will be disappointed, for it is a fact that a great proportion of the Constitutional party are friendly to the present Convention, especially to its worthy and excellent head. Jonathan Bayard Smith, it is said, receives 2000 pounds from his office and his brother-in-law, George Bryan, 600 pounds."

The announcement of the gathering of this opposition brought forth, four days later, in the *Gazetteer* (August 12) an indignant letter from "Tar and Feathers", who said:

"Your paper of the eighth instant informs the public that a system of opposition is beginning to the new Federal Constitution in the Supreme Court of two gentlemen who are at the head of the Constitutional party. How men can oppose what they have never seen nor know nothing about, I cannot tell. But if it is really true that these men are at work to defeat the good intended for this country by a Continental Government, before they see it — then all they will say, after it is made public, should go for nothing. It would be well for these men to think of the fate of Hutchinson, Tryon, Galloway and other Crown officers, who lost their offices and estates by opposing the general inclinations of the people. It would be prudent in the Honorable Judge to think of the fate of Carlisle and Roberts, who lost their lives by his hand for acting contrary to the sentiments of a majority of the good people of Pennsylvania. Times are critical. Our laborers are distressed for want of work. Our trade is dull and our farmers are torn to pieces for taxes. Under these circumstances, is it not cruel for men who are revelling in the sweets of fat offices to try to prevent the Government of the Convention, which shall put everything to rights, from having fair play among us?"

A Georgia paper was quoted in *Freeman's Journal* this day, as saying that "at present, one of the chief pillars of a Republican Government is wanting with the Americans — the principle of cohesion; and this arises, not only from the defects of their Constitutional system, but from the nature of their local situation." Signs that, in Massachusetts also, the fears of the emphatic adherents to State Sovereignty were being aroused, may be seen from an article in the *Salem Mercury* (August 7), announcing mistakenly, that the Convention had unanimously agreed on its new plan of Government:

"It is said, the Federal Convention have unanimously agreed on a scheme of Continental Government, adapted to the circumstances, habits, and necessities of the people, and which will speedily be presented to the several Legislatures for their acceptance and ratification. The principal difficulty will now be to have it freely adopted by

the people. And on this account, we should have nothing
to apprehend, were it not that some people, for some reason or another, have started objections to giving power
out of their hands, as they term it, lest the liberties of the
people be endangered. It hath unhappily been the case,
when measures have been proposed in the Assemblies of
the States evidently calculated for the benefit of individual
and confederate States, for some to mount the political
hobby horse and set up the cry of — Liberty! On these
occasions, we frequently hear of our forefathers coming
to this howling wilderness for liberty, and, if we grant
money or power to Congress, our liberties will be in danger — that Congress are profuse, etc. It is undoubtedly
the duty of a free people to be tenacious of their liberties
and guard against encroachments. But does it follow
that we should be suspicious of every publick measure,
or publick character? The suggestions that it would be
dangerous to grant money or power to Congress, or to establish a National Government adequate to National purposes,
are unmanly and unreasonable."

The *Gazette*, this day, pointed out that a leading
source of opposition to the new Constitution would be
found in the State officials whose powers might be
lessened, "upwards of 2000 men being employed in the
Legislative parts of our 13 Governments and ten times
that number in Executive."

"Besides the expence of this little army of rulers, their
wisdom decreases in proportion as their numbers increase.
. . . These facts should prepare us to adopt the frugal
and wise Federal Government which it is expected is now
preparing for the United States. . . . It will enable us to
support government and pay our debts by imposts and
excise, without unequal and oppressive land taxes which
are so injurious to agriculture, — and lastly it will extin-
guish State parties which are so detrimental to social happiness. . . . It is with singular pleasure we inform our
readers that a Society is now forming in this city for the

encouragement and establishment of useful arts and manufactures, by which means the industrious poor will be employed in our city, and arts and manufactures protected and rewarded in every part of the country.   Until we manufacture more, it is an absurdity to celebrate the Fourth of July as the birthday of our Independence.   We are still a dependent people."

To counteract the apparently growing sentiment in favor of the State Sovereignties as against a stronger Federal Government, a very able and exhaustive series of articles (over twenty in number) now began to appear in the newspapers of several States signed "A Foreign Spectator."   Until the publication in the fall and winter of 1787–1788 of the papers entitled *The Federalist*, written by Jay, Madison, and Hamilton, these articles by "A Foreign Spectator" were the most effective and the most important arguments in behalf of the newly planned Government.   The first article, published in the *Gazetteer*, August 6, 7, 8, was entitled "An Essay on the Means of Promoting Federal Sentiments in the United States." [1]   It said:

"The people of a Federal Republic stand in the double relation, as citizens of a particular State and citizens of the United States; in the former they think and act for their respective Republics, in the latter for the whole Confederacy.   As Federal subjects, it is their duty to promote the general interest, to regard their own State only a member of the Union — and to allow it only a just proportion.   Those rights of the Federal Republic and of each particular State, which are defined by the Articles of Confederation, must be faithfully supported.   The Federal allegiance is supreme and obligates every person to be an enemy of his own State, if it should prove treacherous to the Union.   In cases not clearly defined by the

[1] See *Independent Gazetteer*, from August 6 to September 22, 1787; *New York Daily Advertiser*, from August 14 to October 25, 1787; and many other newspapers in the different States.

Constitution, or when the occasional surrender of a right is very beneficial to the Confederacy, or another State, a general condescension and a Federal affection are very salutary. In America, an excessive love of liberty and the novelty of a Federal Constitution combine to render great numbers averse from the so necessary and rational government of a Supreme Congress, though it has proved so worthy of the public trust."

THURSDAY, AUGUST 9, 1787

IN CONVENTION

Congressional Elections

A regulation with respect to the Congressional elections, adopted in the Convention on this day, gave rise to but slight debate; though it became one of the chief causes for opposition to the Constitution on its submission to the States for ratification.

The Committee of Detail had provided in its Report that:

"The times and places and manner of holding the election of the members of each House shall be prescribed by the Legislature of each State; but their provisions concerning them may, at any time, be altered by the Legislature of the United States."

Madison and G. Morris thought that this provision ought at least to be confined to election of members of the House of Representatives; since, as to the Senate, the right of the Legislatures to elect members of that body must necessarily include the right to regulate the times, places, and manner of election. The Convention, however, did not concur with this view. Charles Pinckney and Rutledge moved to reject the power of Congress to alter the provisions made by the States; but Madison, Gorham, King, and G. Morris contended that such a power was absolutely necessary; for as Madison said:

"The necessity of a General Government supposes that the State Legislatures will sometimes fail or refuse to consult the common interest, at the expense of their local conveniency or prejudices. . . . The Legislatures of the States ought not to have the uncontrouled right of regulating the times, places and manner of holding elections. These were words of great latitude. It was impossible to foresee all the abuses that might be made of the discretionary power. . . . It seemed as improper in principle . . . to give over the election of the Representatives of the people in the General Legislature, as it would be to give to the latter a like power over the election of their Representatives in the State Legislatures."

The Convention supported Madison's view. Read of Delaware then suggested an amendment to vest in Congress the power "not only to alter the provisions of the States, but to make regulations in case the States should fail or refuse altogether", and this was adopted. In the closing sessions, on September 14, the Convention voted to add at the end of this section the words "except as to the places of choosing Senators", in order to "exempt the seats of Government in the States from the power of Congress"; and thus it was made impossible for Congress to require a State Legislature in electing Senators to convene at any other place than that fixed by the Legislature itself. The provisions on this whole subject, as finally adopted, are now contained in Article I, section 4, of the Constitution, as follows:

"The times, places and manner of holding elections for Senators and Representatives, shall be prescribed in each State by the Legislature thereof; but the Congress may at any time by law make or alter such regulations, except as to the places of chusing Senators."

From the slight debate in the Convention, it would appear that the delegates did not realize the great extension of authority over the States which was thus given to the National Government. In the contests in the State Conventions of 1788, however, this provision was made one of the principal objects of attack upon the Constitution; and as Luther Martin (who was absent in New York on this day) said later, in his report to the Maryland Legislature, it was regarded as "a provision expressly looking to, and I have no doubt designed for, the utter extinction and abolition of all State Governments." [1]

One other provision regarding the Senate, made by the Committee of Detail in its Report, aroused some discussion on this August 9, viz. that: "Vacancies may be supplied by the Executive until the next meeting of the Legislature." Wilson urged that this was not only unnecessary, but also that "it removes the appointment too far from the people, the Executives in most of the States being elected by the Legislatures." He thus once more evinced his devotion to popular government; for, he said, he had "always thought the appointment of the Executive by the Legislative department wrong; so it was still more so that the Executive should elect into the Legislative department." His objection, however, met with no support. Madison then moved to amend so as to provide that:

"Vacancies happening by refusals to accept, resignations or otherwise may be supplied by the Legislature of the State in the representation of which such vacancies

[1] *Elliot's Debates*, I, 361. A letter by "Cornelius" in the *Hampshire Gazette* (Mass.) Dec. 11, 18, 1787, gives a good idea of the fears as to this clause: "This power being vested in the Congress may enable them, from time to time, to throw the elections into such particular parts of the several States where the dispositions of the people shall appear to be the most subservient to the wishes and views of that honorable body. . . . Should it so happen (as it probably will) that the major part of the Members of Congress should be elected in and near the seaport towns, there would in that case naturally arise strong inducements for fixing the places for holding elections in such towns or within their vicinity. This would effectually exclude the distant parts of the several States, and the bulk of the landed interest, from an equal share in that government in which they are deeply interested."

shall happen, or by the Executive thereof, until the next meeting of the Legislature."

This amendment was accepted by the Convention, and, in altered phraseology, it appears in the final draft of the Constitution, as Article I, section 3, clause 2:

"And if vacancies happen by resignation, or otherwise, during the recess of the Legislature of any State, the Executive thereof may make temporary appointments until the next meeting of the Legislature, which shall then fill such vacancies."

OUT OF CONVENTION

Washington noted:

"In Convention. Dined at Mr. Swanwick's and spent the afternoon in my own room, reading letters and accts. from home."

The *Gazetteer* published a letter from Petersburgh, Virginia, in support of the Convention:

"Let there be generous and candid concessions, free from local prejudices, such as shall support and maintain on a liberal scale the government and dignity of the Empire. Let Congress be vested with an independent power over the States, without violating the religious tenets or customs of any particular State or in the quiet enjoyment of such territory or rights as shall be ascertained by the general establishment. Let the States yield to Congress the power of regulating our commerce, that by a uniform system we may preserve a genuine alliance of mutual friendship and free intercourse of trade with each other. But I forbear. The Grand Federal Convention, it is hoped, will act wisely; for on their determination alone, and our acquiescence, depends our future happiness and prosperity, and if there lives a man, equal to so arduous a task, it is a Washington."

FRIDAY, AUGUST 10, 1787

IN CONVENTION

Qualifications of Members of Congress

Having, on August 8, agreed upon the section regulating the qualifications of those who were to vote for members of Congress, and having voted against requiring possession of freehold in land as a qualification, the Convention now, on this day, settled the qualifications to be possessed by Representatives and Senators. Its action was a striking example of liberal and democratic views, and in contrast to the conservative provisions in the State Constitutions; for those Constitutions, adopted between 1776 and 1784, required not only religious and residential but also property qualifications.[1]

When Randolph introduced his Resolutions on May 29, they provided for no qualification except that of age. In the Committee of the Whole, on June 12, a minimum age of thirty years was fixed for the Senate, but no limit for the House. When the Convention had discussed the Committee's Report, on June 22, Mason moved that twenty-five years be required as an age qualification for members of the House. "His political opinions at the age of twenty-one," said he, "were too crude and erroneous to merit an influence on public measures. It had been said that Congress had proved a good school for our young men. It might be so, for anything he knew; but if it were, he chose that they should bear the expence of their own education." [2] Wilson said that he was against "abridging the right of election in any shape", that the motion

---

[1] See tables in *Constitutional History of the American People* (1898), by Francis N. Thorpe, I, 70–77; *History of the United States* (1912), by Edward Channing, III.

[2] It is to be noted that in the English Parliament, twenty-one years was the age qualification; though Fox, Shaftesbury, and others actually sat at nineteen years of age.

"tended to damp the efforts of genius and of laudable ambition"; and he cited the signal services of Pitt and Lord Bolingbroke in the public service before the age of twenty-five. Mason's motion, however, was carried. On June 25, the Convention had agreed without dissent to the thirty year age qualification for Senators. It may be noted that under the New Hampshire and South Carolina State Constitutions, there was a thirty year age qualification for Senators; in the other States, in general, twenty-five years. The Committee of Detail, in its Report, made no change in the age requirements; and the Convention adopted them on August 8.

The Committee did, however, provide for two additional qualifications — United States citizenship for three years for a member of the House; and four years, for a Senator; also residence within the State for which each should be chosen. In establishing these qualifications the Committee followed the requirements of the State Constitutions then in force. For a State Representative, South Carolina required residence of three years; Pennsylvania and New Hampshire, two years; Massachusetts, New Jersey, Maryland, North Carolina, and Georgia, one year; Delaware and Virginia unspecified terms of residence in the county; New York, no provision. For a State Senator, New Hampshire required residence of seven years; Massachusetts and South Carolina, five years; Maryland, three years; New York, New Jersey, North Carolina, one year; Delaware and Virginia prescribed no definite time; Pennsylvania and Georgia had no Senate.

When the requirements proposed by the Committee of Detail were debated on August 8, considerable fear was evinced by the delegates lest the doors of office should be too readily opened to foreigners; and on motion of George Mason and G. Morris, it was voted to require seven years' citizenship for members of the House.

Considerable discussion arose on the question of residence. Sherman, Madison, and Wilson wished to substitute the word "inhabitant" for "resident." Madison thought that both terms were "vague", but that the latter was "least so in common acceptation, and would not exclude persons absent occasionally for a considerable time on public or private business." He stated that "great disputes had been raised in Virginia concerning the meaning of residence as a qualification of Representatives, which were determined more according to the affection or dislike to the man in question than to any fixt interpretation of the word." Mercer said that in Maryland also there had been violent disputes as to the meaning of the term "residence." It was apparently felt that "resident" might imply physical presence, while "inhabitant" would signify simply legal domicile. Wilson thought it important that the expression used should not be so strict as to exclude persons who might be physically absent from their States attending sessions of Congress. Dickinson proposed that the requirement should be "inhabitant actually resident for [blank] years", as "this would render the meaning less indeterminate." Rutledge wished to provide for a previous residence of seven years within the State; but Madison, in opposition, suggested that this might deprive the new States in the West of any representation, and Read and Mercer pointed out that such a provision "would interweave local prejudices and State distinctions in the very Constitution which is meant to cure them." Ellsworth and Dickinson thought that one year's residence would be sufficient. Mason thought seven years' residence too long but that the valuable principle should be maintained. "If residence be not required," said he, "rich men of neighboring States may employ with success the means of corruption in some particular district and thereby get into the public councils after having failed in their own State," as in the boroughs in England. A motion by Butler and Rutledge of South Carolina to require three years' "previous inhabitancy" was voted down; and so was a motion for one year's, made by Ellsworth and Mason. Accordingly, it was left, as it appears in Article I, section 2, of the final draft of the Constitution — simply that "no person shall be a Representative . . . who shall not, when elected, be an inhabitant of that State in which he shall be chosen."

On August 9, an attempt was made to require a longer term of citizenship for Senators than the four years proposed in the Report of the Committee of Detail. G. Morris proposed to make this fourteen years, saying: "As to those philosophical gentlemen, those citizens of the world as they call themselves, he owned he did not wish to see any of them in our public councils; he would not trust them; the men who can shake off their attachments to their own country can never love any other; these attachments are the wholesome prejudices which uphold all Governments." [1] And Charles Pinckney and Pierce Butler supported him, on the ground that as the Senate was to "have the power of making treaties and managing our foreign affairs, there is peculiar danger and impropriety in opening its doors to those who have foreign attachments." The reason for fixing the period at fourteen years was evidently to make it certain that the office should, at the outset of the Government at least, be confined to persons who had been here before the Revolution. The proposal, however, was strongly opposed. Ellsworth thought it would discourage "mer-

[1] According to the *Notes* of Rufus King, G. Morris said: "Foreigners cannot learn our laws or understand our Constitution under fourteen years. Seven years are requisite to learn to be a shoemaker, and double this term will be necessary to learn to be an American Legislator."

itorious aliens from emigrating to this country."
Madison and Franklin also disliked giving such "a
tincture of illiberality" to the new Constitution.
Wilson, who had been born in Scotland, pointed out
that he might be "incapacitated from holding a place
under the very Constitution which he had shared in the
trust of making" and said that "to be appointed to a
place may be matter of indifference.   To be incapable
of being appointed is a circumstance grating and
mortifying."   Morris' motion for fourteen years' citizenship and General Pinckney's for ten years' were
defeated, and finally nine years' was agreed to, after
Williamson urged that, as the Convention had fixed
seven years' for members of the House, it was more
necessary to guard the Senate, in which "bribery and
cabal can be more easily practiced", since its numbers
would be so small.[1]

After voting on age and residence qualifications for
members of Congress, the Convention was now confronted with a proposal on which its decision was of
great significance.   Almost all the State Constitutions
required members of their Legislatures to possess
considerable property.   A State Senator was required
in South Carolina to have a freehold of 2000 pounds in
value; in New Jersey and Maryland, 1000 pounds in
real and personal property; in Massachusetts, freehold
of 300 pounds or 600 pounds in personal property; in
New Hampshire, freehold of 200 pounds; North
Carolina, freehold of 300 acres; in Virginia, Delaware,
and New York, freehold of no limited amount.   A
State Representative was required in South Carolina

[1] On August 13, the Convention having voted to reconsider the question as to
length of citizenship for Members of the House, James Wilson and Randolph moved
to require four years instead of seven; Madison also concurred; Gerry and Pierce
Butler, on the other hand, wished to confine eligibility to natives; and Williamson
wanted nine years.   Wilson pointed out that of the Pennsylvania delegates, Robert
Morris, Fitzsimmons, and himself were not natives.   Wilson's attempt to lessen
the citizenship requirements for both House and Senate were decisively defeated.

to have 500 pounds in real estate; in New Jersey and
Maryland, 500 pounds real and personal; in New
Hampshire, 100 pounds freehold; in Massachusetts,
100 pounds freehold or 200 pounds other property; in
Georgia, 250 acres or 250 pounds; in Delaware and
Virginia, a freehold of no limited amount; in Pennsylvania, he must be a taxpayer; New York alone had no
property qualification. With these qualifications required in the States, it would have been natural if the
Convention had prescribed similar ones in the new
Constitution. But, as will be seen, more liberal and
democratic ideas prevailed.[1] Early in the sessions, on
June 26, George Mason had suggested "the propriety
of annexing to the office of Senator a qualification of
property"; for Mason was one of a small group who
thought that "one important object in constituting the
Senate was to secure the right of property" — a theory
which was rejected by the Convention. On July 26,
Mason had moved that "the Committee of Detail be
instructed to receive a clause requiring certain qualifications of landed property . . . in members of the
Legislature. . . ." Charles Pinckney and General
Charles C. Pinckney had moved to extend these
qualifications to both the Judiciary and the Executive.
In the debate, Dickinson said that "he doubted the
policy of interweaving into a Republican Constitution
a veneration for wealth. He had always understood
that a veneration for poverty and virtue were the
objects of republican encouragement. It seemed improper that any man of merit should be subjected to

---

[1] *Constitutional History of the United States* (1901), by Francis N. Thorpe, I, 464.
For a defense of property as the basis of government, see *Proceedings and Debates
of the Virginia State Convention of 1829–1830*, 277 *et seq.*, and especially the remarks
of James Monroe, James Madison, John Marshall, Philip P. Barbour, and Abel P.
Upshur. See also the remarks of Daniel Webster, John Adams, and Judge Story
in the Massachusetts Convention of 1820, and of Chancellor Kent, Rufus King,
Martin Van Buren, and Ambrose Spencer in the New York Constitutional Convention of 1821. See also *The Suffrage Franchise in the Thirteen English Colonies in
America* (1905), by A. E. McKinley.

disabilities in a Republic where merit was understood
to form the great title to public trust, honors and
rewards." Gerry (who later refused to sign and
opposed the adoption of the Constitution) favored
property as a qualification, saying: "If property be
one object of Government, provisions for securing it
cannot be improper." Madison and King thought that
if property was to be any qualification, it should not
be confined to "landed property", since this would
exclude the commercial and manufacturing classes;
and Madison observed that the "unjust laws of the
States had proceeded" more from the landed interest
than from any other source, meaning by this that the
landed interest were largely the farmers and owners of
land on the frontier who favored paper money and stay
laws hindering collection of debts. After striking out
the word "landed", the Convention, by a vote of eight
to three (Connecticut, Pennsylvania, and Delaware
voting no), had adopted Mason's proposal to instruct
the Committee of Detail to report a property qualification. In accord with this instruction, the Committee's Report of August 6 provided that: "The
Legislature of the United States shall have authority
to establish such uniform qualifications of the members
of each House, with regard to property, as to the said
Legislature shall seem expedient." When this was
debated, on this August 10, Charles Pinckney said that
"he was opposed to the establishment of an undue
aristocratic influence in the Constitution, but he
thought it essential that the members of the Legislature,
the Executive, and the Judges should be possessed of
competent property to make them independent and
respectable." He moved that the President and
Judges be required to possess clear, unincumbered
estates to an [unfixed] amount. Rutledge concurred.
On the other hand, the wise Doctor Franklin "expressed

his dislike of everything that tended to debase the spirit of the common people. If honesty was often the companion of wealth, and if poverty was exposed to peculiar temptations, it was not less true that the possession of property increased the desire for more property. Some of the greatest rogues he was ever acquainted with, were the richest rogues. . . . This Constitution will be much read and attended to in Europe, and if it should betray a great partiality to the rich will not only hurt us in the esteem of the most liberal and enlightened men there, but discourage the common people from removing into this country."

Pinckney's motion was (as Madison states) "rejected by so general a *no* that the States were not called." Ellsworth, always zealous for the rights of the States, wished to leave the whole matter of qualifications to the State Legislatures. G. Morris, on the other hand, moved to give Congress unlimited power to fix qualifications. This motion was defeated. And thereupon, the Convention rejected the clause as reported by the Committee, thus refusing to establish any property qualification. In this way, for the third time, the sharp issue between property and non-property was decided against the former by the Convention.[1]

On this same day, August 10, the Convention, without debate or dissent, agreed to the section reported by the Committee of Detail which provided that:

"Each House shall be the judge of the elections, returns and qualifications of its own members."

[1] Timothy Pickering, writing to Charles Tillinghast, Dec. 24, 1787, pointed out that the charges made by the opponents of the Constitution that it established an aristocracy, were absurd, since hereditary rights, titles of nobility, and property qualifications were all excluded, a fact which "manifests the marked regard of the Convention to preserve the equal rights of the people, without suffering mere wealth to hold the smallest pre-eminence over poverty attended with virtue and abilities. It deserves, indeed, particular notice that while several of the State Constitutions prescribe a certain degree of property as indispensable qualifications for office, this which is proposed for the United States throws the door wide open for the entrance of *every man* who enjoys the confidence of his fellow citizens." *Pickering Papers MSS.*, V, 412, in Mass. Hist. Soc. Library.

The meaning of this provision (which became Article I, section 5, of the Constitution as finally drafted) is clearly shown, if taken in connection with the action of the Convention on the proposed property qualifications. As above stated, the Committee's Report provided that Congress should have power "to establish such uniform qualifications of the members of each House with regard to property as to the said Legislature shall seem expedient." When G. Morris moved to strike out the words "with regard to property", the effect of this, if adopted, would have been to allow Congress to establish any qualifications which it deemed expedient. Williamson and Madison strongly opposed this. Madison said that it would vest "an improper and dangerous power in the Legislature", and that the qualifications of the elected were "fundamental articles in a Republican Government and ought to be fixed by the Constitution." If the Legislature could regulate them, "it can by degrees subvert the Constitution . . . by limiting the number capable of being elected. . . . Qualifications founded on artificial distinctions may be devised by the stronger, in order to keep out partisans of a weaker faction." He also pointed out "the British Parliament possessed the power of regulating the qualifications . . . of the elected and the abuse they had made of it was a lesson worthy of our attention." They had made changes in qualifications "subservient to their own views or to the views of political or religious parties." [1]   The Con-

---

[1] Madison's reference was undoubtedly to the famous election case of John Wilkes, in England, who had been rejected as a member by the House of Commons, on Feb. 3, Feb. 16, March 18, and April 13, 1769, for the reason that he had been earlier expelled by the House on Jan. 19, 1764.   On May 3, 1782, the House of Commons expunged the resolution passed by it, Feb. 17, 1769, which read as follows: "Mr. Wilkes, having been in this session of Parliament, expelled the House, was and is incapable of being elected a member to serve in the present Parliament."   For the best accounts of the Wilkes episode, see Mahan's *History of England*, V, 349 et seq.; *History of the English Parliament* (1892), by G. Barnett Smith, I, 361–369; *The Law and Custom of the Constitution* (4th ed. 1909), by Sir William R. Anson, I,

vention evidently concurred in these views; for it defeated the proposal to give to Congress power to establish qualifications in general, by a vote of seven States to four; and it also defeated the proposal for a property qualification, by a vote of seven States to three. Such action would seem to make it clear that the Convention did not intend to grant to a single branch of Congress, either to the House or to the Senate, the right to establish any qualifications for its members, other than those qualifications established by the Constitution itself, viz., age, citizenship, and residence. For certainly it did not intend that a single branch of Congress should possess a power which the Convention had expressly refused to vest in the whole Congress.[1] As the Constitution, as then drafted, expressly set forth the qualifications of age, citizenship, and residence, and as the Convention refused to grant to Congress power to establish qualifications in general, the maxim *expressio unius exclusio alterius* would seem to apply. It is to be noted especially that Dickinson of Delaware, on July 26, expressed his opposition to "any recital of qualifications in the Constitution" at all on this very ground; for, said he, "it was impossible to make a compleat one and a partial one would by implication tie up the hands of the Legislature from supplying the omission." The Committee of Detail

78 *et seq.*, 168–172; *A Treatise on the Law, Privileges, Proceedings and Usage of Parliament* (12th ed. 1917), by Sir Thomas Erskine, May, pp. 26 *et seq.*; *Cooley's Blackstone* (1872), Book I, p. 162, note 18; *Parliamentary History of England* (1813), XVI, pp. 540–587.

[1] It is to be noted that at least four amendments to the Constitution have been proposed to the qualifications for members of Congress specifically prescribed by the Constitution: to make officers and stockholders of the Bank of the United States ineligible, *2d Cong., 2d Sess.*, March 2, 1793; to make Government contractors ineligible, *9th Cong., 1st Sess.*, March 29, 1806; *10th Cong., 1st Sess.*, March 1, 1808; *24th Cong., 1st Sess.*, Feb. 13, 1836. The New York ratifying Convention in 1788, and the Massachusetts and Connecticut Legislatures in 1798, recommended an amendment making naturalized foreigners ineligible, as did the Legislatures of Massachusetts and Connecticut, in 1815, following the recommendation of the Hartford Convention. *Proposed Amendments to the Constitution, 1789–1889* (1897), by Herman V. Ames.

had differed from Dickinson's view and had made
express provision as to qualifications. And to this
express provision, Dickinson's argument was undoubtedly applicable that the recital of these qualifications did "by implication tie up the hands of the
Legislature from supplying" any further qualifications.
Wilson, on this August 10, recognized this to be the
effect; for he said, if the section giving power to
Congress to establish property qualifications remained
in the Constitution, "this particular power would
constructively exclude every other power of regulating qualifications." The elimination of all power in
Congress to fix qualifications clearly left the provisions of the Constitution itself as the sole source of
qualifications.[1]

[1] An argument to the contrary has been made based on the fact that the qualifications, as reported by the Committee of Detail on August 6, were expressed affirmatively, thus: "Every member of the House of Representatives shall be of the age
of twenty-five years at least; shall have been a citizen in the United States for at
least three years before his election; and shall be at the time of his election a resident
of the State in which he shall be chosen" (and similarly as to Senators); whereas,
as finally drafted by the Committee of Style on September 12, they were expressed
negatively as follows: "No person shall be a representative who shall not have
attained to the age of twenty-five years and been seven years a citizen of the United
States, and who shall not, when elected, be an inhabitant of that State in which he
shall be chosen" (and similarly as to Senators). The argument is made that
this change, while giving to each House unlimited power to establish qualifications, simply imposed an obligation on them not to admit any persons having the
specified *disqualifications*.

It is to be noted, however, that the Committee of Style had no authority from
the Convention to make alterations of substance in the Constitution as voted by
the Convention, nor did it purport to do so; and certainly the Convention had no
belief, after September 12, that any important change was, in fact, made in the provisions as to qualifications adopted by it on August 10. That there was no difference in legal effect between a qualification expressed affirmatively and one expressed
negatively may be seen from the fact that the Constitution of Massachusetts of
1780 contained affirmative qualifications for Representatives and exactly similar
negative qualifications for Senators as follows: "Every member of the House of
Representatives . . . for one year at least next preceding his election shall have
been an inhabitant of and have been seized in his own right of a freehold of the value
of one hundred pounds within the town he shall be chosen to represent, or any
taxable estate of two hundred pounds." "No person shall be capable of being
elected as a Senator who is not seized of his own right of a freehold, within this
commonwealth, of the value of three hundred pounds at least, or possessed of personal estate to the value of six hundred pounds at least, or both to the amount of
the same sum, and who has not been an inhabitant of this Commonwealth for the
space of five years immediately preceding his election, and at the time of his elec-

It is, moreover, especially to be noted that the provision that "each House shall be the judge of . . . the qualifications of its own members" did not originate with this Convention. Such a provision was found in the State Constitutions of Delaware, Maryland, Massachusetts, New Hampshire, New Jersey, North Carolina, Pennsylvania, and South Carolina. It was taken originally from William Penn's charter to Pennsylvania of 1701, which provided that the Assembly "shall have power to choose a Speaker and their other officers, and shall be judges of the qualifications and elections of their own members." Each of the State Constitutions contained provisions establishing many qualifications for members of the Legislature — residence, age, religion, property, and others (qualifications expressed in both affirmative and negative terms); and it was with reference to possession of such qualifications that their Legislatures were authorized to judge as to their members. There is, so far as appears, no instance in which a State Legislature, having such a provision in its Constitution, undertook to exclude any member for lack of qualifications other than those required by such Constitution.[1] In the Constitutions of Massachusetts

tion he shall be an inhabitant in the district for which he shall be chosen." And in each case the Massachusetts Constitution termed them "qualifications" and empowered the House and Senate to judge them, as follows: "The Senate shall be the final judge of the elections, returns and qualifications of their own members as pointed out in the Constitution." "The House shall be the final judge of the elections, returns and qualifications of their own members as pointed out in the Constitution."

So, too, in the State Constitutions of New Hampshire of 1784, Pennsylvania of 1776, and South Carolina of 1778, the qualifications of members of the Legislature are expressed in the negative phraseology thus: "No person shall be capable of being elected" — "no person shall be eligible to sit", etc.

[1] In 1780 in the State of Virginia, which had no provision in its Constitution on this subject, the House of Delegates refused to admit John Breckenridge as a member on the ground that he was a minor (aged 19); but its action was apparently based on the fact that he could not qualify under the provision of the State Constitution that a member must be "such men as actually resided in and are freeholders of the same, and are qualified according to law."

It was stated in *The Federalist* (No. 66) by Hamilton that: "The qualifications

and New Hampshire, it was specifically stated that the qualifications of which the Legislature was to "judge" were to be "the qualifications of their own members *as pointed out in the Constitution.*"

That the Convention was far from wishing to give the Houses of Congress power by a majority vote to establish any qualification which they chose for admission of members, is seen by the fact that on this same day, August 10, it voted to alter a provision reported by the Committee of Detail that: "Each House may determine the rules of its proceedings, may punish its members for disorderly behaviour; and may expel a member." Madison, observing "that the right of expulsion was too important to be exercised by a bare majority of a quorum; and in emergencies of faction might be dangerously abused", moved that expulsion should be allowed only with the concurrence of two thirds of the members. Randolph, Mason, and Carroll agreed with him; and it was unanimously voted (the vote of Pennsylvania being divided). It is difficult to conceive that the Convention in so requiring a two thirds vote to expel was, at the same time, willing to allow each House to exclude a member by a majority vote, for any reason which it should deem fit.

While the refusal to make any property qualification for Representatives and Senators was a striking example of the liberal sentiment pervading the Convention, and

of the person who may choose or be chosen, as has been remarked on another occasion, are defined and fixed in the Constitution; and are unalterable by the Legislature." So also in *The Federalist* (No. 52) it was said that "the qualifications of the elected . . . being at the same time more susceptible of uniformity have been properly considered and regulated by the Convention."

It may be noted, on the other hand, that during the contest over the ratification of the Constitution, at least one Antifederalist writer in Massachusetts believed that the Congress was given by the Constitution unlimited power to fix qualifications. Thus "Cornelius", in *Hampshire Gazette*, Dec. 11, 18, 1787, wrote: "By this Federal Constitution, each House is to be the judge not only of the elections and returns, but also of the *qualifications* of its members, and that, without any other rule than such as they themselves may prescribe. This power in Congress, I take to be equal to that of a negative on elections in general."

while it represented a much more democratic tendency than had appeared in the State Constitutions, all of which contained such property qualifications, the Convention omitted requiring one other qualification, of even greater significance in showing its determination to frame a liberal form of government. Under the State Constitutions, a religious qualification was required of Representatives in the Legislature in every State except New York and Virginia. Thus, in New Hampshire, New Jersey, South Carolina, North Carolina, and Georgia, he was required to be a Protestant; in Massachusetts and Maryland, of the Christian religion; in Pennsylvania, a Protestant, and having a belief in God and the inspiration of the Scriptures; in Delaware having a belief in the Trinity and in the inspiration of the Scriptures.[1] The Convention, having all the religious requirements of the States before it, and knowing that, under them Catholics, Jews, and

[1] See *History of the United States* (1912), by Edward Channing, III; *Constitutional History of the American People* (1898), by Francis N. Thorpe, I, 70: "No State at this time pursued a political practice which would now be considered liberal. In one way or another, Church and State were united. Unitarians, Jews and Roman Catholics were not allowed to enjoy the privilege granted to others who were described as religiously qualified. New York was most tolerant of the right to private opinion. When the Constitution of Pennsylvania was forming in 1776, it was proposed to restrict membership in the Assembly, and indeed the right to vote and hold office to those who, on oath or affirmation professed 'faith in God the Father and in Jesus Christ His eternal son the true God, and in the Holy Spirit, one God, blessed forever more;' and who acknowledged the Holy Scriptures of the Old and New Testament to be given by Divine inspiration. Franklin, who was President of the Convention, expressed the opinion, in private correspondence, four years later, that the clause requiring Members of Assembly to declare their belief that the whole of the Bible is given by Divine inspiration might better have been omitted. 'I opposed the clause,' said he, 'but being overpowered by numbers and fearing more might in future times be grafted on it, I prevailed in having the additional clause adopted "that no further or more extended profession of faith should ever be exacted." . . . The evil of it was the less as no inhabitant nor any officer of government, except the members of assembly, was obliged to make that declaration.' *Works of Benjamin Franklin* (Bigelow's ed.), XII, 140, Franklin to Dr. Richard Price, Oct. 9, 1780. For the origin of the movement and the attempt to secure other religious qualifications in this Constitution, see the letter of Reverend Henry M. Muhlenberg, October 2, 1776, giving an account of a conference of the Philadelphia clergy, who feared that the Commonwealth was to be ruled 'by Jews, Turks, Spinozists, Deists, and perverted Naturalists', in the *Pennsylvania Magazine of History and Biography*, April, 1898, p. 129–131."

even members of some Protestant denominations were excluded from admission to State Legislatures, deliberately determined that there should be no such illiberal discriminations under the National Government. The credit for this notable step is due to Charles Pinckney of South Carolina. Neither the Randolph Plan nor the Paterson Plan of Government contained any provision on the subject. On August 20, however, Pinckney submitted a proposition that : "No religious test or qualification shall ever be annexed to any oath of office under the authority of the United States." The Committee of Detail, to which this was referred, made no report upon it. Accordingly, when the section of the Constitution relative to oaths, as reported by that Committee on August 6, came up for consideration of the Convention, on August 30, Pinckney moved that there be added to it the following broad pronouncement: "but no religious test shall ever be required as a qualification to any office or public trust under the authority of the United States." Although Roger Sherman thought it unnecessary, saying that the prevailing liberality was a sufficient security against such tests, the Convention adopted it without a dissenting vote. Thus, not only Representatives and Senators, but also all public officers of the United States, were freed from any religious qualifications.

SATURDAY, AUGUST 11, 1787

IN CONVENTION

Adjournments of Congress

The Report of the Committee of Detail of August 6 had provided that:

"Neither House, without the consent of the other, shall adjourn for more than three days, nor to any other place than that at which the two Houses are sitting. . . . He (the President) may convene them (the Congress) on extraordinary occasions."

"In case of disagreement between the two Houses, with regard to the time of adjournment, he may adjourn them to such time as he thinks proper."

The right of a Legislature to adjourn of its own volition, without the necessity of assent by the Executive and without right in the Executive to require its adjournment, is an important Legislative authority.[1] In the Colonies, there had been many struggles between the popular Assemblies and the Royal Governors over the latter's exercise of power to prorogue or dissolve the former. Hence, when the State Constitutions were framed, complete power over their own sittings was reserved to the Legislatures. Virginia, New Jersey, Delaware, Pennsylvania, Maryland, and North Carolina allowed either branch of the Legislature to "adjourn at pleasure"; New Hampshire and Massachusetts provided that neither should adjourn for more than two days (and South Carolina, for more than three days) without the consent of the other. It was the provision in these latter States which the Committee copied. The State Constitutions of Delaware, Pennsylvania, Maryland, New York, South Carolina, Massachusetts, and New Hampshire allowed the Executive, however, to convene the Legislature "before the time to which they stand adjourned"; and this authority the Committee also adopted. When the Convention debated these provisions on this day, the discussion was confined to the advisability of allowing the Houses to change the place or location of their sessions. The many transits of the Congress of the Confederation from Philadelphia, Princeton, Trenton, Annapolis, and New York, between 1782 and 1786, had impressed the dele-

[1] See *The Evolution of the Constitution of the United States* (1910), by Sydney George Fisher, pp. 135–136.

gates with the disadvantages of such "mutability."
Many desired that there should be no possibility of a
change in location, except by a duly enacted law; and
the section as reported by the Committees was accepted, on this August 11, with slight verbal changes.

Privileges of Congress

One other important privilege of the Legislature was
carefully guarded, in the provision in the Report of the
Committee of Detail that:

"Freedom of speech and debate in the Legislature shall
not be impeached or questioned in any Court or place out
of the Legislature; and the members of each House shall,
in all cases except treason, felony and breach of the peace,
be privileged from arrest during their attendance at Congress, and in going to and returning from it."

These were rights which were derived directly from
the provisions in England pertaining to Parliament.[1]
The Massachusetts and New Hampshire State Constitutions also had provided that:

"The freedom of deliberation, speech and debate, in
either House of the Legislature is so essential to the rights
of the people, that it cannot be the foundation of any accusation or prosecution, action or complaint in any other
Court or place whatsoever.

. . . And no member of the House of Representatives
shall be arrested, or held to bail on mesne process, during
his going into, returning from, or his attending the General
Assembly."

The Maryland State Constitution provided that:

"Freedom of speech and debates or proceedings in the
Legislature ought not to be impeached in any other Court
of Judicature."

And the Articles of Confederation provided that:

[1] See *Sources of the Constitutions of the United States* (1894), by C. Ellis Stevens.

"Freedom of speech and debate shall be allowed in Congress nor shall anything done in Congress be impeached or questioned out of it.

. . . The members of Congress shall be protected in their persons from arrests and imprisonments during the time of their going to and from, and attendance in Congress, except for treason, felony, or breach of the peace."

The recommendations of the Committee of Detail were adopted, without debate (August 10). In the Report of the Committee of Style on September 12, and in the final draft of the Constitution, they appear in compressed form, as Article I, section 6, clause 1.

Journals of Congress

The Committee of Detail had provided in its Report that:

"The House of Representatives, and the Senate, when it shall be acting in a Legislative capacity, shall keep a journal of their proceedings, and shall, from time to time, publish them; and the yeas and nays of the members of each House, on any question, shall at the desire of one fifth part of the members present be entered on the Journal."

In England, for several hundred years, secrecy of Legislative proceedings had been the general rule. It was not until 1641 that provisions for a record of transactions was made by the issue of the "Diurnal Occurrences of Parliament"; but no publication of speeches was even then allowed. In 1680, an Act was passed requiring an authorized publication of votes and proceedings; but until 1771, Parliament regarded public reports of speeches and debates as illegal.[1]

The Articles of Confederation had required the Congress to:[2]

---

[1] See *Sources of the Constitution of the United States* (1894), by C. Ellis Stevens, pp. 107–108.

[2] It is to be noted that the Congress of the Confederation expressly refused to vote for open sessions. On April 23, 1783, a motion by James Wilson, seconded by

"publish the Journal of their proceedings monthly, except such parts thereof relating to treaties, alliances or military operations, as in their judgment require secrecy; and the yeas and nays of the delegates of each State on any question shall be entered on the Journal, when it is desired by any delegate; and the delegates of a State, or any of them, at his or their request, shall be furnished with a transcript of the said Journal, except such parts as are above excepted, to lay before the Legislatures of the several States."

When the Convention debated this section in the Report of the Committee of Detail, on August 10 and 11, G. Morris, Carroll, and Randolph thought that if the yeas and nays were proper at all, any individual ought to be authorized to call for them. Gorham, Ellsworth, and Sherman thought the recording of yeas and nays at all, as objectionable and misleading to the people, since "the reasons governing the votes never appear along with them." G. Morris and Wilson answered that if reasons were to be entered, this privilege must be allowed to the majority as well as to the minority, and thereby the Journal would, "like the records of a Court, be filled with replications, rejoinders, etc." A motion to allow any member to enter his dissent was defeated. Gerry then moved to strike out "when it shall be acting in its Legislative capacity", and to insert "such parts thereof as in their judgment require secrecy." Madison and Rutledge moved as a substitute:

"that each House shall keep a Journal of its proceedings, and shall publish the same from time to time; except such part of the proceedings of the Senate, when acting not in its Legislative capacity, as may be judged by that House to require secrecy."

Alexander Hamilton, that "whereas it is of importance in every free country that the conduct and sentiments of those to whom the direction of public affairs is committed should be publicly known; resolved, that in future the doors of Congress shall be open, unless otherwise ordered by a vote or by the rules of the House", was rejected by a vote of seven States to one (Pennsylvania being the dissenting State, and Virginia being divided).

This motion was rejected, some delegates objecting to the implication that the Senate might act in some capacity other than Legislative — which it was, nevertheless, undoubtedly to do. Ellsworth and Sherman, moreover, thought it unnecessary, as "the Legislature will not fail to publish their proceedings from time to time", and "the Legislature might be trusted in this case, if in any." Wilson, however, thought that "the people have a right to know what their agents are doing or have done, and it should not be in the option of the Legislature to conceal their proceedings"; and that as this provision was now in the Articles of Confederation, its omission might be regarded as a suspicious circumstance. Mason also thought that it "would give a just alarm to the people, to make a conclave of their Legislature." Finally, the Convention voted to require publication of the Journals of each House "except such parts as may in their judgment require secrecy."

OUT OF CONVENTION

Washington noted:

"In Convention. Dined at the Cold Spring Club at Springsbury and after tea returned and spent the evening at home."

A New York despatch of this date expressed the view that the people would undoubtedly adopt the new Constitution, though State officials and interested factions might oppose: [1]

"Some timid, or perhaps *interested*, politicians have expressed apprehensions that the Federal Government will not be adopted by the States or the people. Such persons do not know or recollect the good sense of the Americans, who, under pressing circumstances, in the year 1775, adopted the resolutions of Congress and in the year 1776, the Declaration of Independence. For neither of these

[1] Reprinted in *Boston Gazette*, Aug. 20; *Connecticut Courant*, Aug. 20; *Maryland Journal*, Aug. 14, 1787; and in other papers.

were the citizens of America half so well prepared as they are now for a vigorous Federal Government; it is probable some of the States will object to it, and certain factions composed of salary and perquisite men may object to it in all the States; but (as was the case with the resolutions of Congress and the Declaration of Independence) truth and public safety will finally prevail over fell interest and faction. America will be the delight of her friends and citizens, and the envy, admiration and example of the whole world."

The same views were expressed in a despatch from New Hampshire about this time : [1]

"'As the heart panteth after the cooling water brook' so does every citizen of this State pant after a reform in Government, not only a local but a Foederal reform, and this, we have reason to hope, will be effected, notwithstanding the arts that are or may be used in New York and Rhode Island to oppose it. . . . The characters residing in those two States who have uniformly opposed a Foederal reform are well known. It would be well for them to desist from their nefarious schemes. The united force of America is against them. The bolts of vengeance are forging — tremble, ye workers of iniquity, and no longer oppose the salvation of your country, lest speedy destruction come upon you and you fall into the pit which your own hands have digged."

Edward Carrington, a Member of Congress from Virginia, wrote from New York this day, to Madison :

"The departure of North Carolina and Georgia left us only 7 States, and the day before yesterday we lost another in the decampment of Doctor Holton (of Massachusetts). . . . The President has been requested to write to the States unrepresented, pressing upon them the objects which require the attendance of their delegations, and urging them to come forward. Amongst those objects is that of the report of the Convention, which, it is supposed, is now in the state of parturition. This bantling

<hr/>

[1] *Pennsylvania Journal,* Aug. 18, 1787, despatch from Portsmouth, N. H., Aug. 7.

must receive the blessing of Congress this session, or, I fear, it will expire before the new one will assemble. Every experiment has its critical stages, which must be taken as they occur, or the whole will fail. The people's expectations are rising with the progress of this work, but will desert it, should it remain long with Congress. Permit me to suggest one idea as to the mode of obtaining the accession of the States to the new plan of Government. Let the Convention appoint one day, say the first of May, upon which a Convention appointed by the people shall be held in each State for the purpose of accepting or rejecting, *in toto*, the project. Supposing an act of the ordinary Legislature to be equally authentic, which would not be true, yet many reasons present themselves in favor of special Conventions. Many men would be admitted who are excluded from the Legislatures. The business would be taken up unclogged with any other. And it would effectually call the attention of all the people to the object as seriously affecting them. All the States being in Convention at the same time, opportunities of speculating upon the views of each other would be cut off. The project should be decided upon without an attempt to alter it. You have doubtless found it difficult to reconcile the different opinions in your body. Will it not be impossible then, to reconcile those which will arise amongst numerous Assemblies in the different States? It is possible there never may be a general consent to the project, as it goes out; but it is absolutely certain there will never be an agreement in amendments. It is the lot of but few to be able to discern the remote principles upon which their happiness and prosperity essentially depend."

SUNDAY, AUGUST 12, 1787

Washington noted in his diary : [1]

"Dined at Bush-hill with Mr. William Hamilton. Spent the evening at home writing letters."

[1] It is interesting to note that, the day before, August 11, the *Herald* had described a highway robbery by two men with cudgels which occurred on land leading

Assembly." [1] A Philadelphia despatch to a Boston paper, this day, said : [2]

"The Convention, I am told, have unanimously agreed on a system for the future Government of the United States which will speedily be laid before the several Legislatures for their acceptance and ratification. What this system is, is not yet known but to the framers of it, but that it will be a system founded on justice and equity in which the rights of citizens will be properly balanced, considering the characters who formed it, none can doubt. That, consistent with these, it may be energetic, none can but wish."

Elbridge Gerry wrote, this day, to General James Warren in Massachusetts :

"It is out of my power, in return for the information you have given me, to inform you of our proceedings in Convention, but I think they will be complete in a month or six weeks, perhaps sooner. Whenever they shall be matured, I sincerely hope they will be such as you and I can approve, and that they will not be engrafted with principles of mutability, corruption or despotism — principles which some, you and I know, would not dislike to find in our National Constitution."

On this day, there was published, for the first time in Philadelphia, a despatch from New Haven, Connecticut, dated August 2, which contained a report of a most extraordinary nature, to the effect that a movement for a monarchy was spreading in the country : [3]

"A circular letter is handing about the country recommending a kingly Government for these States. The writer

---

[1] *Pennsylvania Herald*, Aug. 15, 1787.

[2] *Pennsylvania Gazette*, Aug. 15; *Independent Chronicle*, Aug. 19, 1787.

[3] See *Massachusetts Centinel*, Aug. 8, quoting *New Haven Gazette* (Conn.) of Aug. 2; *Independent Gazetteer*, Aug. 14; *Pennsylvania Gazette*, Aug. 15; *Independent Chronicle*, Aug. 16, 1787; and numerous other papers throughout the country.

The Bishop of Osnaburgh, referred to in this story, was Frederick, Duke of York, born in 1763, second son of George III, and Secular Bishop of Osnaburgh, a town in the Prussian Province of Hanover. See especially George Ticknor Curtis' *History of the Constitution* (1858), II, 492-494.

proposes to send to England for the Bishop of Osnaburgh, second son of the King of Great Britain, and have him crowned King over this continent. We have found by experience, says he, that we have not wit enough to govern ourselves — that all our declamation and parade about Republicanism, Liberty, Property and the Rights of Man are mere stuff and nonsense, and that it is high time for us to tread back the wayward path we have walked in these twelve years. This plan, we are told, gains friends and partisans rapidly, and it surely is necessary for the great body of the people to be on their guard. The Federal Convention may save us from this worst of curses (a Royal Government), if we are wise enough to adopt their recommendations when they shall be communicated to us."

This story was copied in newspapers throughout the States and caused some perturbation; and an anecdote appearing in the *Gazetteer* shows that it was given consideration, even in Philadelphia : [1]

"On taking down the *Crown* of Christ Church steeple, which sometime since had been much injured by lightning, one of the bystanders asked what they were going to do with it. He was told it was to be repaired and put up immediately. 'I guess,' says an arch boy, who had been very attentive to the query and answer, 'they had better wait till the Convention breaks up and know first what they recommend.'"

Alexander Hamilton, in New York, started an investigation of the sources of the story, and wrote to Col. Jeremiah Wadsworth in Connecticut : [2]

"The enclosed is said to be the copy of a letter circulating in your State. The history of its appearance among us is that it was sent by one Whitmore, of Stratford, formerly in the Paymaster General's office, to one James Reynolds of this city. I am at a loss clearly to understand

---

[1] *Independent Gazetteer*, Aug. 18, 1787.

[2] Hamilton to Wadsworth, Aug. 20, 1787; Wadsworth to Hamilton, Aug. 26, 1787; Col. David Humphreys to Hamilton, Sept. 16, 1787.

its object, and have some suspicion that it has been fabricated to excite jealousy against the Convention, with a view at an opposition to their recommendations. At all events, I wish, if possible, to trace its source and send it to you for that purpose. Whitmore must of course say where he got it, and by pursuing the information we may at last come at the author. Let me know the political connections of this man and the complexion of the people most active in the circulation of the letter. Be so good as to attend to this inquiry somewhat particularly, as I have different reasons of some moment for setting it on foot."

Wadsworth replied to Hamilton's inquiry, as follows:

"I received your favor this day, with the inclosed copy of a letter said to be circulating in this State. Some time since, a paragraph in the New Haven paper hinted at such a letter, and appeared to be written to scare the antifederal party or alarm them, and I believed it was well intended, as it seemed to be meant to prepare them to comply with the doings of the Convention — least worse befell them — but the close of this letter appears to be calculated for other purposes. Wetmore has always associated with Mr.
who wished well to America and a good Government, he is half brother to the spirited Federal writer in our papers who signs himself Cato — and if he has really written or circulated the letter in question I am quite at a loss to know his intentions. I have communicated this matter to Col. Humphrey in confidence who is on his way to New Haven (where Wetmore lives, tho formerly of Stratford) he will enquire carefully into the matter and write you. He has lived in the same house with Wetmore and can easily fathom him. Wetmore is naturally sanguine, has some talents, and I believe is enterprizing — but fickle. Who the active people in this business are, I have yet to learn, as it certainly has not circulated hereabouts. But from Humphrey, you may expect to know all that is true in Wetmore's neighborhood."

And Col. David Humphreys of Connecticut also wrote to Hamilton:

"Our friend, Col. Wadsworth, has communicated to me a letter in which you made enquiries respecting a political letter that has lately circulated in this State. I arrived in this town yesterday and have since conversed with several intelligent persons on the subject. It appears to have been printed in a Fairfield paper as long ago as the 25th of July. I have not been able to trace it to its source. Mr. Wetmore informs me that when he first saw this letter, it was in the hands of one Jared Mansfield, who, I believe, has formerly been reputed a Loyalist. Indeed it seems to have been received and circulated with avidity by that class of people, whether it was fabricated by them or not. I think, however, there is little doubt that it was manufactured in this State. I demanded of Mr. Wetmore what he thought were the wishes and objects of the writer of that letter; he said he believed it might be written principally for the amusement of the author and perhaps with some view to learn whether the people were not absolutely indifferent to all government and dead to all political sentiment. Before I saw the letter in question, a paragraph had been published by Mr. Meigs, giving an account of it and attempting to excite the apprehension of the Antifederalists, with an idea that the most disastrous consequences are to be expected, unless we shall accept the proceedings of the Convention. Some think this was the real design of that fictitious performance; but others, with more reason, that it was intended to feel the public pulse and to discover whether the public mind would be startled with propositions of Royalty. The quondam Tories have undoubtedly conceived hopes of a future union with Great Britain, from the inefficiency of our Government and the tumults which prevailed in Massachusetts during the last winter. I saw a letter written at that period, by a clergyman of considerable reputation in Nova Scotia to a person of eminence in this State, stating the impossibility of our being happy under our present

Constitution and proposing (now we could think and argue calmly on all the consequences) that the efforts of the moderate, the virtuous, and the brave should be exerted to effect a re-union with the parent State. He mentioned, among other things, how instrumental the Cincinnati might be, and how much it would redound to their emolument. It seems, by a conversation I have had there, that the ultimate practicability of introducing the Bishop of Osnaburgh is not a novel idea among those who were formerly termed Loyalists. Ever since the peace it has been occasionally talked of and wished for. Yesterday, where I dined, half jest, half earnest, he was given as the first toast. I leave you now, my dear friend, to reflect how ripe we are for the most mad and ruinous projects that can be suggested, especially when, in addition to this view, we take into consideration how thoroughly the patriotic part of the community, the friends of an efficient Government, are discouraged with the present system and irritated at the popular demagogues who are determined to keep themselves in office at the risque of everything. Thence apprehensions are formed, that tho' the measures proposed by the Convention may not be equal to the wishes of the most enlightened and virtuous, yet that they will be too high-toned to be adopted by our popular Assemblies. Should that happen our political ship will be left afloat on a sea of chance, without a rudder as well as without a pilot. I am happy to see you have (some of you) had the honest boldness to attack in a public paper, the Antifederal dogmas of a great personage in your State [Gov. Clinton]. Go on and prosper. Were the men of talents and honesty throughout the Continent properly combined into one phalanx, I am confident they would be competent to hew their way thro' all opposition. Were there no little jealousies, bickerings, and unworthy sinister views to divert them from their object, they might by perseverance establish a Government calculated to promote the happiness of mankind and to make the Revolution a blessing instead of a curse."

Meanwhile, the accuracy of the report was denied by members of the Convention; and for the first time they, unofficially, authorized a public statement to be made, which appeared in the *Gazette*, August 15, as follows:[1]

"We are well informed that many letters have been written to the members of the Federal Convention from different quarters, respecting the reports, idly of circulating, that it is intended to establish a monarchical government to send for the Bishop of Osnaburgh, etc. etc. — to which it has been uniformly answered, 'Tho we cannot affirmatively tell you what we are doing; we can, negatively tell you what we are not doing — we never once thought of a King.'"

It is certain that there were no members of the Convention who actually favored a monarchy in this country, though it is possible that the attitude of Alexander Hamilton and George Read, who advocated an extremely "high-toned" form of Government with an Executive and a Senate elected for life, gave some color to a belief on the part of some in their monarchical tendencies.[2] That there were delegates who regarded their attitude with suspicion is shown by a note made by James McHenry, on his return from Maryland on August 4, with reference to his fellow-delegate, John F. Mercer:[3]

---

[1] See also *Pennsylvania Herald*, Aug. 18; *Pennsylvania Journal*, Aug. 22; *Boston Gazette*, Aug. 27; *Salem Mercury*, Aug. 28, 1787; and many other papers.

[2] In later years, there were intimations that at one time Nathaniel Gorham of Massachusetts had leanings in that direction, but the proof of this story is extremely slight. See *Prince Henry of Prussia and the Regency of the United States 1786*, by R. Krauel, *Amer. Hist. Rev.* (1911), XVII, 114; *A Study of Monarchical Tendencies in the United States from 1776 to 1801* (1922), by Louise B. Dunbar.

[3] Daniel Carroll wrote to Madison, May 28, 1788 (*Doc. Hist.*, IV, 636): "It has come to light that Luther Martin, in his tavern harangues among the Members during the sitting of that Assembly, had informed many of them that more than twenty Members of the Convention were in favor of a Kingly Government, and that he received the information from Mr. McHenry who had a list of their names on the first printed report of the Committee of Detail. This positive assertion under the weight of Mr. McHenry's name had the effect I have mentioned [defeat of Carroll for Congress]. Some time after the breaking up of the Assembly, being informed of what Martin had said, I wrote to Mr. McHenry who gave for answer,

"Saw Mr. Mercer make out a list of the member's names who had attended or were attending in Convention, with for and against marked opposite most of them — asked carelessly what question occasioned his being so particular, upon which he told me, laughing, that it was no question but that those marked with 'A' were for a king. I then asked him how he knew that, to which he said, 'No matter, the thing is so.' I took a copy with his permission. . . ."

On the other hand, Abraham Baldwin in giving an account of the Convention four months later said that the delegates agreed in vesting in the President as much power "as could be, consistently with guarding against all possibility of his ascending in a tract of years or ages to Despotism or Monarchy — of which all were cautious. *Nor did it appear that any Members in Convention had the least idea of insidiously laying the foundation of a future Monarchy* . . . but were unanimously guarded and firm against everything of this ultimate tendency." [1] Madison himself later wrote that the determination of the delegates to provide an adequate National Government was strengthened by their belief that much of the opposition to the Convention came from men imbued with "monarchical or aristocratical predilections." [2]

that, seeing a list of names on Mr. Mercer's report, he copied it, and asked him what the words *for* and *against* meant, who replied, '*for* a Kingly Government, *against* it.' I wrote to Mr. McHenry that as I had been injured by his name being mentioned, I desired he would take a proper occasion whilst the [State] Convention was sitting of having justice done me. He has answered that on speaking to Mercer on the subject, he told him that he meant a National Government, to which McHenry says, 'I do not know what you *meant*, but you *said* a Kingly Government.' This, Mercer denies and has given from under his hand that he 'neither said Kingly or National Government.' I have a letter from Luther Martin, wherein he says he had the information from McHenry, without Mercer being mentioned, who told him he might rely on the persons being, as marked, for a Kingly Government. Thus, this matter rests at present. It is to be settled between McHenry and Martin on one point, and him and Mercer on another."

[1] *The Literary Diary of Ezra Stiles* (1901), III, December 21, 1787 — see Appendix E.

[2] *Writings of James Madison* (Hunt's ed.), IX, Madison to John G. Jackson, Dec. 27, 1821.

"The disposition to give to the new system all the vigour consistent with Republican principles, was not a little stimulated by a backwardness in some quarters towards a Convention for the purpose, which was ascribed to a secret dislike to popular Government and a hope that delay would bring it more into disgrace and pave the way for a form of Government more congenial with monarchical or aristocratical predilections."

And Jefferson, eleven years later, recorded "a very remarkable fact indeed in our history", which had been related to him by Abraham Baldwin, a delegate from Georgia.[1] Though Baldwin's information was undoubtedly inaccurate, his statement is an example of what men then believed:

"Before the establishment of our present Government, a very extensive combination had taken place in New York and the Eastern States among that description of people who were partly monarchical in principle, or frightened with Shays rebellion and the impotence of the old Congress. Delegates in different places had actually had consultations on the subject of seizing on the powers of a Government and establishing them by force, had corresponded with one another, and had sent a deputy to Gen. Washington to solicit his coöperation. He calculated too well to join them. The new Convention was in the meantime proposed by Virginia and appointed. These people believed it impossible the States should ever agree on a Government, as this must include the impost and all the other powers which the States had a thousand times refused to the general authority. They thereafter let the proposed Convention go on, not doubting its failure and confiding that on its failure would be a still more favorable moment for their enterprise. They therefore wished it to fail, and especially when Hamilton, their leader, brought forward his plan of Government, failed entirely in carrying it and retired in disgust from the Convention. His associates

---

[1] *Writings of Thomas Jefferson* (Ford's ed.), I, " The Anas ", Jan. 5, 1798.

then took every method to prevent any form of Government being agreed to. But the well intentioned never ceased trying first one thing, then another, till they could get something agreed to. The final passage and adoption of the Constitution completely defeated the views of the combination and saved us from an attempt to establish a Government over us by force. This fact throws a blaze of light on the conduct of several members from New York and the Eastern States in the Convention at Annapolis and the Grand Convention. At that of Annapolis, several Eastern members most vehemently opposed Madison's proposition for a more general Convention with more general powers. They wished things to get more and more into confusion, to justify the violent measure they proposed. The idea of establishing a Government by reasoning and agreement they publicly ridiculed, as an Utopian project, visionary and unexampled."

On this day, August 13, there was also published another false report as to the Convention, in the shape of a letter "from a Gentleman in Philadelphia to his Friend in Charleston", dated July 4. It is of curious interest, as showing conclusively how well the delegates had preserved secrecy prior to that date; for, while it purported to give specific facts as to matters being considered by the Convention, not a single fact referred to was accurate : [1]

"You requested me, in your last, to inform you of the state of our markets and politics in general; which, in my last, I treated of in brief, when I only advised you of the nature of the business at the opening of the Convention; but many matters have been proposed and debated on since — and although secrecy was agreed on, it is credited by some of the first informed men in this city that amongst the matters now under consideration are —

A continuance of the Foederal Government, and to

[1] *New York Daily Advertiser*, Aug. 13, 1787; see also *Massachusetts Centinel*, Aug. 29, 1787, and other papers.

include the State of Vermont. To establish a revenue for 25 years (easy in its collection) of 5 per cent on all imports, $2\frac{1}{2}$ per cent on all exports, on such articles as are not produced in any of the British provinces — the 5 per cent to be appropriated to the payment of our foreign and domestic debts; the $2\frac{1}{2}$ per cent for the expenses of keeping up a small land force and navy. A poll tax of one shilling per head on all whites, and two shillings on all other inhabitants, to be applied for granting bounties on ships built in the United States and on every ton of shipping employed in the fisheries. And, as many of our present difficulties arise from the imbecillity of the inhabitants to pay their debts — that it be strongly recommended to each State to pass laws for paying off all debts contracted before the 1st of October, 1784, by installments of one, two, three, four and five years, giving security. That serious application be made for the free navigation of the Mississippi, according to the treaty of peace. That no new States be established until the public debt is paid off. Five hundred troops to be raised and kept in each State, the half on the sea coast and the other half on the frontiers. That three frigates of forty guns be built immediately. Congress to be called the General Assembly of the United States and to sit six months in the year.

No doubt much more is talked of, but as these seem leading points I hand them to you; and shall, whenever I have good grounds to go on, keep informing you of what I learn, particularly on matters of commerce. Have just heard from undoubted authority that a member of the Convention will propose next week that no slave whatever be imported into any of the States for the term of twenty-five years."

TUESDAY, AUGUST 14, 1787

IN CONVENTION

Compensation of Members of Congress

On this day, the Convention took up a section relating to Congress, reported by the Committee of Detail as follows:

allowed.) [1] Ellsworth had again moved that they "be paid by their respective States", saying that: "If the Senate was meant to strengthen the Government, it ought to have the confidence of the States; the States will have an interest in keeping up a representation, and will make such provision for supporting the members as will ensure their attendance." (It is to be recalled that at this stage in the sessions, the Convention had voted that the Senate should be appointed by the State Legislatures but had not agreed to an equality of votes by the States.) Madison pointed out that Ellsworth's proposal would "be a departure from a fundamental principle, and subverting the end intended by allowing the Senate a duration of six years." They would, if this motion should be agreed to, hold their places "during the pleasure of the State Legislatures." The motion, he said, would make the Senate like the Congress under the Confederation, "the mere agents and advocates of State interests and views, instead of being the impartial umpires and guardians of justice and general good." Ellsworth's motion had then been defeated by another close vote of five to six (Connecticut, New York, New Jersey, South Carolina, and Georgia voting for it). Having thus shown that it believed in payment of the Senate by the National Government, the Convention had voted to strike out the words "to be paid out of the public treasury" — evidently with the view that if nothing should be said on the subject, "it would silently devolve on the National Treasury to support the National Legislature." [2]

The Convention having thus twice expressly defeated Ellsworth's proposal that the States should pay the members of the Congress; and having submitted to the

---

[1] Butler and Rutledge had also favored this in the Committee of the Whole, June 12.

[2] See note by Madison in the debates of June 22.

Committee of Detail a resolution containing express provision for payments of members of the House "out of the publick treasury", it must have astonished the delegates to find that the rejected proposal was recommended by the Committee. And when, on August 14, they took up this subject, they must have been equally astonished to hear Ellsworth himself state that, on further reflection, he was satisfied "that too much dependence on the States would be produced by this mode of payment", and that he would move to have his own proposal again rejected. Mason pointed out that if the Committee's suggestion were accepted, both Houses of Congress would be made "instruments of the politics of the States, whatever they may be." Carroll said that "the new Government in the form proposed by the Committee was nothing more than a second edition of Congress (*i.e.*, the Congress of the Confederation) in two volumes instead of one." Dickinson assumed that "all were convinced of the necessity of making the General Government independent of the prejudices, passions and improper views of the State Legislatures. . . . If the General Government should be left dependent on the State Legislatures it would be happy for us if we had never met in this room." The complete divergence between the points of view of the two factions in the Convention — the Nationalists and the States' Rights adherents — was fully and concisely illustrated in a colloquy between Luther Martin and his Maryland colleague, Daniel Carroll. "As the Senate is to represent the States, the members of it ought to be paid by the States," said the former, to which the latter replied: "The Senate was to represent and manage the affairs of the whole and not to be the advocates of State interests. They ought not to be dependent on nor paid by the States." The Convention then decided by the decisive vote of nine to two (Massachusetts and South

Carolina dissenting) that salaries be paid out of the National Treasury.

There then arose a difficult question which had already been broached on June 12 and 22, and left undecided at that date: Should the Constitution itself fix the amount of the salaries? Madison had, at the earlier date, thought that to leave the Congress "to fix their own wages was an indecent thing and might, in time, prove a dangerous one." He suggested a salary fixed according to the price of wheat or some other standard-priced article. Ellsworth now, on August 14, suggested that the Constitution fix a salary of five dollars per day, saying that while he "was not unwilling to trust the Legislature with authority to regulate their own wages, he well knew that an unlimited discretion for that purpose would produce strong, tho perhaps not insuperable, objections," to the Constitution. G. Morris thought that the amount should be left to the discretion of Congress, as "there could be no reason to fear that they would overpay themselves." Sherman said that he was not afraid that the Congress "would make their own wages too high, but too low, so that men ever so fit could not serve unless they were at the same time rich"; and he favored fixing a moderate allowance of five dollars a day with a right in the States to add to it. Jacob Broom of Delaware saw no danger in letting Congress fix its own salaries, since the State Legislatures fixed their own "and no complaint had been made of it." Madison favored fixing in the Constitution a maximum and minimum salary, not to be altered by Congress. Dickinson proposed that the Congress should pass an act every twelve years setting the amount of salaries. After listening to all these diverse views, the Convention decisively defeated Ellsworth's proposal of five dollars per day, and then voted to vest complete power in Congress by inserting the words "to be ascertained by law." And this provision, so settled, became Article One, section 6, clause 1, of the Constitution as finally adopted.

OUT OF CONVENTION

Jefferson wrote from Paris, this day, to Joseph Jones in Virginia, advocating a form of Government such as the Convention was already planning. It is to be noted that, at this time, Jefferson particularly desired a Federal Judiciary :

"I wish to see our States made one as to all foreign, and several as to all domestic matters, a peaceable mode of compulsion over the States given to Congress, and the powers of this body divided, as in the States, into three departments, Legislative, Executive, and Judiciary. It is my opinion the want of the latter organization has already done more harm than all the other Federal defects put together, and that every evil almost may be traced to that source; but with all the defects of our Constitutions, whether general or particular, the comparison of our Governments with those of Europe, are like a comparison of heaven and hell; England, like the earth, may be allowed to take the intermediate station."

On this day, also, Jefferson wrote to Washington :

"I remain in hopes of great and good effects from the decision of the Assembly over which you are presiding. To make our States one as to all foreign concerns, preserve them several as to all merely domestic, to give to the Federal head some peaceable mode of enforcing its just authority, to organize that head into Legislative, Executive, and Judiciary departments, a great desiderata in our Federal Constitution. Yet, with all its defects, and with all these of our particular Governments, the inconveniences resulting from them are so light, in comparison with those existing in every other Government on earth, that our citizens may certainly be considered as in the happiest political situation which exists."

To Adams, he wrote later (August 30) that except for the adoption of a secrecy rule by the Convention, he had no doubt that "all their other measures will be good and wise. It is really an assembly of demigods." [1]

General Knox wrote, this day, to General Washington:

"Influenced by motives of delicacy I have hitherto forborne the pleasure, my dear Sir, of writing to you since my return from Philadelphia. I have been apprehensive that the stages of the business of the Convention might leak out, and be made an ill use of, by some people. I have therefore been anxious that you should escape the possibility of imputation. But as the objects seem now to be brought to a point, I take the liberty to indulge myself in communicating with you. Although I frankly confess that the existence of the State Governments is an insuperable evil in a National point of view, yet I do not see how in this stage of the business they could be annihilated — and perhaps, while they continue, the frame of Government could not with propriety be much higher toned than the one proposed. It is so infinitely preferable to the present Constitution, and gives such a bias to a proper line of conduct in future that I think all men anxious for a National Government should zealously embrace it. The education, genius, and habits of men on this Continent are so various even at this moment, and of consequence their views of the same subject so different, that I am satisfied with the result of the Convention, although it is short of my wishes and of my judgment. But when I find men of the purest intentions concur in embracing a system which, on the highest deliberation, seems to be the best which can be obtained, under present circumstances, I am convinced of the propriety of its being strenuously supported by all those who have wished for a National Republic of higher and more durable powers. I am persuaded that the address of the Convention to accompany their propositions will be couched in the most persuasive terms. I feel anxious that there should be the fullest representation in Congress, in order that the propositions should receive their warmest concurrence and strongest impulse."

---

[1] Jefferson wrote, Aug. 15, 1787, to Count del Verni that: "Doctor Franklin and other the greatest characters of America are members of it." *Doc. Hist.*, IV, 252.

CHAPTER EIGHT

POWERS OF CONGRESS

WEDNESDAY, AUGUST 15, 1787

IN CONVENTION

Presidential Veto

The Convention had by this time disposed of most of the provisions regulating the two Houses of Congress. Two only remained for consideration; one, the question whether the Senate should have power equally with the House to originate money bills, was postponed (see *infra* under date of September 8); the other was the important question, how far a bill passed by the two Houses should be subject to Executive veto. Under the original vote by the Committee of the Whole, on June 4, the President was given power of veto, and "on a motion for enabling two thirds of each branch of the Legislature to overrule the revisionary check, it passed in the affirmative." The power was stated as follows, in the Report of the Committee of the Whole on Randolph's Resolution, on June 13:

"Resolved, that the National Executive shall have a right to negative any Legislative Act which shall not be afterwards passed by two thirds of each branch of the National Legislature."

As adopted by the Convention on July 21, it read:

"Resolved, that the National Executive shall have a right to negative any Legislative Act which shall not be afterwards passed, unless by two third parts of each branch of the National Legislature."

It seems clear that the intention was that the two thirds required should be two thirds of the entire membership of each branch. A similar requirement for two thirds in connection with another subject was undoubtedly interpreted as meaning two thirds of the whole membership. Thus, on July 18, Madison moved that the Judges should be nominated by the Executive, "and such nominations should become an appointment if not disagreed to within   days by two thirds of the second branch." On July 21, Madison argued that "in case of any flagrant partiality or error in the nomination, it might be fairly presumed that two thirds of the second branch would join in putting a negative on it." Gerry said that it appeared to him, "a strong objection that two thirds of the Senate were required to reject a nomination of the Executive." Madison "observed that he was not anxious that two thirds should be necessary to disagree to a nomination. . . . He was content to obviate the objection last made and accordingly so varied the motion as to let a majority reject." Though the motion was lost, it is clear that both Madison and Gerry were referring to two thirds of the whole Senate and to a majority of the whole Senate, and not to two thirds or a majority of a quorum of the Senate. When, however, the Committee of Detail made its Report, on August 6, it introduced an element of doubt in connection with the two thirds requirement in the veto power. In formulating this power, the Committee adopted, almost *verbatim*, the provisions of the Massachusetts State Constitution as to the manner in which the President should return the bill with his objections to the House, in which it originated : [1]

"But if after such reconsideration, two thirds of that House shall, notwithstanding the objections of the President, agree to pass it, it shall, together with his objections be sent to the other House, by which it shall likewise be reconsidered, and if approved by two thirds of the other House also, it shall become a law."

In the same Report, however, the Committee provided also that: "In each House, a majority of the members shall be a quorum to do business." This gave rise to a doubt as to the interpretation of the words "two thirds of that House" in the previous clause. Did they mean two thirds of the total membership of the House, or two thirds of the quorum?

On this August 15, the Convention took up this veto power. Madison, for the third time, attempted to obtain sanction for his favorite plan of associating the Judges with the President in a revision of bills passed by the Legislature. His motion was again opposed by Gerry, Charles Pinckney, and Sherman, the latter two stating that they "disapproved of Judges meddling in politics and parties." And it was defeated by a vote of eight States to three. G. Morris now again advocated giving to the President an absolute and unlimited veto power; for he felt that with a President elected by Congress (as at that stage of the Convention it was

---

[1] The Massachusetts State Constitution of 1780 provided that: "If after such consideration, two thirds of the said Senate or House of Representatives shall, notwithstanding the said objection, agree to pass the same, it shall, together with the objections, be sent to the other branch of the Legislature, where it shall also be reconsidered, and if approved by two thirds of the members present, shall have the force of law." See also the New York Constitution of 1777.

provided), "the tendency of the Legislative authority
to usurp on the Executive" would not be sufficiently
checked by a limited veto capable of being overridden
by the Congress. Wilson also was "most apprehensive
of a dissolution of the Government, from the Legislature swallowing up all the other powers"; he feared
that they had not guarded "against the danger on this
side by a sufficient self-defensive power either to the
Executive or Judiciary Department." As this subject
had already been discussed very thoroughly on several
occasions, the delegates became impatient at any suggestions for further debate. Rutledge "complained of
the tediousness of the proceedings"; Ellsworth said
that "we grow more and more skeptical as we proceed",
and that "if we do not decide soon, we shall be unable
to come to any decision." Williamson, however, sharing the views that the President's power needed to be
strengthened, moved that three fourths of each House
be required to overrule a veto instead of two thirds,
and this proposal was accepted. A month later, on
September 12, in the closing days of the Convention,
Williamson moved to reconsider his own proposal,
which, he said, "puts too much power in the President."
As the Convention had, by that date, agreed to election
of the President by electors instead of by Congress, it
became less necessary to guard against encroachments
by Congress on the Presidential power. Accordingly,
he moved to restore the two thirds requirement. G.
Morris opposed the motion. He dwelt on "the danger
to the public interest from the instability of the laws",
as the greatest evil to be guarded against; and he stated
that: "It is the interest of the distant States to prefer
three fourths, as they will be oftenest absent and need
the interposing check of the President." And, said he,
sagely, "the excess rather than the deficiency of laws
was to be dreaded." Williamson also said that he was

"less afraid of too few than of too many laws", but that he was "most of all afraid that the repeal of bad law might be rendered too difficult by requiring three fourths to overcome the dissent of the President." Hamilton stated that, as a matter of fact, in New York two thirds "had been ineffectual either where a popular object or a Legislative faction operated." Madison again emphasized the danger of Legislative injustice and encroachments. Mason, on the other hand, said that his "leading view was to guard against too great impediment to the repeal of laws." Reconsideration was finally voted, and the requirement of two thirds of each House of Congress was restored.

No delegate seems at that time to have raised the question whether the two thirds meant two thirds of the whole membership of each House or only two thirds of a quorum or of those members present. It is evident, however, that G. Morris considered that two thirds of the whole membership was to be required, for in the discussion, he said: "Considering the difference between the two proportions numerically, it amounts in one House to two members only; and in the other to not more than five according to the numbers of which the Legislature is at first to be composed." And Mason said: "As to the numerical argument of Mr. Gouverneur Morris, little was necessary to understand that three fourths was more than two thirds, whatever the numbers of the Legislature might be." Clearly, these two delegates believed that the two thirds was to be two thirds of the whole House, for they referred only to the "numbers" of which the whole Legislature was to be composed. The numbers of the House had been fixed at sixty-five, of which two thirds would be forty-four and three fourths would be forty-nine — a difference of five, as pointed out by Morris. On the theory that a proportion of a quorum was all that was to be required (a quorum being thirty-three), two thirds would be twenty-two and three fourths would be twenty-five — a difference of but three — which would not at all agree with Morris' figuring. And that two thirds of the whole number were required to override a veto and to adopt a Constitutional Amendment was stated explicitly by G. Morris, in a letter written by him in 1804.[1] Luther Martin evidently shared the same view, for later, in a criticism of the Presidential veto provision he said : "It was urged that even if he was given a negative, it ought not to be of so great extent as that given by the system, since his single voice is to countervail the whole of either branch, and any number less than two thirds of the other." [2] So far as the debates show, it would appear that the delegates intended to require two thirds of the whole membership of the House finally considering the veto. And it may be noted, also, that though the New York and the Massachusetts State Constitutions contained the words "if approved by two thirds of the members present", and though the Committee of Detail copied, in its Report, the rest of the provision in these State Constitutions

---

[1] *Life of Gouverneur Morris* (1832), by Jared Sparks, III, 198, Morris to Uriah Tracy, Jan. 5, 1804: "There remain three cases in which two thirds of the whole number are required. These are, first, the expulsion of a member; secondly, the passage of a law disapproved of by the President; and thirdly, amendments to the Constitution. In these three cases a provision is carefully made to defend the people against themselves, or, in other words, against that violence of party spirit, which has hitherto proved fatal to republican government. The constitutional restriction presumes, that to a measure of indispensable necessity, or even of great utility, two thirds of the whole number of Senators and Representatives would agree, and that, if they should not, no great danger would ensue. The public business might go on, though a member of the legislature should be unworthy of his seat. Neither would the Union materially suffer from the want of a particular law, especially of a law rejected by the first magistrate."

[2] *The Genuine Information* (1788), by Luther Martin. On the other hand, Daniel Carroll of Maryland may have understood that only two thirds of the quorum was required, for on August 15, 1787, arguing for a greater Presidential veto power, he said: "When the negative to be overruled by two thirds only was agreed to, the quorum was not fixed. He remarked that as a majority was now to be the quorum, seventeen in the larger and eight in the smaller house might carry points."

almost *verbatim*, it apparently deliberately omitted the words "by two thirds of the members present" and substituted "by two thirds of the other House."

It is also to be noted that the delegates were fully aware of the difference between two thirds of the membership, and two thirds of the members present; for on five distinct subjects, they expressly used the words "of the members present."   (1) The Report of the Committee of Eleven, on September 4, as to the treaty-making power provided specifically that: "No treaty shall be made without the consent of two thirds of the members present." This remained unaltered in the Report of the Committee of Style, on September 12, and in the final draft of the Constitution. Referring to this provision, Gerry, on September 8, pointed out that two thirds of the members present — a majority being a quorum — might make it possible for a treaty to be passed by a representation of not one fifth of the people; and he moved that: "No treaty be made without the consent of two thirds of *all the members of the Senate*." Sherman also moved "that no treaty be made without a majority *of the whole number of the Senate*." Both motions were rejected. Madison moved that a quorum of the Senate consist of two thirds of all the members. This also was rejected. Hence, it appears that the delegates knew how to say "members present" when they meant "members present." (2) The Report of the Committee of Eleven, on September 4, as to trial of impeachments by the Senate, provided that: "No person shall be convicted without the concurrence of two thirds of the members present." This remained unaltered in the Report of the Committee of Style on September 12, and in the final draft of the Constitution. (3) The Report of the Committee of Detail of August 6 provided in Article VI, section 7, that: "The yeas and nays of the members of each

House, on any question, shall at the desire of one fifth part of the members present, be entered on the journal." This was repeated unchanged in the Report of the Committee of Style on September 12 and in the final draft of the Constitution. (4) On August 24, in the debate on the election of the President by the Legislature, Charles Pinckney moved to insert: "to which election a majority of the votes of the members present shall be required." (5) The Report of the Committee of Detail on August 6 provided in Article XVII that: "New States . . . may be admitted by the Legislature into this Government; but to such admission the consent of two thirds of the members present in each House shall be necessary." This provision was never voted on, since a substitute was proposed on August 29.

It is interesting to note also that a requirement for a vote of more than a majority had been proposed in connection with other subjects during the debates. Thus, on August 21, in the debate over prohibition against export duties, Madison moved that the clause reported by the Committee of Detail, on August 6, be amended, by inserting after the words, "no tax or duty shall be laid by the Legislature on articles exported from any States", the words, "unless by consent of two thirds of the Legislature." Langdon had already suggested "requiring the concurrence of two thirds or three fourths of the Legislature." The motion was lost; but it would seem that Madison intended two thirds of the whole Legislature and not two thirds of a quorum or of those present; for his intention was to protect the Southern States from export duties imposed by a majority of the Northern States — the latter not having a two thirds representation in the House or Senate. But if only two thirds of a quorum was meant, Madison's object would not have been obtained; for it was wholly possible that the Northern States might

at any time have two thirds of a quorum in both House
and Senate. The same considerations apply to a motion, on August 29, by Charles Pinckney, that: "No
Act of the Legislature for the purpose of regulating the
commerce of the United States with foreign powers
or among the several States shall be passed without the
assent of two thirds of the members of each House."
There is evidence as to what he meant by "two thirds
of the members of each House"; for McHenry in his
Notes states that on August 24, "Mr. C. Pinckney gave
notice that he would move that the consent of three
fourths *of the whole Legislature* be necessary to the
enacting of a law respecting the regulation of trade or
the formation of a navigation act." [1] On the other
hand, a similar motion by George Mason on September
15, that: "No law in nature of a navigation act be
passed before the year 1808 without the consent of
two thirds of each branch of the Legislature" seems to
have been interpreted differently by Mason himself, for
McHenry in his *Notes* states that: "Mr. Mason moved
in substance that no navigation act be passed without
the concurrence of two thirds *of the members present in
each House";* and Mason himself in the objections
which he formally embodied to the State of Virginia,
after the signing of the Constitution, wrote: [2]

"By requiring only a majority to make all commercial
and navigation laws, the five Southern States (whose produce
and circumstances are totally different from those of the
eight Northern and Eastern States) will be ruined . . .
whereas, requiring two thirds of the members present in both
Houses, would have produced mutual moderation, promoted

---

[1] It is to be noted, however, that in Randolph's first draft of a Constitution in
the Committee of Detail, he had a clause amended in Rutledge's handwriting: "A
navigation act shall not be passed but with the consent of two thirds of the members
present of the Senate and the like number of the House of Representatives." See
The Growth of the Constitution (1900), by William M. Meigs.

[2] *Elliot's Debates*, I, 495.

the general interest, and removed an insuperable objection to the adoption of the government."

In connection with the question of the meaning of two thirds of the whole membership, there may be cited Madison's remark in the debate on August 10, over the question of the power of the branches of the Legislature to expel members. In the Report of the Committee of Detail of August 6, it had been provided that: "Each House may determine the rules of its proceedings; may punish its members for disorderly behaviour; and may expel a member." It had also been provided that: "In each House, a majority of the members shall constitute a quorum to do business." This latter section had been agreed to by the Convention; but as to the former section, Madison "observed that the right of expulsion was too important to be exercised by a bare majority of a quorum; and in emergencies might be dangerously abused"; and he moved accordingly, that "with the concurrence of two thirds" might be inserted between "may" and "expel." This was voted; and in the final draft of the Constitution it became part of Article I, section 3.

The practical construction by Congress itself of the intention of the framers has differed from the interpretation given by G. Morris in 1804; and the whole question was finally settled, in 1919, by the Supreme Court in *Missouri Pacific Railroad* v. *Kansas* (248 U. S. 276) — a case involving the passage of the Webb-Kenyon liquor law of 1913 — in which case, it was held that a Presidential veto might be overridden by a vote of two thirds of the members present, even if such vote did not constitute two thirds of the whole membership.[1]

One other question has arisen in connection with the veto power.

[1] For a complete consideration of the whole veto question, see *The Veto Power* (1890), by Edward Campbell Mason.

Following a similar clause in the Constitution of Massachusetts, the Committee of Detail provided that: "If any bill shall not be returned by the President within seven days after it shall have been presented to him, it shall be a law, unless the Legislature, by their adjournment, prevent its return; in which case it shall not be a law." The Convention accepted this provision, after changing "seven days" to ten. The Committee of Style, in its Report of September 12, slightly modified it, so as to read as it appears in the final draft of the Constitution in Article I, section 7:

"If any bill shall not be returned by the President within ten days (Sundays excepted) after it shall have been presented to him, the same shall be a law, in like manner as if he had signed it, unless the Congress by their adjournment prevent its return in which case it shall not be a law."

It has been held by the Court of Claims (though not as yet by the Supreme Court) that an "adjournment" of a session of the Congress as well as a final adjournment of the Congress will cause a bill to fail to become a law, if it is not signed by the President within ten days after it shall have been presented to him.[1]

OUT OF CONVENTION

The *Gazette* said this day:

"It is to be hoped (says another correspondent) that the Convention will not lessen the safety, dignity or usefulness of their present Government by any imprudent accommodation to the present temper or prejudices of the uninformed part of the community. It is on wise and good men only they can depend to support their measures. They ought to be

---

[1] Since, affirmed in *The Okanogan, etc. Tribes* v. *United States* (1929) 279 U. S. 655. In *La Abia, etc. Co.* v. *United States* (1899) 178 U. S. 423, it was held that the President may sign a bill during a recess of Congress, and in *Edwards* v. *United States* (1932) 286 U. S. 482, after adjournment of Congress, if signature is within ten days of presentation of the bill.

pleased — their principles ought to be consulted or they cannot concur in establishing the new Government."

Washington wrote, this day, to Lafayette:

"The present expectation of the members is, that it will end about the first of next month; when, or as soon after as it shall be in my power, I will communicate the result of our long deliberation to you. . . . The disturbances in Massachusetts have subsided; but there are seeds of discontent in every part of this Union, ready to produce other disorders if the wisdom of the present Convention should not be able to devise, and the good sense of the people be found ready to adopt, a more vigorous and energetic Government, than the one under which we now live; for the present, from experience, has been found too feeble and inadequate to give that security which our liberties and property render absolutely essential, and which the fulfillment of public faith loudly requires. Vain is it to look for respect from abroad, or tranquillity at home — vain is it to murmur at the detention of our Western Posts, or complain of the restriction of our commerce — vain are the attempts to remedy the evil complained of by Mr. Dumas to discharge the interest due on foreign loans, or satisfy the claims of foreign officers, the neglect of doing which is a high impeachment of our National character, and is hurtful to the feelings of every well wisher to this Country, in and out of it — vain is it to talk of chastising the Algirenes, or doing ourselves justice in any other respect, till the wisdom and force of the Union can be more concentrated, and better applied."

THURSDAY, AUGUST 16, 1787

IN CONVENTION

The Taxing Power and the General Welfare Clause

The Convention now took up the powers which should be vested in Congress. It will be recalled that instead of the very broad outline of authority theretofore voted by the Convention, the Committee of Detail

reported eighteen specific powers. The first of these
was that which constituted the vital and essential spark
in the new system of Government — authority in Congress to levy and collect taxes. Without this power,
any Government of any description is helpless.
Rightly did the advocates of the Constitution in the
Virginia State Convention of 1788 describe it as the
"lungs", the "nerves", the "soul" of the new Government. Ability to function depends on ability to obtain
the means for functioning. It is a farce, said Randolph,
to give power to a Government and to withhold the
means of executing. Hitherto, the United States had
been dependent, for the payment of its debts, upon
voluntary compliance by the States with requisitions
for funds made upon them by Congress. Congress had
no power to levy taxes upon the individual citizens to
obtain such funds to pay debts. Neither had it any
power to force the States to levy taxes or otherwise
comply with requisitions. Hence, it had, for some
time, become evident to those who sought to "render
the Federal Constitution adequate to the exigencies of
Government and the preservation of the Union", in the
words of the vote of Congress of February 21, 1787 —
both to those who wished only to amend the Articles,
as well as to those who wished to frame an entirely new
Government — that the one absolutely necessary function to be imparted was that of taxation.[1] Even the
New Jersey Plan submitted by Paterson, June 15,
granted to Congress power to "pass acts for raising a
revenue" by laying import duties and by stamp taxes.
Accordingly, when the Committee of Detail drafted
the Article conferring specific and limited authority
upon Congress, the very first power so vested was:

[1] Ezra Stiles, President of Yale College, recorded in his diary, Dec. 21, 1787:
"It appeared that they were pretty unanimous in the following ideas . . . that a
certain portion or degree of dominion as to laws and revenue . . . was necessary
to be ceded by individual States to the authority of the National Council."

"The Legislature of the United States shall have the power to lay and collect taxes, duties, imposts and excises" (excepting by a later provision, export duties and taxes or duties on import or migration of slaves). So clear was the necessity of this provision, that the Convention, on this August 16, voted for it with no State dissenting.[1] The power would probably have remained as phrased on that day, if it had not been for the anxiety of the delegates on another subject — an anxiety productive of a change which has caused this General Welfare Clause to be a bone of contention. So vigorously contested has been its interpretation during the political and constitutional history of this country, and so grave has been, and still may be, its effect upon that history, that a detailed description of the manner in which its final phraseology was arrived at is absolutely necessary for its proper comprehension.

Two days after this power to tax had been agreed to by the Convention, Rutledge and Charles Pinckney of South Carolina, and Gerry and King of Massachusetts called attention (on August 18) to the fact that the new frame of a Constitution contained no specific provision for payment of the already incurred public debt; and Pinckney moved to confer two additional powers upon Congress, viz.: "to secure the payment of the public debt", and "to secure all creditors under the new Constitution from a violation of the public faith when pledged by the authority of the Legislature." This motion was referred to the Committee of Detail. Rutledge then moved that a Grand Committee (of one delegate from each State) be appointed to consider the necessity and expediency of assumption by the United States of all the State debts, since such debts had been,

[1] In the closing sessions of the Convention, on September 14, the following clause was added, without debate or dissent: "but all such duties, imposts and excises shall be uniform through the United States."

he said, "contracted in the common defence." [1] As the States were to be called on now to surrender to the United States their rights to tax imports, it would be politic to conciliate them to the new Constitution, "by disburdening the people of the State debts." King also remarked that "besides the consideration of justice and policy . . . the State creditors, an active and formidable party, would otherwise be opposed to a plan which transferred to the Union the best resources of the States without transferring the State debts at the same time." The State creditors had generally been "the strongest foes to propositions in the past to give to Congress power to levy impost duties." The Grand Committee, appointed under Rutledge's motion, reported, three days later (August 21), through Governor William Livingston of New Jersey, recommending the following new power:

"The Legislature of the United States shall have power to fulfill the engagements which have been entered into by Congress, and to discharge as well the debts of the United States, as the debts incurred by the several States during the late war, for the common defence and general welfare."

It was in this Report, and in connection with engagements and debts already incurred, that the phrase "for the common defence and general welfare" thus first occurred in connection with any specific provision of the new Constitution. The proposal was debated, on August 22. Ellsworth thought the power unnecessary, since the United States, having entered into engagements by Congress as their agents, "will hereafter be bound to fulfil them by their new agents." Randolph, on the other hand, thought that "though the United

---

[1] The Committee consisted of: John Langdon of New Hampshire, Rufus King of Massachusetts, Roger Sherman of Connecticut, William Livingston of New Jersey, George Clymer of Pennsylvania, John Dickinson of Delaware, James McHenry of Maryland, George Mason of Virginia, Hugh Williamson of North Carolina, Charles C. Pinckney of South Carolina, and Abraham Baldwin of Georgia.

States will be bound, the new Government will have no authority in the case, unless it be given them" — a striking, though erroneous statement of the view that there would have been no implied power to pay prior debts. Madison thought the power should be given in order "to prevent misconstruction"; and Gerry also thought it "essential that some explicit provision should be made . . . so that no pretext might remain for getting rid of the public engagements." It is evident that the delegates were imbued with an intense feeling that there should be no doubt as to the fulfillment by the new Government of its obligation to creditors. Repudiation, scaling down of debts, and payment in depreciated currency had been rampant in some States; and the delegates were determined that it should be made clear in the new Constitution that no one should question the integrity of the new Government. Accordingly, G. Morris moved that instead of authorizing Congress, the Constitution should require Congress to pay the debts, as follows: "The Legislature *shall* discharge the debts and fulfil the engagements of the United States." And this motion was carried, without a dissenting vote.

It will be noted that the new clause reported by Governor Livingston included a power in Congress to pay State debts hitherto incurred, as well as United States debts. Neither on August 21, 22, nor 23 was there any motion made on this question of State debts, nor any debate (save a speech by Gerry, on August 21, opposing the proposal as likely to excite great opposition to the Constitution on the part of the States which had already done the most to clear off their debts).[1]

[1] It is to be noted that Elbridge Gerry, in a speech in the House, Feb. 25, 1790 (*Annals of Congress, 1st Cong., 2d Sess.*, p. 1360), said that the provision for assumption of State debts would have been accepted by the Convention if it had applied to debts already paid off by the States; see also speech of Madison in the House, April 22, 1790.

Alexander Hamilton wrote to Edward Carrington, May 26, 1792: "The question of an assumption of the State debts by the United States was in discussion when

As to the debts of the United States, the Convention, on August 23, voted to prefix to the taxing power section already adopted by it on August 22, a provision requiring Congress to pay these debts, as follows:

"The Legislature *shall* fulfil the engagements and discharge the debts of the United States and shall have the power to lay and collect taxes, duties, imposts and excises."

And the clause as so amended was agreed to. Pierce Butler of South Carolina asked for a reconsideration so as to provide for discrimination between payment of debts to original holders of securities and payment to "bloodsuckers who had speculated on the distresses of others and bought up securities at heavy discounts"; the question was accordingly reopened on August 25. He wanted to leave the door open to the Government to buy up the securities and he feared lest the requirement that it *shall* discharge the debts would preclude it from doing anything but pay them in full. He also feared lest the provision might be deemed to extend to all the old Continental paper, payment of some of which had been expressly repudiated except at the depreciated ratio of forty to one. It is important to notice the arguments; for they illustrated the great confusion which later existed in the debates in the State Conventions over the adoption of the Constitution. The many misunderstandings on the subject of these old debts and the effect of the new Constitution upon them led to much of the opposition to ratification. Mason now made the objection that "the use of the word *shall* will beget speculation and increase the pestilent practice

the Convention that framed the present Government was sitting at Philadelphia, and in a long conversation with Mr. Madison in an afternoon's walk, I well remember that we were perfectly agreed on the expediency and propriety of such a measure; though we were both of opinion that it would be more advisable to make it a measure of administration than an article of Constitution, from the impolicy of multiplying obstacles to its reception on collateral details." *Works of Alexander Hamilton* (Lodge's ed.), IX, 515.

of stockjobbing"; and pointed out that there was "a great distinction between original creditors and those who purchased fraudulently of the ignorant and distressed." He admitted, however, that those who bought Government securities in the open market, even at a depreciation, might be entitled to payment of the face value, though there would be a difficulty in drawing the line in such cases. Gerry and G. Morris opposed Mason's view; they still thought that there should be an express requirement of Congress to pay the debts and doubted whether the public faith would admit of anything but payment of the full face value; and lest the charge should be made against them that they were actuated by personal and interested motives, G. Morris stated that he, himself, "never had become a public creditor, that he might urge with more propriety the compliance with public faith", and Gerry said that "for himself he had no interest in the question, being not possessed of more of the securities than would, by the interest, pay his taxes." [1] The matter was finally adjusted by a compromise clause, suggested by Randolph and favored by Butler of South Carolina and Johnson of Connecticut, which, instead of imposing a requirement on Congress, presented a solemn declaration that : [2]

"All debts contracted and engagements entered into by or under the authority of Congress shall be as valid against the

---

[1] Charles A. Beard in his *An Economic Interpretation of the Constitution* (1913), p. 97, gives figures which would apparently show that Gerry owned at some time considerable amounts of securities issued by the Massachusetts and the Pennsylvania Loan Offices, but it does not appear that he owned them at this date; and writing in the *Massachusetts Centinel*, Jan. 5, 1788, in reply to charges made by Ellsworth in *Connecticut Courant*, Dec. 24, 1787, Gerry denied that he owned "the value of ten pounds in Continental money" or that he had exchanged Continental for State securities.

[2] The Committee on Style, on September 12, proposed a slight change whereby "by or under the authority of Congress" became "before the adoption of this Constitution." This was necessary because the word "Congress" might refer to either the Congress of the Confederation or the Congress of the Constitution. In this form, it became Article VI, clause one, of the final Constitution.

United States under this Constitution as under the Confederation."

The whole intent of this provision was to leave to creditors, after the Constitution should be adopted, precisely the same rights as they had before; and neither to increase nor to diminish those rights. It is highly important to note this fact that the Constitution made absolutely no change in the status of the Government debt, but left the public creditors in exactly the same legal position in which they were under the Confederation. Congress, after the adoption of the new Constitution, would have no greater (and no less) obligation to redeem the Government securities than it had prior to that adoption. The power of Congress to pay in full or to scale down the debt as to purchasers of securities at a discount remained unaffected by this provision in the Constitution.[1] When, however, the ratification of the Constitution was debated in the State Conventions, a wrong interpretation was placed on this clause; and much of the opposition to the Constitution itself was based on the mistaken view that security holders were given by it a privileged position. And, in recent years, the same mistaken idea has given rise to the theory that the delegates framed the Constitution, in this respect, to favor the propertied class. The fact was that the new Congress was as free to deal with the subject under the new Government as under the old, either to pay in full at the face value, or not, as it should deem right and equitable. The only differ-

---

[1] Thus, Madison said in the Virginia State Convention that this clause meant that "there should be no change with respect to claims by this political alteration, and that the public would stand, with respect to their creditors, as before. He thought that the validity of claims ought not to diminish by the adoption of the Constitution. But, however, it could not increase the demands on the public." And George Nicholas said: "The new Government will give the holders the same power of recovery as the old one. . . . On the will of Congress alone the payment depends. Cannot they decide according to real equity?" *Elliot's Debates*, III, 471–473, 476, 480.

ence was that the new Congress was to have the financial resources with which to pay both old and new debts; whereas, before, owing to failure of the States to pay their quotas, it lacked such means.

Having eliminated the express requirement on Congress to pay the debts of the United States, the question now was presented whether there ought not to be an express provision that the taxes which the Convention had empowered Congress to lay, might be laid for the purpose of paying these old debts. The Committee of Detail, on August 22, had already reported (with reference to the motions made by Charles Pinckney, on August 18) that it was desirable to add to the first clause of section 1 of the Legislative Article, the words: "for payment of the debts and necessary expenses of the United States." Following out this idea, and concurring with Randolph's view as to the necessity of an express power, Sherman of Connecticut, on August 25, stated that he "thought it necessary to connect with the clause for laying taxes, duties, etc., an express provision for the object of the old debts"; and accordingly, he moved to add to the power "to levy and collect taxes, duties, imposts and excises", the words "for the payment of said debts and for the defraying the expences that shall be incurred for the common defence and general welfare." This proposal was intended to cover future expences as well as past debts (although the words "said debts" were ambiguous, since no reference to any "debts" was contained in the clause as it then stood). This motion, however, was defeated "as being unnecessary" (according to Madison's report); and this action apparently showed that the Convention disagreed with Randolph's belief that the Congress would have no implied power to pay the old debts by means of a levy of taxes. It would seem that this action should have finally disposed of the whole subject. But there still remained to be acted upon that portion of Governor Livingston's report of August 21 giving to Congress power to assume payment of State debts incurred during the War. As the Convention had taken no action on this, it was referred, on August 31 (together with all other matters not acted upon), to a Committee of eleven, headed by Judge Brearley of New Jersey. This Committee made a report on September 4, in which, ignoring the question of payment of State debts by Congress, it recommended the very change proposed by Sherman on August 25, but rejected by the Convention as unnecessary; viz., that the first clause of the section granting powers should read:

"The Legislature shall have power to lay and collect taxes, duties, imposts and excises, to pay the debts and provide for the common defence and general welfare of the United States."

This restored the *express* power to levy taxes for the purpose of paying the prior debts of the United States, which both Randolph and Sherman had previously stated that they considered to be a necessary provision. The clause thus changed was agreed to by the Convention without debate or dissent, on this same day, September 4. It is clear that the phrase "to pay the debts" referred solely to the prior debts of the United States and not to those which might be incurred by Congress under the new Constitution in the exercise of the new powers vested in it by that instrument. For, as Madison wrote later:[1]

"A special provision in this mode could not have been necessary for the debts of the new Congress; for a power to provide money and a power to perform certain acts, of which money is the ordinary and appropriate means, must, of course, carry with them a power to pay the expence of performing

[1] Madison to Andrew Stevenson, Nov. 17, 1830.

the act.   Nor was any special provision for debts proposed,
till the case of the Revolutionary debts was brought into
view, and it is a fair presumption from the course of the varied
propositions which have been noticed that but for the old
debts and their association with the terms 'common defence
and general welfare', the clause would have remained as
reported in the first draft of a Constitution expressing
generally a power in Congress 'to lay and collect taxes,
duties, imposts and excises' without any addition of the
phrase, 'to provide for the common defence and general
welfare.'   With this addition, indeed, the language of the
clause being in conformity with that of the clause in the
Articles of Confederation, it would be qualified as in those
Articles by the specification of powers subjoined to it."

It is equally clear that no delegate, at that time, conceived that the phraseology recommended by the Committee was, in any way, altering or expanding the *power*
to levy taxes which had theretofore been voted, except
to extend the application of that power to these prior
debts.   The whole intent of the change was evidently
to make the power to levy taxes for the purpose of paying these old debts an *express* power, instead of leaving
it to be *implied* or doubtful.   The question arises : Why,
then, did the Committee insert the additional words,
"and provide for the common defence and general welfare of the United States" ?   In Governor Livingston's
Committee Report of August 21, these words had been
used with reference to prior debts, and merely described them as having been incurred during the late
war "for the common defence and general welfare."
The probable reason for their insertion by Judge Brearley's Committee was as follows.[1]   Had the Convention
simply voted that Congress should have "power to lay
and collect taxes, duties, imposts and excises, to *pay*

[1] See especially *Judge Story's Position on the so-called General Welfare Clause*, by
Henry St. George Tucker, *American Bar Association Journal* (July–August, 1927),
XIII.

the debts of the United States", and had it stopped there, such a provision might have been construed as giving Congress the power to levy and collect taxes to pay the old debts and only for that purpose. Some words evidently had to be added that would make clear the power of Congress to levy taxes for all the National purposes set forth in the grants of power subsequently specified in this section. Evidently the Committee selected these words, "to provide for the common defence and general welfare", as comprising all the other purposes for which Congress was to be empowered to levy and collect taxes. They selected these words as embracing all the subsequent limited grants of power which the Committee of Detail, in its Report of August 6, had specified as constituting that amount of common defence and general welfare which the National Government ought to control and as to which it ought to have power of legislation. In other words, the phrase "to provide for the general welfare" is merely a general description of the amount of welfare which was to be accomplished by carrying out those enumerated and limited powers vested in Congress — and no others.[1]

Such would seem to have been the evident intention of the delegates in using these words. Two other interpretations, however, have, in later years, been given to this clause — one of which has been definitely abandoned, but the other of which is the prevailing interpretation at the present time.

---

[1] It is to be especially noted that the Committee and the Convention, when they adopted, on September 4, the taxing clause with these words in it, did not borrow the words from the Preamble to the Constitution, though it has frequently been stated by historians, legal writers, and statesmen that they did so borrow. For the Preamble, on that date, did not contain these words, and they were not inserted until September 12, in the Report of the Committee on Style. On September 3, these words were borrowed from the Articles of Confederation, in which they were words of mere general import, containing no grant of power; and clearly, when used in this taxing clause, they were intended to be equally devoid of grant of power and to be simply descriptive, in general, of the remaining grants of power vested in the same section.

In the early years following the adoption of the Constitution, a few statesmen who advocated extreme, Nationalistic power contended that the words "to pay the debts and provide for the common defence and general welfare of the United States" constituted a separate, independent, and substantial power of Congress, and were not to be construed as integrally a part of the power to lay taxes. Such an interpretation has been long demolished — the final blow to it being given by Judge Story, in 1833, in his *Commentaries on the Constitution*.[1] For to use his own impressive words:

"The Constitution was, from its very origin, contemplated to be the frame of a National Government, of special and enumerated powers, and not of general and unlimited powers. This is apparent, as will be presently seen from the history of the proceedings of the Convention which framed it; and it has formed the admitted basis of all legislative and judicial reasoning upon it, ever since it was put into operation, by all who have been its open friends and advocates, as well as by all who have been its enemies and opponents. If the clause, 'to pay the debts and provide for the common defence and general welfare of the United States', is construed to be an independent and substantive grant of power, it not only renders wholly unimportant and unnecessary the subsequent enumeration of specific powers, but it plainly extends far beyond them and creates a general authority in Congress to pass all laws which they may deem for the common defence or general welfare. Under such circumstances, the Constitution *would practically create an unlimited National Government.* The enumerated powers would tend to embarrassment and confusion, since they would only give rise to doubts as to the true extent of the general power, or of the enumerated powers."

Story conclusively established that the words "*to* pay the debts, etc." meant precisely the same as if they

[1] See *Commentaries on the Constitution* (1833), by Joseph Story, I, sections 906–911.

read " *in order to* pay the debts, etc. ", and that payment
of debts, etc., was to be construed as merely descriptive
of one of the ends and purposes for which Congress was
granted the power to levy taxes.   It is unnecessary to
discuss this further, as Story's reasoning is everywhere
now accepted.

The second interpretation, however, has been the
one on which Congress has, in practice, long acted,
though it is contrary to what, as above explained, was
probably the intention of the delegates.   The subsequent practice of Congress has gained most of its
strength from the support given to it by Judge Story,
who, after disposing of the theory that the General
Welfare Clause vested an independent and distinct
power in Congress, adopted, himself, the following
interpretation : that the power to levy taxes was
granted for the purpose of paying the public debts and
providing for the common defence and general welfare ;
that Congress may lay a tax in order to pay for anything which it can reasonably deem to be for the common defence and general welfare ; that so long as the
object is one of "general" as opposed to "local" welfare, Congress may tax and appropriate money for it ;
and that Congress is clothed with the power of determining what is the common defence and general
welfare.[1]

Judge Story's construction has, in fact, resulted in
vesting Congress with a power practically unlimited in
its scope.   This construction, moreover, produces an
anomalous result, viz. ; that though Congress has no
power to create, construct, or administer a specific
instrumentality unless the power be granted in the
Constitution, it may, nevertheless, appropriate money

---

[1] See also letter of John Quincy Adams to Andrew Stevenson, published in the
National Intelligencer, July 12, 1832, and comments upon it in *Mass. Hist. Soc.
Proc., 2d Series* (1905), XIX, 504.

(later reconsidered); to constitute inferior tribunals of the United States; to make rules as to captures on land and water; and to define and punish piracies and felonies committed on the high seas, counterfeiting the securities and current coin of the United States, and offences against the law of Nations.

Of all these powers, possibly the most important in its effect upon the promotion of union among the States was the authority to establish an uniform rule of naturalization. Confusion, misunderstanding, and injustice had resulted from the fact that hitherto each State had legislated for itself and according to its own views as to the admission of foreigners to citizenship. There had been great diversity of treatment; and as Chief Justice Taney later said: "The nature of our institutions under the Federal Government made it a matter of absolute necessity that this power should be confided to the Government of the Union . . . a necessity so obvious that no statesman could have overlooked it. . . . Its sole object was to prevent one State from forcing upon all the others and upon the General Government, persons as citizens whom they were unwilling to admit as such." [1]

Besides this important power, the Convention voted to vest Congress with the power to regulate commerce (which is discussed *infra*), and with the power to declare war — the word "declare" being substituted on motion of Madison and Gerry, for "make" as reported by the Committee.[2] The grant of the war making power to the Legislature constituted an innovation in Govern-

---

[1] See Taney, C. J., in *Passenger Cases* (1849), 7 Howard pp. 482–483. See also *The Law of the American Constitution* (1922), by Charles K. Burdick, pp. 322–323; *The Federalist*, No. 42. It is to be noted that Madison reports no vote of acceptance of this power; but an affirmative vote in its favor appears in the Journal of the Convention, under date of August 16.

[2] This change was adopted in order to reserve to the President the power to repel sudden attacks. "The Executive should be able to repel, and not commence, war," said Roger Sherman.

ment.[1] In all other countries that power had been
vested in the Executive.   Pierce Butler of South Carolina favored vesting this power in the President, since
he "will have all the requisite qualities and will not
make war but when the Nation will support it" — to
which Gerry retorted that he "never expected to hear
in a Republic a motion to empower the Executive alone
to declare war."   Charles Pinckney, expressing the
view that the proceedings of the Legislature "were too
slow", its meetings too infrequent, and its composition
"too numerous for such deliberations", favored vesting
the war power in the Senate as "more acquainted with
foreign affairs and most capable of proper resolutions",
especially since the Senate (at this stage in the sessions)
was vested with the power to make treaties, and "it
would be singular for one authority to make war, and
another peace."   No support was given to either of
these proposals.[2]   The extent of this power of Congress
to declare war has been defined by the Supreme Court:
"that every contention by force between two nations,
in external matters, under the authority of their respective governments is not only war, but public war."   In
recent years, Congress has acquiesced in the assumption by the President of a certain part of this war
power.[3]

OUT OF CONVENTION

The *Gazetteer* published a letter, signed "Meanwell",
suggesting that the Convention, when it had finished its

[1] Jefferson wrote to Madison, Sept. 6, 1789: "We have already given, in
example, one effectual check to the dog of war, by transferring the power of letting
him loose from the Executive to the Legislative body, from those who are to spend
to those who are to pay."

[2] *Talbot* v. *Seamen* (1801), 1 Cranch 1: "The whole powers of war being, by the
Constitution of the United States vested in Congress. . . ."   *Bas* v. *Tingy* (1800),
4 Dallas 37, 400, see also *The Prize Cases* (1863), 2 Black 635, 668: "By the Constitution, Congress alone has the power to declare a national or foreign war. . . .
He (the President) has no power to initiate or declare a war against a foreign nation
or a domestic State."

[3] See especially *Executive Assumption of the War-Making Power*, by Albert H.
Putney, *National University Law Rev.* (1927), VII.

draft should only adjourn so as to be ready to meet again to consider any changes. "We have now sitting," he said, "a Convention which, I am persuaded, would have done honor to the State of Greece and Rome in their highest glory. . . . Every honest man will readily agree with me in opinion, that our future political safety and happiness depends on the results of their present deliberations." [1]

SATURDAY, AUGUST 18, 1787

IN CONVENTION

Powers of Congress over the Army and Navy

On this day, Madison and Charles Pinckney submitted twenty additional powers, "as proper to be added to those of the Legislature." These were referred to the Committee of Detail for consideration. The Convention also voted to refer to a "Grand Committee" of eleven, consideration of the subjects of assumption of State debts, and power of the National Government over the State militias.

Three further powers to Congress were voted, viz.: "to raise and support armies"; "to provide and maintain a navy"; and "to make rules for the government and regulation of the land and naval forces." This latter power had not been suggested by the Committee of Detail; but as it was contained in the old Articles of Confederation, it was now voted. Discussion of the former power developed the old jealousy of the American Colonies and States against the maintenance of standing armies in time of peace. Gerry called attention to the lack of any check against this, and said that "the people were jealous on this head, and great opposition to the plan would spring from such an omission." He thought an army in time of peace to be dangerous,

[1] *New York Daily Advertiser*, Aug. 23, 1787.

and he moved that "in time of peace the army shall not consist of more than   men", suggesting that 2000 or 3000 should be sufficient.   Luther Martin supported him.   At this point in the Convention, as later narrated by General Mercer, General Washington, who was in the Chair and therefore could offer no motion, turned to a delegate who stood near and in a whisper made the satirical suggestion that he move to amend the motion so as to provide that "no foreign enemy should invade the United States at any time, with more than three thousand troops." [1]   To the same effect, General Pinckney asked "whether no troops were ever to be raised until an attack should be made upon us"; and Dayton observed that "preparations for war are generally made in peace; and a standing force of some sort may, for aught we know, become unavoidable."   Gerry's motion was unanimously rejected.   On September 5, Judge Brearley's Committee proposed to add to the clause granting to Congress the power "to raise and support armies", the further proviso "but no appropriation of money to that use shall be for a longer term than two years."   This provision was an example of the same apprehensions which had been felt in England and which led to the provisions contained in the Mutiny Acts making army appropriations annually.   It was adopted without dissent, though Gerry expressed his opposition on the ground that "it implied there was to be a standing army, which he inveighed against as dangerous to liberty, as unnecessary even for so great an extent of country as this, as, if necessary, that some restriction on the number and duration ought to be provided."   Moreover, said he, this is not a proper time for "such an innovation", and "the people will not bear it."   Sherman also stated that he would like "a reasonable restriction on the number and continuance

[1] Quoted by Paul Wilstach in *Patriots off Their Pedestals* (1927).

of an army in time of peace." Following the action on August 18, a warm debate took place on the proposed power of Congress over the State militia. The subject was referred to a Committee (as discussed *infra*, under date of August 23).

As illustrations of the deep seated sentiments then prevalent, it may be noted that the Massachusetts members of Congress had written to their State Legislature, June 4, 1784, that (with the other New England members), they had given vigorous opposition to any power in Congress to raise standing armies in time of peace, on the ground that it was unconstitutional and that the militia was "the constitutional and only safe defence of Republican Government;" and Richard Henry Lee had written to James Monroe, January 5, 1787, that: "You are perfectly right in your observation concerning the consequence of a standing army — that it has constantly terminated in the destruction of liberty. It has not only *been* constantly so, but I think it clear, from the construction of human nature, that it *will* always be so. . . . A well regulated militia is indeed the best defence and only proper security for a free people to venture upon."

The Convention had now been in session three months, and members were desirous of returning home. Accordingly, it was voted that the meetings thereafter begin at 10 A.M., and last until 4 P.M. — this being the proposal of Rutledge of South Carolina, who remarked on "the probable impatience of the public and the extreme anxiety of many members of the Convention to bring the business to an end." A week later, on August 24, the Convention repealed this vote and again fixed the hour of adjournment at 3 P.M., as the later hour had seriously interfered with the dinner hour then prevailing in Philadelphia.

OUT OF CONVENTION

Washington noted:

"In Convention. Dined at Chief Justice McKean's. Spent the afternoon and evening at my lodgings."

SUNDAY, AUGUST 19, 1787

Washington noted:

"In company with Mr. Powell rode up to the White Marsh, traversed my old Incampment, and contemplated on the dangers which threatened the American Army at that place. Dined at Germantown, visited Mr. Blair McClenegan, drank tea at Mr. Peter's and returned to Philadelphia in the evening."

The slow progress of the Convention and the diversity of views prevailing were the subjects of a letter which Washington wrote, this day, to General Henry Knox:

"By *slow*, I wish I could add, and *sure* movements, the business of the Convention progresses but to say when it will end, or what will be the result, is more than I dare venture to do and therefore shall hazard no opinion thereon. If some thing good does not proceed from the session, the defects cannot with propriety be charged to the hurry with which the business has been conducted, notwithstanding which many things may be forgot, some of them not well digested, and others from the contrariety of sentiments with which such a body is pervaded become a mere nihility. Yet I wish a disposition may be found in Congress, the several State Legislatures and the community at large, to adopt the Government which may be agreed on in Convention, because I am fully persuaded it is the best that can be obtained at the present moment under such diversity of ideas as prevail."

expressly to execute these powers, that the sweeping clause, as it has been affectedly called, authorizes the National Legislature to pass all necessary and proper laws."

And Madison wrote:

"Had the Convention attempted a positive enumeration of the powers necessary and proper for carrying their other powers into effect, the attempt would have involved a complete digest of laws on every subject to which the Constitution relates, accommodated, too, not only to the existing state of things, but to all the possible changes which futurity may produce; for in every new application of a general power, the particular powers which are the means of attaining the object of the general powers, must always necessarily vary with that object, and be often properly varied whilst the object remains the same. . . . Had the Constitution been silent on this head, there can be no doubt that all the particular powers requisite as means of executing the general powers would have resulted to the Government, by unavoidable implication. No axiom is more clearly established in law, or in reason, than that wherever the end is required, the means are authorized; wherever a general power to do a thing is given, every particular power necessary for doing it is included. . . ."

The delegates further understood that if there should arise any doubt as to whether any particular law passed by Congress was "necessary and proper", the question whether or not such law came within the Constitutional power of Congress was ultimately to be decided by the Supreme Court. For in no other way could the specific grants to Congress and the restrictions upon Congress be enforced and kept within the bounds set by the Constitution. This was well explained by George Nicholas later, in the Virginia Convention: "But who is to determine the extent of such powers? I say, the same power which in all well regulated communities, determines the extent of Legislative powers. If they exceed these powers, the Judiciary will declare it void." [1] And as Madison wrote in *The Federalist:*

"If it be asked, what is to be the consequence, in case Congress shall misconstrue this part of the Constitution, and exercise powers not warranted by its true meaning, I answer — the same as if they should misconstrue or enlarge any other power vested in them ; as if the general power had been reduced to particulars and any one of these were to be violated — the same, in short, as if the State Legislatures should violate their respective constitutional authorities. In the first instance, the success of the usurpation will depend on the Executive and Judiciary departments, which are to expound and give effect to the Legislative acts."

Treason

Having completed their work on the powers of Congress, with the exception of the power over taxation and over commerce, the Convention, on this August 20, now took up a subject which the Committee had included in the Article relating to the Congress (though it concerned the Judiciary as well) — namely : What should constitute the crime of treason, how should it be proved, and how should it be punished ? [2] The section reported by the Committee had practically adopted the definition of the crime of treason as fixed by the Statute of Edward III in England in 1352 (without its later extensions) ; and embodied the provisions against conviction except on testimony of "two witnesses to the same overt act", which was contained in the old English statute of Edward VI, in 1552. After considerable discussion and verbal amendments, this section was voted by the Convention ; and it became Article III, section 3, of the final draft of the Constitution. As an extreme assertion of States' Rights doc-

---

[1] *Elliot's Debates,* III, 443.

[2] In the final draft of the Constitution, the Committee of Style very properly transferred the treason section from the Legislative Article to the Judiciary Article III, section 3.

"From 10 to 4 are the invariable hours of session, and as much unanimity as can be expected prevails. Yet I believe the business will not be completed in less than a month from this time. . . . Your Excellency is not now to be informed that I am not at liberty to explain the particulars of the mode of Government that the Convention have in contemplation, but I will venture to assure you that it will be such a form of Government as I believe will be readily adopted by the several States, because I believe it will be such as will be their respective interest to adopt."

At the same time, one of the departing members, Alexander Martin, wrote to Governor Caswell:

". . . Much time has been employed in drawing the outlines of the subjects of their deliberations, in which as much unanimity has prevailed as could be well expected from so many sentiments arising in twelve independent Sovereign Bodies; Rhode Island not having deigned to keep company with her sister States on this occasion. The Convention, after having agreed on some great principles in the Government of the Union, adjourned for a few days, having appointed a Committee composed of the following gentlemen, to wit: Mr. Rutledge of South Carolina, Mr. Randolph of Virginia, Mr. Elsworth of Connecticut, Mr. Wilson of Pennsylvania and Mr. Gorham of Massachusetts, to detail or render more explicit the chief subjects of their discussion; on the Report of these gentlemen the Convention again met, and are now employed taking up the same paragraph by paragraph, and so slow is the progress that I am doubtful the business will not be fully reduced to system and finished before the middle of September next, if then. . . . Though I have not told your Excellency affirmatively what the Convention have done, I can tell you negatively what they have not done. They are not about to create a King as hath been represented unfavourably in some of the Eastern States, so that you are not to expect the Bishop Osnaburg or any prince or great man of the world to rule in this country.

the state and nature of my business, I felt myself fully at liberty to return, especially as North Carolina was so fully and respectably represented."

The public curiosity will no doubt be gratified at the next Assembly, perhaps before."

On this day, Hamilton (who had been absent from the Convention from June 29 to August 13, and who was again in New York) wrote to Rufus King:

"Since my arrival here, I have written to my colleagues, informing them if either of them would come down, I would accompany him to Philadelphia; so much for the sake of propriety and public opinion. In the meantime, if any material alteration should happen to be made in the plan now before the Convention, I will be obliged to you for a communication of it. I will also be obliged to you to let me know when your conclusion is at hand, for I would choose to be present at that time."

Eight days later, Hamilton wrote again to King from New York:

"I wrote you some days since to request you to inform me when there was a prospect of your finishing, as I intended to be with you, for certain reasons, before the conclusion. It is whispered here that some late changes in your scheme have taken place which give it a higher tone. Is this the case? I leave town today to attend a circuit in a neighboring county, from which I shall return the last of the week, and shall be glad to find a line from you explanatory of the period of the probable termination of your business."

These letters are notable, for they show how slight an interest Hamilton was taking and how little part he was playing in the Convention, after June 29. His name appears in Madison's *Notes*, as taking part in the debates only on August 13, September 6, 8, 10, and on the final day. Gouverneur Morris, who was one of his closest friends, wrote later that he "had little share in forming the Constitution; he believed the republican government to be radically defective. . . . Hamilton hated republican government, because he confounded it with democratical government; and he detested the latter, because he believed it would end in despotism and be in the meantime destructive to public morality." [1]

TUESDAY, AUGUST 21, 1787

IN CONVENTION

Direct Taxes

While the power of taxation in general was vested in Congress, there was one form which those who favored the sovereignty of the States had been exceedingly loath to part with — the power to impose direct taxes, that is, land taxes and poll taxes. Nevertheless, it was rightly insisted by those who favored an adequate National Government that a limitation of its power to impose any form of tax required by the necessity or the emergency of the moment would weaken the Government's resources and would thereby impair its credit. "Whatever may be the visionary and fanciful conclusions of political sceptics," said Randolph in the Virginia State Convention, "the credit of a nation will be found coextensive with its ability to raise money." [2] It was pointed out that direct taxes were only necessary and would only be levied in time of war or other emergency, after reliance on import duties and excises had failed. That this argument was valid was later shown, when, in the Civil War and in the World War, the Gov-

---

[1] *Diary and Letters of Gouverneur Morris* (1889), II, 523, 531.

[2] *Elliot's Debates*, III, 121–122; see speeches of Madison and Nicholas, *ibid.*, 95–96, 99, 248, 306–307; and see speeches of Mason, Henry, Monroe, Grayson in opposition to the power to levy direct taxes, *ibid.*, 31, 57–58, 216, 280.

Jefferson wrote to Washington, Dec. 4, 1788: "Calculation has convinced me that circumstances may arise, and probably will arise, wherein all the resources of taxation will be necessary for the safety of the State. . . . War requires every resource of taxation and credit. The power of making war often prevents it; and in our case would give efficacy to our desire for peace." Writing to Francis Hopkinson, March 13, 1789, Jefferson said that he approved of the qualified negative on laws given to the Executive, and the power of taxation given to Congress: "I thought at first that the latter might have been limited. A little reflection soon convinced me it ought not to be."

ernment would have been badly crippled had it lacked the power to levy that form of direct tax known as the income tax.[1]

The first mention of direct taxes occurred in the midst of the debate over giving Congress the power to change the representation of the States on the basis of wealth or number of inhabitants. On July 12, G. Morris, who feared lest the Southern States should come into power in Congress and should vote to themselves an increase in Representatives by providing for inclusion of their full number of slaves in their census population, moved to add to the grant of taxing power the following proviso: "that direct taxation ought to be in proportion to representation." One object of this was to ensure that the South should incur increase of taxation with any increase of representation. But another reason for the provision weighed heavily with Morris and other Eastern delegates, namely, the fear lest the new Western States, which were likely to increase rapidly in population but not in wealth, might seek to enact taxes which would fall in undue proportion on the property of the Eastern States.[2] The Southern States admitted the justice of Morris' motion, and it was voted. Through suggestions made by Ellsworth, Ran-

[1] The income tax (though a direct tax) was not levied as the framers of the Constitution intended, since the Sixteenth Amendment specifically authorized its levy without the apportionment required by the original Constitution in case of a direct tax. It may be pointed out, however, that there is no evidence that the framers ever thought of an income tax at all, or considered it as coming within the category of direct taxes.

[2] *Bancroft* (II, 83) comments on this motion by Morris: "In this short interlude, by the temerity of one man, the United States were precluded from deriving an equitable revenue from real property. Morris soon saw what evil he had wrought, but he vainly strove to retrieve it." On July 24, G. Morris said that he "hoped the Committee would strike out the whole of the clause proportioning direct taxation to representation. He had only meant it as a bridge to assist us over a certain gulph; having passed the gulph the bridge may be removed. He thought the principle laid down with so much strictness liable to strong objections." Madison, in a note, explains this statement as follows, that G. Morris' "object was to lessen the eagerness on one side for, and the opposition on the other to, the share of representation claimed by the Southern States on account of the negroes."

dolph, and Wilson, the proposal was made more specific, to the effect that both direct taxation and representation should be proportioned to the States, according to the total whites and three fifths of the black inhabitants. Gerry thought that it would be difficult to levy the taxes on this principle; but Ellsworth stated "in case of a poll tax, there would be no difficulty"; and that in other cases "the sum allotted to a State may be levied without difficulty, according to the plan used by the State in raising its own supplies." [1] Even after this clear recognition that the new Government would possess and exercise power to levy direct taxes, Roger Sherman of Connecticut, as early as July 16, in favoring a specific enumeration of the powers of Congress, made a statement of his idea of the powers which ought to be conferred "including the power of levying taxes on trade but not the power of direct taxation."

The Committee of Detail, in its Report of August 6, gave to Congress a general power to levy taxes, but provided that the proportions of direct taxation should be regulated by the respective populations of the States, including all whites and three fifths of all others (except Indians not paying taxes) — the population to be fixed by a decennial census; and it also provided that capitation taxes (*i.e.*, poll taxes) be regulated in the same manner. The provision that taxation and representation should go hand in hand had already been so thor-

[1] Edmund Randolph said in the Virginia State Convention, in answer to the attacks made on the power to levy direct taxes: "Congress is only to say on what subject the tax is to be laid. It is a matter of very little consequence how it will be imposed, since it must be clearly laid on the most productive article in each particular State. . . . Representatives and taxes go hand in hand. According to the one, will the other be regulated. The number of Representatives is determined by the number of inhabitants; they have nothing to do but lay the taxes accordingly. . . . When any sum is necessary for the General Government, every State will immediately know its exact proportion of it, from the number of their people and Representatives; nor can it be doubted that the tax will be laid on each State, in the manner that will best accommodate the people of such State, as thereby it will be raised with more facility; for an oppressive mode can never be so productive as the most easy for the people." *Elliot's Debates*, III, 121–122.

oughly debated in July, that no further discussion seemed now necessary; but a question asked by King of Massachusetts, on August 20, was of a great pertinence: "What was the precise meaning of direct taxation?" he inquired; and Madison states that "no one answered." Had there been any answer by the delegates, and an expression of their understanding of what constituted a direct tax, it is probable that the noted *Income Tax Cases*, which so excited the country in 1895, and in which the Supreme Court held that an income tax was a direct tax, would never have occurred; and the Sixteenth Amendment might have been unnecessary. On August 21, the Convention agreed to the direct tax provision, Delaware being the only dissenting State. Thereupon, Luther Martin of Maryland stated that: "The power of taxation is most likely to be criticised by the public. Direct taxation should not be used but in case of absolute necessity; and then the States will be best judges of the mode." Accordingly, he moved the following (seconded by McHenry of Maryland):

"Whenever the Legislature of the United States shall find it necessary that revenue should be raised by direct taxation, having apportioned the same, according to the above rule, on the several States, requisitions shall be made of the respective States to pay into the Continental Treasury, their respective quotas within a time in the said requisitions specified, and in case of any of the States failing to comply with such requisitions, then and then only to devise and pass acts directing the mode and authorizing the collection of the same."

This proposal (taken directly from the Paterson Plan proposed on June 15) constituted, in part, a reversion to the old method of taxation under the Articles of Confederation — namely, the levying of quotas on the States, instead of a direct levy on individuals and collection by officers of the National Government. It was contrary to the entire theory of the Government which the Convention had thus far adopted. It is not remarkable, therefore, that at this late stage in the sessions, the Convention should have rejected the motion, without debate and by the decisive vote of eight States to one (New Jersey alone voting for it, and Maryland being divided).

That the vesting of this power in Congress aroused such comparatively little opposition in the Convention was due to two causes — first, the general belief that, without it, the new Government would not possess the resources and financial credit needed to maintain itself in an emergency; second, an implied understanding that the power, even though granted, would probably be seldom used.[1] It is interesting to note, on the other hand, that Rufus King of Massachusetts later said in a speech in the Senate that the Northern States anticipated that Congress would utilize direct taxes as a method for obtaining ordinary revenue, and would in this way relieve those States which would bear the chief burden if taxes should be confined to customs and excises; and that it was only because of this belief that the Northern States were induced to agree to a representation in Congress of three fifths of the slaves of the Southern States.[2]

The Report of the Committee of Detail of August 6 made a separate and specific provision as to that form of direct tax known as a "capitation tax", *i.e.*, a poll tax,

---

[1] Congress levied a direct tax of $2,000,000 on real estate and slaves, by the Act of July 14, 1798, c. 75 (1 Stat. 597), assessed and collected by Federal officials; it levied a direct tax of $20,000,000 on real estate by the Act of Aug. 5, 1861, c. 45 (12 Stat. 294), assessed and collected by Federal officials; and it levied by the Act of Aug. 27, 1894, c. 349 (28 Stat. 58), an income tax, which was held to be a direct tax and therefore unconstitutional because levied without apportionment among the States. See *Pollock* v. *Farmers Loan and Trust Co.* (1895), 158 U. S. 601.

[2] See *Life and Correspondence of Rufus King*, VI, 697–700, speech in the Senate, March, 1819.

to the effect that such a tax must also be apportioned according to the census population. It was stated that one reason for this was to protect the Southern States by preventing Congress from enforcing a general emancipation of slaves by a special poll tax on slaves.[1] That the right to impose a poll tax should have been granted to Congress at all was a remarkable fact and evinced the determination of the Convention to vest the new Government with complete power to obtain an adequate revenue from every possible source. No tax had been more unpopular in the States or regarded as more unequal in its incidence. "The cause of the present commotion (the Shays Rebellion), the worm at the root of the tree . . . is the shocking mode of taxation which cramps industry by oppressing the poor. . . . Capitation taxes in all countries have done the same mischief. . . . We must change a system . . . which has hitherto introduced nothing but misery and sedition," a writer in a Boston paper had said.[2] The provision, however, that like other direct taxes, it must be apportioned among the States according to population, rendered it an impracticable tax to levy and Congress has never imposed such a Federal poll tax. The Convention did not act upon this specific provision until

[1] See *Bancroft*, II, 164.

[2] See *Freeman's Journal*, March 4, 1787; see also *Pennsylvania Gazette*, April 8, 1787: "Agriculture is the basis of National wealth and prosperity. The utmost encouragement therefore should be given to it. A cultivated farm should never pay a direct tax. All taxes should be by impost or customs."

George Mason said in the Virginia State Convention (*Elliot's Debates*, III, 264), that a poll tax is "of all taxes the most grievous, because it falls light on the rich and heavy on the poor. It is most oppressive, for if the rich man is taxed, he can only retrench his superfluities; but the consequence to the poor man is that it increases his misery. That they will lay the most simple taxes and such as are easiest to collect is highly probable, nay absolutely certain."

Governor George Clinton ("Cato") in *New York Journal*, Dec. 6, 1787, spoke thus of a poll tax: "This much admired principle, when stripped of its mystery, will in this case appear to be no less than a basis for an odious poll tax, the offspring of despotic governments, a thing so detestable that the State of Maryland in their bill of rights declares 'that the levying taxes by the poll is grievous and oppressive and ought to be abolished.' A poll tax is at all times oppressive to the poor, and their greatest misfortune will consist in having more prolific wives than the rich."

September 13, when, after an altogether superfluous amendment offered by George Read, it was accepted. The two provisions as to direct taxes became Article I, section 2, clause 3, and Article I, section 9, clause 4, of the Constitution as finally adopted.

OUT OF CONVENTION

David Brearley of New Jersey wrote this day, to his fellow delegate, William Paterson, expressing the hope that he would return to the Convention, from which he had been absent for five weeks: [1]

"I was in hopes after the Committee had reported, that we should have been able to have published by the first of September. At present I see no prospect for our getting through before the latter end of that month. Every article is again argued over, with as much earnestness and obstinacy as before it was committed. We have lately made a rule to meet at ten and sit 'till four, which is punctually complied with. Cannot you come down and assist us? We have many reasons for desiring this; our duty, in the manner we now sit, is quite too hard for three, but a much stronger reason is, that we actually stand in need of your abilities."

General Henry Knox wrote to Mrs. Mercy Warren in Massachusetts: [2]

"I look forward to the period of publication with a degree of anxiety. I am persuaded that some ardent and intelligent spirits may regard the proposition of the Convention as inadequate to remedy the evils of our situation; while others and a greater majority too will be apt at first blush to consider the proposed Government too high-toned. But if the characters of the Convention be duly estimated, and the nature and circumstances of the society, I flatter myself, the Government proposed will be accepted by the multitude as the best that can be obtained at present."

---

[1] *Studies in the History of the Federal Convention*, by J. F. Jameson, *Amer. Hist. Ass. Report* (1902), I.

[2] *Mass. Hist. Soc. Coll.* (1925), LXIII, *Warren-Adams Letters*, II, 297.

WEDNESDAY, AUGUST 22, 1787

IN CONVENTION

Restraints on the Powers of Congress

On this day, the Convention took up the provisions made by the Committee of Detail on two inflammable subjects — the powers of Congress to impose export duties, and taxes or duties on the importation of slaves, which had already been discussed on the previous day, August 21. As the debate became exceedingly bitter (as discussed *infra* under date of August 29), the whole matter, together with the provisions as to navigation acts, were referred to a Committee consisting of one member from each State, headed by Governor Livingston of New Jersey.[1]

The Report of the Committee of Detail, on August 6, besides enumerating the specific powers vested in Congress, contained the following restrictions or prohibitions upon the exercise of power by Congress: (1) against an export tax; (2) against a tax or prohibition on migration or importation of slaves; (3) against a capitation tax, unless laid in proportion to the census of the States; (4) against a navigation act, unless passed by two thirds of each House; (5) against grant of any title of nobility (this prohibition being laid on the United States and not merely on Congress).

In addition to these five restrictions, many others were urged during the debates in the Convention. The first new proposal was made, on this August 22, by Gerry of Massachusetts and McHenry of Maryland that: "The Legislature shall pass no bill of attainder nor any ex post facto law." There was some opposi-

[1] The other members were Langdon of New Hampshire, King of Massachusetts, Johnson of Connecticut, Clymer of Pennsylvania, Dickinson of Delaware, L. Martin of Maryland, Madison of Virginia, Williamson of North Carolina, C. C. Pinckney of South Carolina, and Baldwin of Georgia.

tion, on the ground that the provision was unnecessary and implied "an improper suspicion" of Congress. G. Morris, Wilson, and Dr. Johnson thought it "an unnecessary guard, as the principles of justice, law, etc., were a perpetual bar to such. To say that the Legislature shall not pass an ex post facto law, is the same as to declare that they shall not do a thing contrary to common sense — that they shall not cause that to be crime which is no crime." [1] Hugh Williamson of North Carolina, however, pointed out that such a prohibitory clause was in the Constitution of that State, and "tho it has been violated, it has done good there, and may do good here, because the Judges can take hold of it." The remark is significant, as showing the understanding of delegates that these restrictions in the Constitution were to be enforced by action of the National Judiciary. Gerry's motion was agreed to, and became Article I, section 9, clause 3, of the Constitution.

At the very end of the Convention, on September 14, Mason of Virginia moved to eliminate the prohibition against passage of ex post facto laws, fearing that the phrase might apply to civil cases as well as to criminal, and urging that "no Legislature ever did or can altogether avoid them in civil cases." Gerry, on the other hand, wanted to extend the prohibition specifically to civil cases. Mason's motion was defeated, unanimously. The reason why Mason and a few other delegates were opposed to prohibiting Congress from passing ex post facto laws applicable to civil cases does not appear in Madison's *Notes*, but is made very plain in the debates in the Virginia State Convention in 1788. Much hostility was prevalent throughout the country to the holders of Continental securities purchased at a discount; and it was hotly contended that Congress ought never to authorize the payment of such securities

[1] As reported in McHenry's *Notes*.

at their face value. Mason and Patrick Henry were fearful lest the effect of the ex post facto clause might be to prevent Congress in the future from scaling down the Government debt and from making provision for payment to holders at the price paid by these holders. They feared also that the restriction on the States against passing ex post facto laws or laws impairing the obligation of contracts might have similar effect in preventing State legislation scaling down payment of State securities as against speculators holding such securities. As ex post facto laws undoubtedly applied only to criminal legislation, there was no basis for their fears; but the opposition to this provision of the Constitution, whether groundless or not, was violent.[1]

An important restraint was urged by Charles Pinckney, on August 28, when he moved that the privilege of habeas corpus "should not be suspended but on the most urgent occasions, and then only for a limited time not exceeding twelve months." This provision he took *verbatim* from the State Constitution of Massachusetts, which, with New Hampshire, had been the only States to make such a provision. Wilson and Rutledge thought that the right to habeas corpus should be inviolable and never suspended. G. Morris made the following substitute motion, which was adopted (see Article I, section 9, clause 2):

"The privilege of the writ of habeas corpus shall not be suspended; unless where in cases of rebellion or invasion the public safety may require it."

[1] See especially speeches of Patrick Henry and George Mason, and the replies by James Madison, George Nicholas, and Edmund Randolph in the Virginia State Convention, *Elliot's Debates*, III, 471–480; and speech of J. Galloway in the North Carolina Convention, *ibid.*, IV, 190. An amendment to the Constitution was proposed by North Carolina to guard against the feared result, as follows: "That Congress shall not, directly or indirectly, either by themselves or through the Judiciary, interfere with any of the States in the redemption of paper money already emitted, and now in circulation, or in liquidating and discharging the public securities of any of the States, but each and every State shall have the exclusive right of making such laws and regulations for the above purposes as they shall think proper."

The Committee of Style, in its Report of September 12, changed the word "where" to "when." It also inserted this provision in the section which contained the other prohibitions on the exercise of powers by Congress — thus apparently recognizing that the power to suspend the writ of habeas corpus was to be exercised by Congress in the cases not therein prohibited.

A still further restriction on the power of Congress, and of the United States in general, was suggested by Charles Pinckney, and adopted on August 30, as follows:

"No religious test shall ever be required as a qualification to any office or public trust under the authority of the United States." [1]

A further restriction on the power of Congress was proposed on August 18, by Charles Pinckney, as follows:

"Funds which shall be appropriated for payment of public creditors shall not, during the time of such appropriation, be diverted or applied to any other purpose, and that the Committee prepare a clause or clauses for restraining the Legislature of the United States from establishing a perpetual revenue."

And on August 20, Pinckney proposed that:

"The military shall always be subordinate to the civil power and no grants of money shall be made by the Legislature for supporting military land forces for more than one year at a time."

These two proposals were considered by the Committee of Detail to which they were referred; and it reported on August 22 that the following addition be made to the clause authorizing Congress to levy taxes:

"For payment of the debts and necessary expenses of the United States; provided that no law for raising any branch

[1] In the final draft of the Constitution, the words "the authority of" were eliminated.

such a provision was unnecessary, because of the fact that the Constitution contained no grant of power to Congress to legislate on any of the subjects which a Bill of Rights would comprise; and, as Hamilton said later (in *The Federalist*, No. 81), in explaining the omission of a Bill of Rights: "I go further and affirm that Bills of Rights are not only unnecessary in the proposed Constitution but would even be dangerous. They would contain various exceptions to powers not granted, and on this very account would afford a colorable pretext to claim more than were granted. For why declare that things shall not be done, which there is no power to do?" Similar explanations of the omission were given in the State Conventions which ratified the Constitution in 1787 and 1788, by James Wilson and other ardent supporters; but while these explanations were undoubtedly earnest and thoroughly sincere, they were highly inadequate. The framers of the Constitution failed to appreciate the scope of the Necessary and Proper Clause which they had adopted. They failed to see that while possibly there were no specific powers vested in Congress to infringe the freedom of speech or of the press, or to impose unreasonable search and seizure without search warrant, legislation which would so operate might be enacted in the necessary and proper execution of one of the specific powers. For instance, in the collection of taxes, Congress (unless restrained by a Bill of Rights) might order an unreasonable seizure without search warrant, as a necessary and proper means of executing the taxing power.[1]

The omission of a Bill of Rights became the chief object of attack upon the Constitution, and quite

---

[1] As James Monroe said in the Virginia State Convention, relative to the effect of the Necessary and Proper Clause on the lack of a Bill of Rights: "By this general, unqualified power, they may infringe not only on the trial by jury, but the liberty of the press and every right that is not expressly secured or excepted from that general power." *Elliot's Debates*, III, 218.

naturally and rightly so. And it is especially interesting to note that the people themselves, in those early days, understood that it was by means of the Judiciary and its power to hold laws unconstitutional that the provisions of a Bill of Rights were to be enforced. Thus, in a letter written to the editor of the *Independent Gazetteer* (a paper opposing the Constitution) as early as October, 1787, an argument was made for such a Bill of Rights " under which we might contend against any assumption of undue power and appeal to the Judicial branch of the Government to protect us by their judgments." Another writer said, in December: "Now, Mr. Oswald, I thought it was a Bill of Rights ascertaining the bounds of Legislative power that gave the Judges a right to say when the laws were unconstitutional and void." [1] It was the assurance that its omission would be supplied by Amendments to the Constitution which made possible the ratification of the Constitution by the necessary number of States in 1788.[2]

OUT OF CONVENTION

Washington noted:

"In Convention. Dined at Mr. Morris's farm at the Hill's. Visited Mr. Powell's in the evening."

It is singular that Washington made no mention of the most striking event which took place on this day, as to which Dr. William Samuel Johnson referred in his diary, as follows: "Fine. In Convention. Fitches Steamboat." This brief reference was to the trial trip on the Delaware River made by John Fitch's newly invented steamboat. In the preceding winter, the Legislature of Pennsylvania had passed an Act grant-

---

[1] See *Independent Gazetteer*, Oct. 7, 1787, letter of "Old Whig"; *ibid.*, Dec. 11, 1787, letter of "One of the People."

[2] See *Congress, the Constitution, and the Supreme Court* (1925), by Charles Warren.

ing to Fitch "the sole right and advantage of making and employing the steamboat by him lately invented, for a limited time." [1]   And its method of operation had been described in the *Columbian Magazine* in December, 1786, as follows: "Each revolution of the axletree moves twelve oars five and a half feet. As six oars come out of the water, six more enter the water, which makes a stroke similar to the paddle of a canoe." At the trial trip on this day (as Fitch recorded in his Journal) nearly all the members of the Convention were present. "Governor Randolph of Virginia was pleased to give the invention countenance"; and Dr. Johnson, on the next day, sent to Fitch the following note: "Dr. Johnson presents his compliments to Mr. Fitch and assures him that the exhibition yesterday gave the gentlemen present much satisfaction. He, himself, and he doubts not, the other gentlemen, will always be happy to give him every countenance and encouragement in their power which his ingenuity and industry entitle him to." [2]   An entry in the diary of Ezra Stiles, president of Yale College, five days later, reported that: "Judge Ellsworth, a member of the Federal Convention just returned from Philadelphia, visited me, and tells me the Convention will not rise under three weeks. He there saw a steam engine for rowing boats against the stream invented by Mr. Fitch of Windsor in Connecticut. He was on board the boat and saw the experiment succeed." [3]   On the other hand, the most

[1] The *Pennsylvania Herald*, Jan. 3, 1787, printed an advertisement; "Just Published — The Columbian Magazine for Dec. 1786, embellished with a Plan of Mr. Fitch's steamboat."

[2] *Life of John Fitch* (1857), by Thompson Westcott, p. 192; *Diary of Ezra Stiles*, Aug. 27, 1787; *History of the People of the United States*, by John Bach McMaster, I, 432–435.

[3] That there was scepticism and joking over this invention is recorded by J. P. Brissot de Warville, who recorded in his *New Travels in the United States of America*, that on September 1, 1788: "I went to see an experiment near the Delaware on a boat, the object of which is to ascend rivers against the current. The inventor was Mr. Fitch who had formed a company to support the expense. One of the most zealous associates is Mr. Thornton. . . . I doubt not but physically speaking this

eminent American inventor of that era, Benjamin Franklin, did not attend this experiment and had no faith in its practicality (as he wrote to Jean de Crève-cœur a few months later).[1]　That the public had little interest in it is shown by the fact that no Philadelphia newspaper published a single item as to this momentous event in steam navigation; though the *Herald* of this date found space enough to publish: "It is a curious fact that a large green turtle was lately caught in the Delaware near Trenton."　On this very day, however, when this Fitch steamboat was the warning sign of the future decay of the wooden ship, the *Herald*, noting the decay of shipbuilding "manifest through the Continent, but particularly at New York, where a traveller informs us, there is but one small vessel on the stocks", never-theless expressed the hope that "this, as well as every other art, will soon be revived by the natural influence of a regular and efficient Government."

James McClurg wrote to Madison from Virginia, this day:

"I have still some hope that I shall hear from you of the reinstatement of the Negative — as it is certainly the only means by which the several Legislatures can be restrained from disturbing the order and harmony of the whole, and the Government rendered properly national and one.　I should

machine may produce part of the effects which are expected from it, but I doubt its utility in commerce. . . . I saw (Mr. Thornton) assailed by railleries on account of the steamboat.　These railleries appear to me very ill placed.　The obstacles to be conquered by genius are everywhere so considerable, the encouragement so flexible, and the necessity of supplying the want of hard labour in America so evident, that I cannot, without indignation, see the Americans discouraging by their sarcasms the generous efforts of one of their fellow citizens."

[1] Franklin wrote to Crèvecœur, Feb. 16, 1788: "I have received your favor of Jan. 30, respecting Mr. Fitch's steamboat and asking my opinion of it.　Not being able to go much abroad I have never seen it, and tho I never doubted that the force of steam properly applied might be sufficient to move a boat against the current in most rivers, yet when I considered the first cost of such a machine as the fire engine, the necessity of it being accompanied constantly by a skillful engineer to work it and to repair it on occasion, and the room it would take up in the boat, I confess I feared that the advantage would not be such as to bring the invention into use." *Franklin Papers MSS.*, VIII, in Library of Congress.

suppose that some of its former opponents must by this time have seen the necessity of advocating it, if they wish to support their own principles."

The newspapers continued to show much interest in the progress of the Convention, and the *Packet* said, this day:

"The profound secrecy hitherto observed by the Convention we cannot help considering as a happy omen; as it demonstrated that the spirit of party on any great and essential point cannot have arisen to any height."

The *Gazette* commented favorably on the Convention as follows: [1]

"The punctuality with which the members of the Convention assemble every day at a certain hour and the long time they spend in the deliberations of each day (sometimes seven hours) are proofs among other things, how much they are entitled to the universal confidence of the people of America. Such a body of enlightened and honest men perhaps never before met for political purposes, in any country upon the face of the earth."

And it published two letters from correspondents of a similar tone:

"The long and peaceable session of the present august Convention and the general determination among all classes of people to receive the Government they are now framing (says a correspondent) indicates degrees of order and good sense in the Americans that have seldom appeared in other countries. . . . It is to be hoped (says another correspondent) that the name of Congress will be laid aside in the new Federal Government. There is an involuntary propensity among mankind to associate ideas — and who can hear of the word Congress without associating with it the ideas of weakness, instability, slender powers, in some instances of faction, of continental money, of the forty for one measure,

---

[1] See also *Pennsylvania Journal*, Aug. 30; *Massachusetts Centinel*, Sept. 1; *Boston Gazette*, Sept. 3; *Connecticut Courant*, Sept. 3; *New York Daily Advertiser*, Aug. 17, 27; *Salem Mercury*, Sept. 4, 1787.

of tender laws, and lastly, of a pendulum vibrating for near two years between Annapolis and New York. Names have an influence upon things. The Assembly of the States would perhaps better designate the new and extensive powers to be vested in the Federal Government. . . . There is nothing calls more loudly upon each of the States to adopt the new frame of Federal Government than the situation of Rhode Island. The fate of that State must soon be the fate of every State in the Union, if not prevented by a strong Federal power."

Evidences of the importance which was attached to the Convention in Europe were also appearing from time to time in the newspapers.

The *Gazetteer* stated, this day : [1]

"Private letters from Europe mention that the oppressed and persecuted in every country look with great eagerness to the United States in the present awful crisis of their affairs. Should the new Federal Government be adopted, thousands would embark immediately for America. Holland would pour in, with her merchants, a large quantity of cash among us. Germany and Ireland would send us colonies of cultivators of the earth; while England and Scotland would fill our towns and cities with industrious mechanicks and manufactures. With the liberties, safety, population, and glory of our country, all depending upon the adoption of a National Government, that man must be a greater enemy to his country than Hutchinson or Arnold, who, for selfish or party purposes, advises his countrymen to reject it. One of the first objects with the National Government to be elected under the new Constitution, it is said, will be to

---

[1] See also *Pennsylvania Journal*, Aug. 25; *New York Daily Advertiser*, Aug. 29; *Salem Mercury*, Sept. 4, 1787.

As early as June, Philadelphia despatches reported a letter "from a gentleman in the County of Roscommon in Ireland to his brother in this city" : "You express very sanguine hopes of a termination to these unhappy disputes, from an improvement to take place in the Confederation under the wisdom of a Grand Convention to assemble in May next. This measure is the general topick at every table, and the earliest toast after dinner, through this and the neighboring counties, is, 'success to their deliberations.' I trust in God, you will enable me to be the first to carry round the result of their Councils." *New York Daily Advertiser*, June 27; *Massachusetts Centinel*, July 4, 1787.

provide funds for the payment of the National debt, and thereby to restore the credit of the United States, which has been so much impaired by the individual States. Every holder of a publick security of any kind is therefore deeply interested in the cordial reception and speedy establishment of a vigorous Continental Government. By letters and private accounts from most of the counties in Pennsylvania, we learn, that the good people of this State, of all parties, are alike prepared and disposed to receive the new Federal Government. It is remarkable that Pennsylvania has, in every great and necessary measure, set an example of a Federal disposition to all the States."

The *Gazette* printed later the following extract from a letter written from London, in July: [1]

"We long to hear what your Grand Convention is doing. The friends of America have been much distressed to hear of the evils which you have brought on yourselves by the weakness of your Governments. . . . Union alone will save you and disappoint your enemies. If your Convention gives you a strong Government and you have wisdom enough to adopt it, you will half depopulate this country by emigration; for thousands are waiting only to see whether a Shays will seize your supreme power by force or whether you will as an enlightened and free people chuse a Washington — a Hancock or a Franklin to be the legal head of your country."

Despite these optimistic views of the new Constitution, the rumblings of opposition which had been heard in New York, and evidence of which had appeared in Pennsylvania, as commented on, two weeks earlier in a Philadelphia paper, again were made evident by a letter which appeared, this day, in *Freeman's Gazette.*[2] It

---

[1] *Pennsylvania Gazette*, Sept. 26, 1787.

[2] *Freeman's Gazette*, Aug. 22, 1787, letter of "Z". A satirical "Chronicle" in *Freeman's Gazette*, Oct. 17, 1787, referred to "Robert, the Cofferer" [Morris], "James the Caledonian" [Wilson], "Thomas the Roman" [Mifflin], "George the Clumberian" [Clymer], and "Gouvero, the Cunning Man" [G. Morris]. It stated that Jared [Ingersoll] was also appointed to the delegation, though not of the "Sheepfold"; and it stated that "Benjamin of the House of Frankland" [Franklin] who was "highly reverenced by the people" had been appointed to give respect

contended that the Pennsylvania delegation were representatives of a "Junto", consisting merely of opponents of the State Constitution, adherents of the Bank, supporters of a State poll tax, and advocates of unlimited license to import foreign goods :

"As the Convention was looked up to with eager expectation for the relief of our distresses and embarrassments, and as much will probably depend upon the unanimity with which the people shall receive their decisions, it was of great importance to secure the hearty concurrence of so considerable a State as that of Pennsylvania. For this end, the Junto have confined the choice of delegates for this great State to the City of Philadelphia and almost exclusively to their own narrow party in the city — for even the venerable Franklin was excluded, in their first choice. One thing alone consoles us for the disappointment we have sustained in so very partial a representation. They have included in the delegation a man who is not even a citizen of this State, whose interest lies in another State [probably G. Morris] but who has the sublime merit of being the ready tool of the great head of the Junto. The people on the borders of the Susquehannah and the Ohio will be gratified to the extent of their wishes, when they find that they are represented by a citizen of New York. Should anything a little unpalatable appear in the proceedings of the Convention, which nevertheless it may be proper to receive for the sake of the great good which will result from the whole, the numerous people of this State in all its different and extensive parts, when they reflect how fully they have been represented in the Convention, will no doubt think themselves bound in honour to promote all its measures."

In reply to this satirical attack, several letters were later published in the Philadelphia papers pointing out

to their council. "Now they considered that Benjamin was an old man and full of days and that his body was feeble and bowed down with years, and they supposed that his outgoings to the meetings of the deputies of the tribe would not be frequent ; and the thing which Robert [Morris] had proposed pleased them well and it was done as he desired."

that if all the delegates came from that city, it was due to the fact that the Legislature was urged, by the very men who now complained, to choose only men from Philadelphia and its surroundings who might readily be able to attend the Convention; and that a place had been offered on the delegation to the chief complainant (William Findley) and declined by him because no salary was attached. It was also pointed out that five of the delegation, Franklin, Ingersoll, Robert Morris, Clymer, and Mifflin had received the practically unanimous vote of the Legislature.[1]

THURSDAY, AUGUST 23, 1787

IN CONVENTION

Power of Congress over the Militia

On this day, the Convention were confronted with another question involving State sovereignty and State jealousy. On August 18, Mason of Virginia had moved to vest in Congress an additional power not proposed in the Report of the Committee of Detail, as follows: "to make laws for the regulation and discipline of the militia of the several States, reserving to the States the appointment of officers." He stated that "he considered uniformity as necessary in the regulation of the militia throughout the Union." General Charles C. Pinckney and Butler of South Carolina instanced "serious mischiefs" during the war, owing to dissimilarity in the State militias, and said that the States

---

[1] See *Independent Gazetteer*, Aug. 30, 1787, letter of "Halter"; *Pennsylvania Gazette*, Oct. 10, 1787, letter of "Foederal Constitution." The vote of the Pennsylvania Legislature appointing the delegates had been as follows: Total vote sixty-three, Robert Morris, sixty-three, Mifflin, sixty-three, Clymer, sixty-three, Ingersoll, sixty-one, Fitzsimmons, thirty-seven, Wilson, thirty-five, G. Morris, thirty-three, who were elected; and Thomas McKean, twenty-six, Charles Pettit, twenty-five, John Bayard, twenty-five, Franklin, ten, W. Findley, two. Franklin was not at first chosen "because of a misunderstanding as to his willingness to serve." He was later nominated as an additional eighth delegate and unanimously elected.

"would never keep up a proper discipline." Madison said that regulation of the militia so naturally appertained to the authority charged with the public defence that it did not seem in its nature to be divisible between two distinct authorities. Langdon of New Hampshire "saw no more reason to be afraid of the General Government than of the State Governments." Charles Pinckney said that the power was not such a one as could be abused. He had, however, "scanty faith in the militia", and thought the National Government must have, in addition, a "real military force." The United States, he said, "had been making an experiment without such a force, and we see the consequence in their rapid approaches towards anarchy" (referring to the Shays Rebellion in Massachusetts). The proposal, however, had aroused very bitter opposition from the ardent adherents of State Sovereignty. Ellsworth, Sherman, Dickinson, and Gerry were sure that States would not and should not relinquish control of their own militia. Ellsworth said that the General Government "could not sufficiently pervade the Union for such a purpose, nor could it accommodate itself to the local genius of the people. It must be vain to ask the States to give the militia out of their hands." Gerry said that he "thought this the last point remaining to be surrendered. If it be agreed to by the Convention, the plan will have as black a mark as was set on Cain. He had no such confidence in the General Government as some gentlemen professed, and believed it would be found that the States have not." The whole subject had been referred to a Special Grand Committee of one from each State which had already been appointed to consider the question of assumption of State debts.[1] This Committee reported on this

---

[1] The Committee consisted of Langdon of New Hampshire, King of Massachusetts, Sherman of Connecticut, Livingston of New Jersey, Clymer of Pennsylvania,

August 21, through Governor William Livingston, recommending the grant of power to the Congress, to discharge the debts of the United States as well as the State debts incurred during the war "for the common defence and general welfare"; and also a power

"to make laws for organizing, arming and disciplining the militia and for governing such part of them as may be employed in the service of the United States, reserving to the States respectively, the appointment of the officers, and the authority of training the militia according to the discipline prescribed by the United States."

The grave difficulties which General Washington and the Continental Congress had confronted in dealing with the State militias during the war had made a profound impression on all responsible statesmen; and this was intended to obviate future embarrassments. The proposal was at once hotly debated. "This power in the United States is making the States drill-sergeants," said Gerry. "He as lief let the citizens of Massachusetts be disarmed as to take the command from the States and subject them to the General Legislature. It would be regarded as a system of despotism. . . . He warned the Convention against pushing the experiment too far. Some people will support a plan of vigorous Government at every risk. Others of a more democratic cast will oppose it with equal determination; and a civil war may be produced by the conflict." Dayton, Ellsworth, Sherman, and Luther Martin agreed with him.[1] Langdon expressed the

---

Dickinson of Delaware, McHenry of Maryland, Mason of Virginia, Williamson of North Carolina, Gen. C. C. Pinckney of South Carolina, and Baldwin of Georgia.

[1] "It was urged that if . . . the power over the militia should be taken away from the States and also given to the General Government, it ought to be considered as the last *coup de grace* to the State Governments; that it must be the most convincing proof the advocates of this system design the destruction of the State Governments, and that no professions to the contrary ought to be trusted." *The Genuine Information*, by Luther Martin, *Elliot's Debates*, I, 372.

more patriotic view, saying that he could not understand this feeling of jealousy : "The General and State Governments are not enemies to each other, but different institutions for the good of the people of America. As one of the people, he could say : The National Government is mine. The State Government is mine. In transferring power from one to the other, I only take out of my left hand what it cannot so well use, and put it into my right hand where it can be better used." Madison said that "the discipline of the militia is evidently a National concern and ought to be provided for by a National Constitution. . . . As the greatest danger is that of disunion of the States, it is necessary to guard against it by sufficient powers to the common Government; and as the greatest danger to liberty is from large standing armies, it is best to prevent them, by an effectual provision for a good militia." Randolph said that while he was "for trammelling the General Government wherever there was danger, here there could be none." The clause was finally voted by the Convention, and appears in Article I, section 8, of the Constitution.

Having asserted this power of Congress over the States, so objectionable to the adherents of State Sovereignty, the Convention, on this day, proceeded to adopt an amendment, moved by Rutledge, to the Article which established the supremacy of the National laws and treaties over State Constitutions and laws, by adding the provision that *the National Constitution and* laws should so constitute "the supreme law of the several States." This apparently seemed to Luther Martin of Maryland the final blow at the sovereign rights of the States; and at about this stage in the Convention, as narrated by him later, conferences were held in the evenings between Martin, Mason, Gerry, some of the New Jersey, Delaware, and Connecticut delegates, and a delegate from South Carolina, to discuss how the States might be preserved : [1]

"Some time in the month of August, a number of members who considered the system as then under consideration and likely to be adopted, extremely exceptionable, and of a tendency to destroy the rights and liberties of the United States, thought it advisable to meet together in the evenings, in order to have accommodation of sentiments, and to concert a plan of Conventional opposition to and amendment of, that system, so as, if possible, to render it less dangerous. Mr. Gerry was the first who proposed this measure to me — and that before any meeting had taken place — and wished we might assemble at my lodgings ; but not having a room convenient, we fixed upon another place. Then Mr. Gerry and Mr. Mason did hold meetings ; but with them also met the delegates from New Jersey and Connecticut, a part of the delegation from Delaware, an honorable member from South Carolina and myself. Those were the only 'private meetings' that ever I knew or heard to be held by Mr. Gerry and Mr. Mason — meetings at which I myself attended until I left the Convention, and of which the sole object was, *not* to aggrandize the *great* at the expense of the *small*, but to protect and preserve, if possible, the existence and essential rights of *all* the States and the liberty and freedom of their citizens."

And it was at about this stage in the sessions that Luther Martin had a conversation with Washington, as reported by him as follows :

"In desultory conversation . . . one morning, before our honorable President took the chair, he was observing how unhappy it would be should there be such a diversity of sentiment as to cause any members to oppose the system when they returned to their States ; on that occasion, I replied that I was confident no State in the Union would more readily accede to a proper system of Government than Maryland, but that the system under consideration was of

---

[1] Letters of Luther Martin in *Maryland Journal*, March 18, 21, 1788.

such a nature that I never could recommend it for acceptance, and that I thought the State never ought to adopt it, and expressed my firm belief that it never would."

OUT OF CONVENTION

A striking article appeared this day in the *New York Daily Advertiser*, warning people against believing the idle rumors circulated about the Convention, and deploring the opposition in New York: [1]

"The States of America yet remain in statu quo — no communication having been received from the Federal Convention to clear away the tenebrous clouds which have so long been pendant on our political hemisphere. Extracts of letters, pieces, and paragraphs innumerable, have filled the papers upon the probable result of their National consultations; but as the most absolute secrecy has been maintained by that august assembly, these paragraphs, etc., must be viewed as idle — the chimeras of the several political fancies which brought them forth. It is a subject of no trifling moment to reflect (if reports can be credited) that there is a certain class of inhabitants not a thousand miles from this State who have determined what course to steer; what part to act, let the recommendations of the Convention be what they may. Against such a curse to the community, against such a class of people — Good Lord deliver us."

[1] See also *Massachusetts Centinel*, Aug. 29; *New Hampshire Spy*, Sept. 1, 1787. An example of the guesses as to the actions of the Convention is seen in an extract from a letter from a gentleman in New York, dated Aug. 24, saying: "The Convention will not rise until the middle of October — a Governor General — a Legislative Council — a Senate — better than the present but not so good as could be wished." *Massachusetts Centinel*, Sept. 8, 1787.

CHAPTER NINE

The President, the Judiciary, and the States

FRIDAY, AUGUST 24, 1787

IN CONVENTION

Mode of Election of the President

The Convention turned now to consideration of the provisions in the Report of the Committee of Detail relating to the Executive branch of the new Government; and, of course, the first question of importance that presented itself was the much debated method of election of the President. The old problems whether choice should be by the Congress or by the people, which had already occupied the minds of the delegates on ten separate days, now arose once more. An effort by Carroll and Wilson to secure choice by the people was defeated, only two States, Pennsylvania and Delaware, supporting them. G. Morris then delivered a strong speech on the dangers of choice by the Legislature, as leading to cabal and corruption in elections and to Legislative tyranny. "If the Legislature have the Executive dependent on them, they can perpetuate and support their usurpations by the influence of tax gatherers and other officers, by fleets, armies, etc."

To guard against these evils, he moved that the President be elected by electors chosen by the people of the several States. This method, it will be recalled, had already been defeated on June 2, by a vote of two States to eight; election by electors appointed by the Legislatures had been adopted on July 19, and then later rejected on July 24. Now, however, it appeared that the sentiment of the delegates was drifting in favor of such a solution, for Morris' motion was voted for by five States (Connecticut, New Jersey, Pennsylvania, Delaware, and Virginia) as against six States opposed. The probable reason for this change was a previous vote which had been taken on this day, which evidently seriously disturbed the delegates from the small States. The Committee of Detail had proposed in its Report that the President "shall be elected by ballot by the Legislature"; but it had omitted to say how this ballot should be taken. Rutledge of South Carolina, on this day, had moved that the two Houses of Congress ballot jointly, instead of separately. This suggestion at once stirred Sherman of Connecticut to the defence of the small States; for such a proposal would vastly lessen the influence which the latter would have, if the Senate, in which each State had an equal vote, could vote separately from the House and thus exercise a negative on the House's choice of President. Dayton concurred with Sherman in believing that a joint ballot would in fact give the appointment of President to the House. Wilson, Langdon, and Madison supported Rutledge's motion; and it had been carried by the vote of seven States to four. The loss of the influence of the small States in the Legislative election of President, thus brought about, probably induced them to regard favorably some other method of election of that official. The Convention, however, decided, once more, to postpone further action on the whole matter.

"No increase, or diminution shall be made so as to affect the persons actually in office at the time of such increase or diminution." Paterson's Plan contained a like provision. When the Convention had considered this subject on July 18, G. Morris had moved to strike out the words "increase or", since an increase of salary by the Legislature "would not create any improper dependence in the Judges." Franklin urged that, as money became more plentiful, manners and style of living altered, the country more populous, and the business of the Courts increasing, their salaries ought to be susceptible of increase. Madison, on the other hand, thought that: "Whenever an increase is wished by the Judges or may be in agitation in the Legislature, an undue complaisance in the former may be felt towards the latter. If, at such a crisis, there should be in Court suits to which leading members of the Legislature may be parties, the Judges will be in a situation which ought not to be suffered if it can be prevented." Increase of business, he thought, could be provided for by an increase in the numbers of the Court; fluctuations in the value of money could be provided against by taking for a standard of salaries, wheat or some other thing of permanent value. Madison's argument had not appealed to the Convention; and the words "increase or" had been stricken out on July 18. A motion to reinsert them, made by Madison and McHenry of Maryland on this August 27, was defeated.[1] General Pinckney, in opposing the motion, recognized that "the importance of the Judiciary will require men of the first talents; large salaries will, therefore, be necessary, larger than the United States can allow in the first instance." Madison and Randolph then moved that

---

[1] It may be noted that, on this day, on a discussion of this important subject of the Judiciary, the States of Massachusetts, New Jersey, North Carolina, and Georgia were all absent. The States who were present voted 5 to 1 against Madison, with Maryland divided.

Judges' salaries should not be increased "by any Act of the Legislature which shall operate before the expiration of three years after the passing thereof." This was also defeated.

The Convention then took up the subjects of jurisdiction over which the judicial power of the Court was to extend. It will be recalled that it had voted, on July 18, an extraordinarily broad jurisdiction extending "to cases arising under the laws passed by the General Legislature and to such other questions as involve the National peace and harmony" — but with the intention that this language should be later made more precise by express enumeration. Randolph, in the draft prepared by him as a basis for a Constitution to be submitted to the Committee of Detail, had considerably narrowed the above jurisdiction, by providing that the Congress might determine and "assign" the Court's jurisdiction in certain classes of cases involving the National peace and harmony. This would have left the Supreme Court dependent for most of its power upon the will of the Legislature. Evidently, this proposal met with no favor from the Committee. Randolph's draft, however, is interesting as the source of some of the specific subjects of jurisdiction finally adopted. It was as follows:

"The jurisdiction of the Supreme Tribunal shall extend:
1. to all cases arising under laws passed by the General Legislature.
2. to impeachments of officers and
3. to such other cases as the National Legislature may assign, as involving the National peace and harmony
   in the collection of the revenue
   in disputes between citizens of different States
   in disputes between different States
   in disputes in which subjects or citizens of other countries are concerned."

To this were added in Rutledge's handwriting: "in disputes between a State and a citizen or citizens of another State" and "in cases of admiralty jurisdiction."[1] Using this draft as a basis, and adopting parts of the Judiciary provisions of Charles Pinckney's Plan and of Paterson's Plan (see under date of July 18), the Committee had provided that the jurisdiction of the Supreme Court should extend to specific subjects as follows:[2]

(*a*) to all cases arising under laws passed by the Legislature of the United States.

(*b*) to all cases affecting Ambassadors, other Public Ministers, and Consuls.

(*c*) to the trial of impeachments of officers of the United States.

(*d*) to all cases of admiralty and maritime jurisdiction.

(*e*) to controversies between two or more States (except such as shall regard territory or jurisdiction.)

(*f*) to controversies between a State and citizens of another State.

(*g*) to controversies between citizens of different States.[3]

(*h*) to controversies between a State or the citizens thereof and foreign States, citizens, or subjects.

In all cases affecting Ambassadors, Public Ministers and Consuls; or "in which a State shall be a party",

[1] It is singular that admiralty jurisdiction was not contained in Randolph's original draft, for Madison had written to Randolph, April 8, 1787: "It seems at least essential that an appeal should be to some National tribunal in all cases which concern foreigners or inhabitants of other States. The admiralty jurisdiction may be fully submitted to the National Government"; and to Washington, Madison had written, April 16, 1787: "The admiralty jurisdiction seems to fall entirely within the purview of the National Government."

[2] This section as to the Judiciary is in almost the exact form which James Wilson had sketched out in the Committee. See *Farrand*, II, 172.

[3] For a very thorough and illuminating history and discussion of the jurisdiction over controversies between citizens of different States, and the reasons for granting it, see *The Historic Basis of Diversity Jurisdiction*, by Henry J. Friendly, *Harv. Law Rev.* (1928), XLI.

the Court was to have original jurisdiction; in all other cases it was to hear the case simply on appeal, "with such exceptions and under such regulations as the Legislature shall make." It is an extraordinary fact that these subjects of jurisdiction produced very little debate and few amendments.[1]

Jurisdiction over trial of impeachment of officers of the United States, provided for by the Committee, was postponed (and at a later date was stricken out, when the power was vested in the Senate). An additional jurisdiction was given (on motion of Madison and G. Morris) over "controversies to which the United States shall be a party." A limited proposal to the effect was found in Paterson's Plan of June 15, that "provision ought to be made for hearing and deciding upon all disputes arising between the United States and individual States respecting territory." [2]

Charles Pinckney also (on August 20) had moved to add to the Committee of Detail's Report, the following: "The jurisdiction of the Supreme Court shall be extended to all controversies between the United States and an individual State, or the United States and the citizens of an individual State"; and the Committee (on August 22) had recommended that jurisdiction be added over controversies "between the United States and an individual State or the United States and an individual person." No action was ever taken on this; and Madison's motion on this August 27 was evidently adopted as a substitute for the Committee's recommendation and was probably intended to cover the same

---

[1] Abraham Baldwin of Georgia in an interview with President Stiles of Yale College, in December, 1787, said that the delegates had been "unanimous also in the expediency and necessity of a Supreme Judiciary Tribunal of universal jurisdiction, in controversies of a legal nature between States, revenue, and appellate causes, between subjects of foreign or different States." *The Literary Diary of Ezra Stiles* (1901), III.

[2] This does not appear in the version of Paterson's Plan given in Madison's *Notes*, but appears in the Journal, and see *Documentary History of the Constitution*.

was, of course, that the States were impliedly forbidden to exercise those powers which were granted to Congress; any such exercise by the States would be in conflict with the National Constitution; and being so in conflict, all Courts (whether State or National) must hold them to be invalid, since the Constitution was declared to be the supreme law of the land. But on the other hand, it followed, equally of course, that all powers which were not specifically vested in Congress were denied to Congress and remained in the States. Therefore, if it was desired that the States should not exercise any powers not granted to Congress, there must be a specific prohibition of such powers to the States. Hence, the Committee embodied in its Report two Articles comprising such prohibitions. Some of these had appeared in the old Articles of Confederation — such as the restrictions against States entering into treaties, engaging in war, granting titles of nobility, keeping troops or ships in time of peace, entering into compacts with other States without consent of Congress, etc. There were, however, five new prohibitions now inserted by the Committee: (*a*) No State shall coin money; (*b*) or grant letters of marque and reprisal; (*c*) no State without the consent of the Legislature of the United States shall emit bills of credit; (*d*) or make anything but specie a tender in payment of debts; (*e*) or lay imposts or duties on imports.

These prohibitions on the States were first considered by the Convention on this August 28. The restraints contained in the old Articles of Confederation against keeping troops or ships of war in time of peace, and against engaging in any war unless in case of actual invasion by the enemy or imminent danger of such invasion, and against granting titles of nobility, were adopted without debate. The Articles had also contained restrictions on the States as to entering into "any conference, agreement, alliance, or treaty with any foreign power" or into "any treaty, confederation, or alliance whatever between them" without the consent of Congress. These were now adopted, in a broader form, the States being prohibited absolutely from entering into "any treaty, alliance or Confederation", and being prohibited without the consent of Congress from entering into "any agreement or compact with another State." [1]

A motion made by Rutledge for a new restriction forbidding States to pass bills of attainder was accepted without debate.

The most important action on this day, however, was that which the Convention took on the prohibition against emitting bills of credit and making anything but specie legal tender. As an able historian has recently said: "The economic history of the States between the Revolution and the adoption of the Constitution is compressed in the two prohibitions against paper money and against impairing the obligation of contract." [2] There was little divergence of opinion in the Convention, Luther Martin of Maryland being one of the few opponents of this restriction on the States. The leading statesmen of all political factions were united in sentiment against paper money. Richard Henry Lee, William Grayson, Patrick Henry, and Elbridge Gerry, who opposed the Constitution, did not differ from Washington and Madison on this subject.[3] They were convinced that in the interest of common honesty the States must be prohibited from

[1] See especially *Bancroft*, II, 141.

[2] See *An Economic Interpretation of the Constitution* (1913), by Charles A. Beard, pp. 179 *et seq.*

[3] Washington to Madison, Grayson to Madison, May 28, 1786; see also *A Memoir of the Life of William Livingston* (1833), by Theodore Sedgwick, Jr., letter of Livingston of Jan. 19, 1789; see also *Letters of Richard Henry Lee* (ed. by J. C. Ballagh, 1914), II, 419 *et seq. Bancroft*, I, 239, II, 136; see also Washington to Jabez Bowen, Jan. 9, 1787.

further legislation of this kind. Washington, writing to Madison, said: "These and such like things are extremely hurtful and may be reckoned among the principal sources of the evils and corruption of the present day; and this too, without accomplishing the object in view; for if we mean to be honest, debts and taxes must be paid with the substance and not the shadow"; and to a citizen of Rhode Island, he wrote in 1787: "Paper money has had the effect in your State that it ever will have, to ruin commerce, oppress the honest, and open a door to every species of fraud and injustice." William Grayson of Virginia (an opponent of the Constitution) wrote to Madison in 1786: "Congress should have the power of preventing States from cheating one another, as well as their own citizens, by means of paper money." Governor William Livingston of New Jersey, wrote: "No Acts of Assembly have hitherto been able to reconcile me to cheating according to law, or convinced me that human legislators can alter the immutable duties of morality." William Paterson had written in 1786: "An increase of paper money if it be a tender, will destroy what little credit is left; will bewilder conscience in the maze of dishonest speculations; will allure some and constrain others into the perpetuation of knavish tricks, will turn vice into legal virtue; and will sanctify iniquity by law." Richard Henry Lee, writing to George Mason, at the outset of the Convention, on May 15, had urged "that the right of making paper shall be exclusively vested in Congress"; and he added: "This appears to me to be a restraint of the last importance to the peace and happiness of the Union and of every part of it. Knaves assure, and fools believe, that calling paper 'money' and making it tender is the way to be rich and happy; thus the national mind is kept in continual disturbance by the intrigues of wicked men for fraudulent purposes, for speculating designs. This would be a great step towards correcting morals and suppressing legislative frauds, which, of all frauds, is the most fatal to Society." Patrick Henry, an opponent of the Constitution, termed paper money "the bane of the country." [1]

It was with such motives impelling them to prevent the States in the future from departing from standards of honest dealing that the delegates, on this August 28, took up the subject. The Committee's Report had restricted the States from passing legal tender laws without the consent of Congress. Wilson and Sherman now moved to make the prohibition absolute. Gorham of Massachusetts thought that "an absolute prohibition would arouse the most desperate opposition" from the partisans of paper money. Sherman stated that this was "a favorable crisis for crushing paper money. If the consent of the Legislatures would authorize emissions of it, the friends of paper money would make every exertion to get into the Legislature to authorize it." The motion was carried, however, the only dissenting vote cast being that of Virginia.[2]

The Convention then was asked to perfect their action in favor of honesty and morality, by adding a prohibition on the States which would put an end to statutes enacting laws for special individuals, setting aside Court judgments, repealing vested rights, altering corporate charters, staying the bringing or prose-

[1] *Elliot's Debates*, III, 156. It is to be noted that in Massachusetts, New Hampshire, Connecticut, Maryland, Delaware, and Virginia, legal tender paper money laws had been defeated in the Legislature. In all the other States such money had been issued as late as the year 1786.

[2] Ellsworth and Sherman in their official letter to Connecticut explained the intent of the Convention, saying: "The restraint on the Legislatures of the several States, respecting emitting bills of credit, making anything but money a tender in payment of debts, or impairing the obligation of contracts by ex post facto laws, was thought necessary as a security to commerce, in which the interest of foreigners as well as of the citizens of different States may be affected." *Elliot's Debates*, I, 491, 492.

cution of suits, preventing foreclosure of mortgages, altering the terms of contracts, and allowing tender in payment of debts of something other than that contracted for.[1] The State Legislatures had hitherto passed such laws in abundant measure, and the situation was graphically described later by Chief Justice Marshall in one of his most noted decisions, as follows : [2]

"The power of changing the relative situation of debtor and creditor, of interfering with contracts, a power which comes home to every man, touches the interest of all, and controls the conduct of every individual in those things which he supposes to be proper for his own exclusive management, had been used to such an excess by the State Legislatures as to break in upon the ordinary intercôurse of society and destroy all confidence between man and man. The mischief had become so great, so alarming, as not only to impair commercial intercourse and threaten the existence of credit, but to sap the morals of the people and destroy the sanctity of private faith. To guard against the continuance of the evil was an object of deep interest with all the truly wise as well as virtuous of this great community, and was one of the important benefits expected from a reform of the government."

To obviate the conditions thus described, King of Massachusetts proposed the insertion of a new restric-

---

[1] These practices by the State Legislatures had been the subject of frequent complaint in the newspapers. A letter from "A Freeman" published in *Independent Gazetteer*, March 16, 1787, condemned this conduct: "In no instance have the Legislatures of America deviated so much from the liberty held forth in the Constitutions as in attempting to set aside the operation of general and established laws in favor of individuals. Complaints have been heard from several of the States of their Assembly's interfering in private concerns which no ways belonged to them, but was in fact usurping the powers of the Executive and Judicial branches of the government. Personal property ought to be held as sacred as personal liberty. . . . " Throughout the spring of 1787, the Philadelphia newspapers were filled with detailed reports of the excited debates in the Pennsylvania Legislature over the question of the repeal of the charter of the Bank of North America and over its re-incorporation — a debate which must be especially borne in mind in considering later the adoption by the Federal Convention of the clause in the Constitution forbidding a State to impair the obligation of contracts. See *Pennsylvania Herald*, Jan. 3, 6, 10, 13, 17, 20, May 17, 18, 1787.

[2] *Ogden* v. *Saunders* (1827), 12 Wheaton, 213.

tion on the States. Only six weeks before (on July 13), Congress in New York had passed the famous Northwest Territory Ordinance; and in this Ordinance there had been inserted the following clause (drafted probably by Richard Henry Lee and Nathan Dane): "And in the just preservation of rights and property, it is understood and declared that no law ought ever to be made or have force in the said territory that shall in any manner interfere with or affect private contracts or any agreements, bona fide and without fraud, previously formed."[1] King now moved to insert these very words in the Constitution. Wilson and Madison supported his motion. Mason and G. Morris, however, believed that it went too far in interfering with the powers of the States. Mason thought that "cases will happen that cannot be foreseen where some kind of interference will be proper and essential", and he mentioned the case of limiting the period of bringing actions on debts. "There are a thousand laws relating to bringing actions, limitations of actions and which affect contracts," said Morris; and he added the significant remark that "the Judicial power of the United States will be a protection in cases within their jurisdiction", thus implying that the Federal Courts would hold such legislation invalid, even without any express restriction in the Constitution. There was also a genuine belief by some delegates that, under some circumstances and in financial crises, such stay and tender laws might be necessary to avert calamitous loss to debtors. For, as Luther Martin said later, in his letter to the Maryland Legislature: "I considered that there might be times

---

[1] *Bancroft*, II, 113, states that this clause "bears in every word the impress of the mind of Richard Henry Lee"; and that "he hated paper money and therefore had entreated his friends in the Convention at Philadelphia to take from the States the right of issuing it"; and that "contemporary evidence points to R. H. Lee as one with whom he (Nathan Dane) must at least divide the honor of originating this clause."

of such great public calamity and distress, and of such extreme scarcity of specie, as should render it the duty of a Government for the preservation of even the most valuable part of its citizens, in some measure to interfere in their favour, by passing laws totally or practically stopping Courts of justice or authorizing the debtor to pay by installments or by delivering up his property to his creditors at a reasonable and honest valuation. The times have been such as to render regulations of this kind necessary in most or all of the States, to prevent the wealthy creditor and the moneyed man from totally destroying the poor though industrious debtor. Such times may again arrive." [1] Madison "admitted that inconveniences might arise from such a prohibition ", but he thought that on the whole they would be "overbalanced by the utility of it." And Randolph's views, though not expressed until later in the Virginia State Convention, were that this provision was an essential one, "because it must be promotive of virtue and justice and preventive of injustice and fraud. If we take a review of the calamities which have befallen our reputation as a people, we shall find they have been produced by frequent interferences of the State Legislatures with private contracts. If you inspect the great cornerstone of republicanism, you will find it to be justice and honor." [2] The other delegates had been deeply impressed by the disastrous social and economic effects of the stay and tender laws which had been enacted by most of the States between 1780 and 1786, and they decided to make similar legislation impossible in the future. They narrowed King's motion, however, by adopting the suggestion of Rutledge of South Carolina that the States be forbidden to pass "retrospective laws"; and this word "retrospective" was apparently intended to include laws both of a crim-

[1] *Elliot's Debates*, I, 376.   [2] *Elliot's Debates*, III, 478, 479.

inal and civil nature.[1] On August 29, evidently in
consequence of some discussion (not reported by
Madison), John Dickinson "mentioned to the House
that, on examining Blackstone's *Commentaries*, he
found that the term, ex post facto, related to criminal
cases only; that they would not consequently restrain
the States from retrospective laws in civil cases, and
that some further provision for the purpose would be
requisite." Noting this fact, the Committee of Style,
in its final draft of the Constitution September 12,
changed the word "restrospective" adopted by the
Convention to "ex post facto", and also added a
prohibition against "laws altering or impairing the
obligation of contracts."[2] In this manner, provision was
made against retrospective laws in both criminal and
civil cases.[3] On September 14, the wording of this
section so drafted by the Committee of Style was
changed so as to omit from the prohibition the word
"altering" and to confine it to "impairing the obligation of contracts."[4] (It may be noted that Elbridge
Gerry of Massachusetts believed that "Congress ought

[1] It should be noted that Madison asked on August 28, in reply to Wilson's
statement that the intention was only to prohibit "retrospective interferences":
"Is not that already done by the prohibition of ex post facto laws, which would
oblige the Judges to declare such interferences null and void?"   As the prohibition
against ex post facto laws which had been theretofore adopted by the Convention
applied only to Congress and not to the States, Madison's remark was a definite
recognition of the power and duty of the Judiciary to hold an act of Congress unconstitutional and void.

[2] In making this change of language, the Committee evidently did not intend
to lessen the scope of the prohibition against retrospective laws; but it did in fact
do so; for the Supreme Court held, later, in *Saterlee* v. *Matthewson* (1829), 2 Peters
380, that there were many kinds of retrospective laws which did not come within
the meaning of ex post facto laws, or laws impairing obligation of contract, and
which were, therefore, not forbidden by this clause of the Constitution as it was
finally drafted.

[3] As Judge William Johnson said in *Ogden* v. *Saunders* (1827), 12 Wheaton, p.
286: "By classing bills of attainder, ex post facto laws and laws impairing the obligation of contracts together, the general intent becomes very apparent; it is a
general provision against arbitrary and tyrannical legislation over existing rights,
whether of person or property."

[4] It is not known who made the change in phraseology from "interfere with or
affect private contracts" in the Northwest Territory Ordinance to "impair the

to be laid under the like prohibitions" and made a motion to that effect; but it was not seconded, and hence never acted upon by the Convention.)

The next prohibition on the States which the Convention took up on August 28, was that against laying imposts or duties on imports without the consent of Congress. Madison moved to make this prohibition absolute, for, as he pointed out, encouragement of manufactures by any particular State would require duties on imports from the other States as well as from foreign countries and this "would revive all the mischiefs experienced from the want of a General Government over commerce"; moreover, as the States interested in this power "by which they could tax the imports of their neighbors passing through their markets" would be in the majority in Congress, they could give the consent of Congress, to the injury of New Jersey and North Carolina. The Convention, however, thought an absolute prohibition unnecessary and voted against the motion. A similar motion by Madison to restrict the States from laying embargoes was defeated, G. Morris stating very truly that the provision was unnecessary, since the power of regulating trade between State and State, already vested in Congress, was sufficient to deal with the subject.

A motion by King to prohibit State laws laying export taxes or duties without the consent of the Congress was

---

obligation of contracts" in the Constitution; but John M. Shirley in *The Dartmouth College Causes* (1879), pp. 213–214, contends with much forceful argument that it was probably James Wilson.

Charles G. Haines, arguing in *Ogden* v. *Saunders* in 1824, states that in the Virginia Convention, Patrick Henry, George Mason, and George Nicholas "considered the expressions ex post facto laws and laws impairing the obligation of contracts as meaning the same thing, and as relating to the redemption of Continental money and calculated to gratify the cupidity of speculation. Mr. Madison corrected these erroneous impressions; and Governor Randolph, after he had correctly defined the legal and technical meaning of the term ex post facto law, as presented by the common-law writers, also speaks of the wholesome prohibition relating to contracts."

of preserving that State's rights to levy taxes for maintenance of navigation in Chesapeake Bay. McHenry
and Carroll now moved that:

"No State shall be restrained from laying duties of tonnage for the purpose of clearing harbours and erecting light
houses."

Madison was of opinion that under the power of
Congress to regulate commerce the States would be
without authority to lay tonnage duties; and he stated
that he was "more and more convinced that the regulation of commerce was in its nature indivisible and
ought to be wholly under one authority." Sherman
added that: "the power of the United States to regulate
trade being supreme, can controul interferences of the
State regulations when such interferences happen; so
that there is no danger to be apprehended from a concurrent jurisdiction." Langdon of New Hampshire
insisted that "the regulation of tonnage was an essential
part of the regulation of trade, and that the States ought
to have nothing to do with it." [1] The desires of Maryland finally were partially complied with, by allowing
State tonnage duties with the consent of Congress; and
the following clause was adopted:

"No State shall lay any duty on tonnage without the consent of Congress."

Three further provisions relating to the States, somewhat in the nature of limitations on State authority,
may also be noted.

(1) The Committee of Detail, in its Report of August
6, had included the following Article: [2]

[1] On August 31, in considering the report of the Committee of Eleven made on
August 28, providing that "all tonnage, duties, imposts and excises laid by the
Legislature (Congress) shall be uniform throughout the United States, the word
"tonnage" was struck out by the Convention, as comprehended in "duties." This
was a clear interpretation of the power of Congress to impose "duties" as including
power to levy "tonnage" duties.

[2] Charles Pinckney, in a speech in the House, Feb. 13, 1821 (*Annals of Congress,
16th Cong., 2d Sess.*), claimed the authorship of the article: "Having been made by

" The citizens of each State shall be entitled to all privileges and immunities of citizens in the several States."

This was taken almost *verbatim* from the Articles of Confederation, which provided that:

"The better to secure and perpetuate mutual friendship and intercourse among the people of the different States in this Union, the free inhabitants of each of these States, paupers, vagabonds and fugitives from justice excepted, shall be entitled to all privileges and immunities of free citizens in the several States; and the people of each State shall have free ingress and regress to and from any other State, and shall enjoy therein all the privileges of trade and commerce, subject to the same duties, impositions and restrictions as the inhabitants thereof respectively, provided that such restriction shall not extend so far as to prevent the removal of property imported into any State, to any other State, of which the owner is an inhabitant."

The Committee's Report was agreed to by the Convention, on August 29; and it became Article IV, section 2, clause 1, of the final Constitution. General Pinckney of South Carolina, however, stated that "he was not satisfied with it. He seemed to wish some provision should be included in favor of property in slaves." The provision so desired by him was undoubtedly the latter portion of the Articles of Confederation, which, though phrased in general terms, was intended to apply to slave property, and which did not appear in the Committee's Report in express terms. It is interesting to note that, later, the power of Congress over commerce between the States was held by the Supreme Court to protect these rights as to slave property so guarded by the Articles of Confederation.

me it is supposed I must know or perfectly recollect what I meant by it. In answer, I say that at the time I drew that Constitution, I perfectly knew that there did not then exist such a thing in the Union, as a black or colored citizen, nor could I then have conceived it possible that such a thing could have ever existed in it; nor, notwithstanding all that has been said on the subject, do I now believe one does exist in it."

(2) The Committee of Detail had also reported the following Article XV:

"Any person charged with treason, felony, or high misdemeanour in any State, who shall flee from justice, and shall be found in any other State, shall, on demand of the Executive power of the State from which he fled, be delivered up and removed to the State having jurisdiction of the offence."

This provision was taken *verbatim* from Article IV of the Articles of Confederation. This was also agreed to by the Convention on August 28, the words "other crime" being substituted for "high misdemeanour." Here again the slavery issue arose, when Butler and Charles Pinckney of South Carolina moved that "fugitive slaves and servants be delivered up like criminals." When objection was raised that this would oblige a State Governor to deliver up slaves at the public expense and that the public ought not to be called upon to surrender a slave any more than a horse, the motion was withdrawn; it was renewed on the next day, August 29, in another form:

"If any person bound to service or labor in any of the United States shall escape into another State, he or she shall not be discharged from such service or labor, in consequence of any regulations subsisting in the State to which they escape, but shall be delivered up to the person justly claiming their service or labor."

The Convention agreed to this without a dissenting vote; and it is to be noted that this action was taken immediately following the vote by which the Convention agreed to the compromise as to importation of slaves. The two votes constituted a triumph for the Southern States. The Committee of Style in reporting the final draft of the Constitution, on September 12, re-worded this clause as follows:

"No person legally held to service or labour in one State, escaping into another, shall in consequence of regulations

CHAPTER TEN

COMMERCE AND NEW STATES

WEDNESDAY, AUGUST 29, 1787

IN CONVENTION

Regulation of Commerce — Export Duties — The Slavery Compromise

After the power of taxation, the next most essential authority vested in Congress by the Report of the Committee of Detail was that of regulation of commerce. The refusal by the States to surrender such power to the Congress of the Confederation not only had disabled that body from paying the National debts but also had aroused great dissension between the States because of State legislation imposing duties and commercial burdens on goods introduced from other States as well as from foreign countries.[1] "If there was any one object

---

[1] Even while the Convention was sitting, New Jersey had passed a statute taxing the lighthouse at Sandy Hook, owned by New York but situated on New Jersey land — this statute being in retaliation for a law of New York imposing entrance

riding over every other in the adoption of the Constitution, it was to keep the commercial intercourse among the States free from all invidious and partial restraints," said Judge Johnson in the great Steamboat Monopoly Case, in 1824.[1] "Most of our political evils may be traced to our commercial ones, as most of our moral may to our political," Madison had written, March 18, 1786; and on this point, men were very generally agreed.[2] It must be remembered, however,

and clearance fees for vessels from or bound to Connecticut and New Jersey similar to those imposed on vessels from foreign ports. See Acts of New Jersey, c. 29, June 1, 1787; Acts of New York, c. 81, April 11, 1787. Similar legislation by Virginia had been repealed in the spring of 1787 — see a Boston despatch in *Pennsylvania Journal*, May 5, 1787; "The commercial intercourse between the Eastern States and Virginia has for some time past been affected by the revenue laws of that State which imposed like duties upon the importation of other articles manufactured in the Eastern States, with those laid on such goods imported from foreign nations. It is with satisfaction that we are authorized to inform the public that these duties are entirely abolished by a law passed at the last session of the Legislature in Virginia."

[1] *Gibbons* v. *Ogden* (1824), 9 Wheaton 231.

[2] Chief Justice Marshall said in *Brown* v. *Maryland* (1827), 12 Wheaton 438, 439: "From the vast inequality between the different States of the Confederacy as to commercial advantages, few subjects were viewed with deeper interest, or excited more irritation, than the manner in which the several States exercised or seemed disposed to exercise, the power of laying duties on imports. From motives which were deemed sufficient by the statesmen of that day, the general power of taxation, indispensably necessary as it was, and jealous as the States were of any encroachments on it, was so far abridged as to forbid them to touch imports or exports, with the single exception which has been noticed. . . ." (445, 446) "The oppressed and degraded state of commerce previous to the adoption of the Constitution can scarcely be forgotten. It was regulated by foreign nations with a single view to their own interests; and our disunited efforts to counteract their restrictions were rendered impotent by want of combination. Congress, indeed, possessed the power of making treaties; but the inability of the Federal Government to enforce them had become so apparent as to render that power in a great degree useless. Those who felt the injury arising from this state of things, and those who were capable of estimating the influence of commerce on the prosperity of nations, perceived the necessity of giving the control over this important subject to a single government. It may be doubted whether any of the evils proceeding from the feebleness of the Federal Government contributed more to that great revolution which introduced the present system, than the deep and general conviction that commerce ought to be regulated by Congress. It is not, therefore, matter of surprise, that the grant should be as extensive as the mischief, and should comprehend all foreign commerce and all commerce among the States. To construe the power so as to impair its efficacy, would tend to defeat an object, in the attainment of which the American public took, and justly took, that strong interest which arose from a full conviction of its necessity. What, then, is the just extent of a power to regulate commerce with foreign nations, and among the several States?"

that in the Southern States there were still some who regarded a relinquishment of power over commerce as "dangerous in the extreme", since their want of ships and seamen "would expose their freightage and produce to a most pernicious and destructive monopoly" and place them at the mercy of the Eastern States.[1]

Nevertheless in the Continental Congress, as early as July 13, 1785, a Committee consisting of Monroe, Spaight, Houston, Johnson, and King (all of whom except Monroe were members of the Convention) had reported that Congress should be vested with the power

"of regulating the trade of the States as well with foreign nations as with each other, and of laying such imposts and duties upon imports and exports as may be necessary for the purpose . . . provided also that the Legislative power of the several States shall not be restrained from prohibiting the importation or exportation of any species of goods or commodities whatever."

The sub-committee of Congress, in August, 1786 (headed by Charles Pinckney), had recommended that the States grant to Congress

"sole and exclusive power of regulating the trade of the States as well with foreign nations and with each other, and of laying such prohibitions and such imposts and duties upon imports and exports as may be necessary for the purpose, provided the citizens of the States shall in no instance be subjected to pay higher duties and imposts than those imposed on the subjects of foreign powers; provided also that all such duties as may be imposed shall be collected under such regulations as the United States in Congress assembled shall establish consistent with the Constitutions of the States respectively, and to accrue to the use of the State in which the same shall be payable; provided, also,

[1] For expression of the Southern view, see Richard Henry Lee to Madison, Aug. 11, 1786, *Life of James Madison* (1859), by William C. Rives, II, 31–34, 41; and see the views of the Maryland delegation on the power, quoted *supra* under date of August 7, 1787.

that the Legislative power of the several States shall not be restrained from laying embargoes in time of scarcity."

The Report of the Committee of Detail of August 6 now contained three separate sections on this subject of regulation of commerce, the first of which was:

"The Legislature of the United States shall have the power . . . to regulate commerce with foreign nations and among the several States."

This clause was adopted without any dissent on this August 16; and at that time, at least, there seems to have been no doubt as to its meaning. The violent differences of opinion which arose during the first half of the Nineteenth Century as to what the term "commerce" included, and as to whether the power to "regulate" was exclusive in Congress or exercisable by the States until Congress should act, were apparently not in the least foreseen by the members of the Convention.[1] A debate did arise, however, over the further recommendation in the Report of the Committee of Detail that "no tax or duty shall be laid by the Legislature on articles exported from any State." Here, there was

---

[1] Judge Wayne in 1849, in the *Passenger Cases*, 7 Howard, p. 416, said: "Now what commerce was in fact, at least so far as European nations were concerned, had been settled beyond all dispute before our separation from the mother country. It was well known to the framers of the Constitution, in all its extent and variety. Hard denials of many of its privileges had taught them what it was. They were familiar with the many valuable works upon trade and international law which were written and published, and which had been circulated in England and in the Colonies from the early part of the last century up to the beginning of the Revolution. It is not too much to say that our controversies with the mother country upon the subject had given to the statesmen in America in that day more accurate knowledge of all that concerned trade in all its branches and rights, and a more prompt use of it for any occasion, than is now known or could be used by the statesmen and jurists of our own time. Their knowledge, then, may well be invoked to measure the constitutional power of Congress to regulate commerce."

As to whether the power of Congress was exclusive or concurrent, an argument at one time was based on the fact that in the Report of the Committee of Detail the wording was that Congress "shall have the power", while, as finally drafted by the Committee of Style of September 12, it became that Congress "shall have power" (omitting the word "the"), — see argument of Thomas Addis Emmet in *Gibbons* v. *Ogden*, 9 Wheaton, pp. 85-86. No significance has been given by the Court to this change of wording.

revealed, even more sharply than before, the serious geographical division in the Convention. As before pointed out, Madison, King, G. Morris, and others had already voiced the view that the real difference of interests in the Convention lay not between the large and the small States but between the Northern and the Southern. "The institution of slavery and its consequences formed the line of discrimination," Madison had said. As early as July 10, General Charles C. Pinckney, in discussing the Great Compromise as to representation in the House, said that if the Southern States "are to form so considerable a minority and the regulation of trade is to be given to the General Government they will be nothing more than overseers for the Northern States." And G. Morris, on July 13, expressed the fear that if the South was to be given the representation desired by it in the House, there would be "such a transfer of power from the maritime to the interior and landed interest" and "such an oppression of commerce", that he would be obliged to vote for what he termed "the vicious principle" of equality in the Senate, "in order to provide some defence for the Northern States." Morris and Gerry, on July 14 also, had expressed the fear that the Southern States would join with the new Western States in oppressing the commerce of the Eastern States. The question of a prohibition of taxes and duties on exports now brought these sectional differences into an outbreak in the Convention.

It is to be noted, as a preliminary to consideration of this clash, that the Committee's proposal to forbid export duties was a very radical departure from the theory and practice theretofore prevailing in governmental taxation. As has been well said : "To attempt to organize a Government without the power to tax exports was an innovation. From time immemorial, every nation had taxed whatever productions of its soil its inhabitants might presume to export. In the old economy, its maxim was to tax exports but to admit imports free." [1] The prohibition of export duty now inserted in the new Constitution was not based, however, on any change in economic theory but on purely political and sectional conditions. The South, being agricultural and having three great crops which grew nowhere else, — tobacco, rice, and indigo, — feared that the possession of this power by Congress would enable the North to discriminate against it, by a tax which would operate only on the peculiarly Southern articles of export. This fear had been expressed early in the Convention. Madison, on July 11, had said that "it seemed to be understood on all hands" that future taxes by the new Government would be principally levied on imports and exports; and, said he prophetically, "the extent and fertility of the Western soil will for a long time give to agriculture a preference over manufactures," and thus they would pay their share by taxes on exports, and the imports destined to them would also be taxed. This remark had alarmed General Pinckney, who, on July 12, described the great extent of South Carolina's exports and urged that a clause be inserted prohibiting export taxes; on July 24, he warned the Convention that if the Committee to draft the new Constitution failed to insert "some security to the Southern States against an emancipation of slaves and taxes on exports, he should be bound by duty to his State to vote against their Report."

[1] *Constitutional History of the United States* (1901), by Francis N. Thorpe, I, 515–516: "The mercantile system had long ruled the world; but about the time of the American Revolution, it received a deadly blow, in that judgment, which many thoughtful men shared, delivered by Adam Smith against the system, in his *Wealth of Nations*. But any departure from the old system seemed to many of the members altogether too venturesome, and few opposed the grant of power to Congress to tax exports on the economic grounds advanced by Smith. Others opposed it for political reasons, fearing lest the General Government might thereby fall under the control of a few commercial States, to whom the remainder of the Union might be compelled to pay tribute."

It was natural that the Southern States should have felt thus strongly on the subject; for they had no manufacturing, no shipbuilding or shipowning, and little mercantile interests; they were entirely dependent on the profits of exportation of their crops, largely raised by slave labor. On the other hand, there were many men in the North who felt that if slaves were to be imported free of tax, and if slaves were to be counted in the representation of the South in Congress, then the exports produced by slave labor should be taxable. The Committee of Detail (composed of two Southerners — Rutledge and Randolph — and three Northerners — Gorham, Ellsworth, and Wilson) had yielded entirely to the South in its Report on this subject.

The debate on export taxes took place on August 16 and 21. Those opposing the Committee's Report and favoring the power of Congress to impose such taxes were G. Morris, Madison, Wilson, Dickinson, and Fitzsimmons; those opposed to such taxes were Gerry, Rutledge, Butler, Mercer, Sherman, Ellsworth, Carroll, Williamson, and Mason. Ellsworth summed up the arguments against allowing such a power: "It will discourage industry, as taxes on imports discourage luxury; the produce of different States is such as to prevent uniformity in such taxes; it will engender incurable jealousies." Butler of South Carolina strenuously opposed the power as "unjust and alarming to the staple States." Gerry thought that the Convention had given to the General Government already "more power than we know how will be exercised." Mason pointed out that the eight Northern States had been given disproportionate power in the Congress, and that the Southern States "had therefore good ground for their suspicions." On the other hand, Mason's colleague from Virginia, Madison, contending as always that "we ought to be governed by National and permanent views", favored the grant of this power to Congress. Wilson also thought that "to deny this power is to take from the Common Government half the regulation of trade." It was his opinion that a power over exports might be more effectual than that over imports in obtaining beneficial treaties of commerce. The arguments of those who favored restricted power in Congress, however, prevailed; and the Convention voted for the Committee's Report prohibiting Congress from imposing export duties, by a vote of seven States to four (New Hampshire, New Jersey, Delaware, and Pennsylvania voting no). (It may be noted that the Virginia delegation split, General Washington and Madison voting no, and in favor of export taxes.) During this debate, one of the leading arguments of those who wanted Congressional power over exports was, that its denial would leave the power with the separate States, and that this would simply continue the disastrous conditions then prevailing, whereby each shipping State was able to tax heavily the produce of other States forced to be. exported through the taxing State — New York thus being able to profit greatly at the expense of New Jersey and Connecticut, and Virginia at the expense of North Carolina and Maryland. This argument became entirely invalid, when the Convention voted, on a subsequent day (August 28), to insert a clause prohibiting the States, as well as the United States, from imposing export taxes.

The vesting in Congress of a general power to regulate commerce and the prohibition to it of a power to impose export duties did not by any means settle or dispose of the whole question. A grave crisis was still hanging over the Convention, in connection with commerce of a special form, to wit, slaves. The Southern States, having won a victory in securing the prohibition of export duties, at once became insistent on the adoption of the other clause designed for their particular benefit. The Committee of Detail, in its Report of August 6, had included in the export duty section, a prohibition of a tax or duty "on the migration or importation of such persons as the several States shall think proper to admit; nor shall such migration or importation be prohibited." It will be noted that though the word "slaves" was not used, this section was intended to apply to them. Hitherto, the highly inflammable topic of slavery had been touched upon in the debates only from the economic and political standpoints. Its other aspect, however, could no longer be avoided. And on August 21, Luther Martin moved to vest power in Congress to tax or even to forbid the importation of slaves. He contended that the provision whereby three fifths of the slaves were to be counted in determining the representation of the Southern States in Congress was an encouragement to the slave traffic, and hence that it was unreasonable that this traffic should be freed from taxation. He also urged that "it was inconsistent with the principles of the Revolution and dishonorable to the American character to have such a feature in the Constitution." Many delegates, both of the North and South, were extremely anxious that the moral side of slavery should not be discussed. Ellsworth of Connecticut said that: "The morality or wisdom of slavery are considerations belonging to the States themselves. . . . The old Confederation had not meddled with this point, and he did not see any greater necessity for bringing it within the policy of the new one. . . . Let us not intermeddle. Slavery, in time, will not be a speck in our country." His colleague, Roger Sherman, said that while he disapproved of the slave trade, he thought it expedient to leave to the States the completion of the process of abolition of slavery which was already going on. Abraham Baldwin, of Georgia, said that the subject was "of a local nature" and not "a National object to be dealt with by the National Government", and that if left to herself, Georgia "may probably put a stop to the evil." John Rutledge of South Carolina said that "religion and humanity had nothing to do with the question"; and both he and General Pinckney said that the Southern States would never accept the new Government, if it should prohibit the slave trade. "The people of the States will never be such fools as to give up so important an interest." Hugh Williamson of North Carolina also thought that "the Southern States could not be members of the Union" if the clause should be rejected, and that it was wrong to force anything down, not absolutely necessary, or to which any State must disagree. On the other side, George Mason of Virginia made a powerful argument against "this infernal traffic" in slaves and the disastrous effect of slavery economically, since it discouraged arts and manufactures and prevented migration and use of white labor; and he stated that he held it "essential in every point of view that the General Government should have power to prevent the increase of slavery." Wilson and Randolph agreed with Mason. Langdon of New Hampshire said that "he could not with a good conscience leave it to the States." Dickinson of Delaware considered that "on every principle of honor and safety" the Constitution should not authorize the slave trade. "The true question was, whether the National happiness would be promoted or impeded by the importation, and this question ought to be left to the National Government, not to the States particularly interested." Gerry of Massachusetts "thought we had nothing to do with the conduct of the States as to slaves, but ought to be careful not to give any sanction to it"; and his colleague, King, saying that he thought that "the subject should be considered in a political light only", pointed out that the exemption of slaves from duty whilst every other subject of import was dutiable would produce an inequality "that could not fail to strike the commercial sagacity of the Northern and Middle States."

The flat and threatening statement of the Southern States that they would not accept the Constitution without this clause, however, made it evident that nothing could be accomplished by insistence of either side on their full demands. Evidently, some compromise must be arrived at. Accordingly, General Pinckney, Rutledge, Read, Randolph, and G. Morris favored the reference of the whole subject of export taxes, slave trade, and navigation acts, to a Committee. Morris said that "these things may form a bargain among the Northern and Southern States"; and Randolph expressed the hope that "some middle ground might, if possible, be found", since he would "sooner risk the Constitution" than agree to this clause. On the other hand, Gorham of Massachusetts and Ellsworth favored adopting the plan as it stood. The former took pains to point out that "the Eastern States had no motive to Union, but a commercial one"; that they were not afraid of external danger and did not need the aid of the South. Ellsworth's speech clearly showed the critical situation in the Convention :

"This widening of opinions has a threatening aspect. If we do not agree on this middle and moderate ground, he was afraid we should lose two States, with such others as may be disposed to stand aloof, should fly into a variety of shapes and directions, and most probably into several Confederations and not without bloodshed."

Finally, the whole subject was referred to a Committee of Eleven (one from each State) — the Southern members being Madison, Williamson, General Pinckney, and Baldwin. This Committee reported, on August 24, a series of proposals which constituted a second crucial compromise by the Convention — Congress was to be forbidden power until the year 1800 to prohibit "the migration or importation of such persons as the several States now existing shall think proper to admit. . . . But a tax or duty may be imposed on such migration or importation at a rate not exceeding the average of the duties laid on imports"; the provision requiring assent of two thirds of each House for the passage of a navigation act was to be stricken out; the provision prohibiting the laying of a capitation tax unless in proportion to the census was to be retained.

On August 25, the first part of the Compromise Report was taken up, and after General Pinckney (against Madison's opposition) had secured the extension of the prohibition on Congress until the year 1808, it was accepted by a vote of seven States to four (New Jersey, Pennsylvania, Delaware, and Virginia voting against it). In this vote, it will be noted, the Northern and the Southern States were joined against the Middle States. It will also be noted that the use of the word "slaves" was still sedulously omitted; and Luther Martin, in his message to the Maryland Legislature, later, bitterly commented upon this fact, saying: "The design of this clause is to prevent the General Government from prohibiting the importation of slaves; but the same reasons which caused them to strike out the word 'National', and not admit the word 'stamps' influenced them here to guard against the word 'slaves.' They anxiously sought to avoid the admission of expressions which might be odious to the ears of Americans, though they were willing to admit into their system those things which the expressions signified."[1]

---

[1] *Elliot's Debates*, I, 372, 373. One other word of doubtful meaning was contained in this prohibition on the power of Congress, viz., the word "migration."

That part of the Report which allowed a tax on importation of slaves was strongly opposed by Sherman, G. Morris, and Madison on the ground that it was "wrong to admit in the Constitution the idea that there could be property in men", to be taxed like imports of other goods. General Pinckney admitted that this provision was the price which the Southern States had paid for obtaining the first part of the compromise. Finally, the Convention changed this part so as to read: "But a tax or duty may be imposed on such importation not exceeding ten dollars for each person." Four days later, August 29, the Convention took up the part of the Committee's Compromise Report which eliminated the requirement of a two thirds vote for the passage of any navigation act by Congress. Obtaining this cession had been a decided victory for the Northern States, and a severe defeat for the South. To understand the importance of the issue, it must be recollected that the term "navigation act", while in general applying to any regulation of commerce, had a particular significance at that date. The principal form of such acts, then familiar to Americans, were those obnoxious statutes of Great Britain which confined shipment of goods to English-built and English-owned ships. The Southern States, which neither built nor owned ships, were extremely apprehensive lest the Northern States, having control of Congress by a majority vote, might pass a similar act requiring all American exports and imports to be carried in American ships. (Such statutes

During the excited debates in 1819–1820, over the admission of Missouri as a State, a question arose as to its interpretation, and Charles Pinckney said in the House that it applied only to the entrance of free whites from foreign countries and that the intent was to encourage immigration of whites; see *16th Cong. 1st Sess.*, 1311–1318, Feb. 14, 1820. But see also Madison to Webster, Nov. 27, 1819; Madison to Monroe, Feb. 10, 1820, as to a different interpretation. In the famous *Passenger Cases* (7 Howard, 283), decided in 1849, there may be found the fullest discussion on the intent of the framers; but no final decision was reached, as the Judges differed vitally on the question whether or not it was to be interpreted as applying solely to slaves.

had been enacted by the New England States in 1784 and 1785.)   Enactment by Congress of such legislation might deprive the South of the privilege of conducting its commerce, as then carried on, in English ships, and might thus enhance freights.[1]   Accordingly, when this part of the compromise was reached, Charles Pinckney made a proposal (seconded by Luther Martin), which, if adopted, would have overthrown the whole work of the Convention.   He moved that Congress should have no power to enact any regulation of commerce (whether navigation acts or otherwise) except with the assent of two thirds of the members of each House. He said that there were five distinct commercial interests which "would be a source of oppressive regulations, if no check to a bare majority should be provided" — the fisheries and West India trade, belonging to New England — wheat and flour of New Jersey and Pennsylvania — tobacco of Maryland, Virginia, and North Carolina — rice and indigo of South Carolina and Georgia — and New York's interest being for free trade.   It is impossible to understand properly the fight over the adoption of the Constitution in the Convention, or over its ratification outside, unless this fear of the South at Northern domination of its commerce is thoroughly realized.   It had long existed and was strongly expressed in letters by Richard Henry Lee.[2]   As early as 1785, writing to Madison, he had said:

[1] " The limitations thus far considered were theoretically important, but those placed upon the control of commerce were of direct practical concern.   New England and the Middle States were the commercial and shipping sections of the country.   To require that all American products should be carried in American built and American manned vessels would have been a great stimulus to shipbuilding and commerce.   But the South was a producing section.   It had to have markets for its raw materials and it therefore needed free intercourse with the outside world. Such restrictions as had been laid on the Colonies by the British government before American independence were greatly dreaded.   Also to meet its labor problems, the South needed an increasing number of slaves."   *The Framing of the Constitution* (1913), by Max Farrand, p. 147.

[2] *The Letters of Richard Henry Lee* (J. C. Ballagh, ed.), III, letters of Aug. 4, Oct. 10, 1785.

". . . It seems to me clear beyond doubt that the giving Congress a power to legislate over the trade of the Union would be dangerous in the extreme to the five Southern or staple States, whose want of ships and seamen would expose their freightage and their produce to a most pernicious and destructive monopoly.   With such a power eight States in the Union would be stimulated by extreme interest to shut close the door of monopoly, that by the exclusion of all rivals, whether for the purchasing of our produce or freighting it, both these might be at the mercy of our East and North.   The spirit of commerce throughout the world is a spirit of avarice, and could not fail to act as above stated. What little difficulty there would be in drawing over one of the 5 to join the 8 interested States would be very discernible to those who have marked the progress of intrigue in Congress."

And again he wrote :

"So essential is the difference between the Northern and Southern productions and circumstances relative to commerce that it is not easy to adopt any system that would well accord with all; and the staple States would be feelingly alive to the proposed plan of vesting powers absolute for the restraint and regulation of commerce in a body of Representatives whose constituents are very differently circumstanced.   Intrigue and coalition among the Northern staple States, taking advantage of the disunion and inattention of the South, might fix a ruinous monopoly upon the trade and production of the staple States that have not ships or seamen for the exportation of their valuable productions. . . . I am free, therefore, to own that I think it both safest and best to give no such power to Congress. . . . A contrary one (plan) would, I verily believe, be more hurtful, much more hurtful to us than even the crabbed, selfish system of Great Britain."

The debate which arose over Pinckney's proposal was one of the most important during the whole Convention.   Only Randolph and Mason of Virginia and

Williamson of North Carolina favored Pinckney's
motion. His own colleagues, General Pinckney, Butler,
and Rutledge, opposed it; so did Spaight of North
Carolina, Madison of Virginia, Clymer, Wilson, and G.
Morris of Pennsylvania, Sherman of Connecticut, and
Gorham of Massachusetts — Madison's speech being
particularly effective in seeking to prove how groundless
were the fears of the South that the other States would
seek to injure its trade. Gorham made a somewhat
truculent speech; for, after maintaining the improb-
ability of a combination between the North and Middle
States against the South, he said that while he "depre-
cated the consequences of disunion, but if it should
take place, it was the Southern part of the Continent
that had the most reason to dread them. The Eastern
States were not led to strengthen the Union by fear for
their own safety." General Pinckney made an interesting confession of his conversion from his prejudice
against the Eastern delegates, saying:

"It was the true interest of the Southern States to have
no regulation of commerce; but considering the loss brought
on the commerce of the Eastern States by the Revolution,
their liberal conduct towards the views of South Carolina
[viz., in agreeing to permission to import slaves until 1808],
and the interests the weak Southern States had in being
united with the strong Eastern States, he thought it proper
that no fetters should be imposed on the power of making
commercial regulations; and that his constituents, though
prejudiced against the Eastern States, would be reconciled
to this liberality. He had himself prejudices against the
Eastern States before he came here, but would acknowledge
that he had found them as liberal and candid as any men
whatever."

His colleague, Pierce Butler, while saying that he
would vote against Charles Pinckney's motion, since
he was "desirous of conciliating the affections of the

Eastern States", took occasion to point out again the conditions which had been apparent throughout the Convention, namely, that "he considered the interests of these (the Southern States) and of the Eastern States to be as different as the interests of Russia and Turkey." And, said Luther Martin later: "I found the Eastern States, notwithstanding their aversion to slavery, were very willing to indulge the Southern States, at least with a temporary liberty to prosecute the slave trade, provided the Southern States would, in their turn, gratify them by laying no restrictions on navigation acts." [1]

Charles Pinckney's motion was rejected by vote of seven States to four, Maryland, Virginia, North Carolina, and Georgia voting for it. Thereupon, the Committee's Report was accepted; and this great compromise became embodied in the Constitution, when, on September 15, the Convention defeated an attempt by Mason to reverse its action by moving that: "No law in the nature of a navigation act be passed before the year 1808, without the consent of two thirds of each branch of the Legislature", Mason arguing that a bare majority ought not to have power to enhance the freights and "enable a few rich merchants in Philadelphia, New York, and Boston to monopolize the staples of the Southern States."

While the compromise of July 16 between the large and small States has been generally regarded as the crucial one of the Convention, it is probable that this present compromise between the Southern and the Northern States had fully as potent effect upon the form which the Constitution finally assumed; for it is certain that after this date (August 29), the most

---

[1] *Elliot's Debates*, I, 373. For a valuable description of the compromise, see George Ticknor Curtis' *History of the Constitution*, II, 301-317. See also Madison to Robert Welsh, Nov. 27, 1817.

difficult problems which had hitherto split the delegates were swiftly resolved. In this connection, a statement made by George Mason to Jefferson, a few years later, is enlightening : [1]

"The Constitution as agreed to till a fortnight before the Convention rose was such a one as he would have set his hand and heart to. 1. The President was to be elected for 7 years, then ineligible for 7 more. 2. Rotation in the Senate. 3. A vote of 2/3 in the Legislature on particular subjects and expressly on that of navigation. The 3 New England States were constantly with us in all questions . . . so that it was these three States with the 5 Southern ones against Pennsylvania, Jersey and Delaware. With respect to the importation of slaves, it was left to Congress. This disturbed the two Southernmost States who knew that Congress would immediately suppress the importation of slaves. Those two States therefore struck up a bargain with the three New England States. If they would join to admit slaves for some years, the two Southernmost States would join in changing the clause which required the 2/3 of the Legislature in any vote. It was done. These articles were changed accordingly, and from that moment the two Southern States and the three Northern ones joined Pennsylvania, Jersey and Delaware and made the majority 8 to 3, against us instead of 8 to 3 for us, as it had been thro' the whole Convention. Under this coalition, the great principles of the Constitution were changed in the last days of the Convention."

It is to be noted that while this compromise involved the attitudes of the delegates towards slavery, that subject had not then the importance as a moral question which it bore later in our history ; and it did not bulk so large in the Convention as some historians have supposed. This has been strikingly commented upon by Farrand, in describing the compromises of the Constitution. He has pointed out that the early histor-

[1] *Writings of Thomas Jefferson* (Ford's ed.), I, 237, "The Anas", Sept. 30, 1792.

ical accounts of the Constitution appeared soon after the publication of Madison's *Notes* in 1840, and just at the period when slavery was becoming our chief political problem.   It was not surprising, therefore, that early historians placed an undue emphasis on the part which slavery played in the Federal Convention, and that later writers have followed them.[1]   Hence, while giving overweight to the concession on slavery made by the North, historians have underestimated the importance of the concession made on commerce by the South.[2]   Had Pinckney's proposal been adopted, requiring a two thirds vote of Congress for all laws regulating commerce, the course of American history would have been vitally changed.   Enactment of protective tariffs might have been practically impossible.   The whole political relations between the South and the North growing out of commercial legislation would have been changed.   The Nullification movement in the 1830's,

[1] "Take, for example, Richard Hildreth's *History of the United States*. The third volume which covers the period of the Revolution and the Confederation appeared in 1849.   In the chapter that is devoted to the formation of the Federal Constitution, one third is taken up with the slavery debates; and of the 'three great compromises' that he notices two are slavery compromises. The second volume of G. T. Curtis's *History of the Constitution* was published in 1858. Although Curtis does not neglect, as Hildreth did, the other features of the Convention's work, and although he corrects Hildreth's misapprehension that the counting of three fifths of the slaves was the essential feature of the compromise in which both representation and direct taxation were to be apportioned according to population, he distinctly exaggerates the importance of the slavery questions, and he chooses the same provisions as the 'grand compromises of the Constitution.' . . . Even Bancroft failed to appreciate the significance of the Federal Convention's action in at least two cases to which particular attention is to be given in this article . . . the admission of new States and the method of electing the President." *Compromises of the Constitution*, by Max Farrand, *Amer. Hist. Rev.* (1904), p. 479.

[2] George Ticknor Curtis in his *History of the Constitution*, II, 306–307, said: "The just and candid voice of History has also to thank the Southern statesmen who consented to this arrangement for having clothed a majority of the two Houses with a full commercial power.   They felt, and truly felt, that this was a great concession.   But they looked at what they had gained."

George McDuffie of South Carolina said in a speech in the Senate, in 1830: "These interests then stand diametrically and irreconcilably opposed to each other. The interest, the pecuniary interest, of the Northern manufacturer is directly promoted by every increase of taxes imposed on Southern commerce; and it is unnecessary to add that the interest of the Southern planter is promoted by every diminution of the taxes imposed on the productions of his industry."

which arose out of opposition to a Northern tariff, might not have occurred.

The compromise arrived at on this August 29 did not complete the action of the Convention on the subject of commerce. There were still some delegates who feared lest the broad power "to regulate commerce" might be exercised by Congress to the injury of the States. Maryland had long been apprehensive that Congress "might favor the ports of particular States by requiring vessels destined to or from other States to enter and clear thereat"; and accordingly, her delegates, Carroll and Luther Martin, had moved, on August 25, that:

"The Legislature of the United States shall not oblige vessels belonging to citizens thereof, or to foreigners, to enter or pay duties or imposts in any other State than in that to which they may be bound, or to clear out in any other than the State in which their cargoes may be laden on board; nor shall any privilege or immunity be granted to any vessels on entering or clearing out, or paying duties or imposts in one State in preference to another."

For, as Martin stated later in his letter to the Legislature: "Without such a provision, it would have been in the power of the General Government to compel all ships sailing into or out of the Chesapeake to clear and enter at Norfolk, or some port in Virginia — a regulation which would be extremely injurious to our commerce, but which would, if considered merely as to the interests of the Union, perhaps not be thought unreasonable since it would render the collection of the revenues arising from commerce more certain and less expensive." Gorham of Massachusetts, on the other hand, thought that the National revenue "might be defeated, if vessels could run up long rivers, through the jurisdiction of different States without being required to enter, with the opportunity of landing and selling their cargoes by the way." Another Maryland delegate, James McHenry, and General Pinckney of South Carolina moved as a substitute:

"Should it be judged by the Legislature of the United States that one or more ports for collecting duties or imposts other than those ports of entrance and clearance already established by the respective States, should be established, the Legislature of the United States shall signify the same to the Executives of the respective States, ascertaining the number of such ports adjudged necessary; to be laid by the said Executives before the Legislatures of the States at their next session; and the Legislature of the United States shall not have the power of fixing or establishing the particular ports for collecting duties or imposts in any State, except the Legislature of such State shall neglect to fix and establish the same during their first session to be held after such notification by the Legislature of the United States to the Executive of such State."

They also proposed the following:

"All duties, imposts, and excises, prohibitions or restraints laid or made by the Legislature of the United States shall be uniform and equal throughout the United States."

These propositions had been considered of such vital importance that they had been referred to a Special Committee of one from each State, elected by ballot. This Committee had reported, through Sherman of Connecticut, on August 28, the following limitation on the power of Congress over commerce:

"nor shall any regulation of commerce or revenue give preference to the ports of one State over those of another, or oblige vessels bound to or from any State to enter, clear or pay duties in another, and all tonnage, duties, imposts and excises laid by the Legislature shall be uniform throughout the United States."

On August 31, two days after the compromise, though objections were raised that this provision would facilitate smuggling, the Convention agreed to it (the word "tonnage" being struck out, as comprehended in the word "duties").[1] It will be noted that all the limitations, thus adopted, were intended to allay the same fears that had caused the Convention to prohibit Congress from imposing export duties — namely, the fear lest Congress might discriminate against certain of the States. The constant expression of this feeling by various delegates makes it singular that when the Committee of Style reported the final draft of the Constitution, on September 12, it entirely omitted to include this provision voted on August 31; and the Convention was obliged to pass a vote on September 14, to remedy the omission. In engrossing the final document, the provision against preference to ports became part of Article I, section 9, being inserted after "no tax or duty shall be laid on articles exported from any States"; and the provision as to uniformity became part of Article I, section 8, relating to the power to lay and collect taxes.

One further topic connected with the power over commerce should be noted. It is a singular thing that the Report of the Committee of Detail contained no provision relating to the relations of the new Government to the Indians. The Articles of Confederation had vested in Congress the "sole and exclusive right and power of . . . regulating the trade and managing all affairs with the Indians, not members of any of the States, provided that the Legislative right of any State within its own limits be not infringed or violated."

---

[1] Hugh Williamson of North Carolina, in a speech on the cod fisheries bounties bill, in the House, February 7, 1792, explained that the "clear and obvious intention" of this clause was "that Congress might not have the power of imposing unequal burdens — that it might not be in their power to gratify one part of the Union by oppressing another. It appeared possible, and not very improbable, that the time might come when, by greater cohesion, by more unanimity, by more address, the Representatives of one part of the Union might attempt to impose unequal taxes or to relieve their constituents at the expense of the people."

This clause with its reservation of rights to the States had been productive of serious trouble; and the States had dealt with and regulated the Indians with great freedom, and with little regard to Congress or to the interests of other States or of the Nation. Accordingly, Madison, on August 18, moved to supply this serious omission made by the Committee, by proposing an additional extremely broad power in Congress: "to regulate affairs with the Indians, as well within as without the limits of the United States." The Committee of Detail, on August 22, reported this, in a much restricted form, by adding at the end of the clause granting power to Congress " to regulate commerce with foreign nations and among the several States" the further words "and with Indians, within the limits of any State, not subject to the laws thereof." This not being acted upon, Judge Brearley from the Committee on postponed matters reported, on September 4, that the power be given to Congress to regulate commerce with the Indians, by adding the following simple words, "and with the Indian tribes." This was agreed to without dissent, on that day.

OUT OF CONVENTION

The *Gazette* stated, this day, that commerce and industry were at a standstill throughout the country, awaiting the action of the Convention, in framing a more adequate form of Government: [1]

"Every enterprize, public as well as private, in the United States (says a correspondent) seems suspended till it is known what kind of Government we are to receive from our National Convention. The States neglect their roads and canals, till they see whether those necessary improvements will not become the objects of a National Government. Trading

---

[1] *Pennsylvania Gazette*, Aug. 29, 1787; see also *Independent Chronicle*, Sept. 20, 1787.

and manufacturing companies suspend their voyages and manufactures, till they see how far their commerce will be protected and promoted by a National system of commercial regulations.   The lawful usurer locks up or buries his specie, till he sees whether the new Frame of Government will deliver him from the curse or fear of paper money and the tender laws.   The wealthy farmer views a plantation with desire for one of his sons, but declines to empty his chest of his hard dollars for it, till he is sure it will not in a few years be taken from him by the enormous weight of State Governments and taxes.   The public creditor, who, from the deranged state of finances in every State, and their total inability to support their partial funding systems, has reason to fear that his certificates will perish in his hands, now places all his hope of justice in an enlightened and stable National Government. The embarrassed farmer and the oppressed tenant, who wish to become free and independent by emigrating to a frontier county, wait to see whether they shall be protected by a National force from the Indians and by a National system of taxation from the more terrible pest of State and county tax gatherers.   In short, the pulse of industry, ingenuity, and enterprize in every occupation of man now stands still in the United States, and every look and wish and hope is only *to* and every prayer to Heaven that has for its object the safety of your country is only *for*, the present august National Convention."

THURSDAY, AUGUST 30, 1787

IN CONVENTION

Admission of New States

On this day, the Convention disposed of a question which the pending situation of the United States with reference to its Western Territory rendered of great importance.

Randolph's original Resolution had provided:

"For the admission of States lawfully arising within the limits of the United States, whether from a voluntary junction of Government and Territory or otherwise, with the consent of a number of voices in the National Legislature less than the whole."

This constituted a proposal to allow admission of new States by vote (possibly a majority vote) of Congress, rather than to require nine States to agree to the admission. It was a very radical change from the Articles of Confederation which had provided that:

" Canada acceding to this Confederation, and joining in the measures of the United States, shall be admitted into, and entitled to all the advantages of this Union; but no other colony shall be admitted into the same, unless such admission be agreed to by nine States."

Under this provision of the Confederation, there had been great diversity of opinion whether it was possible to admit any portions of one of the thirteen States, as a new State. Admission of Vermont, Franklin, and Kentucky had been bitterly resisted, on this ground.[1] It is singular, therefore, that when Randolph's proposal had been considered in Committee of the Whole, on June 5, and again by the Convention on July 18, it had been agreed to without debate. In spite of this apparent unanimity on the subject, however, the debates on other questions had developed considerable hostile sentiment as to admission of new States. For many years past, the subject of Spain's exclusion of Americans from free navigation of the Mississippi River had been greatly agitating the Southern States, especially Virginia and North Carolina, whose western lands comprised the later States of Kentucky and

---

[1] George Mason wrote to Edmund Randolph, Oct. 19, 1782: "Congress are properly the delegates of the different States, with powers defined and limited by the Articles of Confederation. These they cannot be permitted to exceed, without establishing an arbitrary and tyrannical aristocracy. . . . There is not a single word in the Articles of Confederation giving Congress a power of limiting, dividing or parcelling out any of the thirteen States or of erecting new ones." *George Mason Papers MSS*, in Library of Congress.

Tennessee. Insistence on American rights in the River and opposition to any treaty with Spain which did not recognize them had been the source of sharp political and sectional divisions in Congress from 1778 to 1786. In recent years, the Eastern States in Congress had, to a certain extent, antagonized the South by their lukewarm attitude on this question; and there was little doubt that the Eastern States, with their commercial and shipbuilding interests, were averse to the growth of population in the West and to the consequent increasing diversion of commerce down the Mississippi. Jealousy of future Western States had been especially prominent in the discussion of July 5 and 6 on the subject of regulating the proportionate representation of the States in the House of Representatives. A strong sentiment had always existed in the old Colonies and in many of the thirteen States against allowing to the "back country" — the frontier settlements of each State which consisted largely of foreigners and of pioneers — a Legislative representation equal to that possessed by the older settled portions of the State.[1] Such a representative inequality had prevailed to a considerable extent in Pennsylvania Virginia, and the Carolinas. As this system had worked in Pennsylvania to keep political power in the hands of the older portions, G. Morris of Pennsylvania, supported by the delegates from South Carolina and Massachusetts, now sought to apply the same principle to the representation in the National Legislature from the future States in the West. To accomplish this end, he had opposed the proposal made by the Committee, on July 5 and 9, that the Legislature should have power to regulate the number of Representatives from new States. If the Legislature was to have any such power, he favored

[1] *Compromises of the Constitution*, by Max Farrand, *Amer. Hist. Rev.* (1904) p. 479 *et seq.*

apportioning Representatives according to the wealth
of the States, instead of according to population, so
that the increasingly populous Western States might
not be enabled to outweigh the less populous but more
wealthy States on the seaboard. He had said (July 5)
that he looked forward "to that range of new States
which would soon be formed in the West. He thought
the rule of representation ought to be so fixed as to
secure to the Atlantic States a prevalence in the
National Councils"; and he urged this extraordinary
argument that: "The new States will know less of
the public interest; will have an interest in many
respects different; in particular will be less scrupulous
of involving the community in wars, the burdens and
operations of which would fall chiefly on the maritime
States." He advocated permanently fixing the
representation which each new State should have, so
that the maritime States might never be outvoted.
Rutledge of South Carolina had shared the same views,
stating (July 11) that as the Western States would not
be able to contribute in taxes in proportion to their
numbers, they should not, therefore, be represented in
that proportion. Gorham of Massachusetts, on the
other hand, had argued the inconvenience of fixing
definitely the number of Representatives, and pointed
out that the Kentucky and the Maine districts were
already about to become separate States, and "he hoped
to see all the States made small by proper divisions,
instead of their becoming formidable, as was apprehended, to the small States. King of Massachusetts,
advocating that wealth be taken into consideration
in representation, had pointed out that Congress had
already, by a Resolve of April 23, 1784 (framed by
Thomas Jefferson), "impoliticly" laid out the Northwest Territory into ten possible States, each to be
admitted when having the number of inhabitants

possessed by the smallest States in the Union, by which "ten new votes may be added without a greater addition of inhabitants than are represented by the single vote of Pennsylvania." G. Morris had repeated his forebodings (July 11) as to "the danger of throwing such a preponderancy into the Western scale"; he had suggested that "in time the Western people would outnumber the Atlantic States", and had stated that "he wished therefore to put it in the power of the latter to keep a majority of votes in their own hands." He had said that: "The busy haunts of men not the remote wilderness are the proper school of political talents. If the Western people get the power into their hands, they will ruin the Atlantic interests. The back members are always most averse to the best measures." This policy of discrimination against new Western States, however, had been strongly opposed by Mason of Virginia, who had said (July 11) that: "If the Western States are to be admitted into the Union, they must be treated as equals and subjected to no degrading discriminations. They will have the same pride and other passions which we have, and will either not unite with or will speedily revolt from the Union, if they are not in all respects placed on an equal footing with their brethren." And he added, with great foresight, that "he did not know but that in time they would be both more numerous and more wealthy than their Atlantic brethren; the extent and fertility of their soil made this probable." Randolph of Virginia had agreed with Mason that it was entirely "inadmissable that a larger and more populous district of America should hereafter have less representation than a smaller and less populous district. If a fair representation of the people be not secured, the injustice of the Government will shake it to its foundations." Madison also had said (July 11) that "with regard to the Western States he was clear and firm in opinion that no unfavorable distinctions were admissible, either in point of justice or policy." [1]

Meanwhile, after these discussions had taken place in the Convention as to the policy of admitting new States, Congress, on July 13, had passed the Northwest Territory Ordinance providing for five new States carved from the lands north of the Ohio River, and for "their admission to a share in the Federal councils on an equal footing with the original States." [2] The Convention, on July 23, having undoubted knowledge of the adoption of that Ordinance by Congress, accepted Randolph's original Resolution as to the admission of new States — but without making any provision one way or the other, as to their admission on an equality with the present States. The Committee of Detail, however, in its Report of August 6, altered the provisions of the Convention's previous vote, evidently bearing in mind the provisions of the Ordinance, as well as the views in favor of equality of States expressed by the Virginia members in the above debates, so as to provide that:

"New States lawfully constituted or established within the limits of the United States may be admitted, by the Legislature, into this Government; but to such admission, the consent of two thirds of the members present in each House shall be necessary. If a new State shall arise within

[1] That a failure to grant equality in the admission of the new States, like that which was striving for Statehood in the Kentucky District of Virginia, might have resulted in a separation of such States from the Union, and that the new Federal Government was looked forward to as a protection to such new States, may be seen from a letter published, at this time, in the *Independent Chronicle* (Boston), July 19, 1787: "What feuds, what discords do we behold from the several quarters of the United States! While those in the east only *appear* to be dying away, new and accumulated evils seem to be gathering in the West. The treaty with Spain relative to the navigation of the Mississippi has set the people on the falls of the Ohio, etc., into a political frenzy; the general voice of the Western Community (who, it is said, can raise 20,000 militia) is 'Equal liberty with the thirteen States or a breach of peace and a new alliance.' . . . These circumstances greatly corroborate the necessity of an immediate efficient Federal Government."

[2] This Ordinance was published in full for the first time in Philadelphia, in the *Pennsylvania Herald*, July 25, 1787.

the limits of any of the present States, the consent of the Legislatures of such States shall be also necessary to its admission. If the admission be consented to, the new States shall be admitted on the same terms with the original States. But the Legislature may make conditions with the new States concerning the public debt which shall be then subsisting."

This newly drafted Article was first debated on August 29, immediately after the conclusion of the compromise between the South and the East as to the commerce clause and the importation of slaves. G. Morris at once moved to strike out the provision that new States be admitted on equal terms with the original States, stating that he did not wish "to throw the power into their hands." Langdon of New Hampshire and Williamson of North Carolina concurred. Madison opposed, insisting that the Western States "neither would nor ought to submit to a Union which degraded them from an equal rank with other States"; and Mason and Sherman agreed with him. Morris' motion, however, was carried by a decisive vote, only Maryland and Virginia voting against it. It is highly probable that this result was reached as a part of the price which South Carolina paid to Pennsylvania for securing the slavery compromise. Any express declaration of the equality of the new States with the old was thus excluded from the Constitution. Fortunately, however, in spite of this decisive action of the Convention, the principle has been restored by the consistent practice of Congress. And the Supreme Court in a case in 1911 has said that: "The constitutional equality of the States is essential to the harmonious operation of the scheme upon which the Republic was organized." [1]

---

[1] *Coyle* v. *Oklahoma* (1911), 221 U. S. 559, 580, per Lurton, J. The statement is sound, though historically inaccurate as an interpretation of the vote of the Conven-

After their victory on the equality question, Morris and John Dickinson then moved a complete new draft of the whole Article, eliminating the provision for a two thirds vote by Congress. The debate now turned in a new direction. Luther Martin of Maryland, Langdon of New Hampshire, and Dickinson of Delaware opposed the requirement of the consent of the State to the creation of a new State within its limits, on the ground that this might prevent the creation of Kentucky, Vermont, Maine, and Tennessee as States, and thus force the people of those districts to continue against their will under the States then governing them. Wilson and many others, on the other hand, took the position that "nothing would give greater or juster alarm than the doctrine that a political society is to be torn asunder without its own consent." The motion made by Morris and Dickinson was carried on this August 30; and (compressed in phraseology by the Committee on Style in its Report of September 12) it became Article IV, section 3, of the Constitution as follows:

"New States may be admitted by the Congress into this Union; but no new State shall be formed or erected within the jurisdiction of any other State; nor any State be formed by the junction of two or more States, or parts of States, without the consent of the Legislatures of the States concerned as well as of the Congress."

Because of the lack of explicitness in the phrasing of this section, the question was presented whether the

tion. See especially as to equality of new States, *The Law of the American Constitution* (1922), by Charles K. Burdick, pp. 307–311, 438–439.

Note that in *Illinois Central R. R.* v. *Illinois* (1892), 146 U. S. 387, Judge Field said: "The State of Illinois was admitted into the Union in 1818 on an equal footing with the original States in all respects. Such was one of the conditions of the cession of the territory northwest of the Ohio River, out of which the State was formed. But the equality prescribed would have existed if it had not been thus stipulated. There can be no distinction between the several States of the Union in the character of the jurisdiction, sovereignty and dominion which they may possess and exercise over persons and subjects within their respective limits."

Constitution permitted the creation of new States from territory which was not within the United States at the time of its ratification. Seventeen years later, in 1804, and just after the annexation of Louisiana, G. Morris, the drafter of the section, wrote to a friend: "Your inquiry . . . is substantially whether the Congress can admit, as a new State, territory which did not belong to the United States when the Constitution was made. In my opinion, they cannot. I always thought that when we should acquire Canada and Louisiana, it would be proper to govern them as provinces and allow them no voice in our council. In wording the third section of the fourth Article, I went as far as circumstances would permit, to establish the exclusion. Candor obliges me to add my belief that had it been more pointedly expressed, a strong opposition would have been made." [1] Fortunately, in this case of creation of States from newly acquired territory as in the other case of admission of new States on equality, the views held by Morris were not followed by the United States Government in its subsequent action; and any ambiguity in the phrasing of this section has now been made entirely clear by the interpretation given to it in practice.

The Territories

When this action was completed on the subject of admission of new States, the Convention proceeded to consider another motion by G. Morris on a subject which clearly demanded attention and settlement —

---

[1] *Life of Gouverneur Morris* (1832), by Jared Sparks, III, 192; cited in *Dred Scott v. Sandford* (1857), 19 Howard 507, per Judge Campbell. William Plumer of New Hampshire said in the Senate, Feb. 18, 1805, in the Louisiana debate: "I think we cannot admit a new partner formed from without the limits of the United States into the Union, without the previous consent of each partner composing the form first obtained." See *Memorandum of Proceedings in the United States Senate, 1803–1809* (1923), by William Plumer, p. 293, the speech not being reported in the *Annals of Congress*.

namely, the power of the Congress over territory of the United States before its becoming a State or States.[1] The Articles of Confederation had not contemplated and had made no reference to the owning of territory by the United States itself. Yet when the various States had ceded to the United States the Western lands claimed by them (New York in 1781; Virginia in 1784; Massachusetts in 1785; and Connecticut in 1786) it had been necessary for Congress to exercise powers of government over them, even though no such power was expressly granted by the Articles. The passage of the Northwest Territory Ordinance by Congress on July 13, 1787, making elaborate provisions for the government of lands north of the Ohio River and east of the Mississippi and for its division into not less than three nor more than five new States, each to be admitted as a State when possessing more than 60,000 inhabitants, made it clearly necessary that any new Constitution should deal with this question.[2] For the action of Congress in passing this Ordinance was as ultra-legal as the adoption of the Declaration of Independence itself. Madison, perceiving that the Committee of Detail in its Report of August 6 had made no provision for the situation, had submitted, on August 18, a motion for vesting additional powers in Congress, viz., "to dispose of the unappropriated lands of the United States", and "to institute temporary governments for new States arising therein." These being referred to the Committee of Detail, that Committee had reported, on August 22, a substitute for them couched in such language as to give to Congress an extraordinarily broad authority:

[1] On this subject, see especially *The Law of the American Constitution* (1922), by Charles K. Burdick.

[2] See *Legal History of the Northwest Territory Ordinance*, by J. M. Merriam, *Amer. Antiq. Soc. Proc.* (April, 1898); *History of the United States* (1912), by Edward Channing, III.

"to provide, as may become necessary, from time to time, for the well managing and securing the common property and general interests and welfare of the United States in such manner as shall not interfere with the governments of individual States, in matters which respect only their internal police, or for which their individual authorities may be competent."

Such power "to provide for the . . . general interests and welfare of the United States", had it been voted by the Convention, would have given to Congress practically unrestricted scope of legislation; and the whole theory of a National Government with strictly limited authority would have been dissipated. The Convention, however, took no action on this proposal; but G. Morris, on this August 30, reverted to the more limited powers suggested by Madison, and moved the following that:

"The Legislature shall have power to dispose of and make all needful rules and regulations respecting the territory or other property belonging to the United States; and nothing in this Constitution contained, shall be so construed as to prejudice any claims either of the United States or of any particular State."

The latter part of the motion was intended to calm the fears of those who thought that by requiring consent of a State to erection of a new State within its jurisdiction, the Constitution might be favoring the claims of some State to vacant lands ceded to the United States by the treaty of peace with Great Britain. Morris' motion was carried, with only one dissenting vote (that of Maryland); and it became the second clause of Article V, section 3, of the Constitution. In this way, this vastly important clause, under which the United States has governed all its territorial possessions, came into being, almost as an afterthought and towards the end of the Convention.[1]

[1] On the subject of the power of Congress over the territories and new States, see especially George Ticknor Curtis' *History of the Constitution* (1858), II, 341-358.

Guaranty of Protection to the States

After thus providing for new States and for territorial possessions, the Convention, on this August 30, finally determined the degree of protection which the new Government should afford to the States comprising it. It was evident to all that it must possess some means to deal with such a situation as had recently arisen in Massachusetts during the Shays Rebellion in the winter of 1786–87. When, in that disturbance, it had seemed probable that the State might not be able to suppress the insurrection by means of its own forces, and many men had urged that Congress send Continental troops to the aid of the State, there had been bitter opposition to such a measure. The power of Congress to take such a step had been vehemently challenged and denied. The serious plight, therefore, in which a State might find itself, if unable to cope alone with an armed uprising within its limits and if Congress could not act, had suggested to the framers of the draft for a Constitution, the necessity of making some provision against such a contingency. Accordingly, Randolph in his Resolutions of May 29 had provided: "That a Republican Government and the territory of each State, except in the instance of a voluntary junction of Government and territory, ought to be guaranteed by the United States to each State." This Resolution had been considered in Committee of the Whole on June 11, at which time opposition had arisen to guaranteeing the "territory" of the States (in view of the fact that there existed many conflicting claims to the same territory by different States). Accordingly, it had been redrafted so as to provide that "a Republican Constitution and its existing laws ought to be guaranteed to each State by the United States." In this form, it had been agreed to without dissent. When the subject had been considered by the Convention on July 18, active discussion had arisen. G. Morris was unwilling that existing State laws should be guaranteed, and instanced objectionable laws in Rhode Island. William Houstoun of Georgia was afraid of perpetuating existing State Constitutions, and instanced that of his own State as a very bad one. Randolph pointed out that the Resolutions had two purposes — to secure Republican Government, and to suppress domestic commotions. Gorham of Massachusetts and Carroll of Maryland contended that if a rebellion existed in the country the General Government should interpose and end it. Rutledge thought that Congress would have the power, even without the insertion of any such guarantee. Martin of Maryland, always insistent on State Sovereignty, was "for leaving the States to suppress rebellions themselves." Finally, a substitute motion by Wilson had been adopted without dissent: "That a Republican form of Government shall be guaranteed to each State and that each State shall be protected against foreign and domestic violence."

When the Committee of Detail made its Report, on August 6, it changed this vote, to appease the States' Rights delegates, as follows: "The United States shall guaranty to each State a Republican form of Government; and shall protect each State against foreign invasion, and, on the application of its Legislature, against domestic violence." The Committee's Report also vested in Congress the specific power "to subdue a rebellion in any State, on the application of its Legislature." This latter power had been debated by the Convention on August 17, at which time Charles Pinckney had moved to strike out the words "on the application of its Legislature." This had at once aroused the States' Rights delegates. Martin of Maryland opposed it, "as giving a dangerous and unnecessary power"; and Gerry of Massachusetts said that he was "against letting loose the myrmidons of the United States on a State without its consent . . . more blood would have spilt in Massachusetts in the late insurrection, if the General Authority had intermeddled." On the other hand, Langdon of New Hampshire concurred with Pinckney and thought that "the apprehension of the National force will have a salutary effect in preventing insurrections." So also, G. Morris thought that: "We are acting a very strange part. We first form a strong man to protect us, and at the same time wish to tie his hands behind him. The Legislature may surely be trusted with such a power to preserve the public tranquillity." Ellsworth of Connecticut thought that in many cases the General Government ought not to be able to interpose without being called upon; but he was willing that the call might come from the State Governor as well as the State Legislature. Morris retorted that the Governor himself might be at the head of the Rebellion. Ellsworth then had proposed that Congress might act alone when the State Legislature could not meet. After voting this change, the Convention had then proceeded to reject the whole power. And so Congress was left without any authority to suppress a rebellion in a State.

The question came up again, however, on this August 30, when the Convention considered the other Articles in the Report of the Committee of Detail which provided for a guaranty to the States of a Republican form of Government and protection against foreign invasion, and, on the application of its Legislature, against domestic violence. An attempt was now made again to strike out the words "on the application of its Legislature", on motion of Dickinson of Delaware, who said that he thought it "of essential importance to the tranquillity of the United States that they should *in all cases* suppress domestic violence", and that such violence might possibly proceed from the State Legislature itself or from disputes between the two branches where such existed. Dickinson's motion was voted down. The Convention, however, was willing to vote to add the words "or on the application of the Executive", Dickinson pointing out that the occasion itself might hinder the Legislature from meeting, and hence from making the application. The Committee of Style, in its Report of September 12, redrafted this clause, so as to read:

"The United States shall guarantee to every State in this Union a republican form of Government, and shall protect each of them against invasion; and on application of the Legislature or Executive, against domestic violence."

On September 15, the words "when the Legislature cannot be convened", were inserted after the word "Executive", and in this form it became Article IV, section 4, of the Constitution, as finally adopted. (It may be noted that the Convention had, on August 30, deliberately defeated a motion by Luther Martin to add, after the word "Executive", the words "in the recess of the Legislature.") In view of the fact that the Convention expressly rejected the proposed power to Congress to suppress a rebellion in a State, its action in adopting this Article IV, section 4, left an open question whether the power vested in that Article was to be exercised by Congress or by the President.

OUT OF CONVENTION

Dr. Benjamin Rush wrote from Philadelphia to Timothy Pickering, this day: [1]

"The new Federal Government like a new Continental waggon will overset our State dung cart, with all its dirty

[1] *Pickering Papers MSS*, in Mass. Hist. Soc. Library.

contents (reverend and irreverend) and thereby restore order and happiness to Pennsylvania. From the conversations of the members of the Convention, there is reason to believe the Federal Constitution will be wise, vigorous, safe, free, and full of dignity. General Washington, it is said, will be placed at the head of the new Government, or in the stile of my simile, will drive the new waggon."

A reflection of the economic conditions existing in Maryland appeared in a Baltimore letter published, this day, in the newspapers: [1]

"How are the times with you? Here they are bad enough. No money in circulation, and consequently no trade. The expectation of the people seem to be fixed on the Grand Convention, now in your metropolis. But nothing has transpired."

A Philadelphia despatch of this date in various papers in other States pointed out that the depressed economic conditions of the country could not all be cured by the action of the Convention: [2]

"It is laughable to observe the strange whims and ideas of people in respect to the Grand Convention and their proceedings. It is taken for granted by the generality that something is accidentally wrong in our political machine, which a little skill and contrivance may alone put to rights by the magick of a few resolves upon paper; not considering that the evils and confusion we experience have originated in a great measure with the people themselves and by them only can be eventually rectified. A long course of frugality, disuse of foreign luxuries, encouragement of industry, application to agriculture, attention to home manufactures and a spirit of union and national sobriety can alone place us in the respectable rank of rich and florishing nations, a situation which we all pant for, but the price of which very few are willing to pay."

[1] *Independent Chronicle* (Boston), Aug. 30, 1787.
[2] *Freeman's Journal*, Aug. 29; *Pennsylvania Herald*, Sept. 1; *New York Daily Advertiser*, Sept. 6; *Massachusetts Centinel*, Sept. 12; *Independent Chronicle* (Boston) Sept. 13, 1787.

A New York paper of two days earlier commented on the conditions in the shipping industry there : [1]

"It is a fact as notorious as lamentable that there is not at present a single vessel of any kind building in our ship-yards. What must be the consequence — that our ship carpenters, our merchants, our seamen and laborers and a number of artists must all be out of employ and foreigners engross all our trade. This is a most serious and alarming circumstance and evidently shows the necessity and policy of our adopting such measures as will effectually revive this valuable branch of business."

FRIDAY, AUGUST 31, 1787

IN CONVENTION

Ratification of the Constitution

It will be recalled that on July 23, after a vigorous and determined fight, the Nationalists in the Convention had prevailed in their contention that the new Constitution must be ratified by Conventions elected by the people of the States rather than by the State Legislatures. The new Government must rest on as broad a foundation of popular vote and acceptance as was then practicable. When the Committee of Detail made its Report of August 6, it provided a detailed mode of ratification of the new Government in two Articles, as follows :

XXI. The ratifications of   States shall be sufficient for organizing this Constitution.

XXII. This Constitution shall be laid before the United States in Congress assembled, for their approbation, and it is the opinion of this Convention, that it should be afterwards submitted to a Convention chosen in each State under the recommendation of its Legislature, in order to receive the ratification of such Convention.

[1] *New York Daily Advertiser*, Aug. 28, 1787.

When these provisions were acted on by the Convention, on August 30 and 31, the momentous step was taken which settled the fate of the Articles of Confederation. Under that document, all thirteen States had agreed that it should be "inviolably observed by every State and the Union shall be perpetual", unless alterations should be agreed to by the Legislature of every State. It was now proposed that States to a number less than thirteen might reject their obligations under these Articles and might form a new Government. This would, in fact, constitute a peaceful revolution. But the delegates were now fully prepared to recommend such action. Carroll and Luther Martin, however, still insisted on ratification of this new Constitution by thirteen States, since "unanimity was necessary to dissolve the existing Confederacy." Sherman agreed, but was willing to propose ratification by ten States. Randolph and Butler proposed nine; Wilson, seven. One difficulty now loomed up; for, as Madison pointed out, if seven, eight, or nine States should be able to organize the Constitution, it "might be put in force over the whole body of the people, though less than a majority of them should ratify it." Butler, on the other hand, said that "he revolted at the idea that one or two States should restrain the rest from consulting their safety." Wilson also, replying to Madison's objection, maintained that: "As the Constitution now stands, the States only which ratify can be bound; we must in this case go to the original powers of Society; the house on fire must be extinguished without a scrupulous regard to ordinary rights." King now offered a remedy to Madison's objection, by moving that, at the end of the provision for ratification after the words "for organizing the Constitution", there be inserted the words "between the said States." This would confine the operation of the new Government simply to those States which should ratify it. This motion was agreed to.

The question then arose, on this August 31, as to the mode of ratification. G. Morris moved that the States be left, each to pursue the particular mode of ratification desired by it — his object, as he said, being "to facilitate the adoption of the plan by leaving the modes approved by the several State Conventions to be followed." This suggestion was made to appease the Maryland delegates, who contended that as the new Constitution would alter their State Constitution's provisions and as their State Constitution prescribed the mode of its own alteration, they could not vote for any other provision. The upholders of the more democratic plan rallied against Morris' proposal. Madison once more brought the attention of the delegates back to fundamental principles. "The people," he said, "were in fact the fountain of all power, and by resorting to them, all difficulties were got over. They could alter Constitutions as they chose. It was a principle in the Bills of Rights that first principles might be resorted to."

King also said that, though the Massachusetts State Constitution was unalterable until the year 1790, "this was no difficulty with him. The State must have contemplated a recurrence to first principles before they sent delegates to this Convention." These arguments for popular sovereignty prevailed and G. Morris' motion was defeated. It was then voted, on this August 31, that the new Government be organized after ratification by nine States. G. Morris and Charles Pinckney then moved to strike out the requirement that the new Constitution receive the approbation of Congress before being submitted to the State Conventions. This motion was carried. Another motion by Morris, urging that the State Legislatures should call Conventions "as speedily as circumstances will permit" was lost, Luther Martin saying that the people would not ratify "unless hurried into it by surprise." [1] Gerry now moved to postpone action on the whole subject. This proposal brought some support from Mason and Randolph of Virginia, both of whom, though hearty supporters of the proposed Constitution in the opening days of the Convention, had become less and less enthusiastic. Mason now said that "he would sooner chop off his right hand than put it to the Constitution as it now stands"; and both he and Randolph wished that the draft might be submitted to another General Convention, after the State Conventions had been allowed to propose amendments. These statements brought forth from G. Morris the pungent retort that he too would be glad to see another Convention "that will have the firmness to provide a vigorous Government, which we are afraid to do." This passage-at-arms well illustrated the fact that the Constitution, as it then stood, was too "high-toned" to suit the States' Rights delegates and too conservative

---

[1] A fuller account of this episode was written by Martin in the *Maryland Journal*, March 21, 1788: "Not more than two days before I left Philadelphia (September 4) a delegate from Pennsylvania urged most strenuously that the Convention ought to hasten their deliberations to a conclusion, assigning as a reason that the Assembly of Pennsylvania was just then about to meet, and that it would be of the greatest importance to bring the system before that session of the Legislature, in order that a Convention of the State might be immediately called to ratify it, before the enemies of the system would have an opportunity of making the people acquainted with their objections, at the same time declaring that if the matter should be delayed, and the people have time to hear the variety of objections which would be made to it by its opposers, he thought it doubtful whether that State or any other State in the Union would adopt it. As soon as the honourable Member took his seat, I rose and observed that I was precisely of the same opinion, that the people of America never would, nor did I think they ought, to adopt the system if they had time to consider and understand it; whereas, a proneness for novelty and change, a conviction that some alteration was necessary, and a confidence in the Members who composed the Convention might possibly procure its adoption, if brought hastily before them; but that these sentiments induced me to wish that a very different line of conduct should be pursued from that recommended by the honourable Member. I wished the people to have every opportunity of information, as I thought it much preferable that a bad system should be rejected at first, than hastily adopted and afterwards be unavailingly repented of."

to suit the Nationalists. That it so appeared to the leaders of the two factions was a fortunate circumstance; for had it represented the extreme views of either side, it would probably never have been signed by the delegates or adopted by the peoples of the States.

Having declined to make any further modification of the mode of ratification proposed by the Committee of Detail, the Convention accepted it, only Maryland dissenting. Ten days later, on September 10, on Gerry's motion to reconsider the whole proposal, the Convention again refused to insert a requirement that the new Constitution receive "the approbation of Congress" before its submission to the States. Though Alexander Hamilton supported Gerry, the majority of the delegates refused to accept the proposal, agreeing with Wilson and Fitzsimmons of Pennsylvania in their statements that such a requirement had been struck out "in order to save Congress from the necessity of an act inconsistent with the Articles of Confederation under which they held their authority." And, said they: "After spending four or five months in the laborious and arduous task of forming a Government for our country, we are ourselves at the close throwing insuperable obstacles in the way of its success." Apart from their desire to base the new Government entirely on the people, these men knew well the practical difficulty of obtaining the assent of Congress; for in that body Rhode Island would have a vote (though not represented in this Convention); and New York, two of whose delegates had left the Convention, would certainly vote against the new Constitution; and Maryland was likely to do so. The Committee of Style, in reporting the final draft of the Constitution, on September 12, compressed the subject of ratification into the following Article (entirely omitting any reference to Congress):

"The ratification of the conventions of nine States shall be sufficient for the establishment of this Constitution between the States so ratifying the same."

And on September 13, this Committee reported the following resolution:

"Resolved, that the preceding Constitution be laid before the United States in Congress assembled, and that it is the opinion of this Convention that it should afterwards be submitted to a Convention of delegates chosen in each State by the people thereof, under the recommendation of its Legislature, for their assent and ratification; and that each Convention asserting and ratifying the same should give notice thereof to the United States in Congress assembled."

The resolution also provided that when nine States should have ratified the Congress of the Confederation should fix a day for elections of President and of the new Congress under the Constitution. Randolph and Mason made a last attempt to have the Convention agree that "amendments to the plan might be offered by the State Conventions, which should be submitted to and finally decided on by another General Convention", and stated that unless this were adopted they could not sign. The Convention, however, voted against this proposal, unanimously.

OUT OF CONVENTION

Washington noted:

"Dined at home, Mr. Morris's, and with a party went to Lansdale [Lansdowne] and drank tea with Mr. and Mrs. Penn."

SATURDAY, SEPTEMBER 1, 1787

IN CONVENTION

On this day, the Convention took no action except to receive two Reports from Special Committees.

SUNDAY, SEPTEMBER 2, 1787

Washington noted :

"Rode to Mr. Bartram's and other places in the country, and drank tea at Mr. Gray's (Gray's Ferry) and returned to the city in the evening."

To John Jay, in New York, Washington wrote, this day :

"I regret not having had it in my power to visit New York during the adjournment of the Convention, last month — Not foreseeing with any precision the period at which it was likely to take place or the length of it, I had put my carriage in the hands of a workman to be repaired and had not the means of moving during the recess, but with, or the curtesy of, others. I thank you for the hints contained in your letter."

MONDAY, SEPTEMBER 3, 1787

IN CONVENTION

Eligibility of Members of Congress to Office

The question of the eligibility of members of the National Legislature to office under the State and National Governments gave the Convention considerable concern — and aroused a degree of warmth which, at the present day, it is difficult to understand. It was largely due to the resentment and jealousies which had been created in some of the States over the appointments made by the Congress under the Confederation of many of its own members to diplomatic and executive positions. There was also a fear lest the new Government might follow the example of Great Britain "where men got into Parliament that they might get offices for themselves or their friends — a source of the corruption that ruined their Government." [1]

---

[1] See Pierce Butler, June 22, 1787.

The Articles of Confederation had provided that a State delegate should not be "capable of holding any office under the United States for which he, or another for his benefit receives any salary, fees or emoluments of any kind." Randolph, in his Resolutions of May 29, had taken over this provision, with very great extensions, as follows: "To be ineligible to any office established by a particular State, or under the authority of the United States, except those peculiarly belonging to the functions of the first (second) branch during the term of service, and for the space of   years after its expiration." This resolution had been considered by the Committee of the Whole on June 12. A motion to strike out ineligibility to State offices had been defeated by a close vote. The blank as to term of years after service was filled by "one", after an attempt to make it "three" had been unsuccessful.

A further ineligibility of members of Congress to re-election which was proposed by Randolph, however, met with opposition. This brought up the whole theory of rotation in office — a subject on which there had been much division of opinion in the States. In Massachusetts particularly, rotation had been made a frequent issue in gubernatorial and other campaigns. The older statesmen of pre-Revolutionary times were devoted to the theory — which had been embodied in the Articles of Confederation — to wit, that no State delegate should be "capable of being a delegate for more than three years in any term of six years." The provision had worked very badly in Congress and had served to prevent the re-election of delegates just at a time when they were becoming most valuable to their States. This had been notably the case with reference to James Madison himself. Nevertheless, Massachusetts had been so attached to the principle that its Legislature had passed a resolution instructing its

delegates not to depart from the rotation established
in the Article, nor to agree in any case to give to members of Congress a capacity to hold offices under the
Government.[1]

The Resolutions submitted by Randolph on May 29
had contained the provision of the Articles in the
following form: that members of the Legislature
should be "incapable of re-election for the space of
after the expiration" of their term of service, and
Randolph had added a new and striking provision,
viz., that they were to be "subject to recall." The
Committee of the Whole, however, without debate or
dissent voted on motion of Charles Pinckney to eliminate this whole provision. When the Convention had
debated the Committee's report on June 22, King and
Gorham of Massachusetts moved to reconsider the vote
as to ineligibility to State and National offices, as
unnecessary and injurious; Wilson declared himself
as opposed to such disqualifications as "fettering elections and discouraging merit." Mason, however,
regarded it "as a corner stone in the fabric", and cited
the creation by Congress of a multiplicity of foreign
embassies, as an example of the temptation to create
offices later to be filled by members of Congress.
Gorham's motion was defeated. On June 23, the
Convention had decided to strike out the ineligibility
of members of the House of Representatives to State
offices, Charles Pinckney and Sherman arguing the
needlessness of such a fetter on the National Legislature.
Madison attempted, unsuccessfully, to get the ineligibility to National office limited to "such offices only
as should be established or the emoluments thereof

---

[1] See speech of Gerry, August 14, 1787, who said that this Resolve of the Massachusetts Legislature had been repealed after the Congress of the Confederation had
on February 21, 1787, recommended to the States to send delegates to the Convention, since "the State thought it proper to comply in an unqualified manner. The
sense of the State, however, was still the same."

augmented by the Legislature of the United States during the time of their being members." Rutledge of South Carolina, Mason, Sherman, and Gerry had argued that the Legislature must be preserved "as pure as possible by shutting the door against appointments of its own members to offices, which was one source of its corruption." Wilson, on the other hand, concurred with Madison, and said that the "proper cure for corruption in the Legislature was to take from it the power of appointing to office." (It will be recalled that, at this time, power of appointment to offices was vested in the State Legislatures under many of the State Constitutions; and that Randolph's Plan for the new National Constitution contemplated appointment of the Judges by the National Legislature). Madison and Wilson also argued strongly that it was "impolitic to add fresh objections to the Legislative service" by such absolute disqualification of its members, and thus to discourage the best citizens from engaging in the public service. A compromise between Madison's views and Sherman's had been arrived at, by which the ineligibility to National office was retained during the term for which they were elected, but the extension to one year thereafter was stricken out. It is to be noted that the Convention had refused to take this same action as to the Senate; and on June 26, it had voted to make members of that body ineligible to appointment to office during their terms, and also for one year thereafter. These provisions had been left intact in the Report of the Committee of Detail of August 6; but they met with long and emphatic opposition when they were again discussed, on August 14. Charles Pinckney argued that the proposal was degrading to the members of the Legislature, and would be found inconvenient and impolitic in practice, "because the Legislature would cease to be a magnet to the first talents and abilities." He moved as a substitute that acceptance of an office should merely vacate the seat of a member. G. Morris and Wilson concurred, the latter stating, that "nothing seemed to be wanting to prostrate the National Legislature but to render its members ineligible to National offices, and by that means take away its power of attracting those talents which were necessary to give weight to the Government and to render it useful to the people." On the other hand, Randolph, Mason, Sherman, Ellsworth, Gerry, John F. Mercer of Maryland, and Williamson were hotly opposed to changing this provision and especially to allowing members of the Senate to be appointed to office. They argued that most of the corrupt measures in the State Legislatures were traceable to office hunting, and Mercer asked: "What led to the appointment of this Convention? The corruption and mutability of the Legislative Councils of the States."

It was evident that the delegates by a large majority were opposed to allowing members of Congress to be eligible to appointment to office. Foreseeing defeat, the South Carolina members suggested postponing the whole subject until the Convention should finally determine the powers of the Senate, "when it would be more easy to judge of the expediency of allowing officers of State to be chosen out of that body." On September 1, the Special Committee on postponed matters reported, through Judge Brearley, a slight compromise in the following form:

"The members of each House shall be ineligible to any civil office under the authority of the United States during the time for which they shall respectively be elected, and no person holding an office under the United States shall be a member of either House during his continuance in office."

This only changed the previous proposal by eliminating the ineligibility of Senators for one year after their term of office. When this was taken up, on September 3, Charles Pinckney moved as a substitute the following:

"The members of each House shall be incapable of holding any office under the United States for which they or any other for their benefit, receive any salary, fees or emoluments of any kind, and the acceptance of such office shall vacate their seats respectively."

This was practically the provision contained in the Articles of Confederation. He said that he was "opposed to an ineligibility of members to office and therefore wished to restrain the proposition to a mere incompatibility." His proposal received little support. Mason said that ineligibility would keep out corruption "by excluding office hunters." Sherman stated that he was "for entirely incapacitating members of the Legislature. He thought their eligibility to offices would give too much influence to the Executive." Gerry thought that "the eligibility of members would have the effect of opening batteries against good officers, in order to drive them out and make way for members of the Legislature." Gorham, on the other hand, said that: "The experience of the State Governments, where there was no such ineligibility, proved that it was not necessary; on the contrary, that the eligibility was among the inducements for fit men to enter into the Legislative service." Abraham Baldwin of Georgia replied that: "The example of the States was not applicable. The Legislatures there are so numerous that an exclusion of their members would not leave proper men for offices. The case would be otherwise in the General Government." Finally, when matters appeared to have reached a perfect impasse, a compromise suggestion made by Rufus King, taken up and elaborated by Hugh Williamson, and embodying the precise motion which Madison had made as early as June 23, was adopted by the Convention as its final action on this much disputed question, as follows:

"The members of each House shall be ineligible to any civil office under the authority of the United States, created, or the emoluments whereof shall have been increased during the time for which they shall respectively be elected — and no person holding any office under the United States shall be a member of either House during his continuance in office."

The adoption of this motion by five States to four, was brought about by a division of the delegates from Georgia, Connecticut, New Jersey, Maryland, and South Carolina maintaining their opposition to the end.

The great importance which was attached to the ineligibility of members of Congress to be appointed to office under the National Government was due, in part, as pointed out above, to the resentment of the delegates towards some of the appointments which had been made by the Congress under the Confederation; but it was chiefly due to the fear lest the President should combine with the Congress in corrupt bargains as to his appointments. When the Convention finally decided that the President should be chosen by electors and not by Congress itself, the grounds for this fear were lessened, but not entirely removed. The views, however, of the strong minority are of interest, as expressed by Martin in his letter to the Maryland Legislature:[1]

"It was said — and in my opinion justly — that no good reason could be assigned why a Senator or Representative should be incapacitated to hold office in his own Government,

[1] *Elliot's Debates*, I, 366.

since it can bind him only more closely to his State and attach him the more to its interests, which, as its Representative, he is bound to consult and sacredly guard as far as it is consistent with the welfare of the Union. . . . But we sacredly endeavoured to preserve all that part of the Resolution which prevented them from being eligible to offices under the United States, as we considered it essentially necessary to preserve the integrity, independence and dignity of the Legislature, and to secure its members from corruption. . . . As the system is now reported, the President having the power to nominate to all offices, it must be evident that there is no possible security for the integrity and independence of the Legislature, but that they are most unduly placed under the influence of the President and exposed to bribery and corruption. . . . That vacating the seat of the person who was appointed to office made way for the admission of a new Member, who would come there as desirous to obtain office as he whom he succeeded, and as ready to pay the price necessary to obtain it; in fine, that it would be only driving away the flies that were filled to make room for those that were hungry. . . . As to the exception that they cannot be appointed to offices created by themselves or the emoluments of which are by themselves increased, it is certainly of little consequence since they may easily evade it by creating new offices to which may be appointed the persons who fill the offices before created, and thereby vacancies will be made, which may be filled by the members who for that purpose have created the new offices."

OUT OF CONVENTION

It is interesting to note that though Washington had displayed no interest in the experimental trip of the steamboat, ten days before, he now paid considerable attention to the invention of a new machine called a mangle:

"In Convention.   Visited a Machine at Doctr. Franklin's (called a Mangle) for pressing, in place of ironing, clothes as from the wash.   Which Machine from the facility with which it despatches business is well calculated for table cloths and such articles as have not pleats and irregular foldings and would be very useful in all large families. Dined, drank tea and spent the evening at Mr. Morris's."

A striking letter on the subject of a Federal Government was written, this day, to John Adams in London by Richard Henry Lee (then attending Congress in New York as a Member from Virginia) — of interest in view of Lee's opposition to the Constitution as finally drafted:

"The present Federal system, however well calculated it might have been for its designed ends, if the States had done their duty, under the almost total neglect of that duty has been found quite inefficient and ineffectual. The Government must be both Legislative and Executive, with the former power paramount to the State Legislatures, in certain respects essential to Federal purposes. I think there is no doubt but that this Legislature will be recommended, to consist of the triple balance, if I may use the expression, to signify a compound of the three simple forms acting independently, but forming a joint determination. The Executive (which will be part of the Legislative) to have more duration, and power enlarged beyond the present. This seems to be the plan expected, and generally spoken of. I say expected, because the Convention is yet sitting, and will continue to do so until the middle of this month. I was appointed to that Assembly, but being a Member of Congress, where the plan of Convention must be approved, there appeared an inconsistency for members of the former to have session in the latter, and so pass judgment at New York upon their opinion at Philadelphia. I, therefore, declined going to the Convention."

CHAPTER ELEVEN

THE PRESIDENT AND VICE PRESIDENT

TUESDAY, SEPTEMBER 4, 1787

IN CONVENTION

Report of Committee on Election of President

This day was made memorable by the presentation of a Report by Judge Brearley's Committee on postponed matters, which finally solved the difficult and long-contested question of the method of election of the President. As great credit is due to this Committee for this remarkable achievement as was awarded to the Committee which framed the first great compromise, exactly two months prior.[1] The result of its deliber-

---

[1] A glance at the composition of the Committee discloses the reason for its success, consisting as it did of almost the ablest men from each State. King of Massachusetts, Sherman of Connecticut, Brearley of New Jersey, G. Morris of Pennsylvania, Dickinson of Delaware, Carroll of Maryland, Madison of Virginia, Williamson of North Carolina, Butler of South Carolina, Baldwin of Georgia, and Gilman of New Hampshire.

ations was in the nature of a compromise between those who favored increased power in the Executive and those who favored the Senate. It provided for a President with a term of four years, but with no restriction as to eligibility to re-election; he was to be appointed by electors, equal in number to the Senators and Representatives from each State and chosen by each State in a mode to be decided by it; the electors to vote by ballot for two persons, one of whom at least should not be an inhabitant of the same State as the electors; these votes were to be sent sealed to the United States Senate which should count them and declare such person as received a majority vote to be elected the President; if two persons should have had an equal number of votes, the Senate was to elect and also if no person should have a majority of the votes the Senate should elect a President from the five highest. The Committee's plan provided for a new official never heretofore suggested in the debates to be termed the Vice President, this office to be filled in every case by the person having the greatest number of votes, after the choice of President. The method of choice by electors was taken from a similar provision in the Maryland Constitution in the choice of Senators. The office of Vice President was suggested by the existence of a similar office in several of the States — Delaware and New Jersey had a Vice President; Massachusetts, Virginia, New York, and South Carolina, a Lieutenant Governor; and as in those States, so here, the Vice President was to be *ex officio* President of the Senate. The qualifications for the President were that he must be a natural born citizen (or a citizen at the time of the adoption of the Constitution), thirty-five years of age and resident fourteen years within the United States. A provision was made for impeachment of the President, and for exercise of his powers

and duties by the Vice President, in case of removal
of the President after conviction on impeachment,
death, absence, resignation, or inability to discharge
the powers or duties of his office. The President was
vested with powers of appointment (including appointments of Judges and Ambassadors which hitherto had
been reserved to the Senate by the Convention) ; but,
as a compensation to the Senate, its advice and consent
had to be obtained to all appointments made by the
President. The treaty-making power was taken away
from the Senate, and was vested in the President in
concurrence with two thirds of the members present
of the Senate; and the power of the Senate was
increased, by vesting it with power to try impeachments — a power theretofore given by the Convention
to the Supreme Court. The chief thing of importance
to note in this Report is that it appealed to the small
States by the increased power it gave to the Senate,
through its possible final choice of the President;
while it appealed to the large States, by giving to them,
by virtue of their larger representation in the body of
electors, a greater influence in naming the five candidates from whom the Senate must eventually choose.

As soon as this Report was rendered, the Convention
took up the portion of it relating to election of the
President. It is not known who was its author, but
G. Morris announced the reasons impelling the Committee. "Nobody had appeared to be satisfied with
an appointment by the Legislature," he said, because
of "the danger of intrigue and faction" and "the
opportunity for cabal" ; all were agreed on the "indispensable necessity of making the Executive independent." There seemed to be no great opposition to the
new compromise, except to that part which placed the
eventual power of election in the Senate. Wilson,
Charles Pinckney, Williamson, Randolph, and Mason

thought this to be dangerous. The chance that any person would receive a majority of electoral votes was considered slight. Mason believed that it would be left to the Senate to choose, nineteen times in twenty; though Baldwin suggested, very wisely, that "the increasing intercourse among the people of the States would render important characters less and less unknown and the Senate would consequently be less and less likely to have the eventual appointment thrown into their hands." The Committee's Report, however, was too important to be acted on in one day, and further consideration was postponed, "that each member might take a copy of the remainder of it."

OUT OF CONVENTION

Madison wrote to James Madison, Sr., this day: that "the Convention has not yet broken up, but its session will probably continue but a short time longer. Its proceedings are still under the injunction of secrecy. . . . As soon as the tie of secrecy is dissolved, I will forward the proceedings of the Convention."

WEDNESDAY, SEPTEMBER 5, 1787

IN CONVENTION

Power of Congress over the District of Columbia, and over Patents and Copyrights

The power of Congress to legislate for the District of Columbia was inserted in the Constitution on this day, in accordance with a Report of Judge Brearley's Committee on postponed matters. It had originated in a suggestion submitted by Madison on August 18, that Congress be given various additional powers, among them:

"To exercise exclusively Legislative authority at the seat of the General Government, and over a district around the same, not exceeding   square miles; the consent of the

Legislature of the State or States comprizing the same, being first obtained."

This was referred to the Committee of Detail; but that Committee did not act upon it. Brearley's Committee, on September 5, redrafted it in the following form:

"To exercise exclusive legislation in all cases whatsoever over such district (not exceeding ten miles square) as may by cession of particular States and the acceptance of the Legislature become the seat of the Government of the United States, and to exercise like authority over all places purchased for the erection of forts, magazines, arsenals, dockyards, and other needful buildings."

When the Convention took this up, fear of extension of the National authority was again displayed over the latter part of the proposed power; and Gerry contended that it "might be made use of to enslave any particular State by buying up its territory, and that the strongholds proposed would be a means of awing the States into an undue obedience to the General Government." Accordingly, to allay the fears of the States at absorption of their territory, Gerry's colleague, King, proposed that, after the words "over all places purchased", there be inserted the words "by the consent of the Legislature of the States." G. Morris seconded this motion; and the Convention agreed to the power, with this amendment.

Another additional power, originally proposed both by Madison and Pinckney on August 18, was adopted on this September 5, in the form drafted by Judge Brearley's Committee, as follows: "To promote the progress of science and useful arts by securing for limited times to authors and inventors, the exclusive right to their respective writings and discoveries." [1]

---

[1] Madison's draft was: "to secure to literary authors their copyright for a limited time"; and "to encourage by premiums and provisions, the advancement

OUT OF CONVENTION

Washington noted :

" Dined at Mrs. House's and drank tea at Mr. Bingham's."

On this day, the Pennsylvania State Assembly, which had adjourned in the preceding March, met in the State house and, owing to the occupancy of its regular room by the Federal Convention, adjourned (according to its official Minutes) to meet in a "chamber above stairs." [1]

Jacob Hiltzheimer, a member of the Assembly, wrote in his diary :

"Took a ride with the Hon. Mr. Langdon in his phaeton. In the afternoon met the Assembly at the State House in the lower room, and adjourned to meet tomorrow at half past nine o'clock in the upper room, leaving the lower room as before to the gentlemen of the Convention."

These entries as to adjournment present an historical mystery. For, on July 13, Dr. Manasseh Cutler, on his visit to Philadelphia, had found the Federal Con-

of useful knowledge and discoveries." Charles Pinckney proposed the following additional powers: "to grant patents for useful inventions" and "to secure to authors exclusive rights for a certain time."

[1] It is recorded in the Minutes of the Assembly as follows: "Mr. Speaker informed the House, that the Honorable Convention of the United States, during the recess of the House, had met in the room appropriated to the use of the General Assembly, and that the session of the Convention would probably not be closed before the end of next week, and requested to know what order the House would be pleased to take on the subject. Thereupon, resolved that this House do adjourn to meet in the chamber above stairs tomorrow at half past nine o'clock A.M." In *Constitution of the United States* (1924) by James M. Beck, p. 350, another transcript of this vote is given which varies in phraseology, as follows: "The honorable Mr. Speaker represented to the House, that the room they usually sat in was, at present, occupied by the Federal Convention, whose sitting had been prolonged beyond the time expected — therefore the room above had been fitted up, in order to accommodate either House or the Convention as should be determined most eligible. Whereupon, ordered, that when the House adjourns, it shall be to the room upstairs." In the *Pennsylvania Packet*, Sept. 5, 1787, and in the *Independent Gazetteer*, Sept. 10, 1787, it is stated, under date of Wednesday, September 6, 1787: "The House met and having appointed a Committee to inform the Executive Council that they were ready to receive any communication adjourned till tomorrow morning at half past 9 o'clock." The Assembly convened again on September 6 and 7, and adjourned from September 8 to September 10 at 3 P.M. See *Pennsylvania Packet*, Sept. 13, 1787.

vention then sitting in a room upstairs in the State House and over the hall where the Declaration of Independence was signed. Apparently, at some time after July 13, the Convention must have moved downstairs — but when or why this move occurred cannot be known, for there is no mention of it in any contemporary or later writing. One of the most curious lapses in history is the omission from all official records of any statement as to the particular room or rooms in which the Convention was held.[1]

A Philadelphia despatch of this date to a New York paper, referred to possible sources of opposition to the new Government : [2]

"Every State has its Shays, who, either with their pens or tongues, or offices, are endeavoring to effect what Shays in vain attempted with his sword. In one of the States, this demagogue tries to persuade the people that it is dangerous to increase the powers of Congress; in another, he denies the authority of the Convention to redress our National grievances; in a third he whispers distrust, saying the States will not adopt the new Frame of Government, in a fourth he says the State Constitutions and the officers who act under them are of divine right and can be altered by no human power, and of course considers all attempts to restore order and Government in the United States as a 'laughable' thing; in a fifth, he opposes a general Confederacy and urges the division of the States into three small Confederacies, that he may the more easily place himself at the head of one of these. The

---

[1] The only references in Madison's *Notes of Debates*, as to the place of session were on May 25, when, referring to Franklin, he stated that "the season of the rain did not permit him to venture to the Convention Chamber"; and on Aug. 14, when Dickinson was reported as saying: "If the General Government should be dependent on the State Legislatures, it would be happy for us if we had never met in this Room." See also Cutler's diary, *supra* p. 304; and statement by John T. Watson in his *Annals of Philadelphia in the Olden Times* (1845), I, 402: "The Convention which met to form the Constitution of the United States met upstairs, and at the same time the street pavement along Chestnut St., was covered with earth to silence the rattling of wheels." (Watson made this statement, as he says, on the authority "of an elderly gentleman"; but in the first edition of Watson's book in 1830, this statement from the "elderly gentleman" did not appear.)

[2] *New York Daily Advertiser*, Sept. 8, 1787.

spirit and wickedness of Shays is in each of these principles and measures. Let Americans be wise."

Freeman's Journal published, this day, a letter from Connecticut, dated August 21 : [1]

"The year 1787 may justly be denominated the year of discontents and apprehension. Every man is a politician; and everyone is so sore, either in reality or imagination, that a bystander can scarcely venture to laugh without hurting the feelings of some one honest citizen or another. The conduct of Shays had for a long time been a source of ill humor among the patriotic; our impatience to know what the Grand Convention is about has made us no less snappish to each other for more than two months past; and he must be a Democratus himself who would venture to smile, when the decay of our trade is brought upon the carpet."

THURSDAY, SEPTEMBER 6, 1787

IN CONVENTION

Method of Election of the President

On September 5, Rutledge and Charles Pinckney of South Carolina opposed the Report as to the election of President, fearing that the electors "will not have sufficient knowledge of the fittest men and will be swayed by attachment to the eminent men of their respective States"; and also apprehending that a President chosen by the Senate would be "the mere creature of that body." They also still continued to hold out for a seven year term, with ineligibility to re-election. Mason and Williamson also thought that "referring the appointment to the Senate lays a certain foundation for corruption and aristocracy"; and Randolph thought that the influence of the Senate in the election of President would, in addition to its other powers, "convert that body into a real and dangerous

---

[1] Reprinted in *Independent Gazetteer* and *Pennsylvania Herald*, Sept. 8, 1787.

aristocracy." G. Morris thought that this point was being overstressed, and that it was probable that a majority of the electors would unite on the same man, so that the election would not be thrown into the Senate. Madison agreed with him that there would be a "concerted effort of the large States to make the appointment in the first instance conclusive." Wilson and Dickinson moved for final election by the whole Congress instead of by the Senate, in case a majority of the electors failed to choose a President; but their motion was defeated. The debate continued on this September 6. Wilson announced his agreement with Randolph that, if the Senate was to have power to try impeachments and share in making treaties and appointments as well as power to elect a President, it might be "dangerous, in its tendency to aristocracy." According to the plan as it now stands, he said, "the President will not be the man of the people as he ought to be, but the minion of the Senate." Clymer and Williamson agreed with him. Hamilton now stepped forward and announced the statesmanlike position which he had determined to adopt. He stated that he did not "agree with those persons who say they will vote against the Report, because they cannot get all parts of it to please them", and that he would take "any system which promises to save America from the dangers with which she is threatened." [1] The Convention was now ready to come to a final disposition of this question. It first settled the much debated point as to the length of the President's term of office. It will be recalled that the seven year term had been fixed, only when coupled with a provision for no re-election. Hence, though the Committee's Report contained no reference whatever to eligibility to re-election, an attempt was now made to fix the term at seven years. This was

[1] As reported in McHenry's *Notes*.

defeated, as was a motion for six years; and the four year term suggested by the Committee was accepted. The provision for an eventual election by the Senate, in case of failure of choice by the electors was also accepted. Roger Sherman of Connecticut then made an ingenious compromise suggestion which seemed to conciliate those who feared the Senate — namely, that the eventual election be by the House of Representatives, each State to have one vote. This suggestion preserved the influence of the small States, but removed the objection that the same body which was to try impeachments and confirm appointments ought not to share in the election. This motion was carried, with only one State dissenting (Delaware).[1] And so there came to an end the long and hardest fought battle of the whole Convention.[2] It is to be noted that the delegates evidently thought that the electorate would seldom choose, and that normally the election would be made by the House. Though the problem of the mode of choice of President was the most difficult of solution of any of the tasks before the Convention, it was, as Hamilton said in *The Federalist* (No. 78), "almost the only part of the system, of any consequence, which . . . escaped without severe censure"; and Richard Henry Lee, the most ardent opponent of the Constitution, wrote in his *Letters of a Federal Farmer* that "the election of both Vice President and President seems to be properly secured." This method of electing the President, however, remained in operation less than

---

[1] A slight addition was made on motion of Gerry on September 7, 1787, to the effect that if the election went into the House, a quorum should consist of a member or members from two thirds of the States and that a concurrence of a majority of all the States should be necessary to make choice of a President.

[2] Madison wrote to George Hay, Aug. 23, 1823: "The difficulty of finding an unexceptionable process for appointing the Executive Organ of a Government such as that of the United States was deeply felt by the Convention; and as the final arrangement of it took place in the latter stage of the Session, it was not exempt from a degree of the hurrying influence produced by fatigue and impatience in all such bodies; tho' the degree was much less than usually prevails in them."

twenty years. The famous tie vote in the House of Representatives in 1800–1801, which so long made impossible any choice between Burr and Jefferson, brought about the Twelfth Amendment in 1804. Under this Amendment, briefly stated, the electors were to cast their votes for a specific person as President and for another specific person as Vice President; and if no person received a majority of votes for President, the House chose the President from the three highest on the list of those voted for by the electors for President; and in case no person had a majority for Vice President, the Senate chose from the two having the highest number of votes; and if by any chance the House failed to choose a President by the fourth of March, then the Vice President "shall act as President as in the case of death or other constitutional disability of the President."

OUT OF CONVENTION

Washington noted:

"In Convention. Dined at Doctr. James Hutchinson's and spent the afternoon and evening at home, Mr. Morris's."

Jacob Hiltzheimer wrote in his diary:

"Forenoon, met the Assembly at State House in the upper room. In the afternoon, went with the Hon. Mr. Langdon and Hon. Mr. Sherman down to the banks of the Schuylkill; had a drink of punch, and then took a small round, home."

The *Packet* said that: "We hear that the Convention propose to adjourn next week after laying America under such obligations to them for their long, painful and disinterested labours, to establish her liberty upon a permanent basis, as no time will ever cancel." And it published a letter saying:

"The year 1776 is celebrated, says a correspondent, for a revolution in favour of liberty. The year 1787, it is expected will be celebrated with equal joy for a revolution in favour of Government. The impatience with which all classes of people wait to receive the new Federal Constitution can only be equalled by their zealous determination to support it."

On this day, Madison wrote to Jefferson, a summary of the plan thus far adopted :

"As the Convention will shortly rise, I should feel little scruple in disclosing what will be public here, before it could reach you, were it practicable for me to guard by cypher against an intermediate discovery. But I am deprived of this resource by the shortness of the interval between the receipt of your letter of June 20, and the date of this. This is the first day which has been free from Committee service, both before and after the hours of the House, and the last that is allowed me by the time advertised for the sailing of the packet. The Convention consists now as it has generally done of eleven States. There has been no intermission of its session since a House was formed; except an interval of about ten days allowed a Committee appointed to detail the general propositions agreed on in the House. The term of its dissolution cannot be more than one or two weeks distant. A Government will probably be submitted to the people of the States, consisting of a President cloathed with Executive power; a Senate chosen by the Legislatures, and another House chosen by the people of the States, jointly possessing the Legislative power; and a regular Judiciary establishment. The mode of constituting the Executive is among the few points not yet finally settled. . . . These are the outlines. The extent of them may perhaps surprize you. I hazard an opinion nevertheless that the plan, should it be adopted, will neither effectually answer its National object, nor prevent the local mischiefs which everywhere excite disgusts against the State Governments. The grounds of this opinion will be the subject of a future letter. . . . Nothing can exceed the universal anxiety for the event of the meeting here. Reports and conjectures abound concerning the nature of the plan which is to be proposed. The public however is certainly in the dark with regard to it. The Convention is equally in the dark as to the reception which may be given to it on its publication. All the prepossessions are on the right side, but it may well be expected that certain characters will wage war against any reform whatever. My own idea is that the public mind will now or in a very little time receive anything that promises stability to the public councils and security to private rights, and that no regard ought to be had to local prejudices or temporary considerations. If the present moment be lost, it is hard to say what may be our fate. . . . Mr. Wythe has never returned to us. His lady whose illness carried him away, died some time after he got home."

FRIDAY, SEPTEMBER 7, 1787

IN CONVENTION

The Vice President

As before noted, the office of a Vice President who should be ex-officio President of the Senate was an entirely new proposal, when provided for in the Report of the Committee of September 4. No hint as to the necessity or desirability of such an officer had been previously made in the Convention. The necessity of providing for a Vice President seems to have arisen from two sources. First, there must be some way of disposing of that one of the two candidates for whom the electors were required to vote, and who should receive the second largest vote; second, there must be some impartial person to preside over the Senate, without taking a member of that body and thus depriving a State of its two votes, thereby reducing its equality. The latter reason was interestingly set forth by William R. Davie in the North Carolina State Convention, in 1788: "It was in the Senate that the several political interests of the States were to be preserved and where all their powers were to be perfectly balanced. The commercial jealousy between the Eastern and Southern

States had a principal share in this business. It might happen in important cases that the voices would be equally divided. . . . It would then be necessary to have some person who should determine the question as impartially as possible. . . . From the nature of his election and office, he represents no one State in particular, but all the States . . . the officer and representative of the Union. . . . These, I believe, are the principles upon which the Convention formed this officer." [1]

When the Vice President was debated in the Convention, on this day, little enthusiasm was expressed for such an officer. Randolph was opposed to the provision. Mason "thought the office of Vice President an encroachment on the rights of the Senate and that it mixed too much the Legislative and Executive which . . . ought to be kept as separate as possible." [2] Gerry was "against having any Vice President"; and he thought that a Vice President as head of the Senate would be practically equivalent to putting the President himself there, owing to "the close intimacy that must subsist between the President and Vice President." As to the suggested danger from this "close intimacy", G. Morris made the sage reply (highly prophetic of the future course of our history) that "the Vice President then will be the first heir apparent that ever loved his father." Sherman also stated that he saw no danger in a Vice President acting as head of the Senate, and unless this officer should so act, then a member of the

---

[1] *Elliot's Debates*, IV, 42–43.

[2] Mason, in the Virginia State Convention, said: "The Vice President appears to me to be not only an unnecessary, but a dangerous officer. He is, contrary to the usual course of parliamentary proceedings, to be President of the Senate;" and both Mason and Monroe objected to the Vice President's having a casting vote in case of a tie, since this would give to the State from which he came three votes instead of two, in the Senate. There was similar opposition to the Vice President's sharing in the legislative power, in the North Carolina State Convention. *Elliot's Debates*, III, IV.

Senate must be chosen, which would deprive him of his vote (except in case of an equal division.) It is to be noted that the whole discussion on the subject of the Vice President centred on his status as a Legislative officer.[1] There being no further debate, the Convention adopted the Committee's proposal, Massachusetts alone voting in the negative.

It is singular that there was no discussion as to the chief part which the Vice President has, in fact, played in history, that is, to his succession in case of the death of the President. It would seem, however, that the delegates probably contemplated that, in such case, the Vice President would only perform the duties of President until a new election for President should be held; and that he would not *ipso facto* become President. The Special Committee in its Report of September 4 provided:

"In case of his [the President's] removal as aforesaid, death, absence, resignation or inability to discharge the powers or duties of his office, the Vice President shall exercise those powers and duties until another President be chosen, or until the inability of the President be removed."

The Report of the Committee of Detail of August 6 had contained the same provision, except that the

---

[1] In view of the experiment made by President Harding, in inviting Vice President Coolidge to sit in the Cabinet meetings, it is interesting to note Jefferson's views on this subject. Writing to Madison, Jan. 22, 1797, he said: "My letters inform me that Mr. Adams speaks of me with great friendship, and with satisfaction in the prospect of administering the Government in concurrence with me. . . . As to participating in the administration, if by that he meant the Executive Cabinet, both duty and inclination will shut that door to me. . . . As to duty, the Constitution will know me only as the member of a Legislative body; and its principle is, that of a separation of Legislative, Executive and Judiciary functions, except in cases specified. If this principle be not expressed in direct terms, yet it is clearly the spirit of the Constitution, and it ought to be so commented and acted on by every friend to free government." And writing to E. Gerry, May 3, 1797, he said: "Those who endeavor to separate us are probably excited by the fear that I might have influence on the Executive councils; but when they shall know that I consider my office as constitutionally confined to Legislative functions, and I could not take any part whatever in Executive consultations even were it proposed, their fears may perhaps subside."

President of the Senate was to be the successor. When that Report had been debated on August 27, Dickinson remarked that it was "too vague", and he asked: "What is the extent of the term 'disability', and who is to be the judge of it?" This was a very pertinent inquiry, and the failure of the Convention to answer it by express provision may well produce complications, as was seen at the time of President Wilson's illness and apparent incapacity to act, in 1919. One other defect in the Report of the Special Committee was pointed out by McHenry (who was a member of the Committee) in his *Notes*, as follows: "No provision in the above for a new election in case of the death or removal of the President." [1] In the Report of the Committee of Style, the phraseology of the Special Committee's Report was changed as follows:

"In case of the removal of the President from office, or of his death, resignation, or inability to discharge the powers and duties of the said office, the same shall devolve on the Vice President. . . ."

The ambiguity of the language raised the doubt whether it was the "said office", or the "powers and duties" which were to "devolve" on the Vice President.[2] And

---

[1] George Mason, in the Virginia State Convention, pointed out as one of the defects in the Constitution: "There is no provision for a speedy election of another President, when the former is dead or removed." *Elliot's Debates*, III, 487.

The Report of the Committee of Detail of August 6 had contained a provision as to the President, as follows: "In case of his removal as aforesaid, death, resignation, or disability to discharge the powers and duties of his office, the President of the Senate shall exercise those powers and duties, until another President of the United States be chosen; or until the disability of the President be removed." When this was debated, on August 27, G. Morris objected to the President of the Senate as a successor, and suggested the Chief Justice. (Note that Ellsworth, Aug. 18, made first reference to a Chief Justice.) Madison suggested that "the Executive powers during a vacancy be administered by the persons composing the Council to the President." Williamson suggested "that the Legislature ought to have power to provide for occasional successors," and he moved to postpone the whole subject. Dickinson seconded the motion, remarking that the provision was "too vague" and that no definition was given of "disability."

[2] On the death of President William Henry Harrison, April 4, 1841, the Vice President, John Tyler, took the oath "to faithfully execute the office of President of the United States." William Cranch, Chief Justice of the Circuit Court of the

since no express provision was made by the Convention, the question first arose on the death of President Harrison, in 1841 : What was the Vice President after the death of the President? Was he merely acting President, or did he become President in fact and in law? The former was probably the intention of the delegates; the latter has been established in practice (by Tyler, Fillmore, Johnson, Arthur, Roosevelt, and Coolidge). It is clear that in at least one case, the delegates contemplated the possibility of a special election for President, *i.e.*, in the event of the death of both President and Vice President. To provide for this contingency, Randolph moved, on September 7, that:

"The Legislature may declare by law what officer of the United States shall act as President in case of the death, resignation, or disability of the President and Vice President; and such officer shall act accordingly until the time of electing a President shall arrive."

Madison then "observed that this, as worded, would prevent a supply of the vacancy by an intermediate election of the President", thus clearly expressing his

District of Columbia, administered the oath and made the following interesting certificate as to Tyler's view: "I . . . certify that the above named John Tyler personally appeared before me this day, and although he deems himself qualified to perform the duties and exercise the powers and office of President on the death of William Henry Harrison, late President of the United States, without any other oath than that which he has taken as Vice President, yet, as doubts may arise, and for greater caution, took and subscribed the foregoing oath before me." It would appear from this statement by Tyler that he, at first, took the position that he did not become President, but remained only Vice President acting as President. But he very soon changed his view, and assumed the right to act as President.

It is to be noted that when the 12th Amendment was adopted, its framers interpreted the Constitution as meaning that the Vice President should only *act* as President in case of the latter's death, for that Amendment provided that if the House should not choose a President before the 4th of March, "then the Vice President shall act as President *as in the case of the death or other Constitutional disability of the President.*"

It would seem to be clear that in the case of a "disability" of the President, which "disability" might later be removed, the Vice President, while acting in the interim and until the President re-assumed his functions, would not become President. The Constitution does not by its language differentiate the position of the Vice President, when acting by reason of death from his position when acting by reason of disability.

belief that when both President and Vice President were dead, there might or should be an election of President prior to the date when "the time of electing a President shall arrive." G. Morris agreed with him, and on their motion, the Randolph proposal was amended, so as to read, "until such disability be removed, or a President shall be elected." As so amended, it was agreed to, though Madison notes that "it seemed to be an objection with some that according to the process established for chusing the Executive, there would be difficulty in effecting it at other than the fixed periods." It is to be noted that the Committee of Style, in its Report of September 12, ignored this vote and restored Randolph's original proposal, as follows:

"And the Congress may by law provide for the case of removal, death, resignation or inability, both of the President and Vice President, declaring what officer shall then act as a President, and such officer shall act accordingly, until the disability be removed, or the period of chusing another President arrive."

On September 15, the Convention voted to restore the wording of the vote of September 7, and to change the words "or the period of chusing another President arrive" into "or a President shall be elected." This pointed change and reversal of the Committee of Style's action clearly denote the intention of the delegates that there might be a special election of President in the contingency provided for; and Madison so stated, in the Virginia State Convention.[1]

[1] *Elliot's Debates*, III, 487: "When the President and Vice President die, the election of another President will immediately take place."

In accordance with this view, Congress, by the Act of March 11, 1792, provided that if the offices of both President and Vice President should become vacant, the Secretary of State should notify the Executives of all the States and issue a call for appointment of electors within thirty-four days preceding the first Wednesday of December ensuing, providing that two months should elapse between the latter day and the date of the call, and if two months should not elapse then the election to be held in the next December.

Qualifications of the President

Neither Randolph in his original Resolutions of May 29, nor the Committee of Detail in its Report of August 6, made any provision as to age or residential qualifications of the President. Rutledge for the Committee proposed, on August 22, that the President "shall be of the age of thirty-five years, and a citizen of the United States and shall have been an inhabitant thereof for twenty-one years." The Special Committee's Report of September 4, provided that:

"No person except a natural born citizen or a citizen of the United States at the time of the adoption of this Constitution shall be eligible to the office of President; nor shall any person be elected to that office, who shall be under the age of thirty-five years, and who has not been in the whole, at least fourteen years a resident within the United States."

It will be noted that the provision for residence cut down the requirement from twenty-one to fourteen years "in the whole." Apparently, the period of fourteen years was taken from Gouverneur Morris' suggestion (on August 9) of that period for citizenship of Senators, by reason of "the danger of admitting strangers into our public councils" — the object being to require citizenship in this country prior to the Revolution. The Committee of Style, in its Report of September 12, omitted the words "in the whole" and thereby produced a doubt as to whether a change of meaning was intended, and as to whether the fourteen years were to be consecutive, prior to election:

"Neither shall any person be eligible to that office who shall not have attained to the age of thirty-five years, and been fourteen years a resident within the United States."

President's Power of Appointment

Having settled the method of election, term of office, and qualifications of the President and of the Vice

President, the Convention was now ready to consider the increased authority which the Committee had recommended to be vested in the President — and first the power to appoint Ambassadors and other Public Ministers, and Judges of the Supreme Court. Randolph's original Resolutions of May 29 had given to the Executive no power to appoint officers, but such a power had been voted by the Committee of the Whole on June 1. Randolph's Resolutions had given to the National Legislature the appointment of Judges, following the practice of the State Constitutions under which the State Legislatures appointed the Judges, except in New Hampshire, Massachusetts, and New York. When the Committee of the Whole had considered this provision on June 5, both Wilson and Madison opposed choice of Judges by the Legislature, saying that there was danger of intrigue and partiality in so numerous a body, and that it would not be capable of passing upon the requisite qualifications. On June 13, Madison had proposed appointment by the Senate as being a "less numerous and more select body"; and this had been agreed to. Paterson, in his New Jersey Plan of June 15, had proposed appointment of the Federal Judiciary by the Executive. When the Convention had debated the question on July 18, Wilson and G. Morris had moved appointment by the Executive alone, while Gorham, Madison, and Randolph favored appointment by the Executive with the advice and consent of the Senate. Both motions had been defeated. On July 31, discussion had been resumed, when Madison proposed appointment by the Executive unless two thirds of the Senate should disagree; he had formerly proposed appointment by the Senate, he said, but that was at a stage when the Senate was to be elected by the people and not as now (under the compromise) by the State Legislatures equally from each State. Now if

the Senate alone had the power, a minority of the
people, though a majority of the States, might appoint
the Judges — an unjustifiable proceeding, since the
actions of the Judiciary were "to relate to the people
rather than to the States", and also "the appointments
would be thrown entirely into the hands of the Northern States", and "a perpetual ground of jealousy and
discontent would be furnished to the Southern States."
G. Morris supported Madison; but Gerry and Mason
opposed any appointment by the Executive as "a dangerous prerogative. It might even give him an influence over the Judiciary Department itself." The Convention had voted against the proposal and retained
the Senate as the appointing power for the Judges.

When the Committee of Detail reported, on August
6, it gave to the President the power to "appoint
officers in all cases not otherwise provided for by this
Constitution"; and to the Senate, it gave the appointment not only of Judges of the Supreme Court, but also
of Ambassadors. This power had been again opposed
by G. Morris (on August 23) on the ground that the
Senate was too numerous for the purpose, and subject
to cabal — also that as the Senate was to try impeachments of Judges of the Supreme Court, it ought not also
to fill the vacancies "which its own decrees were to
create." So the matter stood when the Special Committee made its report, on September 4, proposing to
vest the President with two new powers — to make
treaties and "to appoint Ambassadors and other
Public Ministers, Judges of the Supreme Court and all
other officers of the United States, whose appointments
are not otherwise herein provided for." This proposal
took away from the Senate its exclusive power to
appoint such Judges and Ambassadors; but, as a compensation, it required the advice and consent of the
Senate to the appointment not only of these officers

but of all other officers (theretofore to be appointed solely by the Executive). As the proposed change undoubtedly increased the power of the Senate, it aroused much antagonism, when considered by the Convention on September 6 and 7, both from those who feared enhanced importance of the Senate, and from those who opposed any blend of the Executive and the Legislative branches. Wilson contended that it was a dangerous step towards aristocracy, destroying the independence of the Executive. "The President will not be the man of the people as he ought to be, but the minion of the Senate", and he stated that the Senate, possessing this triple power to make treaties, to try impeachments, and to concur in appointments, and acting thus as a combined Legislative, Judiciary, and Executive, would "depress the other branch of the Legislature and aggrandize themselves in proportion." This fear, in which Charles Pinckney and Gerry concurred, was somewhat accurately prophetic of the subsequent development of the Senate's position. The Committee's proposal, however, was adopted; and so power was vested in the President, in concurrence with the Senate, to appoint all officers of the United States, "whose appointments are not otherwise provided for", in the Constitution. This phraseology was still open to the objection that the President was left free to create officers not provided for by Congress. The objection had been obviated by votes adopted by the Convention on August 24; and it was again obviated on the last working day of the Convention, September 15, by adding after "not otherwise provided for", the words "and which shall be established by law"; and also by adding thereafter, "but the Congress may by law vest the appointment of such inferior officers as they think proper in the President alone, in the Courts of law, or in the heads of Departments."

A most singular failure on the part of the Convention was the omission to make any express provision relative to the power of the President to make removals from office. Although the removal power was the subject of intensive debate in the first session of the First Congress in 1789, and frequently in subsequent Congresses, no definitive decision that this power inhered in the President as the Executive was ever made until the Supreme Court so held in the year 1926.[1]

President's Cabinet

On this September 7, the Convention voted the following additional power to the President, as proposed by the Special Committee in its Report of September 4:

"may require the opinion in writing of the principal officer in each of the Executive Departments, upon any subject relating to the duties of their respective offices."

It is from this clause that the institution known as the President's Cabinet has developed, though the Constitution itself makes no provision for such an institution or for those functionings known as Cabinet meetings, and the word "Cabinet" was never used by anyone in the debates in the Convention.[2] In fact, the clause, unexplained, seems to have little meaning or importance. Its explanation is: that it is the bare remnant of the much advocated proposal to provide a Council for the Executive. Its history in the making of the Constitution is as follows. In Colonial days, the charter of each Royal Province or Colony provided for a Council, whose members were usually appointed by the Assembly, subject to the veto of the Royal Gov-

---

[1] *Myers* v. *United States* (1926), 272 U. S. 52.

[2] See *The President's Cabinet* (1912), by H. Barrett Learned; *The President's Cabinet*, by John A. Fairlie, *Amer. Pol. Sci. Rev.* (1913), VII. The first use of the words "Cabinet" was by Charles Pinckney, in October, 1787, in his pamphlet *Observations on the Plan of Government*, in which he said: "By this means, our Government will possess, what it has always wanted, but never yet had, a Cabinet Council."

ernor. This Council though intended by the Crown as a check upon the Assembly, frequently became a curb upon the Governor himself, constituting usually a second branch of the Legislature. From this Provincial Council, there were developed the State Senates under the early State Constitutions. Some States, however, in addition to a Senate made provision for a separate Privy Council (usually chosen by the Legislature), to advise the Governor — Delaware, Maryland, Massachusetts, New Hampshire, North Carolina, South Carolina, Georgia, and Virginia.[1] In Pennsylvania, a Council was elected by the people. In New Jersey, the Senate passed on acts of the Executive; and in New York, all appointments by the Executive were to be confirmed by the Senate. Neither Randolph nor Paterson had included in their Plans for a new Government any proposal for such a Council to advise the Executive; nor did either of them make any reference to "Executive Departments." Charles Pinckney, however, in the Plan submitted by him on May 29, had proposed, as one of the "powers and duties" of the President, that "he shall have a right to advise with the heads of the different Departments as his Council." Pinckney also proposed that Congress "shall institute offices and appoint officers for the Departments of Foreign Affairs, War, Treasury, and Admiralty"; and he proposed a "Council of Revision consisting of the President, Secretary for Foreign Affairs, Secretary of War, Heads of the Departments of Treasury and Admiralty, or any two of them together with the President." In the Convention's proceedings, the earliest suggestion of a Council had been made by Gerry, during the first debate over the Executive, on June 1,

---

[1] The North Carolina Constitution provided for a "Council of State who shall advise the Governor in the execution of his office"; the Virginia Constitution provided for a "Privy Council to assist in the administration of government."

when he "favored the policy of annexing a Council to the Executive in order to give weight and inspire confidence." On June 4, Sherman of Connecticut remarked that in all the States there was "a Council of advice, without which the first Magistrate could not act", and he thought it necessary "in order to attract the confidence of the people." Wilson, on the other hand, said that a Council "oftener serves to cover, more than prevent, malpractices." Franklin, who was opposed to an Executive power of veto, thought that "if the Executive was to have a Council, such a power would be less objectionable." On June 6, Charles Pinckney, in opposing the joining of the Judiciary with the President in a power to veto, observed that at first he had favored "joining the heads of the principal departments, the Secretary at War, of Foreign Affairs, etc., in the Council of Revision. He had, however, relinquished the idea, from a consideration that these could be called in by the Executive Magistrate whenever he pleased to consult them." This was the first reference to "principal departments"; and Pinckney undoubtedly had in mind only those departments which he had proposed in his Plan of May 29. Hamilton, on June 18, in his "Sketch of a Government" had provided for appointment by the Executive of the "heads or chief officers of the department of Finance, War and Foreign Affairs." Nothing further had been said or done on the subject until August 18, when Ellsworth "observed that a Council had not yet been provided for the President"; and he suggested one composed of the President of the Senate, the Chief Justice, and the Ministers as they might be established for the departments of Foreign and Domestic Affairs, War, Finance, and Marine, who should advise but not conclude the President. Charles Pinckney (who had made the original proposal for a similar body) urged that the matter be laid over, as Gouverneur Morris had already planned to make such a proposal. "His own idea," he said, "was that the President should be authorized to call for advice or not, as he might chuse. Give him an able Council and it will thwart him; a weak one, and he will shelter himself under their sanction." Gerry, who had been the first man to favor a Council, now said that he was against letting the Chief Justice or "the heads of the departments, particularly of finance, have anything to do in business connected with legislation." Two days later, on August 20, G. Morris, seconded by Pinckney, had submitted an elaborate proposal for a "Council of State to assist the President in conducting the public affairs" — to consist of the Chief Justice "who shall from time to time recommend such alterations and additions to the laws of the United States as may in his opinion be necessary to the due administration of justice, and such as may promote useful learning and inculcate sound morality throughout the Union", and the Secretary of Domestic Affairs, Commerce and Finance, Secretaries of Foreign Affairs, War, and Marine (the duties of each being expressly set forth), with the further provision that: "The President may from time to time submit any matter to the discussion of the Council of State, and he may require the written opinions of any one or more of the members; but he shall in all cases exercise his own judgment, and either conform to such opinions or not as he may think proper; and every officer above mentioned shall be responsible for his opinion on the affairs relating to his particular Department." This elaborate proposal was referred without debate, to the Committee of Detail, which, on August 22, through Rutledge reported a modification of the Morris-Pinckney proposal as follows:

"The President of the United States shall have a Privy Council which shall consist of the President of the Senate, the Speaker of the House of Representatives, the Chief Justice of the Supreme Court, and the principal officer in the respective departments of Foreign Affairs, Domestic Affairs, War, Marine, and Finance, as such departments of office shall from time to time be established, whose duty it shall be to advise him in matters respecting the execution of his office, which he shall think proper to lay before them; but their advice shall not conclude him, nor affect his responsibility for the measures which he shall adopt."

This Report (eliminating the President of the Senate, the Speaker and the Chief Justice) foreshadowed the Cabinet as it in fact developed. It is a singular fact that no vote was ever taken on it by the Convention.[1] Meanwhile, on September 4, the Special Committee on postponed matters, in reporting through Judge Brearley the new plan for the election of President, recommended vesting in him the power "to require the opinion in writing of the principal officer in each of the Executive Departments upon any subject relating to the duties of their respective offices." No definition was made of the term "Executive Departments"; but it undoubtedly referred to those mentioned in Rutledge's Report of August 22. When the Convention considered this particular power, on this September 7, Mason, who from the outset had feared Executive power, said that he was averse to vesting so dangerous a power as that of appointment in either the President alone, or in the Legislature; and he favored giving the power to a Privy Council for the President, composed of six members for six years to be chosen by the Senate — two each from the Eastern, Middle, and Southern States. Wilson, who was also opposed to blending the Legislative power of the Senate with the Executive in the appointment of officers, said that he would prefer

---

[1] Its pendency, however, caused G. Morris, on August 27, to object to trial by the Supreme Court of impeachment of the President, "if the first Judge was to be of the Privy Council."

the Council proposed by Mason, provided its advice should not be made obligatory on the President. King of Massachusetts, on the other hand, remarked that most of the inconveniences charged on the Senate would be also incident to any Council of Advice; and he was of opinion that the people "would be alarmed at an unnecessary creation of new Corps which must increase the expense as well as influence of the Government." It is significant that though the Convention had never taken any vote upon the Rutledge proposal for a Privy Council, the delegates had apparently expressed their opinions in private against it, so that Mason was now led to say that "in rejecting a Council to the President, we were about to try an experiment on which the most despotic Governments had never ventured. The Grand Signor himself had his Divan." He moved for the establishment of "an Executive Council as a Council of State for the President", of six members, to be appointed by the Legislature or Senate. Franklin, who still retained a fear of appointments by the President, seconded Mason, saying that "he thought a Council would not only be a check on a bad President, but be a relief to a good one." Madison and Dickinson also favored the proposal. G. Morris replied that: "The question of a Council was considered in the Committee, where it was judged that the President, by persuading his Council to concur in his wrong measures, would acquire their protection for them." This argument was apparently convincing to the Convention, for it voted against Mason, by eight States to three. Accordingly, the Committee's Report giving power to the President to require the opinion in writing of the principal officer in each of the Executive Departments was accepted; and nothing further was heard of a Council. The manner in which this provision was expected to work, and the quite different way in which

it actually developed in practice, are interestingly
shown as follows.[1] James Iredell, in 1788, in answer to
George Mason's objections wrote:

"He is to not be assisted by a Council, summoned to a
jovial dinner perhaps, and giving their opinions according to
the nod of the President; but the opinion is to be given with
the utmost solemnity in writing. No after-equivocation can
explain it away. It must forever speak for itself, and commit
the writer in lasting colors either of fame or infamy or neutral
insignificance, to future ages, as well as the present. From
those written opinions, weighed with care, surely the President can form as good a judgment as if they had been given
by a dozen formal characters carelessly met together on a
slight appointment. And this further advantage would be
derived from the proposed system (which would be wanting
if he had constitutional advice to screen him) — the President must be personally responsible for everything."

On the other hand, Jefferson, writing in 1810, said:

"The ordinary business of every day is done by consultation between the President and the Head of the department
alone to which it belongs. For measures of importance or
difficulty, a consultation is held with the Heads of departments, either assembled, or by taking their opinions separately in conversation or in writing. The latter is most
strictly in the spirit of the Constitution. Because the President, on weighing the advice of all, is left free to make up
an opinion for himself. In this way, they are not brought
together, and it is not necessarily known to any what opinion
the others have given. This was General Washington's
practice for the first two or three years of his administration,
till the affairs of France and England threatened to embroil
us and rendered consideration and discussion desirable. In
these discussions, Hamilton and myself were daily pitted in
the cabinet like two cocks. . . . I practised this last method
because the harmony was so cordial among us all that we

---

[1] *Life and Correspondence of James Iredell* (1858), II, 197; Jefferson to Dr.
Walter Jones, March 5, 1810; Jefferson to Destutt Tracy, Jan. 26, 1811.

never failed, by a contribution of mutual views of the subject, to form an opinion acceptable to the whole. . . . Yet this does, in fact, transform the Executive into a Directory and I hold the other method to be more constitutional."

Oath of the President and Other Officers

The Committee of Detail in its Report of August 6, had provided for the oath to be taken by the President as follows: "I solemnly swear (or affirm) that I will faithfully execute the office of President of the United States"; and in a subsequent article they provided that: "The members of the Legislatures, and the Executive and Judicial officers of the United States, and of the several States, shall be bound to support this Constitution." On August 27, on motion of Mason and Madison, it was voted to add to the President's oath: "and will to the best of my judgment and power preserve, protect and defend the Constitution of the United States." (Wilson thought the general provision as to oaths rendered this addition unnecessary.) The Committee on Style, in its Report of September 12, left the oath as thus amended unchanged. At some time in the closing sessions, however, the phraseology was changed, by striking out the words "to the best of my judgment and power", and by substituting "to the best of my ability", so that the oath in the final draft of the Constitution is: "I do solemnly swear (or affirm) that I will faithfully execute the office of President of the United States, and will to the best of my ability, preserve, protect and defend the Constitution of the United States." It is to be noted that the oath prescribed by the first statute passed in the first session of the First Congress for all other officers of the United States, was simply "to support the Constitution of the United States." [1]

---

[1] See *The Independence of the Executive* (1913), by Grover Cleveland.
The present oath required by the United States statute now in force is: "to

OUT OF CONVENTION

Washington noted :

"In Convention. Dined and spent the afternoon at home (except when riding a few miles)."

Jacob Hiltzheimer wrote in his diary :

"Forenoon went to the State House as usual and nothing of importance being offered, the House adjourned at twelve o'clock to meet tomorrow at half past nine. Dined at General Mifflin's with George Ross and Richard Willing."

SATURDAY, SEPTEMBER 8, 1787

IN CONVENTION

The Treaty-Making Power

Having settled the proposal of the Special Committee of September 4 for joining the Senate and the President in the power over appointments, the Convention now took up the Committee's other compromise suggestion as to a similar junction of authority over treaties.

The treaty-making power had been given no express consideration, either in the Randolph Resolutions of May 29, or by the Convention itself, prior to the appointment of the Committee of Detail. That Committee, in its Report of August 6, proposed vesting this power in the Senate alone. It soon became evident that the Convention viewed this disposition with apprehension. On August 15, in debate over the question of granting to the House sole power to originate revenue bills, G. Mason stated that "he was extremely anxious to take this power from the Senate who could already sell the whole country by means of treaties." John F. Mercer contended that the treaty-making power belonged to the Executive, and ought not to be vested in the Senate ; and he further maintained that

support and defend the Constitution of the United States against all enemies, foreign and domestic . . . bear true faith and allegiance to the same."

treaties "would not be final so as to alter the law of the land, till ratified by Legislative authority." [1] Mason stated that while "he did not say that a treaty would repeal a law, the Senate by means of a treaty might alienate territory, etc. without Legislative sanction. . . . If Spain should possess herself of Georgia, the Senate might by treaty dismember the Union." Gerry likewise, on August 17, said, in urging that Congress be given the power of making peace, that "eight Senators may possibly exercise the power if vested in that body, and fourteen if all should be present; and may consequently give up part of the United States." [2] On August 23, there developed considerable sentiment adverse to the Senate's possession of the treaty-making power, especially from Madison, Wilson, Gorham, and G. Morris. Madison thought that as the President represented the whole people, it was proper that he should "be an agent in treaties", since "the Senate represented the States alone." (This latter statement was a singular one; for those delegates who hitherto had lined up with Madison had frequently insisted that the Senate must not be regarded as representative of the States alone but of the people and the Nation in general.) G. Morris wished to insert a provision that "no treaty shall be binding on the United States which is not ratified by a law." This would have made the Senate a simple negotiator, and the Congress the ratifying

[1] The status of a treaty as a law was recognized on August 23, when the provision of the Report of August 6 by the Committee of Detail, that Congress have power "to call forth the aid of the militia in order to execute the laws of the Union, enforce treaties, suppress insurrection and repel invasions," was amended by striking out the words "enforce treaties"; for, as G. Morris pointed out, the words were "superfluous, since treaties were to be 'laws.'"

The Supreme Court decided, later, that a treaty might repeal a statute of the United States, and that a statute might repeal a treaty. *Foster* v. *Neilson* (1829), 2 Peters 314; *The Cherokee Tobacco Case* (1871), 11 Wall. 616. See esp. *Treaties, Their Making, and Enforcement* (1916, 2d ed.) by Samuel B. Crandall, pp. 153 *et seq.*

[2] See *Crandall, supra*, pp. 161 *et seq.*, 220 *et seq.*; *Moore's Digest of International Law*, V, 172–174, as to cession of territory of a State and of the United States, by treaty.

body; hence, Madison pointed out "the inconvenience of requiring a legal ratification of treaties of alliance for the purpose of war, etc." Gorham also thought it inconvenient if treaties of peace had to be ratified by a statute; and he pointed out "that a Minister could not then be instructed by the Senate who were to appoint him, or if instructed, there could be no certainty that the House of Representatives would agree to confirm what he might agree to under these instructions." [1] G. Morris replied that there would be no inconvenience, since it would simply require foreign powers to send their Ministers here to make treaties; and he stated that he was "not very solicitous to multiply and facilitate treaties. . . . The more difficulty in making treaties, the more value will be set on them." Wilson was inclined to agree with Morris and suggested that unless treaties were required to receive the sanction of Congress, the Senate alone by a treaty might impose an export duty — a thing which the Convention had just prohibited being done by the Congress itself. Dickinson also favored Morris' suggestion, though he pointed out that it would be unfavorable to the small States "which would otherwise have an equal share in making treaties." In the course of this debate, Gorham, in answer to Morris, expressed the curious view that it was not desirable that negotiations of treaties should take place here, but rather through our Ministers abroad, because the Legislature here, if having anything to do with treaties, "will be generally influenced by two or three men, who will be corrupted by the Ambassadors here. In such a Government as ours, it is necessary to guard against the Government itself being seduced." The Convention decided to send the subject back to the Committee.

The debates on the treaty power cannot be under-

[1] As reported in McHenry's *Notes*.

stood without an appreciation of the fact that underlying many of the views expressed was the great question of the freedom of navigation of the Mississippi; and here again was an instance of the division between the Southern and the Eastern interests. The proposal to abandon this right, so dear to the hearts of Virginia and the South, which had been made in Congress in the previous summer and which was still unsettled, had inspired the Southern delegates with a fear lest any provision should be made in the new Constitution which should facilitate such an abandonment, and a consequent possible surrender of the Western territory. Evidently, the Special Committee on September 4, in proposing to vest the treaty making power in the President but only with the advice and consent of two thirds of the Senate present, had in mind to avert these fears. Nevertheless, when its Report was debated on September 6, 7 and 8, considerable opposition was still aroused. Wilson, on September 6, opposing the powers of the Senate as having "a dangerous tendency to aristocracy", pointed out that treaties were to be the "law of the land", and that the power of making treaties involved that of making subsidies, in which case "foreign influence is to be dreaded." On September 7, Wilson renewed the proposal that the House of Representatives be also joined in this power, since "as treaties are to have the operation of laws, they ought to have the sanction of laws also." Sherman replied that the Senate could be safely trusted with the power, and that the necessity of secrecy in the case of treaties would forbid a reference of them to the whole Legislature. Wilson's motion was defeated.

That part of the Committee's Report which provided for consent of "two thirds of the members present" was debated on September 7 and 8. The requirement of two thirds practically restored the provision

of the Articles of Confederation making necessary a
vote of nine States out of thirteen to make a treaty;
the requirement of "members present" obviated the
embarrassment experienced under the Articles, by the
failure of delegates from nine States to attend Congress.
Wilson thought the whole provision objectionable as
placing "in the power of a minority to control the will
of a majority." King thought that though a two thirds
vote was required under the Articles of Confederation,
there was no need now, as an Executive check was
provided which did not exist in the old Congress. Nevertheless, a motion to strike out the two thirds requirement was defeated; so was a motion to require consent
of two thirds of *all the members* of the Senate; so was a
motion to require a majority of the whole number of
the Senate; so was a motion by Madison that two
thirds of all the members constitute a quorum of the
Senate; so was a proposal by Williamson and Gerry
that "no treaty should be made without previous notice
to the members and reasonable time for their attending." During this debate, the Convention had been
willing to concede a point to Madison and others who
thought that peace treaties should be allowed to be
made with less difficulty than other treaties; and on
September 7, it had decided by a unanimous vote to
except peace treaties from the two thirds requirement.
Later on this day, Williamson and Spaight of North
Carolina moved to limit this, by providing that: "No
treaty of peace affecting territorial rights should be
made without the concurrence of two thirds of the
members of the Senate"; and King of Massachusetts
moved to include "all present rights of the United
States." Madison in his *Notes* records no vote on this
motion; but the Journal states that it was voted in
the following form: "But no treaty of peace shall
be entered into whereby the United States shall be

deprived of any of their present territory or rights without the concurrence of two thirds of the members present." Madison then moved that two thirds of the
Senate alone should be authorized to make a peace
treaty, without the concurrence of the President; for,
he argued, "the President would necessarily derive so
much power and importance from a state of war that he
might be tempted, if authorized, to impede a treaty
of peace." Butler was "strenuous for the motion, as
a necessary security against ambitious and corrupt
Presidents." Gorham, on the other hand, thought the
precaution unnecessary; and G. Morris said that no
peace ought to be made without the President, "who
was the general guardian of the National interests."
This second proposal by Madison was rejected. On
September 8, the question of peace treaties was reconsidered. Williamson remarked that "treaties are to
be made in the branch of the Government where there
may be a majority of the States, without a majority
of the people; eight men may be a majority of a quorum
and should not have the power to decide the conditions of peace." Gerry enlarged on the "danger of
putting essential rights of the Union in the hands of so
small a number as a majority of the Senate, representing perhaps not one fifth of the people. The Senate
will be corrupted by foreign influence." He thought
that "in treaties of peace, a greater rather than less
proportion of votes was necessary than in other treaties.
In treaties of peace, the dearest interests will be at
stake, as the fisheries, territories, etc., and there is more
danger to the extremities of the Continent of being sacrificed than in any other occasions." On the other
hand, Wilson contended that if two thirds were to be
required to make peace, "the minority may perpetuate
war against the sense of the majority." And G. Morris
made the singular arguments that: "If two thirds of

the Senate should be required for peace, the Legislature will be unwilling to make war for that reason on account of the fisheries or the Mississippi — the two great objects of the Union. Besides, if a majority of the Senate be for peace and are not allowed to make it, they will be apt to effect their purpose in the more disagreeable mode of negativing the supplies for the war." The Convention decided, however, to reverse its action of the previous day and struck out the exception of peace treaties, thus making treaties of every kind subject to the two thirds provision. Sherman and G. Morris thought that rights established by a peace treaty should not be left to the Senate alone and moved a proviso "that no such rights should be ceded without the sanction of the Legislature." Madison records no vote on this motion.

Few parts of the Constitution aroused more antagonism, later in the State Conventions, than did this treaty provision; but, as already noted, it was opposed not because of political theory but because of fear of its application to existing conditions.[1] That the provision for a two thirds, rather than a majority, vote of the Senate was inserted for the express purpose of calming the fears of Virginia, North Carolina and the West lest the North and East should relinquish the navigation rights on the Mississippi was later directly asserted by Hugh Williamson, a delegate from North Carolina:

"Of all the wrong heads who have started in opposition, none have been mentioned who appear to be so palpably wrong as the people of Kentucky. It is said that some Antifederal in Maryland in the last winter fastened on the ear of General Wilkinson who was accidentally there, and persuaded him that, in case of a new Government, the navigation of the Mississippi would infallibly be given

---

[1] Madison to Jefferson, Oct. 7, 1788; see also Williamson to Madison, June 2, 1788, *Doc. Hist.*, IV; cf., however, *Works of Alexander Hamilton*, VI, 183.

up. Your recollection must certainly enable you to say that there is a proviso in the new system which was inserted for the express purpose of preventing a majority of the Senate, or of the States (which is considered as the same thing) from giving up the Mississippi. It is provided that two thirds of the members present in the Senate shall be required to concur in making treaties, and if the Southern States attend to their duty, this will imply two thirds of the States in the Union together with the President, a security rather better than the present nine States, especially as Vermont and the Province of Maine may be added to the Eastern interest; and you may recollect that when a member, Mr. Wilson, objected to this proviso, saying that in all Governments the majority should govern, it was replied that the navigation of the Mississippi, after what had already happened in Congress, was not to be risqued in the hands of a mere majority, and the objection was withdrawn."

In view of the sentiment which has developed in recent years against requiring more than a majority of the Senate to ratify a treaty, it is interesting to note that, in 1788, much of the opposition to the treaty clause was based on the feeling that the two thirds requirement was too small. Virginia proposed an amendment that "no treaty ceding, contracting, restraining or suspending the territorial rights or claims of the United States or any of them, or their, or any of their rights or claims to fishing in the American seas, or navigating the American rivers shall be but in cases of the most urgent and extreme necessity, nor shall any such treaty be ratified without the concurrence of three fourths of the whole number of the members of both Houses respectively."

Impeachment

The method of appointment, the length of term, and the powers of the President being all disposed of, the

Convention now took up the question of how to get rid of that officer. Randolph's original Resolutions of May 29 had given to the National Judiciary trial of "impeachment of all National officers", but there was no specific provision as to the Executive. On June 2, Dickinson said that it was necessary to place the power of removing somewhere, that he did not like the plan of impeaching great officers of State, and that he suggested removal of the Executive by the National Legislature (which was, at that stage of the Convention, to elect him), on the request of a majority of the Legislatures of individual States. Madison and Wilson opposed such a mixture of the State authorities in the business. It was finally voted that the Executive "be removable on impeachment and conviction of malpractice or neglect of duty"; but it was not definitely stated that the National Legislature should be the impeaching body.

The practice under the State Constitutions then in force differed. In all the States, the lower branch of the Legislature was empowered to impeach. In Virginia and Maryland, the trial was by the Courts; in New York and South Carolina by a special Court consisting of the Senate and the Judges; in the other States, the upper branch of the Legislature tried impeachments. In Virginia and Delaware, the Executive could not be impeached until he was out of office.[1]

[1] In Virginia, the House of Delegates could impeach the Governor after he left office, and all other officers guilty of maladministration, the trial to be in the General Court; Judges of the General Court if impeached were tried in the Court of Appeals. Persons found guilty were disabled from holding office.

In Delaware, the Assembly could impeach the President when out of office, and all other officers guilty of maladministration — the Council to try the impeachment.

In Pennsylvania, the General Assembly might impeach and the President and Council try.

In New York and South Carolina, the lower branch might impeach by a two thirds vote, the trial to be in a Court consisting of the Senate and the Judges — conviction to be had only on assent of two thirds of the members of the Court.

In Massachusetts and New Hampshire, the House of Representatives could impeach and the Senate try.

On June 13, the Committee of the Whole had voted to give to the National Judiciary jurisdiction over "impeachment of National officers", but the Convention, on July 18, struck out this jurisdiction. When the Convention, on July 17 and 20, had debated the report of the Committee of the Whole as to impeachment of the Executive, G. Morris thought that the Executive ought not to be impeachable. "This is a dangerous part of the plan. It will hold him in such dependence that he will be no check on the Legislature, will not be a firm guardian of the people and of the public interest." Pinckney thought (following the Virginia and Delaware Constitutions) that the Executive ought not to be impeachable at all, while in office; and that certainly impeachments should not issue from the Legislature "who would in that case hold them as a rod over the Executive and by that means effectually destroy his independence." King agreed, saying that "he relied on the vigor of the Executive as a great security for the public liberties", that impeachment by the Legislature destroyed the "primitive axiom that the three great departments of Government should be separate and independent; and that an Executive should not be impeachable unless he held office during good behaviour." Mason, on the other hand, thought that no one point was of more importance than the right of impeachment. "Shall any man be over Justice?" he asked. Franklin, Gerry, and Wilson concurred; and Madison thought it "indispensable that some provision should be made for defending the community against the incapacity, negligence, or perfidy of the Chief Executive." Randolph favored a proposal made

In Georgia, the Assembly might impeach; but no provision was made as to trial.

In North Carolina, the General Assembly or the grand jury might impeach; but no specific provision was made as to trial.

In New Jersey, the Assembly might impeach and the Council try.

by Hamilton for impeachment by a tribunal composed of State Judges. At the end of the debate, G. Morris said that his opinion "had been changed by the arguments used in the discussion"; that he was "now sensible of the necessity of impeachments", that our Executive might "be bribed by a greater interest to betray his trust"; that he might be in foreign pay, and that: "This Magistrate is not the King, but the Prime Minister. The people are the King. When we make him amenable to justice, however, we should take care to provide some mode that will not make him dependent on the Legislature." The Convention voted to adopt the recommendation of the Committee of the Whole, that the Executive be removable on impeachment and conviction of malpractice or neglect of duty.[1]

When the Committee of Detail made its Report, on August 6, it recognized the validity of Morris' argument against trial of impeachment by the Legislature which was to appoint the Executive, and it provided for impeachment as follows:

"He shall be removed from his office on impeachment by the House of Representatives, and conviction in the Supreme Court, of treason, bribery, or corruption."

Nothing further was done on this subject until the Report of the Special Committee, on September 4, as to the new plan for choice of President. The evil of appointment and impeachment by the same body being removed by the suggestion of choice of President by electors, the Committee restored impeachment by the National Legislature in the following form:

"He shall be removed from his office on impeachment by the House of Representatives, and conviction by the Senate, for treason or bribery."

[1] On July 21, during the debate on the mode of election of the Executive, G. Morris opposed appointment by the Legislature as the worst of all possible modes, since the Executive "will be the mere creature of it", if it shall have power both to appoint and impeach. (See also G. Morris, July 25.)

And it also provided that:

"The Senate of the United States shall have power to try all impeachments; but no person shall be convicted without the concurrence of two thirds of the members present."

This proposal was debated by the Convention on this September 8.[1] Madison opposed the provision for trial by the Senate instead of by the Supreme Court, as previously fixed, and favored the latter mode. Charles Pinckney thought also that trial by the Senate would make the President too dependent on the Legislature. "If he opposes a favorite law, the two Houses will combine against him, and under the influence of heat and faction throw him out of office." Sherman, on the other hand, thought the Supreme Court "improper to try the President, because the Judges would be appointed by him"; and G. Morris said that: "No other tribunal than the Senate could be trusted. The Supreme Court were too few in number and might be warped or corrupted. He was against a dependence of the Executive on the Legislature, considering the Legislative tyranny the great danger to be apprehended; but there could be no danger that the Senate would say untruly on their oaths that the President was guilty of crimes or facts, especially as in four years he can be turned out." Mason and Gerry thought that the provision for impeachment ought not to be confined simply to treason and bribery, since "treason as defined in the Constitution will not reach many great and dangerous offences." It was proposed that the word "maladministration" be added; but Madison thought that "so vague a term will be equivalent to a tenure during the pleasure of the State." Mason then

[1] James McHenry, in his Report to the Maryland House of Delegates, Nov. 29, 1787 (*Farrand*, III, 144–150), said: "The power of trying impeachments was lodged in this body as more likely to be governed by cool and candid investigation, than by those heats that too often inflame and influence more populous Assemblies."

proposed extending impeachment to "other high crimes and misdemeanors against the State." This amendment was accepted; and the Convention then adopted the Committee's Report, as amended.[1] A question next arose whether other National officers ought to be subject to impeachment. Randolph's original Resolutions of May 29 had given to the National Judiciary "trial of impeachments of all National officers." The Report of the Committee of Detail of August 6 had included within the jurisdiction of the Supreme Court "trial of impeachment of officers of the United States"; but the Convention, on August 27, had postponed action on this subject. On August 22, the Committee of Detail had submitted a supplemental report that "the Judges of the Supreme Court shall be triable by the Senate on impeachment by the House of Representatives"; [2] but it was this suggested power of the Senate to try the Judges which had caused G. Morris and others to oppose appointment of Judges by the Senate, considering it particularly wrong to let the Senate have the filling of vacancies "which its own decrees were to create" (August 23). Now on September 8, the Convention, without debate, extended the provision for impeachment by the House, triable by the Senate, so that "the Vice President and other civil officers of the United States shall be removed from office on impeachment and conviction as aforesaid." These various provisions were reframed by the Committee of Style,

---

[1] No comment was made in this debate as to the provision in the Committee's Report that when the Senate was engaged in the trial of the President of the United States, the Chief Justice should preside instead of the regular *ex officio* President of the Senate, namely, the Vice President of the United States. The propriety of this provision was obvious, in view of the fact that a conviction on impeachment would result in the exercise of the powers and duties of the President by the Vice President.

[2] In the State Constitutions of Massachusetts, Maryland, Delaware, and South Carolina Judges were removable on address of the two Houses of the Legislature, by the Governor; in Pennsylvania, the single-house Legislature could remove the Judges.

September 12, and became Article II, section 3, of the Constitution.

Power to Originate Money Bills

As the Report of the Special Committee of September 4 had disposed of four of the great questions which had divided the Convention — the election of the President, the power of appointment, the treaty-making power, and the power of trial of impeachment — and had settled each by compromises which in their final result were favorable to Senatorial authority, so now this same Committee offered a solution of another very difficult question, by a further suggested compromise, in a supplemental Report of September 5. It will be recalled that a part of the Great Compromise of July 16 as to equality of representation of the small States in the Senate had been the concession to the large States of the right of the House of Representatives to originate all revenue bills, without power in the Senate to alter or amend. This portion of that compromise had been embodied in the Report of the Committee of Detail of August 6, as follows :

"All bills for raising or appropriating money, and for fixing the salaries of the officers of Government, shall originate in the House of Representatives, and shall not be altered or amended by the Senate."

When the Convention had taken this section up for debate, on August 8, G. Morris and Charles Pinckney, though representatives of the large States, moved to strike it out, on the ground that the Senate ought peculiarly to possess this power. Mercer of Maryland, a small State delegate, thought that without this power the equality of votes in the Senate was rendered "ideal and of no consequence." Madison also favored the motion, thinking the power of no consequence to the

House and likely to involve the two branches in "injurious alterations." Mason, Butler, and Ellsworth, on the other hand, opposed the motion, on the ground that it would add to the already too great powers of a Senate and promote an aristocracy, and that the compromise ought to be adhered to. The Convention, however, had proceeded to reverse its former action and had struck out the power by a vote of seven States to four — three of the smaller States, New Jersey, Delaware, and Maryland joining with the larger States of Pennsylvania, Virginia, South Carolina, and Georgia. On the next day, August 9, Randolph of Virginia had moved to reconsider, stating that he thought this vote not only "extremely objectionable" but "as endangering the success of the plan." Williamson of North Carolina said that his State "had agreed to equality in the Senate, merely in consideration that money bills should be confined to the other House, and he was surprised to see the smaller States forsaking the condition on which they had received their equality." Dr. Franklin also considered the two propositions "as essentially connected by the compromise." Mason said that unless this power should be restored to the House, "he should, not from obstinacy, but from duty and conscience, oppose throughout the equality of representation in the Senate." G. Morris, on the other hand, considered the section relating to money bills as "intrinsically bad"; and Wilson said that the two large States of Pennsylvania and Virginia had uniformly voted against it.

It had become evident, at this point, that the Convention was facing another serious crisis; for it appeared probable that the junction of those delegates from the smaller States who were opposed to the provision, with those of the larger States who were equally opposed, might prevail to overturn the whole compromise which had been arrived at with such extreme difficulty, a month prior. Two days later (August 10), Randolph had made an elaborate speech in support of the vesting of this power in the House. It will make the plan "more acceptable to the people, because they will consider the Senate as the more aristocratic body, and will expect that the usual guards against its influence be provided, according to the example in Great Britain." He thought also that the restraint of the Senate from amending was of particular importance. Charles Pinckney had said, in reply, that he had never considered this provision as making any part of the compromise (a singular remark, in view of Williamson's statement that North Carolina had voted for the compromise only because of this provision). The Convention had voted to reconsider, nine States to one, with South Carolina divided. On August 13, Randolph had moved a modified form of power in the House over revenue bills. Again a hot debate had taken place. Madison and Wilson urged that "one of the greatest evils incident to Republican Government was the spirit of contention and faction", which would be promoted by this provision — it being difficult to determine whether a bill sent down by the Senate was or was not an amendment or alteration of a House revenue bill. "Can there be a more fruitful source of dispute, or a kind of dispute more difficult to be settled?" Moreover, why should the Senate be restrained from checking the possible extravagance of the House? On the other hand, Mason, Dickinson, and Gerry agreed on the view that: "Taxation and representation are strongly associated in the minds of the people, and they will not agree that any but their immediate representatives shall meddle with their purse. In short, the acceptance of the plan will inevitably fail, if the Senate be not restrained from originating money bills." "Experience," said Dickinson, "should be our only guide. Reason may mislead us. . . . And has not experience verified the utility of restraining money bills to the immediate representatives of the people?" Randolph and Dickinson both thought also that the people would dislike aristocratic powers given to the Senate. "When this plan goes forth," said Dickinson, "it will be attacked by the popular leaders. Aristocracy will be the watchword, the Shibboleth, among its adversaries. Eight States have inserted in their Constitutions the exclusive right of originating money bills in favor of the popular branch of the Legislature. Most of them, however, allowed the other branch to amend. This he thought would be proper for us to do." [1] And Randolph said that the new Constitution had already enough "numerous and monstrous difficulties to combat. . . . When the people behold in the Senate the countenance of an aristocracy, and in the President the form, at least, of a little Monarch, will not their alarms be sufficiently raised, without taking from their immediate representatives a right which has been so long appropriated to them?" In reply to these arguments, Rutledge of South Carolina had come forward, saying: "Will not the people say that this restriction is but a mere tub to the whale? They cannot but see that it is of no real consequence; and will be more likely to be displeased with it as an attempt to bubble them, than to impute it to a watchfulness over their rights." Finally, the Convention had adhered to its action of August 8, refusing to vest this right in the House, by a vote of four States to seven — Massachusetts, New Hampshire, North Carolina, and Virginia alone supporting

[1] There were, in fact, seven States which had this provision in their State Constitutions. They were Delaware, Maryland, Massachusetts, New Hampshire, New Jersey, South Carolina, and Virginia.

the provisions of the previous compromise. Virginia's vote, which hitherto had been cast against it, was now reversed, through the change made in General Washington's vote, who now deserted Madison and Blair and voted with Randolph and Mason, on the conciliatory ground (as stated by Madison) that though "he disapproved and till now voted against the exclusive privilege [of the House] he gave up his judgment, he said, because it was not of very material weight with him and was made an essential point with others who, if disappointed, might be less cordial in other points of real weight." This expression of view is of great significance in showing the spirit of concession which animated so many of the delegates and without which the Constitution would not have been framed. Following this action, the Convention had then rejected, on August 13, the modified proposal made by Dickinson of Delaware, to vest the exclusive power of origination in the House but giving to the Senate power to amend — a provision which was found in the State Constitutions of Delaware, Massachusetts, and New Hampshire. On the next day, August 14, Williamson of North Carolina referred to the money bill section as dead, but said that "its ghost, he was afraid, would not withstanding haunt us", and that though he "had swallowed the vote of rejection with reluctance, he could not digest it." Following this, Caleb Strong of Massachusetts, on August 15, had proposed a modification of the section, giving each House the right to originate bills, as follows:

"Each House shall possess the right of originating all bills, except bills for raising money for the purposes of revenue, or for appropriating the same and for fixing the salaries of the officers of the Government which shall originate in the House of Representatives; but the Senate may propose or concur with amendments as in other cases."

The phraseology of this power of the Senate to amend was taken from the Massachusetts State Constitution. Williamson now advanced a new argument in favor of this provision, saying that he "was for an efficient and stable Government", but that many would not be in favor of properly strengthening the Senate if it should not be restricted in the case of money bills. "The friends of the Senate would, therefore, lose more than they would gain by refusing to gratify the other side." On this motion, accordingly, it was voted to postpone the whole subject until the powers of the Senate should be fully discussed. This action finally proved to be the solution for the whole difficult and critical problem. On August 21, Mason of Virginia stated that he wished "to know how the proposed amendment as to money bills would be decided, before he agreed to any further points." The Convention, however, was still unready to take any action; but on September 5, a solution of the difficulty was found. Judge Brearley's Special Committee had already recommended that the power of final choice of President be vested in the Senate in case a majority of the electors were not united for any candidate; it now attempted to conciliate those who would be inclined to oppose such an increase of power in the Senate, by proposing as a concession to those delegates from the large States who were unfavorable to the Senate, the suggestion which Caleb Strong had made as to revenue bills, in the following form:

"All bills for raising revenue shall originate in the House of Representatives, and shall be subject to alterations and amendments by the Senate; no money shall be drawn from the Treasury, but in consequence of appropriations made by law."

It will be noted that this proposal differed essentially from the provision voted by the Convention on July 16, as part of the Great Compromise. The latter denied

to the Senate not only the power to originate but also
the power to amend; the present compromise denied
the first power but granted the second (following in
this respect the State Constitutions of Delaware,
Massachusetts, and New Hampshire).[1] This new
compromise satisfied some of the delegates from the
smaller States and some from the larger States, who had
hitherto opposed the origination of revenue bills in the
House; and the provision was accepted by the Convention, on September 8, without any debate and by a
vote of nine States to two (only Delaware and Maryland dissenting).   And thus ended this long and hard
fight over a question which had seriously threatened
to break up the Convention.[2]   That such importance
should have been attached to a matter which today
seems of minor importance, can only be understood by
realizing how deeply the delegates felt, on the one side
or the other, regarding any increase in the powers of
the Senate.   When, however, the large States surrendered on the point of allowing the Senate to amend the
House revenue bills, they really surrendered on the
whole proposition; for, as William Grayson (an opponent of the Constitution) pointed out in the Virginia
State Convention as early as 1788: "The power of
proposing amendments is the same, in effect, as that of

[1] In explanation of the new mode of election of President, G. Morris said, September 5, 1787, that it was the result of a compromise; and King said that "the
influence of the small States in the Senate was somewhat balanced by the influence
of the large States in bringing forward the candidates, and also by the concurrence
of the small States in the Committee in the clause vesting the exclusive origination of
money bills in the House of Representatives."   To this statement, Madison adds
a note: "This explains the compromise mentioned above by Gov'r Morris.   Col.
Mason, Mr. Gerry and other members from large States set great value on this
privilege of originating money bills.   Of this, the members of the small States with
some from the large States who wanted a high mounted Government, endeavored
to avail themselves, by making that privilege the price of arrangements in the Constitution favorable to the small States and to the elevation of the Government."
[2] The words "shall be subject to alterations and amendments by the Senate"
were changed before the vote to "but the Senate may propose or concur with amendments as in other bills" — the latter being the phraseology of the Massachusetts
State Constitution.

originating. The Senate could strike out every word of the bill except the word *whereas*, or any other introductory word, and might substitute new words of their own." [1] Grayson's prophecy constitutes exactly what has taken place, in practice, in the Senate.

OUT OF CONVENTION

Washington noted:

"In Convention. Dined at the Cold Spring, Springsbury, with the Club, and spent the evening at my lodgings."

John Jay wrote, this day, from New York to Jefferson in Paris:

"The Convention will probably rise next week, and their proceedings will probably cause, not only much consideration, but also much discussion, debate, and perhaps heat; for as *docti indoctique scribimus* so *docti indoctique*, disinterested patriots and interested politicians will sit in council and in judgment, both within and without doors. There is, nevertheless, a degree of intelligence and information in the mass of our people, which affords much room for hope that by degrees our affairs will assume a more consistent and pleasing aspect. For my own part, I have long found myself in an awkward situation, seeing much to be done, and enabled to do very little. All we can do is to persevere. If good results, our labor will not be in vain; if not, we shall have done our duty, and that reflection is valuable."

SUNDAY, SEPTEMBER 9, 1787

Washington noted:

"Dined at home Mr. Morris's after making a visit to the Gardoqui [Minister from Spain] who as he says came from New York on a visit to me."

The *Journal* said (September 15):

"On Saturday night last arrived in this city from New York, his Excellency Don Diego de Gardoqui, Minister

[1] *Elliot's Debates*, III, 377.

from his Catholic Majesty to the Honorable the Congress of the United States, on a visit to His Excellency General Washington, previous to his departure for his seat at Mt. Vernon."

Jonathan Dayton wrote to Gen. Elias Dayton: [1]

"We have happily so far finished our business as to be employed in giving it its last polish and preparing it for the public inspection. This, I conclude, may be done in three or four days, at which time the public curiosity and our desire of returning to our respective homes will be equally gratified."

MONDAY, SEPTEMBER 10, 1787

IN CONVENTION

Amendments of the Constitution

On this day, the Convention took up the subject of amendments to the Constitution. It may be noted that provisions for amending the State Constitutions were contained in those of Delaware, Maryland, South Carolina, Pennsylvania, Georgia, Massachusetts, and New Hampshire — the first three States giving power to the Legislature to amend under certain restricted conditions, the latter four States requiring amendments to be made by Conventions of the people.[2] The Articles of Confederation provided for alterations on assent of Congress and of the Legislatures of *all* the States. Randolph's original Resolutions of May 29 had provided:

"That provision ought to be made for the amendment of the Articles of Union, whenever it shall seem necessary, and

---

[1] *Amer. Hist. Ass. Report* (1902) I, 100.

[2] "Provision for the regular and orderly amendment of an instrument of Government first appears in the Pennsylvania Frame of Government of 1683. A similar provision reappears in the Act of Settlement of 1683, the Pennsylvania Frame of 1696, and the Pennsylvania Charter of Privileges of 1701. Each of these documents provides that it shall not be altered, changed or diminished 'without the consent of the Governor . . . and six parts of seven of the Assembly.' No other Colonial charter contained any provision for amendment." *Proposed Amendments to the Constitution, 1789 to 1889*, by Herman V. Ames, *Amer. Hist. Ass. Report for 1896* (1897).

that the assent of the National Legislature ought not to be required thereto."

When this had been taken up by the Committee of the Whole, on June 5, in a discussion whether "provision ought to be made for hereafter amending the system now to be established, without requiring the assent of the National Legislature", Charles Pinckney "doubted the propriety or necessity of it." Gerry, on the other hand, favored it, saying: "The novelty and difficulty of the experiment requires periodical revision. The prospect of such a revision would also give intermediate stability to the Government." And he stated that "nothing had yet happened in the States where this provision existed to prove its impropriety." The Committee, however, had voted to postpone action. On June 11, several delegates said that they "did not see the necessity of the Resolution at all, nor the propriety of making the consent of the National Legislature unnecessary." Mason, however, urged the necessity of such a provision. "The plan now to be formed will certainly be defective, as the Confederation has been found, on trial, to be. Amendments, therefore, will be necessary and it will be better to provide for them in an easy, regular and constitutional way, than to trust to chance and violence. It would be improper to require the consent of the National Legislature, because they may abuse their power and refuse their consent on that very account." The Committee had failed to accept the last part of Mason's argument, but voted as follows:

"That provision ought to be made for the amendments of the Articles of Union, whensoever it shall seem necessary."

This vote of the Committee had been accepted by the Convention, without debate or dissent, on July 23.

Throughout the early period of the sessions, the

delegates had evidently been impressed with the fact that amendments would undoubtedly be necessary; and there had been no intimation that there was any portion of the Constitution which they considered not susceptible of amendment. On June 20, Mason had said that "the Convention, though comprising so many distinguished characters, could not be expected to make a faultless Government, and he would prefer trusting to posterity the amendment of its defects, rather than to push the experiment too far." Gerry said, on July 2, that "accommodation is absolutely necessary and defects may be amended by a future Convention." [1] Ellsworth said, on June 29: "Let a strong Executive, a Judiciary, and Legislative power be created; but let not too much be attempted, by which all may be lost. He was not, in general, a half-way man; yet he preferred doing half the good we could, rather than nothing at all. The other half may be added, when the necessity shall be more fully experienced." And again, on August 8, Ellsworth said that "if the Government should continue so long (150 years) alterations may be made in the Constitution in the manner proposed in a subsequent article."

The Committee of Detail, in its Report of August 6, for the first time made provision as to the manner in which amendments should be proposed, as follows:

"On the application of the Legislatures of two thirds of the States in the Union, for an amendment of this Constitution, the Legislature of the United States shall call a Convention for that purpose."

When the Convention had taken this up, on August 30, G. Morris suggested that the Legislature should be left to call a Convention whenever they pleased; but no one supported his idea and the Article had been adopted in the form proposed by the Committee of

[1] As reported in Yates' *Notes*.

Detail. On this September 10, however, a reconsideration was now voted, on motion of Gerry, who pointed
out, as an objection to the provision, that, since the
Constitution is to be paramount to the State Constitutions, "two thirds of the States may obtain a Convention, a majority of which can bind the Union to
innovations that may subvert the State Constitutions
altogether." Hamilton supported Gerry, but on
another ground. He felt that "an easy mode should
be provided for supplying defects which will probably
appear in the new system, and that the mode proposed
was not adequate." He thought that "the State
Legislatures will not apply for alterations but with a
view to increase their own powers", and that as "the
National Legislature will be the first to perceive and
will be the most sensible to the necessity of amendments, it ought also to be empowered, whenever two
thirds of each branch should concur, to call a Convention." This suggestion was one of the few made by
Hamilton which was embodied in the Constitution.
Madison also thought this Article vague. It did not,
in fact, make clear whether "the Legislatures were to
propose amendments and the Convention was to adopt
them, or whether the Convention was both to propose
and adopt them, or only to propose them for adoption
by some other body or bodies not specified."

Sherman, seconded by Gerry, then moved to add to
the Article, the words, "or the Legislature may propose
amendments to the several States for their approbation, but no amendments shall be binding until consented to by the several States." Wilson wanted to
make consent of two thirds of the States sufficient, and
though his motion to that effect was rejected by the
close vote of five States to six, a later motion by him
to permit three fourths of the States to make an amendment effective was adopted without dissent. Madison,

seconded by Hamilton, then proposed a substitute for the whole Article as follows :

"The Legislature of the United States whenever two thirds of both Houses shall deem necessary, or on the application of two thirds of the Legislatures of the several States, shall propose amendments to this Constitution, which shall be valid to all intents and purposes as part thereof, when the same shall have been ratified by three fourths at least of the Legislatures of the several States, or by Conventions in three fourths thereof, as one or the other mode may be proposed by the Legislature of the United States."

This proposal constituted a great change in the whole system. Instead of providing for a single Convention for the adoption of an amendment, in which, as Gerry had objected, a majority might subvert all Constitutions, the Legislatures of three fourths of the States or Conventions in three fourths of the States must ratify. This portion of Madison's plan was, of course, acceptable to the adherents of State Sovereignty, although it was not so extreme a proposal as that made by Sherman to require unanimous consent of all the several States. Finally, instead of allowing the Congress to propose amendments which (since a majority constituted a quorum in each House) might have resulted in proposal by half of the majority plus one, it was required that "two thirds of both Houses" should deem the amendment necessary. The exact meaning of this phrase "two thirds of both Houses" was not absolutely clear (and it will be considered *infra*).

When the Convention, on September 15, took up the Report of the Committee of Style of September 12 which rephrased this vote, G. Morris moved "to amend the Article so as to require a Convention on application of two thirds of the States." This suggestion was not identical with the provision previously voted on August 30; for under that provision, the Convention to be

called was to act finally on the amendment suggested
by two thirds of the States. By the motion of G.
Morris now, the Convention to be called by Congress
when required by two thirds of the States was simply to
propose amendments for submission later to the States
for adoption. Madison stated that he saw no objection to this suggestion, "except only that difficulties
might arise as to the form, quorum, etc.", in such a
Convention. The Convention adopted the amendment. Sherman again renewed his motion to strike
out the words "three fourths" — which, if accepted,
would have required ratification of an amendment to
be by all the States; but the motion was lost. Gerry
then attempted, unsuccessfully, to strike out the provision for ratification by Conventions in three fourths
of the States. The insertion of this alternative mode
of ratification by Conventions had undoubtedly been
due to the same liberal republican spirit which had
pervaded the framing of the Constitution in other
respects. Elections of delegates to Conventions were
not trammelled by the restrictions which attended
representation in the State Legislatures. Every State
at that time had property and religious qualifications
both for the electors of the State Legislatures, and for
the Representatives and Senators to be elected to the
same; moreover, in some States certain classes of
men, such as clergymen, were entirely excluded from the
Legislature. Hence a much more general representation of the people might then have been expected in a
State Convention than in a State Legislature.[1] More-

[1] Gorham of Massachusetts said (July 23): "In the States, many of the ablest
men are excluded from the Legislatures, but may be elected into a Convention.
Among these may be ranked many of the clergy who are generally friends to good
government. Their services were found to be valuable in the formation and establishment of the Constitution of Massachusetts." On the other hand, Gerry of
Massachusetts, who throughout was opposed to Conventions, said later in a speech
in the House in the First Congress, August 13, 1789: "The Legislatures are elected
by the people. I know no difference between them and Conventions, unless it be

over, though the size of the State Legislatures was limited by the State Constitutions, there was no restriction as to size of Conventions; and Conventions did not present the difficulty of action which the two branches of a Legislature with their varying interests might occasion.   Since the rise, in subsequent years, of universal manhood and womanhood suffrage and the abolition of property qualifications, the necessity of Conventions is at the present time less apparent.   Consideration of an amendment by a Convention, however, presents one advantage which is as applicable today as in 1787, namely, that the submission is to a body chosen for the special purpose of considering the amendment, whereas submission to a Legislature may be to a body elected beforehand on entirely different issues and with no view towards its capacity to pass on the amendment. The evil in the latter condition of affairs has been seen in several of the States which have provided in their State Constitutions that amendments to the United States Constitution shall be acted upon only by a State Legislature elected after submission of the amendment by Congress, or by a popular referendum.   Unfortunately, the United States Supreme Court has held such provisions of no effect, on the ground that the Federal Constitution contains the complete requisites for ratification and that no State can add to them.[1]

One further important action was taken with reference to the subject of amendments.   It will be noted that no restriction whatever was expressed in Madison's motion, as to the kind or extent of amendment which might be proposed.   Unless some implied restriction was to be read into it, amendments might take away or

that the former will generally be composed of men of higher characters than may be expected in Conventions; and in this case, the ratification by the Legislatures would have the preference."

[1] *Hawke* v. *Smith* (1920), 253 U. S. 220; *Rhode Island* v. *Palmer* (1920), 253 U. S. 350.

restrict powers granted to Congress by the Constitution; or might enlarge or add to them; or might contain additional restrictions on the powers of the States, or remove those already imposed, or deny to the States powers which they now retained and reserved under the Constitution; amendments might even alter or upset the great compromise which formed the basis of agreement on a draft of Constitution. The possibility of the latter class of amendment now struck Rutledge of South Carolina with great force. He saw that the compromise over commerce and slave importations might be interfered with. Accordingly, to obviate this, and saying that "he never could agree to give a power, by which the Articles relating to slaves might be altered by the States not interested in that property and prejudiced against them", he moved, on September 10, that there be added to Madison's proposal the following proviso: "Provided that no amendments which may be made prior to year 1808 shall in any manner affect the 4th and 5th sections of the Seventh Article", i.e., the Article embodying the compromise before referred to. The Convention, without debate, agreed to this limitation of the power to amend; and, modified verbally, it appears as Article V of the Constitution. Five days later, on September 15, Sherman of Connecticut awoke to the fact that the terms of the power of amendment were broad enough to upset another one of the compromises, namely, that as to equality of the States in the Senate; and also broad enough to authorize encroachments by the General Government upon the internal affairs of the States. He "expressed his fears that three fourths of the States might be brought to do things fatal to particular States, as abolishing them altogether, or depriving them of their equality in the Senate. He thought it reasonable that the proviso in favor of the State importing slaves should be

extended, so as to provide that no State should be
affected in its internal police or deprived of its equality
in the Senate." And noting the success of Rutledge
in obtaining a proviso to protect the Southern States,
Sherman now moved to attach at the end of the Article,
another proviso, viz. : "that no State shall without its
consent be affected in its internal police, or deprived of
its equal suffrage in the Senate." Madison objected
that : "Begin with these special provisos and every
State will insist on them for their boundaries, exports,
etc." And Mason stated that he thought the whole
plan of amending "exceptionable and dangerous", and
that "no amendments of the proper kind would ever
be obtained by the people if the Government should
become oppressive, as he verily believed would be the
case." Sherman's motion was defeated, receiving the
support of only Connecticut, New Jersey, and Delaware; and a motion then made by Sherman to strike
out the whole Article was also defeated. Thereupon,
in a conciliatory mood, and in order to calm part of
Sherman's fears, G. Morris moved to annex the following proviso : "that no State, without its consent, shall
be deprived of its equal suffrage in the Senate." This
was accepted by the Convention, "this motion being
dictated by the circulating murmurs of the small States,
was agreed to without debate, no one opposing it."
The votes on these motions have considerable significance; for the rejection of Sherman's motion to provide
that no State "without its consent be affected in its
internal police" by any amendment, makes it apparent
that the delegates contemplated the possibility of future
amendments which might affect the internal police of
the States, and were unwilling to bar the proposal of
amendments of such a nature. It is to be noted that,
as to the scope of the power to amend, Madison had
already said (on August 31) that : "The people were,

in fact, the fountain of all power, and by resorting to them all difficulties were got over. They could alter Constitutions as they pleased."

In 1803, the question was raised, for the first time, whether there were any implied limitations upon the power of amendment. Senators Tracy and Plumer, in the debate over the Twelfth Amendment changing the mode of election of President, contended that while "the form and modes of proceeding established by the Constitution may be amended, its principles cannot without violence be changed." "You may upon experiment so modify the Constitution in its practice and operation as to give it, upon its own principles, a more complete effect," said Tracy. "But this [amendment] is an attack upon a fundamental principle established after a long deliberation and by mutual concession, a principle of essential importance to the instrument itself, and an attempt to wrest from the smaller States a vested right and by it to increase the power and influence of the large States."[1] In recent years, a similar contention has been made, in arguments on the validity of the Prohibition Amendment.[2] Another theory has been advanced that amendments of those parts of the Constitution (and of the first ten amendments) which contain rights reserved to the people as distinguished from the States, can only be ratified by Conventions of the people, and that State Legislatures are only competent to ratify amendments relating to the "frame of government."[3] Nothing in the debates in the Convention, or in the State Conventions of 1788, or in the decisions of the Supreme Court, would seem

---

[1] *8th Cong., 1st Sess.,* p. 163, speech of Uriah Tracy in the Senate, Dec. 3, 1803; *William Plumer's Memorandum of Proceedings in the United States Senate* (1923), pp. 54, 55.

[2] See especially *The Law of the American Constitution* (1922), by Charles K. Burdick, pp. 45–50, and authorities cited.

[3] *The Bill of Rights and Its Destruction by Alleged Due Process of Law* (1927), by Henry Wynans Jessup; *Citizen or Subject* (1923), by Francis X. Hennessy.

to afford any basis for discriminating between the various parts or sections of the Constitution, with respect to its amendability.

One other point of significance should be noted in connection with the provisions for amending the Constitution. No delegate appears to have raised the question whether the "two thirds of both Houses" which were required to "deem necessary" an amendment, before its submission to the States for ratification, were to be two thirds of the whole membership of each House or simply two thirds of a quorum present. As a matter of Legislative practice, it appears to have been decided by Congress that two thirds of the members present are all that are required. When the First Congress considered the first ten amendments, the Senate Journals state that they were adopted, "two thirds of the Senators present concurring therein." [1] A similar view was taken of the subject by Congress in 1803, in adopting the Twelfth Amendment. On the other hand, Gouverneur Morris in a letter written at that time expressed his view that the Federal Convention of 1787 had intended to require two thirds of the whole membership of each House.[2] The question was

---

[1] *1st Cong., 1st Sess., Senate Journal*, Sept. 9, 21, 1789, pp. 77, 83.

[2] See discussion *supra*, p. 457. The Twelfth Amendment was adopted in a Senate of thirty-four members by a vote of twenty-two to ten; and in a House of 136 members, by a vote of eighty-four to forty-two (the Speaker casting the deciding vote). G. Morris wrote (*Life of Gouverneur Morris* (1832), by Jared Sparks, III, 198): "The idea that two thirds of the whole number of Senators and of the whole number of Representatives are required by the Constitution to propose an amendment, is certainly correct. There are, I believe only six cases in which the majority of a quorum cannot act. In one of these cases, *viz.* the choice of a President by the House of Representatives, a majority of all the States is required and the reason is evident. In two other cases, which respect only the Senate, two thirds of the members present are required. . . . There remain three cases in which two thirds of the whole number are required. These are, first, the expulsion of a member; secondly, the passage of a law disapproved of by the President; and thirdly, amendments to the Constitution. In these three cases a provision is carefully made to defend the people against themselves, or in other words, against that violence of party spirit, which has hitherto proved fatal to republican government. . . . So in the case of amendments to the Constitution, it was presumed, that America might enjoy a tolerable share of felicity under the existing compact, and that if a

not definitely decided until the Supreme Court, in 1920, in *The Prohibition Cases* (253 U. S. 380, 386), held that a vote of two thirds of the members present in each House was sufficient for the adoption of Constitutional amendments. It is a singular fact that, on so important a subject, the delegates should have left their phraseology open to differing interpretations. That they thoroughly realized the difference between a vote by two thirds of the whole membership and two thirds of the members present is shown by the fact that, in five instances during the Convention they discussed a vote of the "members present." [1] Moreover, when the State Conventions in 1788 proposed amendments to the Constitution, they also were aware of the difference between the two phrases. For Virginia and North Carolina proposed that no commercial treaty should be ratified "without the concurrence of two thirds of the whole number of the Senate", and that no treaty as to territorial or fishing rights might be ratified "without the concurrence of three fourths of the whole number of the members of both Houses respectively"; and New Hampshire proposed that no standing army be kept up in time of peace unless with the consent of three fourths of the members of each branch of Congress. Whereas, on the other hand, other States proposed amendments prohibiting Congress from legislating on certain subjects "without the assent of two thirds of the members present in both Houses", as follows: by

case should arise to point out the necessity of amendment, two thirds of the whole number of each Legislative body would concur in the recommendation."

William Plumer, Senator from New Hampshire, also took this view — see *William Plumer's Memorandum of Proceedings in the United States Senate 1803–1809* (1923), pp. 48–49 (the same speech being reported less amply in *Annals of Congress, 8th Cong., 1st Sess.*, pp. 153 *et seq*). See also speech of Uriah Tracy in the Senate, Dec. 3, 1804, *ibid*, p. 175, in which he said: "Two thirds of both Houses, must, I think, on every fair principle of construction, mean two thirds of all the members. . . . This is a point which, I am told, has never been agitated, but is certainly worthy of attention."

[1] See under date of August 15, *infra*, pp. 457–463.

Virginia and North Carolina, with reference to navigation laws or laws regulating commerce; by Virginia, North Carolina, and New York, with reference to raising or maintaining a standing army in time of peace; by Rhode Island and New York, with reference to borrowing money on the credit of the United States and with reference to declaration of war; by North Carolina, with reference to declaring any State to be in rebellion.

Submission of the Constitution to the States

With its action on the subject of amendments, the Convention concluded its labors on the draft of a Constitution as submitted by the Committee of Detail, six weeks prior; and it was now ready to turn over the result to a Special Committee which had been appointed by ballot on the preceding Saturday, September 8, "to revise the stile of and arrange the article which had been agreed to."

There was one further matter which still had to be disposed of. Gerry, Randolph, Sherman, and others were still insistent that the draft of the Constitution which should be signed by the delegates should be subject to the approval of the existing Congress under the Articles of Confederation as therein required. Hamilton also agreed with them and "thought it wrong to allow nine States to institute a new Government on the ruins of the existing one." The Convention, however, was vigorously opposed to making any change in the plan already adopted of referring the Constitution for approval by Conventions of the people. Edmund Randolph of Virginia then made a final effort, in the shape of a resolution that the plan be submitted to Congress and thence to the State Legislatures, "and from these to State Conventions having power to adopt, reject or amend, the process to close with another

General Convention with full power to adopt or reject the alterations proposed by the State Conventions, and to establish finally the Government." Though seconded by Dr. Franklin, the motion was not acted upon. A motion by Charles Pinckney that the Committee of Style be instructed to prepare an address to the People to accompany the present Constitution was adopted. The Convention then adjourned to await the performance of its task by the Committee.

OUT OF CONVENTION

Dr. James McClurg wrote to Madison from Virginia : "There is said to be a disposition generally prevalent through this State to comply with the plan of the Convention without much scrutiny. . . . I am persuaded that those who sacrifice solid and permanent advantages in this plan, to their idea of the transitory disposition of the people, will condemn themselves hereafter." Jefferson wrote, this day, from Paris, to Dumas : "Our Federal Convention is likely to sit till October. There is a general disposition through the States to adopt what they shall propose, and we may be assured their propositions will be wise, as a more able Assembly never sat in America. Happy for us that when we find our Constitutions defective and insufficient to secure the happiness of our people, we can assemble with all the coolness of philosophers and set it to rights, while every other nation on earth must have recourse to arms to amend or restore their Constitutions."

TUESDAY, SEPTEMBER 11, 1787

The Convention adjourned without doing any business, while waiting for the Report of the Committee of Style.

Washington noted :

"In Convention. Dined at home in a large company with Mr. Gardoqui, drank tea and spent the evening there."

CHAPTER TWELVE

THE FINAL SESSIONS

WEDNESDAY, SEPTEMBER 12, 1787

IN CONVENTION

Report of the Committee of Style

On this day, the Committee of Style (consisting of
Dr. William Samuel Johnson of Connecticut, Alexander
Hamilton of New York, Gouverneur Morris of Pennsylvania, James Madison of Virginia, and Rufus King of
Massachusetts) made its report of a final and revised
draft of a Constitution, printed copies of four folio
pages printed on one side being furnished the delegates.
The twenty-three articles divided into forty-one
sections of the draft reported by the Committee of
Detail on August 6 were compressed into seven articles
with twenty-one sections; the substance of changes,
amendments and additions voted by the Convention
since August 6 were duly embodied, with their language
condensed, clarified, and polished; in a very few
instances changes had been made in the votes of the

Convention; and an entirely new Preamble had been drafted. The credit for the authorship of this draft has been generally given by historians to Gouverneur Morris, based on his own claim and on the authority of Madison. Morris wrote to Timothy Pickering, in 1814 : [1]

"What can a history of the Constitution avail towards interpreting its provisions? This must be done by comparing the plain import of the words with the general tenor and object of the instrument. That instrument was written by the fingers which write this letter. Having rejected redundant and equivocal terms, I believed it to be as clear as our language would permit; excepting, nevertheless, a part of what relates to the Judiciary. On that subject, conflicting opinions had been maintained with so much professional astuteness, that it became necessary to select phrases which, expressing my own notions, would not alarm others, nor shock their self-love; and to the best of my recollection, this was the only part which passed with cavil."

And Madison wrote to Jared Sparks in 1831 : [2]

"The *finish* given to the style and arrangement of the Constitution fairly belongs to the pen of Mr. Morris; the task having been probably handed over to him by the Chairman of the Committee, himself a highly respectable member, with the ready concurrence of the others. A better choice could not have been made, as the performance of the task proved. It is true that the state of the materials, consisting of a reported draught in detail, and subsequent resolutions accurately penned and falling easily in their proper places, was a good preparation for the symmetry and phraseology of the instrument; but there was sufficient room for the talents and taste stamped by the author on the face of it."

It is probable, however, that James Wilson, Morris' colleague from Pennsylvania (though not a member of the Committee), is equally, if not more, entitled to the

[1] G. Morris to T. Pickering, Dec. 22, 1814. *Elliot's Debates*, I, 506.
[2] *Works of James Madison*, IX, 447, Madison to Sparks, April 5, 1831.

honor of making this final draft; for Timothy Pickering, writing in 1828, said that Wilson told him that "its final revision in regard to correctness of style was committed to him", and again that "James Wilson once told me that after the Constitution had been finally settled, it was committed to him to be critically examined respecting its style, in order that the instrument might appear with the most perfect precision and accuracy of language." And Wilson's claim is supported by the account of the Convention given to President Stiles of Yale College in December, 1787, by Abraham Baldwin, a delegate from Georgia, who stated that "Morris and Wilson had the chief hand in the last arrangement and composition." [1]

Accompanying the draft of the Constitution was a draft of a letter "to the United States in Congress Assembled" to be submitted to Congress with the Constitution. The Convention now read it once throughout and afterwards agreed to it by paragraphs.[2] This letter breathes such a spirit of conciliation and toleration that it may well serve as a perfect example of the manner in which the solution of all great governmental problems must be approached.[3] The most striking portions are here reproduced:

"It is obviously impracticable in the Federal Government of these States, to secure all rights of independent sover-

---

[1] *Pickering Papers MSS* in Massachusetts Hist. Soc., Pickering to John Lowell, Jan. 9, 1828; letter of Pickering, March 10, 1828. See also *The Framing of the Constitution* (1913), by Max Farrand, p. 181; *The Literary Diary of Ezra Stiles* (1901), III, Dec. 21, 1787.

[2] See *Journal.*

[3] Madison wrote to Henry Lee, June 25, 1824: "What a metamorphosis would be produced in the code of law, if all its ancient phraseology were to be taken in its modern sense! And that the language of our Constitution is already undergoing interpretations unknown to its founders will, I believe, appear to all unbiased inquirers into the history of its origin and adoption. Not to look farther for an example, take the word 'consolidate' in the Address of the Convention, prefixed to the Constitution. It there and then meant to give strength and solidity to the Union of the States. In its current and controversial application, it means a destruction of the States by transfusing their powers into the Government of the Union."

eignty to each, and yet provide for the interest and safety of all. Individuals entering into society, must give up a share of liberty to preserve the rest. The magnitude of the sacrifice must depend as well on situation and circumstance, as on the object to be obtained. It is at all times difficult to draw with precision the line between those rights which must be surrendered, and those which may be reserved; and on the present occasion, this difficulty was encreased by a difference among the several States as to their situation, extent, habits, and particular interests. In all our deliberations on this subject we kept steadily in our view, that which appears to us the greatest interest of every true American, the consolidation of our Union, in which is involved our prosperity, felicity, safety, perhaps our National existence. This important consideration, seriously and deeply impressed on our minds, led each State in the Convention to be less rigid on points of inferior magnitude than might have been otherwise expected; and thus the Constitution, which we now present is the result of a spirit of amity, and of that mutual deference and concession which the peculiarity of our political situation rendered indispensible."

The remainder of this day was spent in motions, made mostly unsuccessfully, to alter provisions already agreed upon after full debate.

OUT OF CONVENTION

Washington noted for the third time dining with Dr. Franklin:

"In Convention. Dined at the President's and drank tea at Mr. Pine's."

THURSDAY, SEPTEMBER 13, 1787

IN CONVENTION

On this day, as Madison states, "the Report from the Committee of Style and Arrangement was taken up in order to be compared with the Articles of the plan as agreed upon by the House and referred to the

Committee, and to receive the final corrections and sanctions of the Committee." The delegates were now "very impatient" to get through, and tolerated little debate.

OUT OF CONVENTION

Washington noted:

"Attended Convention. Dined at the Vice President's [of Pennsylvania] Charles Biddle's. Drank tea at Mr. Powell's."

It is interesting to note that Biddle in his autobiography said of Washington that: "When he was in Convention, I dined several times in company with him. . . . He was a most elegant figure of a man, with so much dignity of manners that no person whatever could take any improper liberties with him. I have heard Mr. Robert Morris, who was as intimate with him as any man in America, say he was the only man in whose presence he felt any awe. You would seldom see a frown or a smile on his countenance; his air was serious and reflecting, yet I have seen him in the theatre laugh heartily." [1]

The *Herald* published, this day, the following news from the Convention:

"We are well informed that the Foederal Convention will break up tomorrow or the next day, having concluded all their business, except determining upon the proper mode of making their report. Some members propose a general return of their proceedings to Congress; others conceive that, though the requisition of Congress induced the respective Legislatures to adopt the measure, yet as the delegates sit under the authority of the individual States, the return of their proceedings must be made to the power that appointed them."

The newspaper conflict between the parties in New York, which were now becoming known as Federal

---

[1] *Autobiography of Charles Biddle* (1883), p. 284.

and Antifederal, culminated, this day, in a slashing letter in the *New York Independent Journal*, by "Rusticus." This was the first personal attack in any newspaper or otherwise on the members of the Convention or on their characters :

"I cannot but express my indignation at the many illiberal publications which constantly crowd our newspapers, on the subject of politics. It seems by these publications, to be highly criminal, especially at this particular period, for any man to differ in opinion from a certain aristocratic junto, who appear determined by their writings, to silence and traduce every person who will not subscribe to every part of their political creed. In a free country, as this is, every man has an undoubtable right to think for himself, and to express his approbation or disapprobation of public measures, whenever he supposes them consistent or inconsistent with the interest and happiness of the people. If this is not the case, then have we been fighting for a shadow and lavishing our blood and treasure to very little purpose. We are frequently informed by this junto, or their adherents, that the present Convention in Philadelphia is composed of the wisest and best characters in the United States, and that it is next to high treason to lisp a suspicion that such a band of patriots can possibly recommend any system, or measure, inconsistent with the liberty, interest and happiness of those whom they represent. I am very sensible that there are many such characters in that honorable assembly as these writers have mentioned; but at the same time it is well known that there are too many of a very different character — perfect Bashaws (saving a want of power) who would trample on the most sacred rights of the people, without the least reluctance or remorse — men who are possessed of the highest opinion of their own superlative excellence and importance, and who have worked themselves into a belief that Heaven hath formed the bulk of mankind to be mere slaves and vassals to men of their superior genius, birth and fortune. The greatest part of the publications alluded to are artfully calculated to prepare the minds of the people, implicitly to receive any form of government that may be offered them. If this is not the design, why anticipate? If the Convention recommend such measures as are not consistent with the Union, but those that will promote the general interest of the Confederation, and secure the essential rights of the people, every good and virtuous citizen will not only subscribe to them but use all his influence, nay, show every name to carry them into effect. . . ."

Joseph Jones wrote, this day, from Richmond to Madison:

"The continuance of your session and some stories I have heard since my return and on my visit to Alexandria, make me apprehensive there is not that unanimity in your councils I hope for and had been taught to believe. From whence it originated, I know not, but it is whispered here, there is great disagreement among the gentlemen of our delegation, that the General and yourself on a very important question were together, Mr. Mason alone and singular in his opinion and the other two gentlemen holding different sentiments. I asked what was the dispute, and was answered that it respected either the defect in constituting the Convention in not proceeding immediately from the people, or the referring the proceedings of the body to the people for ultimate decision and confirmation."

FRIDAY, SEPTEMBER 14, 1787

IN CONVENTION

Powers Denied to Congress

This day was consumed in perfecting the final draft by minor amendments. There were one or two important changes (all of which have been considered *supra* in connection with the history of the various clauses). There were several votes of rejection of proposed new provisions. Nothing is more striking than the fact that all these votes were taken with very little debate. The delegates were evidently tired and anxious to finish their labor and go home. It will be convenient at this point in the closing days of the Convention, for the sake of giving the complete story, to note the powers proposed by various delegates to be vested in Congress, but which the Convention refused to grant.

(1) The Committee of Detail, in its Report of August 6, had vested in Congress power : "To borrow money and emit bills on the credit of the United States." On August 16, G. Morris and Butler of South Carolina moved to strike out "emit bills on the credit of the United States." Issue of paper money and making it legal tender had been two of the chief evils from which the States had suffered, and the delegates were insistent upon protecting the new National Government from such disaster. Ellsworth of Connecticut "thought this a favorable moment to shut and bar the door against paper money. The mischiefs of the various experiments which had been made were now fresh in the public mind and had excited the disgust of all the respectable part of America. . . . Paper money can in no case be necessary. Give the Government credit, and other resources will offer. The power may do harm, never good." To remove the possibility of paper money, said Wilson, "will have a most salutary effect on the credit of the United States." George Read of Delaware said picturesquely that : "The words, if not struck out, would be as alarming as the mark of the Beast in Revelations." Langdon of New Hampshire said he had "rather reject the whole plan than retain the three words ('and emit bills')." Pierce Butler was urgent for "disarming the Government of such a power." G. Morris thought that an additional argument for rejecting the power was that, if paper emissions be not prohibited, "the monied interest will oppose the plan of Government." Ellsworth also believed that "by withholding the power from the new

Government more friends of influence would be gained to it than by almost anything else." On the other hand, Mason of Virginia said that "though he had a mortal hatred to paper money, yet, as he could not foresee all emergencies, he was unwilling to tie the hands of the Legislature"; and he observed that the War of the Revolution could not have carried on, had such a prohibition existed. Randolph took the same view. John F. Mercer of Maryland stated that he was a friend to paper money, "though in the present state and temper of America, he should neither propose nor approve such a measure"; nevertheless, he was opposed to a prohibition of paper money altogether, and he urged that: "It was impolitic to excite the opposition of all those who were friends to paper money. The people of property would be sure to be on the side of the plan, and it was impolitic to purchase their further attachment with the loss of the opposite class of citizens." Madison suggested that it might be "sufficient to prohibit making them (bills of credit) a tender. This will remove the temptation to emit them with unjust views, and promissory notes in that shape may in some emergencies be best." Gorham replied that, in his view, "the power, as far as it will be necessary or safe, is involved in that of borrowing", and that he considered it wiser to strike out the express power to emit bills of credit, "without inserting any prohibition", relative to legal tender; since "if the words stand, they may suggest and lead to the measure", i.e., to a legal tender measure.

The Convention voted to strike out this power, to "emit bills on the credit of the United States", only two States voting in its favor (New Jersey and Maryland).[1] The views of those who opposed depriving

[1] Madison in a note explains that the vote of Virginia in favor of striking out the power was due to his own acquiescence, as he had become "satisfied that striking

Congress of this power were well expressed by Luther Martin, later, in his report to the Maryland Legislature: [1]

"Against the motion we urged, that it would be improper to deprive Congress of that power; that it would be a novelty unprecedented, to establish a Government which should not have such authority; that it was impossible to look forward into futurity so far as to decide that events might not happen that should render the exercise of such a power absolutely necessary; and that we doubted whether, if a war should take place, it would be impossible for this country to defend itself without having recourse to paper credit. . . . that, considering the administration of the Government would be principally in the hands of the wealthy, there could be little reason to fear an abuse of the power by an unnecessary or injurious exercise of it. But a majority of the Convention, being wise beyond every event, and

out the words would not disable the Government from the use of public notes, as far as they could be safe and proper; and would only cut off the pretext for a paper currency, and particularly for making the bills a tender either for public or private debts."

Bradley, J., in *Knox* v. *Lee* (1871), 12 Wall. 457, gave the following, as his explanation of the vote of the Convention: "The words 'and emit bills' were struck out. But they were struck out with diverse views of members, some deeming them useless and others deeming them hurtful. The result was that they chose to adopt the Constitution as it now stands, without any words either of grant or restriction of power, and it is our duty to construe the instrument by its words, in the light of history, of the general nature of government, and the incidents of sovereignty." Gray, J., in *Juilliard* v. *Greenman* (1884), 110 U. S. 421, stated: "It cannot be known how many of the delegation by whose vote the motion was adopted, intended neither to proclaim nor to deny the power to emit paper money, and were influenced by the argument of Mr. Gorham." On the other hand, Chief Justice Chase in dissent in *Knox* v. *Lee* said: "The whole discussion upon bills of credit proves, beyond all possible question, that the Convention regarded the power to make notes a legal tender as absolutely excluded from the Constitution." See also description of the debate by Clifford, J., dissenting.

[1] *Elliot's Debates*, I, 369–370. It may be noted that Gray, J., rather inaccurately said, in *Juilliard* v. *Greenman* (1884), 110 U. S. 421: "The philippic delivered before the Assembly of Maryland by Mr. Martin . . . can hardly be accepted as satisfactory evidence of the reasons or the motives of the majority of the Convention." James McHenry being later called upon to explain to the House of Delegates of Maryland the principles upon which the Constitution had been based, informed that body that it had been argued that the power to emit bills of credit ought to be left to the State but that "this was overruled by a vast majority as the best security that could be given for the public faith at home and the extension of commerce with foreigners."

being willing to risk any political evil rather than admit the idea of a paper emission in any possible case, refused to trust this authority to a Government to which they were lavishing the most unlimited powers of taxation, and to the mercy of whom they were willing blindly to trust the liberty and property of the citizens of every State in the Union."

It is to be noted that in spite of this action by the Convention on August 16, it was held, many years later, by the Supreme Court of the United States that, under the Necessary and Proper Clause of the Constitution, the power to emit bills of credit and also the power to make them legal tender in payment of private debts were to be implied from the express power "to borrow money", such subsidiary powers being deemed to be appropriate means to carry out that end.[1]

(2) On August 17, the Convention (as already described) rejected a power proposed by the Committee of Detail in its Report of August 6, viz., "to subdue a rebellion in any State on the application of its Legislature", as amended on motion of Madison by adding "against the Government thereof." This action, however, was of slight importance; for the Convention finally adopted another clause which became Article IV, section 4, of the Constitution.

(3) On August 17, the Convention rejected a motion to vest in Congress the power to make peace, which had been advocated by Butler of South Carolina and Gerry of Massachusetts, the latter urging the singular argument that the Senate, if given power to make peace, might "give up part of the United States", as it was a small body and "more liable to be corrupted by an enemy than the whole Legislature."

---

[1] See *Hepburn* v. *Griswold* (1870), 8 Wall. 603; *Knox* v. *Lee* (1871), 12 Wall. 457; *Juilliard* v. *Greenman* (1884), 110 U. S. 421. And as to the subject of this debate, see Bancroft, II, 134–137; Story's *Commentaries on the Constitution*, II, Sec. 1371; *Works of Daniel Webster*, IV, 271; brief of Clarkson N. Potter in *Hepburn* v. *Griswold, supra.*

(4) On August 17, the Convention considered the proposal made by the Committee of Detail in its Report of August 6, to vest in Congress power: "To appoint a Treasurer by ballot." George Read of Delaware moved to reject it, so as to leave the appointment of this officer as of others to the Executive, stating that "the Legislature was an improper body for appointments; those of the State Legislatures were a proof of it." Mason of Virginia, on the other hand, said that since the money belonged to the people, "the Legislature representing the people ought to appoint the keeper of it." The power was voted by the Convention. Later, on September 14, however, Rutledge and General Pinckney, noting that the system worked badly in South Carolina, moved to strike out this power. G. Morris urged that if the Treasurer were not appointed by the Legislature, he would be more narrowly watched and impeached. Gorham and King of Massachusetts and Sherman of Connecticut thought that the Legislative appointment of Treasurer should be retained, as the people "are accustomed and attached to that mode" and "the innovation will multiply objections to the system." The Convention voted, however, to strike out this power.

(5) Charles Pinckney, on August 18, had proposed a power: "To regulate stages on the post roads"; but the Committee of Detail had made no recommendation, as this power was apparently included in the power "to establish post offices and postroads" and "to regulate commerce", already adopted by the Convention.

(6) On August 20, Mason of Virginia moved that Congress be granted power "to enact sumptuary laws", saying: "No Government can be maintained unless the manners be made consonant to it. . . . It was

grant charters of incorporation." This proposed power to charter corporations, however, aroused opposition, the basis of which should be remarked. King expressed a fear that such a power "would be considered in Philadelphia and New York as directed towards the establishment of a bank which had been a subject of contention in those cities", and elsewhere as intended to promote mercantile monopolies. Though Wilson replied that power to create such monopolies were "already included in the power to regulate trade", Mason stated that he was "afraid of monopolies of every sort, which he did not think were by any means implied by the Constitution as supposed by Mr. Wilson."

The motion, when put, was confined to a power to create canals; but even in this limited form it was rejected by the Convention, only Pennsylvania, Virginia, and Georgia voting for it.[1] In view of the colloquy between Mason and Wilson, it is interesting to note that the Convention apparently did not realize that, under the Necessary and Proper Clause, a power to create corporations for certain National purposes was

---

[1] Madison though regarding this vote as a denial of power of Congress over canals expressed the view, in a letter to Reynolds Chapman, Jan. 6, 1831, that Congress ought to possess the power: "Perhaps I ought not to omit the remark that, although I concur in the defect of powers in Congress on the subject of internal improvements, my abstract opinion has been that, in the case of canals particularly, the power would have been properly vested in Congress. It was more than once proposed in the Convention of 1787, and rejected from an apprehension, chiefly, that it might prove an obstacle to the adoption of the Constitution. Such an addition to the Federal powers was thought to be strongly recommended by several considerations, 1: As Congress would possess exclusively the sources of revenue most productive and least unpopular, that body ought to provide and apply the means for the greatest and most costly work. 2. There would be cases when canals would be highly important in a National view, and not so in a local view. 3. Cases where, though highly important in a National view, they might violate the interest, real or supposed, of the State through which they would pass, of which an example might now be cited of the Chesapeake and Delaware Canal, known to have been viewed in an unfavorable light by the State of Delaware. 4. There might be cases where canals, or a chain of canals, would pass through sundry States and create a channel and outlet for their foreign commerce, forming at the same time a ligament for the Union and extending the profitable intercourse of its members, and yet be of hopeless attainment if left to the limited faculties and joint exertions of the States possessing the authority."

implied (as the Supreme Court later held with reference to the charter of the Bank of the United States in *McCulloch* v. *Maryland*, in 1819), and that a similar authority was implied from the clauses giving Congress power to legislate for the district containing the seat of government; and to make needful rules and regulations respecting the territory of the United States. Nor did the Convention realize the extent to which the power to regulate commerce between the States was, in the future, to be construed to expand the National power over canals and other forms of internal improvement, railroads, and other interstate corporations.[1]

During the debate on this proposed power, an interesting episode (not mentioned in Madison's *Notes* or in the Journal of the Convention) was later reported by Jefferson, based on statements by Abraham Baldwin and James Wilson.[2] In describing a conversation at a dinner in 1798, relative to the bill to charter the first Bank of the United States, Baldwin, he said, mentioned at table the following fact :

"When the Bank bill was under discussion in the House of Representatives [in 1791], Judge Wilson came in and was standing by Baldwin. Baldwin reminded him of the following fact which passed in the Grand Convention. Among the enumerated powers given to Congress was one to erect corporations. It was, on debate, struck out. Several particular powers were then proposed. Among others, Robert Morris proposed to give Congress a power to establish a National Bank. Gouverneur Morris opposed it, observing that it was extremely doubtful whether the Constitution they were framing could ever be passed at all by the people of America; that to give it its best chance, however, they should make it as palatable as possible, and put nothing into

---

[1] As late as 1824, Madison was of opinion that the power to construct canals was not intended by the Convention to be included in the power to regulate commerce. See letter to Edward Livingston, April 17, 1824, and see especially speech of Thomas W. Cobb in the Senate, Feb. 23, 1825.

[2] *Writings of Thomas Jefferson* (Ford's ed.), I, 343, "The Anas", March 11, 1798.

wanted the appointment of a Committee to prepare an address to the People. Rutledge objected, because of the delay and the impropriety of addressing the people before it was known whether Congress would support them. Moreover, said he, "the members of the Convention can also explain the reason of what has been done to their respective constituents." The motion was rejected.

Three delegates then took the occasion to state the causes which would impel them to refuse their signature to the new instrument of Government. Edmund Randolph of Virginia — the man who had submitted the original Resolutions embodying the general plan on which the Constitution as framed had been based — expressed "the pain he felt at differing from the body of the Convention, on the great and awful subject of their labors." He had already, on September 10, stated that his objections to the system were: (a) the vesting the Senate with power to try impeachment of the Executive; (b) the large vote required to override the President's veto; (c) the smallness of the House of Representatives; (d) the want of limitation on a standing army; (e) the insertion of the necessary and proper clause; (f) the lack of restraint on the power of Congress to pass navigation acts; (g) the failure to restrict more absolutely the power of the States to impose export duties; (h) the want of a more definite boundary between the powers of Congress and the powers of the States, and between the powers of the National and State Courts respectively; (i) the lack of restraint on the power of the President to pardon for treason; (j) the want of a limit on the power of Congress to fix its own compensation. These defects, he had contended, would cause the plan to "end in tyranny." On this September 15, Randolph now reiterated his fears of the "indefinite and dangerous" powers granted to Congress and stated that he could not sign, unless the Convention should agree that "amendments might be offered by the State Conventions, which should be submitted to and finally decided on by another General Convention." He stated, however, that he would not say whether he would actually oppose the plan when it should be submitted to his own State. His colleague, George Mason, likewise animadverted on "the dangerous power and structure" of the proposed Government, and predicted that it "would end either in monarchy or a tyrannical aristocracy"; but he also stated that he would sign, if a second General Convention might be arranged for. Mason appears to have been particularly disturbed by the changes made in the last fortnight of the sessions.[1] A third delegate, Elbridge Gerry of Massachusetts, then gave as reasons why he should withhold his signature — (a) the duration of the Senate and its ineligibility to appointment to office; (b) the power of the House to conceal its Journals; (c) the power of Congress over the places of election and its unlimited power over its own compensation; (d) the lack of due representation for Massachusetts in the House; (e) the lack of specific provision against monopolies; (f) the provision for representation of three fifths of the slaves; and in addition and as vital, the following failures to secure the rights of citizens, through the presence of the necessary and proper clause, the right to raise armies

---

[1] See conversation with Jefferson, Sept. 30, 1792, in *Writings of Thomas Jefferson* (Ford's ed.), I, 237, quoted *supra*, p. 584. Though refusing to sign, Mason had been a valuable member of the Convention and, as Madison wrote to G. Mason, Jr., Dec. 29, 1827, had "sustained throughout the proceedings of the body, the high character of a powerful reasoner, a profound statesman, and a devoted Republican. My private intercourse with him was an occasional visit to Gunston Hall (on the Potomac) when journeying to and from the North, in which his conversations were always a feast to me." As to the formal draft of his objections to the Constitution, prepared by Mason before he left the Convention, and published in October, 1787, see *Life of George Mason* (1892), by Kate Mason Rowland, III, 182–184; also *Farrand*, III, 367.

and money without limit, and the absence of a guaranty of jury trial in civil cases.

Many of these objections, it will be seen, were not on essential matters, and they did not lie against the general theory or basis of the new Government as a Nation rather than a Confederacy. Moreover, it is to be noted particularly that no one of these opponents of the Constitution raised any objection whatever to the portions of the instrument which some modern writers have supposed were one of the chief objects of the framers in protection of property interests, namely, the sections forbidding the States to issue legal tender paper money, or to impair the obligation of contracts, and the section as to the payment of the United States debts.

In reply, Charles Pinckney said that "these declarations from members so respectable, at the close of this important scene, give a peculiar solemnity to the present moment"; but he contended that nothing but confusion and contrariety could come from the calling of another Convention. He stated that he also was opposed in some degree to the Constitution as drafted, but for very different reasons — notably the "contemptible weakness" and lack of independence of the Executive, and the extent of the power of Congress over commerce. Nevertheless, "apprehending the danger of a general confusion and an ultimate decision by the sword, he should give the plan his support."

The Convention then unanimously rejected Randolph's proposal for a second General Convention; and "on the question to agree to the Constitution, as amended, all the States, ay. The Constitution was then ordered to be engrossed." [1]

The statement made by Pinckney (who had been a strong Nationalist) to the effect that he was "not with-

---

[1] McHenry states in his *Notes*: "Ordered to be engrossed and 500 copies struck."

out objections" to the plan represented the view held, in general, by all the delegates. None of them were entirely satisfied with the work; many were fearful lest the Constitution as agreed upon would prove but a temporary alleviation of evil conditions in the States; but, with very few exceptions, they agreed that its adoption now was essential to preserve the country from ruin. A striking summary of the situation has only recently appeared in print — the account by William Plumer (Senator from New Hampshire) of his conversation in 1806 with Abraham Baldwin (one of the Georgia delegates to the Convention). "He said," wrote Plumer, "that General Washington at that time, in a morning's walk, told him that he did not expect the Constitution would exist more than twenty years. He said that the Convention was more than once upon the point of dissolving without agreeing upon any system. Many believed they had no authority to report a new system, but only to propose amendments to the old Articles of Confederation. Some were for a Government of energy, embracing many objects of legislation — but others to have a more limited authority and to extend to fewer objects. All were better pleased with it, when the propositions were reduced to form and connected together, than they expected." [1]

OUT OF CONVENTION

Washington noted:

"Concluded the business of Convention all to signing the proceedings; to effect which the House sat till 6 o'clock; and adjourned till Monday that the Constitution which it was proposed to offer to the People might be engrossed and a number of printed copies struck off. Dined at Mr. Morris's and spent the evening (at my lodgings) there. Mr. Gardoqui set off for his return to New York this forenoon."

[1] *William Plumer's Memorandum of Proceedings in the United States Senate 1803–1808* (1923), p. 518.

Jacob Hiltzheimer wrote in his diary :

"In the morning went with General Mifflin to see the camel in Shippen's Alley, between Walnut and Spruce Streets, and then attended at the State House. In the afternoon went with my wife to General Mifflin's at the Falls of Schuylkill."

On this day, the Pennsylvania Assembly, being informed that the Constitution had been agreed upon, adjourned to meet on Monday at 3 P.M.

SUNDAY, SEPTEMBER 16, 1787

Washington noted :

"Wrote many letters this forenoon. Dined with Mr. and Mrs. Morris at the Hills and returned to town in the evening."

It is interesting to find that Jefferson, writing on this day from Paris to George Wythe, one of the Virginia delegates, stated as his idea of the principles on which the new Government should be based, the precise principles which the Convention had already embodied in the Constitution :

"You ask me in your letter, what ameliorations I think necessary in our Federal Constitution. It is now too late to answer the questions, and it would always have been presumptuous in me to have done it. Your own ideas and those of the great characters who were to be concerned with you in these discussions will give the law, as they ought to do, to us. My own general idea was that the States should severally preserve their sovereignty in whatever concerns themselves alone, and that whatever may concern another State or any foreign nation should be made a part of the Federal sovereignty; that the exercise of the Federal sovereignty should be divided among three several bodies, Legislative, Executive, and Judiciary, as the State Sovereignties are; and that some peaceable means should be contrived for the Federal head to force compliance on the part of the States."

MONDAY, SEPTEMBER 17, 1787

IN CONVENTION

The Signing of the Constitution

On this day, immediately upon assembling, the Convention heard the engrossed Constitution read; and, thereupon, Doctor Franklin rose with a written speech in his hand, which was read by Wilson — a speech which ought forever to be kept before the eyes of every American legislator, a great speech, in which he asked each man present to doubt somewhat as to his own infallibility and to yield to the common good. In this speech, he echoed (but in more tactful language) that striking letter which Oliver Cromwell wrote to some troublesome Presbyterian preachers, saying : "My brethren, in the name of Christ, I beseech you to think it possible that you *may* be mistaken." In a last effort to bring about unanimous action by the Convention, Franklin uttered these words of wisdom :

"I confess that there are several parts of this Constitution which I do not at present approve, but I am not sure I shall never approve them. For having lived long, I have experienced many instances of being obliged by better information, or fuller consideration, to change opinions even on important subjects, which I once thought right, but found to be otherwise. It is, therefore, that the older I grow, the more apt I am to doubt my own judgment, and to pay more respect to the judgment of others. . . . Thus, I consent, Sir, to this Constitution, because I expect no better, and because I am not sure, that it is not the best. . . . On the whole, Sir, I cannot help expressing a wish that every member of the Convention who may still have objections to it, would, with me, on this occasion doubt a little of his own infallibility, and to make manifest our unanimity, put his name to this instrument."

The newspapers referred to this speech as follows:[1]

"On Monday last, the Federal Convention closed their session by signing the Federal Government. The States, we are told, were *unanimous* in this business. The address of his Excellency Dr. Franklin to the members of the Convention, previously to this solemn transaction (a correspondent assures us) was truly pathetick and extremely sensible. The concurrence of this venerable patriot in this Government and his strong recommendation of it cannot fail of recommending it to all his friends in Pennsylvania."

This speech must have produced some effect upon wavering delegates; for as James McHenry of Maryland wrote in his *Notes:* "It was plain, insinuating, persuasive, and in any event of the system guarded the Doctor's fame." McHenry himself was by no means satisfied with parts of the Constitution, but he wrote at the conclusion of his *Notes*, a statement of the reasons which induced him to sign — a statement which was responsive to Franklin's appeal:

"Being opposed to many parts of the system, I make a remark why I signed it and mean to support it. 1st. I distrust my own judgment, especially as it is opposite to the

---

[1] *Connecticut Courant,* Oct. 1; *Boston Gazette,* Nov. 26, Dec. 3; *Salem Mercury,* Oct. 27, 1788. There are various contemporary statements that Franklin, in signing, did so with tears in his eye. *Salem Mercury,* Oct. 2, 1787. The *New York Morning Post,* Dec. 14, 1787, quoting the above article said: "No wonder he shed a tear, as it is said he did, when he gave his sanction to the new Constitution." General James Warren, writing as "Helvidius Priscus" in *Independent Chronicle,* Dec. 27, 1787, said: "The ancient Doctor, who has always been republican in principle and conduct, doubted, trembled, hesitated, wept and signed." Gen. Warren was in close touch with Elbridge Gerry throughout the Convention and may have learned the fact from him.

Franklin's speech was sent by him to several friends, after the Convention, and was printed in many newspapers. The *Virginia Independent Chronicle,* Dec. 5, 1787, said: "Your readers may depend that the following speech is genuine. The late members of the Foederal Convention who heard it delivered will readily allow it to be so. How it came into my possession is a question which only Dr. Franklin has a right to examine; and however sensibly I might feel his displeasure for thus publishing it without his consent, I think the risque of offending him is overbalanced by the service I may render my country by disseminating those principles it contains of modest deference for the opinion of others. How many States and even families have been thrown into confusion by opiniative obstinacy, which might have long remained united and happy by 'mutual deference and concession.'"

opinion of a majority of gentlemen whose abilities and patriotism are of the first cast; and as I have had already frequent occasions to be convinced that I have not always judged right. 2nd. Alterations may be obtained, it being provided that the concurrence of two thirds of the Congress may at any time introduce them. 3rd. Comparing the inconveniences and evils which we labor under and may experience from the present Confederation, and the little good we may expect from it — with the possible evils and probable benefits and advantages promised us by the new system, I am clear that I ought to give it all the support in my power."

At the conclusion of his speech, Franklin made the motion that the Constitution be signed, and he offered the following as a convenient form, viz., "Done in Convention by the unanimous consent of the States present." "This motion had been drawn by Gouverneur Morris," said Madison, "in order to gain the dissenting members, and put into the hands of Doctor Franklin that it might have the better chance of success." It was felt that delegates who disapproved in part might be willing to sign, if the action should appear to be, not theirs individually, but that of the States whose delegates at various times during the Convention had voted for the various provisions comprising the document.

Prior to the putting of this motion, Gorham of Massachusetts, seconded by his colleague, King, and by Daniel Carroll of Maryland, moved that the clause prescribing the ratio for appointment of Representatives, might be changed so that instead of being 1 to 40,000 inhabitants, it should be 1 to 30,000. This was the last motion made in the Convention, and was prompted by a desire to facilitate the adoption by some of the larger States, which had felt that they sacrificed themselves by agreeing to equality in Senate, and also to appease those who felt that there ought to be a fuller representation of the people. This latter democratic view prompted General Washington to rise in the Convention and make his one and only speech since the opening day.[1] He said now that:

"Although his situation had hitherto restrained him from offering his sentiments on questions depending in the House, and it might be thought, ought now to impose silence on him, yet he could not forbear expressing his wish that the alteration proposed might take place. It was much to be desired that the objections to the plan recommended might be made as few as possible. The smallness of the proportion of Representatives had been considered by many members of the Convention an insufficient security for the rights and interests of the people. He acknowledged that it had always appeared to himself among the exceptionable parts of the plan, and late as the present moment was for admitting amendments, he thought this of so much consequence that it would give him much satisfaction to see it adopted."

Another description of this speech, interestingly to be compared with Madison's account, was given by Abraham Baldwin of Georgia to William Plumer, a few years later, as follows:[2]

"Mr. Baldwin observed that after the instrument was engrossed and ready to be signed, General Washington, then President of the Convention, rose with his pen in his hand, and observed that his duty as presiding officer and his inclination had united in preventing him from taking an active part in the interesting debates of that body — that doubts might exist whether he approved of the instrument or only signed it by order of the Convention — he thought it his duty to remove these doubts by explicitly declaring that tho' he did not consider it a perfect system, yet he approved of it

[1] While Washington took no part in the debates, he was active in voting on all motions made in the Committee of the Whole (over which Gorham presided); and in instances when in the full Convention the vote of Virginia was divided, Madison records Washington's individual vote which was usually cast in concurrence with Madison's views.

[2] William Plumer Memorandum of Proceedings in the United States Senate 1803–1809 (1923), p. 519.

as a man and as a delegate from Virginia. There was, however, one feature in it he wished, even at this late hour, might be changed. It was the only favor he had or would ask of the Convention. That was the representation of the States. 40,000 souls he thought too high a number for a Representative. A State who has from seventy to one hundred Representatives in its Legislature will, if this principle is retained, have not more than two, three, or four Representatives in the House of Representatives in Congress. This principle, to him, appeared anti-republican. He wished the Convention would strike out 40,000 and insert 30,000. To this the Convention unanimously agreed."

Washington's speech was interestingly described in the newspapers of the day as follows : [1]

"The following instance of the influence of a good and great man will, we presume, be acceptable to every reader who loves his country and venerates its darling Hero. In the late Federal Convention, it had been for a long time debated what should be the ratio of representation, and it was carried by considerable majority to make it one for every forty thousand inhabitants. In this form, the matter was sent to the press; but when the subject came for the last time under the consideration of the Convention, and was about to be confirmed by an almost unanimous vote, General Washington rose, and spoke to the following effect : 'Though I am sensible of the impropriety of your chairman's intermingling in your debates, yet I cannot help observing that the small number which constitutes the representative body appears to be a defect in your plan. It would better suit my ideas, and, I believe, it will be more grateful to the wishes of the people, if that number was increased.' The question was immediately put, without a debate, upon a motion that the ratio be one for thirty thousand (as it now stands) and it was unanimously carried. Such was the magick force of this patriot's opinion ! And it adds to the lustre of his virtues that this critical interference (which we are well assured was

---

[1] *Massachusetts Centinel*, Nov. 21, 1787, "Of Our American Fabius."

all the share he had in the business of the late Convention) tended to promote the interest and dignity of *The People.*"

An amusing illustration of the false rumors as to the proceedings in the Convention is found in a letter to a Boston paper, two months later, making the absolutely incorrect statement that Washington took an active part in the discussions : [1]

"A correspondent asks whether the enemies to the new plan ought so frequently to call to their aid 'the scurvy art of lying'; as it is a fact as notorious as it is true that the Great Washington (although *they* shamelessly assert the contrary) was upon his feet two hours at a time in speaking upon some parts of the proposed system ; and by a gentleman who was at Philadelphia at the time the Convention was sitting, information has been received that *He* advocated every part of the plan, with all those rhetorical powers which he possesses in so eminent a degree."

After the acceptance of Gorham's motion, the question was put on the enrollment of the Constitution, in order to be signed. "It was agreed to, all the States answering ay." Before the vote, however, Edmund Randolph rose to explain once more, apologetically, why he declined to sign, "notwithstanding the vast majority and venerable names that would give sanction to its wisdom and its worth." He stated that he "did not mean by this refusal to decide that he should oppose the Constitution without doors. He meant only to keep himself free, to be governed by his duty and should be prescribed by his future judgment." Gouverneur Morris said that he too had objections, but would "take it with all its faults", being willing to abide by the determination of the majority. Hamilton "expressed his anxiety that every member should sign", saying that "no man's ideas were more remote from the Plan

---

[1] *New York Daily Advertiser,* Nov. 30, 1787, Boston despatch, Nov. 20.

than his were known to be; but is it possible to deliberate between anarchy and convulsion on one side, and
the chance of good to be expected from this plan on the
other?" William Blount of North Carolina said he
would not sign as an individual, but under the form
adopted would sign as attesting that the plan was the
unanimous act of the States. Dr. Franklin expressed
his "high sense of obligation" to Randolph for submitting the Plan originally and his hopes that Randolph
would yet concur, in order to "prevent the great
mischief which the refusal of his name might produce."
Randolph replied that though his refusal to sign might
be the "most awful step of his life", it was dictated by
his conscience and his fear that "the holding out this
plan with a final alternative to the People of accepting
or rejecting it *in toto* would really produce the anarchy
and evil convulsions which were apprehended from the
refusals of individuals to sign it." Gerry described
"the painful feelings of his situation" and his fears lest
"civil war may result from the present crisis of the
United States, in view of the divisions in politics
especially in Massachusetts, each violent in the
extreme"; he regretted that the Plan had not taken
"a more mediating shape, in order to abate the heat
and opposition of the parties." General Pinckney said
that he would sign, with a view "to support it with all
his influence, and wished to pledge himself accordingly."
Jared Ingersoll of Pennsylvania now made his first
speech in the Convention, saying that he considered
the signing, not as a pledge to support, but as a recommendation of what, all things considered, was the most
eligible.

On the motion of Dr. Franklin, that the Constitution
now be signed by the delegates, all the States voted aye,
except South Carolina, which was divided. Before the
actual signature took place, King suggested that the

Journals be either destroyed or deposited in the custody of the President, saying that he thought "if suffered to be made public, a bad use would be made of them by those who would wish to prevent the adoption of the Constitution." It was voted that they be so deposited, and that the President "retain the Journal and other papers subject to the order of the Congress, if ever formed under the Constitution." Washington asked whether "copies were to be allowed to the members if applied for." The question, however, was not specifically answered; and the vote was apparently thought to cover the matter.[1]

Thirty-eight of the members then proceeded to sign the instrument, and the signature of the thirty-ninth, John Dickinson (who was absent), was affixed at his request by George Read. Gerry, Mason, and Randolph refused to sign.[2] Hamilton inscribed on the great sheet of parchment the name of each State as the delegations came forward, one after the other, in geographical order.[3]

It was during the signing that Doctor Franklin made his notable reference to the chair (still preserved in Independence Hall), which had been occupied by John Hancock as President of the Continental Congress at the time of the signing of the Declaration of Independence, and in which Washington as presiding officer of the Convention and Gorham as Chairman of the Committee of the Whole had sat in this Convention. As reported by Madison, Franklin said:

[1] James McHenry, in his Report to the Maryland House of Delegates, Nov. 29, 1787 (Farrand, III, 144–150), said: "The Convention having deposited their proceedings with their worthy President, and by a resolve prohibited any copy to be taken, under the idea that nothing but the Constitution thus framed and submitted to the public could come under their consideration, I regret that at this distant period I am unable from memory to give this honorable House so full and accurate information as might possibly be expected on so important and interesting a subject."

[2] See letter of Dickinson to Read, Sept. 15, 1787, Farrand III, 81.

[3] Bancroft, II, 221.

"Whilst the last members were signing it, Doctr. Franklin looking towards the President's chair, at the back of which a rising sun happened to be painted, observed to a few members near him, that painters had found it difficult to distinguish in their art a rising from a setting sun. I have, said he, often and often in course of this session, and the vicissitudes of my hopes and fears as to its issue, looked at that behind the President, without being able to tell whether it was rising or setting; but now at length I have the happiness to know that it is a rising and not a setting sun."

And it was at this time, also, that Washington is reported in the newspapers to have said: "Should the States reject this excellent Constitution, the probability is that an opportunity will never again offer to cancel another in peace — the next will be drawn in blood." [1]

The signing being finished, and Doctor Franklin having concluded his speech, only one thing remained to be done. On September 13, Dr. Johnson had reported from the Committee of Style a draft of a Resolution recommending that the Constitution when adopted should be laid before Congress, and expressing "the opinion of this Convention" that it should be submitted to a Convention of delegates chosen in each State under the recommendation of its Legislature "for their assent and ratification"; that Congress, as soon as the Conventions of nine States should have ratified, should fix a date for election of the new Government; and that after such election "the Congress, together with the President, should, without delay, proceed to execute this Constitution." This Resolution was now voted "by the unanimous order of the Convention." [2] It is to be noted that the delegates thoroughly understood that, in submitting this

---

[1] *Pennsylvania Journal*, Nov. 14, 1787. As Madison does not mention this speech, there is some doubt as to the accuracy of the report.

[2] See *Journals of Congress*, IV, 781, Sept. 28, 1787.

draft of a Constitution to the people of the States, they were exceeding the powers vested in them by the State Legislatures when they first met; but, as James Wilson said later in the Pennsylvania State Convention : "The Federal Convention did not act at all upon the powers given to them by the States, but they proceeded upon original principles, and having framed a Constitution which they thought would promote the happiness of their country, they have submitted it to their considera- tion, who may either adopt or reject it, as they please."

The end of the Convention came about four o'clock in the afternoon, of this September 17, when it "dis- solved itself by adjournment, *sine die*." [1] Later on that afternoon, the Secretary of the Convention, William Jackson, sent to General Washington the following note :

"Major Jackson presents his most respectful compliments to General Washington. He begs leave to request his signature to forty diplomas intended for the Rhode Island Society of the Cincinnati. Major Jackson, after burning all loose scraps of paper which belong to the Convention, will this evening wait upon the General with the journals and other papers which their vote directs to be delivered to his Excellency, Monday evening."

At three o'clock on the same afternoon, the Pennsyl- vania Assembly was holding its daily sitting in another chamber upstairs in Independence Hall; and there the following proceedings took place. [2] "The Speaker presented a letter to the House from their delegates in Convention of the following purport, viz. that they were happy in being able to inform the House that the Convention had agreed upon the Constitution of a

---

[1] See *American Museum* (1788), II, quoting the following newspaper item : "Yesterday afternoon, about four o'clock, the Federal Convention after having concluded the important and difficult task of framing a Federal system of Govern- ment broke up; and many of the delegates we are informed, are already on their way to communicate to the anxious constituents the result of their deliberations."

[2] *Pennsylvania Packet*, Sept. 18; *Pennsylvania Herald*, Sept. 18, 1787.

Federal Government for the United States, and that the delegates were ready to report to the Legislature at any time they should be appointed. Upon motion and special order this letter was taken up for a second reading, when Mr. Fitzsimmons observed that as this measure was essentially interesting to the people, and as it had already exercised a great share of public patience, he should propose that tomorrow morning at 11 o'clock be appointed for receiving the report of the delegates, which being seconded by Mr. Hibley was accordingly agreed to. Mr. Fitzsimmons then mentioned that it was the wish of the delegates to the Federal Convention, after the accomplishment of so arduous a task, to enjoy a social meeting, which on account of the departure of some of them, this evening, had been appointed for today's dinner. He hoped, therefore, that the House would agree to an adjournment, in order that the Speaker and the other members of the House that were delegates might have it in their power to attend this appointment. Accordingly, the House adjourned to meet tomorrow morning at half past nine o'clock."

The social meeting thus referred to, took place that evening, when the members of the Convention met for the last time at the City Tavern for dinner. Some of them had been in Philadelphia continuously for over three months, Madison and Washington since May 14; some of them had been in attendance as Members of Congress in New York at intervals, like Pierce, Few, and Blount; some of them had been absent at their homes for long periods, like Paterson of New Jersey (who had returned to sign, after an absence since July 23), McHenry of Maryland, and Hamilton; some of the very active supporters of the Constitution, for various reasons, had been unable to return to be present for the signature, like Oliver Ellsworth, James

McClurg, William R. Davie, George Wythe, Alexander S. Martin, William Pierce, and Caleb Strong. Only four of the delegates who returned home before the signature are known to have been definitely opposed to the Constitution — Luther Martin and John F. Mercer of Maryland and Robert Yates and John Lansing of New York.[1]

With the conclusion of the dinner at the City Tavern, the delegates dispersed; and Washington made the following impressive entry in his diary, recording the work of this memorable day:

"Met in Convention, when the Constitution received the unanimous assent of 11 States and Colo. Hamilton's from New York (the only delegate from thence in Convention) and was subscribed to by every Member present except Mr. Randolph and Colo. Mason from Virginia, and Mr. Gerry from Massachusetts.

" The business being thus closed, the Members adjourned to the City Tavern, dined together and took a cordial leave of each other; after which I returned to my lodgings, did some business with, and received the papers from the Secretary of the Convention, and retired to meditate on the momentous work which had been executed, after not less than five, for a large part of the time six, and sometimes 7 hours' sitting every day (except) Sundays and the ten days adjournment to give a Committee opportunity and time to arrange the business, for more than four months."

Less impressive but more graphic was the description written, a few weeks later, by some one (not a delegate) whose name is unknown but who was evidently in close touch with the proceedings of the Convention:[2]

---

[1] It may be noted that there were six delegates who were not recorded in Madison's *Notes* as ever making a speech during the whole debates until September 17 — Gilman of New Hampshire; Ingersoll of Pennsylvania; Bassett of Delaware; Blair of Virginia; Blount of North Carolina; and Few of Georgia. Their signatures, however, tested their advocacy.

[2] *Documentary History of the Constitution*, IV, 324; *Farrand*, III, No. 128, letter dated Oct. 11, 1787, a copy of which in Jefferson's handwriting is in the *Jefferson Papers MSS*, in the Library of Congress.

"After four months session, the House broke up, the represented States, eleven and a half, having unanimously agreed to the act handed to you, there were only three dissenting voices; one from New England, a man of sense, but a Grumbletonian. He was of service by objecting to every thing he did not propose. It was of course more canvassed, and some errors corrected. The other two are from Virginia; but Randolph wishes it well and it is thought would have signed it, but he wanted to be on a footing with a popular rival. Both these men sink in the general opinion. No wonder they were opposed to a Washington and Madison. Dr. Franklin has gained much credit within doors from his conduct, and was the person who proposed the general signature. He had prepared his address in writing. The exertion of speaking being too great, they allowed another to read it. The day previous he sent for the Pennsylvania delegates; and it was reported that he did it to acquaint them of his disapprobation of certain points, and the impossibility of agreeing to them; his views were different, he wanted to allay every possible scruple, and make their votes unanimous. . . . The attempt is novel in history; and I can inform you of a more novel one; that I am assured by the gentlemen who served that scarcely a personality, or offensive expression escaped during the whole session. The whole was conducted with a liberality and candor which does them the highest honor. I may pronounce that it will be adopted. . . ."

TUESDAY, SEPTEMBER 18, 1787

On this day, the *Packet* and the *Herald* announced the adjournment of the Convention, as follows (in large type):

"We have the heartfelt pleasure to inform our fellow citizens that the Federal Convention adjourned yesterday, having completed the object of their deliberations, and we hear that Major W. Jackson, the Secretary of that honourable body, leaves this city for New York this morning, in order to lay the great result of their proceedings before the United States in Congress."

The *Gazetteer* said :

"Yesterday afternoon, the Honorable the Convention of the United States closed their deliberations, and we hear the plan of the new Federal Government will, at eleven o'clock this day, be promulgated by our Delegates to the General Assembly of this Commonwealth."

At 11 A.M. on this day, the General Assembly having, on motion of William Findley, appointed Col. Piper and Dr. Moore to introduce the delegates to the Federal Convention at the time appointed for receiving their report, convened for that purpose ; and the ceremony was described in the newspapers as follows : [1]

"Precisely at 11 o'clock, Col. Piper and Dr. Moore introduced his Excellency Dr. Franklin, Robert Morris, George Clymer, James Wilson, Thomas Fitzsimmons, Jared Ingersoll and Governeur Morris, Esquires, the delegates to the Federal Convention, when his Excellency addressed himself to the Speaker to the following effect — 'Sir, we have now the honor to present to this House the Plan of Government for the United States which has been determined upon by the Federal Convention. We sincerely hope and believe that the result of the labors of that honorable body will tend to promote the happiness and prosperity of this Commonwealth in particular and of the United States in general.' Mr. Fitzsimmons then stated the propriety of the report being read by a member of the delegation and proposed the Speaker for that purpose, who accordingly read it to the House. . . . As soon as the Speaker had concluded, Dr. Franklin rose and delivered a letter from the delegates to the House, which being read consisted of a recommendation to the Legislature

[1] *Pennsylvania Herald*, Sept. 20, 1787.

Jacob Hiltzheimer gave in his diary, the following account of the reception of the Constitution by the Assembly: "Sept. 17. In the afternoon attended at the State House, when a communication from our delegates in the Convention was read, informing the House that the Convention had adjourned and that they would be ready tomorrow to lay before the House, their proceedings of a four months' session." "Sept. 18. Forenoon, attended the Assembly as usual. Our delegates to the Convention brought into the Assembly the proceedings of said Convention, signed by thirty nine members, as appears in the same Constitution read by our Speaker, Thomas Mifflin, to the House this day."

'that a law should be immediately passed vesting in the new Congress a tract of land ten miles square by which that body might be induced to fix the seat of Foederal Government in this State — an event that must be highly advantagious to the Commonwealth of Pennsylvania.' "

Another newspaper account was as follows : [1]

"Yesterday the new Frame of Government was reported by the Delegates of Pennsylvania, agreeably to their instructions to the General Assembly of this State and read publickly, in the presence of a large crowd of citizens, who stood in the gallery of the Assembly room, and who testified the highest pleasure in seeing that great work at last perfected, which promises, when adopted, to give security, stability and dignity to the Government of the United States.

The division of the power of the United States into three branches gives the sincerest satisfaction to a great majority of our citizens who have long suffered many inconveniences from being governed by a single Legislature.   All single

---

[1] *Pennsylvania Gazette*, Sept. 19;   *Connecticut Courant*, Oct. 1;   *Salem Mercury*, Oct. 27, 1787.

It is not known in which room in the State House, the Assembly was sitting this day, whether upstairs or downstairs in the Declaration of Independence Chamber; but one thing is certain, viz., that it was a room with a gallery, for the newspapers mentioned "the large crowd of citizens who stood in the gallery of the Assembly room." The *Pennsylvania Herald*, Oct. 2, reporting the proceedings of the General Assembly of Sept. 29, 1787, said: "Mr. McCalmont now made an attempt to withdraw, but a general cry of *stop him*, proceeding from the gallery as well as the House, he paused." Brissot de Warville on his visit, September 6, 1788, described the room in which the Assembly then met, as follows: "There were about fifty members present, seated in chairs inclosed by a balustrade; behind the balustrade is the gallery for spectators." On the other hand, it would not appear that, in 1787, the regular room in which the Assembly sat had any gallery, for in the session of the Assembly held from Oct. 23 to Dec. 30, 1786, Robert Morris had unsuccessfully tried to obtain a provision for galleries in the Assembly Room. See *Independent Gazetteer*, Nov. 27, 1786, stating that: "A motion was made by Mr. G. Clymer to have writing tables introduced into the House, for the convenience of the members; and Mr. Morris wished it had been carried further, so as to include the galleries and sounding boards he had mentioned in the last House, which being put was negatived." It has always been stated that the Pennsylvania State Convention which met to ratify the Constitution sat in the same room in which the Federal Convention met; but it is to be noted that this Pennsylvania Convention also sat in a room in which there was a gallery; for a letter to the *Pennsylvania Packet*, Dec. 8, 1787, describing the latter Convention, said: "I have heard in the gallery the whispers of approbation circulate, as true Federal sentiments have been well expressed or happily introduced by the speakers."

governments are tyrannies — whether they be lodged in one man, a few men, or a large body of the people."

As to the reception of the news in Philadelphia, a correspondent wrote: "Having stepped into a beer-house on Saturday evening last, I perceived the room filled with a number of decent tradesmen who were conversing very freely about the members of the Federal Convention — who, it was said, like good workmen, had finished their work on a Saturday night." [1] And another correspondent wrote: [2]

"I was walking the other day in Second Street and observed a child of five or six years old, with a paper in his hand, and lisping with a smile. 'Here's what the Convention have done.' Last evening I was walking down Arch Street and was struck with the appearance of an old man whose head was covered with hoary locks and whose knees bent beneath the weight of it, stepping to his seat by the door, with a crutch in one hand, and his spectacles and the Federal Constitution in the other. These incidents renewed in my mind, the importance of the present era to one half the world! I was pleased to see all ages anxious to know the result of the deliberation of that illustrious Council whose constituents are designed to govern a World of Freemen. The unthinking youth who cannot realize the importance of government seems to be impressed with a sense of our want of system and union; and the venerable sire who is tottering to the grave feels new life at the prospect of having everything valuable secured to posterity."

Washington wrote, this day, to Jefferson, announcing the completion of the work:

"Yesterday put an end to the business of the Foederal Convention. Inclosed is a copy of the Constitution by it agreed to. Not doubting but that you have participated in the general anxiety which has agitated the mind of your

---

[1] *Independent Gazetteer*, Sept. 21, 1787; *Salem Mercury*, Oct. 2, 1787.
[2] *Pennsylvania Packet*, quoted in *Salem Mercury*, Oct. 9, 1787.

countrymen in this interesting occasion, I shall be excused, I am certain, for this endeavor to relieve you from it."

He also wrote to Lafayette:

"In the midst of hurry, and in the moment of my departure from this city, I address this letter to you. The principal, indeed the only design of it, is to fulfill the promise I made that I would send you the proceedings of the Foederal Convention as soon as the business of it was closed. More than this, circumstanced as I am at present, is not in my power to do. Nor am I inclined to attempt it, as the enclosure must speak for itself and will occupy your thoughts for some time. It is the production of four months deliberation. It is now a child of fortune, to be fostered by some and buffeted by others. What will be the general opinion on, or the reception of it, it is not for me to decide, nor shall I say anything for or against it. If it be good, I suppose it will work its way good — if bad it will recoil on the framers."

Edmund Randolph wrote to Lieutenant Governor Beverly Randolph, this day: [1]

"I do myself the honor of forwarding to the Executive a copy of the National Constitution. Altho the names of Col. Mason and myself are not subscribed, it is not, therefore, to be concluded that we are opposed to its adoption. Our reasons for not subscribing will be better explained at large, and on a personal interview, than by letter. . . . The indisposition of Mrs. Randolph will detain me here until Saturday."

Nicholas Gilman of New Hampshire wrote this day, to Joseph Gilman:

"The important business of the Convention being closed, the Secretary set off this morning to present Congress with a report of their proceedings, which I hope will come before the States in the manner directed, but as some time must necessarily elapse before that can take place, I do myself the pleasure to transmit the enclosed papers for your private satisfaction, forbearing all comments on the plan but that it is the best that could meet the unanimous concurrence of the States in Convention; it was done by bargain and compromise, yet not withstanding its imperfections, on the adoption of it depends (in my feeble judgment) whether we shall become a respectable nation, or a people torn to pieces by intestine commotions and rendered contemptible for ages."

On this day, also, the delegates from North Carolina wrote to Governor Caswell, describing the provisions of the Constitution that appeared favorable to that State; and particular note should be given to the importance which they attached to the compromises relative to representation of three-fifths of the negroes and relative to control of commerce:

"You will observe that the representation in the second branch of the National Legislature is to be according to numbers, that is to say. According to the whole number of white inhabitants added to three fifths of the blacks; you will also observe that during the first three years North Carolina is to have five members in the House of Representatives, which is just one thirteenth part of the whole number in that house and our annual quota of the National debt has not hitherto been fixed quite so high. Doubtless, we have reasons to believe that the citizens of North Carolina are more than a thirteenth part of the whole number in the Union, but the State has never enabled its Delegates in Congress to prove this opinion and hitherto they had not been zealous to magnify the number of their constituents because their quota of the National debt must have been augmented accordingly. We had many things to hope from a National Government and the chief thing we had to fear from such a Government was the risque of unequal or heavy taxation, but we hope you will believe as we do that the Southern States in general and North Carolina in particular are well secured on that head by the proposed system. It is provided in the 9th section of Article the First, that no capitation or other direct tax shall be laid except in proportion to the number of inhabitants, in which number five blacks are only counted as three. If a land tax is laid, we are to pay the same rate, for example; fifty citizens of North Carolina can be taxed no more for all their lands than fifty citizens in one of the Eastern States. This must be greatly in our favour for as most of their farms are small and many twice the value that they possess. When it is also considered that five negroes are only to be charged the same poll tax as three whites the advantage must be considerably increased under the proposed form of Government. The Southern States have also a much better security for the return of slaves who might endeavour to escape than they had under the original Confederation. It is expected a considerable share of the National taxes will be collected by impost, duties and excises; but you will find it provided, in the 8th Section of Article the First, that all duties, imposts and excises shall *be uniform*, throughout the United States. While we were taking so much care to guard ourselves against being overreached and to form rules of taxation that might operate in our favour, it is not to be supposed that our Northern brethren were inattentive to their particular interest. A navigation act or the power to regulate commerce in the hands of the National Government, by which American ships and seamen may be fully employed, is the desirable weight that is thrown into the Northern scale. This is that the Southern States have given in exchange for the advantages we mentioned above; but we beg leave to observe, in the course of this interchange North Carolina does not appear to us to have given up anything, for we are doubtless the most independent of the Southern States; we are able to carry our own produce, and if the spirit of navigation and shipbuilding is cherished in our State, we shall soon be able to carry for our neighbors."

On the afternoon of this eighteenth of September, General Washington left Philadelphia to return to Mount Vernon, as he noted in his diary :

"Finished what private business I had to do in the City this forenoon, took my leave of those families, in wch. I had been most intimate, dined early abt. 1 o'clock at Mr. Morris's, with whom and Gouvr. Morris, I parted at Gray's Ferry, and reached Chester, where we lodged in Company with Mr. Blair, who I invited to a seat in my Chariot carriage; till we should reach Mount Vernon."

After an absence of four months and fourteen days, he reached his home about sunset on September 22. Two days after his return, he wrote to Patrick Henry, the Governor of Virginia, his views as to the work which had been accomplished by the Convention:

"Your own judgment will at once discover the good and the exceptionable parts of it; and your experience of the difficulties, which have ever arisen when attempts have been made to reconcile such variety of interests and local prejudices as pervade the several States, will render explanation unnecessary. I wish the Constitution which is offered had been made more perfect; but I sincerely believe it is the best that could be obtained at this time. And as a Constitutional door is opened for amendment hereafter, the adoption of it, under the present circumstances of the Union, is in my opinion desirable. From a variety of concurring accounts, it appears to me that the political concerns of this country are, in a manner, suspended by a thread, and that the Convention has been looked up to by the reflecting part of the community, with a solicitude which is hardly to be conceived; and, if nothing had been agreed on by that body, anarchy would soon have ensued, the seeds being deeply sown in every soil."

Two weeks later, his attitude towards the new Constitution was reported by a friend visiting at Mount Vernon, as follows: "He is in perfect good health, and looks almost as well as he did twenty years ago. I never saw him so keen for anything in my life as he is for the adoption of the new scheme of Government." [1]

---

[1] Alexander McDonald to Jefferson, Nov. 12, 1787, writing as to his visit of Oct. 5–7. *Writings of George Washington* (Ford's ed.), XI, 169; Madison to Edward Everett, June 3, 1827.

And Madison wrote of him later: "I can testify from my personal knowledge that no member of the Convention appeared to sign the Instrument with more cordiality than he [Washington] did, nor to be more anxious for its ratification. I have indeed the most thorough conviction, from the best evidence, that he never wavered in the part he took in giving it his sanction and support."

That Washington's participation in the Convention and his strong advocacy of its work was to have a vast influence in the ensuing fight for its ratification is seen from many articles and letters in the newspapers and elsewhere. An editorial in a Boston paper addressed him as "illustrious chieftain, immortal sage", and stated: "You have twice saved your country. . . . The unanimity you have secured in your deliberations is an auspicious omen of our future concord and felicity. We anticipate with pleasure the happy effects of your wisdom. The narrow, contracted politics, the sordid envy, the mean jealousy of little minds, the partial views and the local prejudices which have so long retarded the growth of this people will be now annihilated." [1] A Philadelphia paper said: "George Washington, Esq., has already been destined by a thousand

---

[1] *American Herald*, Sept. 30; *Pennsylvania Herald*, Sept. 27, 1787. That many accepted the Constitution on the strength of Washington's and Franklin's signature is undoubted. "A Farmer" writing to the *American Herald* in Boston, January 14, 1788, said: "I doubt much whether they have carefully examined the Constitution. The hypothesis that General Washington and Doctor Franklin made it, is too strong an argument in the minds of many to suffer them to examine, like freemen, for themselves." A letter from a Virginia representative published in the *Maryland Journal*, Dec. 18, 1787, said that "it appears to me the party in favour of the Constitution must prevail; the signature and approbation of our great Washington will give it a preponderancy to weigh down all opposition." Contemporary writings contain rare instances of any unfavorable criticism of Washington. One of the very few is in a letter from Charleston, So. Car., in the *Independent Gazetteer*, April 19, 1788: "As to General Washington, he has much good sense if he would exercise it, but he leans altogether upon others. (We find he did not meddle.) He depends principally upon the Connecticut Poet who was his Aid de Camp (Col. David Humphreys) as an adviser. When this is the case, what dependence can be placed in his judgment, on which I find many weak people did lean, for some time, till the business was opened to them."

voices to fill the place of the first President of the United States, under the new Frame of Government. . . . Can the history of the world show an instance of such a voluntary compact between the deliverer and the delivered of any country, as will probably soon take place in the United States?"

Benjamin Harrison, ex-Governor of Virginia, wrote to Washington, October 4: "I find myself deeply interested in everything that you have had a hand in, or that comes from you; and am so well assured of the solidity of your judgment and the rectitude of your intention that I shall never stick at trifles to conform myself to your opinion." [1] A few weeks later, Gouverneur Morris wrote to him: [2]

"I have observed that your name to the new Constitution has been of infinite service. Indeed, I am convinced that if you had not attended the Convention, and the same paper had been handed out to the world, it would have met with a colder reception, with fewer and weaker advocates, and with more and more strenuous opponents. As it is, should the idea prevail that you will not accept the Presidency, it would prove fatal in many parts. The truth is, that your great and decided superiority leads men willingly to put you in a place which will not add to your personal dignity nor raise you higher than you already stand. But they would not readily put any other person in the same situation."

[1] *Writings of George Washington* (Ford's ed.), XI, 169, Harrison to Washington, Oct. 4, 1787. He continued: "In the present instance, I am so totally uninformed as to the general situation of America that I can form no judgment of the necessity the Convention was under to give us such a Constitution as it has done."

[2] G. Morris to Washington, Oct. 30, 1787. See also Monroe to Jefferson, July 12, 1788: "Be assured, his influence carried this Government; for my own part, I have a boundless confidence in him."

John Jay wrote to Washington, April 21, 1789: "The dissolution of our Governments threw us into a political chaos. Time, wisdom and perseverance will reduce it into form, and give it strength, order and harmony. In this work, you are (in the stile of one of your professions) a master builder, and God grant that you may long continue a free and accepted one."

PART THREE
AFTER THE CONVENTION

CHAPTER ONE

OPPOSITION AND RATIFICATION

One of the most fortunate features of the Constitution was that it was the result of compromises and adjustments and accommodations on the part of the individual delegates — "the result of a spirit of amity and mutual concession" — to use Washington's words.[1] It did not represent the complete supremacy of the views of any particular man or set of men, or of any State or group of States. The claims and interests of neither the North nor the South prevailed. Each had been obliged to sacrifice part of its demands and to subordinate its own advantage to the welfare of the whole country. Moreover, it represented neither an extreme Nationalist point of view nor an extreme States' Rights doctrine. The adherents of each theory had been obliged to yield.

So, too, the discussions throughout the Convention had been based rather on practical than on philosophic lines.[2] The evils to be cured and the benefits to be

[1] Message of President Washington to the House of Representatives on the Jay Treaty, March 30, 1796; see also letter of the Convention of Sept. 17, 1787, to the Congress of the Confederation. Charles A. Beard and Mary R. Beard in their *Rise of American Civilization*, I, 317, phrase this rather strikingly: "In its final form the Constitution, so far as the structure of the Government was concerned was 'a bundle of compromises.' It was more. It was a mosaic of second choices accepted in the interest of union and the substantial benefits to flow from union."

[2] "When one considers the bulk of commentary that has grown up about the Constitution, it is surprising how little political speculation accompanied its making and adoption. It was the work of able lawyers and men of affairs confronting a definite situation rather than of political philosophers." *The Colonial Mind 1620–1800* (1927), by Vernon Laws Purrington. "The question of the nature of the

secured were its chief concern. Hence the desire to push mere theories to their ultimate and logical conclusions — "that passion of small minds" — did not impel or control the delegates. As a result of all these conditions, the Constitution in its final form was not completely satisfactory to any one. This fact again was fortunate; for no one man could claim a complete victory over any other. And it is largely because of this fact that the Constitution has so successfully met the test of time, of changing social and economic circumstances, and of National geographical expansion; for it favored no section of the country and no portion of its population exclusively.

The delegates did not regard their work as perfect; but they were satisfied that no Constitution better adapted to the needs of their country could possibly have been framed, at that time, under all the circumstances.[1] As Roger Sherman said in the House, June 8, 1789: "I do not suppose the Constitution to be perfect. Nor do I imagine if Congress and all the Legislatures on the Continent were to revise it that their united efforts would make it perfect. I do not expect

instrument was discussed in the Convention, not as a philosophy of government, but as a working arrangement." *An Introduction to the Study of the American Constitution* (1926), by Charles E. Martin. "Our Constitution was a practical piece of work for very practical purposes. It arose from the necessity of existing conditions. It was designed to meet certain specific needs, and when those were provided for, the work was done." *The Federal Constitution and the Defects of the Confederation*, by Max Farrand, *Amer. Pol. Sci. Rev.* (1908), II. "No one who has studied the primary material will be ready to assert that men consistently and invariably acted upon a single principle, that they were altogether conscious of the nature and import of what was being done, and that they constantly spoke with logical accuracy of the process. Such consistency and philosophic knowledge do not appear in the affairs of statesmen." *Social Compact and Constitutional Construction*, by Andrew C. McLaughlin, *Amer. Hist. Rev.* (1899), V, 472.

[1] John Adams wrote from London to John Jay, Dec. 16, 1787: "The public mind cannot be occupied about a nobler object than the proposed plan of Government. It appears to be admirably calculated to cement all America in affection and interest as one great Nation. A result of accommodation and compromise cannot be supposed perfectly to coincide with any one's ideas of perfection. But as all the great principles necessary to order, liberty and safety are respected in it, and provision is made for corrections and amendments as they may be found necessary, I confess I hope to hear of its adoption by all the States."

any perfection on this side the grave in the work of man ; but my opinion is that we are not at present in circumstances to make it better."

But while the Constitution was not thus wholly acceptable to the views of any one delegate, undue emphasis must not be laid on the element of compromise. There were many of its essential features on which there was almost complete agreement. This fact has been well set forth in a recent striking history.[1] "If they warmly debated many matters pertaining to means and instrumentalities, they agreed with relative ease that a National Government must be erected and endowed with ample power to defend the country on land and sea, to pay the National debt, to protect private property against agrarian Legislatures, to secure the return of fugitive servants and to uphold the public order against domestic insurrection. This basic fact should not be obscured in any consideration of the long and tempestuous arguments that arose over the form of the new Government and the representation of the States in it."

The views of the delegates themselves as to the difficulties which they felt they had overcome as successfully as possible were interestingly expressed.

Thus, Washington wrote to Col. David Humphreys, October 10, 1787 :

"The Constitution that is submitted is not free from imperfections, but there are as few radical defects in it as could well be expected, considering the heterogeneous mass of which the Convention was composed and the diversity of interests that are to be attended to. As a Constitutional door is opened for future amendments and alterations, I think it would be wise in the people to accept what is offered to them and I wish it may be by as great a majority of them

[1] *The Rise of American Civilization* (1927), by Charles A. Beard and Mary R. Beard, I, 314.

as it was by that of the Convention; but this is hardly to be
expected, because the importance and sinister views of too
many characters will be affected by the change. Much will
depend however upon literary abilities, and the recommendation of it by good pens should be *openly*, I mean, publickly,
afforded in the *Gazettes*. Go matters, however, as they may,
I shall have the consolation to reflect that no objects but the
public good and that peace and harmony which I wished to
see prevail in the Convention, obtruded even for a moment
in my bosom during the whole session, long as it was."

And to his nephew, Bushrod Washington, he wrote,
November 10, 1787, in the same strain:

" The warmest friends and the best supporters the Constitution has, do not contend that it is free from imperfections; but they found them unavoidable, and are sensible,
if evil is likely to arise therefrom, the remedy must come
hereafter; for in the present moment, it is not to be obtained;
and, as there is a Constitutional door open for it, I think the
people (for it is with them to judge) can, as they will have the
advantage of experience on their side, decide with as much
propriety on the alterations and amendments which are
necessary, as ourselves. I do not think we are more inspired,
have more wisdom, or possess more virtue, than those who
will come after us. The power under the Constitution will
always be in the people. It is intrusted for certain defined
purposes, and for a certain limited period, to representatives
of their own choosing; and whenever it is executed contrary
to their interest, or not agreeable to their wishes, their servants can and undoubtedly will be recalled. It is agreed
on all hands, that no Government can be well administered
without powers; yet, the instant these are delegated,
although those who are intrusted with the administration
are no more than the creatures of the people, act as it were
but for a day, and are amenable for every false step they
take, they are, from the moment they receive it, set down
as tyrants; their natures, they would conceive from this,
immediately changed, and that they can have no other
disposition but to oppress. Of these things, in a Government

constituted and guarded as ours is, I have no idea; and do firmly believe, that, whilst many ostensible reasons are assigned to prevent the adoption of it, the real ones are concealed behind the curtains, because they are not of a nature to appear in open day. I believe, further, supposing them pure, that as great evils result from too great jealousy as from the want of it. We need look, I think, no further for proof of this, than to the Constitution of some, if not all, of these States. No man is a warmer advocate for proper restraints and wholesome checks in every department of Government, than I am; but I have never yet been able to discover the propriety of placing it absolutely out of the power of men to render essential services, because a possibility remains of their doing ill."

To Lafayette, he wrote, February 7, 1788: "It appears to me, then, little short of a miracle that the delegates from so many different States (which States you know are also different from each other), in their manners, circumstances and prejudices, should unite in forming a system of National Government, so little liable to well-founded objections." [1]

Benjamin Franklin wrote to his sister, Mrs. Jane Mecom, as to the completion of the Convention's work: [2]

[1] See also Washington to Mrs. Catharine Macaulay Graham, Nov. 16, 1787: "The various and opposite interests which were to be conciliated, the local prejudices which were to be subdued, the diversity of opinions and sentiments which were to be reconciled, and in fine the sacrifices which were necessary to be made on all sides for the general welfare, combined to make it a work of so intricate and difficult a nature that I think it is much to be wondered at that anything could have been produced with such unanimity as the Constitution proposed." See also Washington to Edmund Randolph, Jan. 8, 1788: "There are some things in the new form, I will readily acknowledge which never did, and I am persuaded never will, obtain my cordial approbation; but I then did conceive, and do now most firmly believe that in the aggregate it is the best Constitution that can be obtained at this epoch, and that this or a dissolution of the Union, awaits our choice, and are the only alternatives before us."

[2] Franklin to Mecom, Sept. 26, 1787; to M. LeVeillard, he wrote April 22, 1788: "It is very possible as you suppose, that all the Articles of the proposed new Government will not remain unchanged after the meeting of the new Congress. I am of opinion with you that the two Chambers were not necessary, and I disliked some other articles that are in, and wished for some that are not in the proposed Plan; I nevertheless hope it may be adopted." *Book of the Signers* (1861) by William Brotherhead. To Ferdinand Grand in Paris, he wrote, October 22, 1787: "I send

"The Convention finish'd the 17th instant. I attended the business of it 5 Hours in every day from the beginning, which is something more than four months. You may judge from thence, that my health continues; some tell me I look better, and they suppose the daily exercise of going and returning from the State house has done me good. You will see the Constitution we have propos'd in the papers. The forming of it so as to accommodate all the different interests and views was a difficult task; and perhaps after all, it may not be received with the same unanimity in the different States, that the Convention have given the example of in delivering it out for the consideration. We have, however, done our best, and it must take its chance."

Pierce Butler wrote to his son, Weedon Butler, from New York:[1]

"In passing judgment on it, you must call to mind that we had clashing interests to reconcile — some strong prejudices to encounter, for the same spirit that brought settlers to a certain quarter of this country is still alive in it. View the system then as resulting from a spirit of accommodation to different interests, and not the most perfect one that the Deputies could devise for a country better adapted for the reception of it than America is at this day, or perhaps ever will be. It is a great extent of territory, to be under one free Government; the manners and modes of thinking of the inhabitants differing nearly as much as in different Nations of Europe. If we can secure tranquillity at home, and

you enclos'd the propos'd new Federal Constitution for these States. I was engag'd 4 Months of the last Summer in the Convention that form'd it. It is now sent by Congress to the several States for their confirmation. If it succeeds, I do not see why you might not in Europe carry the project of good Henry the 4th into execution, by forming a Federal Union and one grand Republick of all its different States and Kingdoms, by means of a like Convention, for we had many interests to reconcile."

[1] *Records of the Federal Convention* (1911), by Max Farrand, III, No. 127. To Elbridge Gerry, Butler wrote: "I ardently wished my friend Gerry to think as I did that the Constitution, with all its imperfections, is the only thing that can rescue the States from civil discord and foreign contempt. Reflecting maturely on the little disposition of most of the States to submit to any government, I preferred giving my consent to a trial of the Constitution, with all its imperfections; that there are parts I do not like, you well know." *Life of Elbridge Gerry* (1822), by James T. Austin, II, 59.

respect from abroad, they will be great points gained. We have, as you will see, taken a portion of power from the individual States, to form a General Government for the whole to preserve the Union."

Major William Pierce, who was in attendance in New York as a Member of Congress from Georgia at the time of the signing of the Constitution, wrote to St. George Tucker of Virginia, explaining his views : [1]

"I approve of its principles, and would have signed it with all my heart, had I been present. To say, however, that I consider it perfect would be to make an acknowledgment immediately opposed to my judgment. Perhaps it is the only one that will suit our present situation. The wisdom of the Convention was equal to something greater; but a variety of local circumstances, the inequality of the States, and the dissonant interests of the different parts of the Union made it impossible to give it any other shape or form. . . . Some will oppose it from pride, some from self interest, some from ignorance, but the greater number will be of that class who will oppose it from a dread of its swallowing up the individuality of the States. . . ."

Gouverneur Morris wrote, in January, 1788, that the draft of the Constitution had been "the subject of infinite investigation, disputation and declamation", and that "while some have boasted it as a work from Heaven, others have given it a less righteous origin. I have many reasons to believe that it is the work of plain, honest men, and such I think it will appear. Faulty it must be, for what is perfect? But if adopted, experience will, I believe, show that its faults are just the reverse of what they are supposed to be."

Charles Pinckney said, in the South Carolina Legislature, in 1788 : [2]

"This is the best Government that has ever yet been offered to the world and instead of being alarmed at its

---

[1] *Amer. Hist. Rev.* (1898), III, 313, Pierce to Tucker, Sept. 28, 1787.
[2] *Elliot's Debates*, IV, 261.

consequences we should be astonishingly pleased that one so perfect could have been formed from such discordant and unpromising materials. . . . He confessed, however, that after all that has been said upon the subject, our Constitution was in some measure but an experiment; nor was it possible yet to form a just conclusion as to its practicability."

The following graphic description given by James Wilson to the Pennsylvania State Convention, November 24, 1787, presents the difficulties which the delegates encountered, and the necessity of modelling the new Government to conciliate these divergent views.[1]

"To frame a Government for a single city or State, is a business, both in its importance and facility, widely different from the task entrusted to the Federal Convention, whose prospects were extended not only to thirteen independent and sovereign States, some of which in territorial jurisdiction, population, and resource, equal the most respectable nations of Europe, but likewise to innumerable States yet unformed and to myriads of citizens who in future ages shall inhabit the vast uncultivated regions of the continent. The duties of that body, therefore, were not limited to local or partial considerations, but to the formation of a plan commensurate with a great and valuable portion of the globe. I confess, Sir, that the magnitude of the object before us, filled our minds with awe and apprehension. . . . But the magnitude of the object was equalled by the difficulty of accomplishing it, when we considered the uncommon dexterity and address that were necessary to combat and reconcile the jarring interests that seemed naturally to prevail, in a country which, presenting a coast of 1500 miles to the Atlantic, is composed of thirteen distinct and independent States, varying essentially in their situation and dimensions, and in the number and habits of their citizens — their interests too, in some respects really different, and in many apparently so; but whether really or apparently, such is the constitution of the human

[1] *Pennsylvania and the Federal Constitution* (1888), by J. B. McMaster and F. D. Stone.

mind, they make the same impression, and are prosecuted with equal vigor and perseverance. Can it then be a subject for surprise that, with the sensations indispensably excited by so comprehensive and so arduous an undertaking, we should for a moment yield to despondency, and at length, influenced by the spirit of conciliation, resort to mutual concession, as the only means to obtain the great end for which we were convened? Is it a matter of surprise that where the springs of dissension were so numerous, and so powerful, some force was requisite to impel them to take, in a collected state, a direction different from that which separately they would have pursued? There was another reason, that, in this respect, increased the difficulties of the Federal Convention — the different tempers and disposition of the people for whom they acted. . . . The extent of country for which the new Constitution was required produced another difficulty in the business. . . . These difficulties which embarrassed the Federal Convention are not represented to enhance the merit of surmounting them, but with a more important view to show how unreasonable it is to expect that the plan of Government should correspond with the wishes of all the States, of all the citizens of any one State, or of all the citizens of the united Continent."

Madison, himself, was not wholly satisfied with the results of the labors of the Convention in which he had been so large a factor.[1] Nevertheless, he wrote to Edmund Pendleton, September 20:

"The privilege of franking having ceased with the Convention,[2] I have waited for this opportunity of inclosing

[1] To Philip Mazzei, Madison wrote, a year later, October 8, 1788: "You ask me why I agreed to the Constitution proposed by the Convention of Philadelphia. I answer, because I thought it safe to the liberties of the people, and the best that could be obtained from the jarring interests of States and the miscellaneous opinions of politicians; and because experience has proved that the real danger to America and to liberty lies in the defect of energy and stability in the present establishment of the United States."

[2] A resolution of Congress of April 22, 1787, had been on motion of Edward Carrington of Virginia, seconded by Dr. W. S. Johnson of Connecticut, that members of the Convention should have the "privilege of sending and receiving letters and packets free of postage." *Pennsylvania Gazetteer*, May 11, 1781; *Pennsylvania Journal*, May 12, 1787; *Pennsylvania Packet*, May 16, 1787.

you a copy of the proposed Constitution for the United States. I forbear to make any observations on it, either on the side of its merits or its faults. The best judges of both will be those who can combine with a knowledge of the collective and permanent interest of America, a freedom from the bias resulting from a participation in the work. If the plan proposed be worthy of adoption, the degree of unanimity attained in the Convention is a circumstance as fortunate, as the very respectable dissent on the part of Virginia is a subject of regret. The double object of blending a proper stability and energy in the Government with the essential characters of the republican form, and of tracing a proper line of demarkation between the National and State authorities, was necessarily found to be as difficult as it was desirable, and to admit of an infinite diversity concerning the means among those who were unanimously agreed concerning the end."

And to Jefferson, he wrote, October 24, a long letter of explanation as to the principles embodied in the new Constitution — in which he said that each of the objects which the Convention set itself to accomplish "were pregnant with difficulties. The whole of them together formed a task more difficult than can be conceived by those who were not concerned in the execution of them. Adding to these considerations the natural diversity of human opinions on all new and complicated subjects, it is impossible to conceive the degree of concord which ultimately prevailed as less than a miracle." [1]

Jefferson, though in Paris, had been kept in close touch with the situation by numerous correspondents. At first, he wrote to John Adams, that there were "things in it which stagger all my disposition to subscribe to what such an Assembly has proposed"; and to W. S. Smith, he wrote that: "Our Convention has been too much

---

[1] Jefferson replied, Dec. 20, 1787, giving the views he then entertained, but which he later modified to some extent. See also Jefferson to Madison, Feb. 6, July 31, 1788; Madison to Jefferson, Dec. 9, 1787; Feb. 19, 1788.

impressed by the insurrection of Massachusetts, and on the spur of the moment, they are setting up a kite to keep the barnyard in order." [1] His principal objections were to the omission of a Bill of Rights and to the eligibility of the President to re-election; but as he wrote later to Edward Rutledge: "My confidence is, that there will for a long time be virtue and good sense enough in our countrymen to correct abuses. We can surely boast of having set the world a beautiful example of a Government reformed by reason alone, without bloodshed", and to the Comte de Moustier, he wrote: "I see in this instrument a great deal of good. There are, indeed, some faults which at first revolted me a good deal in the first moment; but we must be contented to travel on towards perfection, step by step." In numerous letters, written during the campaign for ratification, he warmly favored such action, and his attitude was well depicted by him in his *Autobiography* (written in 1821):

"I received a copy early in November and read and contemplated its provisions with great satisfaction. As not a member of the Convention, however, nor probably a single citizen of the Union had approved it in all its parts, so I too found articles which I thought objectionable. . . . I expressed freely in letters to my friends, and most particularly to Mr. Madison and General Washington, my approbations and objections. How the good should be secured and the ill brought to rights was the difficulty. To refer it back to a new Convention might endanger the loss of the whole. My first idea was that the nine States first acting should accept

[1] See especially letters to John Adams, Nov. 13, 1787; W. S. Smith, Nov. 13, 1787; William Carmichael, Dec. 15, 1787; Edward Carrington, Dec. 21, 1787, May 27, June 3, 1788; William S. Smith, Feb. 2, 1788; A. Donald, Feb. 7, 1788; Washington, May 2, 1788; Comte de Moustier, May 17, 1788; Edward Rutledge, July 18, 1788; see also especially Jefferson to Francis Hopkinson, March 13, 1789: "I approved from the first moment, of the great mass of what is in the new Constitution. . . . These my opinions, I wrote, within a few hours after I had read the Constitution, to one or two friends in America. I had not then read one single word printed on the subject."

it unconditionally and thus secure what in it was good, and that the four last should accept on the previous condition that certain amendments should be agreed to; but a better course was devised of accepting the whole and trusting that the good sense and honest intention of our citizens should make the alterations which should be deemed necessary."

The story of the heated opposition to the Constitution which developed within a few months after its signature, and of the bitterly fought contests in the State Conventions which resulted in its ratification by eleven of the thirteen States prior to August, 1788, has been often told.[1] It is unnecessary to repeat the tale here. There are certain phases of that momentous struggle, however, which have not been developed by historians, and which should be noted by anyone who desires to understand the motives and conditions influencing the men of that period in their attitudes towards the Constitution.

Historians have very generally failed to make clear that the Antifederalist party was not something which sprang into being in 1787, for the purpose of opposing the Constitution. It was a party whose sentiments and whose forces and leaders had been solidifying during the previous ten years. It is only when the fight against the Constitution is viewed as the natural result

---

[1] See *The Ratification of the Federal Constitution by the State of New York* (1921), by Clarence E. Miner; *History of the Virginia Federal Convention of 1788*, by H. B. Grigsby, *Virginia Historical Society Collections* (1890–91), N. S. IX, X; *Essays on the Constitutional History of the United States* (1889), ed. by J. F. Jameson, pp. 46–115, as to the Virginia Convention; *Pennsylvania and the Federal Constitution 1787–88* (1888), by J. B. McMaster and F. D. Stone; *Contest over the Ratification of the Federal Constitution in the State of Massachusetts* (1896), by S. P. Harding; *The Geographical Distribution of the Vote of the Thirteen States on the Federal Constitution — 1787–1788*, by O. G. Libby, *Univ. of Wisc. Bulletin Economics, Political Science and History*, Series I, No. 1 (1894); *Maryland's Adoption of the Constitution*, by Bernard C. Steiner, *Amer. Hist. Rev.* (1899), V, 22, 207; *The Confederation and the Constitution* (1905), by Andrew C. McLaughlin, see especially the bibliography; *Life of John Marshall* (1916), by Albert J. Beveridge, I, chapters 8 and 9; *The Fathers of the Constitution* (1921), by Max Farrand; *Writings of James Madison* (Hunt's ed.), V, 1–123, letters from September, 1787, to May, 1788; and see authorities cited on page 6, note 1, of the present book.

of opinions long held by a large portion of the American people in many States that one can make a proper estimate of that fight. And it is only when the strength of the opposition to the Constitution, as framed, is duly understood that one can begin to appreciate the greatness of the triumph of the Constitution over its opponents.

A recent brilliant writer has elaborated the point that the habits of thought of the men of the 1880's and 90's were colored by the influence upon the youth of the 1850's and 60's of the McGuffey school readers.[1] So also, in estimating the factors which have moulded the ways of thinking, and, consequently, the life of Americans, one must by no means omit to consider the important fact, that for about one hundred years after the framing of the Constitution, American history (especially as used in the schools), American biography, and American constitutional law were very largely written by men who had distinct sympathies with the policies and politics of the old Federalist party. These writers have portrayed the Federalists as fighting for principles, while they have described the Antifederalists as indulging only in politics. They have implicitly accepted the political picture which the Federalists drew of their opponents; they have set forth the motives and personalities of the Antifederalists in terms of Federalist charges and characterizations. The result of all this has been to distort the whole situation. Within recent years, a curious reversal of attitude has taken place; and historians of the so-called school of economic determinism now portray the Federalists from the political viewpoint of their opponents, and reproduce the old Antifederalist political charges that the Federalists were all men of property, men impelled by interested economic motives or controlled by their

[1] *Our Times* (1927), by Mark Sullivan, II.

economic environment.   But partisan characterizations
and exaggerations made in a political campaign are
unsafe bases for history.   It is as unfair to the Federalists to depict them as chiefly motivated by selfish,
personal, and economic conditions in their advocacy
of the Constitution, as it was unfair to the Antifederalists to portray them as wholly influenced by similar
conditions, in their opposition.   The fact is, that in
the campaign of 1787–1788 (as in most other political
campaigns), neither side gave to the other any credit
for unselfish convictions or candor or sincerity of
purpose.   The standard Federalist view of their opponents was that written by Oliver Ellsworth of Connecticut in the newspapers, namely, that the Antifederalists were all "men who have lucrative and influential
State offices", "tories, debtors in desperate circumstances, or insurgents", believers only in paper money
and tender acts.[1]   Even Washington himself wrote
that the major part of the Constitution's opponents
were "governed by sinister and self-important motives."
Equally exaggerated were the characterizations of the
Federalists by the Antifederalist writers, who rang the
changes upon the accusation that all who advocated
the adoption of the Constitution were either holders of
public offices, bankers and lawyers and their train of
dependents, members of the Society of the Cincinnati.[2]

While in each party, there were, of course, some
economic causes for its respective attitude, many other
factors were actually determining the course of events.
Party movements and party actions in this country

[1] See also Knox to Washington, Jan. 14, Feb. 14, 1788; Washington to Knox,
Oct. 1787; *Writings of George Washington* (Ford's ed.), XI, 171; *Boston Gazette,*
Nov. 26, 1787; *Independent Gazetteer* (Phil.), Dec. 19, 1787, letter of "Philadel-
phiensis" No. 5; "Cassius" in *Massachusetts Gazette,* Nov. 23, 1787.

[2] See especially letters of "A Republican Federalist", in *Massachusetts Centinel*
Jan. 9, 12, Feb. 6, 1788, as to the establishment of a "baleful aristocracy."   And,
in general, see *Pamphlets on the Constitution* (1788) and *Essays on the Constitution*
(1892), both edited by Paul Leicester Ford, and containing many of the ablest arguments for and against the Constitution.

have seldom possessed that simplicity of cause and motive which the historian delights to attribute to them. The fact is too often ignored that men of different interests and localities may arrive at the same end by different roads; the historian too often finds it easier to apply a theory of a common motive than to trace out the facts as to individual motives.

It has been pointed out in the second chapter of this book that while, in 1787–88, as in every era, there were undoubtedly many men who voted for or against the Constitution because of the effect which they supposed that it would have upon their personal fortunes, nevertheless, the attempt to portray the American people, as a whole, as sharply divided into the classes above enumerated results in a picture drawn on altogether too simple lines to correspond with actual conditions, or, indeed, with human nature. No communities and no States were, in fact, divided into such clearly separated classes. Nor did there exist any great number of either rich or poor. But, as Richard Henry Lee (the leader of the Antifederalists) wrote — while there may have been parties, one composed of debtors and insurgents and the other of a few aristocrats grasping at power, nevertheless, "these two parties are really insignificant compared with the solid, free, and independent part of the community." "Between these two parties is the weight of the community, the men of middling property, men not in debt on the one hand, and men on the other content with republican government and not aiming at immense fortunes, offices, and power." It has also been pointed out that the simplified picture of an economic contest leaves out of consideration the very notable fact that the same class of people in different States took divergent positions as to the Constitution; and also that within the same class of people in each State, there were circumstances and motives pulling in opposite directions. Both with the Federalists in upholding the Constitution, and with the Antifederalists in opposing, economic motives, so far as they were present, had varied effects, even within the same party. But the Antifederalists believed that they had many other reasons for distrusting and attacking the new form of Government; and it is these other reasons, based on deep rooted sentiments, that deserve a consideration which has been too little given to them by historians.

In the first place, it is to be noted that not a few of the objections to the Constitution were purely sectional. Thus, South Carolina and North Carolina feared the commerce clause, believing that it would place their trade entirely in the hands of the Eastern States which alone were the shipowning and shipbuilding States, and which, by virtue of this clause, might secure navigation laws restrictive of commerce to American ships and thus monopolize freights. Virginia and North Carolina, in addition to such fear of the commerce clause, were mortally afraid of the Senate's treaty power, lest it might be exercised to surrender the right to free navigation of the Mississippi which those States deemed vitally important to them. That part of Massachusetts comprised in the Maine district disliked the Constitution, for fear that its adoption would obstruct the admission of that district as a separate State. Racial influence played a part in some States — the Germans of Pennsylvania favoring the Constitution, and the Scotch-Irish being largely opposed. In Connecticut and Rhode Island, religious influences entered into the question — the Baptists being chiefly Federalist.[1] Some of the opposition was personal, attribut-

---

[1] Letters from Rhode Island and Connecticut stated that the Baptists in these States were largely in favor of the Constitution. *New York Daily Advertiser*, Nov. 23, 1787, *Pennsylvania Journal*, November 17, 1787. On the other hand, Madison's father wrote to him, Jan. 30, 1788 (V, 105 note): "The Baptists are now generally opposed to it, as it is said", in Virginia.

able in Virginia to the enmity of the Lee faction towards Gen. Washington, and in Pennsylvania, to hostility to Robert Morris and the Bank of North America.[1]

The geographical division of the opposition has been often pointed out — the fact that the Federalists were largely centred in the seacoast regions, whereas the Antifederalists were strongest in the back country and the frontier portions of the States. Even this division, however, was not universally true. Thus, part of Western Virginia was Federalist, and to that section that party owed the adoption of the Constitution. But when historians attribute this line of cleavage entirely to economic influences, they ignore many other influences of sentiment and otherwise which contributed largely to such a division. They lose sight of the fact that the frontier — the West — throughout the history of this country has always maintained a jealousy of and antagonism to the more settled East; it has always been devoted to local interests and to its individual independence; it has always entertained a suspicion of distant and centralized authority of any kind. It was natural, therefore, that the Western portion of the States, in 1787, should receive with considerable distrust the proposal of a much more centralized Government than had ever before existed in this country. Even before the Revolution, it was the frontier which

---

[1] Oliver Ellsworth in "Letters of a Landholder" in *Connecticut Courant*, Dec. 24, 1787, said: "In Virginia, the opposition wholly originated in two principles: the madness of Mason, and enmity of the Lee faction to Gen. Washington. Had the General not attended the Convention nor given his sentiments respecting the Constitution, the Lee party would undoubtedly have supported it, and Col. Mason would at home have vented his rage to his own negroes and to the winds."

John Chaloner wrote to Hamilton, Dec. 16, 1786, from Philadelphia as to a bank project: "I believe, if adopted, it will so effectually remove the jealousy and apprehension of Government as no longer to cause the Bank to be an object of resentment which was solely occasioned by the influence of a few people had among the stockholders to always nominate and elect the directors who by their continuing to sit as directors did in a great measure influence and command the trade of the City and give a bias to all elections for Assembly or other purposes." *Alexander Hamilton Papers MSS* in Library of Congress.

particularly resented the yoke of Great Britain — and
not for economic reasons, but because, by virtue of its
situation, it insisted on its right to rule itself according to its own views. Moreover, the farming settlements
of the frontier and the small towns distant from the seaboard had few sources of information as to outside conditions, through newspapers, mail, or otherwise; and
when a community was ignorant of the legislation in
other States, which had produced political evils, it was
natural that it should feel a minor interest in the necessity of Union, and that it should preserve a more active
desire for the supremacy of its own particular State.
As has been well said by a recent keen writer on the
Constitution (before quoted) : "Under such conditions,
men's interests naturally centred in their own localities
and the patriotism of many a sturdy Revolutionist
was bounded by the limits of his own State. Why
should those who had taken up arms against the claim
of Parliament to tax them and who had grumbled at
the laws it had passed for the regulation of their trade,
promptly concede these very powers to another central
and remote Government?" And in addition to all
these considerations, a division between the Western
and Eastern portions of the States, in 1787, represented,
to some extent, a division between the less well-informed
and the better informed, rather than a division between
the poor and the well-to-do. Thus, a New Hampshire
paper said, in the spring of 1787: "One great cause of
the discontents of the back country is their total want
of regular intelligence. This gives designing men an
opportunity of forging the grossest falsehoods and
propagating them without fear of detection, there being
no publick newspapers to stare them in the face, and
contradict what they assert." [1] (It is to be noted,

---

[1] A letter "from a gentleman in the Western country" of Pennsylvania, in *Freeman's Gazette*, Oct. 31, 1787, said: "It hath been reported that a number of copies

incidentally, that there was not a single newspaper published west of the Alleghany Mountains until the *Pittsburgh Gazette* was founded in the fall of 1786, and *Kentucky Gazette* in the spring of 1787.)

It has been the practice of historians to depict the Antifederalist party as comprising few men of high character or ability, and as, in general, composed of the lower ranks of the people. Undoubtedly, that party contained a large section of the democratic element; but, here also, it is unsafe to make too broad generalizations; for its composition differed greatly in the various States. In this characterization of the personnel of the Antifederalists, the influence of the Federalist historians from New England is peculiarly apparent; for in New England, the Antifederalists probably included more of the agitator and insurgent type than in any part of the country ; and New England historians have been prone to assume that New England ideas and conditions pervade and control the rest of the country. A fair survey of the situation will satisfy one that the Antifederalist party had its share of "men distinguished alike for their integrity and ability" (as Timothy Pickering, one of their bitterest foes, later admitted).[1]   Among them were Patrick Henry, Benjamin Harrison, George Mason, William Grayson, James Monroe, and Richard Henry Lee of Virginia;

of the proposed Constitution was directed to be printed in the English and German languages to be distributed throughout the State. I wish it were done, that the people might have an opportunity of reading it and judging for themselves. Much time elapses before information can reach the industrious yeomanry of the States that are distant from the seat of Government." A correspondent in *Boston Gazette*, October 1, 1787, writing from Great Barrington in the extreme Western part of Massachusetts, said that: "Convinced that the late irregularities (the Shays Rebellion) have proceeded from want of true information respecting the doings of the General Court here, and the danger they are ever in from the want of a vehicle to convey certain intelligence, they have lately given such encouragement to the establishment of a printing press as to have one erected in Pittsfield for the printing of a newspaper."

[1] Timothy Pickering to Charles Carroll of Carrollton, June 17, 1828, *Pickering Papers MSS*, XVI, 302.

Rawlins Lowndes, Patrick Calhoun, and Aedanus Burke of South Carolina; Luther Martin, John F. Mercer, William Paca, Jeremiah T. Chase, and Samuel Chase of Maryland; George Bryan of Pennsylvania; George Clinton, John Lansing, John Lamb, Melancthon Smith, and Robert Yates of New York; Elbridge Gerry, James Winthrop, Samuel Adams, Benjamin Austin, Gen. James Warren, and Nathan Dane of Massachusetts. As James Madison wrote from New York, October 30, 1787:

"I am truly sorry to find so many respectable names on your list of adversaries to the Federal Constitution. The diversity of opinion on so interesting a subject among men of equal integrity and discernment is at once a melancholy proof of the fallibility of the human judgment and of the imperfect progress yet made in the science of government. Nothing is more common here, and I presume the case must be the same with you, than to see companies of intelligent people equally divided and equally earnest in maintaining, on one side, that the General Government will overwhelm the State Governments, and, on the other hand, that it will be a prey to their encroachments; on one side, that the structure of the Government is too firm and too strong, and, on the other, that it partakes too much of the weakness and instability of the Governments of the particular States. What is the proper conclusion from all this? That unanimity is not to be expected in any great political question; that the danger is probably exaggerated on each side, when an opposite danger is discerned on the opposite side; that if any Constitution is to be established by deliberation and choice, it must be examined with many allowances, and must be compared, *not* with the theory which each individual may frame in his own mind, but with the system which it is meant to take the place of and with any other which there might be a possibility of obtaining."

The Antifederalists of the type mentioned above had a very genuine and profound distrust of what they conceived to be the principles on which the Constitution was framed. As a historian of that day wrote, their objections "were not the result of ignorance; they were made by men of the first abilities in every State, men who were sensible of the necessity of strong and energetic institutions and a strict subordination and obedience to law. Those judicious men were solicitous that everything should be clearly defined; they were jealous of each ambiguity in law or government, or the smallest circumstance that might have a tendency to curtail the Republican system or render ineffectual the sacrifices they had made for the security of civil and religious liberty. . . . They were now apprehensive of being precipitated, without due consideration, into the adoption of a system that might bind them and their posterity, in the chains of despotism."   Richard Henry Lee wrote of his conviction that if the Constitution should be adopted without amendment, "either a tyranny will result from it, or it will be prevented by a civil war." [1] In the perspective of one hundred and forty years, it is difficult now to comprehend why the men of that day were so convinced of the dangers to flow from the document presented to them for adoption. It would seem impossible that a prominent North Carolinian could say, with any seriousness, that: "General Washington was a damned rascal and traitor to his country for putting his hand to such an infamous paper as the new Constitution", or that one of the most distinguished of South Carolinians could solemnly say that the dangers were so evident that "when he ceased to exist, he wished for no other epitaph than to have inscribed on his tomb, 'Here lies the man that opposed the Constitution because it was ruinous to the liberty of America.' " [2] Yet it is undoubtedly a fact that the

[1] R. H. Lee to George Mason, Oct. 1, 1787.

[2] *Life and Correspondence of James Iredell* (1858), II, 224; *Elliot's Debates*, IV, 311, speech of Rawlins Lowndes; Mrs. Mercy Warren, in her *History of the Ameri-*

one fundamental ground on which these Antifederalists opposed the Constitution was their profound belief that it was intended and framed to bring about a consolidation and ultimate destruction of the States and State Sovereignty, and that it was designed to center power in the hands of a limited portion of the community which might thus develop into an aristocracy. They were solemnly convinced that it was a surrender of the liberties they had won in the war. "I most sacredly believe," reported Luther Martin to the Maryland Legislature, "their object is the total abolition of all State Governments and the erection on their ruins of one great and extreme empire." [1] "The new Constitution," wrote a leading Massachusetts Antifederalist, is "intended to, and must, in operation, produce an abolition of the State Governments." It was in vain that James Madison and many others presented the conclusive answers to these fears. Said Madison, in the Virginia State Convention:

"It is urged that its increasing influence will speedily enable it to absorb the State Government. . . . If the General Government were wholly independent of the Governments of the particular States, then indeed usurpation might be expected to the fullest extent. But, sir, on whom does this General Government depend? It derives its authority from these Governments and from the same sources from which their authority is derived. The members of the

can Revolution (1805), III, 364, written only a few years later, said: "Many of the intelligent yeomanry and the great bulk of independent landholders who had tasted the sweets of mediocrity, equality, and liberty, read of every unconditional ratification of the new system in silent anguish, folded the solemn page with a sigh, and wept over the names of the native sons of America who had sold their lives to leave the legacy of freedom to their children. On this appearance of a consolidated Government, which they thought required such important amendments, they feared that a dereliction of some of their choicest privileges might be sealed without duly considering the fatal consequences of too much precipitation."

[1] Maryland Journal, March 21, 1788. A pamphlet entitled Observations on the Proposed Constitution for the United States of America, Clearly Showing it to be a Complete System of Aristocracy and Tyranny and Destructive of the Rights and Liberties of the People, was published in 1788, in New York, 225 copies of which were distributed to the local County Committees of that State.

Federal Government are taken from the same men from whom those of the State Legislature are taken. . . . I do not conceive they will so soon forget the source from whence they derive their political existence."

Logically, this argument was unanswerable. Practically, it was no answer at all — and for a reason which historians have failed to emphasize. The reason is this. The people of one section of the country did not trust the people of other sections; and the jealousies and antagonisms between the South, the Middle States, and the Eastern States were far greater than we now realize. When, therefore, the Antifederalists saw proposed a National Congress in which Representatives of New England, for instance, might combine to impose legislation on the South — or vice versa — they at once assumed that such legislation was bound to be hostile to the interests of their particular section of the country. Running all through the Antifederalist arguments, especially in New York, Virginia, and South Carolina, is the sentiment that the conditions in the various parts of the country were too diverse to admit of regulation by any one body of men. Unless this fact be thoroughly grasped, the extreme fear of a consolidated Government remains inexplicable. The following are a few scattered evidences of this sectional feeling — a jealousy which the united efforts of the States during the war had somewhat allayed, but which still persisted as a vivid influence in post-war politics. One must recall that the men of 1787 were only twelve years removed from the time when John Adams, attending the Second Continental Congress in Philadelphia, wrote that: "We cannot suddenly alter the temper, principles, opinions, or prejudices of men. The characters of gentlemen in the four New England Colonies differ as much from those in the others as that of the common people differs, that is, as much as several distinct nations almost", and that the "gentlemen of other Colonies were habituated to higher notion of themselves and of the distinction between them and the common people than we are. . . . I dread the consequences of this dissimilitude of character, and without the utmost caution on both sides, and the most considerate forbearance with one another, and prudent condescension on both sides, they will certainly be fatal." And Adams' correspondent in Western Massachusetts had written, cautioning him not to strengthen the opinion which prevailed in the other Colonies, that "the Massachusetts gentlemen and especially of the town of Boston do affect to dictate and take the lead in Continental measures, and are apt from an inward vanity and self conceit to assume big and haughty airs." [1] It was only nine years before the Federal Convention met that Henry Laurens of South Carolina, President of Congress, wrote that "party animosity between the Eastern States and the inhabitants of New York is almost coexistent with the inhabitants"; and that Titus Hosmer wrote from Congress to Governor Trumbull of Connecticut that the "old prejudices of North against South, and South against North" were everywhere apparent. Five years before it met, General Greene of Rhode Island wrote as to North Carolina that: "What adds to the misfortunes of this State is that morality is at a low ebb and religion almost held in contempt, which are the great pillars of good Government and sound policy. Where these evils prevail, the laws will be treated with neglect and the magistrate with contempt. Patriotism will have little influence and Government continues without dignity. . . . There will be neither spirit of union or principles of liberty to support our Republican form of

[1] *Works of John Adams* (1858), IX; *Letters of Members of the Continental Congress*, III, IV; *Life and Correspondence of Rufus King*, I.

Government." Only two years before the Convention, Elbridge Gerry of Massachusetts wrote to Rufus King that: "Southern men are continually reprobating the citizens of the Eastern States, and these in turn are ridiculing the others for being fools and empty coxcombs"; and again: "What is the matter with Virginia? Their attachments to their opinions originate, I fear, from mistaken ideas of their own importance. They have certainly many good qualities, but has not their ambition been bribed by artifice and flattery to besiege and undermine their reason and good policy?" In the Federal Convention itself, the sectional cleavage on the subjects debated had been very apparent; and though historians have rather generally dwelt upon the compromises as occurring between the large and the small States, the actual delegates saw more clearly where the real division of interests lay. In the very first month of the session, Madison observed that "it did not lie between the large and small States; it lay between the Northern and Southern"; and Gouverneur Morris of Pennsylvania and Rufus King of Massachusetts repeated this view. Pierce Butler of South Carolina stated that he considered the interests of the Southern States and of the Eastern States "to be as different as the interests of Russia and Turkey." The attitude of one section of the country towards another may also be illustrated by the utterances of three leading Antifederalists, after the Convention.[1] Rawlins Lowndes, in the South Carolina State Convention, argued at length on the "evils which might be apprehended to the South" from the laws that might be passed by Congress, whenever there should be a majority of representatives from the Eastern States, "who

---

[1] "Agrippa" in *Massachusetts Gazette*, and "Cato" in *New York Journal*, see Ford's *Pamphlets on the Constitution; Life of Nathanael Greene* (1871), by George W. Greene, III, 504, Sept. 1, 1783; *Life and Correspondence of Rufus King*, I.

were governed by prejudices and ideas extremely different from ours." James Winthrop, in Massachusetts, wrote that: "The idle and dissolute inhabitants of the South require a different regime from the sober and active people of the North. . . . Many circumstances render us an essentially different people from the inhabitants of the Southern States — the unequal distribution of property, the toleration of slavery, the ignorance and poverty of the lower class, the softness of the climate, and dissoluteness of manners mark their character." And Winthrop further expressed fears of legislation that might be controlled by Pennsylvania — a State, he said, "which in the course of a century has acquired her present extent and population, at the expense of religion and morals. Let any indifferent person judge whether that State, in point of morals, education, energy, is equal to any of the Eastern States." George Clinton, the Antifederalist Governor of New York, expressed himself as convinced that the liberties and industries of the Northern States, "where freedom, independence, industry, equality and frugality are natural to the climate and soil", would be sacrificed by "the people who may compose this National Legislature from the Southern States, in which, from the mildness of the climate, the fertility of the soil, and the value of its productions, wealth is rapidly acquired, and where the same causes naturally lead to luxury, dissipation, and a passion for aristocratic distinction, where slavery is encouraged and liberty of course less respected and protected, who know not what it is to acquire property by their own toil nor to economize with the savings of industry." The general diffusion of such sectional views produced a distrust of any centralized Government which should possess broad powers of legislation over States having such highly divergent interests.

One other fact must be continually borne in mind — that the men of those days, especially the older men, had, less than fifteen years before, been living under the rule of a Parliament and a King claiming uncontrolled power over them. The men of 1787 were removed from the Stamp Act by less than quarter of a century. They had fought, physically as well as intellectually, for liberty of the individual and of their States, for a republican rule; and it was only natural that even the semblance of a return to centralized authority should alarm them. It is in connection with this phase of the situation that a line of division between Antifederalists and Federalists should be noted which has been little commented upon — the line of age. The leaders of the former party were, in general, men of somewhat advanced years — "the old patriots of '75", as they were frequently referred to in the Press. The Federalists, on the other hand, while comprising many of the older generation who considered possible anarchy as worse than a restricted form of republicanism, nevertheless, contained a larger proportion of the young men of the country.[1]

Besides this fundamental fear of a consolidation, three factors served to increase the opposition of the Antifederalists. One was, their failure to understand the meaning and intent of many of the provisions of the Constitution.[2] To an extraordinary extent, misrepresentations and misconstructions were zealously

[1] Thus, of the Antifederalist leaders, Samuel Adams was sixty-five; R. H. Lee, fifty-seven; Patrick Henry, fifty-one; G. Mason, sixty-one; George Bryan, fifty-six; George Clinton, forty-eight; Robert Yates, forty-nine; Samuel Chase, forty-six; E. Gerry, forty-three; L. Martin, forty-three; of the Federalists Madison was thirty-six; Rufus King, thirty-two; McHenry, thirty-two; Hamilton, thirty; C. Pinckney, twenty-nine; W. R. Davie, thirty-one; G. Morris, thirty-five; Fisher Ames, twenty-nine; Ellsworth, thirty-eight.

[2] Madison wrote to Ambrose Madison, Nov. 8, 1787: "I have reason to believe that many objections, as Virginia, proceed from a misconception of the plan or of the causes which produced the objectionable parts of it. . . . My attendance at Philadelphia may enable me to contribute some explanation and information which may be of use."

published and circulated. "Their forte," wrote Washington, "seems to lie in misrepresentation and a desire to inflame the passions and to alarm the fears by noisy declamation, rather than to convince the understanding by sane arguments or fair and impartial statements." [1] It is not necessary, however, to regard these misstatements as intentional, or to term them (as Hamilton did) "a torrent of falsehoods." [2] For there were many equally misleading misrepresentations made by Federalist advocates. The fact is — there was then presented to the people a new and unparalleled form of Government, containing many provisions which had never been contemplated or even envisioned by statesmen or political actors or thinkers of the day. It is small wonder, therefore, that the people at large did not understand, or could not foresee, its probable mode of operation. Time has proved that many of the fears of the Antifederalists were unwarranted; but it has also proved that some of those fears had a sound basis. Moreover, time has proved that some of the arguments of the Federalists were equally unjustified — as, for instance, their denials of any ground for fear lest, under the Constitution, a State might be sued by citizens of another State — a fear that was amply justified when the Supreme Court, only a few years later, held that such a suit would lie.[3] In other words, since it has taken numerous opinions of the Supreme Court, during one hundred and forty years, to develop the meaning of many clauses of the Constitution, one may not lightly impugn the motives of those who misconstrued and misstated their meaning during the excited discussions of the years 1787 and 1788.

[1] Washington to Armstrong, April 25, 1788.

[2] Hamilton to G. Morris, May 19, 1788.

[3] See also an erroneous argument as to the jurisdiction of the Federal Judiciary by Alexander C. Hanson ("Aristides"), *Pamphlets on the Constitution* (1788), and comments on its mistakes by Luther Martin, in *Maryland Journal*, March 28, 1788. See also erroneous interpretation by John Langdon, *supra*, p. 540.

The Federalists themselves contributed greatly to the prevalent misunderstandings, by the policy which the Federal Convention had deliberately adopted of withholding from the public any report of its debates. While, during the Convention, no newspaper criticism of the Secrecy Rule had appeared, there had been symptoms of dissatisfaction in private letters. Jefferson had written from Paris in August that he was "sorry they began their deliberations by so abominable a precedent as that of tying the tongues of their members. Nothing can justify this example but the innocence of their intentions and ignorance of the value of public discussions." After the Convention adjourned, however, this secrecy became the subject of bitter attack in Antifederalist speeches, and in letters and articles in the newspapers.[1] "The injunction of secrecy," wrote a prominent Philadelphian, "was obviously dictated by the genius of aristocracy; it was deemed impolitic to unfold the principles of the intended Government to the people as this would have frustrated the end in view." Another Pennsylvania writer said: "The thick veil of secrecy with which their proceedings have been covered has left us entirely in the dark as to the debates that took place, and the unaccountable suppression of their Journals — the highest insult that could be offered to the majority of the people — shows clearly that the whole plan was entirely the work of an aristocratic majority." A writer in a Massachusetts paper said that the Convention had been afraid lest "their consultations and debates should be viewed by the scrutinizing eye of a free people." And throughout the State ratifying Conventions, there was displayed a very considerable resentment of this secrecy. Viewing the

---

[1] *Independent Gazetteer*, letter of "Centinel", Oct. 3, 1787; letter of "An Officer of the late Continental Army", Nov. 6, 1787; "A Republican Federalist" in *Massachusetts Centinel*, Jan. 2, 1788.

the pros and cons, it would seem now to be unquestionably true that the policy adopted by the Convention was a wise one during the continuance of its sessions. On the other hand, it appears that it would have been far more advantageous to the Federalist cause, had they given ample publicity to the debates as soon as the Convention adjourned. Many of the Antifederalist misunderstandings, misinterpretations, and misrepresentations of the provisions of the new Constitution would have been obviated or cleared away, had the people been made familiar with the arguments adduced on the one side or the other on the particular topic, during the Convention. Furthermore, suppression of the debates and the consequent atmosphere of mystery and suspicion gave a certain color to the charges made by opponents of the work of the Convention, that something unknown and unsuspected underlay the document, which was being "put over" upon the people.

The second factor in maintaining the fears of the Antifederalists was their insistence on measuring the defects of the Constitution by stating hypothetical cases of the most extreme and exaggerated nature, and by assuming that the Congress would necessarily be composed of men bent either on abusing their powers or on using them to the destruction of the interests and in defiance of the wishes of their constituents. Most of the evils thus conjured up were, as a prominent South Carolinian termed them, "phantoms of their own creation." "It is much easier to alarm people than to inform them," wrote William R. Davie to James Iredell.[1] Of the exaggerated views of the evils which the new Constitution would bring about, the following newspaper letter, which was given wide circulation, is an illustration. "Among the blessings of

---

[1] *Life and Correspondence of James Iredell* (1858), II, 217; *Elliot's Debates*, IV, 269, speech of John Julian Pringle.

the new proposed Government our correspondent enumerates the following: 1. The Liberty of the Press abolished. 2. A standing army. 3. A Prussian Militia. 4. No annual elections. 5. Fivefold taxes. 6. No trial by jury in civil cases. 7. General Search Warrants. 8. Excise laws, customs house officers, tide and land waiters, cellar rats, etc. 9. A free importation of negroes for one and twenty years. 10. Appeals to the Supreme Continental Court, where the rich may drag the poor from the furthermost parts of the continent. 11. Election for Pennsylvania held at Pittsburg, or perhaps Wyoming. 12. Poll taxes for our heads, if we chuse to wear them. 13. And *death* if we dare complain." [1] Another letter also widely reprinted gave the "Political Creed of Every Federalist", as follows: "1. Infallibility of the Convention. 2. Ignorance of the People. 3. Non-essentiality of securing the rights of man. 4. Superiority of aristocratic Government. 5. Cowardice of Americans, hence a standing army. 6. Lack of necessity for freedom of the press and trial by jury. 7. The opposition of State officials to the new scheme through selfish motives, though the State Constitutions are not affected. 8. The Constitution is the best form of government ever offered to the world. 9. I believe that to speak, write, read, think, or hear anything against the proposed Government is damnable heresy, execrable rebellion, and high treason against the sovereign majesty of the Convention.

[1] *Independent Gazetteer*, Oct. 6, 1787. See also *New York Journal*, Dec. 17, 1787. Federalist papers printed, as a satirical retort to this alleged Federalist creed, the following, "A Receipt for an Antifederal Essay": "Well-born, nine times — Aristocracy, eighteen times — Liberty of the Press, thirteen times repeated — Liberty of Conscience, once — Negro Slavery, once mentioned — Trial by Jury, seven times — Great Men, six times repeated — Mr. Wilson, forty times, and lastly George Mason's Right Hand in a Cutting box, nineteen times. Put them all together and dish them up at pleasure. These words will bear boiling, roasting or frying — and, what is remarkable of them, they will bear being served, after being once used, a dozen times to the same table and palate." See *Massachusetts Centinel*, Dec. 15, 1787.

. . . And, lastly, I believe that every person who differs from me in belief is an infernal villain." To these Antifederalist exaggerations, sane answers were to be found in the words of John Witherspoon to Iredell that "if we expect a Constitution, the principles of which cannot be violated, we had better, instead of amending that proposed instrument, amend the hearts of men"; and in the words of Pelatiah Webster of Philadelphia, that the Antifederalists founded their objections and fears "on extreme cases or misapplication of supreme powers which may possibly happen under the administration of a wild, weak, or wicked Congress. . . . All institutions are liable to extremes, but ought not to be judged by them; they do not often appear and perhaps never may. But if they should happen in the cases supposed (which God forbid), there is a remedy pointed out in the Constitution itself. . . . At any rate Congress can never get more power than the people will give, or hold it any longer than *they* will permit." [1]

The third factor influencing the Antifederalists was their objection to being forced to swallow the new Constitution whole, without the opportunity of calling a second General Convention to discuss and act upon the amendments which the various State Conventions

---

[1] *Life and Correspondence of James Iredell* (1858) II, 189; *Pamphlets on the Constitution* (1888). Iredell himself said in answer to George Mason's objections (*North Carolina State Gazette*, Jan. 8, 1788): "An imagination indulging itself in chimerical fears, upon the disappointment of a favorite plan, may point out danger arising from any system of Government whatever, even if angels were to have the administration of it, since, I presume, none but the Supreme Being himself is altogether perfect, and of course every other species of beings may abuse any delegated portion of power. This sort of visionary scepticism, therefore, will lead us to this alternative; either to have no Government at all, or to form the best system we can, making allowance for human imperfection."

Johnson, J., in *Ogden* v. *Saunders* (1827), 12 Wheaton 213, 279: "Most of the dangers are imaginary, for the interests of each community, its respect for the opinion of mankind, and a remnant of moral feeling which will not cease to operate in the worst of times, will always present important barriers against the gross violation of principle. How is the General Government itself made up, but of the same materials which separately make up the Governments of the States?"

might think necessary. This element in the opposition has been very generally disregarded by historians; but it had great strength. The failure to provide for such a further Convention was the chief cause of Edmund Randolph's refusal to sign the Constitution; and many of its other opponents, notably Richard Henry Lee and the Massachusetts, New York, and Pennsylvania leaders, would have looked more favorably on the Constitution, had opportunity for consideration of amendments been afforded before its final adoption. "It is certainly the most rash and violent proceeding in the world," wrote Lee, "to cram thus suddenly into men, a business of such infinite moment to the happiness of millions." [1] This argument was the one most forcibly made and the most difficult to answer. The Federalists, however, felt that the simple answer was, that, in view of the difficulty in getting any agreement between divergent interests in the Convention just held, there was no likelihood that any other Convention would reach any better agreement, or adopt any instrument which would obtain more general acceptance. As Washington wrote — in the solution of the problem, there were only two questions to be answered by "men of reflection, candor and information," "Is the Constitution which is submitted by the Convention preferable to the Government (if it can be

[1] Richard Henry Lee to George Mason, Oct. 1, 1787: "Your prediction of what would happen in Congress was exactly verified. It was with us, as with you, this or nothing; and this urged with a most extreme intemperance. The greatness of the powers given and the multitude of places to be created, produces a coalition of Monarchy men, military men, aristocrats, and drones, whose noise, impudence, and zeal exceeds all belief, whilst the commercial plunder of the South stimulates the rapacious trades. In this state of things, the Patriot voice is raised in vain for such changes and securities as reason and experience prove to be necessary against the encroachments of power upon the indispensable rights under which we now act. . . . This Constitution has a great many excellent regulations in it, and if it could be reasonably amended would be a fine system. As it is, I think 'tis past doubt that, if it should be established, either a tyranny will result from it, or it will be prevented by a civil war. I am clearly of opinion with you that it should be sent back with amendments reasonable, and assent to it withheld until such amendments are admitted. . . ."

called one) under which we live? Is it probable that more confidence would, at this time, be placed in another Convention, provided the experiment should be tried, than was placed in the last one, and is it likely that a better agreement would take place thereon?"[1]

From October, 1787, to July, 1788, the Constitution, its advantages and its defects, were the subject of constant and heated discussion by the people throughout the country, except possibly in the more remote regions like Georgia, the Kentucky district, and the thinly settled parts of some of the other States. Contemporary evidence makes it plain that no political topic in our early history ever received so general popular attention.[2] Every prominent newspaper published the

[1] *Writings of George Washington* (Ford's ed.), XI, 171, Washington to Knox, Oct. 1787.

[2] The newspapers contain frequent references to the amount of popular attention being paid to the Constitution. A letter written in March from North Carolina, published in the *Independent Gazetteer*, April 7, 1788, says: "The New Constitution is the general topic in every company. In general, it is exploded . . . an aristocratic government." A letter from Salem County in New Jersey, in the *Pennsylvania Herald*, Oct. 27, 1787, said: "Nothing is talked of here, either in public or private, but the new Constitution. All read, and almost all approve of it." A letter from "a gentleman at Washington Court House near Holstein in Virginia", in *American Herald* (Boston) Jan. 21, 1788, said: "Here I expected to be happily removed from the din of politicks, but even in these remote worlds, the people are deeply engaged in that science. The new Constitution is the subject of universal discussion; a general dissatisfaction with the proceedings of the late Convention prevails here; so much disappointed in their expectations are the people, that they think it more eligible to revert to the tyranny of Britain than bow the neck to domestic tyrants." A letter from one of the Representatives for Frederic County, Va., in *Maryland Journal*, Dec. 18, 1787, said: "Every person who has the least pretence to a knowledge of politics or government is engaged here on the most important subject of the new Federal Constitution, and the most respectable names appear in the number of pros and cons." Rev. Jeremy Belknap of Boston wrote to Ebenezer Hazard, Dec. 8, 1787: "We have been all agog here about the Constitution. The papers teem with Federal and Antifederal pieces." John Jay wrote to John Adams, October 31, 1781, from New York: "The public mind is much occupied by the plan of the Federal Government recommended by the late Convention." Madison wrote to Jefferson, Dec. 9, 1787: "The Constitution proposed by the Convention engrosses almost the whole political attention of America"; and again from New York, Feb. 19, 1788: "The public here continues to be much agitated by the proposed Federal Constitution, and to be attentive to little else." Monroe wrote to Jefferson, April 10, 1788, from Fredericksburg: "The people seem much agitated with this subject in every part of the State." Charles C. Pinckney wrote from South Carolina to Rufus King, May 24, 1788: "The Antifederalists had been most insidiously industrious in prejudicing the minds of our

Constitution in full; and all the newspapers were flooded with letters from both its opponents and its advocates, the Antifederalists predominating in number of contributors. A careful examination of the press at that period discloses the fact that never in American history was so large a proportion of its columns devoted to political argument. The leading arguments for the Constitution were, of course, the letters published in the New York papers (and reproduced to some extent in papers elsewhere), written by Madison, Jay, and Hamilton under the name of "Publius", and printed in book form as *The Federalist*. Owing to the fact, however, that many of the most controverted parts of the Constitution were not treated in these letters until after most of the State Conventions had met, this work had less influence upon the people of that period than has been generally stated.[1] Moreover, they were more suited to the comprehension of statesmen than of the general public. As Maclaine wrote to James Iredell in North Carolina, referring to "Publius": "He is certainly a judicious and ingenious writer, though not well calculated for the common people." [2] Much more

citizens against the Constitution. Pamphlets, speeches, and protests from the minority in Pennsylvania were circulated throughout the State, particularly in the back country." Albert J. Beveridge in his *Life of John Marshall*, I, 320, 325, contended that the people had little knowledge of the Constitution; but the authorities which he cites do not support his theory, except in the remote parts of the country like Kentucky, and like New Hampshire where Tobias Lear wrote to Washington, June 22, 1788: "I was surprised to find that so little information respecting the Constitution had been diffused among the people."

[1] The first letter of *The Federalist* appeared in the *Independent Journal*, in New York, October 27, 1787, and succeeding letters appeared in that paper, in the *New York Packet*, and in the *New York Daily Advertiser*. No. 36 appeared January 7, 1788. The first 36 of the letters were published in book form, March 22, 1788. Nos. 37 to 77 appeared in newspapers between January 8 and April 4, 1788. These, together with eight additional letters relating to the Judiciary and miscellaneous matters, appeared in a printed volume, on May 28, 1788; and these eight additional letters were also published in the newspapers, June 17 to August 15. As to these letters, in general, see letters of Washington to Stuart, Nov. 30, 1787; to Madison, Dec. 7, 1787; to Armstrong, April 25, 1788; to Hamilton, Aug. 28, 1788; see also letters of Madison to Washington, Nov. 18, 1787; to Randolph, Dec. 2, 1787.

[2] *Life and Correspondence of James Iredell* (1858), II, 219, Maclaine to Iredell. March 4, 1788, Tobias Lear wrote to Washington, June 22, 1788, that in New

widespread circulation was given and much greater influence is to be attributed to the *Letters of a Federal Farmer*, written by Richard Henry Lee, and published early in October, 1787, which contained an able and restrained exposition of the Antifederalist arguments.[1]

Such were the conditions and such the situation under which the State Conventions met, one after the other, to consider the ratification of the Constitution. Delaware was the first to ratify on December 7, 1787. The States of Pennsylvania and New Jersey followed in the same month. Georgia and Connecticut ratified in January, 1788. In February, after a long struggle, Massachusetts ratified by a close vote; Maryland ratified in April; South Carolina, in May; New Hampshire in June; Virginia, in June, by a majority of only ten in a total of 168; and New York, in July, by a majority of three in a total of 57. (North Carolina rejected the Constitution in August, 1788, but ratified later in November, 1789; and Rhode Island ratified in 1790).[2]

A brief consideration of the amendments to the Constitution which the Antifederalists desired will throw light on many of their grounds of opposition. It is well known that the State Conventions of Massachusetts, New Hampshire, Virginia, and New York (and later North Carolina and Rhode Island) demanded

Hampshire, "the valuable numbers of 'Publius' are not known." Humphrey Marshall of Kentucky stated, in 1788, that he had never seen a copy of "Publius" in that district of Virginia. *Beveridge*, I, 320, note. On the other hand, A. Stuart wrote from Richmond to Madison, Jan. 14, 1788: "Publius is in general estimation, his greatness is acknowledged universally." And a Senator from Pennsylvania, decidedly anti-Hamiltonian in his views, wrote in his diary, June 12, 1789: "*Mem.* Get, if I can, the *Federalist*, without buying. It is not worth it. . . . (but) it truly was instrumental in procuring the adoption of the Constitution." *Sketches of Debates in the First Senate* (1880), by William Maclay.

[1] Jeremiah Wadsworth of Connecticut wrote to Rufus King, Dec. 16, 1787, that the "Letters of a Federal Farmer" were "written with art and, tho' by no means unanswerable, it is calculated to do much harm." See also Madison to Washington, Dec. 20, 1787.

[2] For details, see Appendix D, *infra*.

amendments, not as a condition of their ratification but on the assumption of a tacit agreement that these or similar amendments should be adopted by the first Congress under the new Government. Besides the fundamental ground of opposition that the Constitution provided for a consolidated Government, there were four other basic fears which were embodied in demands for amendment made by the States or by prominent statesmen. The first was as to the omission of a Bill of Rights and the lack of a definite provision that all powers not expressly granted to the National Government were reserved to the States. The demand for a Bill of Rights was regarded very generally, even by supporters of the Constitution, as justified. The failure to include such a Bill of Rights in the original draft was undoubtedly a grave error of judgment on the part of the framers. And very rightly did Madison himself say, in the First Congress, on proposing the first ten amendments to the Constitution, that the omission of such a Bill of Rights was one of the chief causes of the opposition : "I believe the great mass of the people who opposed it disliked it because it did not contain effectual provisions against the encroachment on particular rights and those safeguards which they have been long accustomed to have interposed between them and the magistrate who exercises the sovereign power." [1]

The second basic objection of the Antifederalists was directed at the eligibility of the President to re-election ; the fear that such re-eligibility might result in an elective monarchy. This embodied the jealousy of Executive power which was a deep seated sentiment in

[1] *1st Cong., 1st Sess.*, June 8, 1789. For a detailed account of the adoption of the first ten amendments by Congress, see *New Light on the History of the Federal Judiciary Act of 1789*, by Charles Warren, *Harv. Law Rev.* (1923), XXXVII. As to the necessity of a Bill of Rights, and of a Judiciary to enforce such rights, see Jefferson to Madison, Dec. 20, 1787; March 15, 1789 (replying to Madison's letters of Oct. 17, Dec. 8, 12, 1788). See also *Congress, the Constitution and the Supreme Court* (1925), by Charles Warren, as to the functions of a Bill of Rights.

the Americans of that day, with its roots running far
into the past. When the political history of the years
1776 to 1786 shall be written (a work which has never
been performed), much consideration must be given to
the part which the autocratic conduct of Robert Morris,
as Superintendent of Finance under the Confederation,
played in arousing fears of Executive usurpations. To
the Antifederalists, the word "Executive" conjured up
the picture of that powerful, determined, and somewhat
arrogant banker and merchant. Moreover, it is to be
noted that, even in the Federal Convention, many of the
strong Nationalists had been reluctant to grant to the
new Executive any extensive authority. And it is a
fact, particularly to be borne in mind, that all the
powers now vested in the President by the Constitution
(with the exception of the treaty making power) were
agreed upon by the Convention, at a stage in the proceedings when it had been decided that the President
should be elected by the Congress and should not be
eligible to re-election. After the powers had been
granted to an official who was to be thus restricted and
made responsible to Congress, the Convention, in the
very closing days of the session, had reversed its decision
as to mode of election, by placing the choice of President
in the hands of popular electors instead of Congress, and
by making such a President capable of re-election.
This fact, very generally overlooked, explains much of
the vigorous insistence which the Antifederalists made,
in the campaign, upon the necessity of such changes in
the Constitution as should make the President ineligible
to re-election. These extensive powers had been
granted to him, they contended, upon the supposition
that he would be checked by Congressional election
and by his legal inability to use them to secure his
re-election. Since this legal inability, on the strength
of which the grant of powers had been made, had been

removed by the final action of the Convention, it was necessary to restore it (so the Antifederalists declared) in order to afford any warrant for the grant of such extensive authority. As it is, said Patrick Henry, "it squints towards monarchy. Your President may easily become King." (Incidentally, the note made by the Reporter of the Virginia State Convention is of curious interest: "Here Mr. Henry strongly and pathetically expatiated on the probability of the President's enslaving America and the horrid consequences that must result.") How extreme were the fears of the President's powers may be seen from what Governor George Clinton of New York, wrote: [1]

". . . He will be surrounded by expectants and courtiers, his power of nomination and influence on all appointments, the strong posts in each State comprised within his superintendence and garrisoned by troops under his direction, his control over the army, militia, and navy, the unrestrained power of granting pardons for treason which may be used to screen from punishment those whom he had secretly instigated to commit the crime and thereby prevent a discovery of his own quiet, his duration in office for four years; these and various other principles evidently prove the truth of the position that if the President is possessed of ambition, he has power and time sufficient to ruin his country. . . . Every American Whig, not long since, bore his emphatic testimony against a monarchical Government . . . and wherein does this President, invested with his power and prerogatives, essentially differ from the King of Great Britain (save as to name, creation of nobility and some immaterial incidents, the creations of absurdity and locality)? . . . The safety of the people in a Republic depends on the share or proportion they have in the Government; but experience ought to teach you that when a man is at the head of an elective Government, invested with great powers, and interested in his re-election, in what circle

[1] "Cato" in *New York Journal*, Nov. 8, 1787.

appointments will be made, by which means an imperfect aristocracy bordering on monarchy may be established."

Throughout the struggle over the adoption of the Constitution, constant emphasis was laid on the dangers which would arise from making the President eligible to re-election, in view of the powers which it was proposed to vest in him. This view was expressed most potently in numerous letters written by Thomas Jefferson to his friends in this country; for that statesman, though heartily in favor of the Constitution, believed that at least two cardinal amendments were needed — the addition of a Bill of Rights and the restriction of the President to a single term.[1] "Reason and experience tell us," he wrote to James Madison, "that the first magistrate will always *be* re-elected, if he *may* be re-elected. He is then an officer for life. . . . The power of removing, every fourth year, by the vote of the people is a power which they will not exercise; and, if they were disposed to exercise, they would not be permitted." And to John Adams, Jefferson wrote: "Once in office and possessing the military force of the Union, without the aid or check of a Council, he (the President) would not be easily dethroned, even if the people could be induced to withdraw their votes for him." But while Jefferson thought that a Constitutional amendment should be at once adopted in this respect, he evidenced

[1] *Writings of Thomas Jefferson* (T. J. Randolph ed., 1830), Jefferson to Adams, Nov. 13, 1787; Jefferson to Madison, Dec. 20, 1787 (a different version of which is given in *Works of Thomas Jefferson*, edited by P. L. Ford); Jefferson to Washington, May 2, 1788. See also Washington to Lafayette, April 28, 1788: "Guarded so effectively as the proposed Constitution is, in respect to the prevention of bribery and undue influence in the choice of President, I confess I differ widely, myself, from Mr. Jefferson and you, as to the necessity or expediency of rotation in that appointment. . . . There cannot, in my judgment, be the least danger that the President will by any practicable intrigue ever be able to continue himself one moment in office, — much less perpetuate himself in it — but in the last stage of corrupted morals and political depravity; and even then there is as much danger that any other species of domination should prevail. Though, when a people shall have become incapable of governing themselves and fit for a master, it is of little consequence from what quarter he comes."

his broad vision and complete faith in the good sense of the American people by writing to General Washington, that he had no doubt that if the evils which he feared should ever take place, the people would remedy them by altering the Constitution. "I was much an enemy to monarchy before I came to Europe. I am ten thousand times more so, since I have seen what they are," he wrote. "There is scarcely an evil in these countries which may not be traced to their King, as its source; nor a good, which is not derived from the small fibres of republicanism existing among them. I can further say, with safety, there is not a crowned head in Europe those talents or merits would entitle him to be elected a vestryman by the people of any parish in America. However, I shall hope that before there is danger of this change taking place in the office of President, the good sense and free spirit of our countrymen will make the changes necessary to prevent. Under this hope, I look forward to the general adoption of the new Constitution with anxiety, as necessary for us under our present circumstances." While the American people did not find it necessary to adopt any amendment as to the Presidential term and powers, and while they have not since found it necessary, yet the old Antifederalist apprehensions as to Executive power still remain alive in the persistence of the anti-third term sentiment. And Jefferson's views on the Executive have been given, to a limited extent, a practical, even if not a Constitutional application.

The third basic objection was directed at the powers of the Senate, especially its treaty-making power. The fourth basic objection was directed at the commerce clause. The South demanded an amendment providing that no statute or treaty regulating commerce should be effective except by a two thirds vote of each branch of Congress; and both North and South demanded

Congress be denied the power to grant exclusive commercial rights. The purpose of the Southern States was to guard against the possibility of navigation laws or other trade regulations being imposed upon them by votes merely of the shipbuilding, shipowning, and importing States of the East. It is interesting to speculate on what would have been the result of such an amendment. One result might have obtained. It might have made impossible any tariff law, designed or tending to be sectional in its effects. As to the demand for an amendment to the commerce clause, forbidding the grant of exclusive rights or charters to trading companies, it is to be noted that the men of that day had witnessed the injurious effects arising from the British exclusive charters to the East India Company and the Hudson's Bay Company and others, and that they were very justifiably apprehensive of vesting Congress with power to create such commercial monopolies. Such monopolies, wrote James Winthrop of Massachusetts, "are injurious to the general commerce, by enhancing prices and destroying that rivalship which is the great stimulus to industry. . . . Exclusive companies are, in trade, pretty much like an aristocracy in Government, and produce nearly as bad effects. . . . They always, by the greatness of their capital, have an undue influence in the Government. In a republick, we ought to guard as much as possible against the predominance of any particular interest. It is the object of Government to protect them all. When commerce is left to take its own course, the advantage of every class will be nearly equal. But when exclusive privileges are given to any class, it will operate to the weakening of some other class connected with them."

Other amendments to the Constitution suggested by the State Conventions were as follows: that the Federal Judiciary be restricted in its jurisdiction so as to eliminate suits between citizens of different States, and to abrogate its appellate jurisdiction over matters of fact which had been decided by a jury; that Congress should have no power to impose a capitation tax, and no power to impose any other direct tax until it was shown that excise and impost taxes would be insufficient and even then not until a State should refuse to comply with requisitions; that no standing army be maintained in time of peace, except by a two thirds vote of Congress; that the States have an increased number of Representatives; that Congress should have no power to regulate the time, place, and manner of holding elections; and that the Journals of Congress should not be secret.

The significant fact is to be noted that not a single amendment was proposed to change any of the provisions of the Constitution which the economic historians allege were inserted to favor the propertied and creditor class — namely, the clauses prohibiting issue of paper money or the impairment of the obligation of contract by stay and tender laws and the like. Yet, if the struggle against the Constitution was, as alleged, a contest between debtor and creditor, property and non-property, certainly some changes would have been demanded in such clauses. It is clear that opposition to the Constitution, if based on paper money sentiment, was not sufficiently strong to make itself felt even in a call for amendments on this subject.[1] Moreover, a

---

[1] Charles C. Pinckney of South Carolina, writing to Rufus King, June 21, 1788, said: "Indeed if we were allowed to pass instalment and valuation laws as heretofore, an Antifederalist would be a rara avis in this State." But it is to be noted that it was not merely the poor who favored such laws, for many of the wealthy planters, heavily in debt, also supported them. Madison wrote to Jefferson, October 17, 1788: "The little pamphlet herewith enclosed will give you a collective view of the alterations which have been proposed by the State Conventions for the new Constitution. Various and numerous as they appear, they certainly omit many of the true grounds of opposition. The articles relating to treaties, to paper money, and to contracts created more enemies than all the errors in the system, positive and negative, put together."

review of the debates in the State Conventions (so far as they were reported) discloses no speeches in favor of paper money, or against the impairment of obligation of contract clause, other than a few in Virginia and in North and South Carolina.   The fact is, that in Massachusetts, New Hampshire, and Connecticut, where the small farmers had considerable representation in the Legislatures (as well as in the Conventions), no paper money laws had been enacted; in New York, New Jersey, Pennsylvania, and Delaware, issues of paper money had practically ceased at the time of the Federal Convention; and in Maryland and Virginia attempts to issue paper money had been defeated.   Moreover, the leading Antifederalists — Richard Henry Lee, Patrick Henry, William Grayson, Elbridge Gerry, Samuel Adams, George Clinton, and most of the other leaders — were vigorously opposed to paper money and to stay and tender laws, and approved of the restrictions in the Constitution on these subjects.   And it is clear that, had all of the Antifederalist leaders been members of the Convention which framed the Constitution, they would have voted with the Federalists to establish the very restrictions on the States against paper money and against impairment of obligation of contract, which were actually inserted in that instrument.   One of the *Letters of a Federal Farmer*, written by Lee, has sometimes been cited in which he expressed the opinion that, had eight or nine men who were appointed members of the Convention attended, "the result of the Convention would not have had the strong tendency to aristocracy now discernable on every part of the plan." [1]   It has been argued from this, that Lee meant

---

[1] This letter of Richard Henry Lee, of October 8, 1787, contains an expression of his high opinion of the most of the delegates to the Federal Convention: "Virginia made a very respectable appointment and placed at the head of it the first man in America.   In this appointment, there was a mixture of political characters, but Pennsylvania appointed principally those men who are esteemed aristocrats.

that the Constitution would have contained less protection to property interests. Such was not Lee's meaning. He was speaking of a political aristocracy, not an economic aristocracy. And the best proof that he had no reference to the securities to property contained in the Constitution is the fact that one of the "eight or nine men" thus referred to was Patrick Henry, who was a vigorous opponent of paper money, and Lee himself was one of the men influential in drafting the very clause against impairment of obligation of contract which was inserted in the Northwest Territory Ordinance in July, 1787, and which the delegates to the Federal Convention copied into the Constitution.[1]

This outline of the objections to the Constitution and of the thorough discussion of its principles which took place in 1787–1788, is necessary to a proper comprehension of one of the reasons for the strength and permanence of the Constitution. Just as it was fortunate that that instrument resulted from compromise and did not embody the complete victory of any one faction, so it was equally fortunate that its final adoption was only secured by a slight margin of votes and

---

. . . Ten other States appointed, and tho they chose men principally connected with commerce and the judicial department, yet they appointed many good republican characters — Had they all attended, we should now see, I am persuaded, a better system presented. The non-attendance of eight or nine men who were appointed members of the Convention, I shall ever consider as a very unfortunate event to the United States. Had they attended, I am pretty clear that the result of the Convention would not have had that strong tendency to aristocracy now discernable on every part of the plan. There would not have been so great an accumulation of powers, especially as to the internal police of this country, in a few hands, as the Constitution reported proposes to vest in them. The young, visionary men and the consolidating aristocracy would have been more restrained than they have been. . . . We shall view the Convention with respect — and at the same time that we reflect there were men of abilities and integrity in it, we must recollect how disproportionately the democratic and aristocratic parts of the community were represented."

[1] Patrick Henry in the Virginia Convention said: "I acknowledge that paper money would be the bane of this country. I detest it. Nothing can justify a people in resorting to it, but extreme necessity. It is at rest, however, in this Commonwealth. It is no longer solicited or advocated." *Elliot's Debates*, III, 156. And see *supra* p. 550.

after bitter and well-argued opposition. As Washington wrote: "Upon the whole, I doubt whether the opposition to the Constitution will not ultimately be productive of more good than evil; it has called forth, in its defence, abilities (which would not perhaps have been otherwise exerted) that have thrown new light upon the source of Government; they have given the rights of man a full and fair discussion, and have explained them in so clear and forcible a manner as cannot fail to make a lasting impression upon those who read the best publications on the subject, and particularly the pieces under the signature of 'Publius.'" Had the Constitution been forced upon the people without thorough argument and keenest dissection of all its principles and details, it is entirely probable that a certain amount of resentment to it would long have lurked in parts of the country and among sections of the people. The fact that the opponents of the Constitution everywhere (except possibly in Pennsylvania, where its ratification was probably rushed through without sufficient debate) had the amplest opportunity to develop, to disseminate, and to argue their objections was a highly beneficial thing. A whole people received an education in the differing political theories of Union and of State independence — of National and of Federal Governments. Knowledge of the principles on which the Constitution was framed and based was spread wide through the country. And that knowledge and that education were imbedded in the American people and handed down to their sons.

When all the arguments for and against the Constitution are considered, when the justification for many of the Antifederalist fears is allowed for, when all the exaggerated accusations and recriminations on the one side and the other are duly discounted, when all the political and economic evils which either existed or were believed then to exist are viewed in historical perspective — the greater becomes the triumph of the Constitution. That instrument becomes the more remarkable, when we perceive that it prevailed, not merely by virtue of the strength of the arguments of its adherents, but also in spite of the weighty arguments of its opponents. What led to this triumph? Largely this. The Antifederalist fight was based on fears and doubts — on the possible evils which might be brought about by this new form of Government; yet (granting that some of their contentions were sound), they had nothing positive to put forward in its place which would adequately meet the situation. The advocates of the Constitution, on the other hand, had a positive plan to remedy existing conditions. The rock on which the Federalists founded their whole argument was, that the Union must be preserved and that it could only be preserved by the adoption of a form of Government based on the principles proposed by them. "I have for some time been persuaded," wrote Madison to Pendleton, February 21, 1788, "that the question on which the proposed Constitution must turn, is the simple one: whether the Union shall or shall not be continued. There is, in my opinion, no middle ground to be taken. The opposition, with some, has disunion assuredly for its object; and, with all, for its real tendency." And writing to Jefferson, he said that it was "the sincere and unanimous wish of the Convention to cherish and preserve the Union of the States. . . . It was generally agreed that the objects of the Union could not be secured by any system founded on the principle of a Confederation of Sovereign States." [1] The sole question, said the Federalists, is: "Shall we have a truly United States? Assume that evils may develop in its operation, is it not better to take the chance of possible future evils

[1] Madison to Jefferson, Oct. 24, 1787.

than to encounter the perfectly certain evils of economic and political disorder and disunion which will follow the failure of the States to accept this Constitution?" To that question, the American people gave the common sense answer, the correct answer. The trouble with the Antifederalists was, not so much that they were wrong as that they were impractical — not so much that their politics were unprincipled, as that they were inadequate to the situation. The triumph of the Constitution was a triumph of political adventure, a triumph of the determination to ignore risks in order to achieve Union.

The great French historian, M. Guizot, once asked James Russell Lowell how long he thought the Republic would endure, to which Lowell replied: "So long as the ideas of the men who made it, continue dominant." [1] President Cleveland said, at the celebration of the one hundredth Anniversary of the signing of the Constitution held in Philadelphia, September 17, 1887: "When we look down one hundred years and see the origin of our Constitution, when we contemplate all its trials and triumphs, when we realize how completely the principles upon which it is based have met every National need and every National peril, how devoutly should we say, with Franklin, 'God governs in the affairs of men', and how solemn should be the thought that to us is delivered this ark of the people's covenant, and to us is given the duty to shield it from impious hands. It comes to us sealed with the test of a century. . . . Another centennial day will come, and millions yet unborn will inquire concerning our stewardship, and the safety of their Constitution. God grant they may find it unimpaired; and as we rejoice today in the patriotism and devotion of those who lived one hundred

[1] *The Independent in Politics* (1888), by James Russell Lowell.

years ago, so may those who follow us rejoice in our fidelity and love of constitutional liberty." To these noble words, Samuel F. Miller, Justice of the Supreme Court of the United States, added this warning: "I should fail of a most important duty if I did not say, on this important occasion, that no amount of wisdom in a Constitution can produce wise government, unless there is a suitable response in the spirit of the people." In this, there was re-echoed the similar warning made by James Madison as to the Constitution, nearly one hundred years before: "The people who are the authors of this blessing must also be its guardians. Their eyes must be ever ready to mark, their voice to pronounce, and their arms to repel or repair, aggressions on the authority of their Constitutions."[1] To enable the people to be its guardians, the people must know its history and its purpose.

That the progress of the age may require amendments to the Constitution is a thing implicit in the document itself. On this subject, Thomas Jefferson wrote the following words, full of wisdom and vision:[2]

"Some men look at Constitutions with sanctimonious reverence, and deem them, like the ark of the covenant, too sacred to be touched. They ascribe to the men of the preceding age a wisdom more than human, and suppose what they did to be beyond amendment. I knew that age well; I belonged to and labored with it. It deserved well of its country. It was very like the present, but without the experience of the present; and forty years of experience in Government is worth a century of book-reading; and this they would say themselves, were they to rise from the dead. I am certainly not an advocate for frequent and untried changes in laws and Constitutions. I think moderate imperfections had better be borne with; because, when once known, we accommodate ourselves to them, and find practical means

---

[1] *National Gazette* (Phil.) Feb. 6, 1792.
[2] Jefferson to Samuel Kerchival, July 12, 1816.

of correcting their ill effects. But I know, also, that laws and institutions must go hand in hand with the progress of the human mind. As that becomes more developed, more enlightened, as new discoveries are made, new truths disclosed, and manners and opinions change with the change of circumstances, institutions must advance also and keep pace with the times."

But amendments, when made, must be consonant with the spirit in which the Constitution was conceived and the principles on which it was founded — otherwise the nature of our republican form of Government may be altered. As a safeguard against assaults upon the political basis of our country, there must be a thorough understanding by the people of the history of its Constitutional birth. To assist this understanding, this book has been written.

CHAPTER TWO

Sources of Knowledge of the Constitution

One hundred and fifty years ago, John Jay, then Chief Justice of New York, said: "Every member of the State ought diligently to read and study the Constitutions of his country and teach the rising generations to be free. By knowing their rights, they will sooner perceive when they are violated and be the better prepared to defend and assert them." These words are as true today as they were then. In the study of the Constitution, it is important to know not only the document itself but the sources from which its interpretation has been derived. For the Constitution, as drafted, was not entirely unambiguous, its provisions have in some respects required interpretation; and the framers knew that this would be so. As Abraham Baldwin of Georgia said in Congress, on March 14, 1796, only nine years after the Convention: [1]

"It was not to disparage the instrument to say that it had not definitely and with precision, absolutely settled everything on which it had spoke. He had sufficient evidence to satisfy his own mind that it was not supposed by the makers of it at the time, but that some subjects were left a little ambiguous and uncertain. It was a great thing to get so many difficult subjects definitely settled at once. The few that were left a little unsettled might, without any great risk, be settled by practice or by amendments in the progress

[1] *4th Cong., 1st Sess.*, p. 537.

of the Government. . . . When he reflected on the immense difficulties and dangers of that trying occasion — the old Government prostrated, and a chance whether a new one could be agreed on, the recollection recalled to him nothing but the most joyful sensations that so many things had been so well settled and that experience had shown there was very little difficulty or danger in settling the rest."

The sources from which interpretations of the meaning of the provisions of the Constitution have been obtained at various times in the past, have been as follows.[1]

First — inspection of the original document itself. The Constitution, as finally engrossed and signed on September 17, 1787, was transmitted on the same day, together with a letter from the Convention in Philadelphia to the Congress sitting in New York under the old Articles of Confederation. The original document remained in the possession of the Secretary of Congress, Charles Thomson, until the new Government was established.[2] On July 24, 1789, President Washington directed Thomson to deliver the "books, records and papers of the late Congress" to Roger Alden, late Deputy Secretary of Congress, to take charge of them in New York. The First Congress, by Act of September 15, 1789, directed that "all books, records, and papers remaining in the Office of the late Secretary of the United States in Congress assembled" be placed in the charge and custody of the new State Department.

---

[1] See also *Bibliography of the Constitution in Pamphlets on the Constitution* (1888), ed. by Paul Leicester Ford.

[2] The ratifications of the Constitution were transmitted to the Congress under the Articles of Confederation and filed with its Secretary. That Congress, by Act of September 13, 1788, provided that electors for President and Vice President under the new Government should be selected on the first Wednesday of January, 1789; that they should give their votes on the first Wednesday of February, and that the new Government should begin in New York on the first Wednesday of March (that day, in 1789, being March 4). No quorum of the new House of Representatives was present until April 1, 1789; and no quorum of the Senate, until April 6. The new President (Washington) took the oath and was inaugurated on April 30.

Alden, however, remained in custody of all these papers until after Thomas Jefferson assumed the duties of the office of Secretary of State, which he accepted on February 14, 1790.[1] When the Government moved from New York to Philadelphia, in 1791, the Constitution was taken back to its place of origin; and it followed the Government and the Secretary of State to Washington, in 1800. In 1814, when the British occupied Washington, the Declaration of Independence and other papers in the State Department were taken out to Leesburg, Virginia, and it is probable that the Constitution was one of these papers. They were returned when President Madison re-occupied Washington.[2] One of the few references to the original document is found in John Quincy Adams' diary, January 11, 1823, when, there being a question raised as to the punctuation of the copy in the printed Journals of the Convention, Adams wrote: "I sent for the original roll of the Constitution itself, and for a copy printed from it in 1820, by my direction and then collated with the roll. The punctuation in no two of the copies were exactly the same." The curious fact may be noted that James Madison himself, as late as 1830, was not fully certain whether the original document was then in the State Department; for, writing to Andrew Stevenson, as to the punctuation of the General Welfare Clause, he said:[3]

"Should it appear that the Document is not there, or that the error has slipped into it, the material in my hands to which you refer will amount, I think, to a proof outweighing even that authority. It would seem strange, if the original Constitution be in the Department of State, that it has

[1] *The Department of State* (1914), by Gaillard Hunt, p. 81.

[2] See letter of Gen. S. Pleasanton, to W. H. Winder, Aug. 7, 1848; *The Declaration of Independence, its History* (1906), by John H. Hazelton.

[3] *Writings of James Madison* (Hunt's ed.), IX, 412, Madison to Stevenson, Nov. 27, 1830.

hitherto escaped notice. But it is to be explained, I presume, by the fact that it was not among the papers relating to the Constitution left with General Washington and there deposited by him; but having been sent from the Convention to the old Congress, lay among the mass of papers handed over, on the expiration of the latter to that Department."

Second — after inspection of the original document, the next source of information as to the Constitution came from its reprints in the newspapers and in pamphlet form in 1787.[1] There appears to have been no formal provision made by the Government of the United States for the promulgation of the Constitution, except by a concurrent resolution of the two Houses of Congress, made during the First Congress, July 6, 1789, whereby it was: "Resolved, that there be prefixed to the publication of the Acts of the present session of Congress a correct copy of the Constitution of Government for the United States." It was later reprinted in the collected editions of the United States Statutes.[2] In those early days, however, comparatively few men were in possession of such books, and there is much evidence of the scanty knowledge of the Constitution which prevailed in remote parts of the country. For instance, in a debate in Congress, December 14, 1798, on the Alien and Sedition Laws, Albert Gallatin of

---

[1] Paul Leicester Ford, in his *Pamphlets on the Constitution* (1888), records pamphlet editions published in 1787 as follows: in New York, two; in Boston, three; in Philadelphia, four; in Hartford, one; in Richmond, ten; and in 1788, one in Poughkeepsie (in Dutch) and one in Albany. He also states that there were many others published which have not been preserved.

[2] The Act of March 3, 1796, provided for including the Constitution in the printing of the statutes. A three volume edition of the statutes was published in 1797, by Richard Folwell; a fourth volume was added in 1799, by Mathew Carey; fifth and sixth volumes in 1803, by William Duane; 7th, 8th, 9th, and 10th volumes in 1811, by Roger G. Weightman. In 1815, a five volume compilation was published by Bioren and Deane, prepared by J. B. Colvin upon the basis of a plan made by Attorney General Richard Rush; and five additional volumes brought the statutes down to 1845. A collection of the statutes, prepared by Joseph Story, was published in 1827. In 1845, a collection of statutes, treaties, etc., in eight volumes was published by Little, Brown and Co.

Pennsylvania, Josiah Parker of Virginia, Richard Sprigg of Maryland, and W. C. A. Claiborne of Tennessee spoke of this ignorance, and the latter said: "It had been conceded by all that the circulation of the Constitution as amended had been very limited, and that the amendments are unknown in some parts of the Union", particularly in the Western country, and that he "should rejoice to see our form of Government in the hands of every freeman in the country."

In 1846, an edition of the Constitution was published in a book (containing also much valuable historical information) by William Hickey, in the preparation of which, for the first time since 1819, a comparison was made with the original document; and the reproduction was duly authenticated as accurate by a certificate from James Buchanan, as Secretary of State. In this book, the author stated that:

"The necessity for a close and continued attention to the execution of a copy of this important instrument became manifest by the use of a printed copy (considered as correct) to print from, which, on being compared with the original, was found to contain several errors in the words, and sixty-five in the punctuation. This circumstance led to a further comparison of copies, in several editions of the laws, printed by different individuals, and it was found that one edition contained 204 and another 176 errors in the punctuation of the Constitution."

The United States Senate in 1847 voted to purchase 12,000 copies of this book; and in 1848, 1850, 1853, and 1854, similar votes were passed; the House of Representatives also in 1854 voting to purchase 38,625 copies. The purpose of these votes was to enable Congress to make wide distribution of the Constitution and accompanying documents. As the Vice President, George M. Dallas, said in writing to the compiler: "Such a fundamental and paramount law in the picture of its origin and in the purity of its text should be placed within the reach of every freeman. It should be found wherever there is a capacity to read; not only in legislative halls, judicial councils, libraries, and colleges, but also in the cabins and steerages of our mariners, at every common school, log hut, factory, or fireside. It should form the fundamental basis of American thought, by being made a perpetually recurring object of memory." [1]

Third — the next sources of information as to the interpretation of the Constitution and the intentions of its framers were the statements, verbal and written, made by the framers themselves. The first account of anything happening in the Convention came in the publication of a pamphlet (reproduced in part in some newspapers) in New York, in October, 1787, by Charles Pinckney of South Carolina, entitled *Observations on the Plan of Government submitted to the Federal Convention in Philadelphia, on the 28th of May, 1787, delivered at different Times in the Course of their Discussions.*[2] Next and most important were the letters written for the newspapers by Madison, Hamilton, and John Jay,

---

[1] Hickey's *Constitution of the United States of America* (1846), letter of Dallas, Feb. 18, 1847. See also letters from Chief Justice Roger B. Taney, Daniel Webster, and many others.

[2] Madison wrote to Washington, Oct. 14, 1787: "I add to it a pamphlet which Mr. Pinckney has submitted to the public, or rather as he professes, to the perusal of his friends, and a printed sheet containing his ideas on a very delicate subject, too delicate in my opinion, to have been properly confided to the press " (*i.e.,* Pinckney's speech in secret session of Congress on the Mississippi River question). Washington replied, October 22: "Mr. C. Pinckney is unwilling (I perceive by the enclosures contained in your favor . . .) to lose any fame that can be acquired by the publication of his sentiments." To Washington, Madison wrote again, Oct. 28: "Mr. C. P's character is, as you observe, well marked by the publications which I enclosed. His printing the secret paper at this time could have no motive but the appetite for expected praise."

Historians seem to be of opinion that very little, if anything, of the alleged speeches contained in this pamphlet were actually delivered in the Convention, but that it was "afterwards dressed up for publication and that certain ideas were inserted which were really the outgrowth of the Convention's work and not original with Pinckney." See *Amer. Hist. Rev.,* IX, 736; *Amer. Hist. Ass. Report* (1902), I, 87 *et seq.*

under the pseudonym of "Publius", in 1787 and 1788, and collected in book form in *The Federalist*. It has ever since been regarded not only as the most important commentary on the Constitution, but also as one of the most valuable works on the theory of political government ever produced. Of it, Washington wrote to Hamilton, August 28, 1788: "When the transient circumstances and fugitive performances which attended this crisis shall have disappeared, that work will merit the notice of posterity because in it are candidly discussed the principles of freedom and the topics of government which will always be interesting to mankind, so long as they shall be connected in civil society." Jefferson wrote to Madison, November 18, 1788: "With respect to *The Federalist*, the three authors had been named to me. I read it with care, pleasure, and improvement, and was satisfied there was nothing in it by one of those hands, and not a great deal by a second. It does the highest honor to the third, as being, in my opinion, the best commentary on the principles of government which ever was written. In some parts of it is discoverable that the author means only to say what may be best said in defence of opinions in which he did not concur. But in general, it establishes firmly the plan of Government. I confess it has rectified me in several points." The classic view of it was expressed by Chief Justice Marshall in a great case, in 1821 : [1]

"The opinion of *The Federalist* has always been considered as of great authority. It is a complete commentary on our Constitution, and is appealed to by all parties in the questions to which that instrument has given birth. Its intrinsic merit entitles it to this high rank, and the part two of its authors performed in framing the Constitution, put it very much in their power to explain the views with which it was framed."

[1] *Cohens* v. *Virginia* (1821), 6 Wheaton, 418.

Nevertheless, it must not be forgotten that *The Federalist* was the work of advocates for a cause, not of non-partisan historians; and Madison himself admitted this; for, writing to Edward Livingston, April 17, 1824, he said that: "It cannot be denied, without forgetting what belongs to human nature, that in consulting the contemporary writings which vindicate and recommend the Constitution, it is fair to keep in mind that the authors might be sometimes influenced by the zeal of advocates." And William Wirt, arguing in the great case of *Gibbons* v. *Ogden* in 1824, spoke of the authors of *The Federalist* as writing a "polemic for the purpose of vindicating the Constitution against popular objections." And as William Lowndes of South Carolina said in 1818: [1]

"*The Federalist* was the composition of three very able men who had great agency in framing the Constitution, in procuring its adoption and afterwards in administering it. It was, too, a contemporary exposition, but the exposition of jealous advocates, anxious to procure the establishment of a Government on which depended the happiness and liberty of the country. Is it to be believed that they never represented a power as less extensive, a limitation as somewhat more strict, than an impartial judge would have pronounced it? If the opinions of Patrick Henry and Mr. Monroe should be read to the Committee as evidence of the just construction of any article of the Constitution, this contemporaneous exposition would weigh but little, nor ought it to weigh. By the apprehensions of the one party, a necessary and well-guarded power was almost magnified into uncontrolled despotism; while the complacency with which the other party were disposed to view their own work, led them to believe its provisions less obnoxious to abuse than they really were. *The Federalist* was written by men yet warm from debates, in which all their ingenuity and talent for refinement had been employed to prove that the powers

[1] *15th Cong., 1st Sess.*, March 10, 1818.

which the Constitution gave were not great enough to be dangerous. That with such powerful disturbing causes, the judgment of these distinguished men, should so often have led to the same construction of the Constitution which cool examination has since confirmed, is a rare testimony of their merit."

The next information as to the intentions of the delegates in framing the Constitution came from the wide publication in the newspapers of the speech of James Wilson, November 24, 1787, in the Pennsylvania State Convention, which (it was stated) "ran through an impression of several thousands, in a few days at Philadelphia, at one shilling each." [1] The next information as to any proceedings in the Convention, particularly as to the part played by Elbridge Gerry, George Mason, and Luther Martin, was contained in letters by Oliver Ellsworth, entitled *Letters of a Landholder*, published in the newspapers from November, 1787, to March, 1788. [2] A most important description of the proceedings of the Federal Convention and of the intentions of the delegates was presented in the report made by Luther Martin, one of the Maryland delegates, to the Legislature of that State, at its request. This report was published in the newspapers, not only in Maryland but in other States, in 1788, and later in pamphlet and book form, under the title *The Genuine Information delivered to the Legislature of the State of Maryland relative to the Proceedings of the General Convention*. [3]

[1] *Massachusetts Centinel*, Dec. 12, 1787.

[2] See *Connecticut Courant*, Nov. 5, 12, 19, 26; Dec. 3, 10, 17, 24, 31, 1787; March 3, 10, 17, 24, 1788. *Maryland Journal*, Feb. 29, 1788.

[3] See *Maryland Gazette*, Dec. 28, 1787, Jan. 1, 4, 8, 11, 15, 18, 22, 29, 1788; Feb. 1, 5, 8. See also *ibid.* Jan. 29, 1788, for letter of Martin to Thomas C. Deye as to the Convention.

A letter from Maryland in *Independent Gazetteer*, May 5, 1788, said that: "When Mr. Martin's speech was published, it was in one newspaper at Baltimore (the extremity of the State) which could be seen by few in the country." A letter from Charleston, South Carolina, in *Independent Gazetteer*, April 19, 1788, said: "Mr. Martin's *Information* is now publishing in our different city papers, and it will

Next came the publications of reports of debates in the State ratifying Conventions in 1788 — published at first partially in a few newspapers, and later in book form.[1] None of the above publications were full or entirely accurate, nor did they have much circulation after 1788. From that year until 1819, the chief knowledge of the proceedings in the Federal Convention came from speeches in Congress made by members who had also been delegates — chiefly Elbridge Gerry of Massachusetts, Abraham Baldwin of Georgia, Jonathan Dayton of New Jersey, James Madison of Virginia,

have great effect, as it is much read." See also *American Herald* (Boston), Feb. 4, 1788. Charles Pinckney ("A Steady and Open Republican") wrote in *State Gazetteer of South Carolina*, May 5, 1788, of "Mr. Martin's long mischievous declaration of the opinion and proceedings of the late General Convention with all his colourings and uncandid insinuations in regard to General Washington and Dr. Franklin." Still further letters as to the Convention by Luther Martin appeared in the *Maryland Journal*, Jan. 18, March 7, 18, 21, 24, 28, April 4, 1788, and in *New York Journal*, June 16, 1788.

As to Martin and John F. Mercer and the Constitution, see John B. Cutting to Jefferson, July 11, 1788, *Mass. Hist. Soc. Proc.* (1903), XVII. Amongst other things, Cutting wrote: "So far did Mr. Martin proceed in his avowed hostility, as even to detail, in the face of decency, before the assembled Legislature of Maryland, the petty dialogues and paltry anecdotes of every description that came to his knowledge in Conventional Committees and private conversations with the respective members of the Convention when at Philadelphia."

[1] *Lloyd's Debates of the Pennsylvania Convention*, containing only speeches of James Wilson and Thomas McKean, were published in 1788; and a book entitled *Commentaries on the Constitution*, containing only the same speeches, was published in 1792. The *Debates in the Massachusetts Convention*, reported by Benjamin Russell of the *Massachusetts Centinel*, were published in 1788 (reprinted in 1808).

The *Debates in the Virginia Convention* were published in 1788, and reprinted (corrected) by David Robertson in 1805. As to this work, George Mason wrote to John Major, July 21, 1788: "You will see the small majority which has ratified the new project. The minority are as respectable for their weight and influence as their number, and it will require the most prudent exertions to keep the people quiet in some parts of the Country. The debates are not yet published; nor is there any cause to expect that they will be authentic; the shorthand man who took them down, being a Federal partizan, they will probably be garbled in some such partial manner as the debates of the Pennsylvania Convention have been by Lloyd." *George Mason Papers MSS* in Library of Congress. Madison also said in Congress, March 20, 1796, that: "In referring to the debates of the State Convention as published, he wished not to be understood as putting entire confidence in the accuracy of them. Even those of Virginia which had probably been taken down by the most skilful hand (whose merit he wished by no means to disparage) contained internal evidence in abundance of chasms and misconceptions of what was said."

The *Debates in the New York Convention* were published, in part, in 1788. The *Debates in the North Carolina Convention*, reported by David Robertson, were published in 1789.

Charles Pinckney of South Carolina, and Rufus King of Massachusetts and New York.[1] As William Vans Murray of Maryland said in the famous Jay Treaty debate in the House, March 22, 1796, urging Madison and Baldwin to state their recollections: "One hundred years hence, should a great question arise upon the Constitution, what would not be the value of that man's intelligence who, allowed to possess integrity and a profound and unimpaired mind . . . and being known to have been in the illustrious body that framed the instrument, should clear up difficulties by his contemporaneous knowledge? . . . To no man's exposition would he listen with more deference." On the other hand, the recollections of the framers were not always accepted as accurate. Thus, as early as September 21, 1789, Fisher Ames of Massachusetts stated in Congress that while he admitted the abilities of James Madison, "he was not disposed to pay implicit deference to that gentleman's exposition of that instrument. There were but a few on the floor who were in Convention, and who could say what was the intention with which every clause was inserted. He was content to take it as he found it." And Elbridge Gerry said in Congress, February 7, 1791: "Are we to depend on the memory of the gentlemen for a history of their debates; and from thence to collect their sense? This would be improper, because the memories of different gentlemen would probably vary, as they had already done with respect to those facts; and if not, the opinions of the individual members who debated are not to be considered as the opinion of the Convention." [2] James Madison, himself, as early as

[1] For a full collection of the statements made by the framers of the Constitution and reported in speeches by either themselves or by men with whom they had communicated, see *The Records of the Federal Convention* (1911), by Max Farrand, III.

[2] John Vining of Delaware also said, February 8, 1791: "Granting that the opinion of the gentleman from Virginia had been the full sense of the members of the

the debate over the Jay Treaty in the House, April 6, 1796, said that:

"After all, whatever veneration might be entertained for the body of men who formed our Constitution, the sense of that body could never be regarded as the oracular guide in expounding the Constitution. As the instrument came from them, it was nothing more than the draft of a plan, nothing but a dead letter, until life and validity were breathed into it by the voice of the people, speaking through the State Conventions. If we were to look, therefore, for the meaning of that instrument beyond the face of the instrument, we must look for it, not in the General Convention which proposed, but in the State Conventions which accepted and ratified it."

This view of the importance of the debates in the Federal Convention has not been adopted by the Supreme Court; and that body has, in many great cases, paid especial attention to those debates as bearing on the interpretation of the Constitution.[1]

As these recollections of the framers were generally voiced in Congress, and as the early debates in Congress were reported in only a few newspapers (the *Register of Debates* containing the collected debates not being published until 1825, and the *Annals of Congress* not until 1834), the general public, prior to 1840, had little means of construing the Constitution. It, however, was known to many men in public life that Madison had made detailed notes of the debates, "taken down

Convention, their opinion at that day is not a sufficient authority by which for Congress at the present time to construe the Constitution."

[1] Of Madison himself as an authority on interpretation of the Constitution, Daniel Webster said, October 3, 1837: "He had as much to do as any man in the framing of the Constitution and as much as any man in administering. Nobody among the living or the dead is more fit to be consulted on a question growing out of it." And John C. Calhoun said, February 18, 1837, that: "We were indebted to Madison at least as much as to any other man for the form of government under which we live. Indeed, he might be said to have done more for our institutions than any man now living or that had gone before him." See *25th Cong., 1st Sess.*, p. 491; *24th Cong., 2d Sess.*, p. 852.

with a labor and exactness beyond comprehension", as Jefferson wrote to John Adams, and publication of these notes had been urged upon Madison, for many years. As early as 1799, he had received word from Jefferson that "a most anxious desire is expressed that you would publish your debates of the Convention. That these measures of the army, navy, and direct tax will bring about a revolution of public sentiment is thought certain, and that the Constitution will then receive a different explanation. Could these debates be ready to appear critically, their effect would be decisive. I beg of you to turn this subject in your mind. The arguments against it will be personal; those in favor of it moral." Madison had replied, however, that the expediency of such publication was "to be well weighed, with an eye to the use of which every part is susceptible." Prior to 1810, he had sent copies to Jefferson, so that "copies in your hands might double the security against destructive casualties",[1] but he deemed it undesirable to publish them at that time. In 1808, Madison himself had been made the subject of political attack by the publication of garbled extracts from notes of the debates of the Convention made by Robert Yates, a New York delegate, and published by E. C. E. Genet in a *Letter to the Electors of President and Vice President of the United States*, by "A Citizen of New York." [2] But even this attack had not stirred him to alter his decision with reference to his own notes.

While full notes of the debates were thus not yet available for publication, the Journals of the Convention remained accessible. When that body adjourned on September 17, 1787, its last vote had been

---

[1] Jefferson to Adams, Aug. 10, 1815; Jefferson to Madison, Jan. 16, 1799; Madison to Jefferson, Sept. 6, 1799; July 17, 1810.

[2] See also Hall's *American Law Journal* (1813), IV.

in response to an inquiry from Washington, "that he retain the Journal and other papers, subject to the order of the Congress, if ever formed under the Constitution." Accordingly, all the papers of the Convention which were preserved were placed in Washington's custody. On March 19, 1796, he, as President, deposited in the State Department 153 pages containing minutes for an official Journal of the Convention kept by William Jackson as Secretary of the Convention, a document of twenty-eight pages containing the Journal of the Committee of the Whole, and one of eight pages and some loose sheets containing the lists of ayes and nays on the various questions debated.[1] In his message to Congress of March 30, 1796, in response to the request of the House that the papers relative to the Jay Treaty be submitted to it, President Washington took occasion to reinforce his views as to the relation of the House to the treaty-making power, by citing a vote of the Convention contained in this Journal, and said: "If other proofs than these and the plain letter of the Constitution itself be necessary to ascertain the point under consideration, they may be found in the Journal of the General Convention, which I have deposited in the office of the Department of State." His action in so citing the contents of Journal aroused some criticism, as being in violation of the Convention's vote as to secrecy; and Madison wrote to Jefferson, April 4, 1796: "According to my memory and that of others, the Journal of the Convention was by a vote deposited with the President to be kept sacred until called for by some competent authority. How can this be reconciled with the use he has made of it? Examine my notes, if you please, at the close of the business and let me

---

[1] Jared Sparks wrote to Madison, Nov. 14, 1831: "It seems to me that your Secretary of the Convention was a very stupid secretary, not to take care of those things better, and to make a better journal than the dry bones which now go by that name." *Life and Writings of Jared Sparks* (1893) by Herbert D. Adams, II, 231.

know what is said on the subject." [1] After that date, it appears that the Journal was open for reference, at least by Members of Congress; for in a speech in the House on the Twelfth Amendment relating to election of the Chief Executive, in 1803, Roger Griswold of Connecticut made the following reference: [2]

"The Journal of the General Convention shows that this subject created more difficulty than any other which fell under the deliberations of that respectable body. . . . After every project had received a deliberate consideration, that body agreed on the plan under which we have successfully practiced for fourteen years."

The first official publication of proceedings of the Convention was made in 1819, when under Resolve of Congress of March 27, 1818, John Quincy Adams, Secretary of State, printed as a Government document such papers as were in his possession, relative to the framing of the Constitution. These included the minutes of the Journal above referred to, and with them there were printed for the first time, the Plans for a Constitution which had been submitted by William Paterson and by Alexander Hamilton, the manuscripts of which were now given to the Government by the executor of the estate of David Brearley (a delegate to the Convention from New Jersey); also the alleged Plan submitted by Charles Pinckney of South Carolina, now furnished by himself on request of John Quincy Adams. [3] The book appeared in the

[1] Jefferson, writing in answer to Madison, April 19, 1796, said: "I have turned to the Conventional history, and enclose you an exact copy of what is there on the subject you mentioned"; and he enclosed copy of the last two pages of the manuscript of Madison's *Notes of Debates*. These pages and the letter were published in 1829, in *Memoirs, Correspondence, Miscellanies of Thomas Jefferson*, edited by Thomas Mann Randolph, this being the first publication of any of Madison's *Notes*, prior to 1840.

[2] *8th Cong., 1st Sess.*, p. 744, Dec. 8, 1803.

[3] For Madison's criticisms as to the accuracy of this Pinckney draft, see his letters to J. K. Paulding, June 6, 1831; Jared Sparks, June 27, Nov. 25, 1831; T. S. Grimke, June 6, 1834; W. A. Duer, June 5, 1835; see also his memorandum in

same year when the great cases on the Constitution were being decided by the United States Supreme Court — the *Dartmouth College Case* and *McCulloch v. Maryland* — and two years before *Cohens v. Virginia* and five years before *Gibbons v. Ogden*.

This publication, however, simply gave the dry bones of the proceedings of the Convention and contained none of the discussions. The first report of actual speeches appeared in 1821, in a book published at Albany, N. Y., entitled *Secret Proceedings and Debates of the Convention at Philadelphia, in the year 1787, for the purpose of forming the Constitution of the United States of America. From Notes taken by the late Robert Yates, Esq., Chief Justice of New York, and copied by John Lansing, Jun., Esq., late Chancellor of that State, Members of that Convention, including 'The Genuine Information' laid before the Legislature of Maryland by Luther Martin, Esquire, then Attorney General of that State and Member of the Same Convention.* As Yates left the Convention, July 10, 1787, these notes covered but a short portion of its work and debates, and they were imperfect and inaccurate.[1] Madison, writing in 1821, said: "I have not yet seen a copy. From the scraps thrown into the newspapers, I cannot doubt that the prejudices of the author guided his pen, and that he has committed egregious errors, at least in relating to others as well as myself." And in 1826, he wrote that Yates and Martin "appear to have reported in angry terms what they had observed with jaundiced eyes." In 1833, he wrote:

Documentary History of the Constitution, V, 417; Journals of Jared Sparks, April 19, 25, 1830; Memoirs of John Quincy Adams, VIII, May 4, 1830.

[1] Madison to John G. Jackson, Dec. 27, 1821; to Thomas Cooper, Dec. 26, 1826; to John Tyler in 1833, replying to Tyler's speech in the Senate of Feb. 6, 1833. To James Robertson, Madison wrote, March 27, 1830, that Judge Yates "though a highly respectable man was a zealous partisan and has committed gross errors in his desultory notes", and that Luther Martin's "feelings had a discoloring effect on his statements."

"So much use has been made of Judge Yates' minutes of the debates in the Convention that I must be allowed to remark that they abound in inaccuracies and are not free from gross errors, some of which do much injustice to the arguments and opinions of particular members. All this may be explained, without a charge of willful misrepresentation, by the very desultory manner in which the notes appear to have been taken, his ear catching particular expressions and losing qualifications of them, and by prejudices giving to his mind all the bias which an honest one could feel. Without impeaching the integrity of Luther Martin, it may be observed of him also that his report of the proceedings of the Convention during his stay in it shows by its colorings that his feelings were but too much mingled with his statements and inferences. There is good ground for believing that Mr. Martin himself became sensible of this and made no secret that, in his Address to the Legislature of his State, he had been betrayed by the irritated state of his mind, into a picture that might do injustice both to the Body and to particular members."

It is only fair to add that, in many particulars, Yates' *Notes* were fuller than Madison's own; but they did undoubtedly contain errors.

In 1828, a few notes of the debates in the Federal Convention taken by William Pierce, a Georgia delegate, and printed in the *Savannah Georgian*, received some local publicity. In 1827–1830, just at the time when the nullification issue was being raised and when the great debates over Constitutional questions were particularly active in the Supreme Court and in the Senate, Jonathan Elliot published his valuable three volume work, *The Debates of the Several State Conventions on the Adoption of the Federal Constitution as Recommended by the General Convention at Philadelphia in 1787.* This book received a warm reception and went into a second edition, of four volumes, in 1836. Its object was well stated by the editor as follows:

"In expounding parts of the Constitution which seems extremely doubtful, the publication of the Proceedings and Debates of the States must be, at least, useful; for what the States really intended to grant to the General Government must be looked for in their acts and in their discussions which manifest their intentions, in a manner peculiarly satisfactory touching Constitutional topics, so frequently the subject of controversy in Congress and in the legal tribunals of the country."

Meanwhile, frequent suggestions were being made to James Madison that he publish his work. The editor of Yates' *Notes*, in 1821, in his preface, expressed the hope and belief that through "the talents and veracity of Mr. Madison, his memories will enrich our annals and that his paternal feelings for *The Federalist* will not affect the rigidity of his narrative as historian." But Madison himself, writing in 1827, stated that he thought posthumous publication best, since "as no personal or party views can then be imputed, they will be read with less of personal or party feelings"; and he pointed out that the time would soon come, as the only framers of the Constitution then alive were Rufus King, William Few, and himself. Six years earlier, he had written that publication "should be delayed till the Constitution should be well settled by practice and till a knowledge of the controversial part of the proceedings of its framers could be turned to no improper account." And in this latter letter, he still expressed the view which he had advanced in Congress in 1796, that the debates on the framing of the Constitution could play little part in interpretation of that instrument, and that the key to its meaning must be found only in the debates of State Conventions which adopted it : [1]

[1] Madison to S. H. Smith, Feb. 2, 1827; to Thomas Ritchie, Sept. 15, 1821. Writing to M. L. Hurlbert, May, 1830, he again said : "But whatever respect may be thought due to the intention of the Convention which prepared and proposed the Constitution, as presumptive evidence of the general understanding at the time of

"As a guide in expounding and applying the provisions of the Constitution, the debates and incidental decisions of the Convention can have no authoritative character. However desirable it be that they should be preserved as a gratification to the laudable curiosity felt by every people to trace the origin and progress of their political institutions, and as a source perhaps of some lights on the science of government, its legitimate meaning of the instrument must be derived from the text itself; or, if a key is to be sought elsewhere, it must not be in the opinion or intentions of the body which planned and proposed the Constitution, but in the sense attached to it by the people in their respective State Conventions where it received all the authority which it possesses."

Nevertheless, Madison saw clearly the historical value of his *Notes*, and in an unfinished Preface which he wrote for them (*circa* 1835), he said that, when he took them, he was not "unaware of the value of such a contribution to the fund of materials for the history of a Constitution on which would be staked the happiness of a people great even in its infancy, and possibly the cause of liberty throughout the world." In his will, dated April 19, 1835, leaving his papers to his wife, Madison wrote that:

"Considering the peculiarity and magnitude of the decision which produced the Convention . . . the characters who composed it, the Constitution which resulted from their deliberation, its effects, during a trial of so many years on the prosperity of the people living under it, and the interest it has inspired among the friends of free Government, it is not an unreasonable inference that a report of its proceedings and discussions . . . will be particularly gratifying to the people of the United States, and to all who take an interest in the progress of political science and the course of true liberty."

the language used, it must be kept in mind that the only authoritative intentions were those of the people of the States, as expressed thro' the Conventions which ratified the Constitution."

Carrying out these views, Mrs. Madison, after her husband's death on June 28, 1836, offered his papers to the Government. There was some difference as to the price to be paid, but finally $30,000 was agreed upon. There was also some controversy over the constitutional power of Congress to make any appropriation for such a purchase. In the debate in the Senate, February 18, 1837, John C. Calhoun, while acknowledging the extreme value of Madison's work, denied the legal power.[1] Asher Robbins of Rhode Island, William C. Preston of South Carolina, John J. Crittenden of Kentucky, and John L. Rives of Virginia took the opposite view, and Daniel Webster said:

". . . It seemed to him that the measure now proposed was of great importance both in connection with the Constitution itself and with the history of its interpretation. . . . A report of such debates from such pen could not be but of the highest importance and its perusal was well calculated to gratify a rational curiosity. It might throw much light on the early interpretation of the Constitution and on the nature and structure of our Government. But while it produced this effect, it could do more than all other things to show to the people of the United States through what conciliation, through what a temper of compromise, through what a just yielding of the judgment of one individual to that of another, through what a spirit of manly and brotherly love that assembly of illustrious men had been enabled finally to agree upon the form of a Constitution for this country."

By Act of March 3, 1837, the Government bought these papers, including the *Notes of the Debates*, and they were first published in 1840, as *The Madison Papers*, edited by Henry D. Gilpin. It is a singular fact that it was not until fifty-three years after the Constitution was signed that the American people were afforded any adequate knowledge of the debates of the Federal Convention. It is also an interesting

[1] *24th Cong., 2d Sess.*

fact that every one of Chief Justice Marshall's great decisions on Constitutional law had been rendered, and all four of the principal books on that subject — Thomas Sergeant's *Constitutional Law* (1822), William Rawle's *A View of the Constitution of the United States* (1825), James Kent's *Commentaries* (1826), and Joseph Story's *Commentaries on the Constitution* (1833) — had been published, prior to the printing of Madison's *Notes*.[1] In studying these early lawbooks, therefore, it is important to bear in mind that they were written without the benefit of the knowledge of the debates.[2]

Fifty-four more years elapsed after 1840 before anything further was known as to the proceedings of the Federal Convention. In 1894, however, rather elaborate notes taken by Rufus King, a delegate from Massachusetts, were published in his *Life and Correspondence*. In 1903, and 1904, the large part which Charles Pinckney of South Carolina played in connection with the form and contents of the Constitution was established on a firm historical foundation by Professor J. Franklin Jameson, who reconstructed

---

[1] In a third edition of his book in 1845, Jonathan Elliot included for the first time, Madison's *Notes*, as a fifth volume. Madison's *Notes* have since been reproduced from the original manuscript; in 1900, in Volume III of the *Documentary History of the Constitution*, issued by the State Department, as *Bulletin No. 9, of the Bureau of Rolls and Library*, under the skilled editing of Andrew Hussey Allen (also as *House Document No. 529, 56th Cong., 2d Sess.*); in 1902, in *The Writings of James Madison*, edited by Gaillard Hunt; in 1911, in *The Records of the Federal Convention of 1787*, edited by Max Farrand; in 1920, in *The Debates in the Federal Convention of 1787*, edited by Gaillard Hunt and James Brown Scott; and in 1927, in the very valuable *House Document No. 398, 69th Congress, 1st Session*, entitled *Documents Illustrative of the Formation of the Union of the American States* (edited by Charles C. Tansill), which also included scattered notes of debates made by other delegates, also many documents prior to 1787, which should be in the possession of every American who desires to trace the sources of the Constitution.

[2] The lack of knowledge of the debates in the Federal Convention was deplored by the noted New York lawyer, Charles G. Haines, arguing in 1824, in *Ogden v. Saunders* (12 Wheaton 213): "What were the intentions of those who framed the Constitution when they inserted in it the provision that 'no State should pass a law impairing the obligation of contracts'? Unhappily for this country and for the general interests of political science, the history of the Convention of 1787 which framed the Constitution of the United States is lost to the world. We are compelled to resort to contemporaneous history in giving a construction to this Constitution." *The Dartmouth College Causes* (1879), by John M. Shirley, p. 206.

Pinckney's Plan for a Constitution in an illuminating article in the *American Historical Review*, which was further strengthened by an article in 1904 by Professor Andrew C. McLaughlin in the same magazine.[1] Scattered notes taken by four other members of the Convention — William Pierce of Georgia, William Paterson of New Jersey, Alexander Hamilton of New York, and James McHenry of Maryland — were published in 1898, 1904, 1905, and 1906.[2] In 1911, Max Farrand published a collection of letters from various delegates to the Federal Convention and other papers bearing upon its work, in volume three of his *Records of the Federal Convention*. In 1912, *The Literary Diary of Ezra Stiles* presented an account of the Convention, as given to Stiles, in December, 1787, in a conversation with Abraham Baldwin, a delegate from Georgia.

Such are the sources of information as to the making of the Constitution. It remains for American citizens to take advantage of them, and to recall that the words written by old George Mason of Virginia into the first Bill of Rights in this country are still true, that: "No free government or the blessings of liberty can be preserved to any people but by . . . frequent recurrence to fundamental principles." Our political system will break down, only when and where the people, for whom and by whom it is intended to be carried on, shall fail to receive a sound education in its principles and in its historical development illustrating its application to and under changing conditions. "Our country," said Edmund Burke, "is not a thing of mere physical locality. It consists, in a great measure, in the ancient order into which we are born."

---

[1] *American Historical Review*, VIII, 509; IX, 735; *Amer. Hist. Ass. Report* (1902), I, 87 *et seq.*; see also *The Mystery of the Pinckney Draught*, by Judge Charles C. Nott, in 1908; and Max Farrand's review of the latter in the *American Historical Review*, XIV.

[2] *American Historical Review*, III, IX, X, XI.

APPENDICES

APPENDIX A

Books Containing Letters Quoted

The letters quoted in this book, except when specific authorities are cited in the footnotes, are to be found in one or more of the following books:

The Records of the Federal Convention of 1787 (1911), by Max Farrand.

Documentary History of the Constitution (1905).

History of the Formation of the Constitution (1882), by George Bancroft.

The Diplomatic Correspondence of the United States, 1783–1789 (1837).

Writings of George Washington (1880–1893), edited by Worthington Chauncey Ford.

The Writings of James Madison (1906–1910), edited by Gaillard Hunt.

The Life and Correspondence of Rufus King (1894–1900), edited by Charles Ray King,

The Works of Thomas Jefferson (1904–1908), edited by Paul Leicester Ford.

The Correspondence and Public Papers of John Jay (1890–1893), edited by Henry Phelps Johnston.

The Writings of James Monroe (1898–1905), edited by Stanislaus Murray Hamilton.

The Works of Alexander Hamilton (1904), edited by Henry Cabot Lodge.

APPENDIX B

THE DELEGATES

Appointments of delegates were as follows.[1]

The Virginia Legislature voted to send delegates, October 16, 1786; and it elected as delegates, December 4, 1786, George Washington, Patrick Henry, Edmund Randolph, John Blair, James Madison, George Mason, and George Wythe; Patrick Henry declined to serve and in his place Governor Edmund Randolph appointed Dr. James McClurg, May 2, 1787. Richard Henry Lee and Thomas Nelson, to whom appointments were offered, also declined to accept.

The New Jersey Legislature voted to send as delegates, November 23, 1787, David Brearley, William Churchill Houston, William Paterson, and John Neilson; on May 18, it added William Livingston and Abraham Clark, and on June 5, Jonathan Dayton; all of whom were commissioned by Governor William Livingston on the above dates respectively; John Neilson declined and Abraham Clark did not attend.

The New Hampshire Legislature voted to send delegates, November 27, 1786, and it chose, on January 17, 1787, John Langdon, Pierce Long, John Sparhawk, and Nicholas Gilman (then its delegates to Congress). By Act of June 27, 1787, it appointed John Langdon, Nicholas Gilman, John Pickering, and Benjamin West (then its delegates to Congress). John Pickering and Benjamin West did not attend.

The Pennsylvania Legislature voted to send as delegates, December 30, 1786, Robert Morris, Thomas Mifflin, George Clymer, G. Morris, Thomas Fitzsimmons, Jared Ingersoll, and James Wilson; and by special Act of March 28, 1787, Benjamin Franklin.

[1] In addition to this list, the *New Haven Gazette*, May 6, June 28, 1787, in publishing alleged full lists of delegates, included Henry Laurens from South Carolina, and George Walton from Georgia.

The North Carolina Legislature voted to send as delegates, January 6, 1787, Governor Richard Caswell, Alexander Martin, William Richardson Davie, Richard Dobbs Spaight, and Willie Jones. Martin, Davie, and Spaight were commissioned by Governor Caswell on April 23. Jones and Caswell declined, and the Governor appointed and commissioned in their places Hugh Williamson on April 3, and William Blount on April 23.

The Delaware Legislature voted to send as delegates, February 3, 1787, George Read, Gunning Bedford, Richard Bassett, John Dickinson, and Jacob Broom, and they were commissioned by Governor Thomas Collins, April 2, 1787.

The Georgia Legislature voted to send as delegates, February 10, 1787, William Few, William Houstoun, William Pierce, Abraham Baldwin, George Walton, and Nathaniel Pendleton, and they were commissioned by Governor George Mathews, April 17, 1787. Walton and Pendleton did not attend.

The New York Legislature voted to send delegates, February 28, 1787; and on March 16, it elected John Lansing, Robert Yates, and Alexander Hamilton.

The South Carolina Legislature voted to send as delegates, March 8, 1787, John Rutledge, Charles Cotesworth Pinckney, Charles Pinckney, and Pierce Butler, and they were commissioned by Governor Thomas Pinckney, April 10.

The Massachusetts Legislature voted to send as delegates, March 10, 1787, Francis Dana, Elbridge Gerry, Nathaniel Gorham, Rufus King, and Caleb Strong, and they were commissioned by Governor James Bowdoin, April 9. Francis Dana did not attend, on account of ill health.

The Maryland Legislature voted to send delegates on April 23, 1787, and elected Robert Hanson Harrison, Charles Carroll of Carrollton, Thomas Sims Lee, Thomas Stone, and Gabriel Duvall — all of whom declined. Their places were filled by the Legislature on May 26, by the appointment of Daniel Carroll, John Francis Mercer, Daniel of St. Thomas Jenifer, Luther Martin, and James McHenry.

The Connecticut Legislature voted to appoint as delegates, May 12, 1787, William Samuel Johnson, Roger Sherman, and Oliver Ellsworth, Roger Sherman being appointed in place of Erastus Wolcott, who declined.

The dates of birth and death of the fifty-five delegates who attended the Convention, and the dates when they first were present and when they left (as far as ascertainable) are as follows.[1]

NEW HAMPSHIRE

JOHN LANGDON (June 25, 1741 — Sept. 18, 1819) — May 23.

NICHOLAS GILMAN (Aug. 3, 1755 — May 2, 1814) — May 23.

MASSACHUSETTS

NATHANIEL GORHAM (May 26, 1738 — June 11, 1796) — May 28.

RUFUS KING (March 24, 1755 — April 29, 1827) — as early as May 21.

ELBRIDGE GERRY (July 17, 1744 — Nov. 23, 1814) — May 29.

CALEB STRONG (Jan. 9, 1745 — Nov. 7, 1819) — May 28; left between Aug. 17 and August 27.

CONNECTICUT

WILLIAM SAMUEL JOHNSON (Oct. 7, 1727 — Nov. 14, 1819) — June 2.

ROGER SHERMAN (April 19, 1721 — July 23, 1793) — May 30.

OLIVER ELLSWORTH (April 29, 1745 — Nov. 26, 1807) — May 28; left after Aug. 23; in New Haven, Aug. 27.

NEW YORK

ALEXANDER HAMILTON (Jan. 11, 1757 — July 12, 1804) — May 19; left June 29; present July 13; in New York, Aug. 20 to Sept. 2.

ROBERT YATES (March 17, 1738 — Sept. 9, 1801) — May 18; left July 10.

JOHN LANSING (Jan. 30, 1754 — 1829) — June 2; left July 10.

NEW JERSEY

WILLIAM LIVINGSTON (Nov. 30, 1723 — July 25, 1790) — June 5; absent July 3–19.

[1] Dates of death and birth are taken from *History of the Celebration of the 100th Anniversary of the Constitution* (1889), by Hampton L. Carson, and *Appleton's Cyclopaedia of American Biography* (1888). Dates of attendance are taken chiefly from *Records of the Federal Convention* (1911), by Max Farrand, III; see also *Studies in the History of the Federal Convention of 1787*, by J. F. Jameson, *Amer. Hist. Ass. Report* (1902), I.

It may be noted that all, with the exception of eight, were born in this country — Hamilton being born in Nevis in the West Indies; Wilson in Scotland; Robert Morris and Davie in England; and Paterson, Fitzsimmons, McHenry, and Butler being of Irish birth.

DAVID BREARLEY (July 11, 1745 — Aug. 19, 1790) — as early as May 25.

WILLIAM PATERSON (1745 — Sept. 9, 1806) — as early as May 25; probably absent from July 23 to Sept. 15.

JONATHAN DAYTON (Oct. 16, 1760 — Oct. 9, 1824) — June 21.

WILLIAM CHURCHILL HOUSTON (1740 — Aug. 12, 1788) — as early as May 25; absent probably after July 17.

PENNSYLVANIA

BENJAMIN FRANKLIN (Jan. 17, 1706 — April 17, 1790) — as early as May 28.

THOMAS MIFFLIN (1744 — Jan. 20, 1800) — as early as May 28.

ROBERT MORRIS (Jan. 20, 1734 — May 8, 1806) — as early as May 25.

GEORGE CLYMER (March 16, 1739 — Jan. 23, 1813) — as early as May 28.

THOMAS FITZSIMMONS (1741 — May 26, 1811) — as early as May 25.

JARED INGERSOLL (1749 or 1750 — Oct. 31, 1822) — as early as May 28.

JAMES WILSON (Sept. 14, 1742 — Aug. 28, 1798) — as early as May 25.

GOUVERNEUR MORRIS (Jan. 31, 1752 — Nov. 6, 1816) — as early as May 25, absent until July 2.

DELAWARE

GEORGE READ (Sept. 17, 1733 — Sept. 21, 1798) — as early as May 19.

GUNNING BEDFORD (1747 — March 30, 1812) — May 28.

JOHN DICKINSON (Nov. 13, 1732 — Feb. 14, 1808) — May 29.

RICHARD BASSETT (April 2, 1745 — Sept. 15, 1815) — as early as May 21.

JACOB BROOM (1752 — April 25, 1810) — as early as May 21.

MARYLAND

JAMES MCHENRY (Nov. 16, 1753 — May 3, 1816) — May 28, absent from June 1 to August 4.

DANIEL CARROLL (July 22, 1730 — May 7, 1796) — July 9.

JOHN FRANCIS MERCER (May 17, 1759 — Aug. 30, 1820) — August 6, probably not present after August 17.

LUTHER MARTIN (Feb. 9, 1748 — July 10, 1826) — June 9, left September 4.

DANIEL OF ST. THOMAS JENIFER (1723 — Nov. 6, 1790) — June 2.

VIRGINIA

GEORGE WASHINGTON (Feb. 22, 1732 — Dec. 14, 1799) — May 14.

EDMUND RANDOLPH (Aug. 10, 1753 — Sept. 12, 1813) — May 15.

JOHN BLAIR (1732 — Aug. 31, 1800) — May 15.

JAMES MADISON (March 16, 1751 — June 28, 1836) — May 14.

GEORGE MASON (1725 or 1726 — Oct. 7, 1792) — May 14.

GEORGE WYTHE (1726 — June 8, 1806) — May 15; left June 4.

JAMES McCLURG (1747 — July 9, 1825) — May 15; left between July 20 and August 5.

NORTH CAROLINA

WILLIAM BLOUNT (March 26, 1749 — March 21, 1800) — June 20; absent from July 2 to August 6.

RICHARD DOBBS SPAIGHT (March 25, 1758 — Sept. 5, 1802) — as early as May 19.

HUGH WILLIAMSON (Dec. 5, 1735 — May 22, 1819) — as early as May 25.

ALEXANDER MARTIN (1740 — November, 1807) — as early as May 25; left at the end of August.

WILLIAM RICHARDSON DAVIE (June 20, 1756 — Nov. 8, 1820) — May 22 or 23; left August 13.

SOUTH CAROLINA

JOHN RUTLEDGE (1739 — July 23, 1800) — May 17.

CHARLES COTESWORTH PINCKNEY (Feb. 25, 1746 — Aug. 16, 1825) — as early as May 25.

CHARLES PINCKNEY (1758 — October 29, 1824) — May 17.

PIERCE BUTLER (July 11, 1744 — Feb. 15, 1822) — as early as May 25.

GEORGIA

WILLIAM FEW ,June 8, 1748 — July 16, 1828) — as early as May 19, absent from July 2 to August 6.

ABRAHAM BALDWIN (Nov. 22, 1754 — March 4, 1807) — June 11.

WILLIAM PIERCE (1740 — 1806) — May 31, absent from July 2 to August 6, and after August 25.

WILLIAM HOUSTOUN (dates unknown) — June 1; probably left July 26.

The following table gives the dates of death of the framers of the Constitution chronologically:

1788 W. C. HOUSTON	1811 T. FITZSIMMONS
1790 D. BREARLEY D. ST. T. JENIFER B. FRANKLIN W. LIVINGSTON	1812 G. BEDFORD 1813 G. CLYMER E. RANDOLPH
1792 G. MASON	1814 N. GILMAN E. GERRY
1793 R. SHERMAN	1815 R. BASSETT
1796 N. GORHAM D. CARROLL	1816 G. MORRIS J. MCHENRY
1798 G. READ J. WILSON	1819 J. LANGDON H. WILLIAMSON C. STRONG
1799 G. WASHINGTON	W. S. JOHNSON
1800 J. RUTLEDGE T. MIFFLIN J. BLAIR W. BLOUNT	1820 W. R. DAVIE 1821 J. F. MERCER
1801 R. YATES	1822 J. INGERSOLL P. BUTLER
1802 R. D. SPAIGHT	1824 J. DAYTON C. PINCKNEY
1804 A. HAMILTON	
1806 G. WYTHE W. PIERCE W. PATERSON R. MORRIS	1825 C. C. PINCKNEY J. MCCLURG 1826 L. MARTIN
1807 O. ELLSWORTH A. MARTIN A. BALDWIN	1827 R. KING 1828 W. FEW W. JACKSON (Secretary)
1808 J. DICKINSON	1829 J. LANSING
1810 J. BROOM	1836 J. MADISON

The date of the death of William Houstoun is uncertain.[1]

[1] James Madison wrote to Jared Sparks, June 1, 1831: "It is quite certain that since the death of Col. Few, I have been the only living signer of the Constitution of the United States. Of the members who were present and did not sign and of those who were present part of the time but had left the Convention, it is equally certain that not one has remained since the death of Mr. Lansing who disappeared so mysteriously not very long ago. I happen also to be the sole survivor of those who were members of the Revolutionary Congress prior to the close of the war, as I have been for some years of the members of the Convention in 1776 which formed the first Constitution for Virginia. Having outlived so many of my contemporaries, I ought not to forget that I may be thought to have outlived myself."

APPENDIX C

COMMENTS ON JOHN ADAMS' BOOK

Madison wrote to Jefferson, June 6, in an uncomplimentary tone as to the book, but admitting its influence:

"Mr. Adams' book which has been in your hands of course has excited a good deal of attention. . . . It will probably be much read in the Eastern States and contribute, with other circumstances, to revive the predilections of this country for the British Constitution. Men of learning find nothing new in it. Men of taste, many things to criticize. And men without either, not a few things which they will not understand. It will, nevertheless, be read and praised, and become a powerful engine in forming the public opinion. The name and character of the author, with the critical situation of our affairs, naturally account for such an effect. The book also has merit, and I wish many of the remarks in it which are unfriendly to republicanism may not receive fresh weight from the operation of our Governments."

John Jay wrote to Adams, May 12, 1787, praising the book, but differing with him as to the adequacy of Congress:

"Accept my thanks for the book you were so kind as to send me. I have read it with pleasure and profit. I do not, however, altogether concur with you in sentiments respecting the efficiency of our great Council, for National purposes, whatever powers more or less, may be given them. In my opinion, a Council *so constituted*, will forever prove inadequate to the object of its institution. . . .

P. S. A new edition of your book is printing in this city, and will be published next week."

On July 4, Jay wrote to Adams:

"Your book gives us many useful lessons. . . . I consider the work as a valuable one, and one that will tend greatly to recommend and establish those principles of Government on which alone the United States can erect any political structure worth the trouble of erecting."

And again on July 28:

"You have, my dear friend, deserved well of your country, and your service and character will be truly estimated, at least by posterity, for they will know more of you than the people of this day. . . . Your book circulates, and does good. It conveys much information on a subject with which we cannot be too intimately acquainted, especially at this period, when the defects of our National Government are under consideration, and when the strongest arguments are necessary to remove prejudices and to correct errors, which, in many instances, design united with ignorance to create, diffuse, and confirm."

Richard Henry Lee wrote to Adams from Congress in New York, September 3:

"On my arrival here, I met with and read with great pleasure, your book on the American Governments. The judicious collection you have made, with your just reflections thereon, have reached America at a great crisis, and will probably have their proper influence in forming the Federal Government now under consideration. Your labor may, therefore, have its reward in the thanks of this and future generations."

Jefferson wrote to Adams, September 28, that judging from the first volume, he thought it "formed to do a great deal of good", and he expressed his views in concurrence with Adams:

"The first principle of a good Government is certainly a distribution of its powers into Executive, Judiciary, and Legislative, and a subdivision of the latter into two or three branches. It is a good step gained when it is proved that the English Constitution, acknowledged to be better than all which have preceded it, is only better, in proportion as it has approached nearer to this distribution of powers. From this, the last step is easy to show, by a comparison of our Constitutions with that of England, how much more perfect they are. The Articles of Confederation is certainly worthy of your pen. It would form a most interesting addition, to show what has been the nature of the Confederations which have existed hitherto, what were their excellencies, and what their defects. A comparison of ours with them would be to the advantage of ours, and would increase the veneration of our countrymen for them. It is a misfortune that they do not sufficiently know the value of their Constitutions, and how much happier they are rendered by them than any other people on earth, by the Governments under which they live."

Some expressions used in Adams' book as to the desirability of having one branch of the Government in which the influence of the "well-born" might be felt gave rise to charges against him of favoring the introduction of aristocracy. Rev. James Madison wrote to Madison, June 11, 1787:

"I am greatly indebted to you for the books you were so good as to send me by Mr. Griffin, particularly the observations of Mr. Adams; not, however, that he has made a convert of me any more than I trust he has of you, to what appears to be the secret design of his work. . . . Is it probable, my dear friend, that all that trouble was taken and shew of learning displayed merely to refute the opinion of Mr. Turgot? . . . Mr. Adams is greatly mortified that our Executives have not a negative upon the Legislature — and thinks the British system of Government beyond comparison the wisest and best ever invented. He must wish them to introduce a similar Government into America. His Executive (which he thinks also should be single) must be a King; the Senate Lords, and the House of Delegates, plebeians, or Commons. . . . Under the mask of attacking Mr. Turgot, he seems insidiously attempting, notwithstanding now and then a saving clause, to overturn our Constitutions, or at least to sow the seeds of discontent. . . . I fear his optics have been too weak to withstand the glass of European Courts. Their own may have corrupted the plain Republican. . . . The truth is, I believe, the outlines of the American Governments are as well drawn, in order to promote public and private happiness and to secure that greatest portion of liberty which we have so successfully contended for as human sagacity could possibly devise. These outlines only require to be skilfully filled up, perhaps in some cases to be somewhat extended; but as to a renunciation of the original plan, I hope in God no honest, or independent man will hesitate. The least that ought to be done surely is to make a fair experiment. This requires time, particularly as we may expect that the rising generation will be much better actors upon the Republican theatre than their predecessors. Besides, time is essentially necessary to give force and energy to any Government."

In the *Pennsylvania Herald*, of September 1, 1787, a Baltimore despatch said: "Our Ambassador, Mr. Adams, having made it necessary to be *well born* in order to be qualified for the higher offices of Government, it has brought the subject under the consideration of several writers whose ideas seem to be very different from this artful and profound politician." In the *Herald*, of July 7, a correspondent had challenged Adams' attack on a single-house Legislature and asked "whether Mr. Adams' work can so properly be called a defence of our Constitutions as an encomium upon the British government?" James McClurg wrote to Madison, Aug. 22, 1787: "A newspaper writer from Prince Edward has promised to investigate and expose the dangerous tendency as well as unsoundness of John Adams' doctrine, supposed to be Mr. (Patrick) Henry. The book is squibbed at in almost every paper." The *Virginia Independent Chronicle*, Aug. 15, 1787, quoted the letter of "Senex" from the *Petersburg Intelligencer*, as follows: "I have read with a great deal of attention Mr. Adams' pretended Defence of the American Constitutions. It is, as far as I can judge, one of the most deep wrought systems of political deception that ever was penned by the ingenuity of man. . . . Americans beware! for if you imbibe a particle of his political poison you are undone forever . . . perhaps prove an eternal ulcer on the body politic of this country." . . .

It is interesting to note Adams' own view of his book; for there were parts of it, criticisms of an excess of democracy in Governments possessing a single branch Legislature, which he thoroughly realized would be distasteful to many unthinking minds. Writing to General James Warren, Adams said [1]:

"The appearance of County Conventions and their resolutions set me upon throwing together some disquisitions concerning our Governments which are now printed. . . . Popularity was never my mistress, nor was I ever or shall I ever be a popular man. This book will make me unpopular. But one thing I know — a man must be sensible of the errors of the People, and upon his guard against them and must run the risque of their displeasure sometimes, or he will never do any good in the long run. I deliver the book up to the mercy of a world that will never show me much mercy, as my confession of political faith unpopular as it may be at present, the time will come, after I am dead, when the system of it in general must be adopted, with bitter repentance that it was not heeded sooner. It is much easier to pull down a Government, in such a conjuncture of affairs as we have seen, than to build up at such a season as the present."

[1] *Warren-Adams Letters,* II, 281, 294, *Mass. Hist. Soc. Coll.* (1925), LXXIII.

APPENDIX D

DELAWARE. The Convention, consisting of thirty members, met December 3, 1787, and ratified the Constitution unanimously, December 7, 1787.

PENNSYLVANIA. The Convention (called by the Act of November 6, 1787), consisting of sixty-nine members, met at Philadelphia on November 21, 1787, with Frederick Augustus Muhlenberg as President. The Constitution was ratified December 12, 1787, by a vote of forty-six to twenty-three.

NEW JERSEY. Under the Act of Oct. 29, 1787, thirty-nine delegates (three chosen from each county) met in Convention at Trenton, Dec. 11, 1787, with John Stevens as President. The Constitution was unanimously ratified December 18, 1787.

GEORGIA. The Convention, consisting of twenty-six members, with John Wheat as President, met at Augusta, December 25, 1787. The Constitution was unanimously ratified, January 2, 1788.

CONNECTICUT. Under the Act of Oct. 16, 1787, the Convention, consisting of one hundred seventy-three members, with Nathan Griswold as President, met at Hartford, on January 1, 1788. The Constitution was ratified by a vote of one hundred twenty-eight to forty on January 9, 1788.

MASSACHUSETTS. Under the Act of October 25, 1787, the Convention, consisting of three hundred sixty-four members, with Governor John Hancock as President, met at Boston, January 9, 1788. The Constitution was ratified by a vote of one hundred eighty-seven to one hundred sixty-eight, February 16, 1788.

MARYLAND. The Convention, consisting of seventy-six delegates (of whom seventy-four attended), with George

Plater as President, met at Annapolis, April 21, 1788. The Constitution was ratified, April 26, 1788, by a vote of sixty-three to eleven.

SOUTH CAROLINA. Under the Act of January 18, 1788, the Convention, to which two hundred thirty-six delegates were chosen, met at Charleston, May 12, 1788, with Governor Thomas Pinckney as President. The Constitution was ratified, May 23, 1788, by a vote of one hundred forty-nine to seventy-three.

NEW HAMPSHIRE. The Convention, consisting of one hundred thirteen delegates, met at Exeter, February 13, 1788, with Governor John Sullivan as President. The Constitution was ratified, June 21, 1788, at Concord, by a vote of fifty-seven to forty-seven.

VIRGINIA. Under Act of October 25, 1787, the Convention met at Richmond on June 2, 1788, consisting of one hundred seventy delegates, with Edmund Pendleton as President. The Constitution was ratified June 25, 1788, by a vote of eighty-nine to seventy-nine.

NEW YORK. The Convention, consisting of sixty-five members, met at Poughkeepsie, June 17, 1788, with Governor George Clinton as President. The Constitution was ratified July 26, 1788, by a vote of thirty to twenty-seven.

NORTH CAROLINA. The Convention, consisting of two hundred twenty-eight members, met at Hillsboro, July 21, 1788. Ratification of the Constitution was rejected, August 4, 1788, by a vote of one hundred ninety-three to seventy-five. It was finally ratified November 21, 1789, by a Convention which met Nov. 16, 1789.

RHODE ISLAND. The Convention, consisting of seventy members, met at South Kingston, March 8, 1790. The Constitution was ratified May 29, 1790, by a vote of thirty-four to thirty-two.

APPENDIX E

ABRAHAM BALDWIN'S ACCOUNT OF THE CONVENTION

In *The Literary Diary of Ezra Stiles* (1901), III, the long account which Abraham Baldwin, a delegate from Georgia, gave to President Stiles of Yale College, is interestingly set forth in various diary entries:

"Sunday, December 9, 1787. The Hon. Abraham Baldwin, a Delegate from Georgia to Congress and to the Convention which lately sat at Philadelphia for the revision of the Foederal Constitution, visited and spent the evening with me, and gave me a full account of the transactions of the Convention. He was formerly a Tutor of Yale College, and is a patriot, an enlightened, sensible, learned man."

December 20, 1787. I spent the evening with Hon. Abraham Baldwin.

December 21, 1787. Mr. Baldwin was one of the Continental Convention at Philadelphia, last summer. He gave me an account of the whole progress in Convention. It appeared that they were pretty unanimous in the following ideas, viz.: 1. In a firm Foederal Government. 2. That this should be very popular, or stand on the People at large. 3. That their object should comprehend all things of common Foederal concern and which individual States could not determine or enforce. 4. That the jurisdiction and Government of each State should be left intire and preserved as inviolate as possible, consistent with the coercive subordination for preserving the Union with firmness. 5. That the present Foederal Government was inadequate to this end. 6. That a certain portion or degree of dominion as to laws and revenue, as well as to treaties with foreign nations, war, and armies, was necessary to be ceded by individual States to the authority of the National Council. 7. That the National Council should consist of two branches, viz. A Senate and Representatives — that the last should be a local representation apportioned to the property and number of inhabitants as far as practicable. That this should be the governing idea — and yet that the distinction of States should be preserved in the House of Representatives as in the Senate. 8. That the Senate stand on the election and distinction of States, as at present in Congress, and tho', like the Representatives, be in some measure proportioned to the number of inhabitants, yet that beside this the vote in Senate should be by States, tho in the House of Representatives the vote should be by plurality of members present indeed, but not by States as States. Hereby, two things are secured — one, that the People at large shall be efficaciously represented, the other that the States as separate States be as also efficaciously represented. 9. That these two Branches combined into one Republican Body be the Supreme Legislature and become vested with the sovereignty of the Confederacy; and have powers of Government and revenue adequate to these ends. 10. As to a President, it appeared to be the opinion of Convention, that he should be a character respectable by the Nations as well as by the Foederal Empire. To this end, that as much power should be given him as could be, consistently with guarding against all possibility of his ascending in a tract of years or ages to Despotism and absolute Monarchy — of which all were cautious. Nor did it appear that any Members in Convention had the least idea of insidiously laying the foundation of a future Monarchy like the European or Asiatic Monarchies either antient or modern; but were unanimously guarded and firm against everything of this ultimate tendency. Accordingly, they meant to give considerable weight as Supreme Executive, but fixt him dependent on the States at large and at all times impeachable. 10 [11]. They vested Congress thus modified with the power of an adequate revenue, by customs on trade, excise, and direct taxation by authority of Congress; as well as with the army, navy, and making war and peace. These were delicate things on which all felt solicitous, and yet all were unanimously convinced that they were necessary. 11 [12]. They were unanimous also in the expediency and necessity of a Supreme Judiciary Tribunal, of universal application in controversies of a legal nature between States, revenue, and appellate causes between subjects of foreign or different States. 12 [13]. The power of appointing Judges and officers of the Supreme Judiciary to be in the Senate.

These and other general and commanding ideas, the members found themselves almost unanimous in. The Representatives would feel for the interests of their respective local representations; and the Senate must feel, not for particular local Districts but a majority of the States or the universal interest.

After some discourses, it was proposed that any and all of the Members should draught their ideas. These were all brought in and examined, and as approved, entered, until all were satisfied they had gone through. Then they reduced these to one sheet (written) of Articles or members of the Constitution. These they considered afresh, sometimes in Committee of the Whole and sometimes in Convention, with subjoyned alterations and additions until August; when they adjourned a few weeks, leaving all to be digested by a Committee of 5, Messrs. Sherman, Ellsworth. On the return of adjournment, the whole digest was printed and every member entered his remarks, alterations, and corrections. These again were committed to a Committee of one Member of each State, of which Mr. Baldwin was one. This maturated the whole. Finally, a Committee of 5, viz. Messrs. Dr. Johnson, Gouverneur Morris, Wilson,   ,   . These reduced it to the form in which it was published. Messrs. Morris and Wilson had the chief hand in the last arrangement and composition. This was completed in September. By this time, several Members were absent, partly Judge Yates of Albany, Mr. Wythe of Virginia, Judge Sherman and Ellsworth. About 42 signed it. Messrs. Mason of Virginia and Gerry of Boston and Governor Randolph refused. Dr. Franklin said he did not entirely approve it, but thought it a good one, did not know but he should hereafter think it the best, on the whole was ready to sign it, and wished all would sign it and that it should be adopted by all the States.

December 24, 1787. Hon. Abraham Baldwin of Augusta in Georgia spent the evening with me. In May 1785, he was elected President of the University in Georgia, ... We conversed on the new Constitution formed by the Convention, on which I have formed this as my opinion — 1. That it is not the most perfect Constitution yet. 2. That it is a very good one and that it is advisable to adopt it. However, 3. That tho much of it will be permanent and lasting, yet much of it will be hereafter altered by future revisions. And 4. That the best one remains to be investigated. When the Convention was proposed, I doubted its expediency. 1. Because I doubted whether our wisest men had yet attained light enough to see and discern the best, and what ought finally to prevail. 2. Neither did I think the People were ripe for the reception of the best one if it could be investigated. And yet, 3. I did not doubt but time and future experience would teach, open and lead us to the best one. And tho we have got a much better one than I expected, and a very good one, yet my judgment still remains as before. I think there is not power enough yet given to Congress for firm Government. Neither can I see how far it is safe to surrender the powers of the States to the Imperial Body without (1) prostrating the Sovereignty of the particular States. (2) Without laying the foundation of the President's growing up into an uncontrollable and absolute monarch. And yet I think the last as well guarded as possible; and I know not whether it is possible to vest Congress with laws, revenues, and army and navy, without endangering the ruin of the interior powers and liberties of the States."

Alexander Hamilton's account of the Convention in his letter to Timothy Pickering, September 18, 1803, should also be given especial attention. "The highest-toned propositions," he wrote, "which I made in the Convention were for a President, Senate and Judges during good behavior — a House of Representatives for three years. . . . I neither recommended nor meditated the annihilation of the State Governments. . . . In the course of the discussions in the Convention, neither the propositions thrown out for debate, nor even those voted in the earlier stages of the deliberations, were considered as evidence of a definitive opinion in the proposer or voter. It appeared to me to be in some sort understood that, with a view to free investigation, experimental propositions might be made, which were to be received merely as suggestions for consideration. Accordingly, it is a fact that my final opinion was against an Executive during good behavior, on account of the increased danger to the public tranquillity incident to the election of a magistrate with this degree of permanence. In the plan of a Constitution which I drew up while the Convention was sitting and which I communicated to Mr. Madison about the close of it, perhaps a day or two after, the office of President has no greater duration than for three years."

APPENDIX F

THE PREAMBLE AND GENERAL WELFARE

In recent years, there has been a contention made in Congress and elsewhere that the phrase "promote the general welfare," used in the Preamble of the Constitution, contained a grant of power to Congress to enact laws for the general welfare. Of course, this is not a fact. As early as 1833, Justice Joseph Story in his *Commentaries on the Constitution*, Section 462, stated that, in law, the Preamble gave no powers to the Government and added in no way to the specific powers contained in the body of the Constitution itself. In 1905, the Supreme Court in *Jacobson* v. *Massachusetts*, 197 U. S. 11, held as follows: "Although that preamble indicates the general purposes for which the people ordained and established the Constitution, it has never been regarded as the source of any substantive power conferred on the government of the United States, or on any of its departments. Such powers embrace only those expressly granted in the body of the Constitution, and such as may be implied from those so granted. Although, therefore, one of the declared objects of the Constitution was to secure the blessings of liberty to all under the sovereign jurisdiction and authority of the United States, no power can be exerted to that end by the United States, unless, apart from the preamble, it be found in some express delegation of power, or in some power to be properly implied therefrom." Professor Westel W. Willoughby, in his *The Constitutional Law of the United States* (2d Ed. 1929), sections 27, 61, says: "The value of the Preamble to the Constitution for purposes of construction is similar to those given to the preamble of an ordinary statute. It may not be relied upon for giving to the body of the instrument a meaning other than that which its language plainly imports, but may be resorted to in cases of ambiguity, where the intention of the framers does not clearly and definitely appear. As Story says: 'The preamble of a statute is a key to open the mind of the makers as to the mischiefs which are to be remedied and the objects which are to be accomplished by the provisions of the statute.' . . . Among the purposes enumerated in its Preamble for the securing of which the Constitution is ordained and established is the promotion of the General Welfare. That the Preamble may, in certain cases, be resorted to for the purpose of determining the meaning of ambiguous provisions in the body of the instrument, but that it may not be viewed as itself a source of Federal power has already been pointed out." See to the same effect *The Constitution of the United States, Its History, Application and Construction* (1910), by David K. Watson, pp. 89–92.

Very early in our history, in a debate on one of the Alien and Sedition bills in the House of Representatives in 1798, the fact that the words "general welfare" in the Preamble and in Article I, Section 8, Clause 1, of the Constitution did not grant any substantive power was pointed out in able speeches by Abraham Baldwin of Georgia (one of the framers of the Constitution), Robert Williams of North Carolina, and Albert Gallatin of Pennsylvania (*Annals of Congress, 5th Cong., 2d Sess.*, June 16, 19, 1798).

INDEX

(No attempt has been made to index herein the numerous speeches made in the Convention by the various delegates.)

DATE DUE